CATIA V5 Tutorials
Mechanism Design & Animation

Release 17

Nader G. Zamani
University of Windsor

Jonathan M. Weaver
University of Detroit Mercy

ISBN: 978-1-58503-440-6

SDC
PUBLICATIONS
Schroff Development Corporation

www.schroff.com
www.schroff-europe.com

Preface

This book of tutorials is intended as a training guide for those who have a basic familiarity with part and assembly modeling in CATIA V5 Release 17 wishing to create and simulate the motion of mechanisms within CATIA Digital Mockup (DMU). The tutorials are written so as to provide a hands-on look at the process of creating an assembly, developing the assembly into a mechanism, and simulating the motion of the mechanism in accordance with some time based inputs. The processes of generating movie files and plots of the kinematics results are covered. The majority of the common joint types are covered. Students majoring in engineering/technology, designers using CATIA V5 in industry, and practicing engineers can easily follow the book and develop a sound yet practical understanding of simulating mechanisms in DMU.

The chapters are designed to be independent of each other allowing the user to pick specific topics of interest without the need to go through the previous chapters.

In order to achieve this independence, there was a need to repeat many topics throughout the workbook. Therefore, we are fully aware of the redundancy introduced in the chapters.

In this workbook, the parts created in CATIA are simple enough that they can be modeled with minimal knowledge of this powerful software. The reason behind the simplicity is not to burden the reader with the part modeling aspects of the software package. However, it is assumed that the user is familiar with the CATIA V5 interface and basic utilities such as sketching and constraining, creating solid models, and manipulating the view (pan/zoom/rotate).

Although the tutorials are based on CATIA Release 17, they can be used for other releases with minor changes made where differences are noticed. The workbook was developed using CATIA in a Windows XP environment. Nevertheless, it can be used for NT and UNIX platforms with no anticipated differences.

Acknowledgements

The authors would like to thank the many students at the University of Windsor and the University of Detroit Mercy who were responsible for the thought behind the writing of this tutorial book and for piloting some of the tutorials. Finally, we would like to thank the Schroff Development Corporation for providing us with the opportunity to publish this book.

NOTES:

Table of Contents

NOTES:

Chapter 1

Introduction

The subject of rigid body dynamics is an integral part of mechanics. In general, dynamics has two distinct branches, kinematics, and kinetics.

The topic of kinematics deals with the motion of objects disregarding the forces that cause the motion. Here, one is interested in studying position, velocity and acceleration. On the other hand, kinetics deals with the forces causing motion and resulting in acceleration.

CATIA's Digital Mock Up workbench has a module known as DMU Kinematics where the former type of dynamic simulations can be performed. However, kinetic analysis is not available in CATIA V5. There are add-on third party packages that can incorporate force calculations in the mechanisms designed in CATIA.

To effectively model mechanisms in DMU Kinematics, one should have a thorough understanding of the various kinematic joint types and their associated effect on system degrees of freedom. When a rigid body in space moves, it can translate in three orthogonal directions (typically considered to be x,y, and z) and rotate about each of these axes (sometimes considered to be roll, pitch, and yaw). Therefore, a rigid body in three dimensional space has six degrees of freedom (dof), three translational and three rotational.

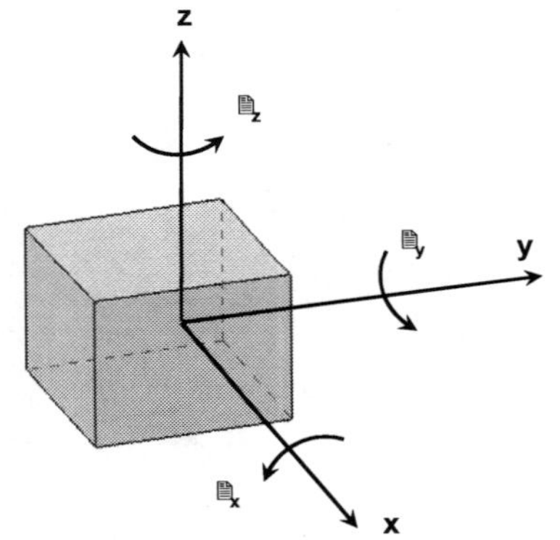

We classify joints in CATIA is as either *simple* or *complex*. We will describe the various simple and complex joint types beginning with the simple ones.

Simple Joints in CATIA:

<u>1- Planar Joint </u>:

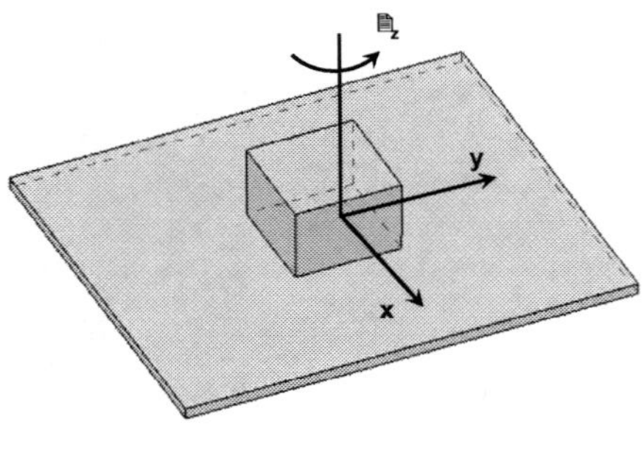

Consider the situation where the above block can slide on a flat plane as displayed on the right.
Here, the position of the block is uniquely determined based on translation in the x,y directions and rotation about the z-axis.

Therefore a planar joint removes one translational dof and two rotational dof. The number of degrees of freedom for a planar joint is three.

2- Prismatic Joint :

In the above situation, if the edge of the block, happens to be translating along the edge of the supporting plane (or any straight line in the plane) without possibility of rotation, it becomes a prismatic joint with a single degree of freedom. All three rotational degrees of freedom and two the three translational degrees of freedom are removed by a prismatic joint.

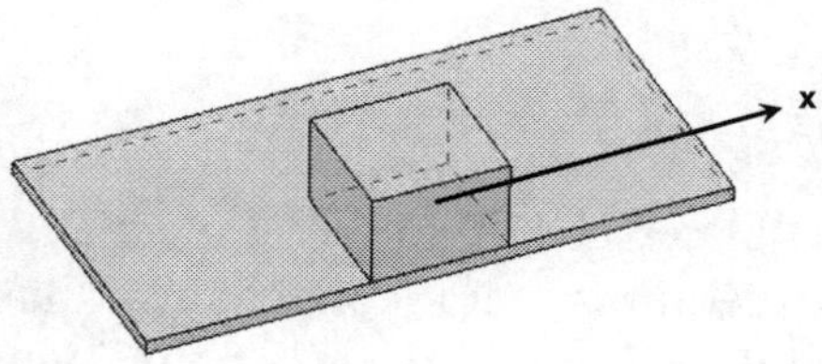

The command for this joint involves the translation.

3- Cylindrical Joint :

Consider the part shown on the right that can slide along the bar and at the same time rotate about the axis of the bar. This constitutes a cylindrical joint with two degrees of freedom. Two of the three rotational degrees of freedom and two of the three translational degrees of freedom are removed, where the axis of the remaining rotation is the same as the axis of the remaining translation.

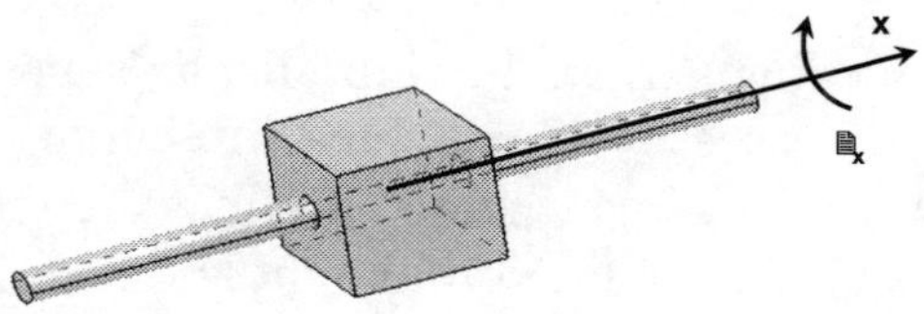

The command with a cylindrical joint involves either the angle of rotation or the translation (or both).

4- Spherical Joint :

A spherical joint removes all translational capabilities and merely has rotational degrees of freedom.
Therefore, a spherical joint has three rotational degrees of freedom.

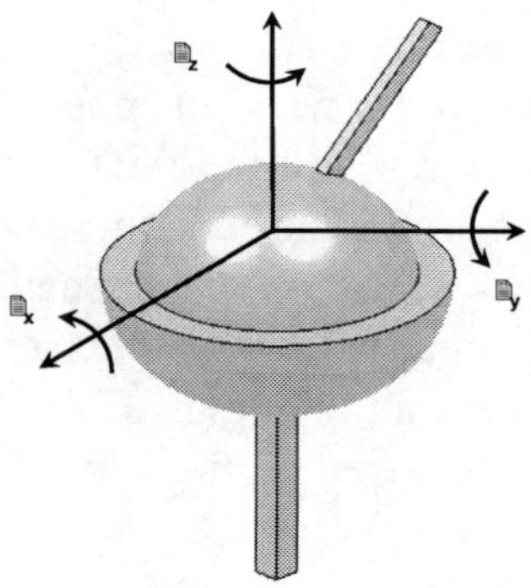

There is no command associated with this joint.

5- Rigid Joint :

A rigid joint is a trivial one where the parts involved in the joint are effectively locked together leaving zero relative degrees of freedom.

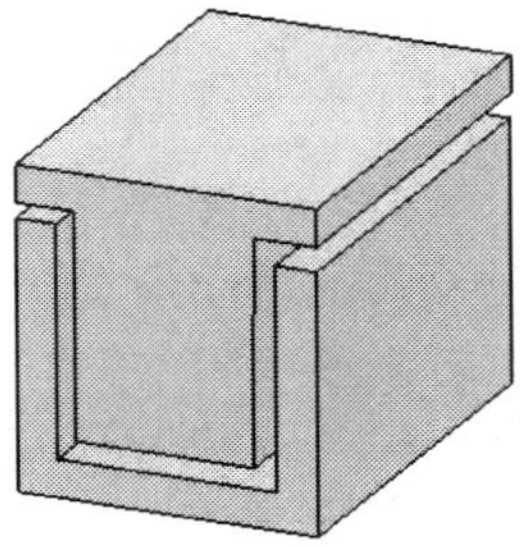

There is no command associated with a rigid joint.

It is also worth noting that mechanism simulation in DMU also requires that the mechanism have one *Fixed Part*, and that the fixed part is essentially locked down as the inertial frame of reference for the mechanism simulation.

Complex Joints in CATIA:

1- Revolute Joint :

The mechanism on the right displays a revolute joint which possesses one degree of freedom, namely a rotation. Two planes and two lines are required for the construction of a revolute joint and the planes must be normal to the axis but may be offset from each other.

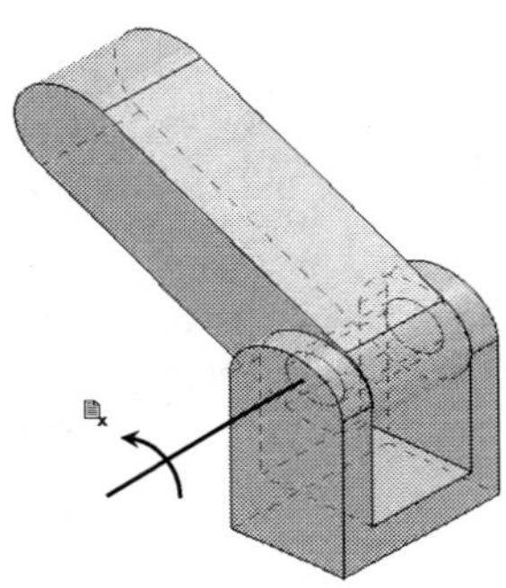

The command for this joint is “Angle”.

2- Gear Joint :

A gear joint is made of two revolute joints. The gear ratio and the direction of rotation can be specified. However, the axes of the revolute joints need to be fixed in space. CATIA requires that the two revolute joints involved in creation of the gear joint share a common part. The involved parts need not be representative of actual gears; the joint simply applies a mathematical relation between the angles of the two involved revolute joints based on the specified ratio.

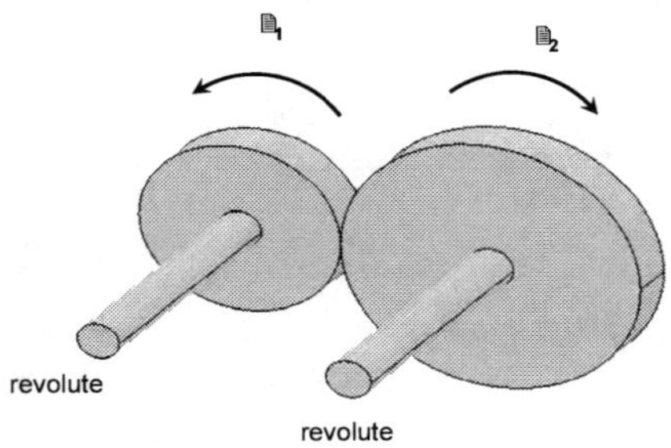

The degree of freedom for the gear joint is one.

The Command with a gear joint involves the angle for one of the revolute joints.

3- Rack Joint  :

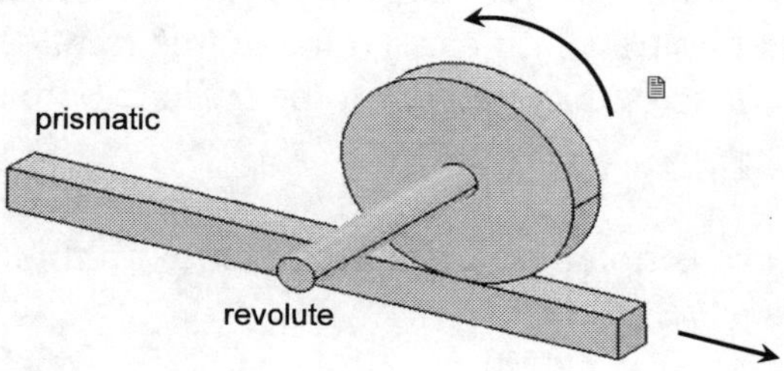

A rack joint is a special case of a gear joint where the radius of curvature of one of the gears is infinite. A rack joint gets built from a revolute and a prismatic joint. The gear ratio in mm per turn and the direction of the rotation can be specified.

Once again, the axis of the revolute joint has to be fixed in space.
The degree of freedom for the rack joint is one – either the translation or the rotation.

The command for a rack joint involves either the rack translation or the revolute joint rotation.

4- Universal Joint  :

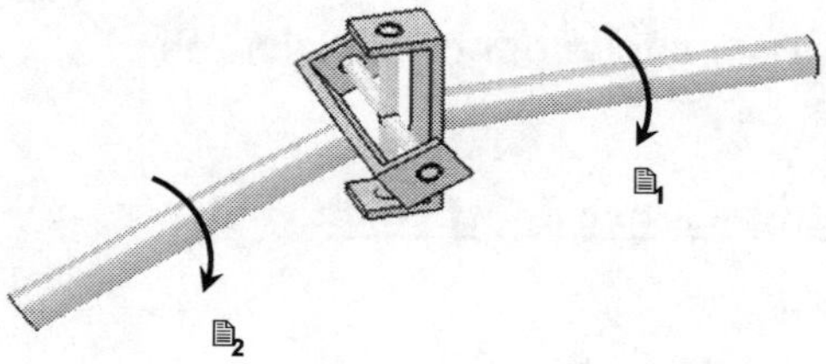

A universal joint enables two shafts to rotate about axes at an angle to each other coupled in a fashion similar to the illustration on the right. Each shaft should already be constrained to its axis with either a revolute or a cylindrical joint. This joint effectively removes all the relative degrees of freedom between the two parts. In other words, one of the two angles of the involved revolute/cylindrical joints may be driven and the other joints angle will be determined from that angle.

There is no command associated with this joint.

5- Screw Joint  :

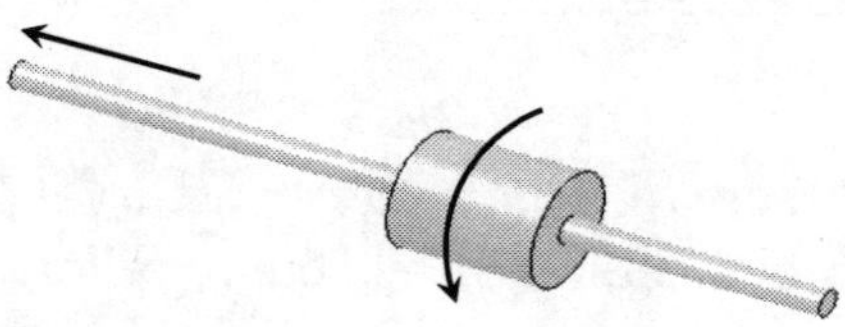

This is a joint involving two coupled degrees of freedom. To specify a screw joint, one needs to specify the axes of the two involved parts and the pitch (linear advance per turn ratio). There is one remaining degree of freedom for a screw joint – either the translation along the axis or the rotation about the axis.

The associated command involves either the rotation angle or the translation length.

6- Point Surface Joint 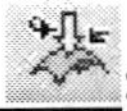:

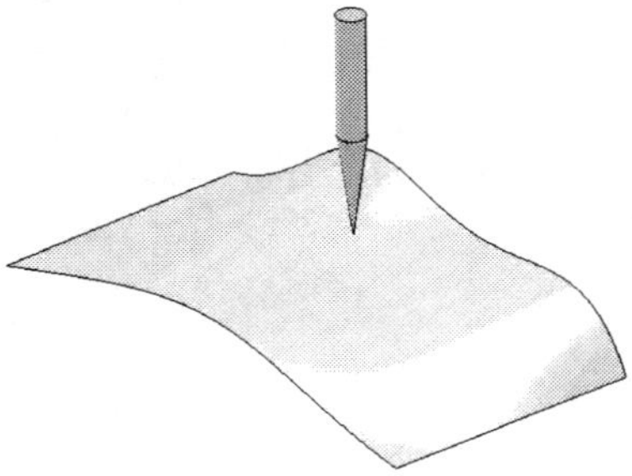

This joint has five degrees of freedom, three rotations and two translations. To make this joint, the point needs to be physically on the surface beforehand.

There is no command associated with this joint.

7- Point Curve Joint :

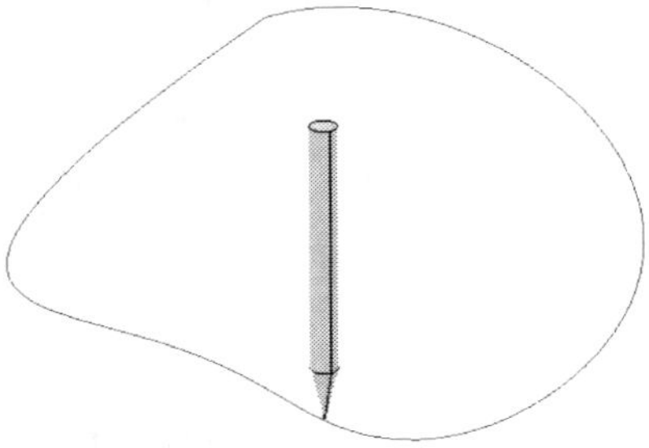

This joint has four degrees of freedom, three rotations and one translation (along the curve). The point needs to be physically on the curve (three dimensional curve) before this joint can be created.

The associated command is length along the curve.

8- Slide Curve Joint :

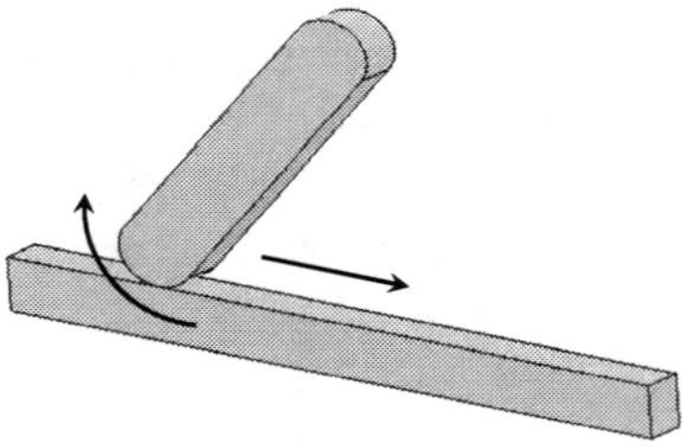

A slide curve joint forces two curves to remain in contact, but allows one curve to slide along the other curve. The two curves must be coincident and tangent at one point before the joint can be created.

There is no command associated with a slide curve Joint.

9- Roll Curve Joint :

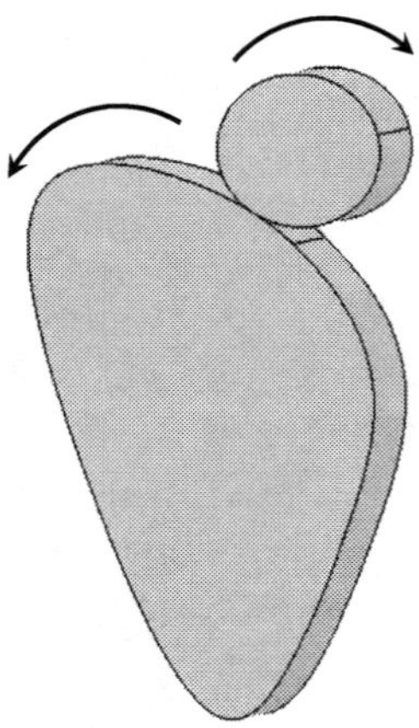

A roll curve joint forces two curves to remain in contact and prohibits sliding of one curve relative to the other. The two curves must be coincident and tangent at one point.

The command associated with the roll curve joint is the length of the translation along the curves to the point of contact.

10- Cable Joint  :

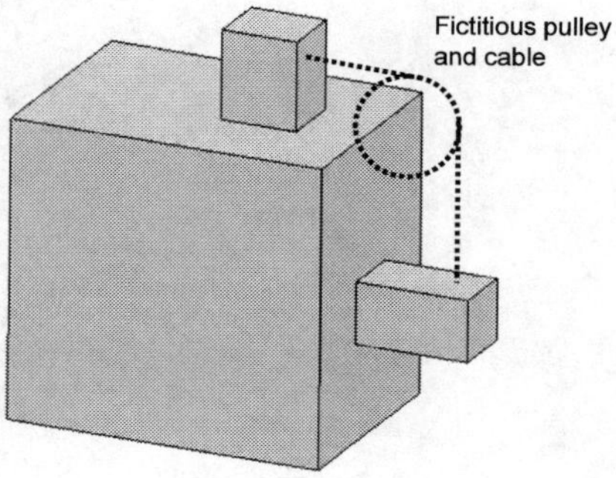

A cable joint can be thought of as a gear joint for two prismatic joints. It associates the length of the two joints by a ratio defined in the joint creation process. The cable and the pulley themselves are fictitious and are not modeled or displayed.

The command associate with this joint is the length of one of the two involved prismatic joints.

Armed with the basic understanding of the various joint types possible in CATIA V5, and assuming you already have a working knowledge of part design and assembly modeling in CATIA V5, you are ready to begin the tutorials.

NOTES:

Chapter 2

A Block with Constant Acceleration along a Prismatic Joint

Introduction

In this tutorial you create a block which accelerates on along a straight line according a user prescribed formula. A prismatic joint is used to simulate this simple mechanism.

1 Problem Statement

The block shown below is starting from rest and accelerating along the base with a constant acceleration of 2 in/s^2. A simple integration of the acceleration term results in the expressions for position and velocity along the base. These expressions are given by $s(t) = t^2$ and $v(t) = 2t$ respectively.

The travel time from one end of the base to the other end is $t = \sqrt{20} \approx 4.47$ s.
In this tutorial, you create the assembly and automatically create the needed joint. The problem under consideration involves a **Prismatic Joint** with the block sliding along the edge maintaining the surface contact.

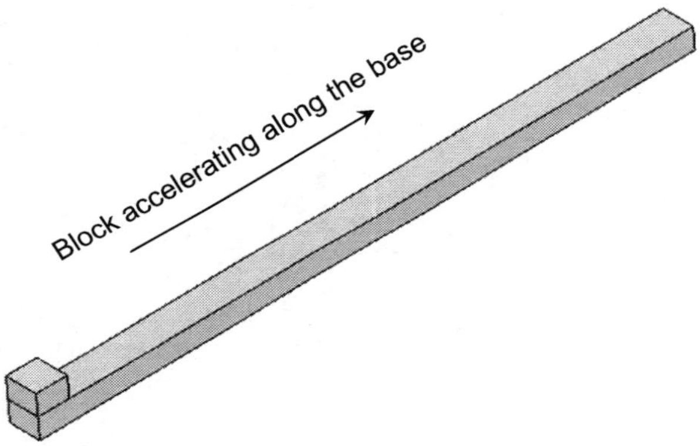

The graphical representation of the position and velocity vs time are provided below, where t is in seconds, s(t) is in inches, and v(t) is in inches per second.

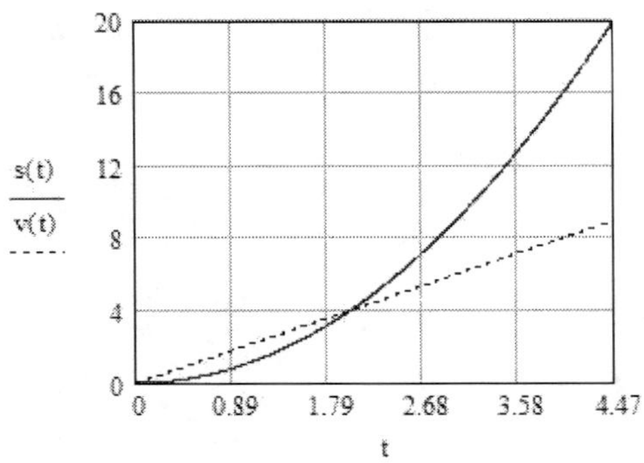

2 Overview of the Tutorial

This tutorial will involve the following steps:

1. Model the two CATIA parts required.
2. Create an assembly (CATIA Product) containing the parts.
3. Constrain the assembly in such a way that the only unconstrained degree of freedom is the translation of the block along the length of the base.
4. Enter the **Digital Mockup** workbench and convert the assembly constraints into a prismatic joint representing the desired translation of the block along the base.
5. Simulate the relative motion of the block along the base without consideration to time (in other words, without implementing the time based kinematics given in the problem statement).
6. Adding a formula to implement the time based kinematics.
7. Simulating the kinematically correct motion and generating plots of the results.

3 Creation of the Assembly in Mechanical Design Solutions

Model two parts named **block** and **base** as shown below with the dimensions being in inches. It is assumed that you are sufficiently familiar with CATIA to model these parts fairly quickly.

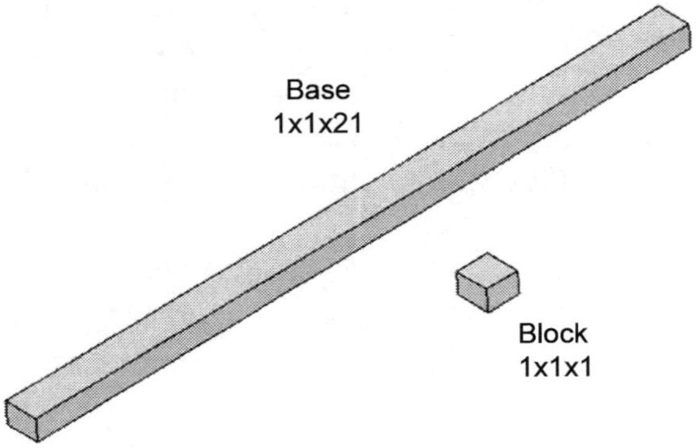

Enter the **Assembly Design** workbench  which can be achieved by different means depending on your CATIA customization. For example, from the standard Windows toolbar, select **File > New** . From the box shown on the right, select **Product**. This moves you to the **Assembly Design** workbench and creates an assembly with the default name **Product.1**.

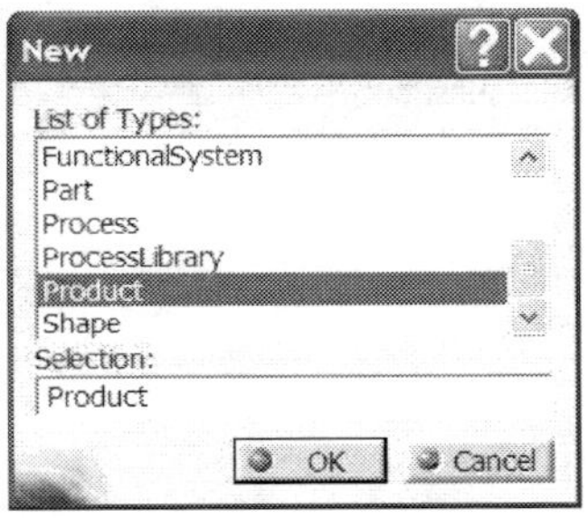

In order to change the default name, move the cursor to **Product.1** in the tree, right click and select **Properties** from the menu list.

From the **Properties** box, select the **Product** tab and in **Part Number** type **accelerating_block**.

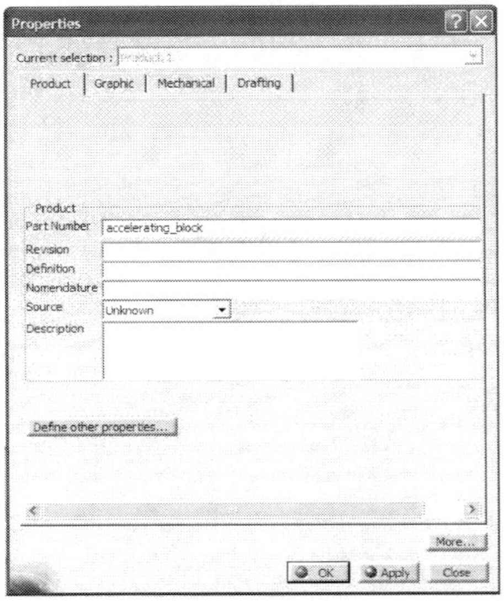

This will be the new product name throughout the chapter. The tree on the top left corner of your computer screen should look as displayed below.

The next step is to insert the existing parts block and base into the assembly just created.

From the standard Windows toolbar, select **Insert > Existing Component**.
From the **File Selection** pop up box choose **base** and **block**. Remember that in CATIA multiple selections are made with the **Ctrl** key.
The tree is modified to indicate that the parts have been inserted.

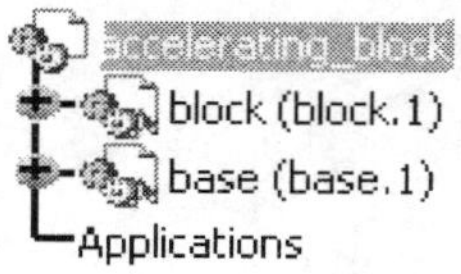

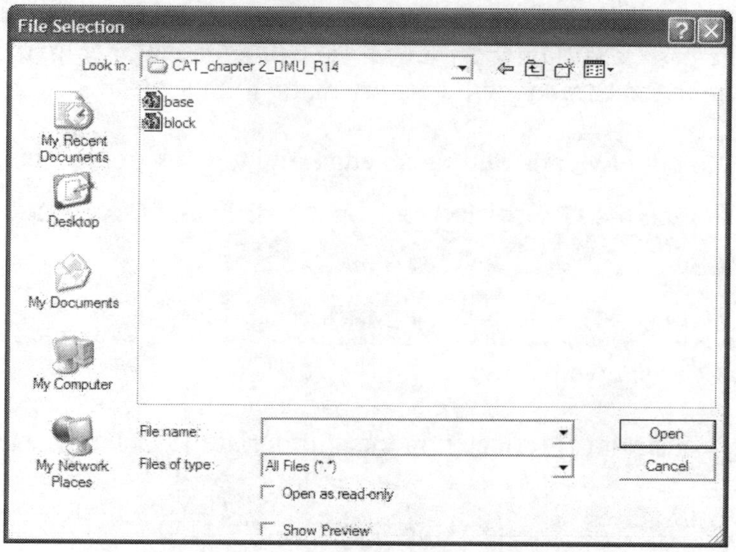

The best way of saving your work is to save the entire assembly.
Double click on the top branch of the tree. This is to ensure that you are in the **Assembly Design** workbench.
Select the **Save** icon . The **Save As** pop up box allows you to rename if desired. The default name is the **accelerating_block** and it will be saved as a **.CATProduct** file.

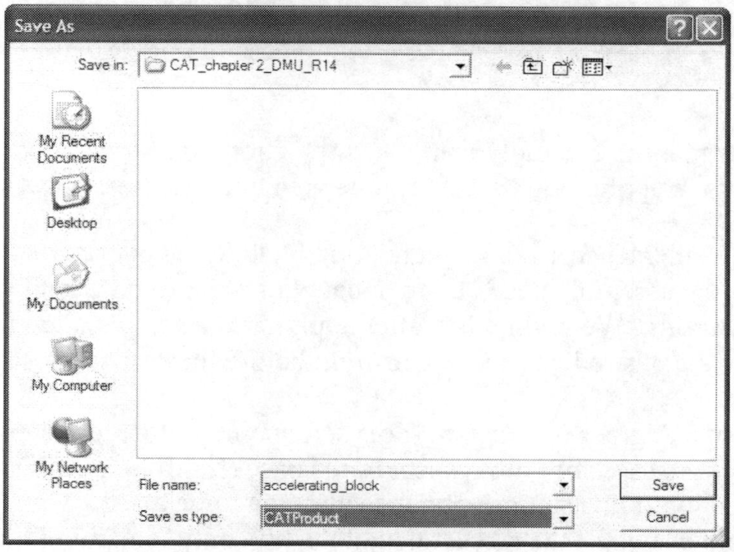

Your next task is to impose assembly constraints. The objective here is twofold: to position the block onto the slider at the desired starting point, and to constrain the assembly in such a way that the assembly constraints can be automatically converted to the appropriate mechanism joint. In this rather simple mechanism, we will want to apply assembly constraints such that the **base** is anchored and the **block** is at its initial position on top of the **base** and constrained to the **base** such that only translation along the length of the base is still unconstrained. The kinematically equivalent mechanism joint to such assembly constraints will be a prismatic joint as desired.

We'll begin by constraining an edge of the block to be coincident with an edge of the base. Pick the **Coincidence** icon  from the **Constraints** toolbar 

. Select the two edges of the **base** and the **block** as shown below.

This constraint is reflected in the appropriate branch of the tree.

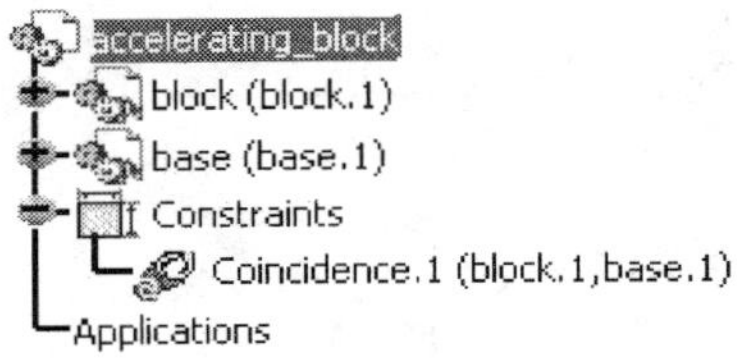

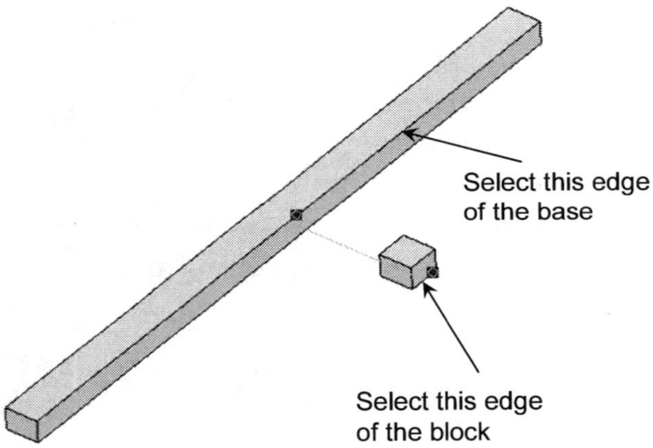

Note that the assembly component positions are not yet updated to reflect the constraint we have applied. This does not happen until the assembly is updated. The image next to the Coincidence.1 branch in the tree includes an overlay of the **Update** icon  to flag that the assembly needs to be updated in order to position the parts consistent with that constraint. We will update after applying the next constraint since it is often easier to pick the desired entities to constrain before they are in close proximity or coincident.

From a degrees of freedom (dof) standpoint, before any constraints were applied, the block had six dof with respect to the base (translations along each of the three axis directions and rotations about each of the three axes). The applied coincidence constraint removes two of the three translations (the only remaining translation is along the line of coincidence) and two of the three rotations (the only remaining rotation is about the line of coincidence).

Next, we will apply a contact constraint between the contacting surfaces of the two parts. This constraint will remove the one remaining rotational dof between the block and the base. Pick the **Contact** icon  from **Constraints** toolbar and select the surfaces shown below. The tree is modified to reflect this constraint.

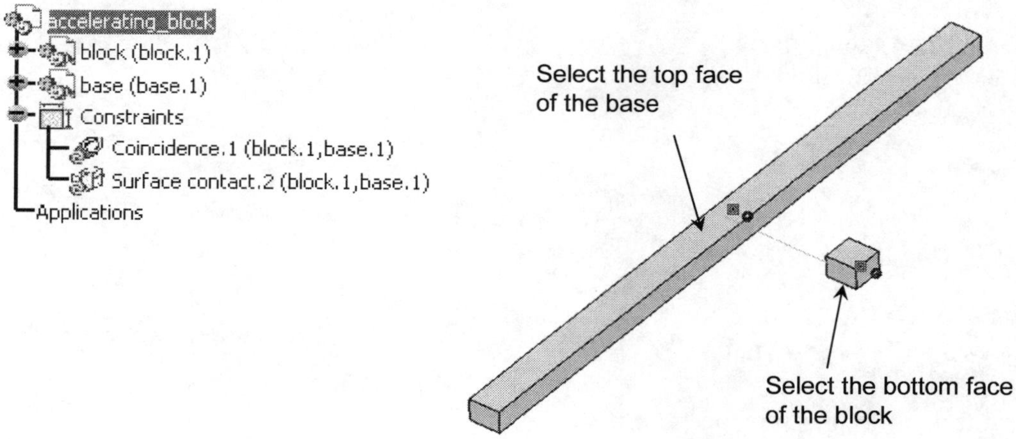

Use the **Update** icon  to position the two parts to be consistent with the applied constraints. The result is as shown below.

Note that the **Update** icon  no longer appears on the constraints branches.

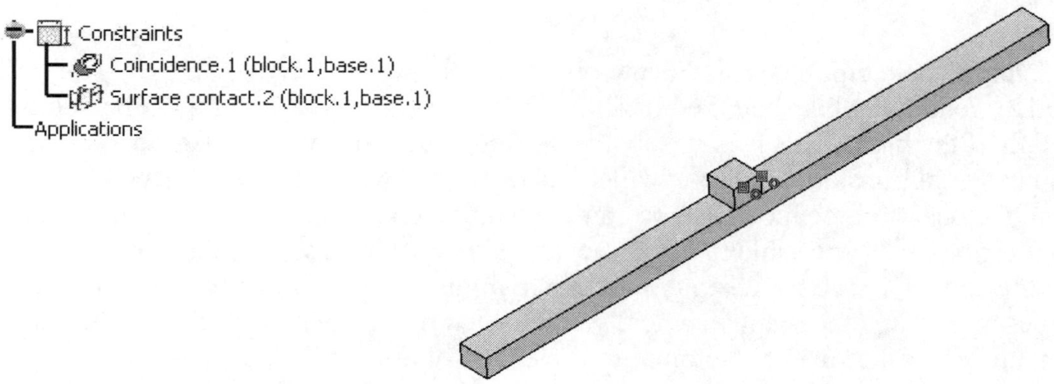

Depending on how your parts were constructed, the block may end up in the middle portion of the base as is shown here. If this is the case, the next step involves creating a temporary constraint to make the vertices coincide thereby positioning the block at the desired starting point at the end of the base. If your block is already at the desired start point at one end of the base you can skip the next step.

Pick the **Coincidence** icon  from **Constraints** toolbar and select the vertices of the two parts as shown below.
The tree is modified to reflect this temporary constraint. Notice that the branch has the **Update** icon  affixed to it.

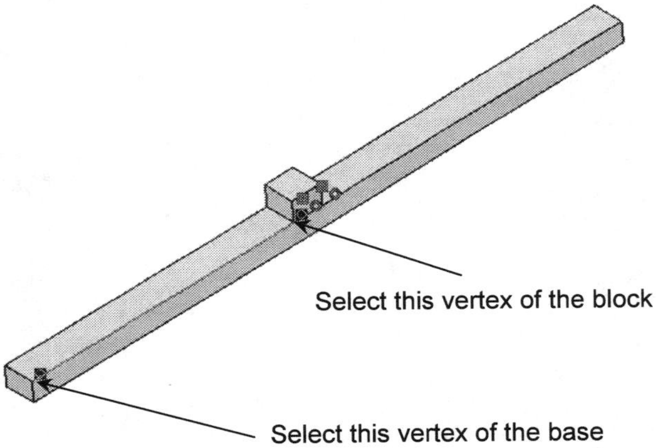

Use the **Update** icon  to position the two parts as shown.

This constraint is no longer needed (and if not removed will result in a later step not working as desired), point the cursor to the **Coincidence.3** constraint branch, right click and delete it.

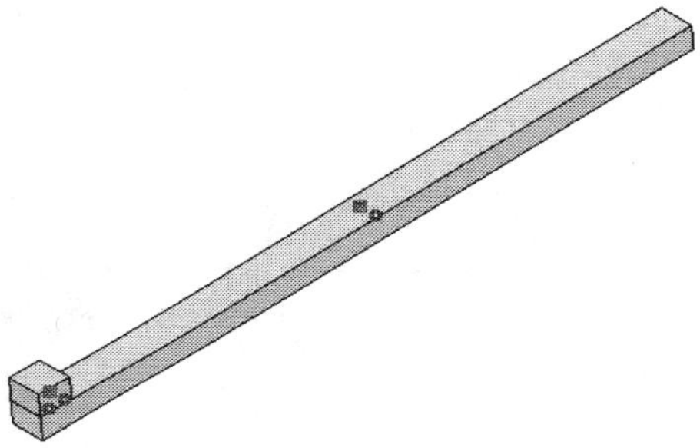

After deleting the temporary coincident constraint between the vertices, the only degree of freedom remaining between the block and the base is a translation of the block along the length of the base. This is precisely the desired situation since we want to simulate one dimensional translation. As we will see shortly, the two assembly constraints applied between the base and the block can be automatically converted to a mechanism prismatic joint. It is not always possible to apply the assembly constraints in such a way as to ensure the conversion to the desired mechanism joints will be automatic. We will see examples of that in later chapters where we will need to create the intended mechanism joints manually rather than by automatic conversion of assembly constraints.

While we have removed all but the one desired translation of the block relative to the base, we have not yet constrained the base such that it is fixed in location and orientation. Next, we will apply an Anchor constraint to lock down the base. Typically, your very first assembly constraint will involve choosing a part to anchor after which you know that the anchored part will not move as your assembly constraints are applied.

Pick the **Anchor** icon from **Constraints** toolbar and select the **base** from the tree or from the screen.

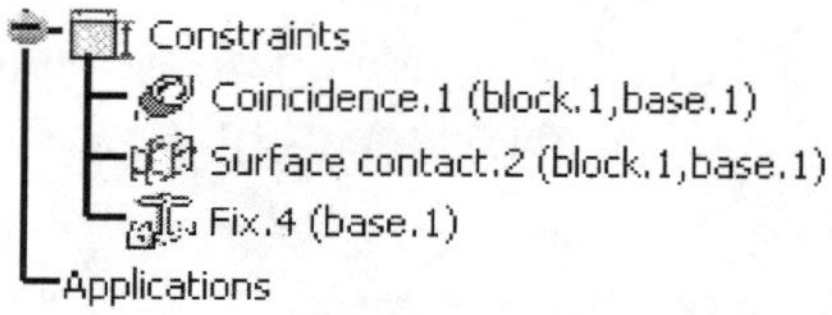

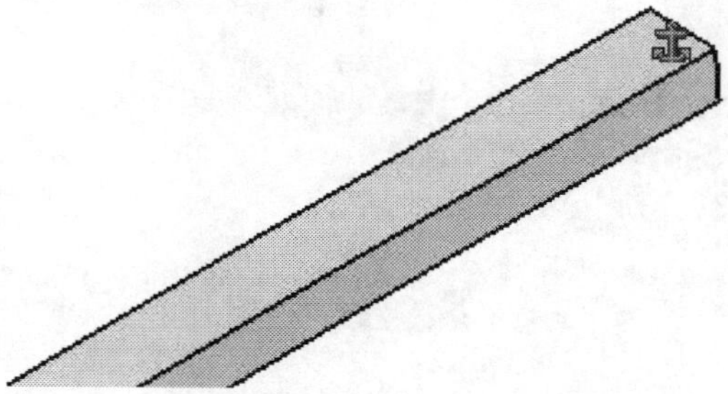

The assembly is complete and we can proceed to the **Digital Mockup** workbench.

4 Creating Joints in the Digital Mockup Workbench

The **Digital Mockup** workbench is quite extensive but we will only deal with the **DMU Kinematics** module. To get there you can use the standard Windows toolbar as shown below. **Start > Digital Mockup > DMU Kinematics**.

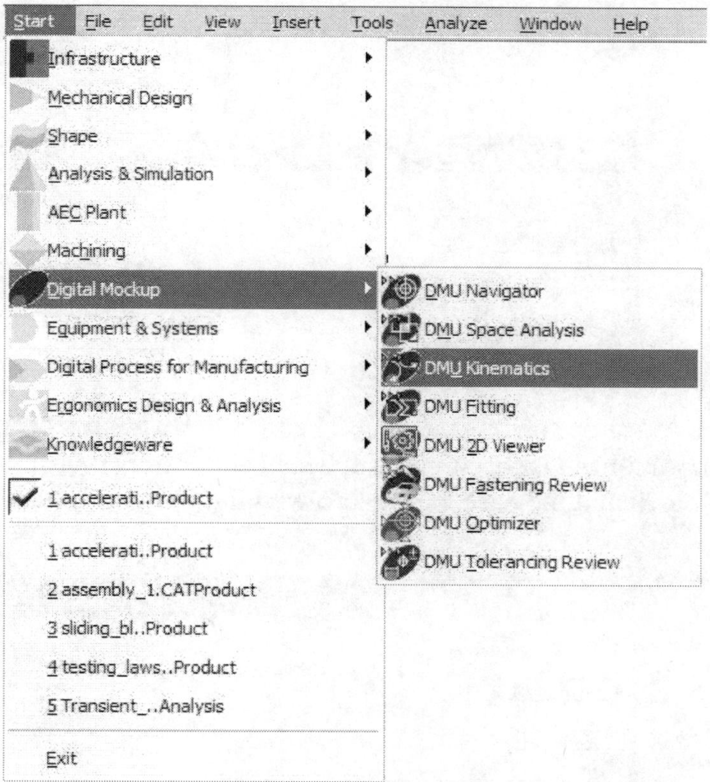

Select the **Assembly Constraints Conversion** icon  from the **DMU Kinematics** toolbar 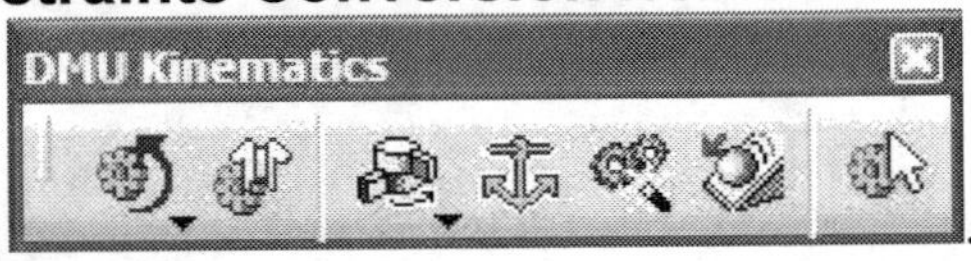

. This icon allows you to create the most common joints automatically from existing assembly constraints. The pop up box below appears.

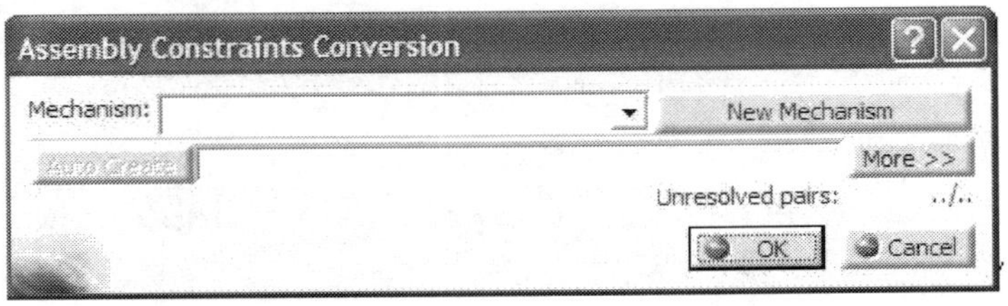

Select the **New Mechanism** button 

.
This leads to another pop up box which allows you to name your mechanism. The default name is **Mechanism.1**. Accept the default name by pressing **OK**.

Note that the box indicates **Unresolved pairs: 1/1**

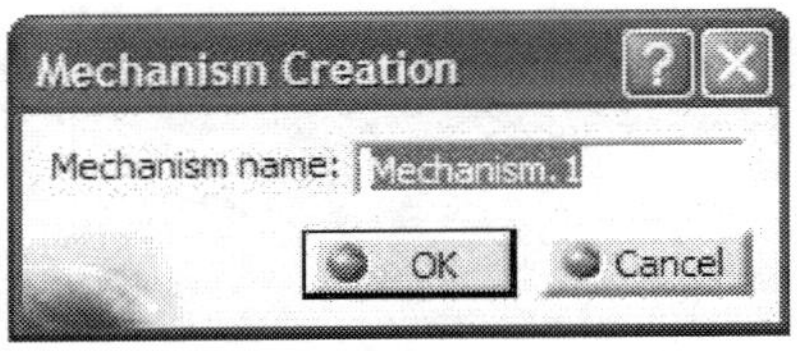

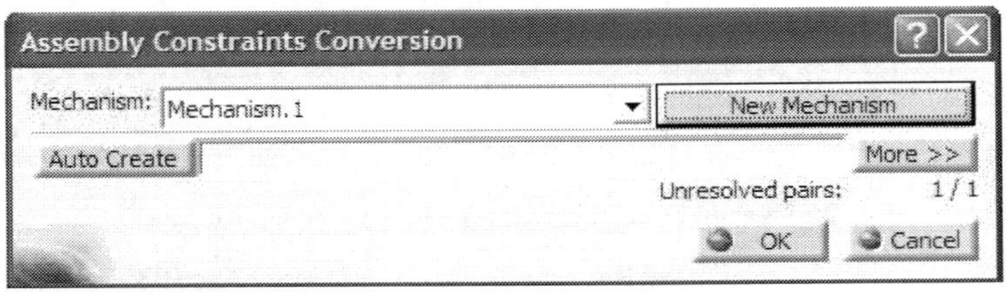

Select the **Auto Create** button 

. Then if the **Unresolved pairs** becomes **0/1**, a mechanism joint has just been made between a pair of parts (in this case our only two parts are the block and the base, so we know a joint has been created between those two parts).

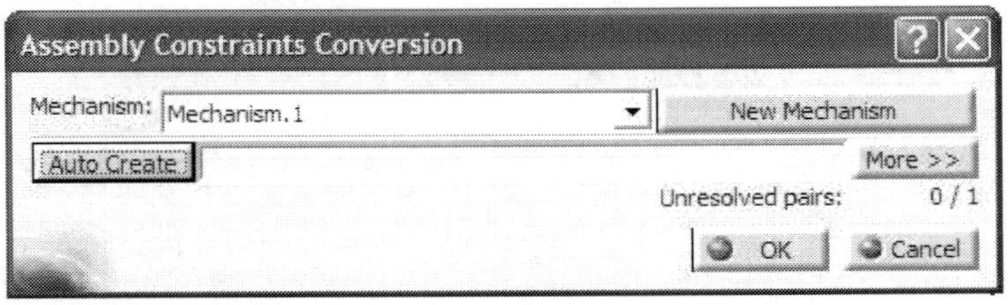

Note that the tree becomes longer by having an **Application** Branch. The expanded tree is displayed below. It clearly indicates the existence of a **Prismatic.1** Joint and a Fixed Part **Fix.4**.

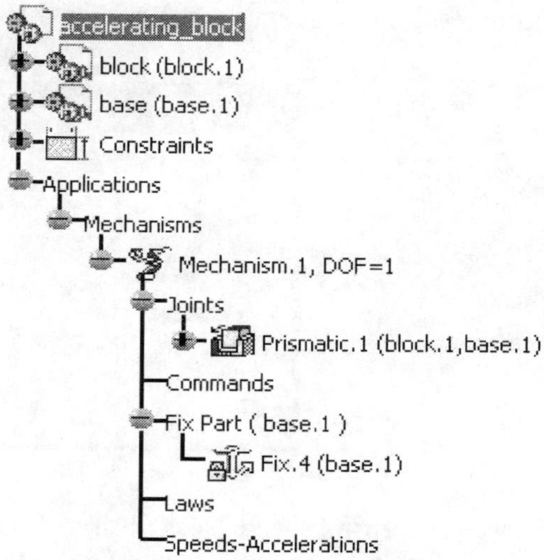

The **DOF** is 1 and it represents the sliding of the block along the base (i.e., motion along the just created prismatic joint).

Note that your prismatic joint was created based on the assembly constraints created earlier and the **Assembly Constraints Conversion** icon 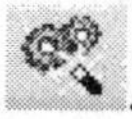.

This joint (and any other joint) can be created directly using the **Kinematics Joints** toolbar shown below.

In order to animate the mechanism, you need to remove the one degree of freedom present. This will be achieved by turning **Prismatic.1** into a **Length driven** joint. Double click on **Prismatic.1** in the tree. The pop up box below appears.

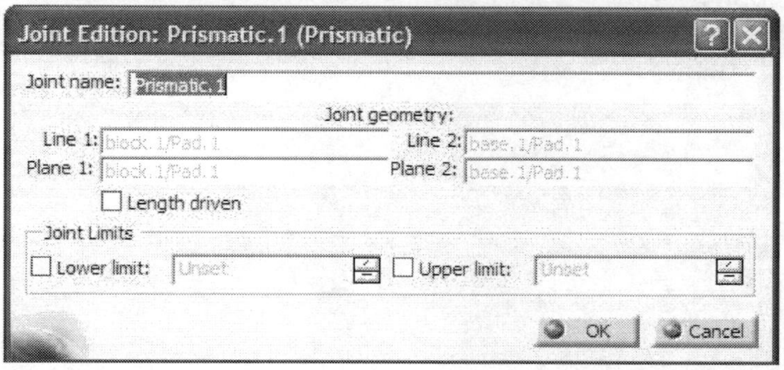

Check the **Length driven** box and change the **Lower limit** and **Upper limit** to read as indicated below. Keep in mind that these limits can also be changed elsewhere.

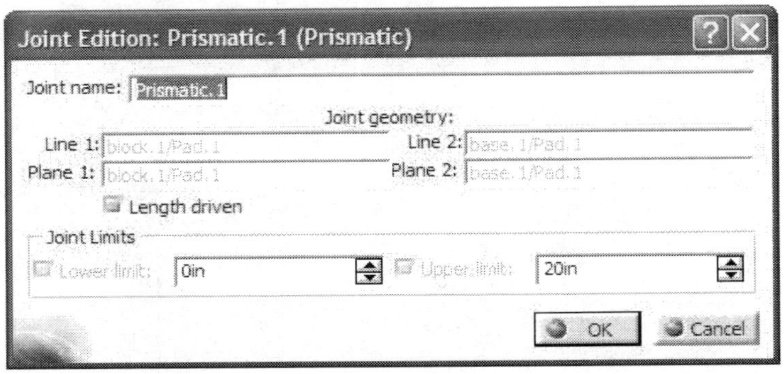

During the animation phase, if your block slides in the wrong direction try **Lower limit= -20in** and **Upper limit =0**.

Upon closing the above box and assuming that everything else was done correctly, the following message appears on the screen.

This indeed is good news.

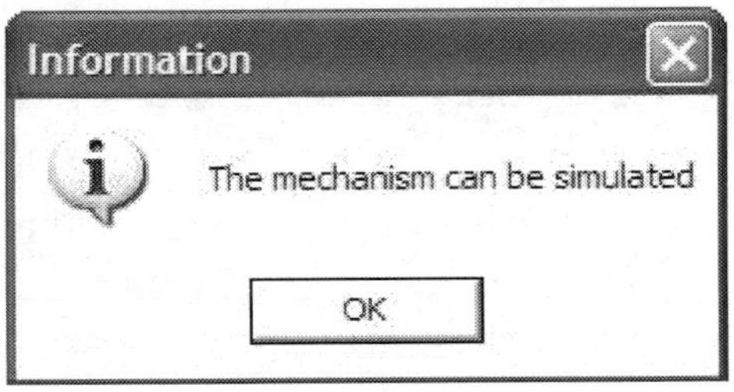

In order to animate the mechanism, there are two ways that one can proceed to simulate the basic motion of the mechanism (without regard to the time parameter). We will illustrate both methods.

Method 1 – Simulation with Commands:

Select the **Simulation with Command** icon  from the **Simulation** toolbar

. The **Kinematics Simulation** pop up box below appears.

Note that by pressing the **Less** <<Less button, the compact version of this box is displayed.

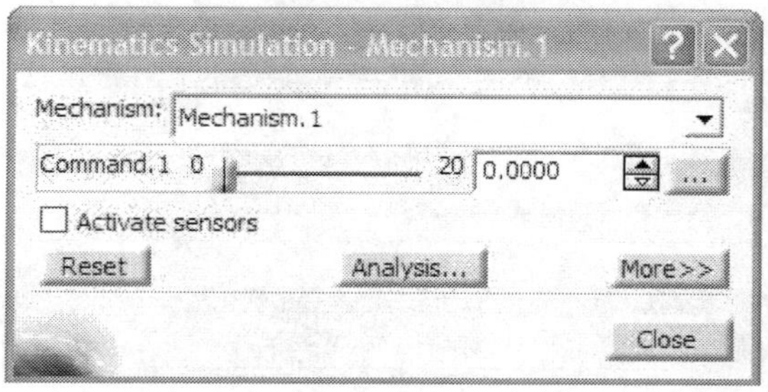

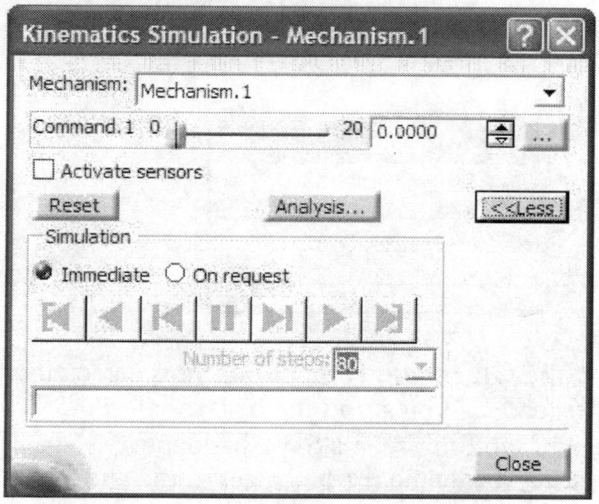

The Upper and Lower limits set earlier are reflected in the scroll bar in the window. In this case the range is 0 in to 20 in. The number of steps represents resolution for capturing the motion. There are two radio buttons present in the full version of the window. If **Immediate** is selected, as the scroll bar is being dragged from the left to right, the motion can be observed on the screen. This is displayed in the next page. Upon reaching the end of the base, use the **Reset** Reset button to return the block to the starting position. This can also be achieved by dragging the scroll bar to the position 0.

Note that the range for the distance traveled can be set by pressing on the button 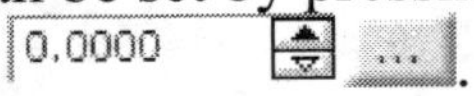.
In the resulting pop up box, the new range can be imposed. Anything larger than 21 inches makes the block pass the other end of the base.

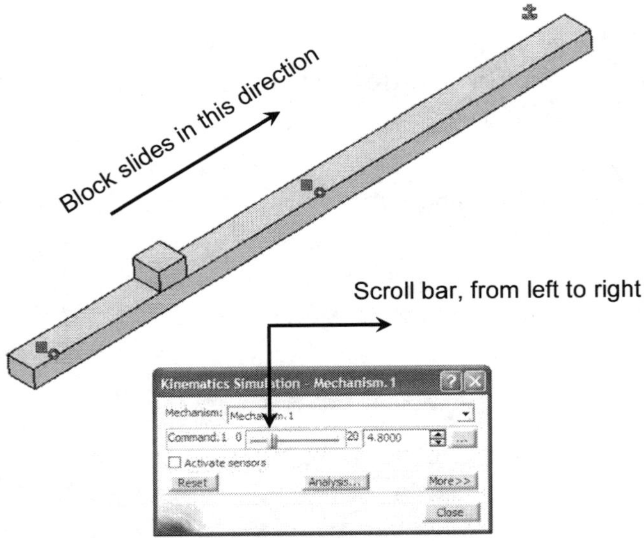

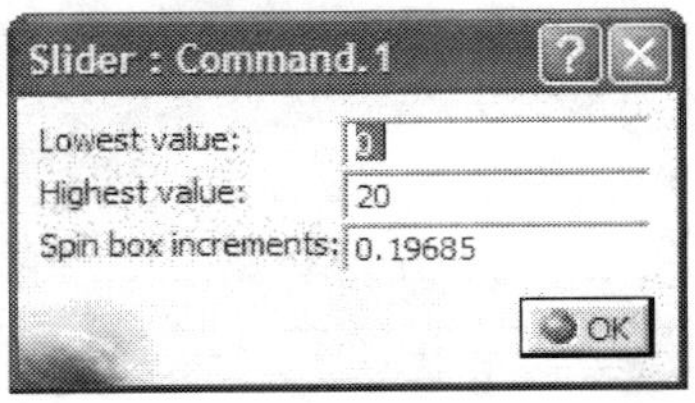

If the **On request** radio button is selected instead, as you scroll the bar from left to right, nothing seems to be happening. However, when the bar reaches the end corresponding to 20 inches, press the  video player button and watch the block travel along the base.

Upon reaching the end of the base, use the **Reset** 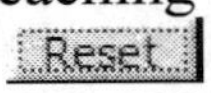 button to return the block to the starting position. This can also be achieved by dragging the scroll bar to the position 0.

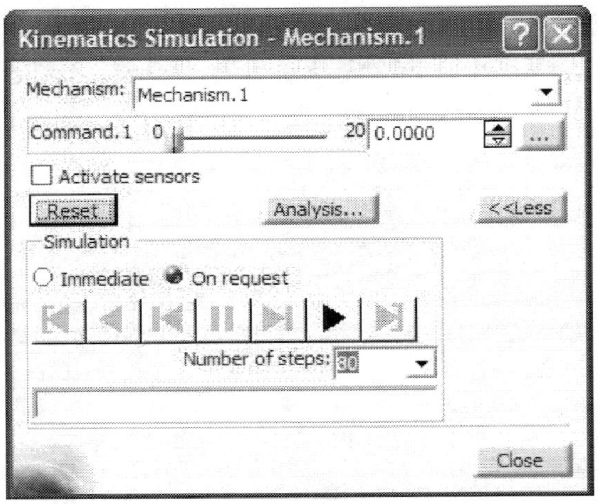

Also note that a **Command.1** has appeared as a branch of the tree.

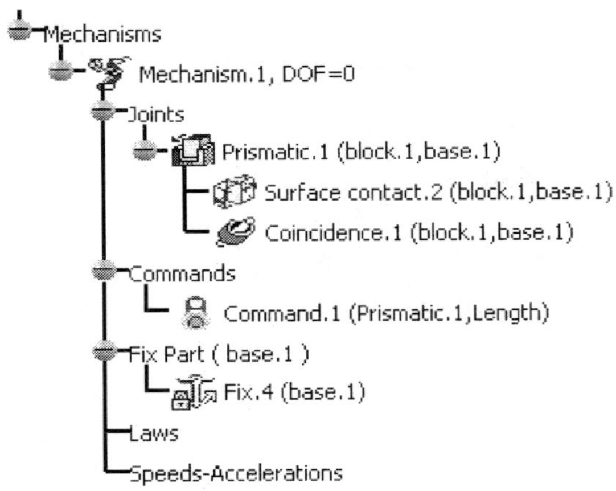

Method 2 – Simulation:

Select the **Simulation** icon  from the **DMU Generic Animation** toolbar 

. This enables you to choose the mechanism to be animated if there are several present. In this case, select Mechanism.1 and close the window.

As soon as the window is closed, a Simulation branch is added to the tree.

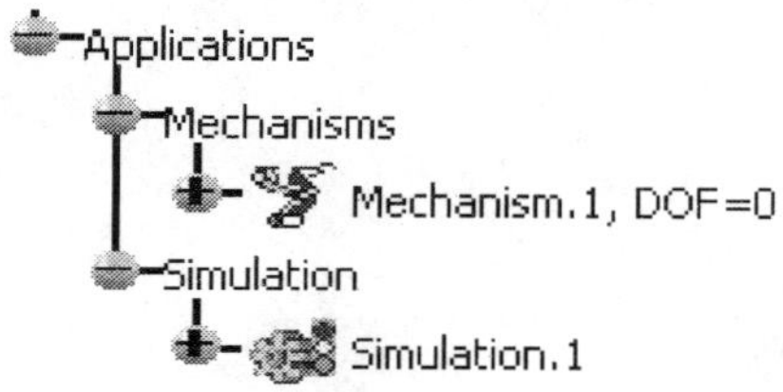

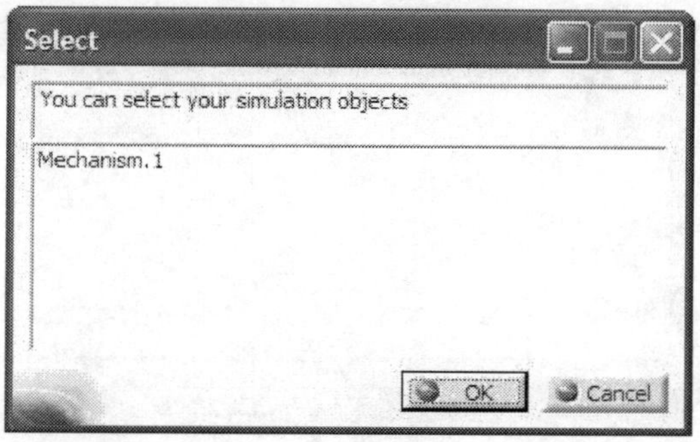

In addition, the two pop up boxes shown below appear.

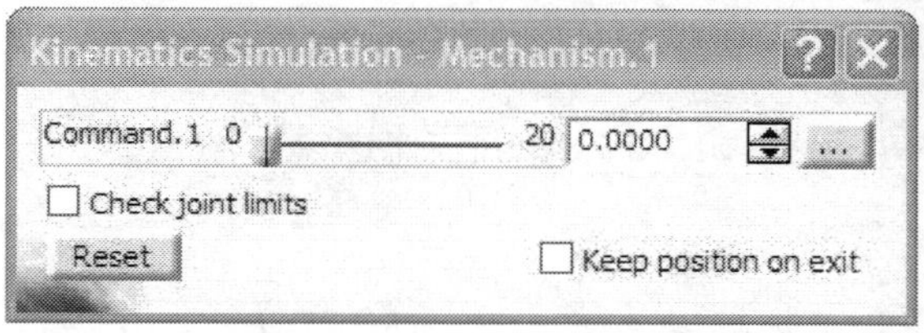

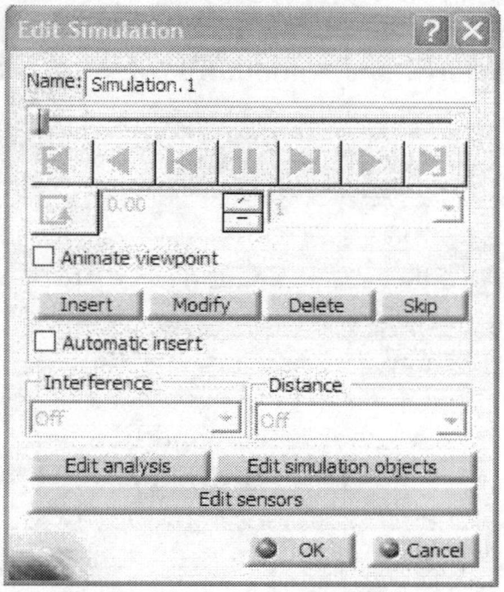

This is very similar to the **Kinematics Simulation** pop up box that appeared in Method 1 above. As you scroll the bar in this toolbar from left to right, the block begins is travel from one end of the base to the other.

When the scroll bar in the **Kinematics Simulation** pop up box reaches the right extreme end, select the **Insert** button 

in the **Edit Simulation** pop up box shown above. This activates the video player buttons shown .

Return the block to its original position by picking the **Jump to Start** button .

Note that the **Change Loop Mode** button  is also active now.

Upon selecting the **Play Forward** button, the block makes a fast jump to the other end of the base.

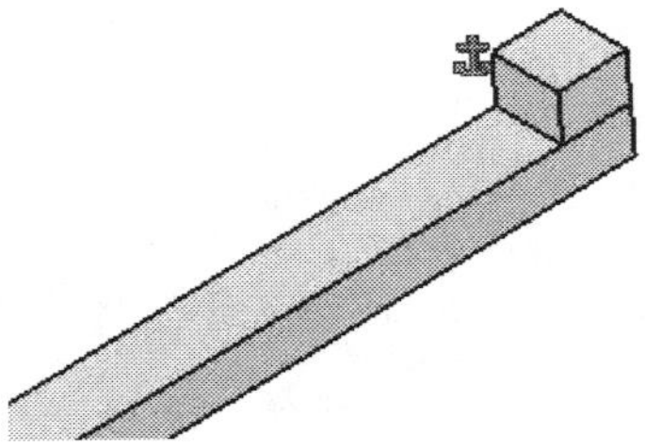

In order to slow down the motion of the block, select a different **interpolation step**, such as 0.04.

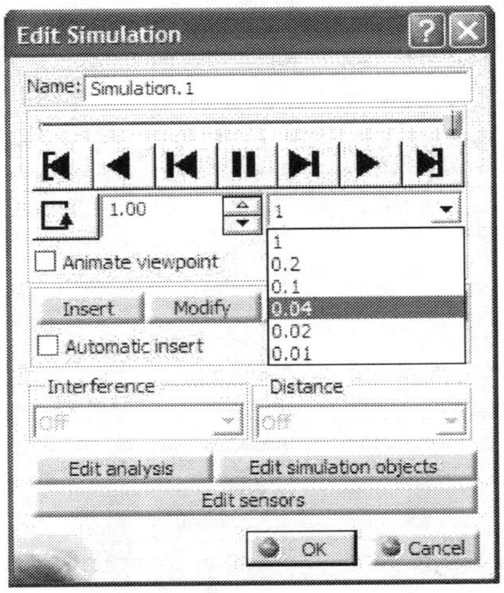

Upon changing the interpolation step to 0.04, return the block to its original position by picking the **Jump to Start** button. Apply **Play Forward** button and observe the slow and smooth translation of the block.

Select the **Compile Simulation** icon from the **Generic Animation** toolbar

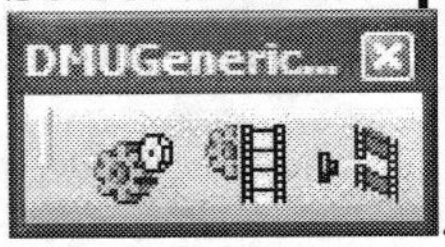

. Choose **Generate an animation file** and press the **File name** button | File name ... | allows you to set the location and name of the animation file to be generated as displayed below.

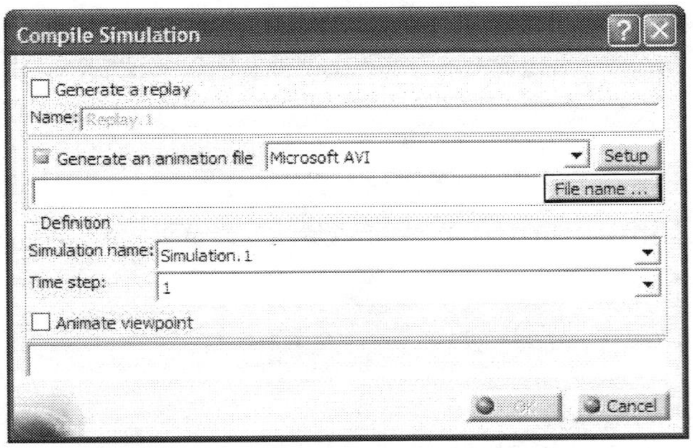

Select a suitable path and file name and change the **Time step** to be 0.04 to produce a slow moving block in an AVI file.

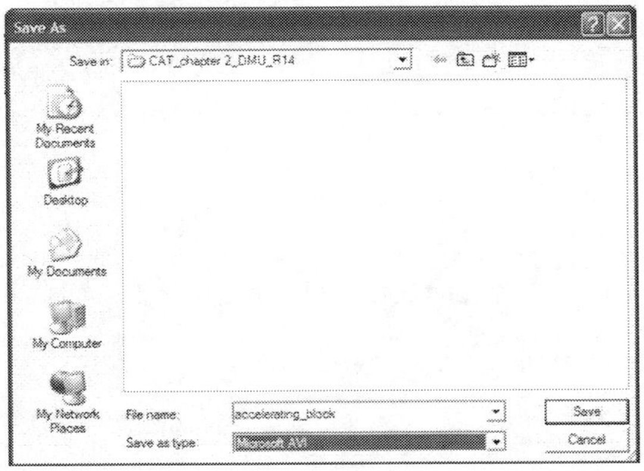

The completed pop up box is displayed for your reference.

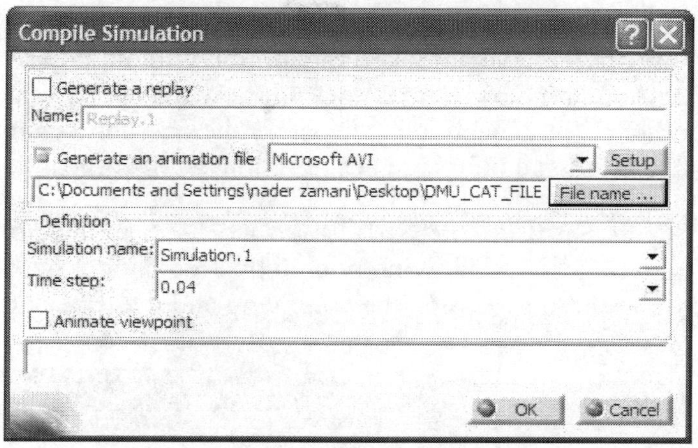

AS the file is being generated, the block slowly translates. The resulting AVI file can be viewed with the Windows Media Player.

In the event that an AVI file is not needed, but one wishes to play the animation, repeatedly, a **Replay** needs to be generated. Therefore, in the **Compile Simulation** box, check the **Generate a replay** button.

Note that in this case most of the previously available options are dimmed out.
A **Replay.1** branch has also been added to the tree.

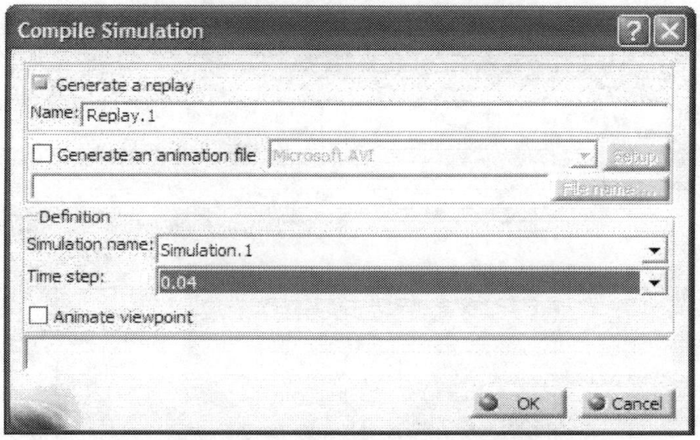

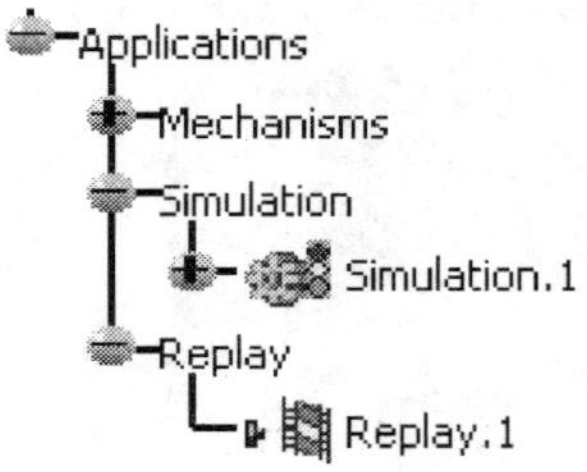

Select the **Replay** icon  from the **Generic Animation** toolbar. Double clock on **Replay.1** in the tree and the **Replay** pop up box appears. Experiment with the different choices of the **Change Loop Mode** buttons . The block can be returned to the original position by picking the **Jump to Start** button .

The **skip ratio** (which is chosen to be x 1 in the right box) controls the speed of the **Replay**.

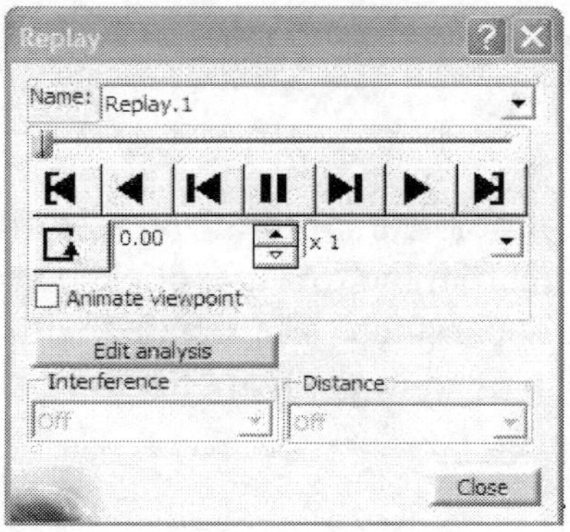

4 Creating Laws in the Motion and Simulating the Desired Kinematics

Thus far you have animated the motion without regard to the time based kinematics specified in the problem. You will now introduce some time based physics into the problem. The objective is to specify the position versus time function. This indirectly specifies the velocity and acceleration versus time.

Click on **Simulation with Laws** icon  in the **Simulation** toolbar. You will get the following pop up box indication that you need to add at least a relation between the command and the time parameter.

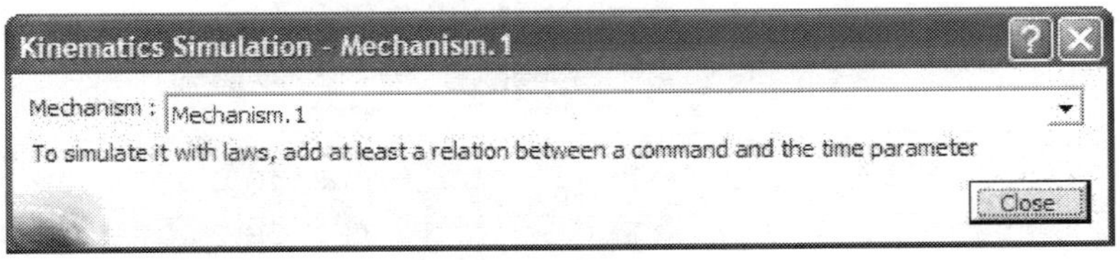

Select the **Formula** icon  from the **Knowledge** toolbar

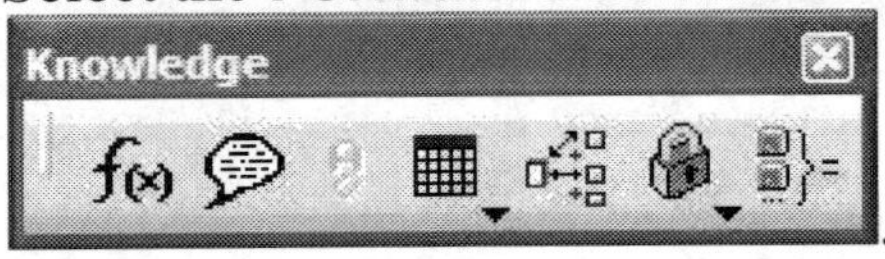

. The pop up box below appears on the screen.

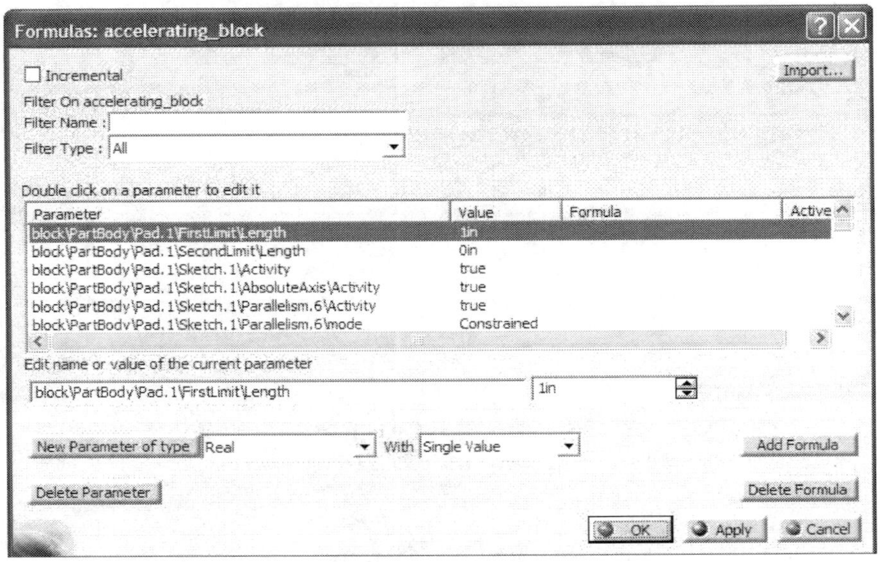

Point the cursor to the **Mechanism.1, DOF=0** branch in the tree and click. The consequence is that only parameters associated with the mechanism are displayed in the **Formulas** box.

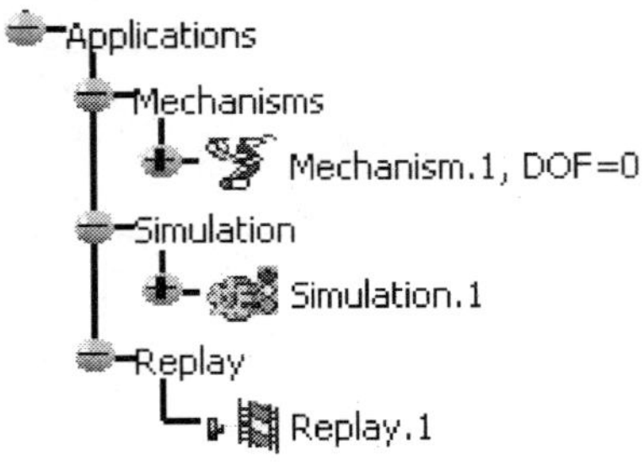

The long list which included all parameters associated with the **accelerating_blockb** assembly is now reduced to two parameters as indicated in the box.

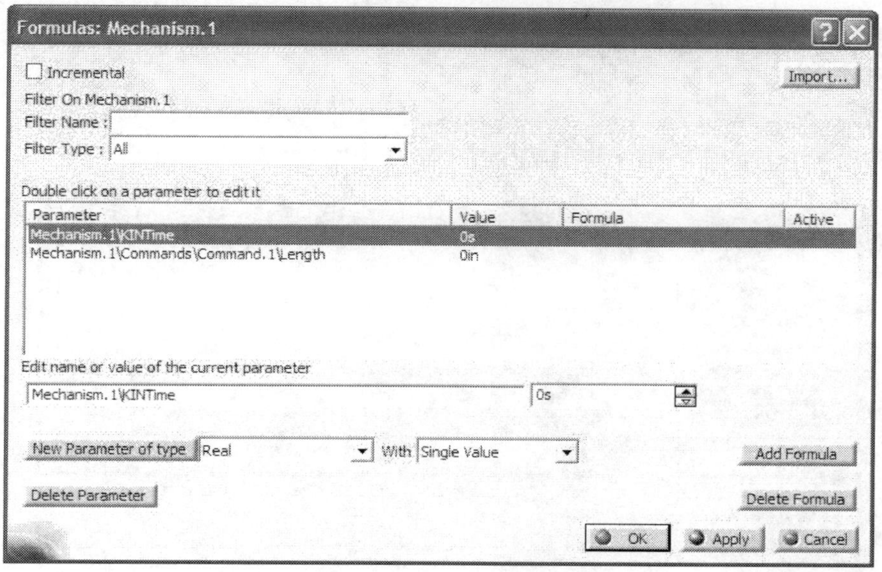

Select the entry **Mechanism.1\Commands\Command.1\Length** and press the **Add Formula** button 

. This action takes you to the **Formula Editor** box.

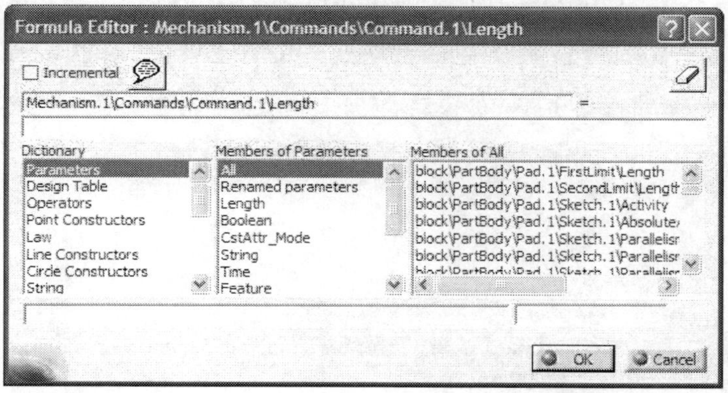

Pick the **Time** entry from the middle column (i.e., **Members of Parameters**).

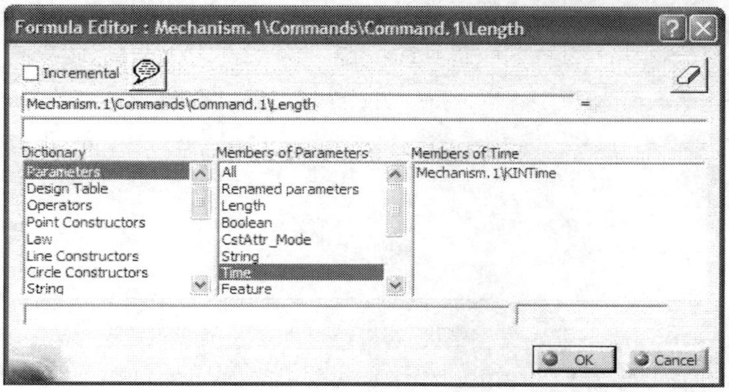

Type in the right hand side of the equality so that the formula becomes as is shown below. The units will be explained shortly.

$$Mechanism.1 \backslash Commands \backslash Command.1 \backslash Length =$$
$$(1in) * (Mechanism.1 \backslash KINTime) **2 / (1s) **2$$

Therefore, the completed **Formula Editor** box becomes

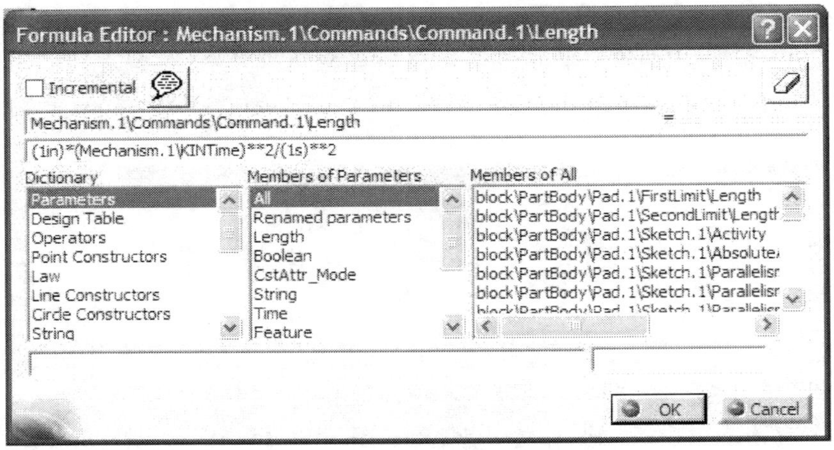

Upon accepting **OK**, the formula is recorded in the **Formulas** pop up box as shown below.

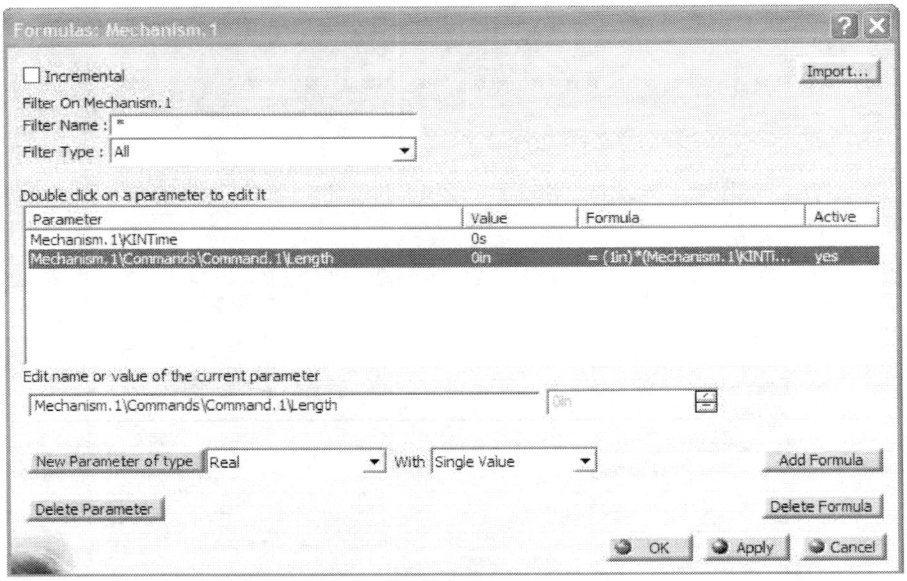

The units on the formula introduced above warrant an explanation. Note that the left hand side of the equality is a Length parameter therefore the entire right hand side should be reducing to inches. This is why, $(Mechanism.1 \backslash KINTime)**2$ has been nondimensionalized by introducing a division by (1s)**2. Here, "s" refers to seconds. Finally, (1in) has been introduced as a term to transform the entire expression to inches. In the event that the formula has different units at the different sides of the equality you will get **Warning** messages such as the one shown below.

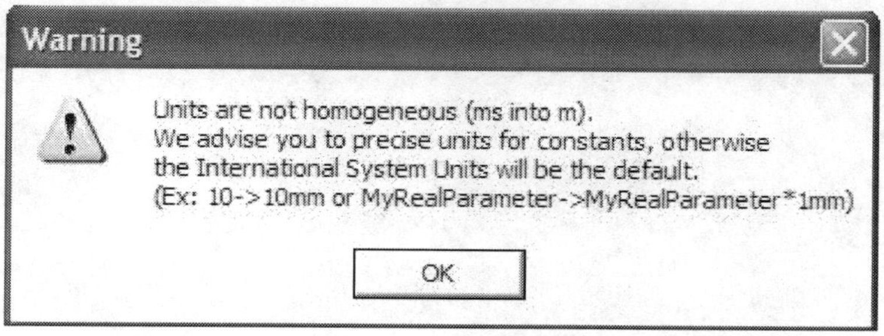

We are spared the warning message because the formula has been properly inputted. Note that the introduced law has appeared in **Law** branch of the tree.

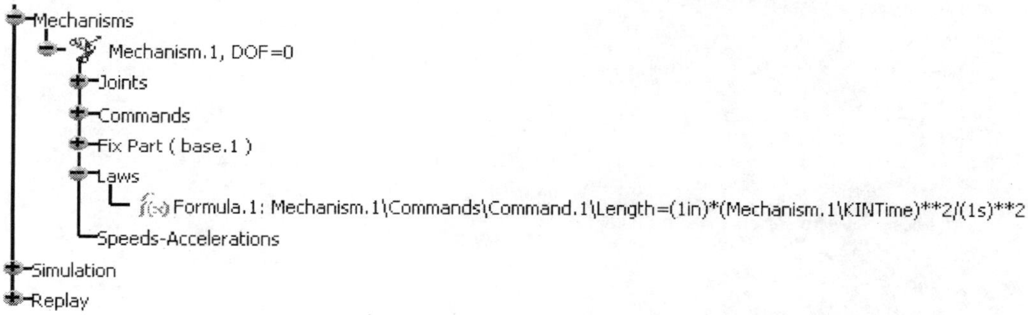

Keep in mind that our interest is to plot the position, velocity and acceleration generated by this motion.

Select the **Speed and Acceleration** icon  from the **DMU Kinematics** toolbar

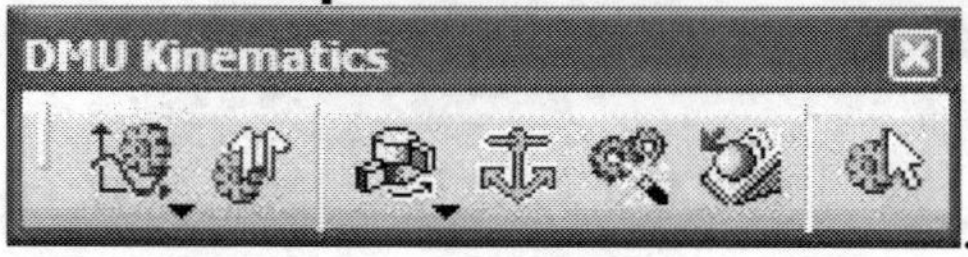

. The pop up box below appears on the Screen.

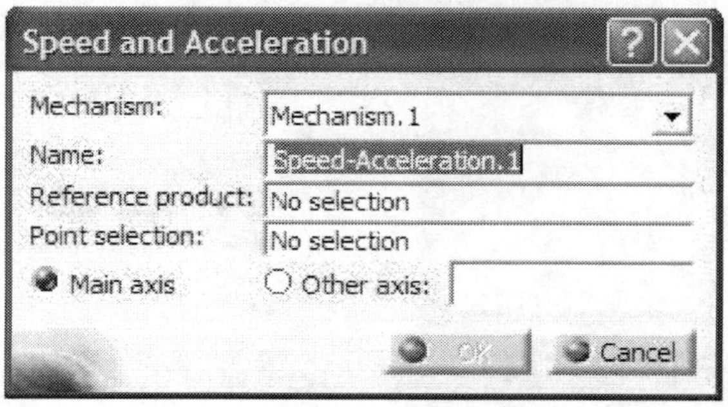

For the **Reference product,** select the **base** from the screen or the tree. For the **Point selection**, pick a vertex on the top corner of the **block** as shown in the sketch below.

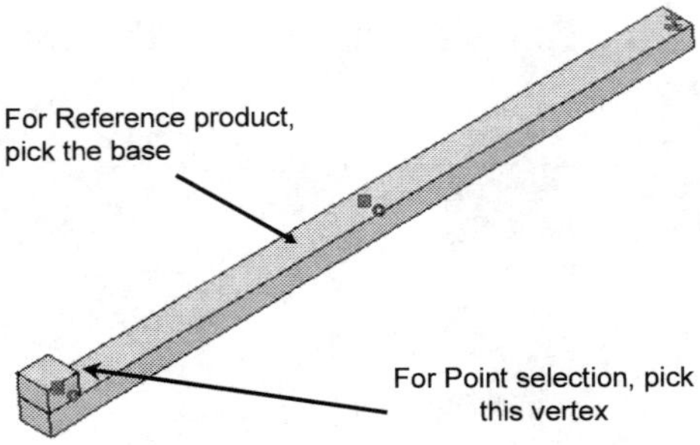

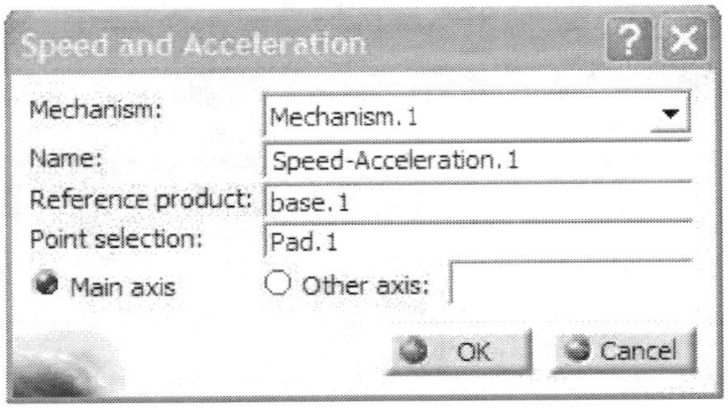

Note that the **Speed and Acceleration.1** has appeared in the tree.

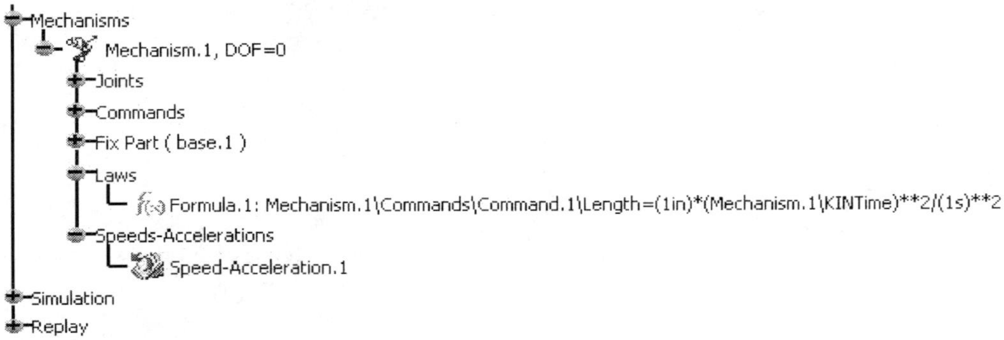

Click on **Simulation with Laws** icon in the **Simulation** toolbar 

. This results in the **Kinematics Simulation** pop up box shown below.

Note that the default time duration is 10 seconds.
To change this value, click on the button [...]. In the resulting pop up box, change the time duration to 4.47s. Recall that this is the time duration for the block to travel 20 in.

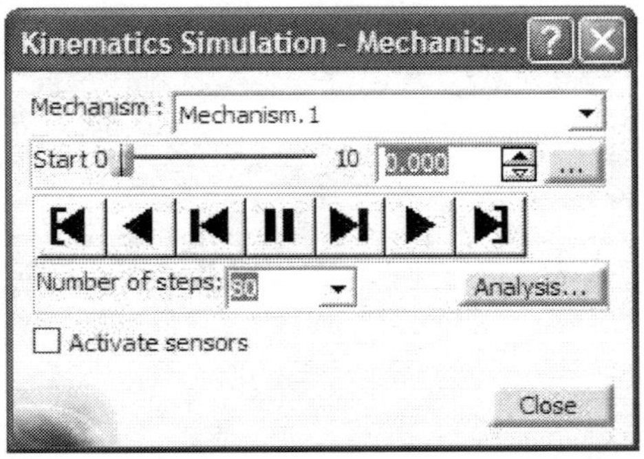

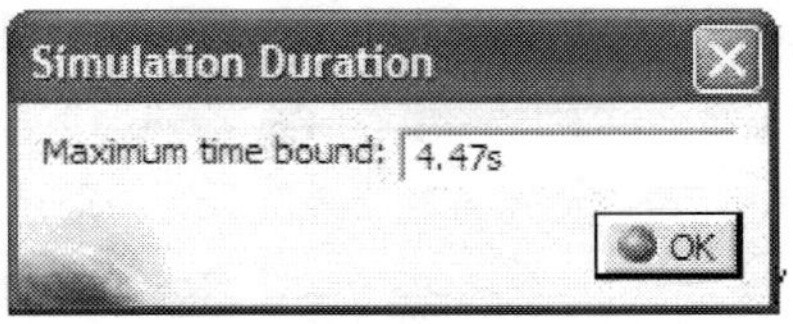

The scroll bar upper limit is now 4.47s.

Check the **Activate sensors** box, at the bottom right corner.

You will next have to make certain selections from the accompanying **Sensors** box.

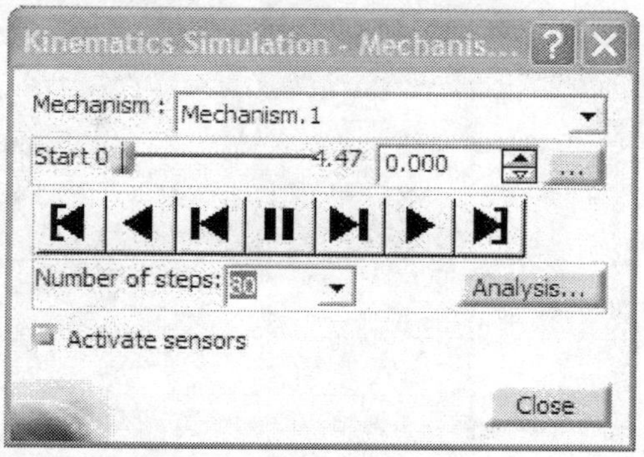

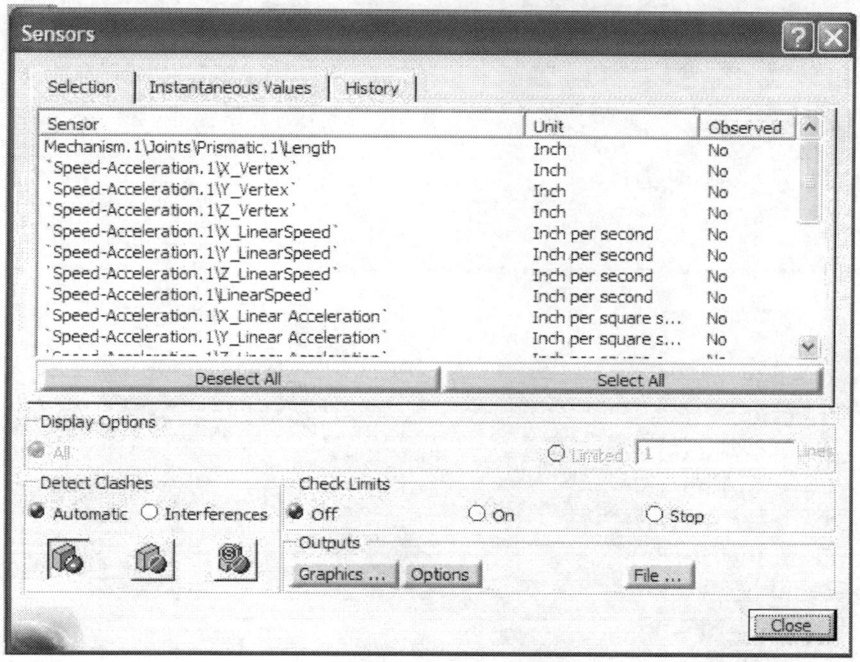

Click on the following items

Mechanism.1\Joints\Prismatic.1\Length
Speed-Acceleration.1\LinearSpeed
Speed-Acceleration.1\LinearAcceleration

As you make these selections, the last column in the **Sensors** box changes to **Yes** for the corresponding items. This is shown in the next page.

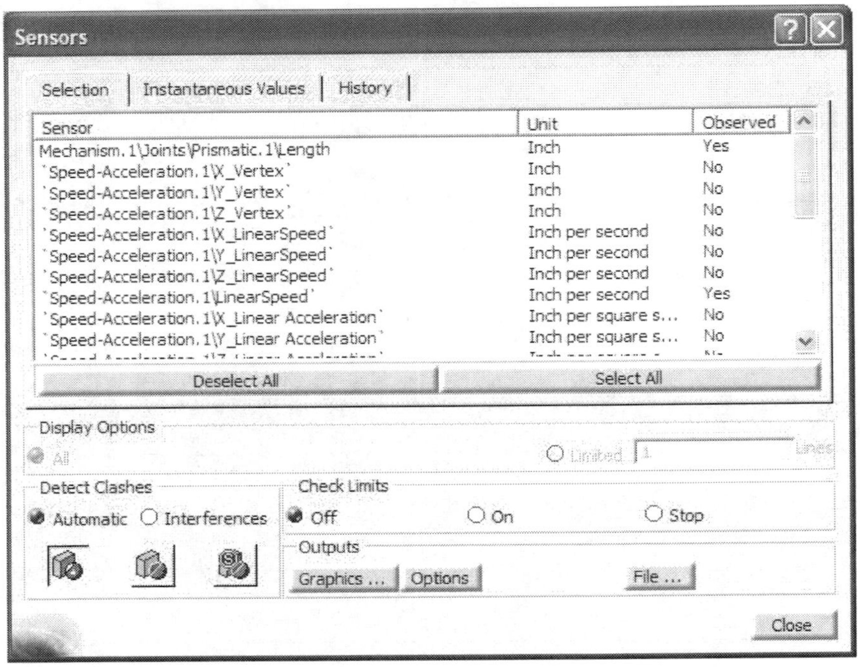

At this point, drag the scroll bar in the **Kinematics Simulation** box. As you do this, the block travels along the base. Once the bar reaches its right extreme point, the block also reaches the end of the base. This corresponds to 4.47 s and traveled distance of 20 in.

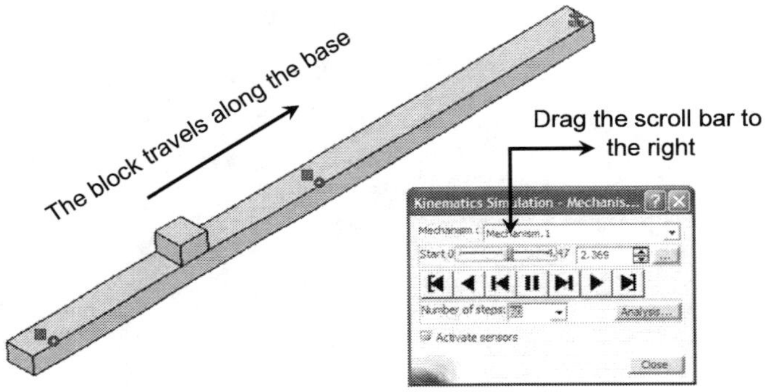

Once the block reaches the end, click on **Graphics** button 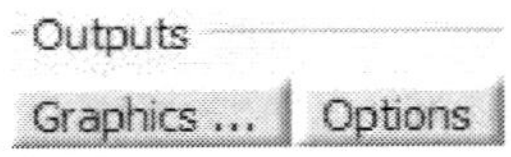 in the **Sensor** box. The result is the plot of the position, velocity and acceleration all on the same axis.

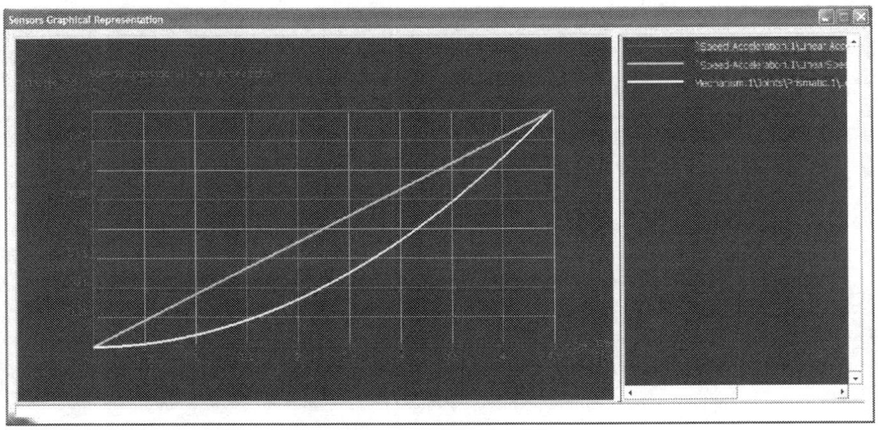

These plots are in perfect agreement with the theoretical results. The plots are deceiving as they all pass though the same point at the top right corner. Note that these plots can be individually looked at by pointing the cursor to them, right clicking, and choosing hide. It is only then that they can be compared with the analytical expressions.

The block can be returned to the original position by picking the **Jump to Start** button . However, this traces another set of graphs that is not desirable. One can use the **History** tab in the **Sensors** pop up box and **Clear** the data.

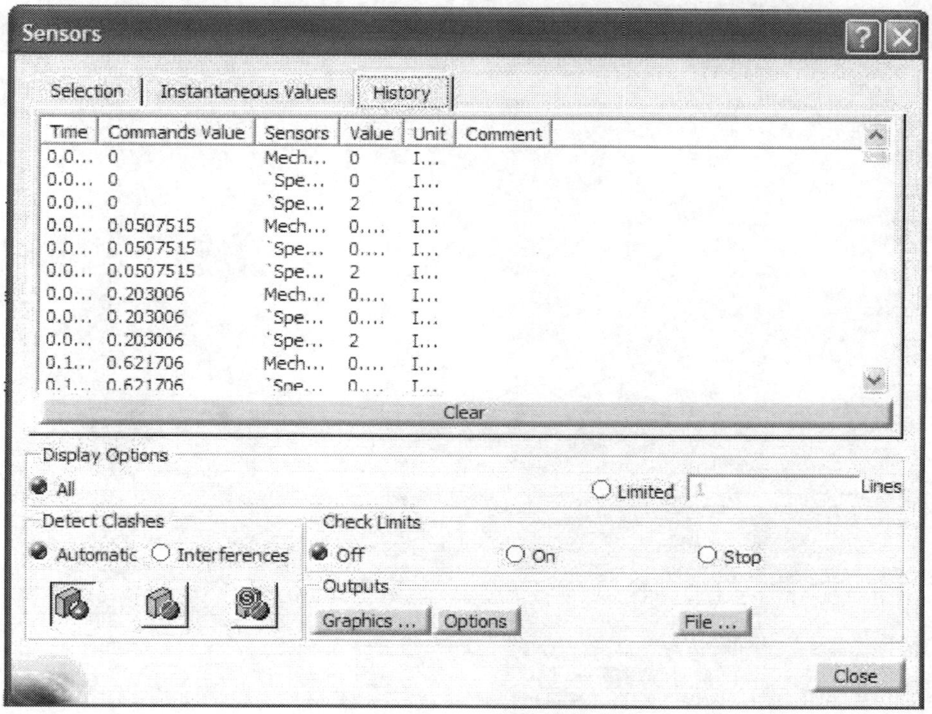

You can now close the **Sensors** box.

This concludes this tutorial.

NOTES:

Chapter 3

An Arm Rotating about a Revolute Joint

Introduction

In this tutorial you create an arm which rotates at a constant angular velocity about an axis. A revolute joint is used to simulate this simple mechanism and plots of the components of velocity and acceleration at the tip of the arm are generated.

1 Problem Statement

The arm of length $R = 5$ inches shown below is rotating at a constant angular velocity of $\omega = 2\pi$ rad/s about the axis AA. Using the x and y axes, one can show that the position, velocity and acceleration at the tip of the arm are dictated by the following expressions.

$$x = R\cos\omega t \qquad \dot{x} = -R\omega\sin\omega t \qquad \ddot{x} = -R\omega^2\cos\omega t$$

$$y = R\sin\omega t \qquad \dot{y} = R\omega\cos\omega t \qquad \ddot{y} = R\omega^2\sin\omega t$$

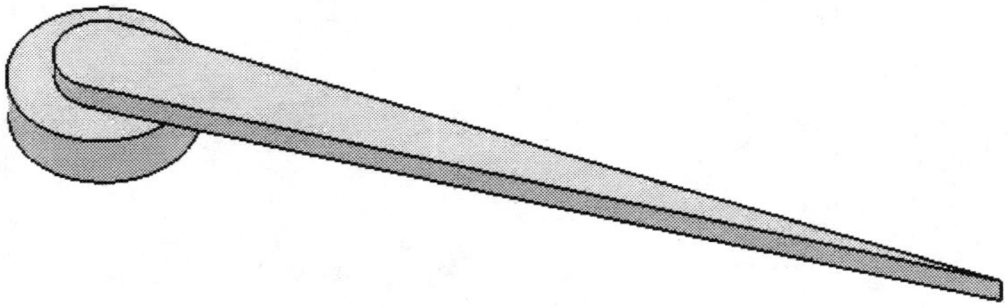

For the parameter values assumed, plots of velocity and acceleration generated in MathCad are displayed below. The units are in/s and in/s^2. Similar plots for the x component of velocity and acceleration will be generated in CATIA later in this tutorial.

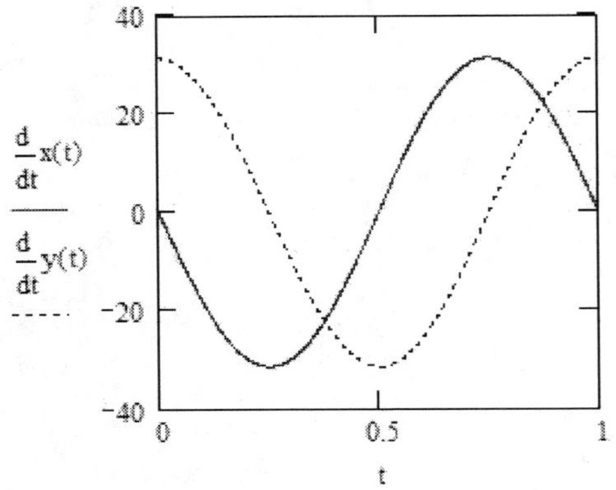

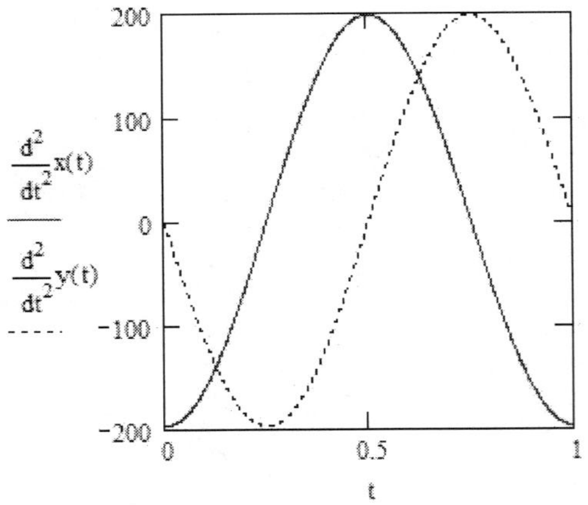

2 Overview of this Tutorial

This tutorial will involve the following steps:

1. Model the two CATIA parts required.
2. Create an assembly (CATIA Product) containing the parts.
3. Constrain the assembly in such a way that the only unconstrained degree of freedom is the rotation of the arm about the axis of the base.
4. Enter the **Digital Mockup** workbench and convert the assembly constraints into a revolute joint representing the desired rotation of the arm about the axis of the base.
5. Simulate the relative motion of the arm base without consideration to time (in other words, without implementing the time based angular velocity given in the problem statement).
6. Adding a formula to implement the time based kinematics.
7. Simulating the desired constant angular velocity motion and generating plots of the results.

3 Creation of the Assembly in Mechanical Design Solutions

Model two parts named **arm** and **base** as shown below with the only critical dimension being R = 5 in. It is assumed that you are sufficiently familiar with CATIA to model these parts fairly quickly.

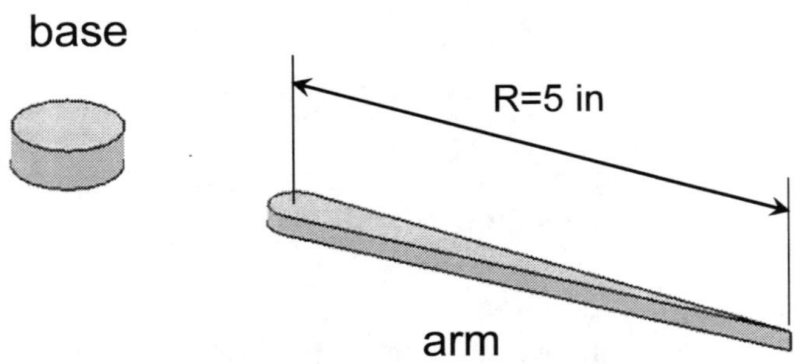

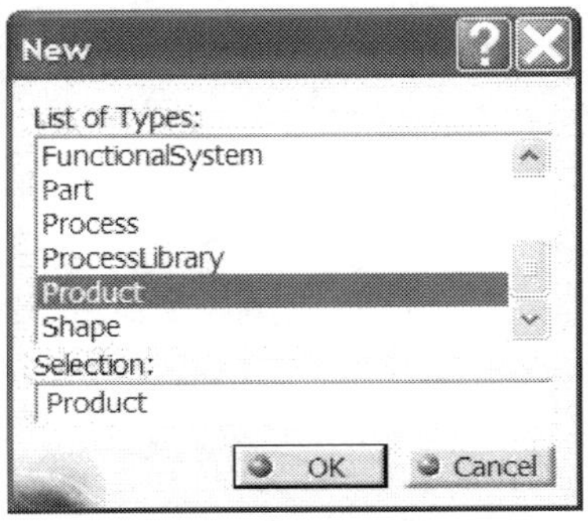

Enter the **Assembly Design** workbench which can be achieved by different means depending on your CATIA customization. For example, from the standard Windows toolbar, select **File > New** . From the box shown on the right, select **Product**. This moves you to the **Assembly Design** workbench and creates an assembly with the default name **Product.1**.

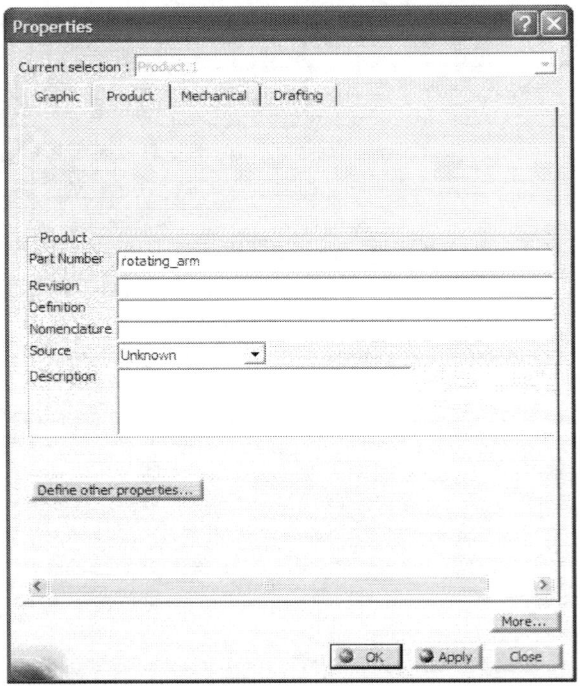

In order to change the default name, move the cursor to **Product.1** in the tree, right click and select **Properties** from the menu list.

From the **Properties** box, select the **Product** tab and in **Part Number** type **rotating_arm**.

This will be the new product name throughout the chapter. The tree on the top left corner of your computer screen should look as displayed below.

The next step is to insert the existing parts block and base into the assembly just created.

From the standard Windows toolbar, select **Insert > Existing Component**.
From the **File Selection** pop up box choose **arm** and **base**. Remember that in CATIA multiple selections are made with the **Ctrl** key.
The tree is modified to indicate that the parts have been inserted.

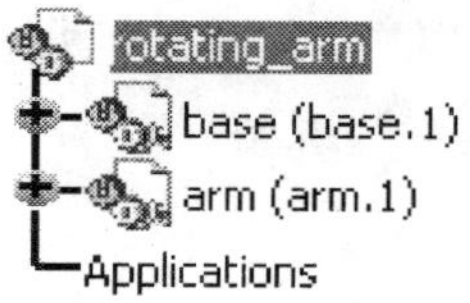

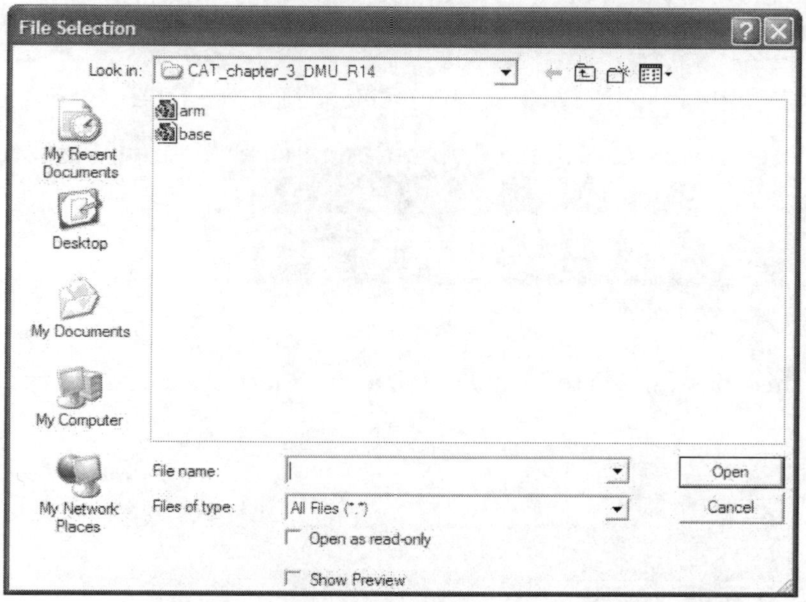

The best way of saving your work is to save the entire assembly.
Double click on the top branch of the tree. This is to ensure that you are in the **Assembly Design** workbench.
Select the **Save** icon . The **Save As** pop up box allows you to rename if desired.
The default name is the **rotating_arm**.

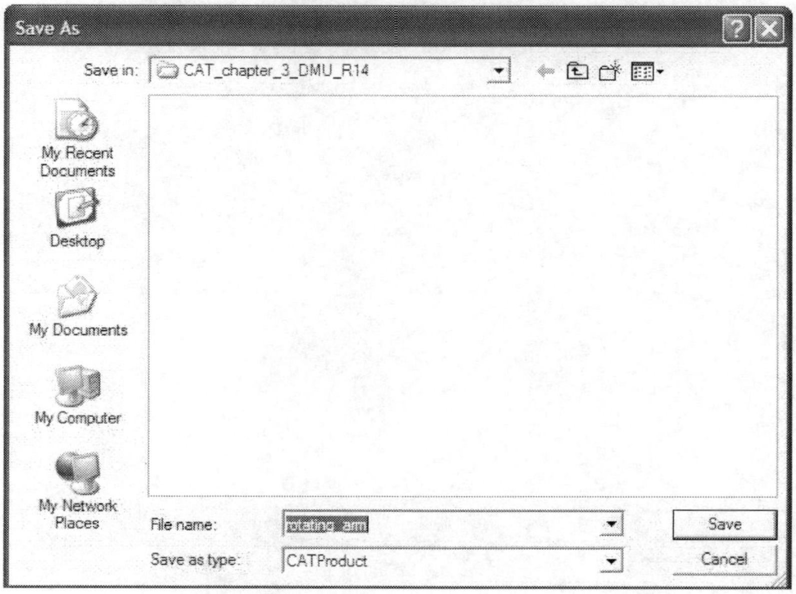

Your next task is to impose assembly constraints. Initially, the arm is free to move with respect to the base in all six degrees of freedom (dof), namely translation along any of the three principle axes and rotation about any of the three axes. The objective in applying the assembly constraints is to remove all these relative dof except for rotation of the axis of the arm about the axis of the base. If this is done properly, CATIA will be able to automatically convert the assembly constraints to a revolute joint in the mechanism.

We will begin by creating a coincidence between the axis of the arm and the axis of the base. To do so, pick the **Coincidence** icon  from **Constraints** toolbar

. Select the axis of the **base** and the **arm** as shown below.

This constraint is reflected in the appropriate branch of the tree.

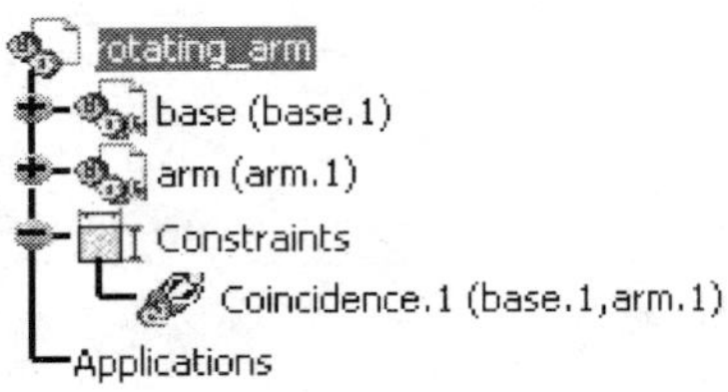

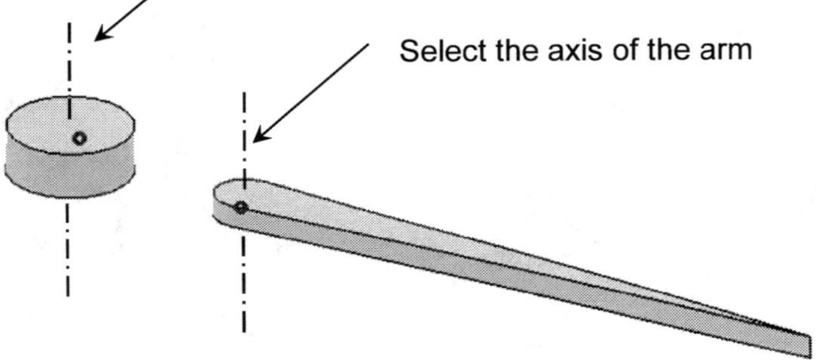

This coincidence constraint just created between the two axes removes all but two relative dof between the arm and the base. The remaining two dof are rotation of the arm about the base (a desired dof), and translation of the axis of the base along the axis of the arm (a dof we wish to remove). A contact constraint between the lower surface of the arm and the upper surface of the base will remove the undesired translation. To create this constraint, pick the **Contact** icon  from **Constraints** toolbar and select the surfaces shown below. The tree is modified to reflect this constraint.

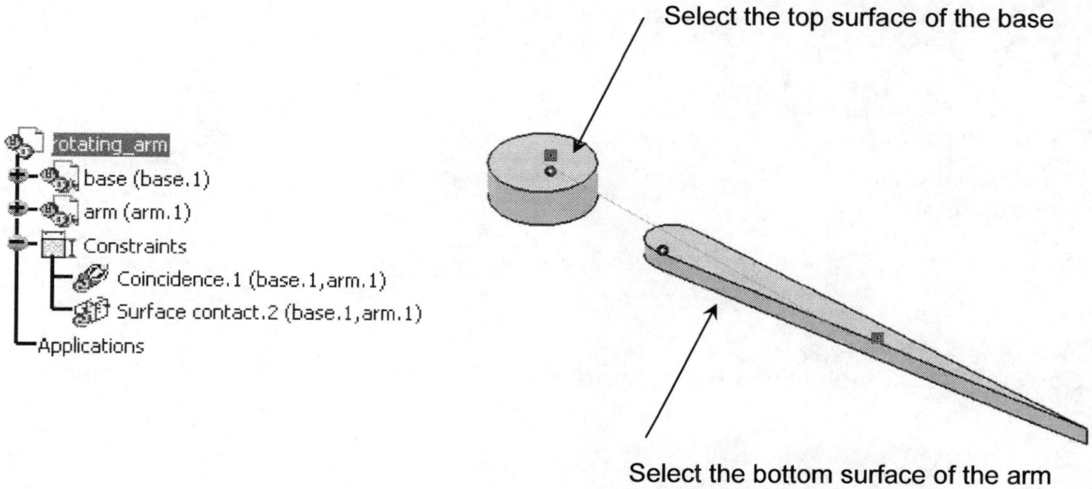

Use **Update** icon  to enforce the two constraints just created resulting in relative position the two parts similar to as shown below.

Note that the **Update** icon  no longer appears on the constraints branches.

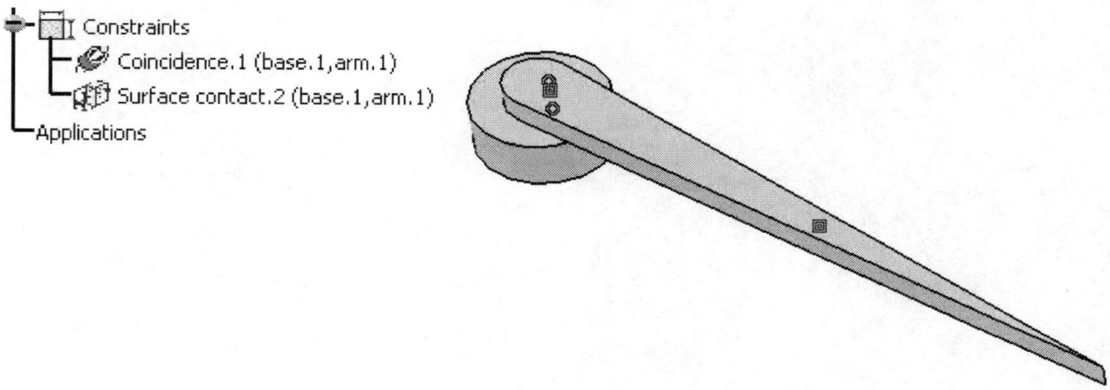

Finally, an anchor constraint will be applied to the fix the position and orientation of the base in space. This constraint could have been applied before the above constraints, but since we did not do so, we will do it now. To apply the anchor constraint, pick the **Anchor** icon from **Constraints** toolbar and select the **base** from the tree or from the screen.

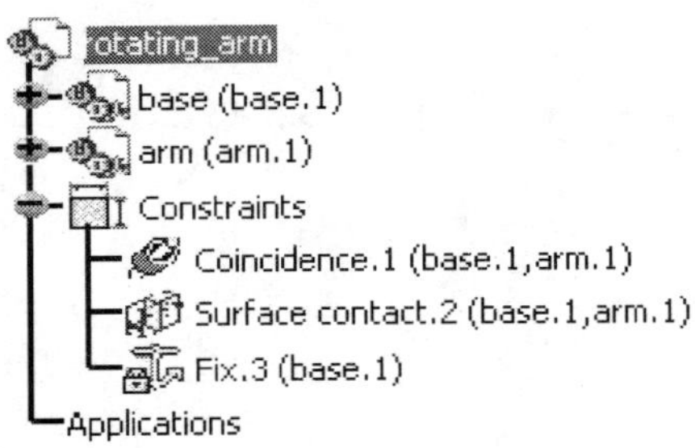

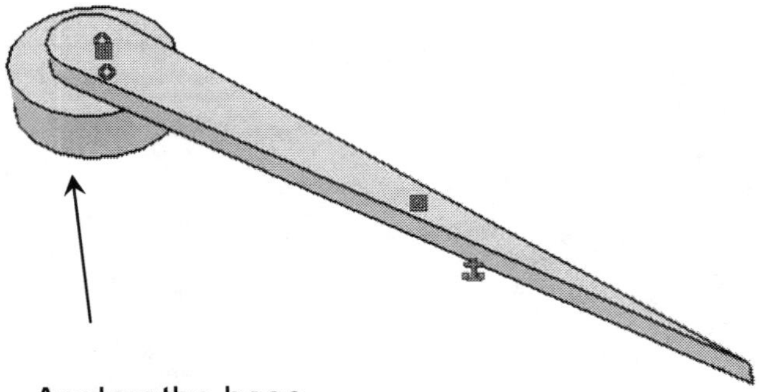

Anchor the base

The assembly is complete and we can proceed to the **Digital Mockup** workbench.

4 Creating Joints in the Digital Mockup Workbench

The **Digital Mockup** workbench is quite extensive but we will only deal with the **DMU Kinematics module**. To get there you can use the standard Windows toolbar as shown below. **Start > Digital Mockup > DMU Kinematics.**

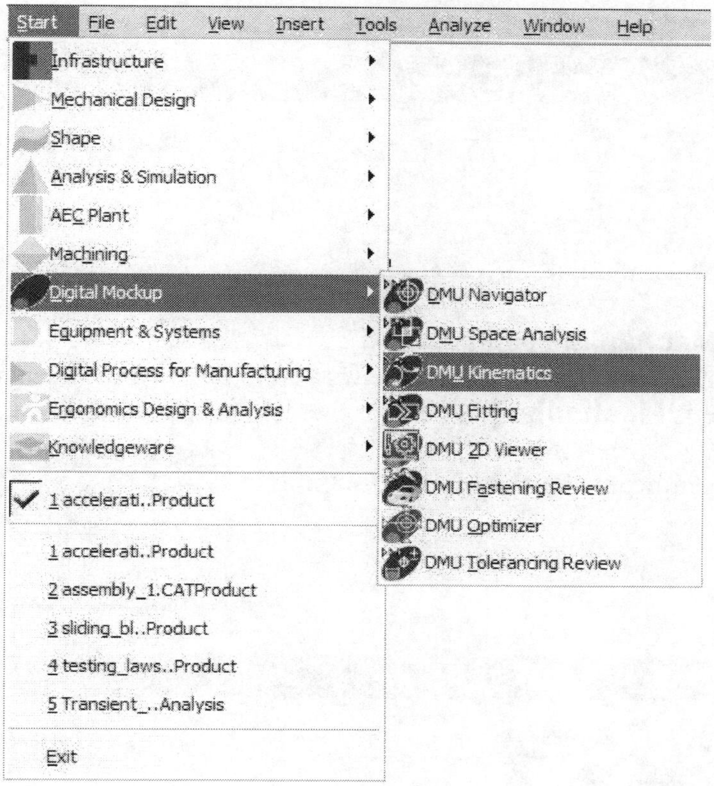

Select the **Assembly Constraints Conversion** icon  from the **DMU Kinematics** toolbar 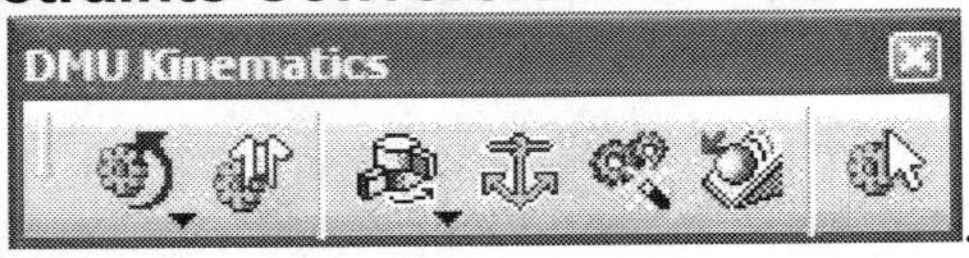

. This icon allows you to create most common joints automatically from the existing assembly constraints. The pop up box below appears.

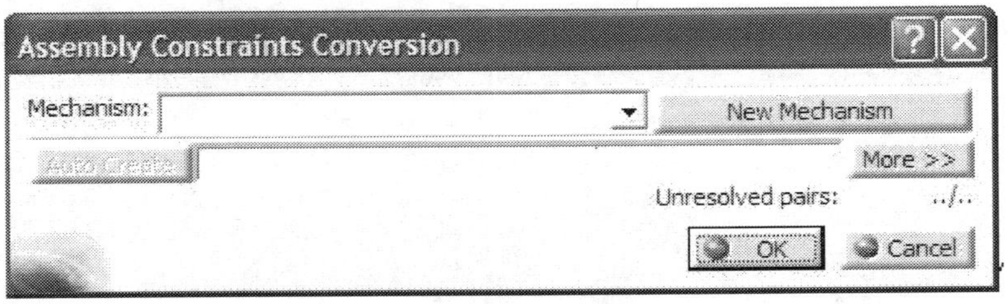

Select the **New Mechanism** button 

.
This leads to another pop up box which allows you to name your mechanism. The default name is **Mechanism.1**. Accept the default name by pressing **OK**.

Note that the box indicates **Unresolved pairs: 1/1**

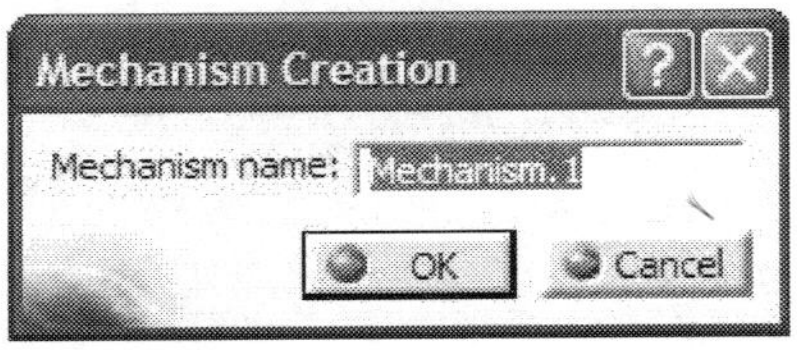

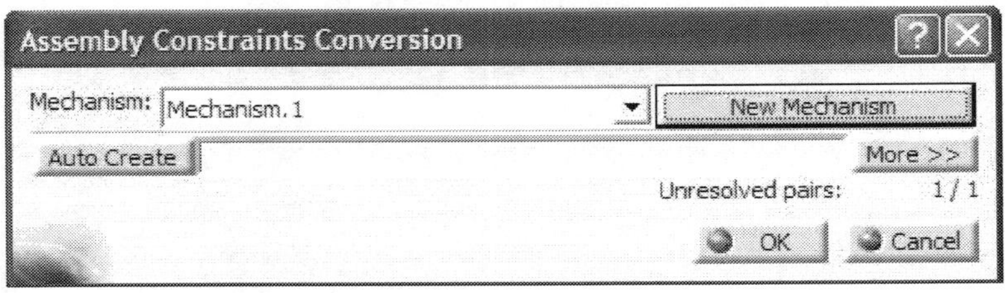

Select the **Auto Create** button 

. Then if the **Unresolved pairs** becomes **0/1**, things are moving in the right direction.

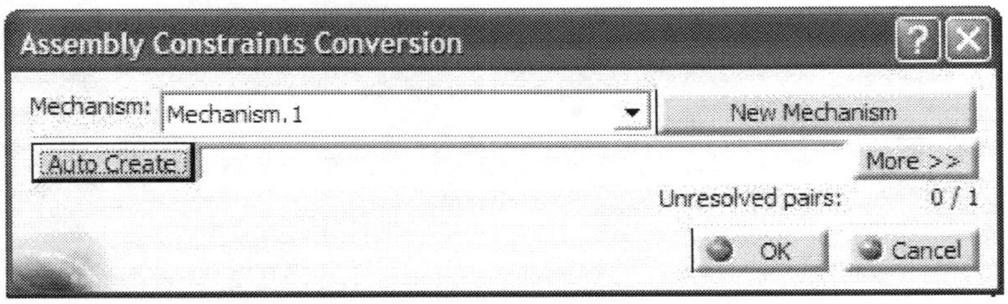

Note that the tree becomes longer by having an **Application** Branch. The expanded tree is displayed below. It clearly indicates the existence of a **Revolute.1** Joint and a Fixed Part **Fix.4**. The **DOF** is 1 which represents the rotation of the arm around the base axis.

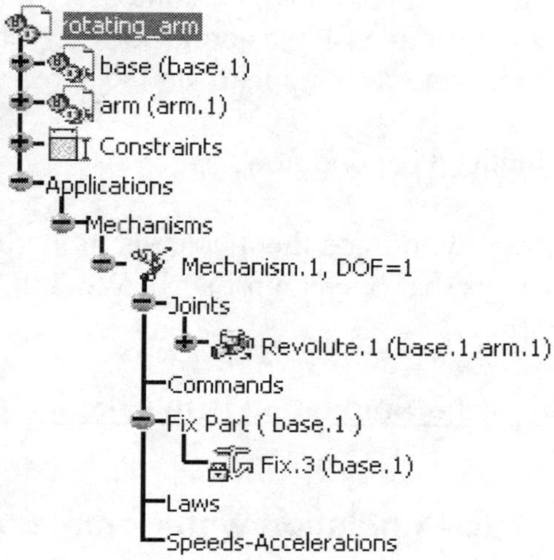

Note that your prismatic joint was created based on the assembly constraints created earlier and the **Assembly Constraints Conversion** icon 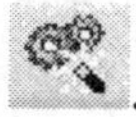.
In the event that automatic assembly constraints conversion does not produce the desired joint or joints, a revolute joint (and any other joint) can be created directly using the **Kinematics Joints** toolbar shown below.

In order to animate the mechanism, you need to remove the one degree of freedom present. This will be achieved by turning **Revolute.1** into an **Angle driven** joint. Double click on **Revolute.1** in the tree. The pop up box below appears.

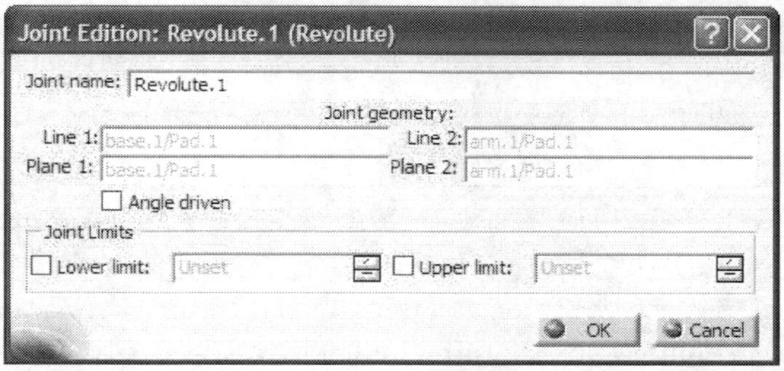

Check the **Angle driven** box and change the **Lower limit** and **Upper limit** to read as indicated below. Keep in mind that these limits can also be changed elsewhere.

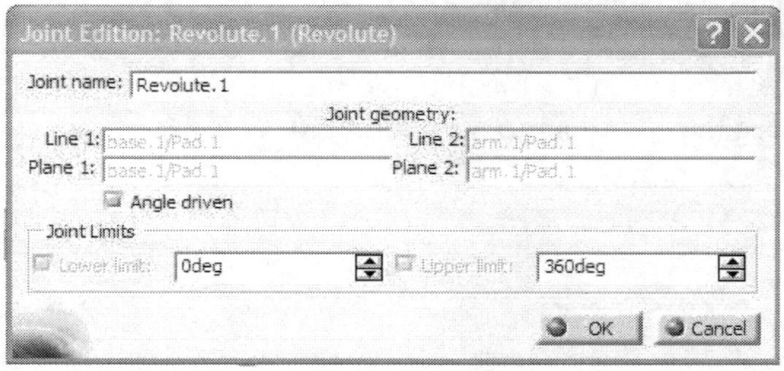

Upon closing the above box and assuming that everything else was done correctly, the following message appears on the screen.

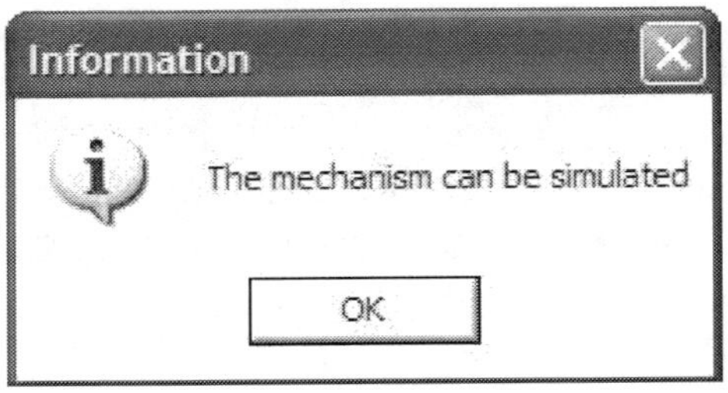

This indeed is good news.

In order to animate the mechanism, there are two ways that one can proceed. We will look at both.

Method 1 – Simulation with Commands:

Select the **Simulation with Command** icon  from the **Simulation** toolbar  . The **Kinematics Simulation** pop up box below appears.

Note that by pressing the **Less**  button, the compact version of this box is displayed.

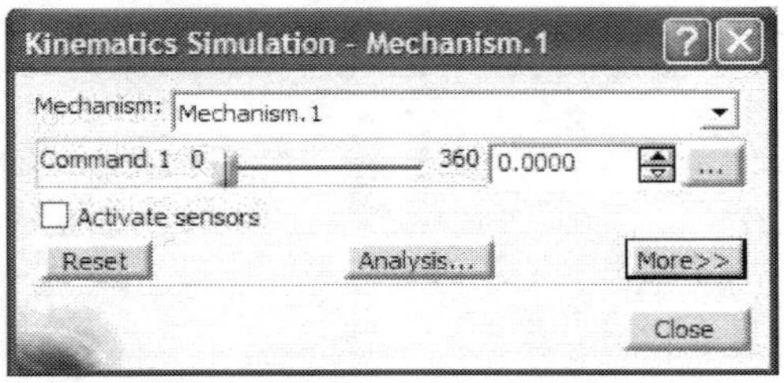

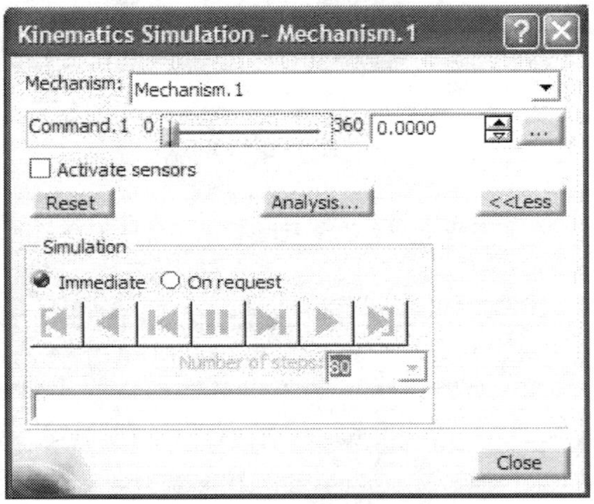

The Upper and Lower limits set earlier of 0 and 360°, respectively, are reflected in the scroll bar in the window. The number of steps represents resolution for capturing the motion. There are two radio buttons present: **Immediate** and **On Request**. If **Immediate** is selected, as the scroll bar is being dragged from the left to right, the motion can be observed on the screen.
This is displayed in the next page. Upon reaching the end of one revolution, use the **Reset** 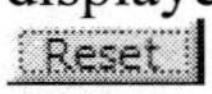 button to return the block to the starting position. This can also be achieved by dragging the scroll bar to the position 0.

Note that the range for the revolute joint can be set by pressing on the button 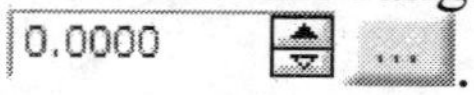.

In the resulting pop up box, the new range can be imposed.

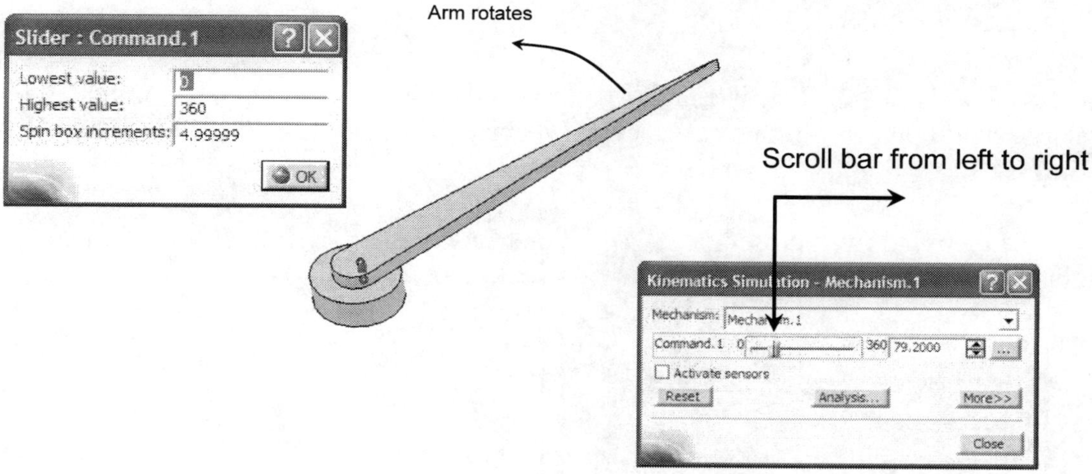

If the **On request** radio button is selected instead, as you scroll the bar from left to right, nothing seems to be happening. However, when the bar reaches then end corresponding to 360˚, press the  video player button and watch the arm rotate around the base.

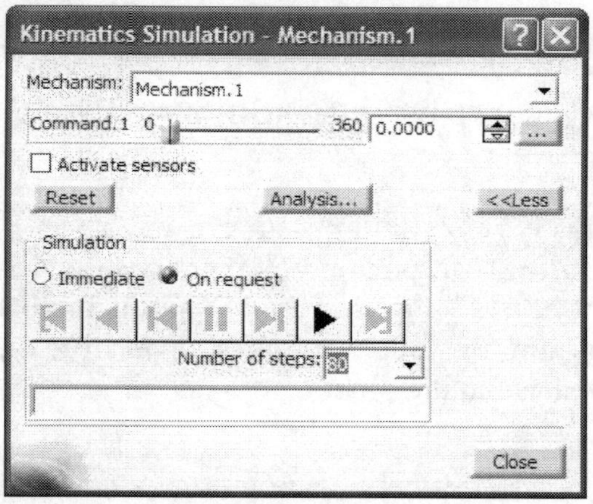

Upon reaching the end of one rotation, use the **Reset**  button to return the block to the starting position. This can also be achieved by dragging the scroll bar to the position 0.

Also note that a **Command.1** has appeared as a branch of the tree.

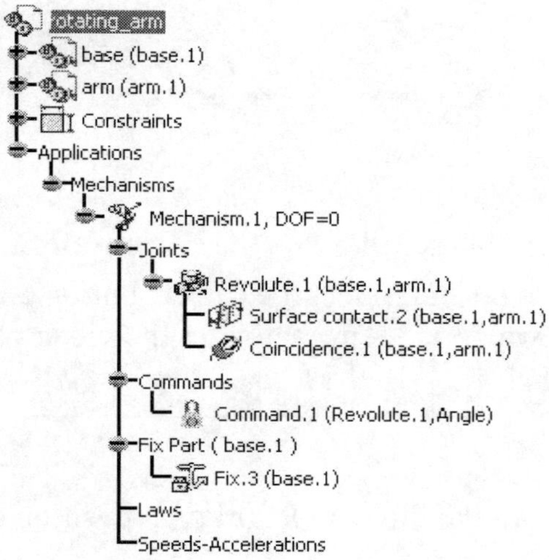

Method 2 – Simulation:

Select the **Simulation** icon  from the **DMU Generic Animation** toolbar 

. This enables you to choose the mechanism to be animated if there are several present. In this case, select Mechanism.1 and close the window by clicking **OK**.

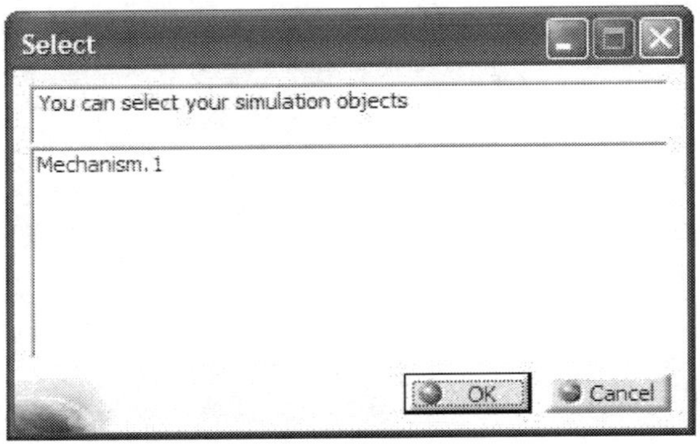

As soon as the window is closed, a Simulation branch is added to the tree.

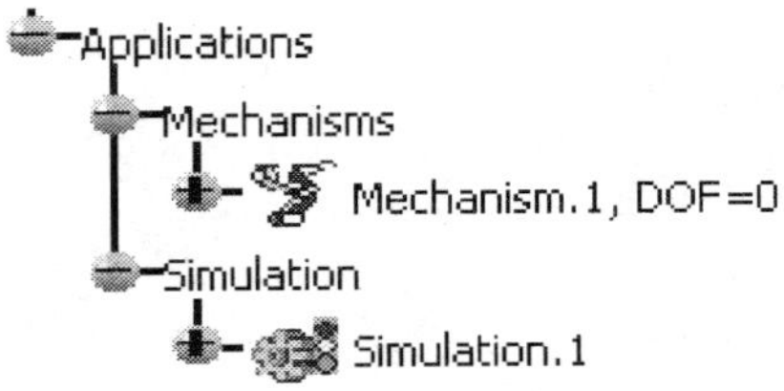

In addition, the two pop up boxes shown below appear.

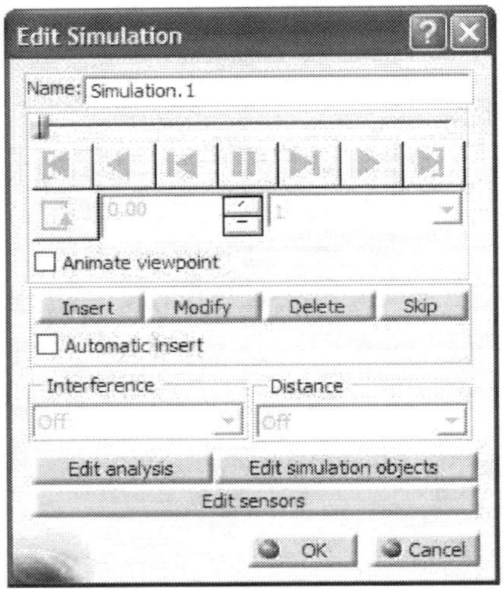

This is very similar to the **Kinematics Simulation** pop up box that appeared in Method 1 above. As you scroll the bar in this toolbar from left to right, the block begins is travel from one end of the base to the other.

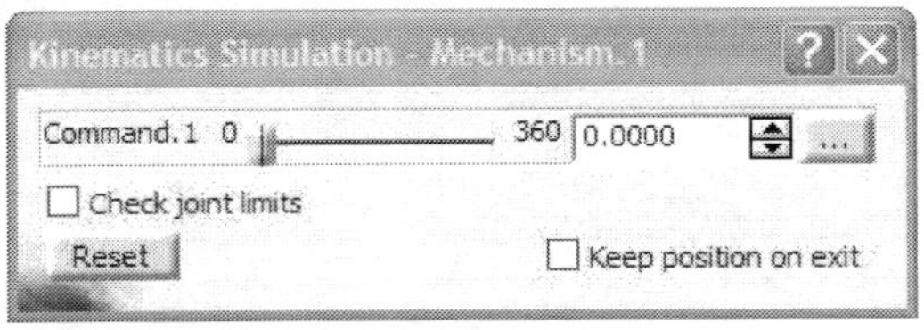

When the scroll bar in the **Kinematics Simulation** pop up box reaches the right extreme end, select the **Insert** button 

in the **Edit Simulation** pop up box shown above. This activates the video player buttons shown 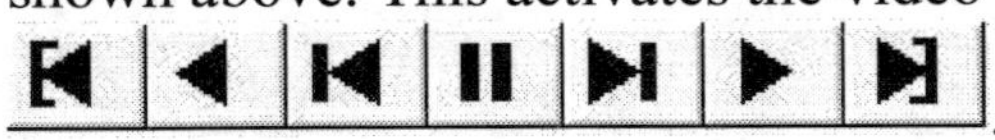.

Return the block to its original position by picking the **Jump to Start** button .

Note that the **Change Loop Mode** button 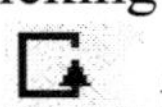 is also active now.

Upon selecting the **Play Forward** button, the arm makes such a fast jump to the end that there does not seem to be any motion.

In order to slow down the motion of the block, select a different **interpolation step**, such as 0.04.

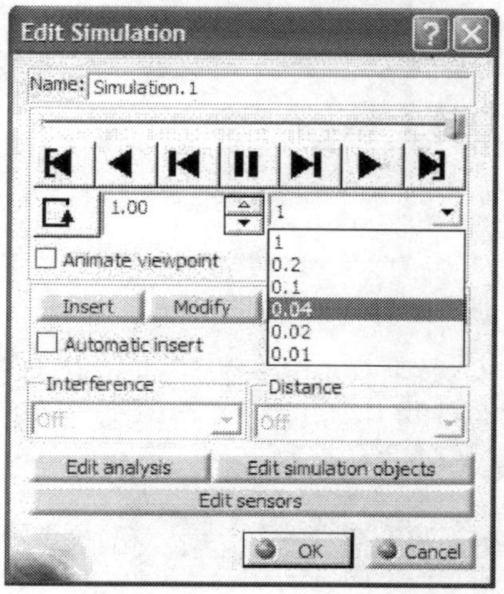

Upon changing the interpolation step to 0.04, return the arm to its original position by picking the **Jump to Start** button. Apply **Play Forward** button and observe the slow and smooth rotation of the arm.

Select the **Compile Simulation** icon from the **Generic Animation** toolbar

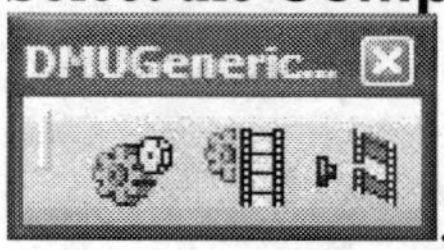

. Pressing the **File name** button File name ... allows you to set the location and name of the animation file to be generated as displayed below.

Select a suitable path and file name and change the **Time step** to be 0.04 to produce a slow moving block in an AVI file.

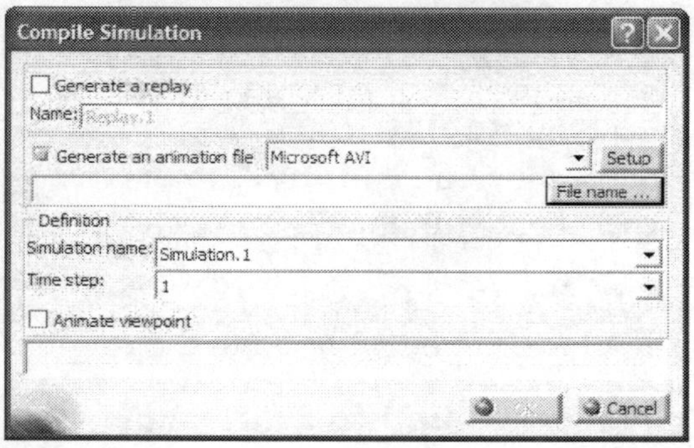

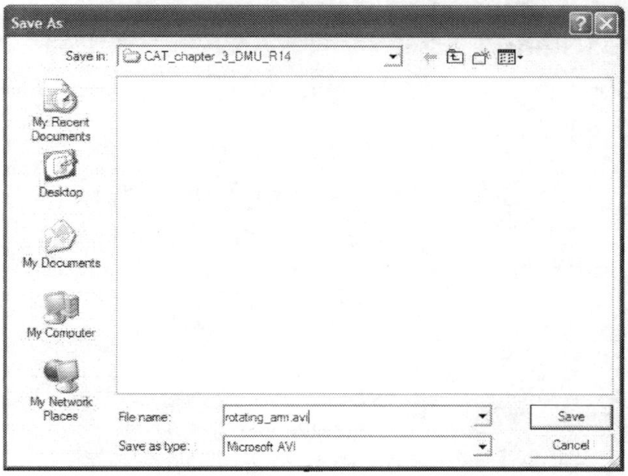

The completed pop up box is displayed for your reference.

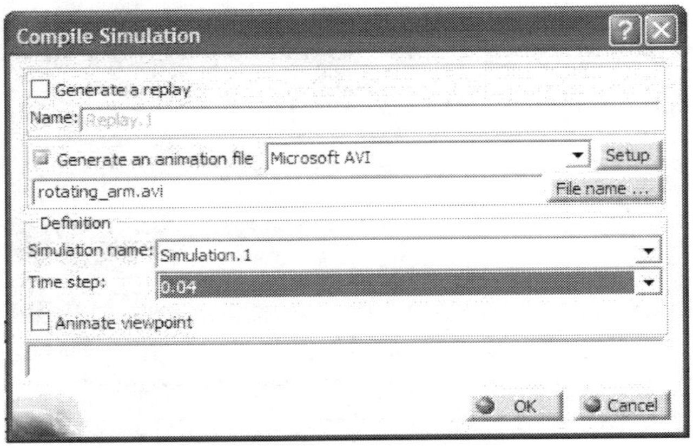

AS the file is being generated, the arm slowly rotates. The resulting AVI file can be viewed with the Windows Media Player.

In the event that an AVI file is not needed, but one wishes to play the animation, repeatedly, a **Replay** needs to be generated. Therefore, in the **Compile Simulation** box, check the **Generate a replay** button.

Note that in this case most of the previously available options are dimmed out. A **Replay.1** branch has also been added to the tree.

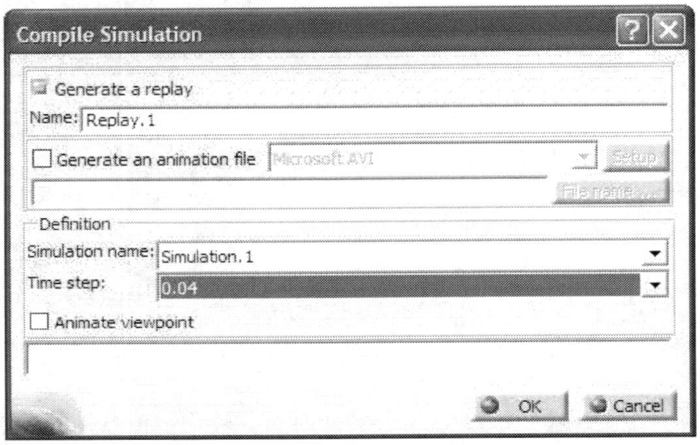

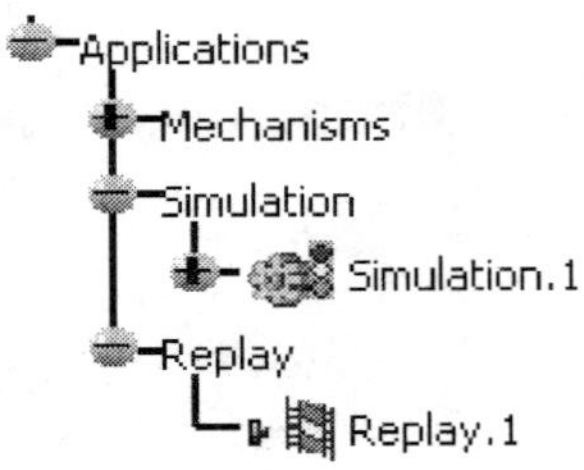

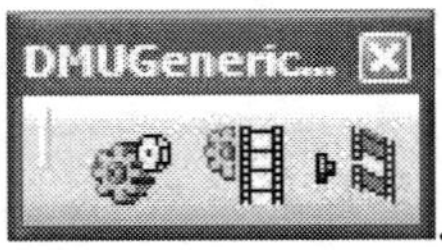

Select the **Replay** icon from the **Generic Animation** toolbar. Double clock on **Replay.1** in the tree and the **Replay** pop up box appears. Experiment with the different choices of the **Change Loop Mode** buttons , , . The block can be returned to the original position by picking the **Jump to Start** button .

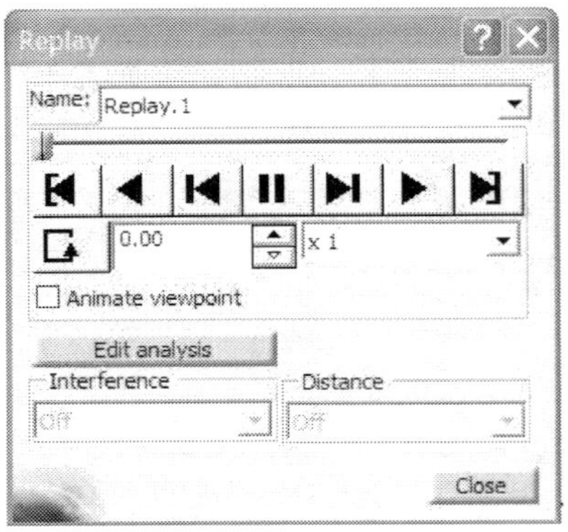

The **skip ratio** (which is chosen to be x1 in the right box) controls the speed of the **Replay**.

5 Creating Laws in the Motion and Simulating the Desired Kinematics

The motion animated this far was not tied to the time parameter or the angular velocity given in the problem statement. You will now introduce some time based physics into the problem. The objective is to specify a constant angular velocity of $\omega = 2\pi$ rad/s.

Click on **Simulation with Laws** icon  in the **Simulation** toolbar 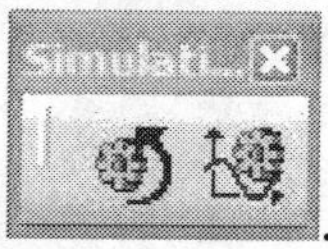

. You will get the following pop up box indication that you need to add at least a relation between the command and the time parameter.

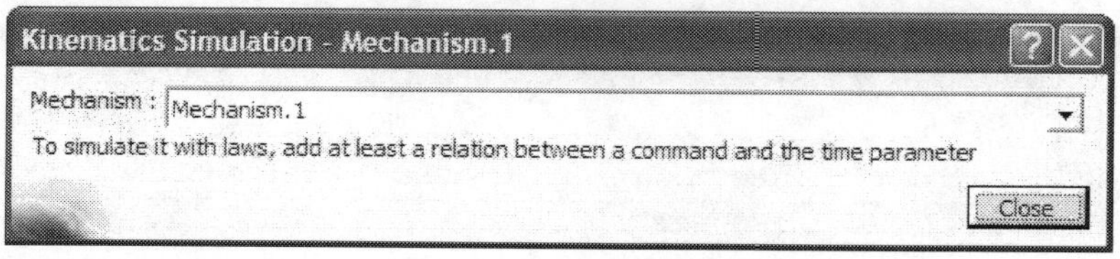

Select the **Formula** icon  from the **Knowledge** toolbar 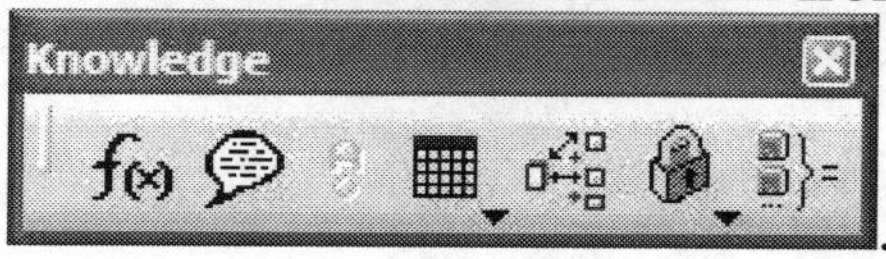

. The pop up box below appears on the screen.

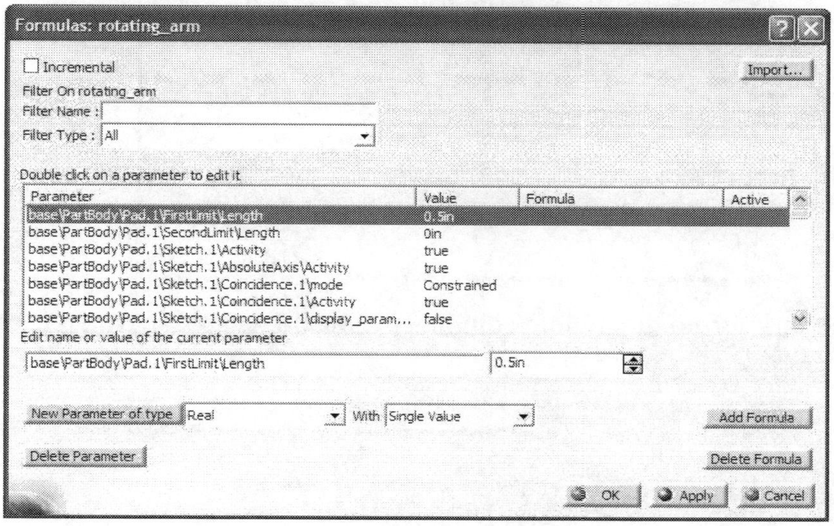

Point the cursor to the **Mechanism.1, DOF=0** branch in the tree and click. The consequence is that only parameters associated with the mechanism are displayed in the **Formulas** box.
The long list is now reduced to two parameters as indicated in the box.

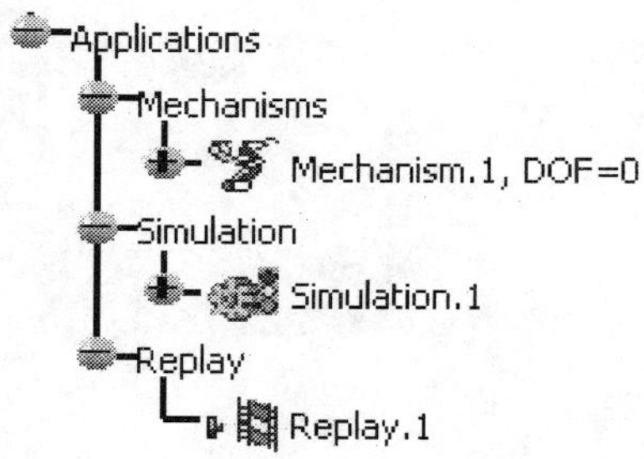

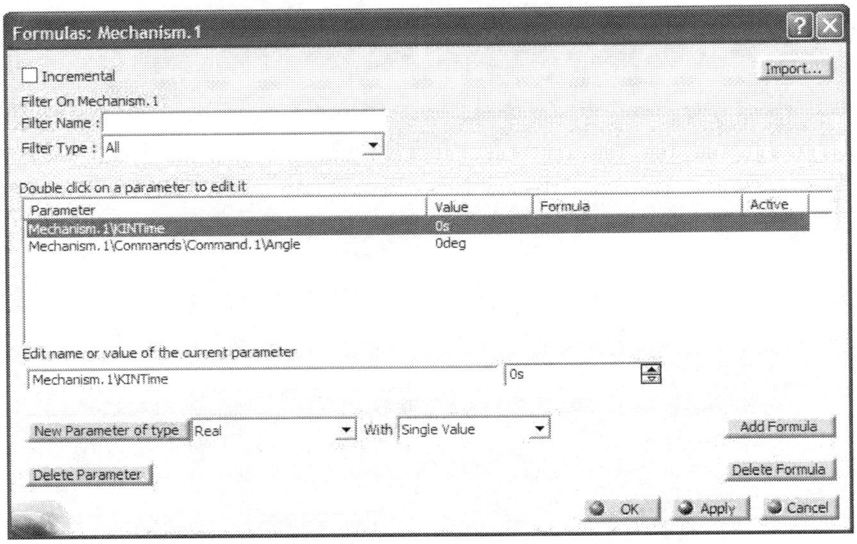

Select the entry **Mechanism.1\Commands\Command.1\Angle** and press the **Add Formula** button Add Formula. This action kicks you to the **Formula Editor** box.

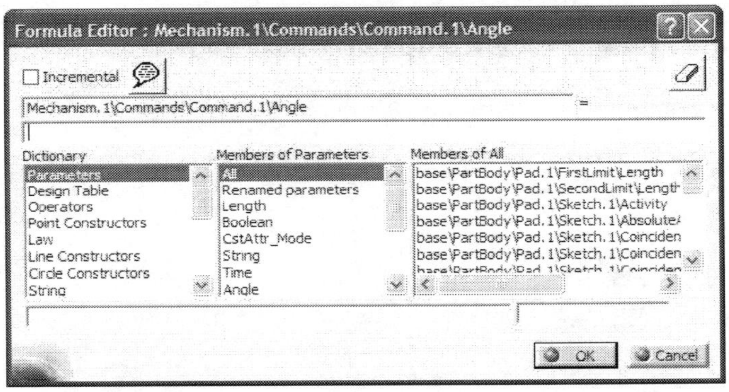

Pick the **Time** entry from the middle column (i.e. **Members of Parameters**).

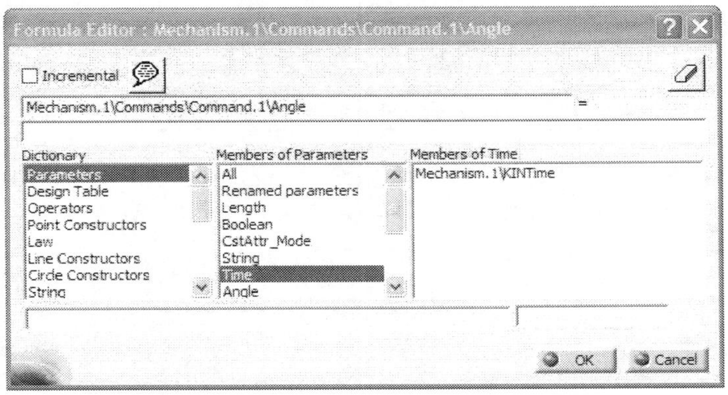

The right hand side of the equality should be such that the formula becomes
$Mechanism.1 \backslash Commands \backslash Command.1 \backslash Angle =$
$(2*PI)*((360\,\text{deg})/(2*PI))*(Mechanism.1 \backslash KINTime)/(1s)$

Therefore, the completed **Formula Editor** box becomes

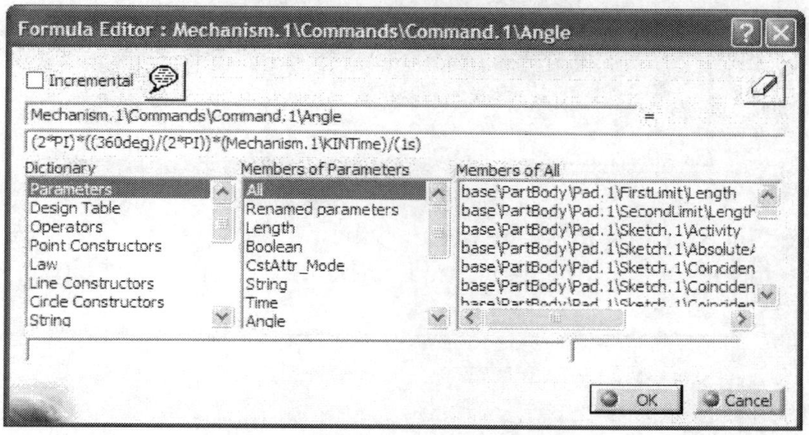

Upon accepting **OK**, the formula is recorded in the **Formulas** pop up box as shown below.

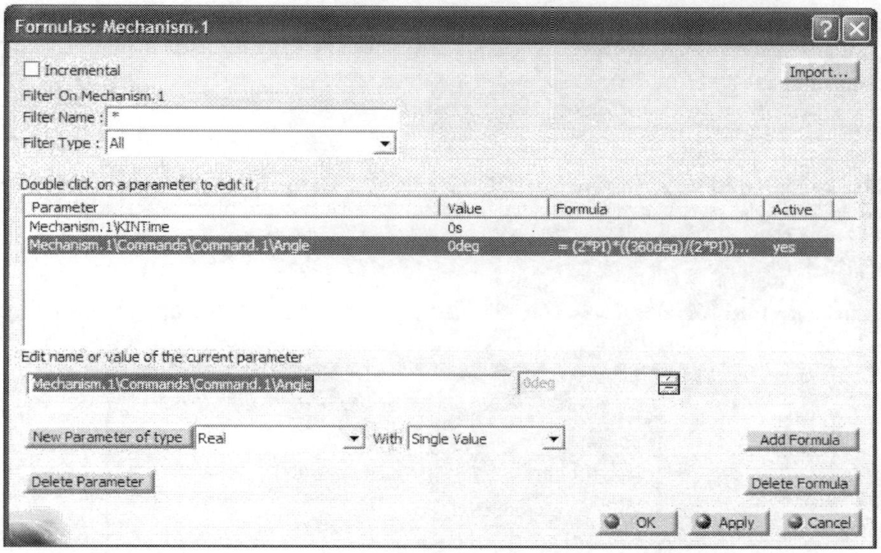

The formula introduced above requires an explanation. Note that the left hand side of the equality is an Angle parameter therefore the entire right hand side should be reducing to an angle in degrees. This is why, $(Mechanism.1 \backslash KINTime)$ has been nondimensionalized by introducing a division by (1s). Here, "s" refers to seconds. Finally, (360 deg) / (2 * PI) has been introduced as a term to transform the given angular velocity which was in radians (per second) into degrees (per second).

In the event that the formula has different units on the different sides of the equality you will get **Warning** messages such as the one shown below.

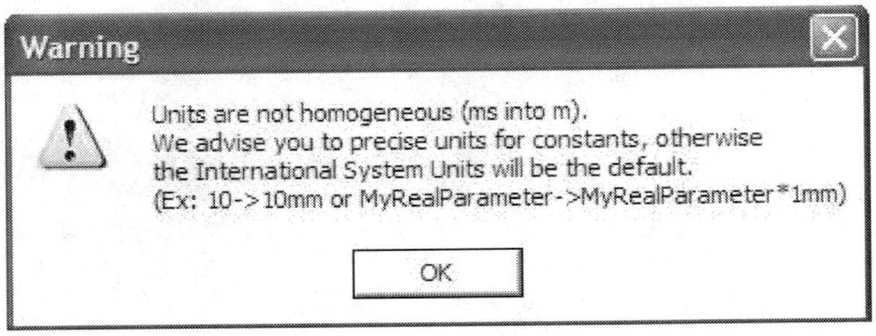

We are spared the warning message because the formula has been properly inputted. Note that the introduced law has appeared in the **Law** branch of the tree.

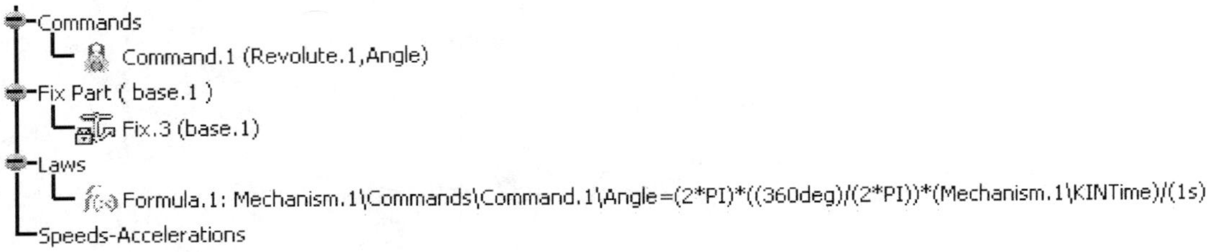

Keep in mind that our interest is to plot the velocity and accelerations of the arm tip generated by this motion.

Select the **Speed and Acceleration** icon  from the **DMU Kinematics** toolbar

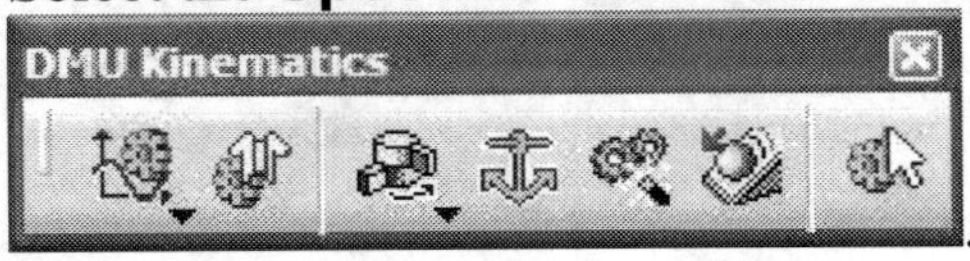

. The pop up box below appears on the Screen.

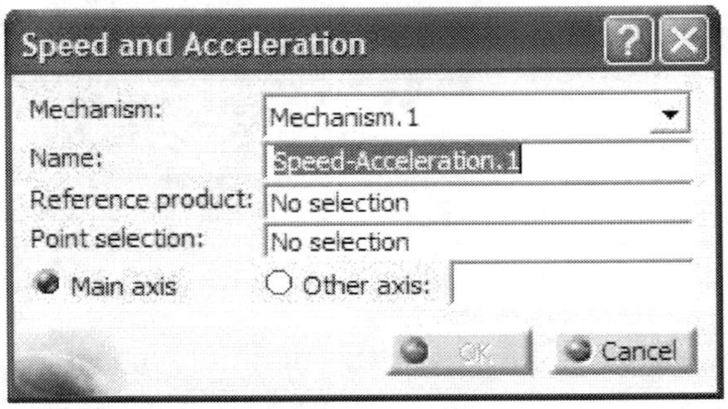

For the **Reference product,** select the **base** from the screen or the tree. For the **Point selection**, pick the vertex of the **block** as shown in the sketch below.

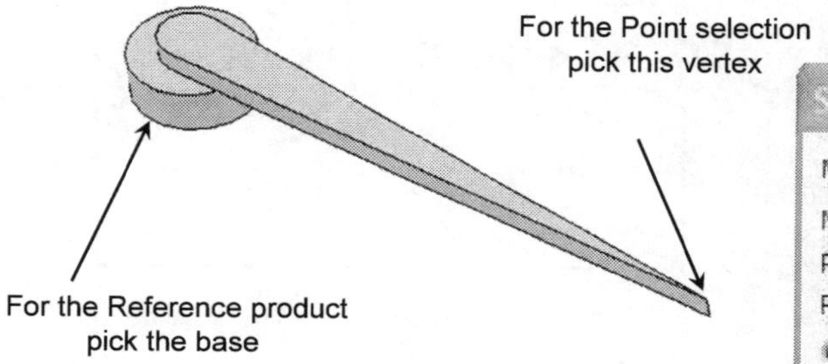

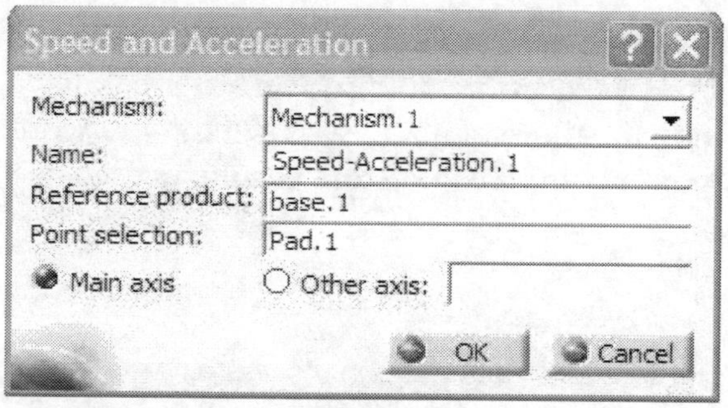

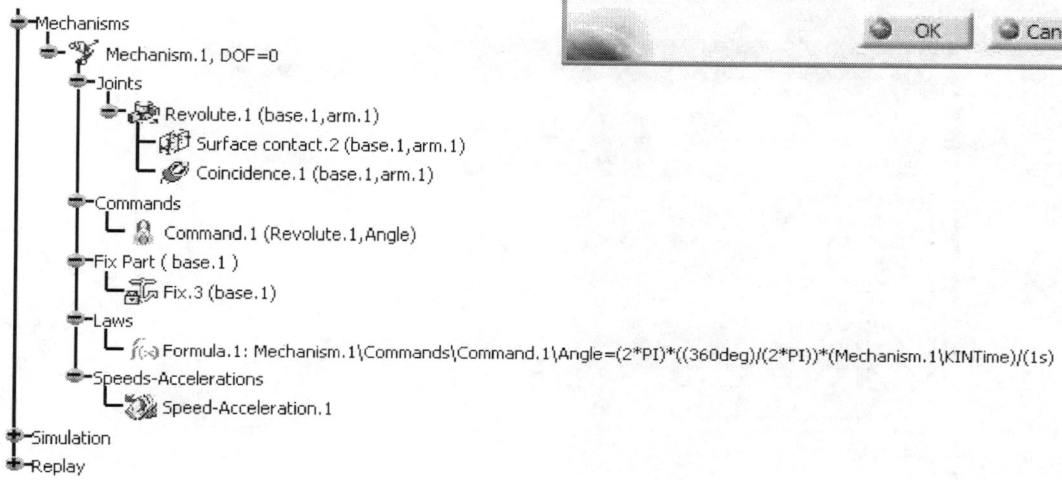

Note that the **Speed and Acceleration.1** has appeared in the tree.

Click on **Simulation with Laws** icon  in the **Simulation** toolbar 

. This results in the **Kinematics Simulation** pop up box shown below.

Note that the default time duration is 10 seconds.
To change this value, click on the button 

. In the resulting pop up box, change the time duration to 1s. Recall that this is the time duration for the arm to make one full revolution at 2π rad/s.

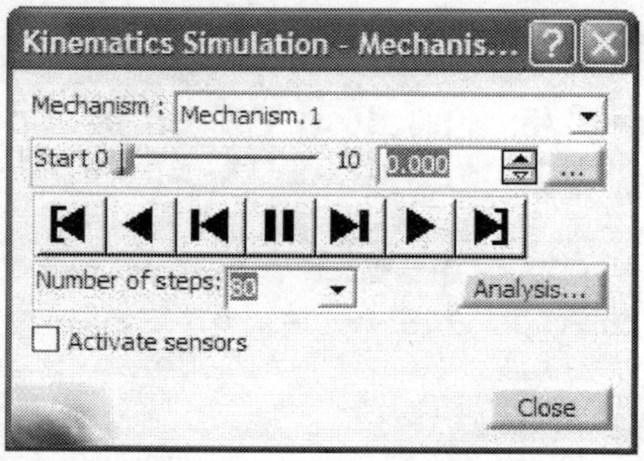

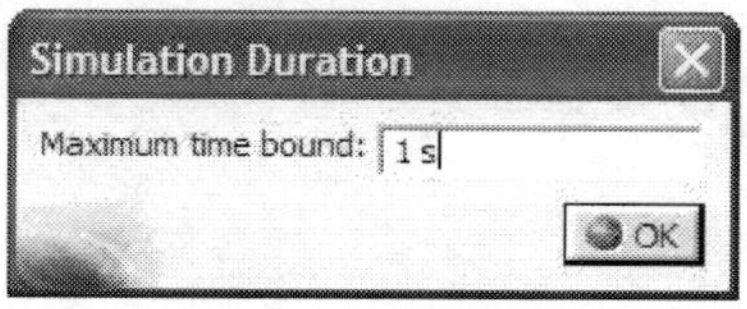

The scroll bar now moves up to 1s.

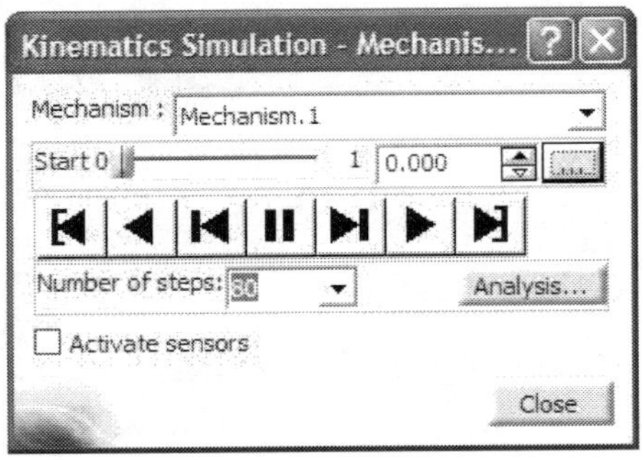

Check the **Activate sensors** box, at the bottom left corner.

You will next have to make certain selections from the accompanying **Sensors** box to indicate the kinematic parameters you would like to compute and store results on.

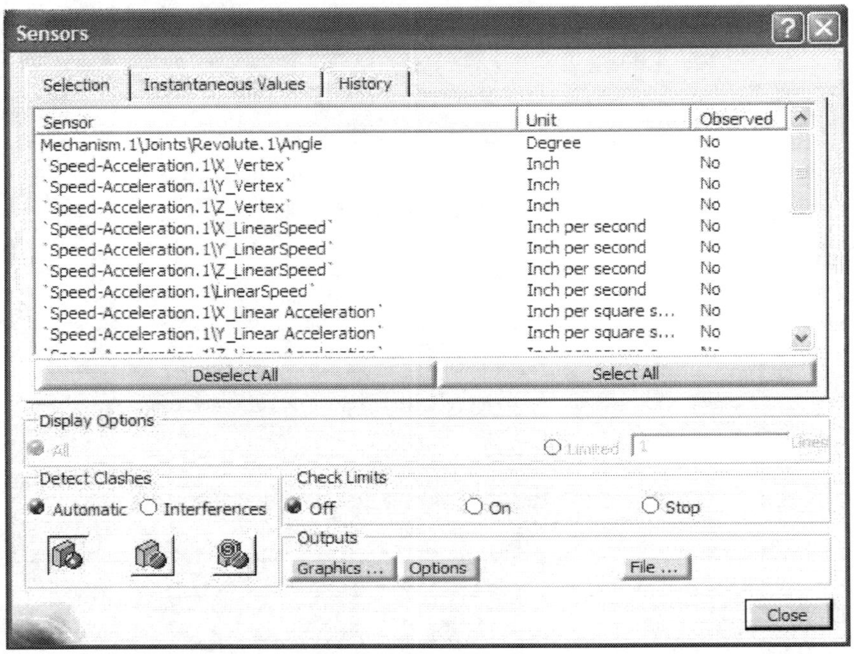

Click on the following items

Speed-Acceleration.1\X_LinearSpeed
Speed-Acceleration.1\X_LinearAcceleration

As you make these selections, the last column in the **Sensors** box, changes to **Yes** for the corresponding items. This is shown in the next page.

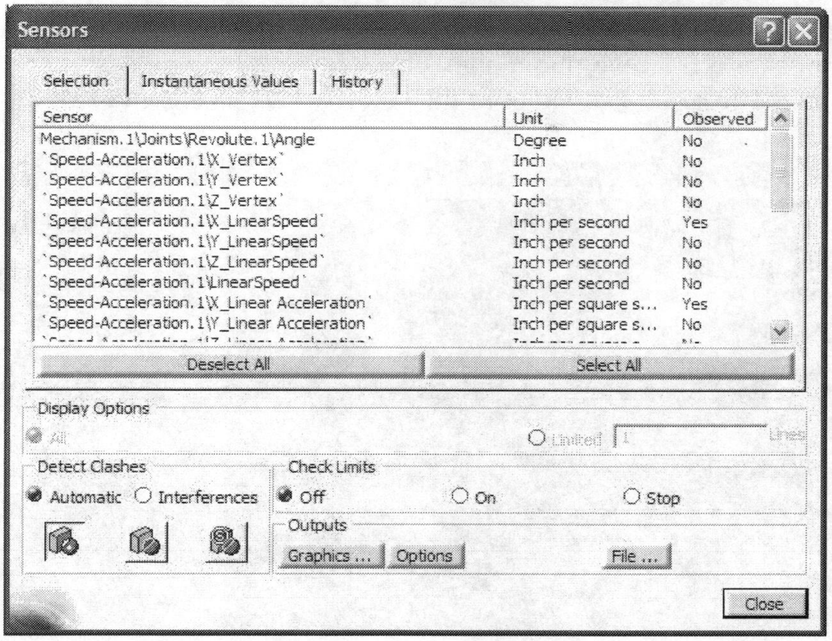

At this point, drag the scroll bar in the **Kinematics Simulation** box. As you do this, the arm rotates about the base. Once the bar reaches its right extreme point, the arm has made one full revolution. This corresponds to 1s and a rotation of 360˚.

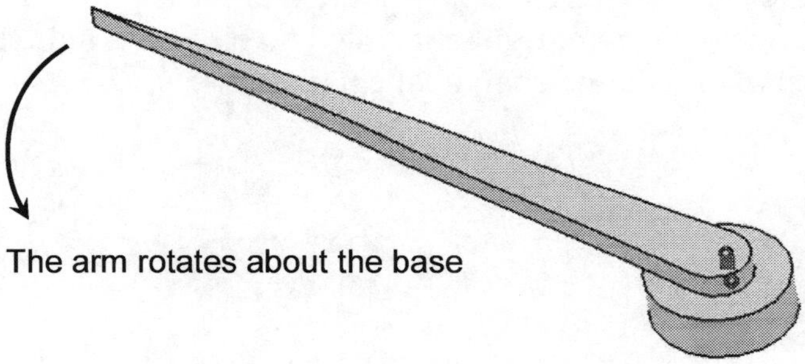

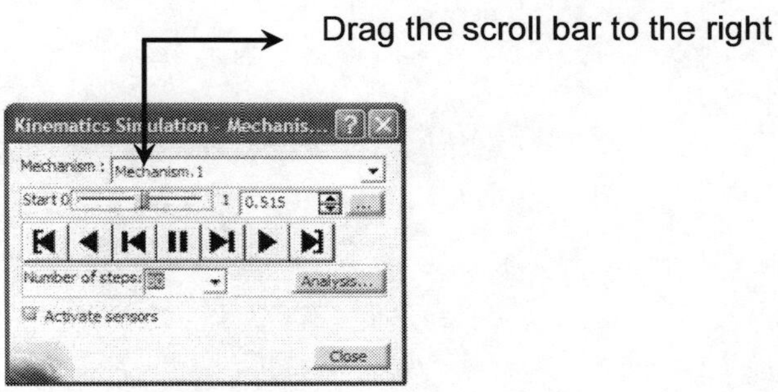

Once the arm makes a full revolution, click on **Graphics** button 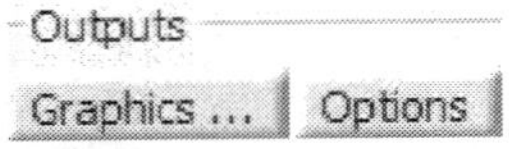

in the **Sensor** box. The result is the plot of the velocity and acceleration all on the same axes.

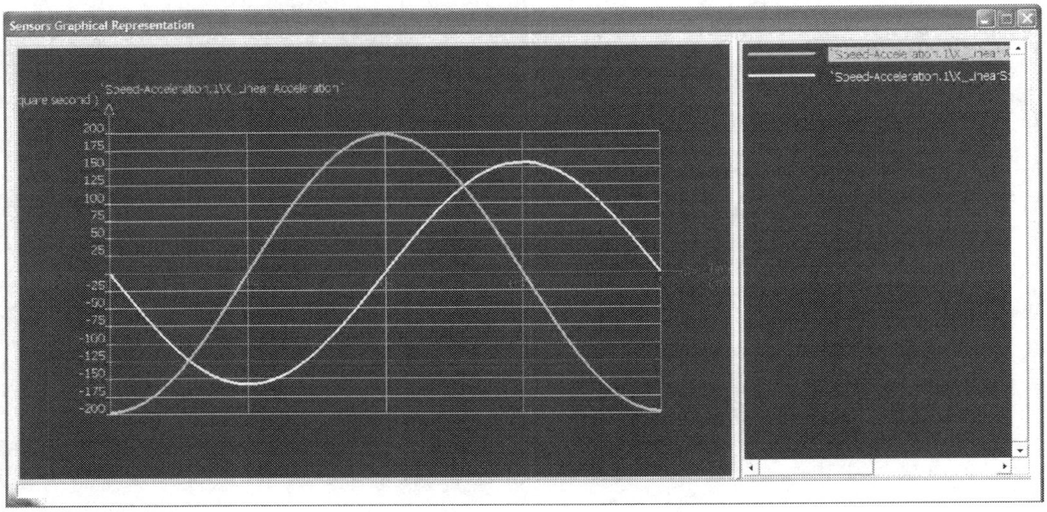

These plots are in perfect agreement with the theoretical results. The plots are deceiving as they have different scales. Note that these plots can be viewed individually by pointing the cursor to them, right clicking, and choosing hide. It is only then that they can be compared with the analytical expressions.

The arm can be returned to the original position by picking the **Jump to Start** button . However, this traces another set of graphs that is not desirable. One can use the **History** tab in the **Sensors** pop up box and **Clear** the data.

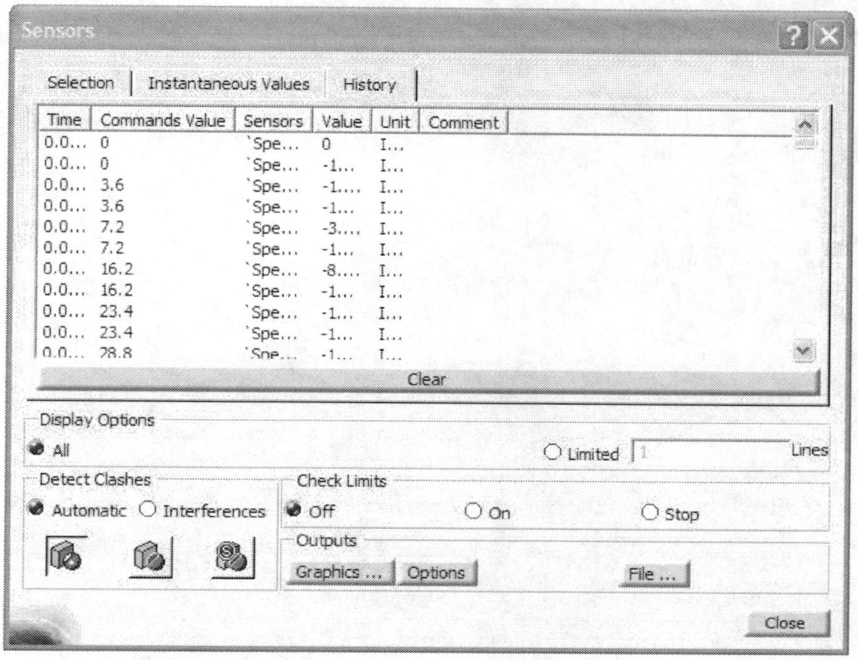

You can now close the **Sensors** box by clicking **OK**.

This concludes this tutorial.

NOTES:

Chapter 4

Slider Crank Mechanism

Introduction

In this tutorial you create a slider crank mechanism using a combination of revolute and cylindrical joints. You will also experiment with additional plotting utilities in CATIA.

1 Problem Statement

A slider crank mechanism, sometimes referred to as a three-bar-linkage, can be thought of as a four bar linkage where one of the links is made infinite in length. The piston based internal combustion is based off of this mechanism. The analytical solution to the kinematics of a slider crank can be found in elementary dynamics textbooks.

In this tutorial, we aim to simulate the slider crank mechanism shown below for constant crank rotation and to generate plots of some of the results, including position, velocity, and acceleration of the slider. The mechanism is constructed by assembling four parts as described later in the tutorial. In CATIA, the number and type of mechanism joints will be determined by the nature of the assembly constraints applied. There are several valid combinations of joints which would produce a kinematically correct simulation of the slider crank mechanism. The most intuitive combination would be three revolute joints and a prismatic joint. From a degrees of freedom standpoint, using three revolute joints and a prismatic joint redundantly constrains the system, although the redundancy does not create a problem unless it is geometrically infeasible, in this tutorial we will choose an alternate combination of joints both to illustrate cylindrical joints and to illustrate that any set of joint which removes the appropriate degrees of freedom while providing the capability to drive the desired motions can be applied. In the approach suggested by this tutorial, the assembly constraints will be applied in such a way that two revolute joints and two cylindrical joints are created reducing the degrees of freedom are reduced to one. This remaining degree of freedom is then removed by declaring the crank joint (one of the cylindrical joints in our approach) as being angle driven. An exercise left to the reader is to create the same mechanism using three revolute joints and one prismatic joint or some other suitable combination of joints. We will use the Multiplot feature available in CATIA is used to create plots of the simulation results where the abscissa is not necessarily the time variable.

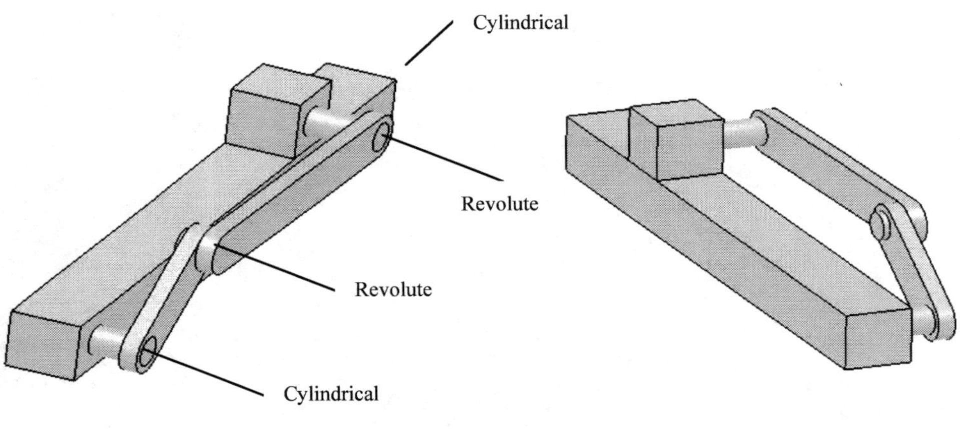

2 Overview of this Tutorial

In this tutorial you will:

1. Model the four CATIA parts required.
2. Create an assembly (CATIA Product) containing the parts.
3. Constrain the assembly in such a way that only one degree of freedom is unconstrained. This remaining degree of freedom can be thought of as rotation of the crank.
4. Enter the **Digital Mockup** workbench and convert the assembly constraints into two revolute and two cylindrical joints.
5. Simulate the relative motion of the arm base without consideration to time (in other words, without implementing the time based angular velocity given in the problem statement).
6. Add a formula to implement the time based kinematics associated with constant angular velocity of the crank.
7. Simulate the desired constant angular velocity motion and generate plots of the kinematic results.

3 Creation of the Assembly in Mechanical Design Solutions

Although the dimensions of the components are irrelevant to the process (but not to the kinematic results), the tutorial details provide some specific dimensions making it easier for the reader to model the appropriate parts and to obtain results similar to those herein. Where specific dimensions are given, it is recommended that you use the indicated values (in inches). Some dimensions of lesser importance are not given; simply estimate those dimensions from the drawing.

In CATIA, model four parts named **base**, **crank**, **conrod**, and **block** as shown below.

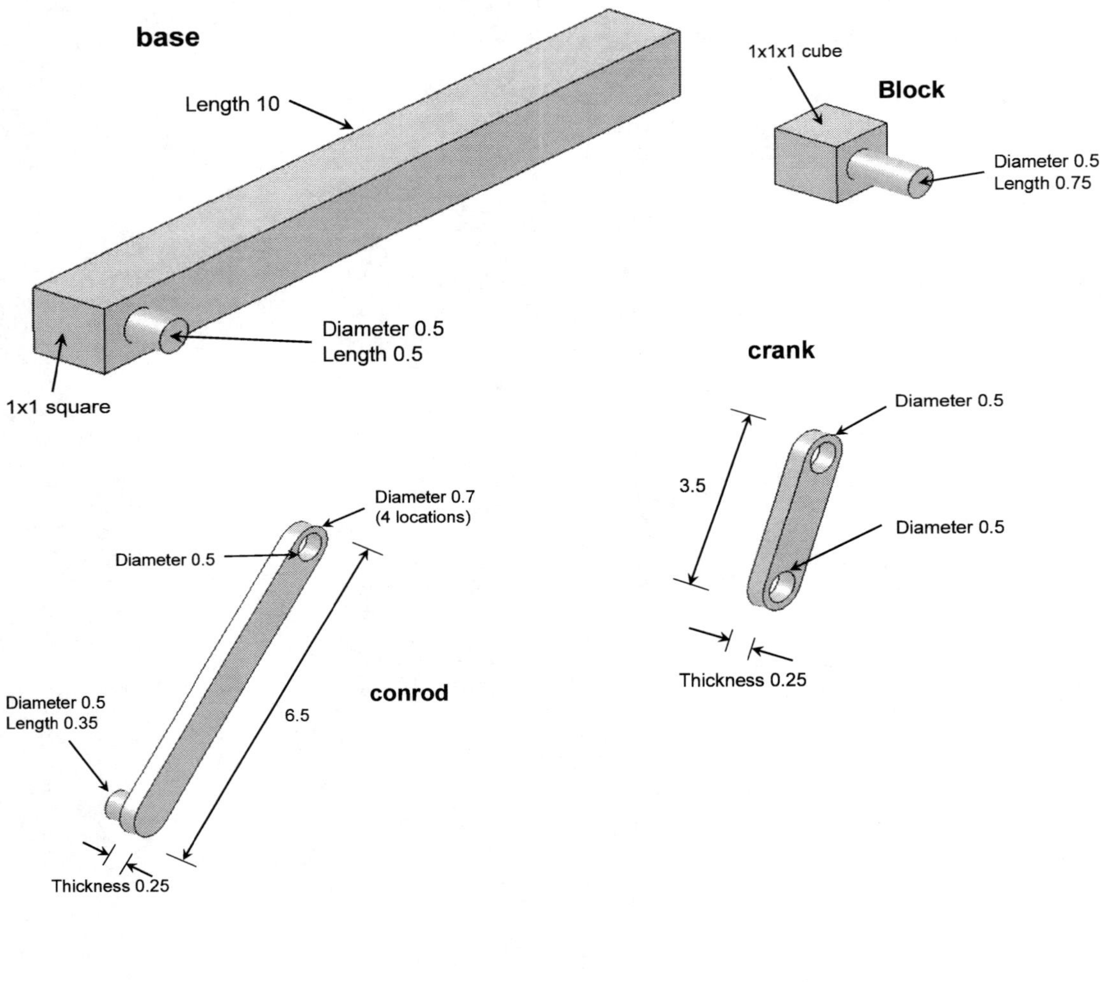

Enter the **Assembly Design** workbench which can be achieved by different means depending on your CATIA customization. For example, from the standard Windows toolbar, select **File > New** .
From the box shown on the right, select **Product**. This moves you to the **Assembly Design** workbench and creates an assembly with the default name **Product.1**.

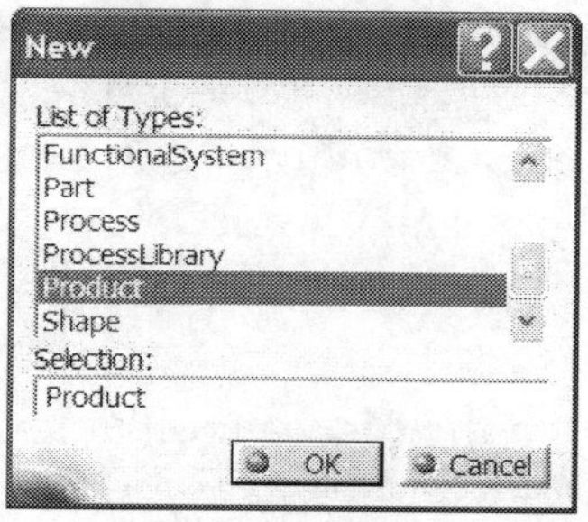

In order to change the default name, move the curser to **Product.1** in the tree, right click and select **Properties** from the menu list.

From the **Properties** box, select the **Product** tab and in **Part Number** type **slider_crank**.

This will be the new product name throughout the chapter. The tree on the top left corner of your computer screen should look as displayed below.

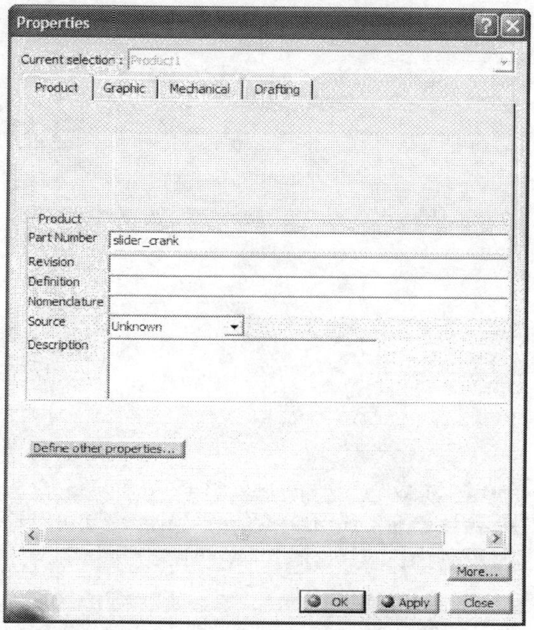

The next step is to insert the existing parts in the assembly just created. From the standard Windows toolbar, select **Insert > Existing Component**.
From the **File Selection** pop up box choose all four parts. Remember that in CATIA multiple selections are made with the **Ctrl** key. The tree is modified to indicate that the parts have been inserted.

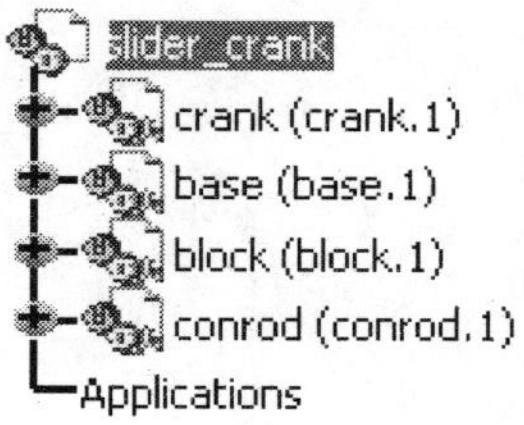

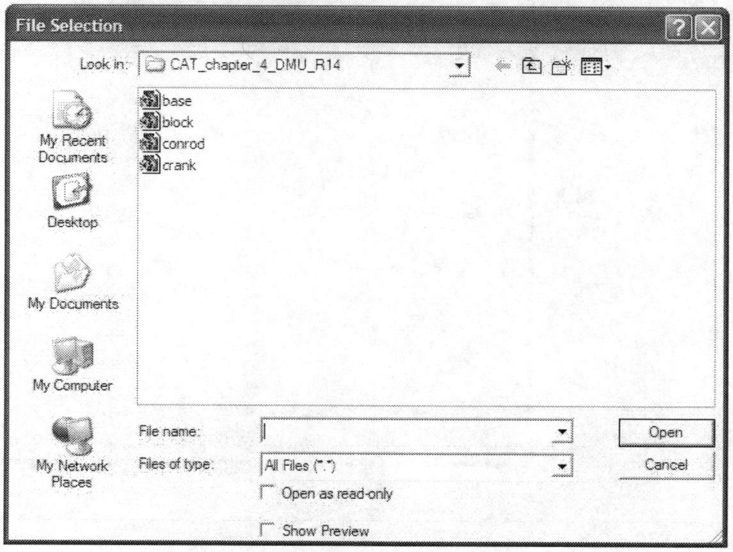

Note that the part names and their instance names were purposely made the same. This practice makes the identification of the assembly constraints a lot easier down the road. Depending on how your parts were created earlier, on the computer screen you have the four parts all clustered around the origin. You may have to use the **Manipulation** icon  in the **Move** toolbar 

to rearrange them as desired.

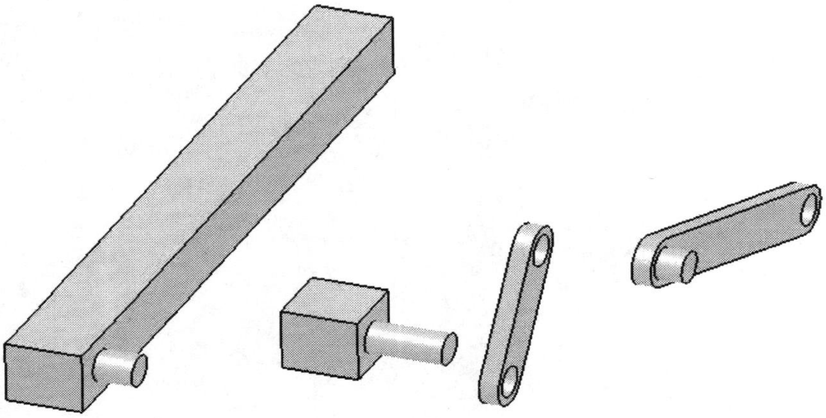

The best way of saving your work is to save the entire assembly.
Double click on the top branch of the tree. This is to ensure that you are in the **Assembly Design** workbench.
Select the **Save** icon . The **Save As** pop up box allows you to rename if desired. The default name is the **slider_crank**.

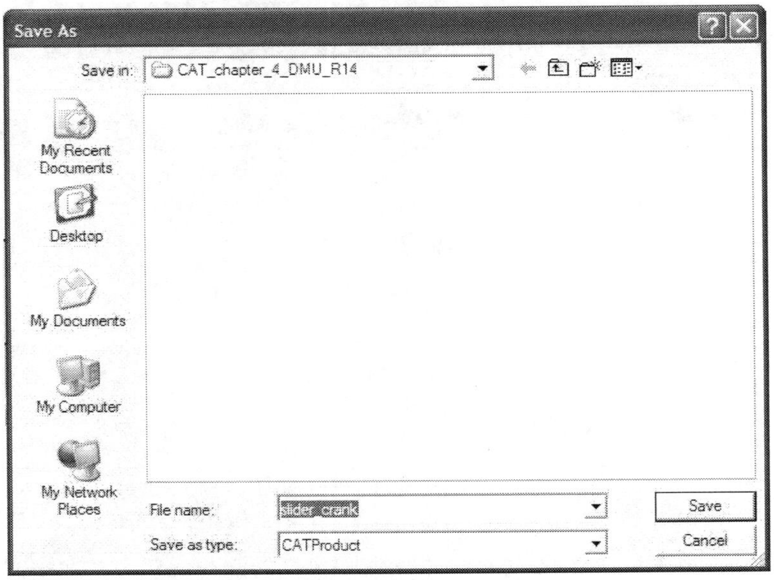

Your next task is to impose assembly constraints.

Pick the **Anchor** icon  from the **Constraints** toolbar and select the **base** from the tree or from the screen. This removes all six degrees of freedom for the base.

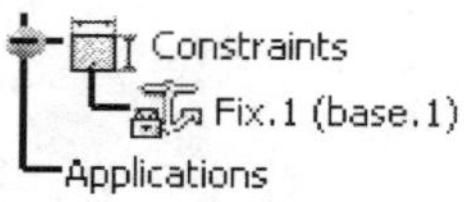

Next, we will create a coincident edge constraint between the base and the block. This removes all dof except for translation along the edge of coincidence and rotation about the edge of coincidence. The two remaining dof are consistent with our desire to create a cylindrical joint between the block and the base. To make the constraint, pick the **Coincidence** icon  from the **Constraints** toolbar

. Select the two edges of the **base** and the **block** as shown below.
This constraint is reflected in the appropriate branch of the tree.

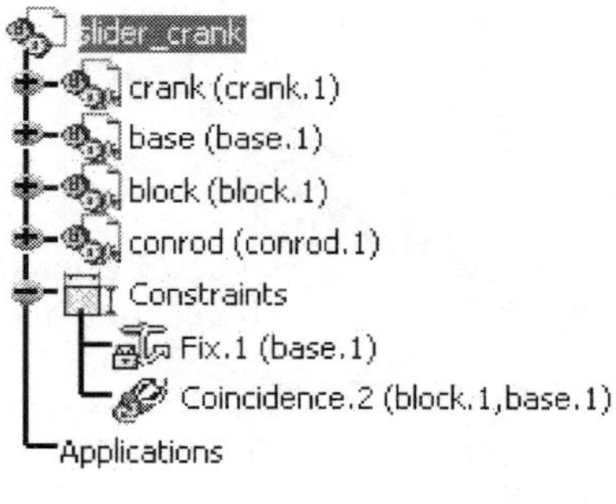

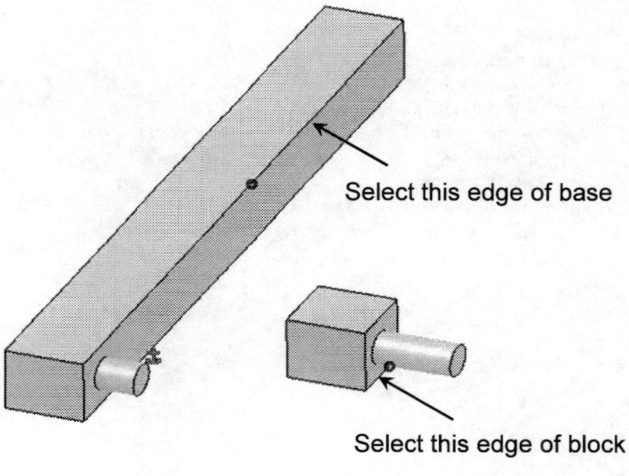

Use **Update** icon  to partially position the two parts as shown.

Note that the **Update** icon  no longer appears on the constraints branches.

Depending on how your parts were constructed the block may end up in a position quite different from what is shown below. You can always use the **Manipulation** icon to position it where desired followed by **Update** if necessary.

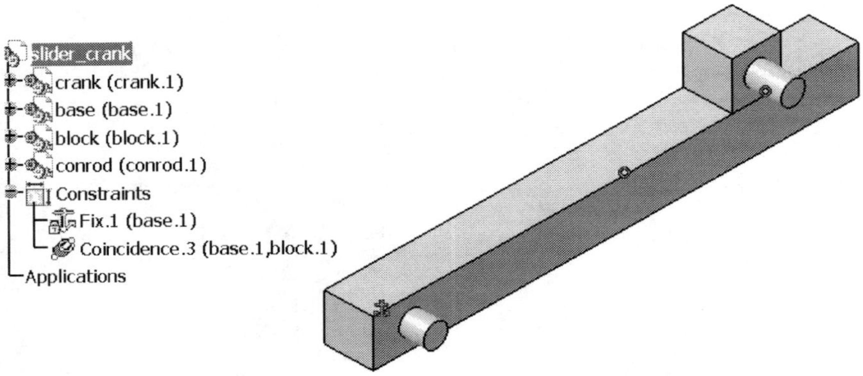

You will now impose assembly constraints between the conrod and the block. Recall that we ultimately wish to create a revolute joint between these two parts, so our assembly constraints need to remove all the dof except for rotation about the axis.

Pick the **Coincidence** icon from **Constraints** toolbar. Select the axes of the two cylindrical surfaces as shown below. Keep in mind that the easy way to locate the axis is to point the cursor to the curved surfaces.

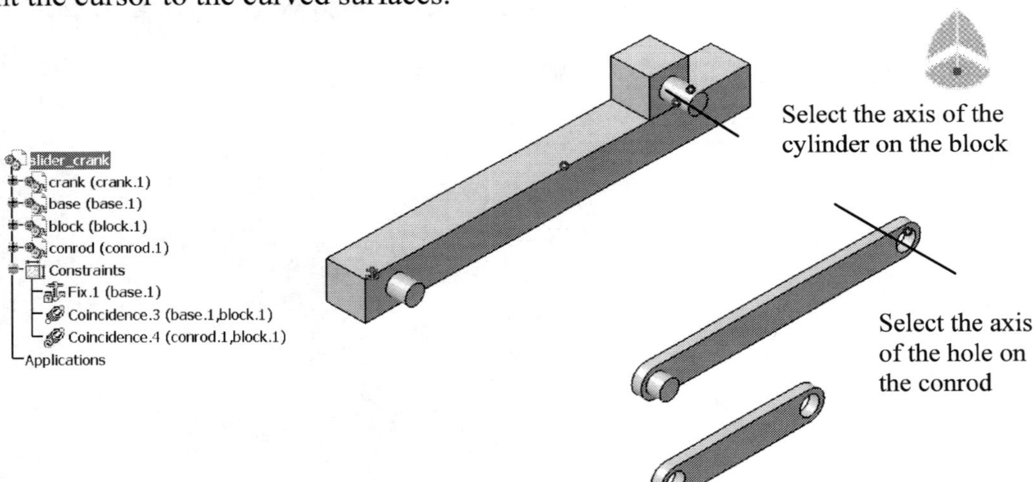

The coincidence constraint just created removes all but two dof between the conrod and the base. The two remaining dof are rotation about the axis (a desired dof) and translation along the axis (a dof we wish to remove in order to produce the desired revolute joint). To remove the translation, pick the **Coincidence** icon from the

Constraints toolbar and select the surfaces shown on the next page. If your parts are originally oriented similar to what is shown, you will need to choose **Same** for the **Orientation** in the **Constraints Definition** box so that the conrod will flip to the desired orientation upon an update. The tree is modified to reflect this constraint.

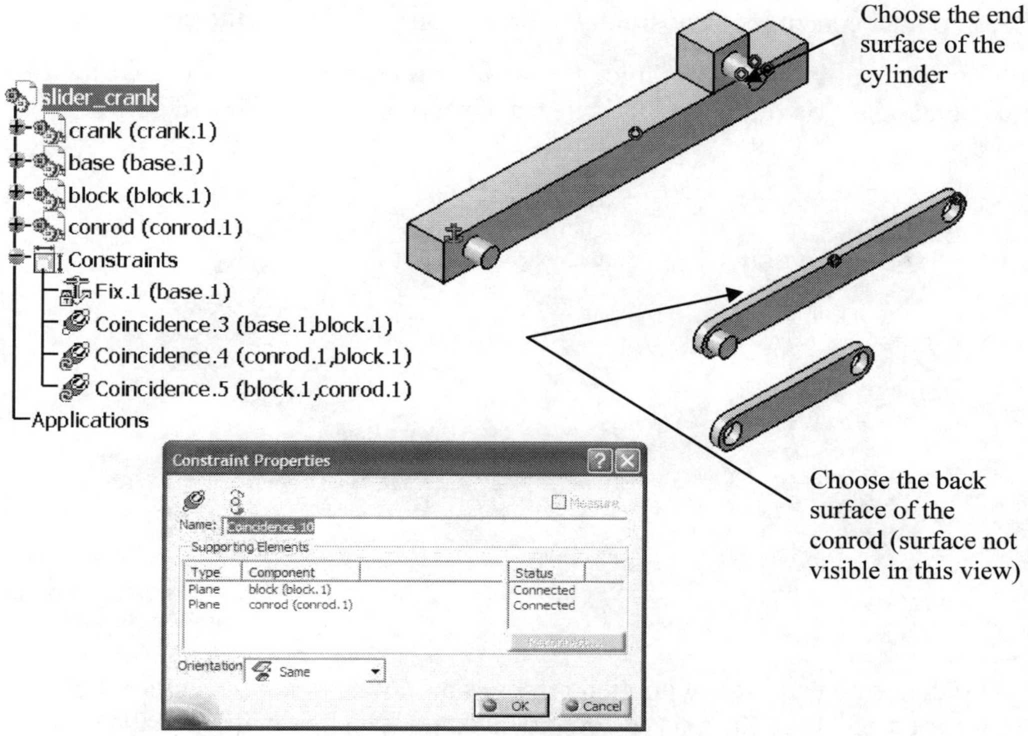

Use **Update** icon  to partially position the two parts as shown below.
Note that upon updating, the conrod may end up in a location which is not convenient for the rest of the assembly. In this situation the **Manipulation** icon  can be used to conveniently rearrange the conrod orientation.

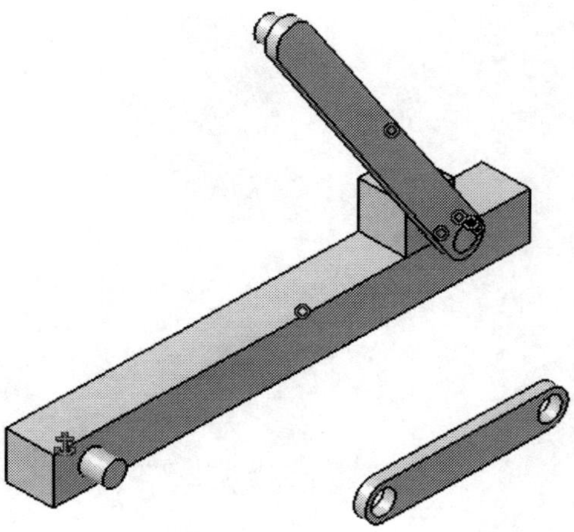

So far, we have created assembly constraints which leave degrees of freedom consistent with a cylindrical joint between the block and the base and a revolute joint between the block and the conrod. Next we will apply assembly constraints consistent with a revolute joint between the conrod and the crank. This will be done with a coincidence constraint between the centerlines of the protrusion on the conrod and the upper hole of the base and a surface contact constraint to position the parts along the axis of the coincidence constraint. To begin this process, pick the **Coincidence** icon from **Constraints** toolbar. Select the axis of the cylindrical surface and the hole as shown below.

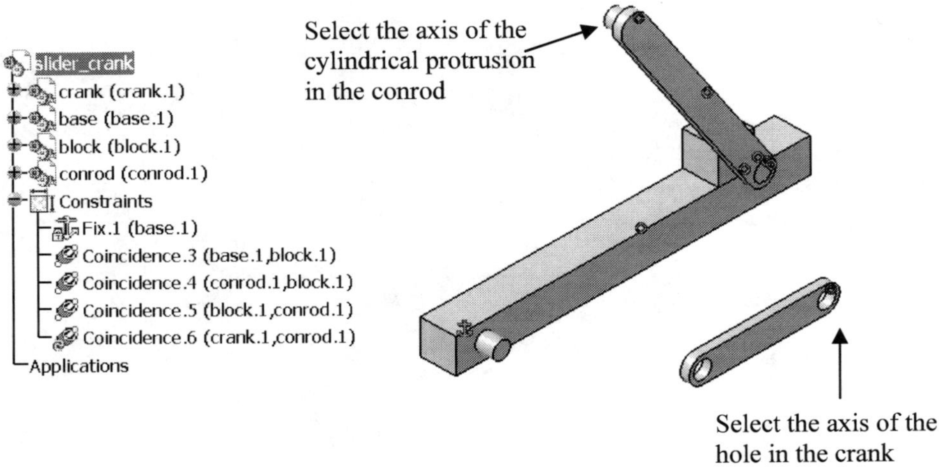

The coincidence constraint just applied removes all dof between the conrod and the crank except for rotation along the axis of coincidence and translation along that axis. To remove the unwanted translational dof, we will use a surface contact constraint (a coincidence constraint could also be applied, but we have chosen to illustrate a contact constraint here). To create the constraint, Pick the **Contact** icon from **Constraints** toolbar and select the surfaces shown in the next page. The tree is modified to reflect this constraint.

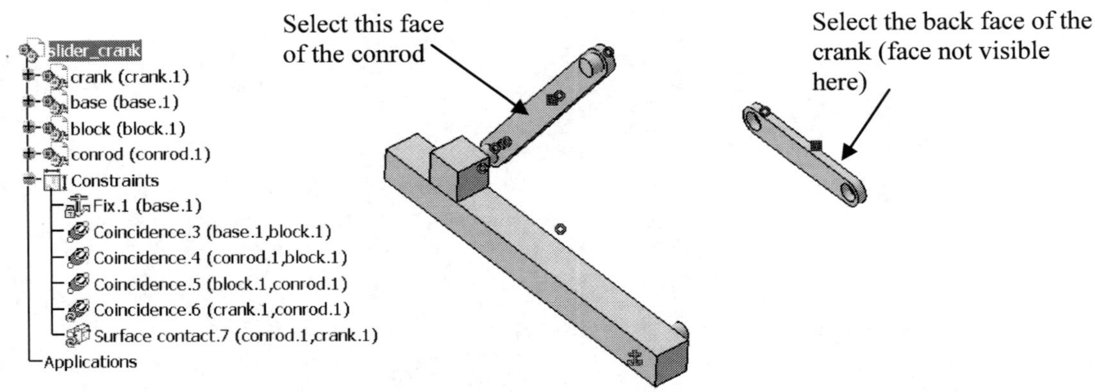

Use **Update** icon  to partially position the two parts as shown.

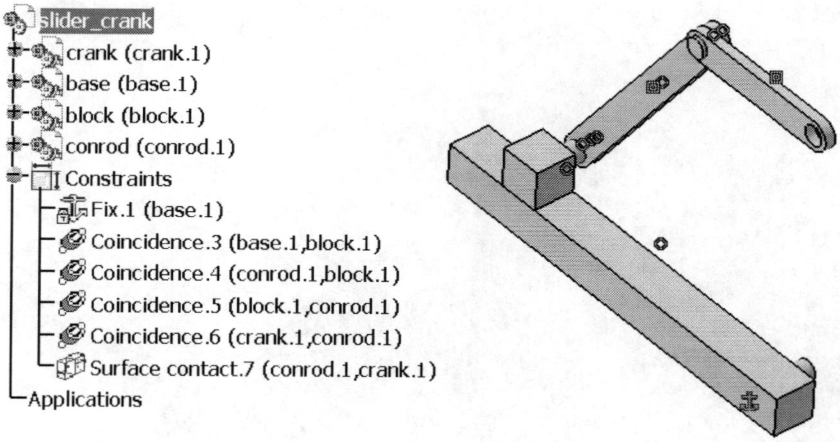

We need to apply one final constraint to locate the lower end of the crank onto the cylindrical protrusion on the base. Pick the **Coincidence** icon  from **Constraints** toolbar. Select the axis of the cylindrical surface and the hole as shown below.

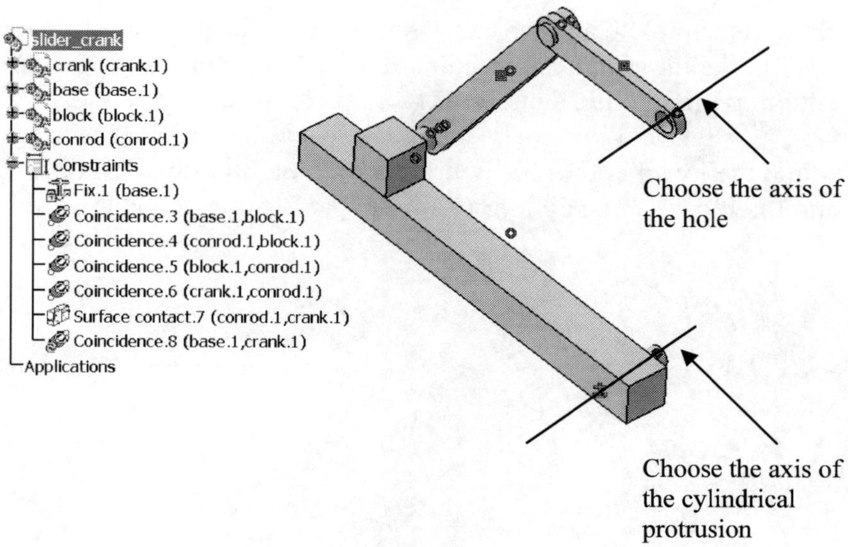

Use **Update** icon  to get the final position of all parts as shown. Note that since we have chosen to create a cylindrical joint between the base and the crank, we do not need to specify a constraint to remove the translation along the axis of coincidence; that translation is effectively removed by the remainder of the assembly constraints.

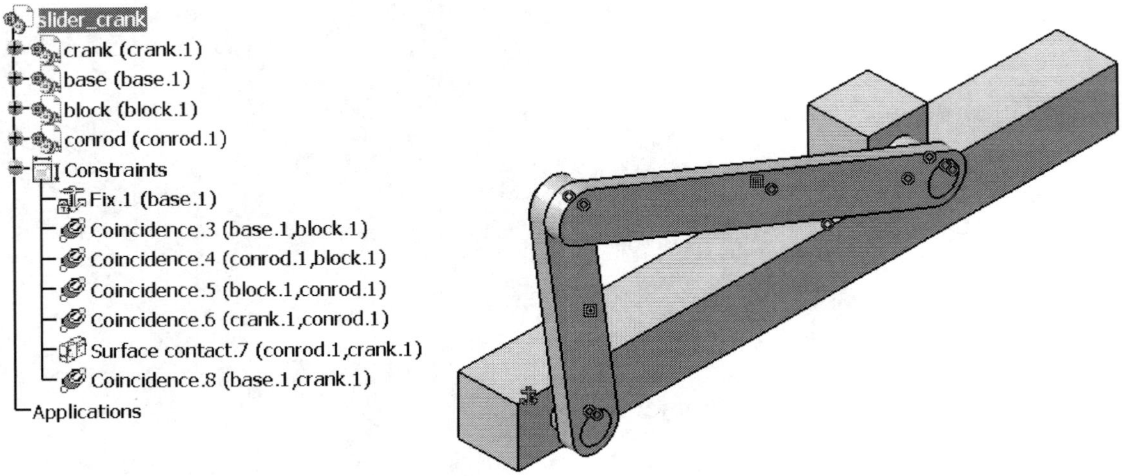

The assembly is complete and we can proceed to the **Digital Mockup** workbench. As you proceed in the tutorial, keep in mind that we have created the assembly constraints with attention to the relative degrees of freedom between the parts in a manner consistent with having a cylindrical joint between the base and the crank, a revolute joint between the crank and the lower end of the conrod, a revolute joint between the upper end of the conrod and the block, and a cylindrical joint between the block and the base.

4 Creating Joints in the Digital Mockup Workbench

The **Digital Mockup** workbench is quite extensive but we will only deal with the **DMU Kinematics module**. To get there you can use the standard Windows toolbar as shown below: **Start > Digital Mockup > DMU Kinematics**.

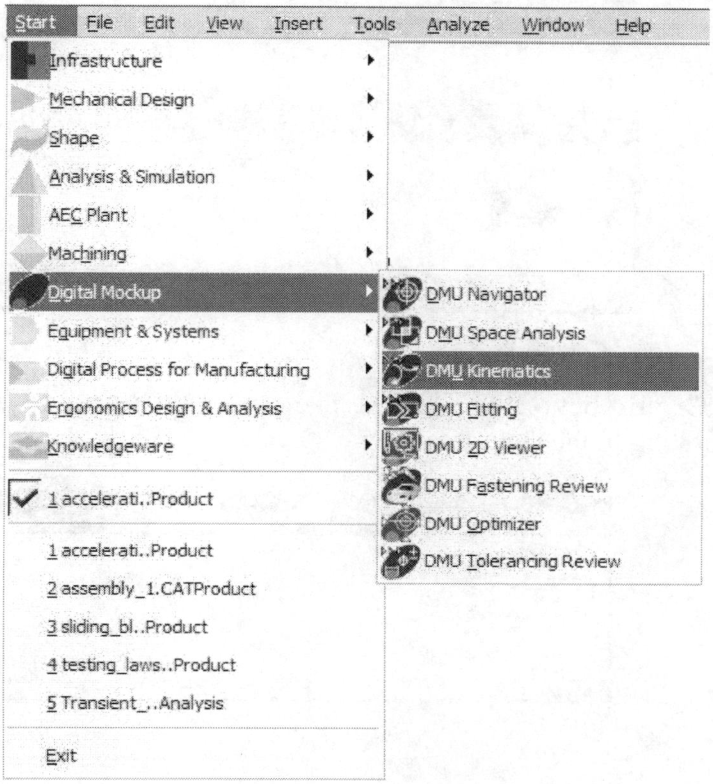

Select the **Assembly Constraints Conversion** icon 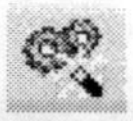 from the **DMU Kinematics** toolbar 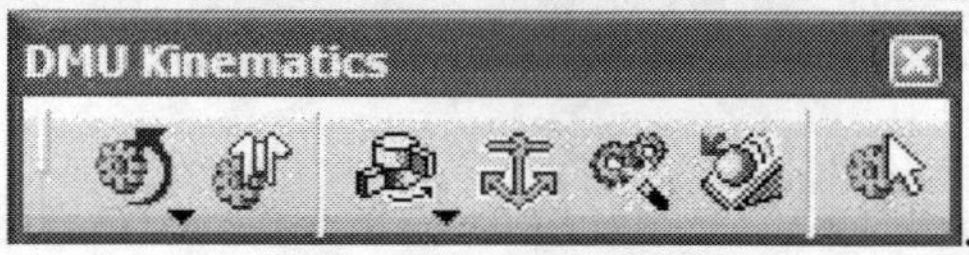

. This icon allows you to create most common joints automatically from the existing assembly constraints.
The pop up box below appears.

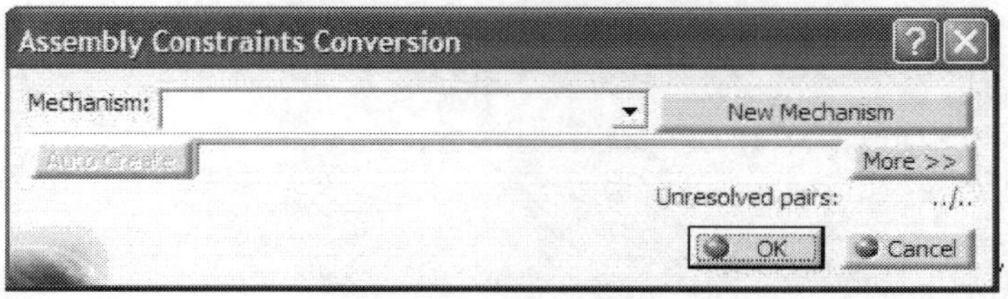

Select the **New Mechanism** button 

.
This leads to another pop up box which allows you to name your mechanism.
The default name is **Mechanism.1**. Accept the default name by pressing **OK**.

Note that the box indicates **Unresolved pairs: 4/4**

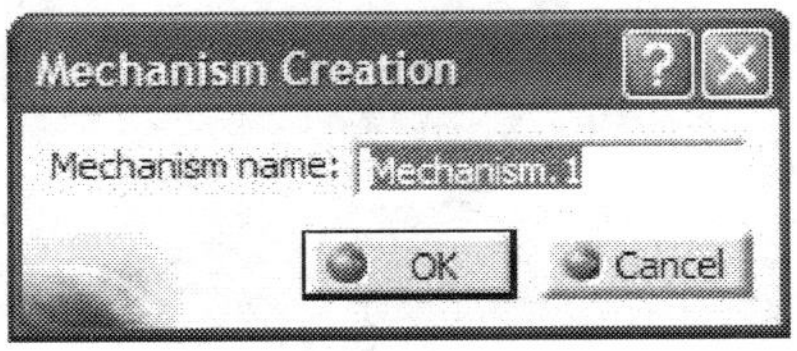

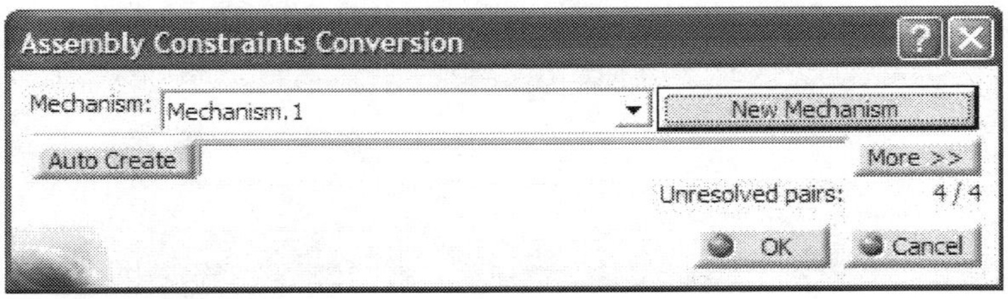

Select the **Auto Create** button 

. Then if the **Unresolved pairs** becomes **0/4**, things are moving in the right direction.

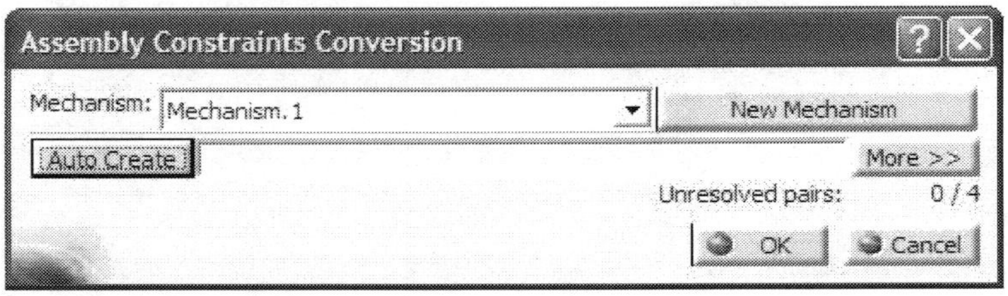

Note that the tree becomes longer by having an **Application** Branch. The expanded tree is displayed below.

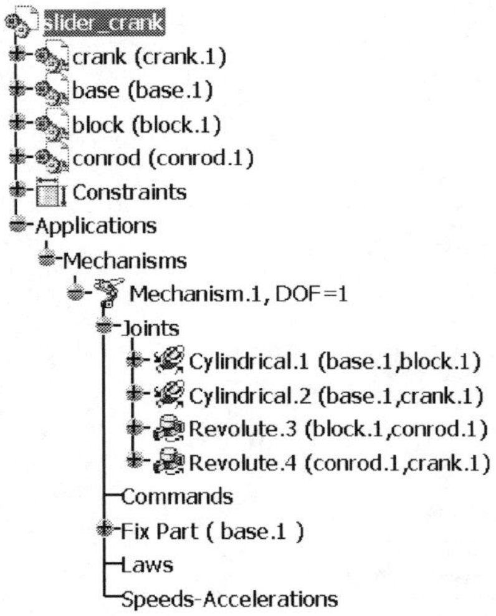

The **DOF** is 1 (if you have dof other than 1, revisit your assembly constraints to make sure they are consistent with those herein, delete your mechanism, then begin this chapter again). This remaining dof can be thought of as the position of the block along the base, or the rotation of the crank about the base. Since we want to drive the crank at constant angular speed, the latter interpretation is appropriate.

Note that because we were careful in creating our assembly constraints consistent with the desired kinematic joints, the desired joints were created based on the assembly constraints created earlier and the **Assembly Constraints Conversion** icon .

All of these joints could also be created directly using the icons in the **Kinematics Joints** toolbar

.

In order to animate the mechanism, you need to remove the one degree of freedom present. This will be achieved by turning **Cylindrical.2** (the joint between the base and the crank) into an **Angle driven** joint.
Note that naming the instances of parts to be the same as the part name makes it easy to identify the joint between any two parts.
Double click on **Cylindrical.2** in the tree. The pop up box below appears.

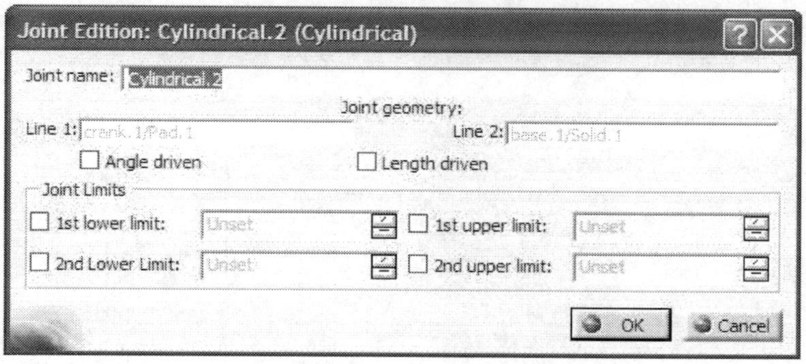

Check the **Angle driven** box. This allows you to change the limits.

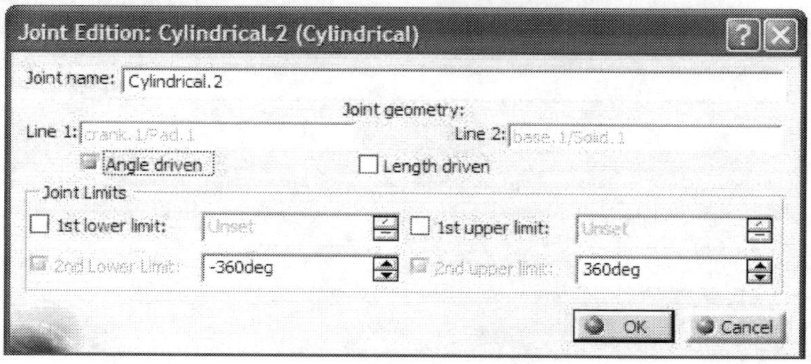

Change the value of **2nd Lower Limit** to be 0.

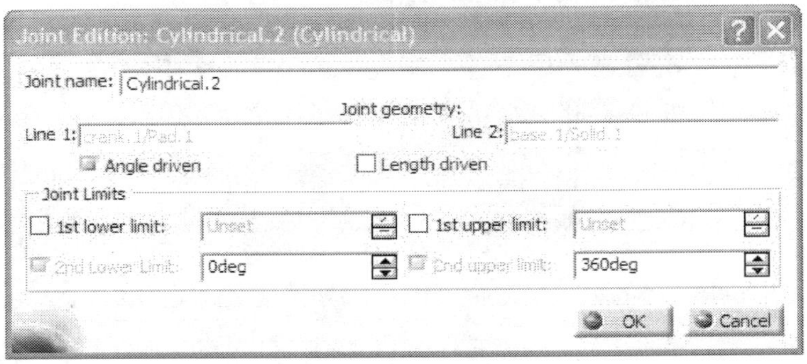

Upon closing the above box and assuming that everything else was done correctly, the following message appears on the screen.

This indeed is good news.

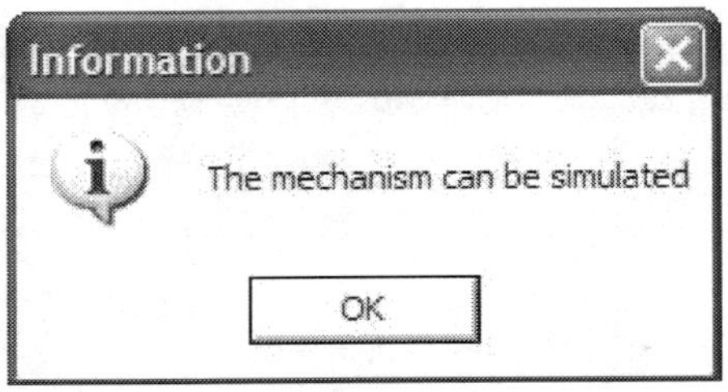

According to CATIA V5 terminology, specifying **Cylindrical.2** as an **Angle driven** joint is synonymous to defining a command. This is observed by the creation of **Command.1** line in the tree.

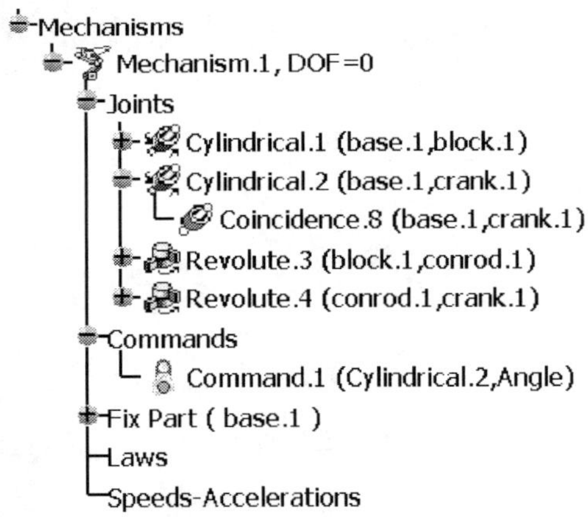

We will now simulate the motion without regard to time based angular velocity. Select the **Simulation** icon  from the **DMU Generic Animation** toolbar

. This enables you to choose the mechanism to be animated if there are several present. In this case, select **Mechanism.1** and close the window.

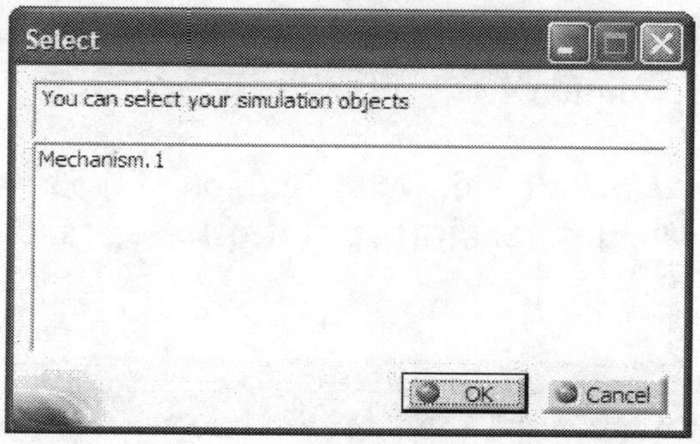

As soon as the window is closed, a Simulation branch is added to the tree.

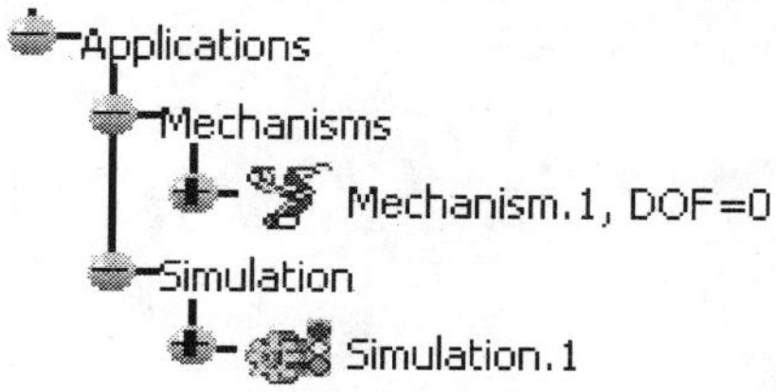

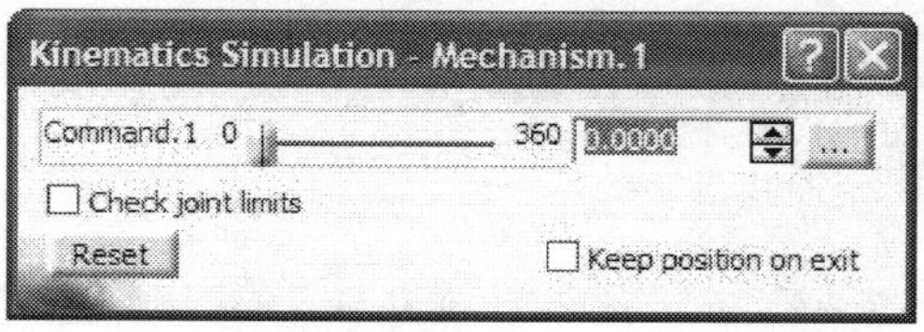

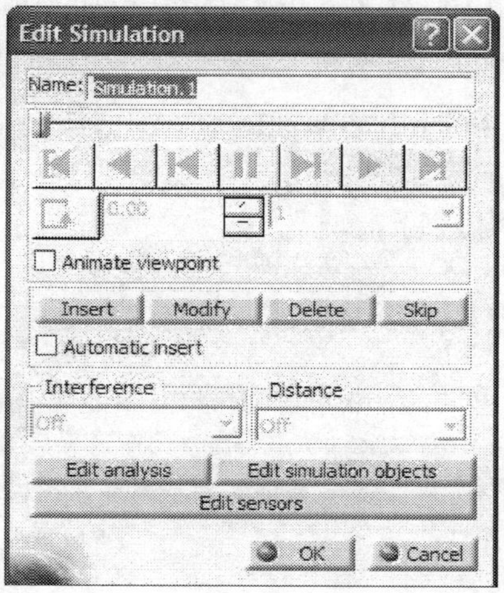

As you scroll the bar in this toolbar from left to right, the crank begins to turn and makes a full 360 degree revolution. Notice that the zero position is simply the initial position of the assembly when the joint was created. Thus, if a particular zero position had been desired, a temporary assembly constraint could have been created earlier to locate the mechanism to the desired zero position. This temporary constraint would need to be deleted before conversion to mechanism joints.

When the scroll bar in the **Kinematics Simulation** pop up box reaches the right extreme end, select the **Insert** button in the **Edit Simulation** pop up box shown above. This activates the video player buttons shown

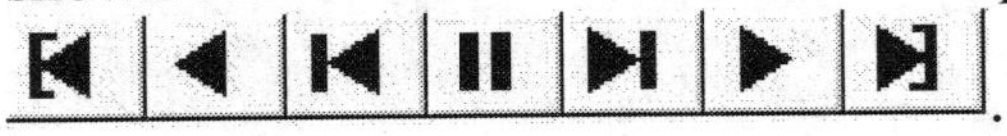

.

Return the block to its original position by picking the **Jump to Start** button .

Note that the **Change Loop Mode** button is also active now.

Upon selecting the **Play Forward** button , the crank makes fast jump completing its revolution.

In order to slow down the motion of the crank, select a different **interpolation step**, such as 0.04.

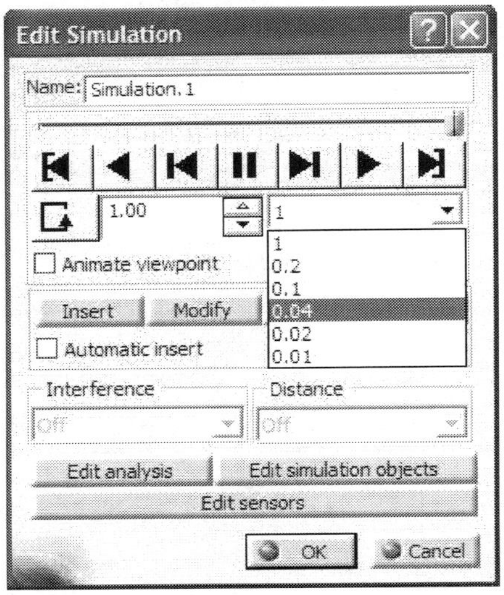

Upon changing the interpolation step to 0 0.04, return the crank to its original position by picking the **Jump to Start** button . Apply **Play Forward** button and observe the slow and smooth rotation of the crank. It is likely that your slider will proceed beyond the end of the block; the entities involved in the joints are treated as infinite. If you wish, you may alter your block dimensions so the slider remains on the block.

Select the **Compile Simulation** icon from the **Generic Animation** toolbar

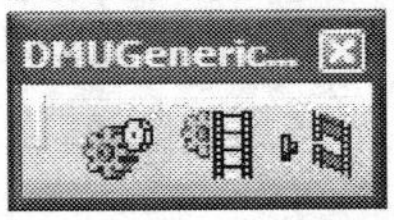

and activate the option **Generate an animation file**. Now, pressing the **File name** button allows you to set the location and name of the animation file to be generated as displayed below.
Select a suitable path and file name and change the **Time step** to be 0.04 to produce a slow moving rotation in an AVI file.

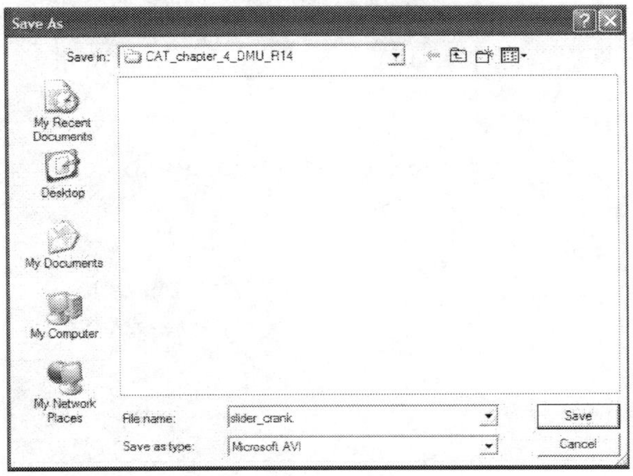

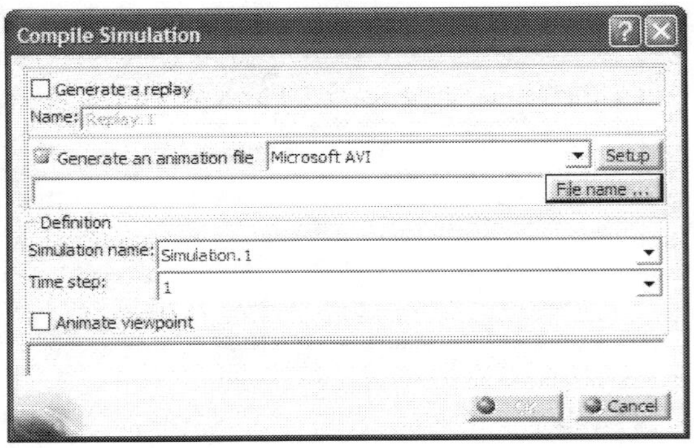

The completed pop up box is displayed for your reference.

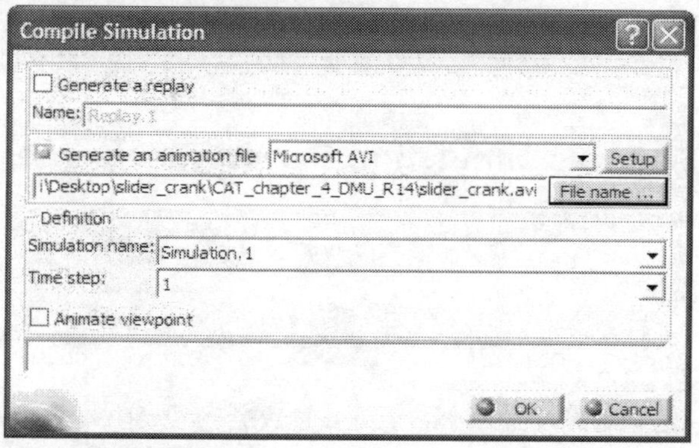

As the file is being generated, the crank slowly rotates. The resulting AVI file can be viewed with the Windows Media Player.

In the event that an AVI file is not needed, but one wishes to play the animation, repeatedly, a **Replay** need be generated. Therefore, in the **Compile Simulation** box, check the **Generate a replay** button.

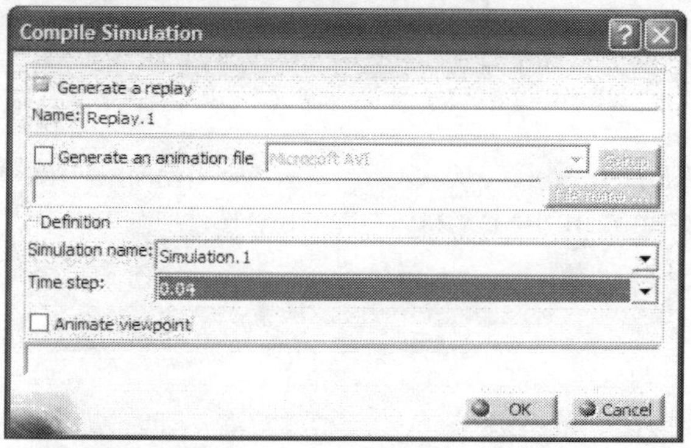

Note that in this case most of the previously available options are dimmed out.

A **Replay.1** branch has also been added to the tree.

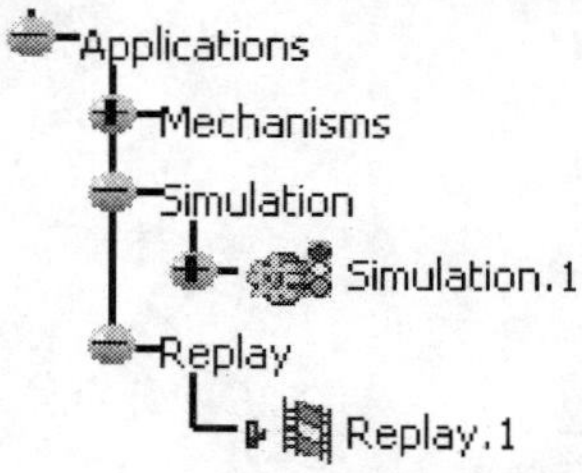

Select the **Replay** icon  from the **Generic Animation** toolbar 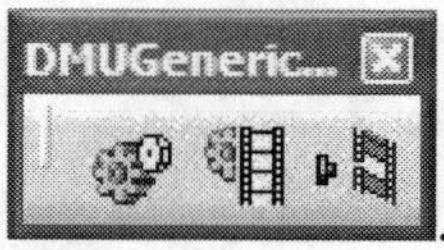.

Double clock on **Replay.1** in the tree and the **Replay** pop up box appears. Experiment with the different choices of the **Change Loop Mode** buttons , , .
The block can be returned to the original position by picking the **Jump to Start** button .

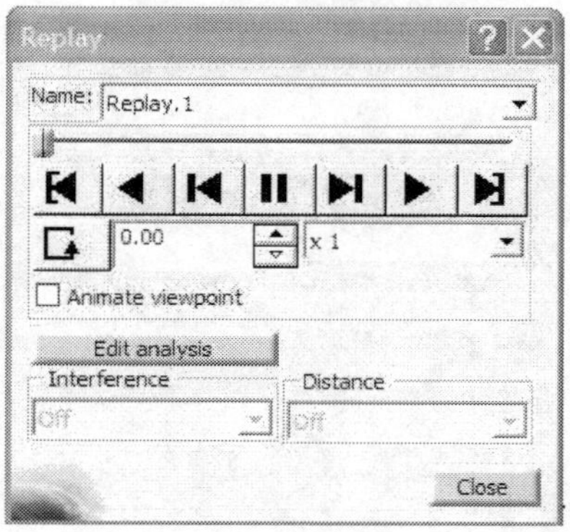

The **skip ratio** (which is chosen to be x1 in the right box) controls the speed of the **Replay**.

Once a **Replay** is generated such as **Replay.1** in the tree above, it can also be played with a different icon.

Select the **Simulation Player** icon  from the **DMUPlayer** toolbar 

.

The outcome is the pop up box above. Use the cursor to pick **Replay.1** from the tree.

The player keys are no longer dimmed out. Use the **Play Forward (Right)** button  to begin the replay.

5 Creating Laws in the Motion

You will now introduce some time based physics into the problem by specifying the crank angular velocity. The objective is to specify the angular position versus time function as a constant 1 revolution/sec (360 degrees/sec).

Click on **Simulation with Laws** icon  in the **Simulation** toolbar. You will get the following pop up box indication that you need to add at least a relation between a command and the time parameter.

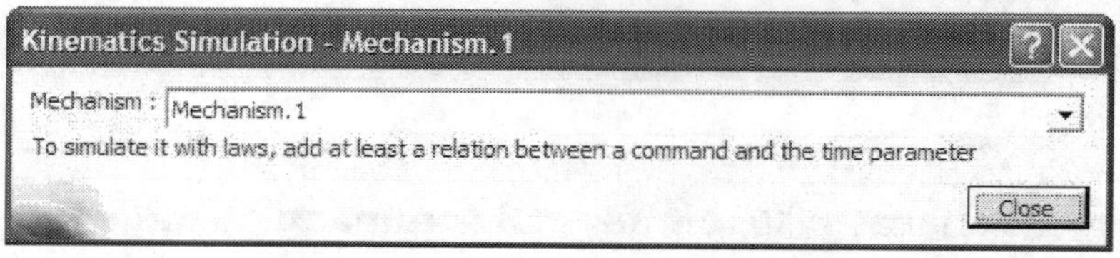

To create the required relation, select the **Formula** icon  from the **Knowledge** toolbar 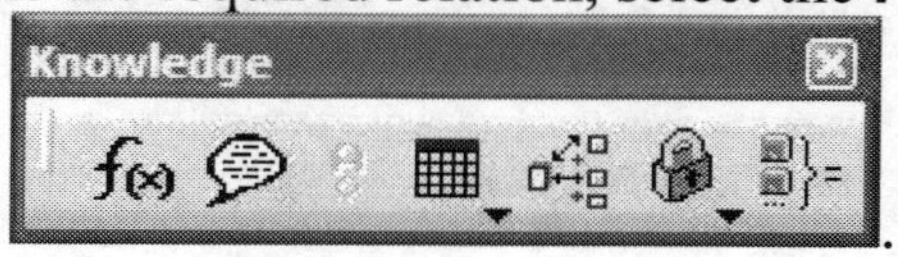. The pop up box below appears on the screen.

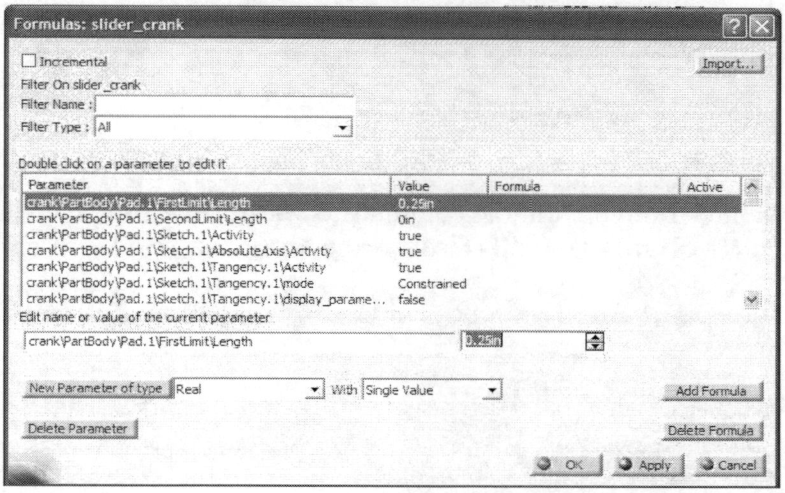

Point the cursor to the **Mechanism.1, DOF=0** branch in the tree and click. The consequence is that only parameters associated with the mechanism are displayed in the **Formulas** box.
The long list is now reduced to two parameters as indicated in the box.

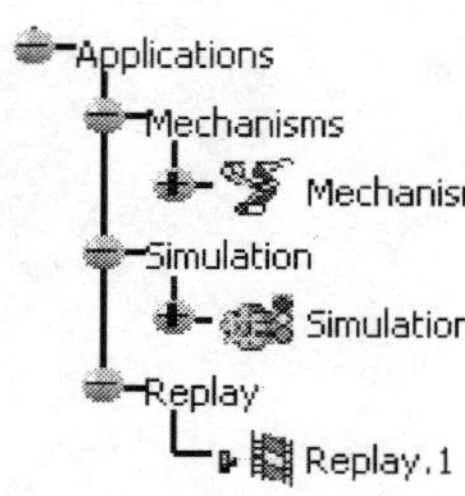

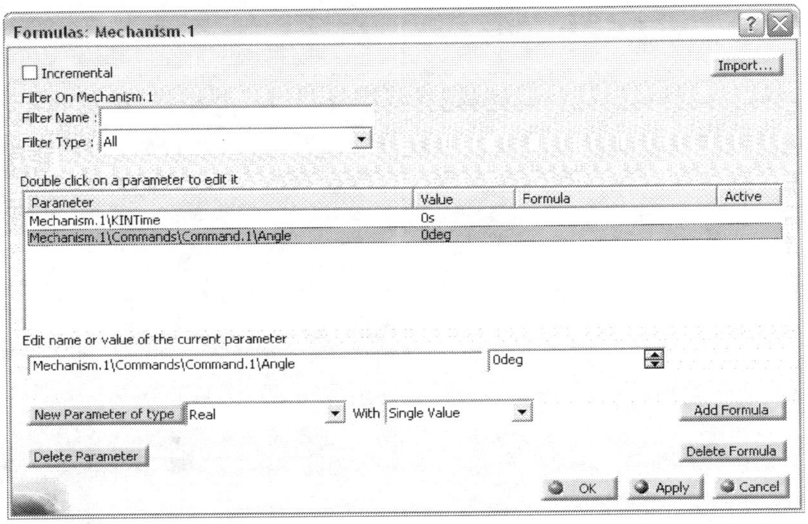

Select the entry **Mechanism.1\Commands\Command.1\Angle** and press the **Add Formula** button Add Formula. This action kicks you to the **Formula Editor** box.

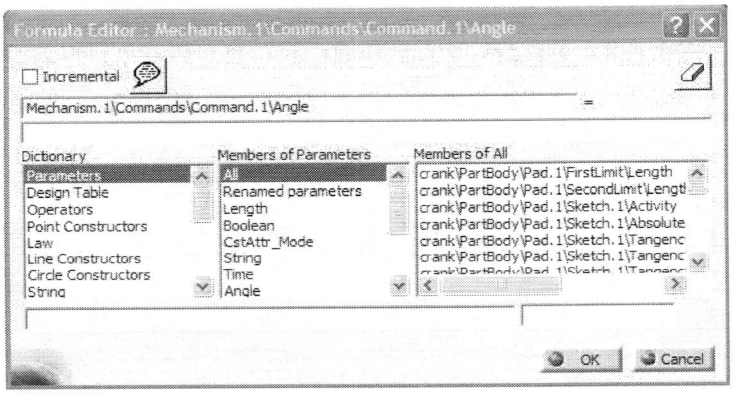

Pick the **Time** entry from the middle column (i.e. **Members of Parameters**) then double click on **Mechanism.1\KINTime** in the **Members of Time** column.

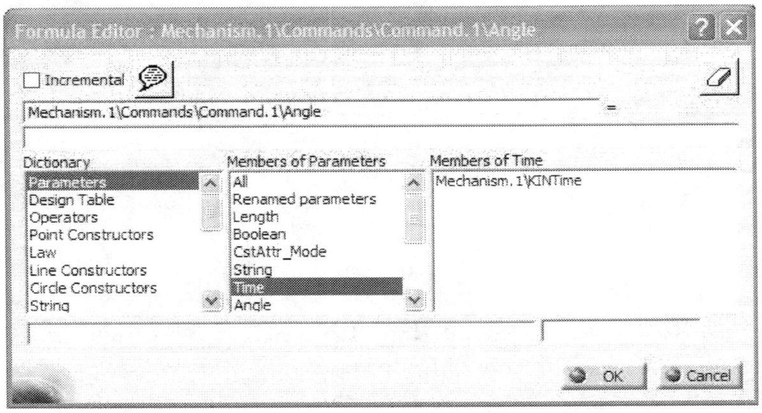

Since angle can be computed as the product of angular velocity (360deg)/(1s) in our case and time, edit the box containing the right hand side of the equality such that the formula becomes:

$$Mechanism.1 \backslash Commands \backslash Command.1 \backslash Angle = (360\,\text{deg})/(1s) * (Mechnism.1 \backslash KINTime)$$

The completed **Formula Editor** box should look as shown below.

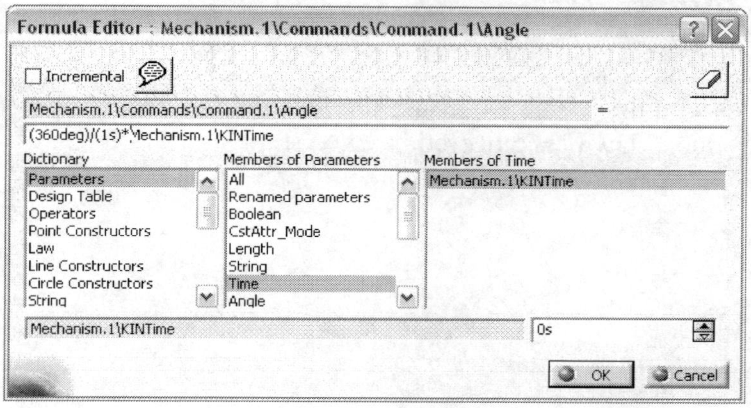

Upon accepting **OK**, the formula is recorded in the **Formulas** pop up box as shown below.

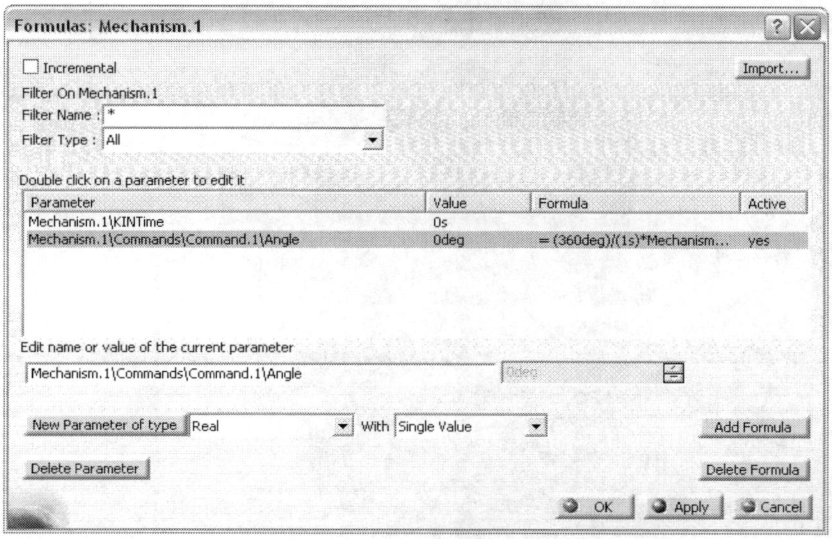

Careful attention must be given to the units when writing formulas involving the kinematic parameters. In the event that the formula has different units at the different sides of the equality you will get **Warning** messages such as the one shown below.

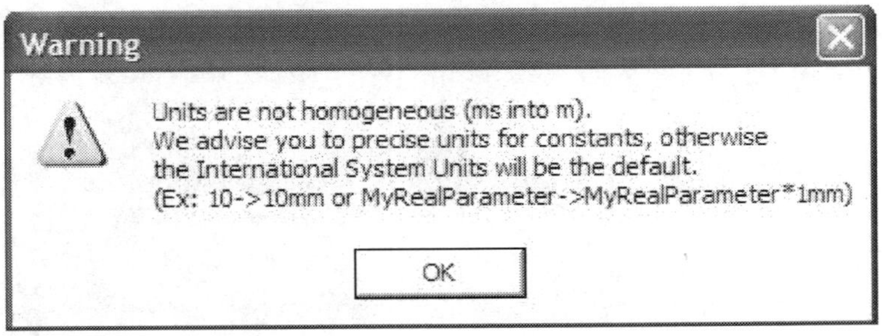

We are spared the warning message because the formula has been properly inputted. Note that the introduced law has appeared in **Law** branch of the tree.

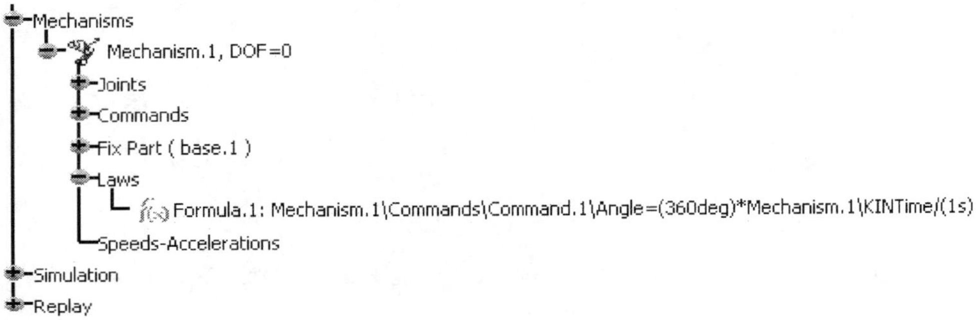

Keep in mind that our interest is to plot the position, velocity and accelerations generated by this motion. To set this up, select the **Speed and Acceleration** icon  from the **DMU Kinematics** toolbar 

. The pop up box below appears on the Screen.

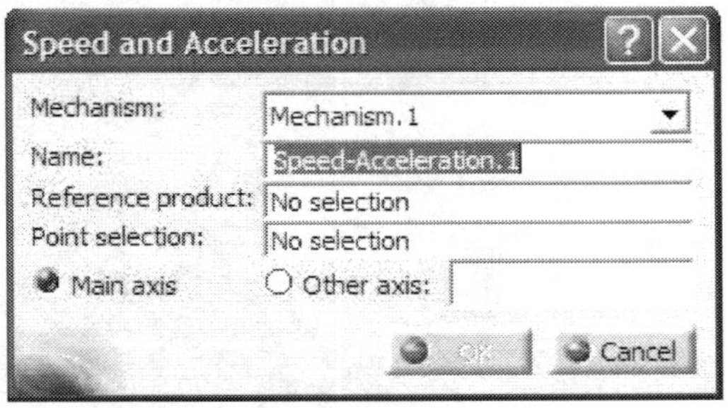

For the **Reference product,** select the **base** from the screen or the tree. For the **Point selection**, pick the vertex of the **block** as shown in the sketch below. This will set up the sensor to record the movement of the chosen point relative to the base (which is fixed).

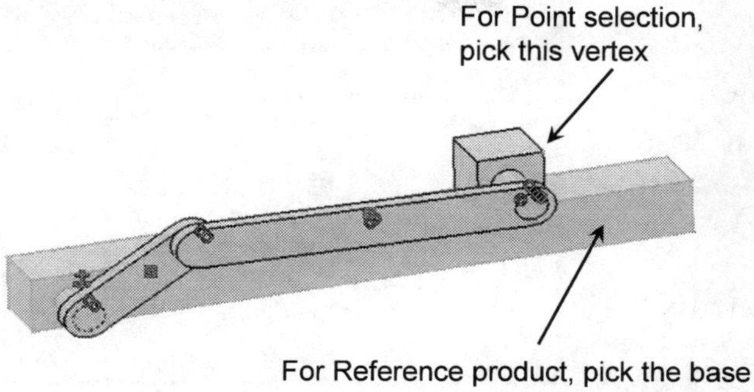

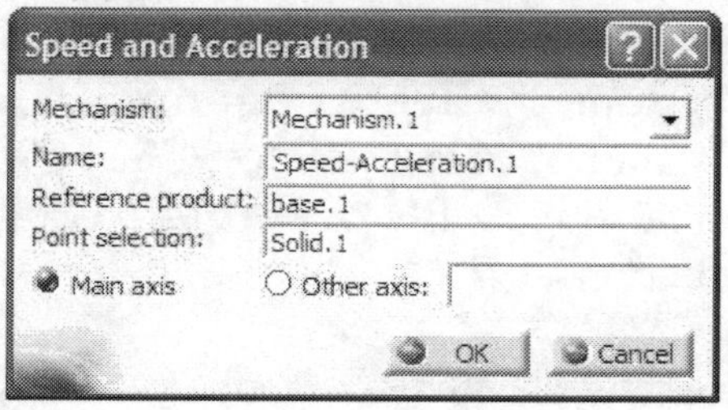

Note that the **Speed and Acceleration.1** has appeared in the tree.

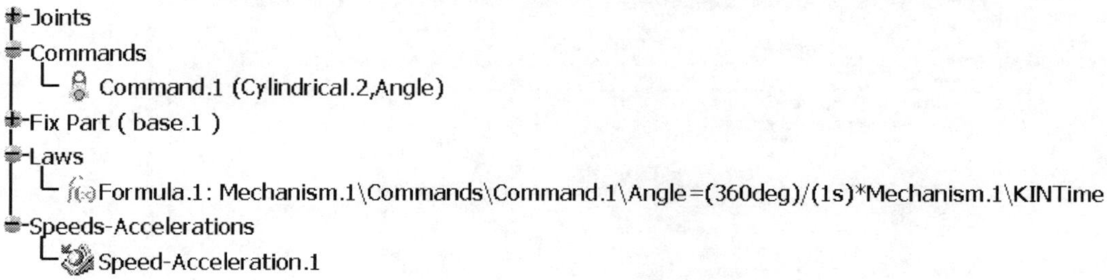

Having entered the required kinematic relation and designated the vertex on the block as the point to collect data on, we will simulate the mechanism. Click on **Simulation with Laws** icon  in the **Simulation** toolbar .
This results in the **Kinematics Simulation** pop up box shown below.

Note that the default time duration is 10 seconds.
To change this value, click on the button 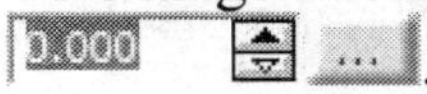. In the resulting pop up box, change the time duration to 1s. This is the time duration for the crank to make one full revolution.

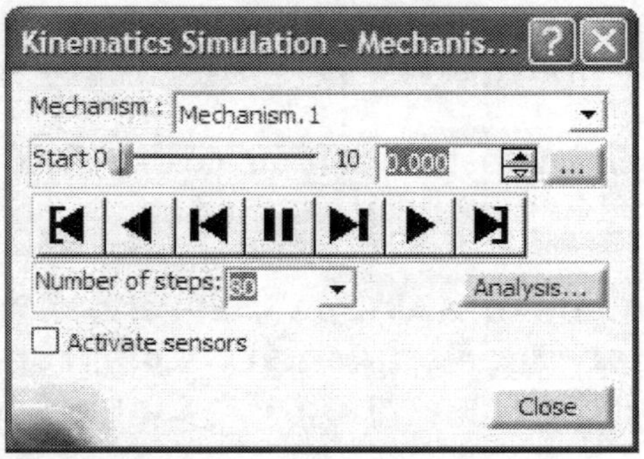

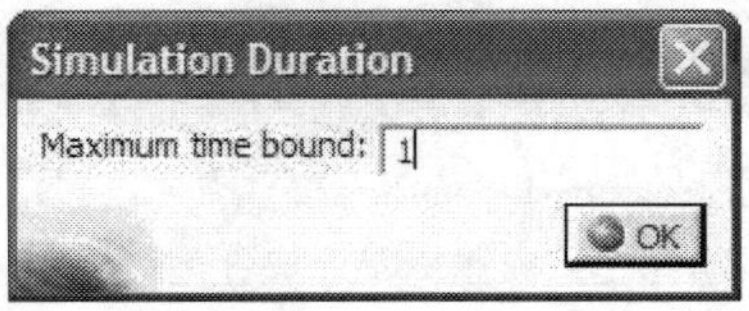

The scroll bar now moves up to 1s.

Check the **Activate sensors** box, at the bottom left corner. (Note: CATIA V5R15 users will also see a **Plot vectors** box in this window).

You will next have to make certain selections from the accompanying **Sensors** box.

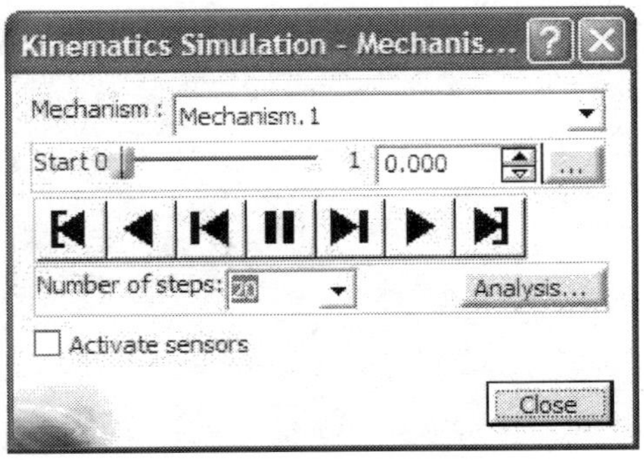

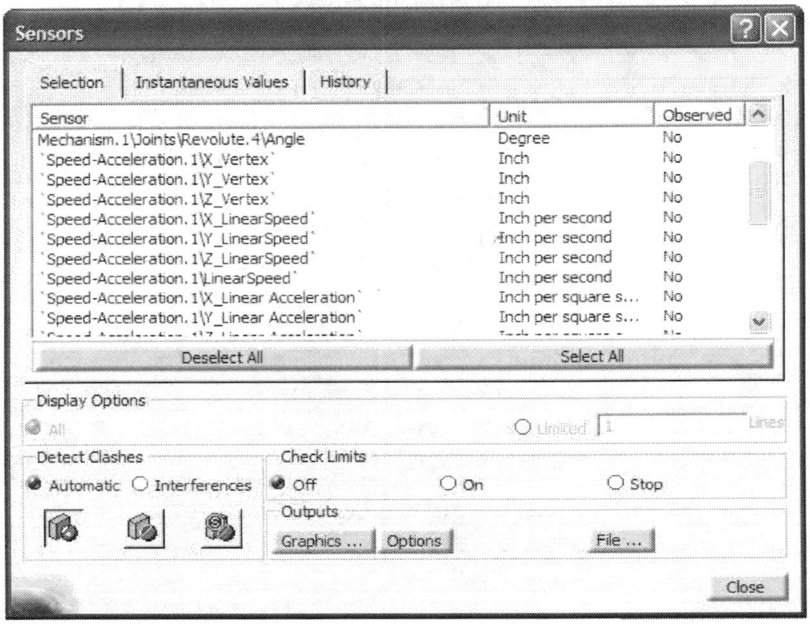

Observing that the coordinate direction of interest is X, click on the following items to record position, velocity, and acceleration of the block:

Mechanism.1\Joints\Cylindrical.1\Length
Speed-Acceleration.1\X_LinearSpeed
Speed-Acceleration.1\X_LinearAcceleration

As you make selections in this window, the last column in the **Sensors** box, changes to **Yes** for the corresponding items. This is shown on the next page. Do not close the **Sensors** box after you have made your selection (leave it open to generate results).

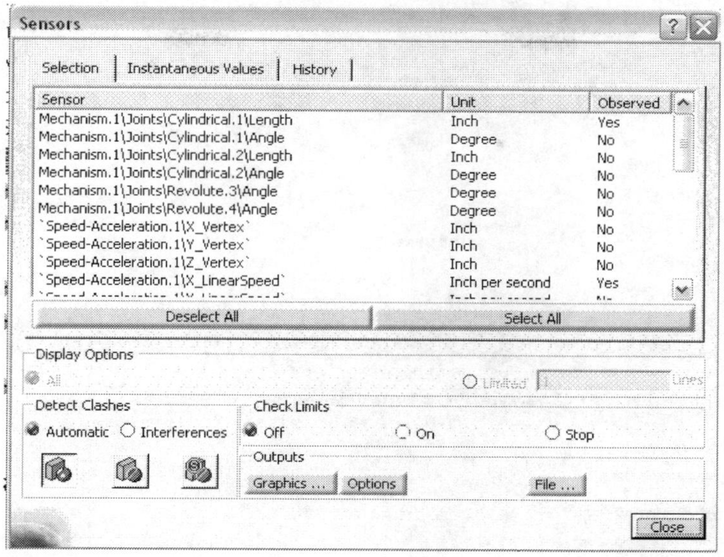

Also, change the **Number of steps to 80**. The larger this number, the smoother the velocity and acceleration plots will be.

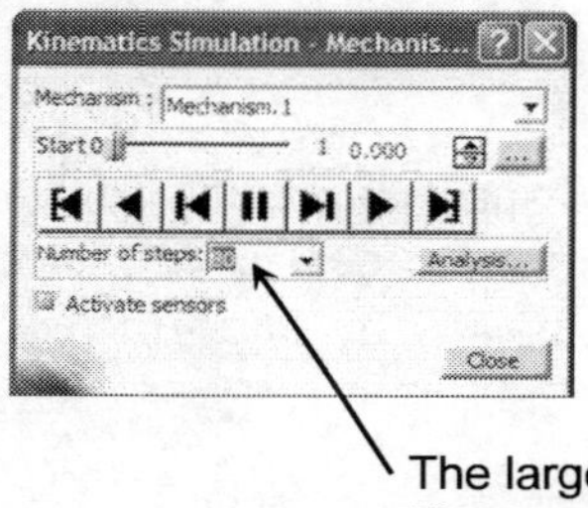

The larger this number,
The smoother the plots

Note: If you haven't already done so, change the default units on position, velocity and acceleration to in, in/s and in/s^2, respectively. This is done in the **Tools, Options, Parameters and Measures** menu shown on the next page.

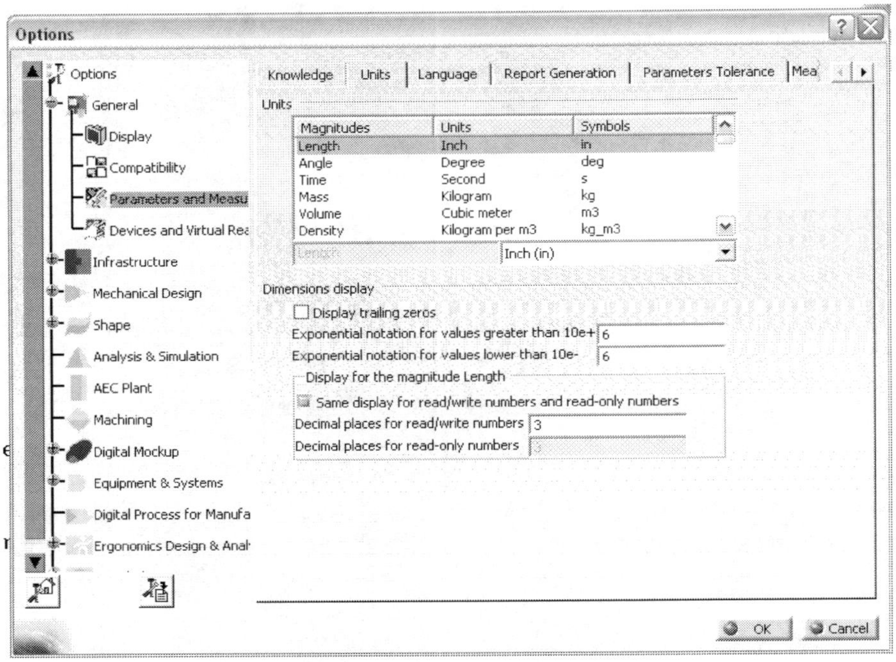

Finally, drag the scroll bar in the **Kinematics Simulation** box. As you do this, the crank rotates and the block travels along the base. Once the bar reaches its right extreme point, the crank has made one full revolution. This corresponds to 1s.

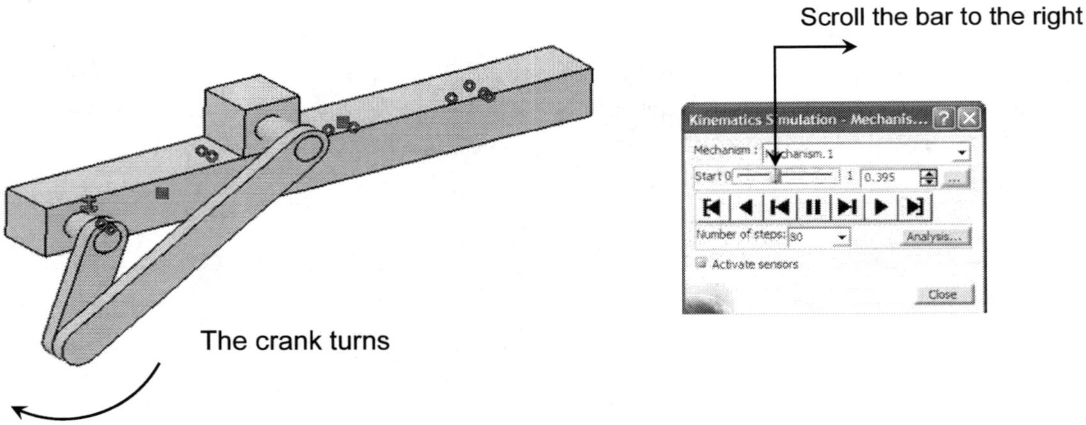

Once the crank reaches the end, click on the **Graphics** button 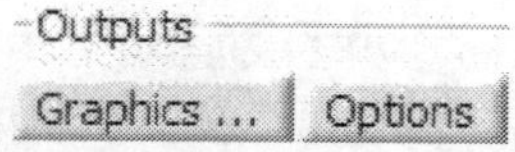

in the **Sensor** box. The result is the plot of the position, velocity and acceleration all on the same axis (but with the vertical axis units corresponding to whichever one of the three outputs is highlighted in the right side of the window). Click on each of the three outputs to see the corresponding axis units for each output. The three plots for position (corresponding to cylindrical joint Length), velocity (X_LinearSpeed), and acceleration (X_Linear_Acceleration) are shown below.

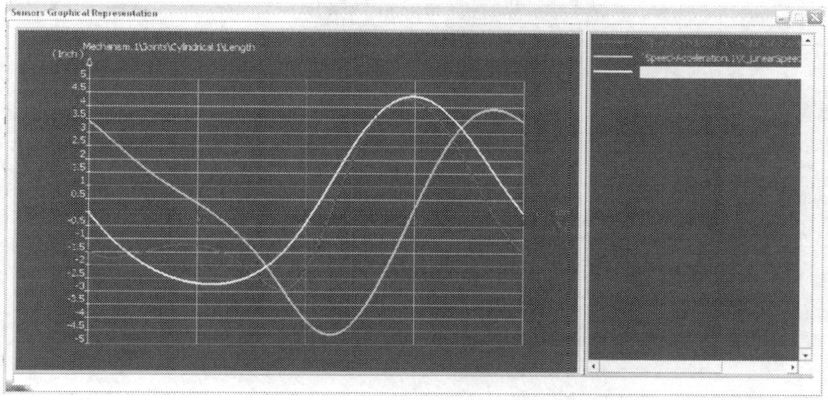

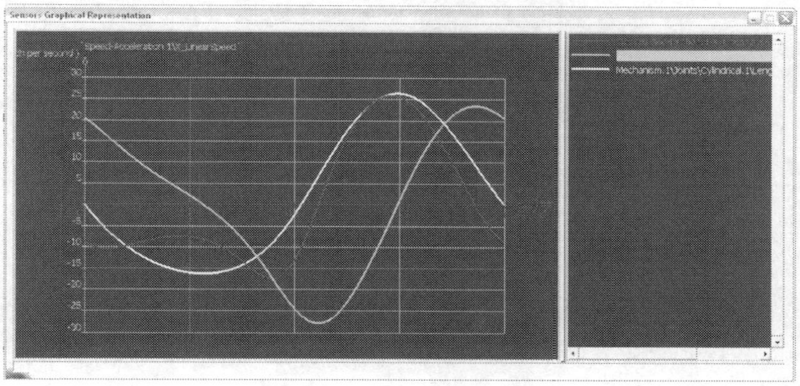

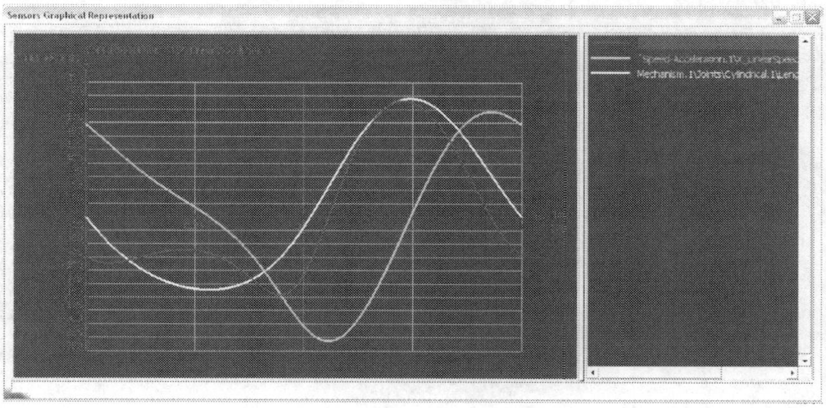

It is not uncommon that you may develop a variety of simulation results before determining exactly how to achieve the desired results. In this case, prior results stored need to be erased. To do this, click on the **History** tab History of the **Sensors** box.

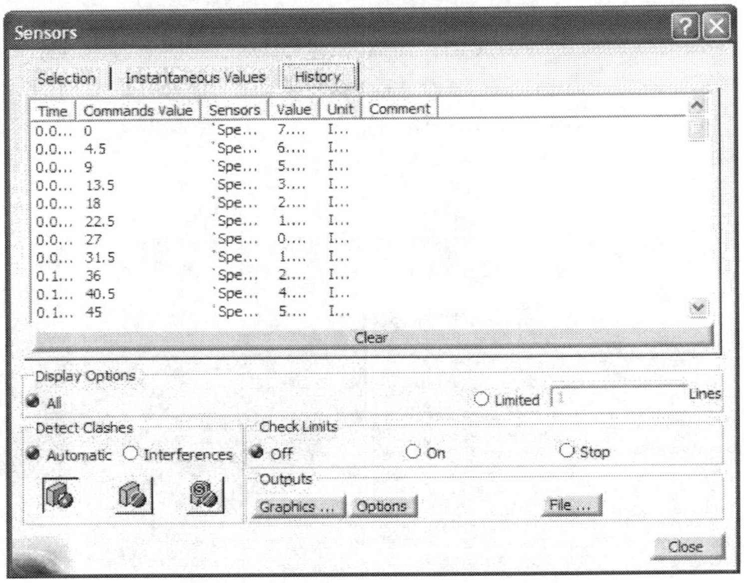

Use the **Clear** key Clear to erase the values generated.

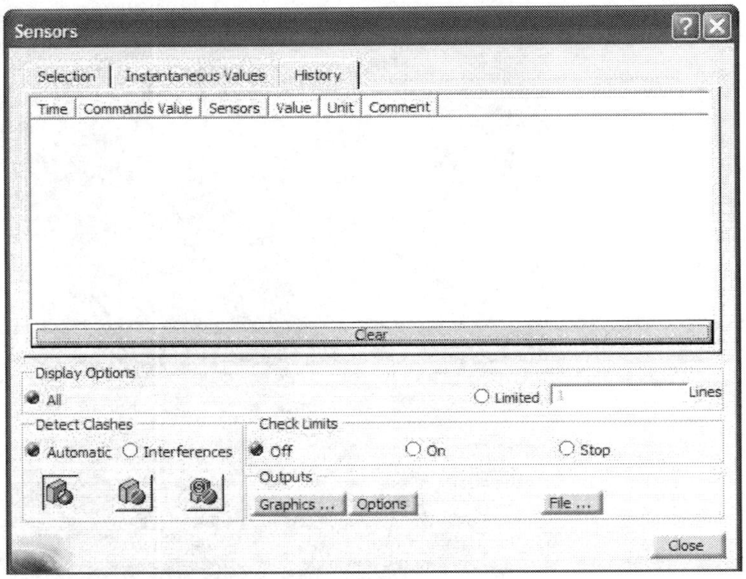

Next, we will create a plot which is not simply versus time. As an illustrative example, we will place a point somewhere along the conrod. For this point, we will plot its linear speed and linear acceleration versus crank angle. It is important to note that DMU computes positive scalars for linear speeds and linear accelerations since it simply computes the magnitude based on the three rectangular components.

First, return to **Part Design** and create a reference point on the conrod at the approximate location as shown below. Return to **DMU**.

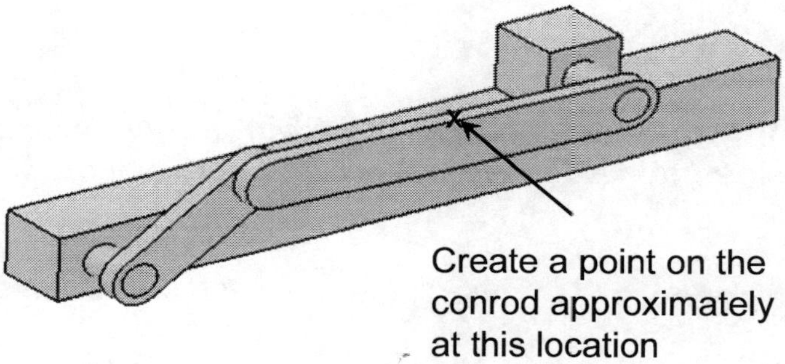

The plan is to generate two plots. The first plot is the speed of the created point against the angular position of the crank. The second plot is the acceleration of the created point against the angular position of the crank.
In order to generate the speed and acceleration data, you need to use the **Speed and Acceleration** icon  from the **DMU Kinematics** toolbar

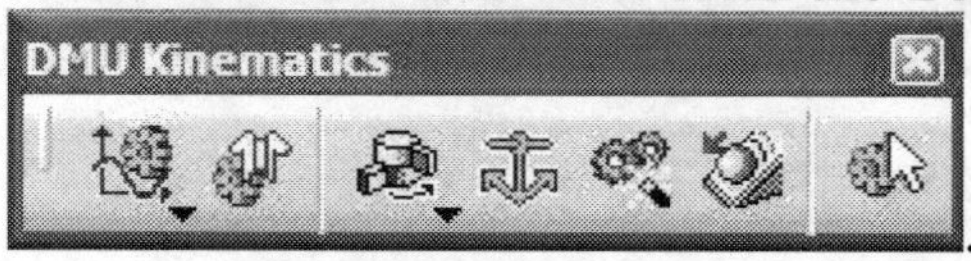

. Click on the icon and in the resulting pop up box make the following selections.
For **Reference product**, pick the base from the screen. For **Reference point,** pick the point that was created earlier on the conrod.

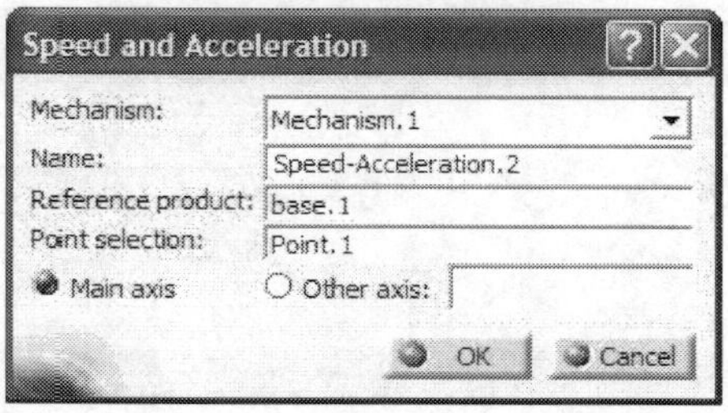

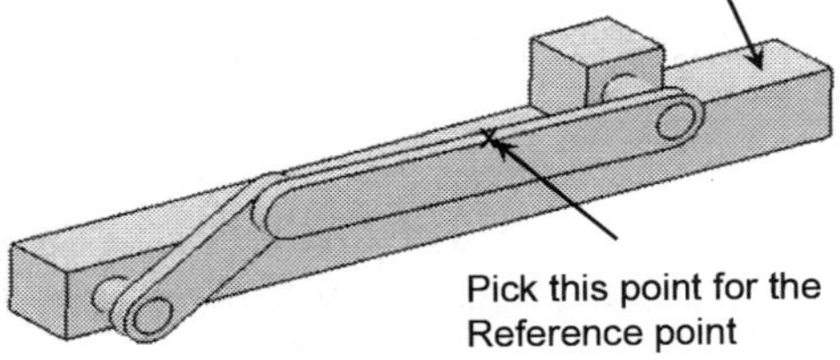

The tree indicates that **Speed-Acceleration.2** is being generated which holds the data for the point on the conrod.

Click on **Simulation with Laws** icon in the **Simulation** toolbar .
This results in the **Kinematics Simulation** pop up box shown below.

Check the **Activate sensors** box, at the bottom left corner.

You will have to make the following selections from the accompanying **Sensors** box.

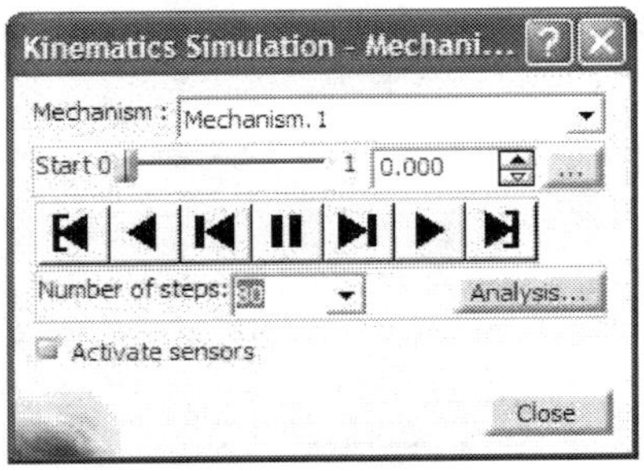

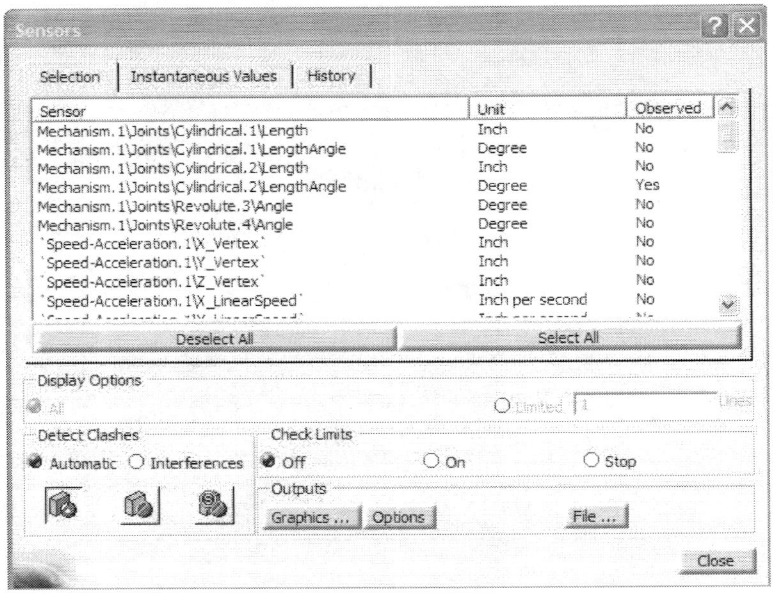

If you scroll down the list, you will notice that the data from **Speed-Acceleration.1** and **Speed-Acceleration.2** are both available.

Click on the **History** tab History of the **Sensors** box and make sure that no data is present. Of course the data can be cleared using the Clear button.

In the **Sensors** box, click on the following line items; be careful as many entries look alike with minor differences.

Mechanism.1\Joints\Cylindrical.2\LengthAngle
Speed-Acceleration.2\LinearSpeed
Speed-Acceleration.2\Linear Acceleration

Note: Depending upon your installation, you may see **Angle** instead of **LengthAngle**.

As you make these selections, the last column in the **Sensors** box, changes to **Yes** for the corresponding items. Be sure you have picked Cylindrical.2 for the angle since this is the cylindrical joint at the crank connection to the base.

Pick the **Options** button Options in the Sensors box. The pop up box shown below appears. Check the **Customized** radio button.

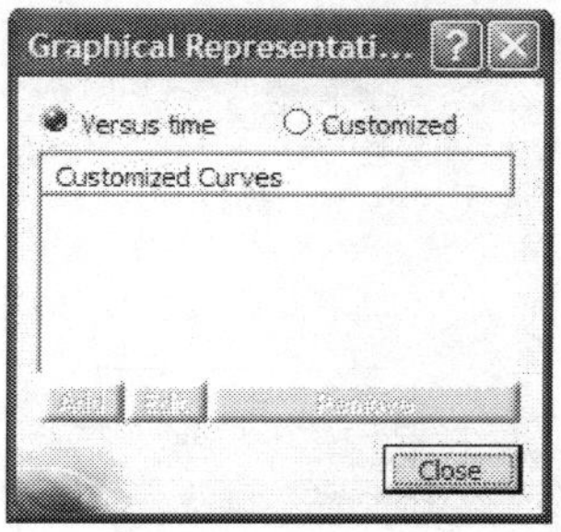

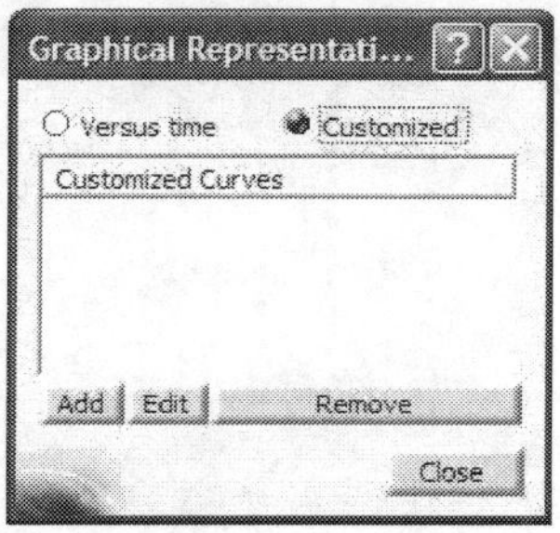

Pick the **Add** button Add.
The **Curve Creation** pop up box appears.

Use the pull down menu to make the following selections.

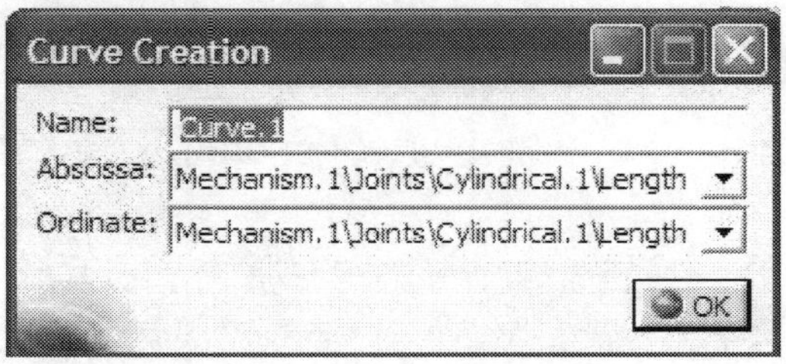

For **Abscissa**, select **Mechanism.1\Joints\Cylindrical.2\LengthAngle**
For **Ordinate**, select **Speed-Acceleration.2\LinearSpeed**

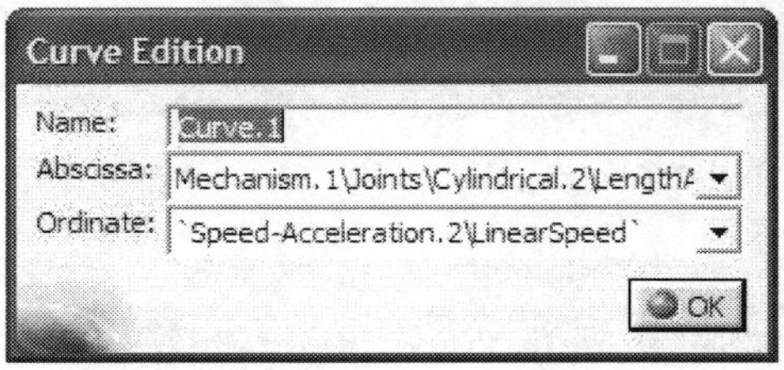

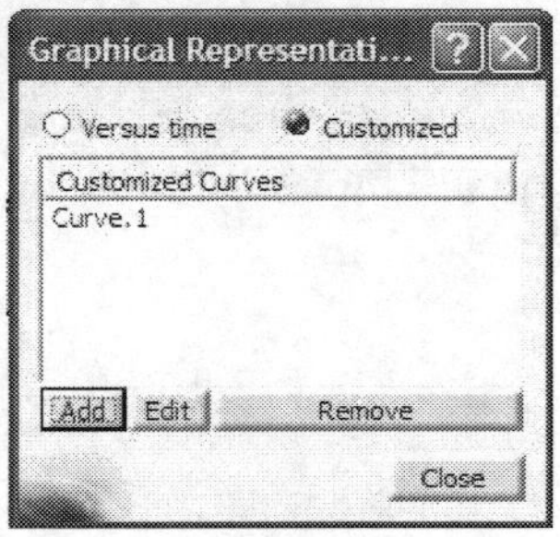

Press **OK** to close the box. Note that **Curve.1** is now setup.

Pick the **Add** button Add once again.
The **Curve Creation** pop up box appears.

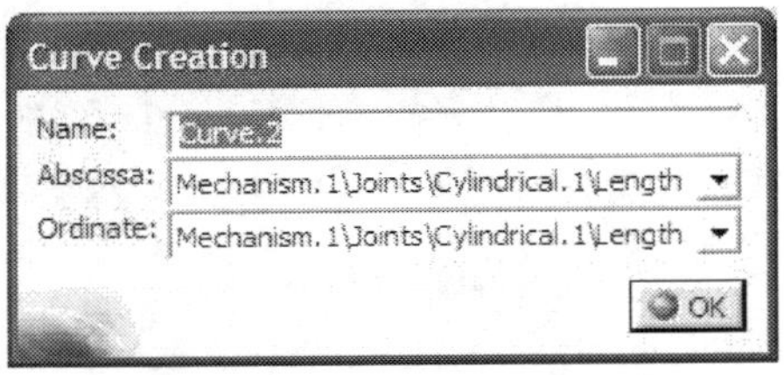

Use the pull down menu to make the following selections.

For **Abscissa**, select **Mechanism.1\Joints\Cylindrical.2\LengthAngle**
For **Ordinate**, select **Speed-Acceleration.2\Linear Acceleration**

Press **OK** to close the box. Note that **Curve.2** is now setup.

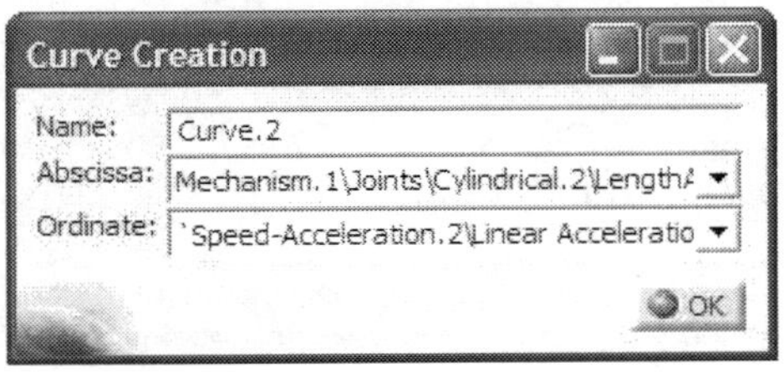

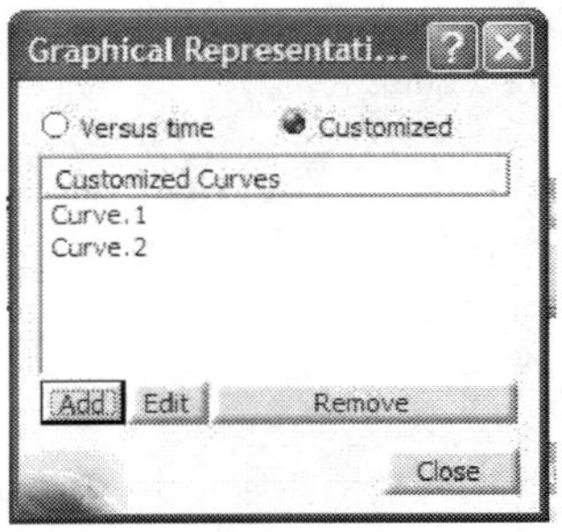

Close the **Graphical Representation** box.

Drag the scroll bar in the Kinematics Simulation box all the way to the right or simply click on ▶.

Drag the scroll bar all the way to the right or simply click on ▶

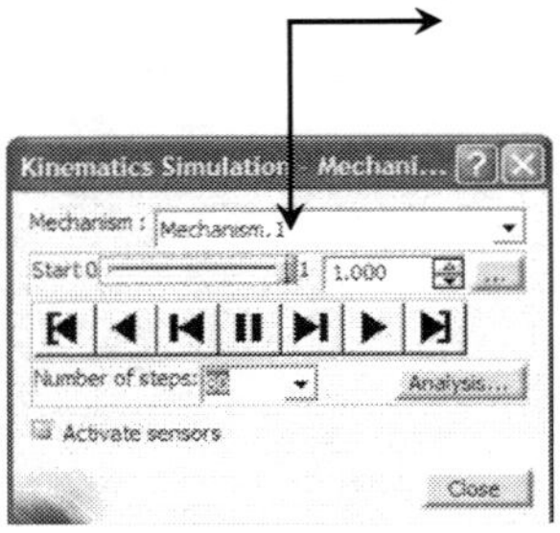

Once the crank reaches the end, click on **Graphics** button Outputs Graphics ... Options in the **Sensor** box. The **Multiplot** window appears and allows you to pick either **Curve.1**, or **Curve.2**.

The plots for **Curve.1** and **Curve.2** are shown on the next page.

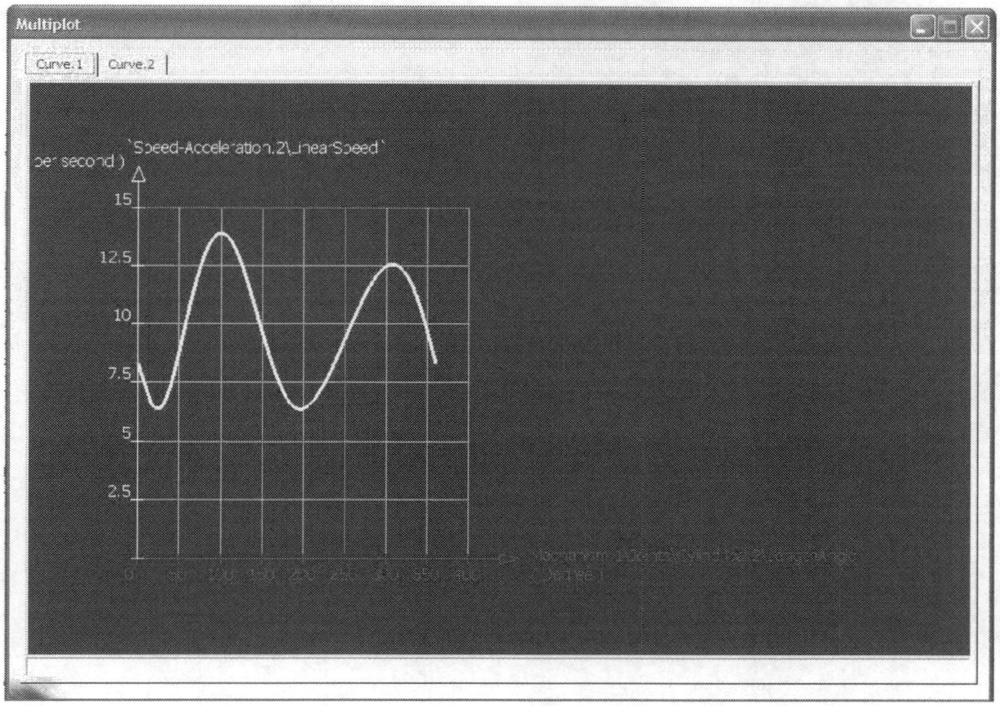
Multiplot
Curve.1
Curve.2
`Speed-Acceleration.2\LinearSpeed`
15
12.5
10
7.5
5
2.5

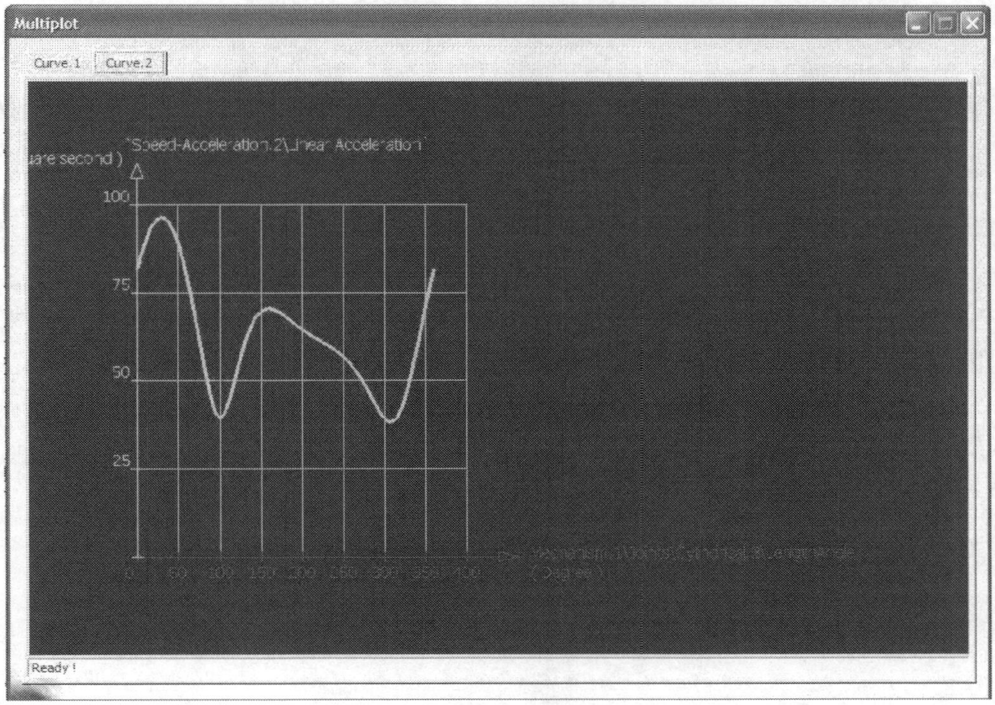
Multiplot
Curve.1
Curve.2
`Speed-Acceleration.2\Linear Acceleration`
100
75
50
25
Ready !

NOTES:

Chapter 5

Sliding Ladder

Introduction

In this tutorial you will model the kinematics of a ladder sliding down a wall. The ladder will be modeled as a solid shaped as shown below. The results obtained can be compared with the theoretical solution derived from the corresponding related rate calculus problem.

To illustrate a few joint types not illustrated in the earlier tutorials, the mechanism will utilize a Point-Curve and a Slide-Curve joint. Also, to illustrate direct joint creation in DMU, the joints will be created manually in DMU rather than through assembly constraint conversion.

1 Problem Statement

The ladder shown slides down the wall while maintaining contact with the wall and the ground. For this simulation, it is assumed that the downward velocity of the top contact point is a given constant of is v_0=10 in/s.

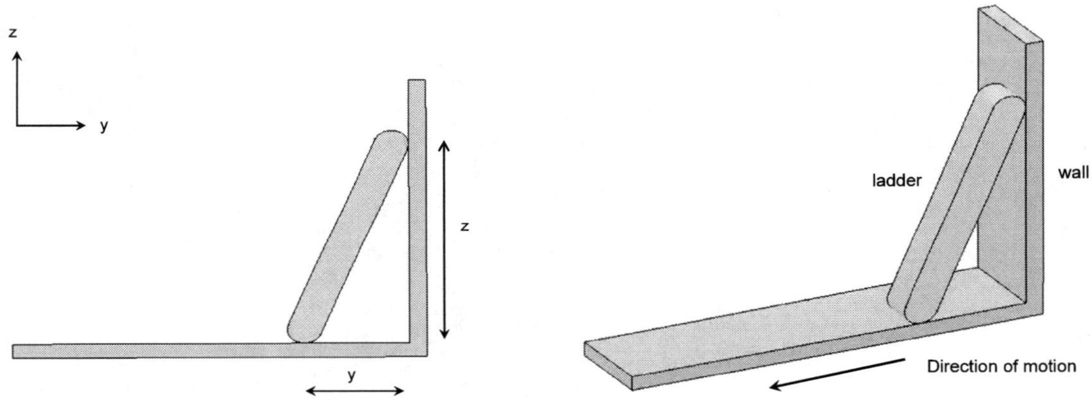

First, we will derive the theoretical solution. Since the length of the ladder L is constant, Pythagorean's theorem implies that $z(t)^2 + y(t)^2 = L^2$. Differentiating both sides gives $z(t)\dot{z}(t) + y(t)\dot{y}(t) = 0$.

The downward velocity being constant leads to $\dot{z} = -v_0$ and $z(t) = z_0 - v_0 t$. In this expression, z_0 refers to the initial z position of the top of the ladder. Substituting this information in the above equation and using $y(t) = \sqrt{L^2 - z(t)^2}$ yields the expressions for velocity and acceleration in the y direction.

$$\dot{y}(t) = \frac{v_0(z_0 - v_0 t)}{\sqrt{L^2 - (z_0 - v_0 t)^2}} \qquad \ddot{y}(t) = \frac{-v_0^{\,2} L^2}{\left[\sqrt{L^2 - (z_0 - v_0 t)^2}\right]^3}$$

The plot of these functions for L=7 in, $z_0 = 5.0$ in, $v_0 = 10$ in/s and $0 \le t \le 0.5$ sec is displayed below.

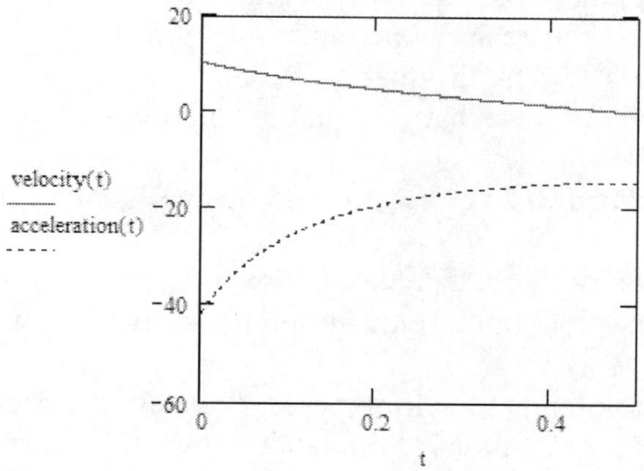

2 Overview of this Tutorial

In this tutorial you will:

1. Model the two CATIA parts required. Some additional reference geometry will be added to facilitate the desired kinematic modeling.
2. Create an assembly (CATIA Product) containing the parts.
3. Constrain the assembly in such a way that the ladder is in its desired starting position.
4. Enter the **Digital Mockup** workbench and manually create a Point-Curve and a Slide-Curve joint.
5. Simulate the motion of the ladder sliding down the wall without consideration to time (in other words, without implementing the known constant velocity given in the problem statement).
6. Add a formula to implement the time based kinematics associated with constant velocity of the top contact point of the ladder down the wall.
7. Simulate the desired constant velocity motion and generate plots of the kinematic results.

3 Creation of the Assembly in Mechanical Design Solutions

Begin by modeling the two CATIA parts named **ladder** and **wall** as shown below with the suggested dimensions in inches. Dimensions not shown are not critical; use any values you wish for those dimensions.

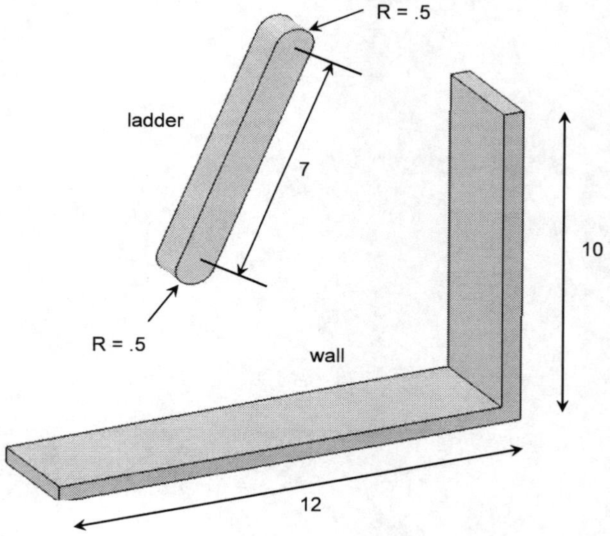

Before assembling the parts, you have to create two reference points on the ladder as indicated below. You also have to create a reference line on the side face of the wall 0.5 in off the plane of the wall. In your mechanism, Point-1 and Line-1 are used to create the Point-Curve joint. Furthermore, the bottom circular edge of the ladder and the bottom edge of the wall are used for the Slide-Curve joint. The purpose of Point-2 is to enable us to measure and plot the velocity and acceleration of the ladder at that location. Although the creation of Point-1, Point-2 and Line-1 is straightforward, we will walk the reader through the steps.

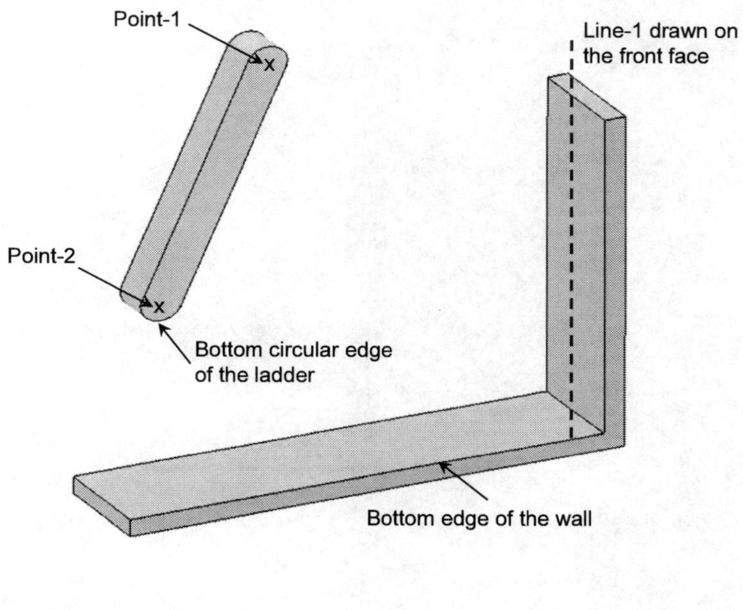

Load the part named **Ladder** into CATIA and enter the **Part Design** workbench  .

Use the **Point** icon  from the **Reference Element** toolbar 

.
In the resulting pop up box for the **Point type** choose **Circle/sphere center**. For **Circle/Sphere**, pick the top circular arc of the ladder as shown. This creates Point-1.

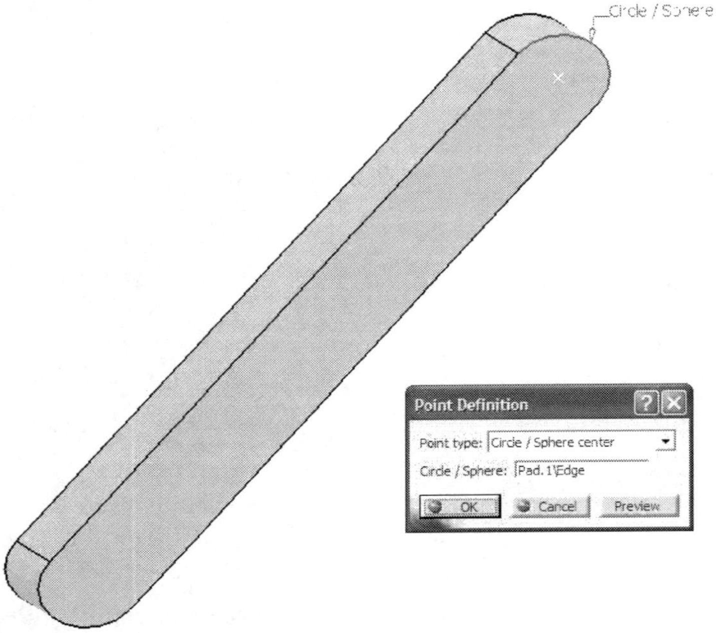

Repeat the same process for the bottom circular arc to create Point-2.

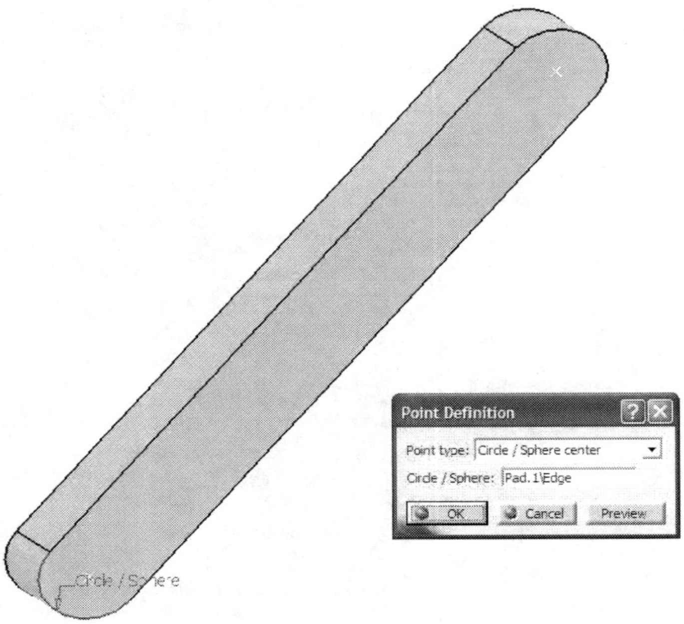

Save the changes in ladder. Note that two points are created and recorded in the specification tree.

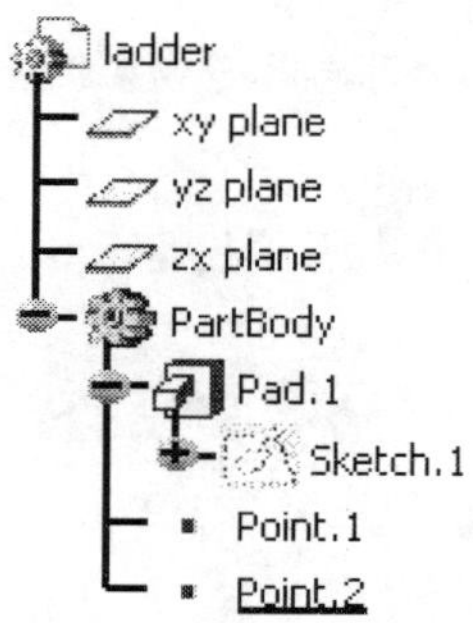

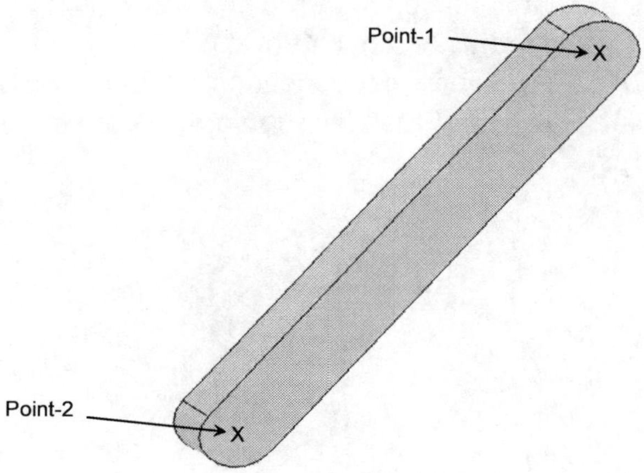

Load the part named **wall** into CATIA and enter the **Part Design** workbench . Use the **Line** icon 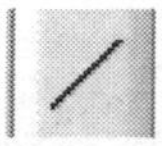 from the **Reference Element** toolbar 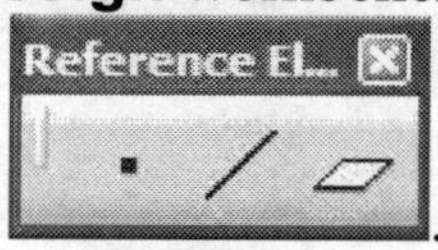.

In the resulting **Line Definition** pop up box for the **Line type** choose **Point-Direction**.
Right-click in the **Point** box of the **Line Definition** box and choose **Create Point**.

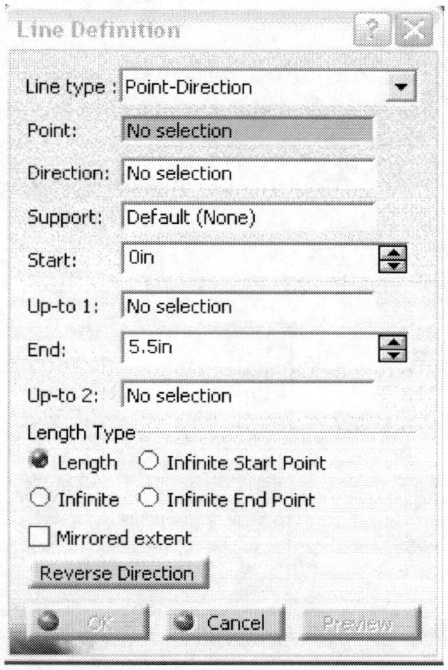

In the **Point Definition** box, choose **On curve** for the **Point type** and complete the dialog box as shown below to create a point 0.5 in offset from the wall along the curve representing the outer side edge of the ground. The 0.5 in dimension is not arbitrary, but rather matches the radius on the end of the ladder. This is done so that when Point 1 on the ladder follows the line we are creating here, the ladder will appear to slide smoothly along the wall. The result thus far should be as shown below.

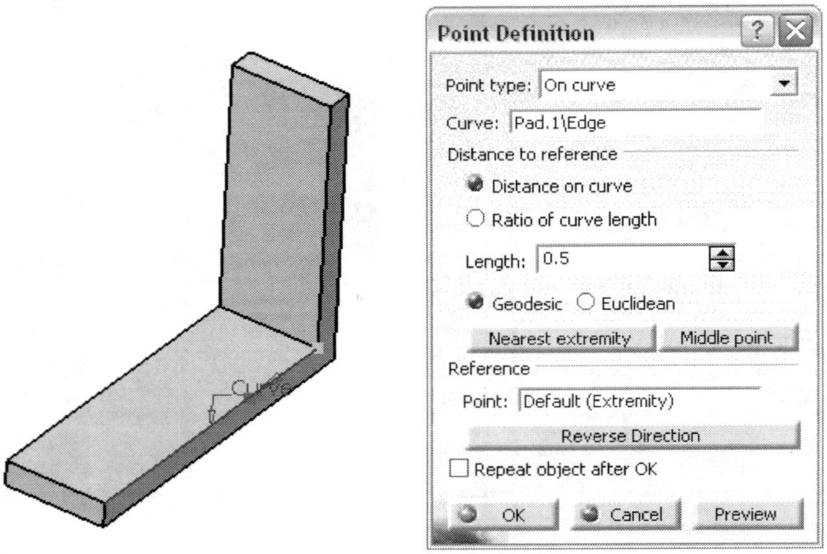

After you **Ok** the **Point Definition** box, you will be returned to the **Line Definition** box. Specify the direction to be along the edge shown below, the **End** distance to be 5.5in, and choose reverse direction as necessary to produce the result shown below. Point 1 created on the ladder will later be made to follow this line created on the wall.

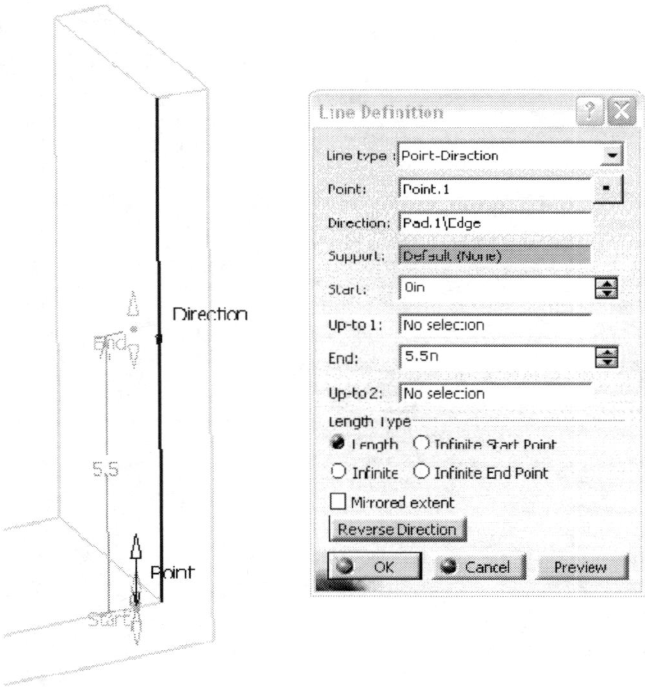

Having added the necessary reference geometry, you are now in a position to assemble the model.

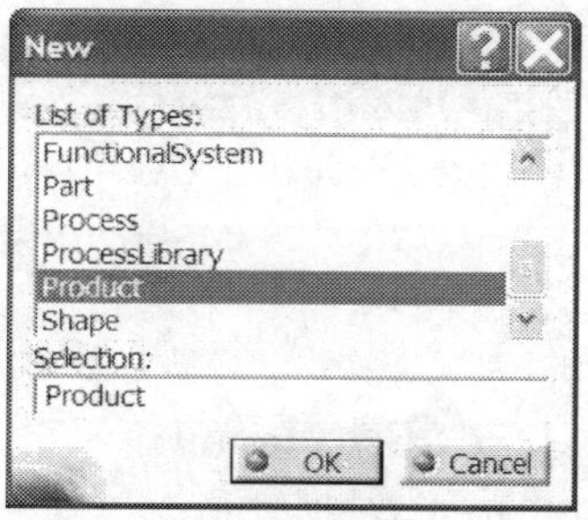

Enter the **Assembly Design** workbench  which can be achieved by different means depending on your CATIA customization. For example, from the standard Windows toolbar, select **File > New** .
From the box shown on the right, select **Product**. This moves you to the **Assembly Design** workbench and creates an assembly with the default name **Product.1**.

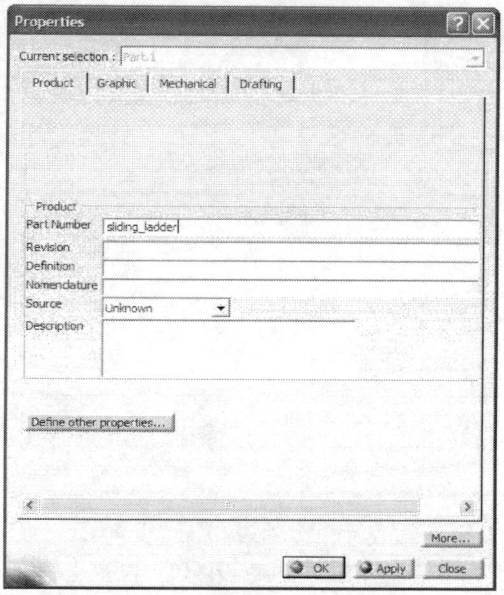

In order to change the default name, move the cursor to **Product.1** in the tree, right click and select **Properties** from the menu list.

From the **Properties** box, select the **Product** tab and in **Part Number** type **sliding_ladder**.

This will be the new product name throughout the chapter. The tree on the top left corner of your computer screen should look as displayed below.

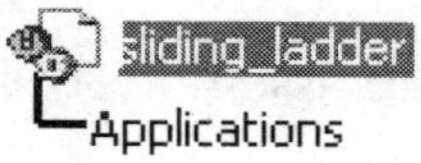

From the standard Windows toolbar, select **Insert > Existing Component**.
From the **File Selection** pop up box choose **ladder** and **block**. Remember that in CATIA multiple selections are made with the **Ctrl** key.
The tree is modified to indicate that the parts have been inserted.

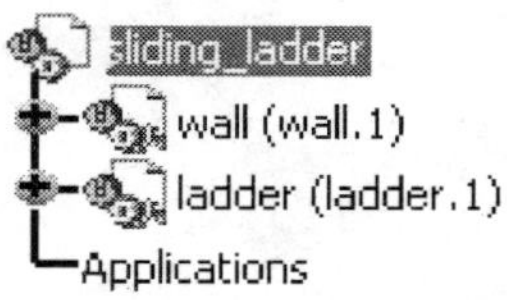

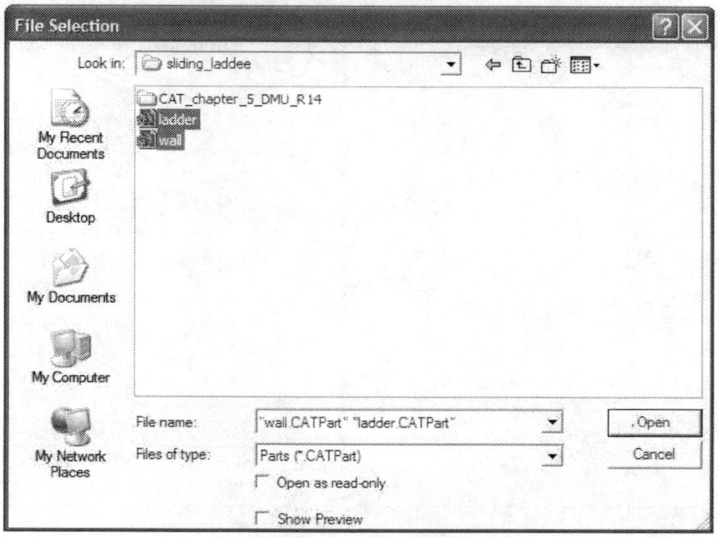

The two parts will show up on the screen. In the event that Point-1, Point-2, and Line-1 are not displayed, they may be hidden. They have to be brought into the **Show** mode. One way to do this is by locating them in the specification tree, right clicking, and selecting **Hide/Show**. The manner in which the reference geometry appears in the specification tree is slightly different in V5R14 versus V5R15, but you should be able to find these entities easily by expanding the tree as needed. You may have to use the **Manipulation** icon  in the **Move** toolbar 

to rearrange the ladder to near the intended start position as shown below.

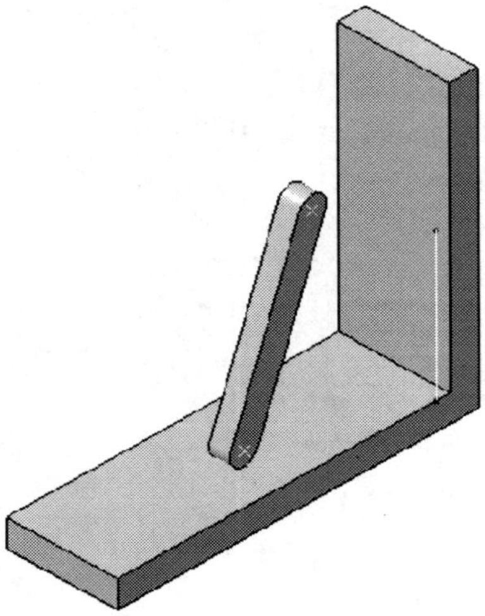

The best way of saving your work is to save the entire assembly.
Double click on the top branch of the tree. This is to ensure that you are in the **Assembly Design** workbench.
Select the **Save** icon . The **Save As** pop up box allows you to rename if desired. The default name is the **sliding_ladder**.

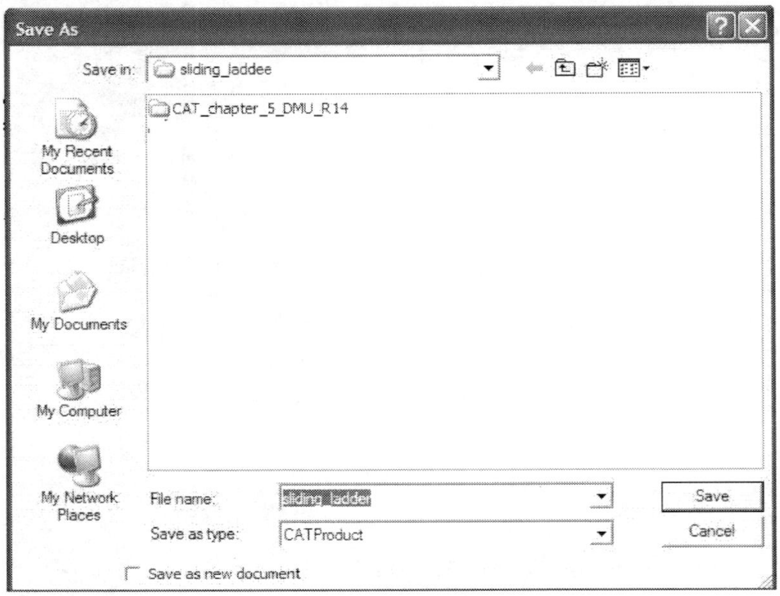

When we go to create the mechanism joints later, it is essential that the ladder already be positioned such that Point 1 on the ladder is coincident with the reference line created on the wall. In fact, Point 1 should be coincident with the upper endpoint of the line so that we know the starting Z is at 5.5 in as desired. Since in this tutorial we will not be using automatic assembly constraints conversion to create the mechanism joint, we can apply some assembly constraints which properly position the ladder at the start point without much regard for remaining (unconstrained) degrees of freedom (dof).

To begin the constraints process, anchor the wall by picking the **Anchor** icon  from **Constraints** toolbar 

and selecting the **wall** from the tree or from the screen.

Next, choose the **Coincident Constraint** icon  from the **Constraints** toolbar and then choose Point 1 and the upper endpoint of Line 1. Do not update yet.

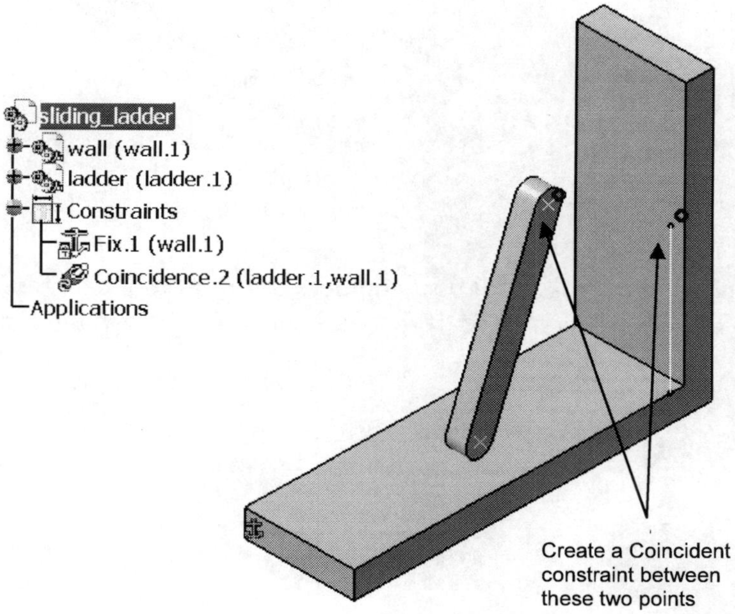

Next we will apply another coincident constraint, this time to ensure the side face of the ladder is coplanar with the side face of the wall. Select the **Coincidence Constraint** icon  from the **Constraints** toolbar. From the screen, select the two planar surfaces shown below. Accept the default orientation of **Same** when making this constraint. Do not update yet.

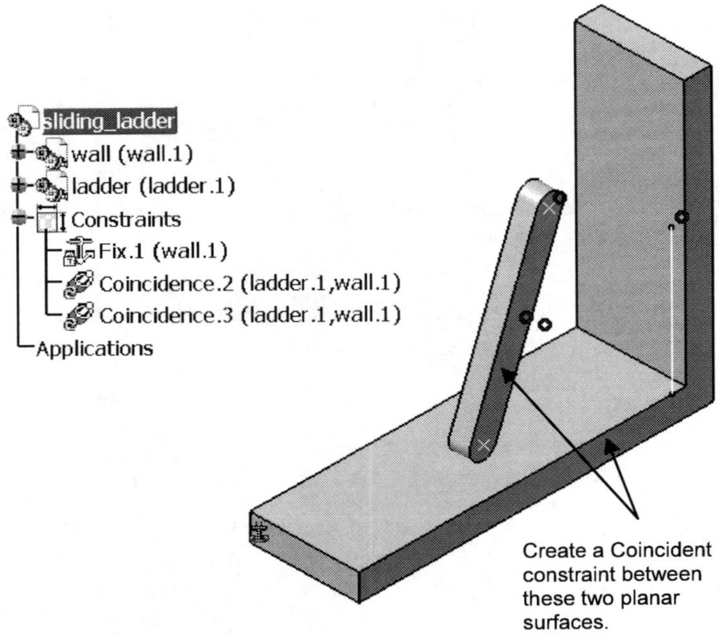

The final constraint we will make will be a contact constraint to locate the bottom of the ladder tangent to the horizontal surface of the wall part (i.e., the ground the ladder is resting on).

Select the **Contact Constraint** icon  from the **Constraints** toolbar. From the screen, select the lower cylindrical surface of the ladder and the upper planar surface of the wall as shown below. To achieve the intended result, you will need to change the orientation to **External** when making this constraint. The three constraints made are reflected in the tree as shown.

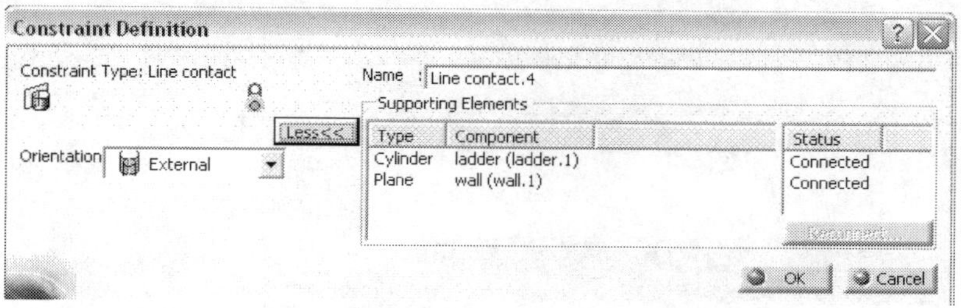

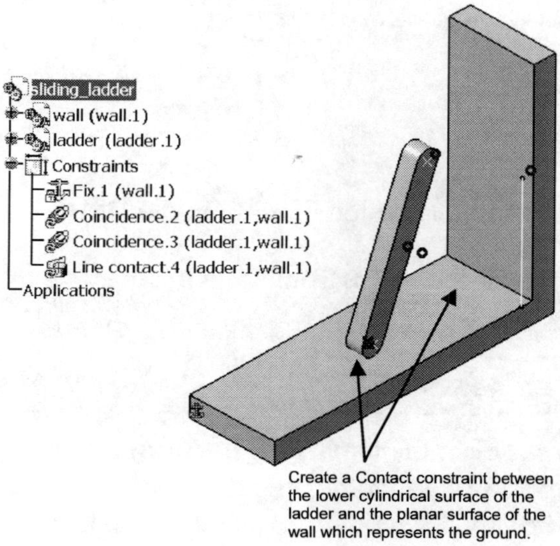

Use the **Update** icon  to rearrange the two parts to the intended starting position as shown below. Since we will be creating the mechanism joints manually rather than by using automatic assembly constraints conversion, these assembly constraints will be ignored in DMU. Their objective of positioning the parts to the intended starting position has been met.

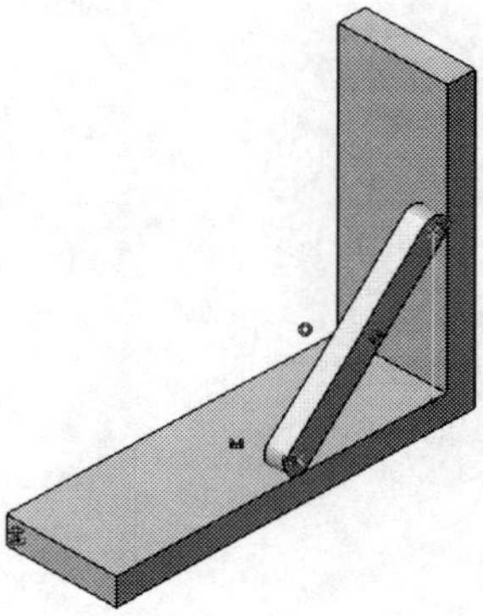

4 Creating Joints in the Digital Mockup Workbench

The **Digital Mockup** workbench is quite extensive but we will only deal with the **DMU Kinematics module**. To get there you can use the standard Windows toolbar as shown below: **Start > Digital Mockup > DMU Kinematics**.

In this tutorial all the joinst will be created directly in the **Digital Mockup** workbench.

Select the **Point Curve Joint** icon  from the **Kinematics Joints** toolbar

In the resulting pop up box, select the **New Mechanism** button 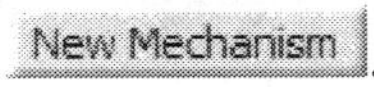

.
The follow up pop up box allows you to rename the mechanism being created. Close the **Mechanism Creation** box by accepting the default name **Mechanism.1**.

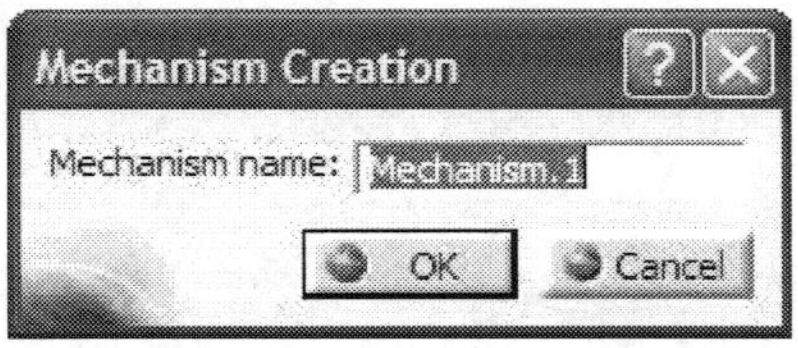

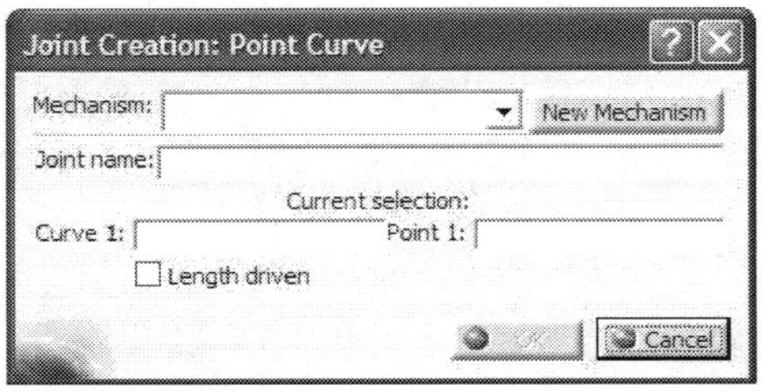

For **Curve 1**, select **Line-1** on the screen and for **Point 1**, pick **Point-1** as indicated in the next page. Close the box by clicking on **OK**. This constraint forces Point 1 to move only along (the infinite) Line 1. Later we will make this joint length driven since the problem statement defines velocity along this line.

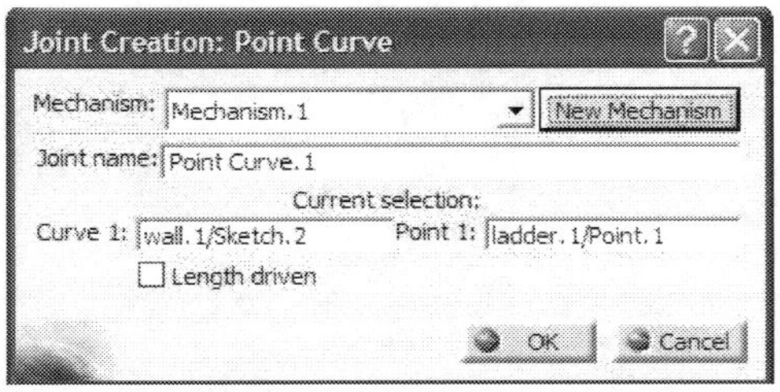

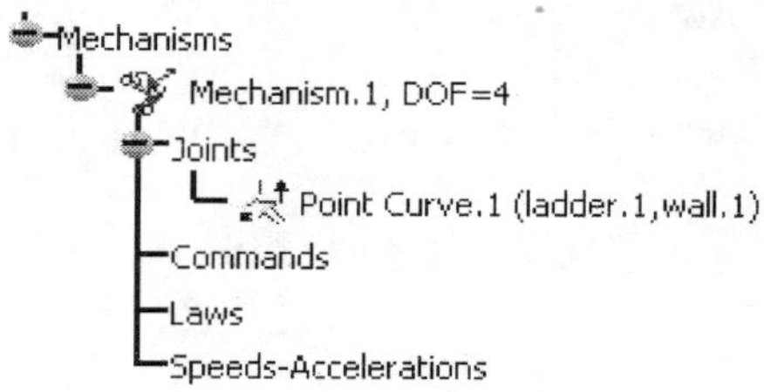

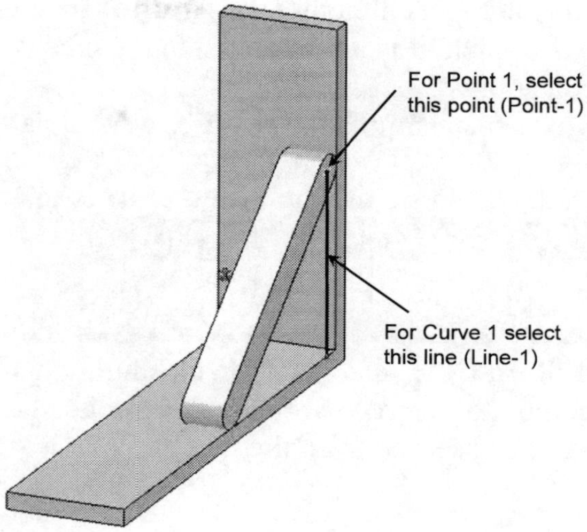

We will create a slide curve joint between the lower cylindrical surface of the ladder and the planar surface of the wall representing the ground. Select the **Slide Curve Joint icon** from the **Kinematics Joints** toolbar.

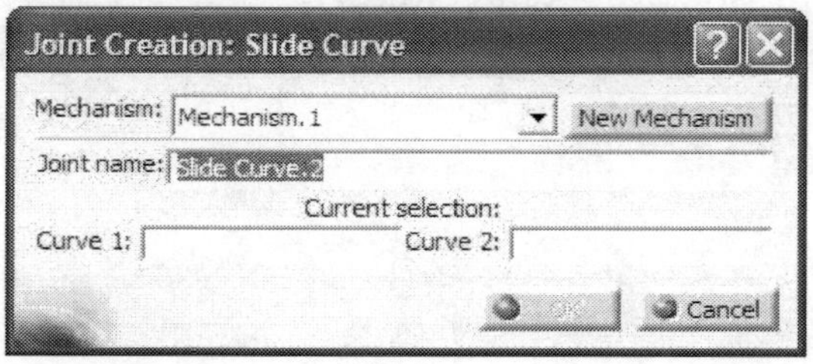

For **Curve 1**, select the bottom edge of the wall. For **Curve 2**, pick the circular edge of the bottom of the ladder.

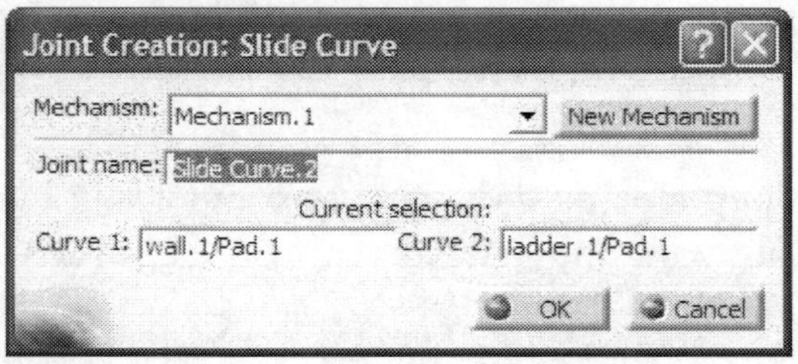

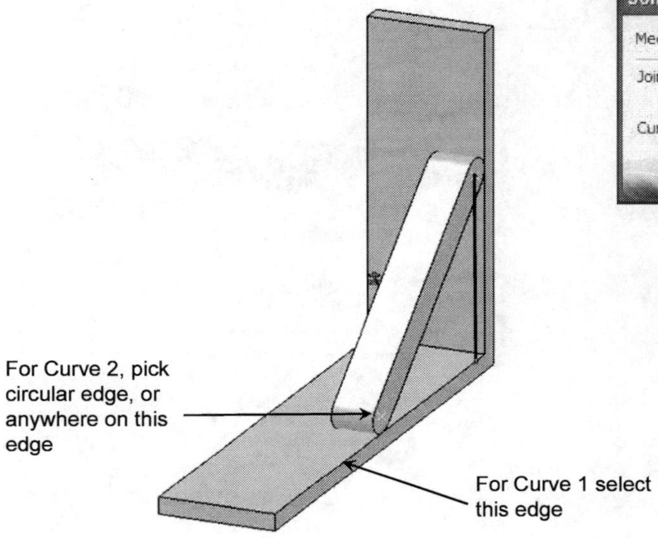

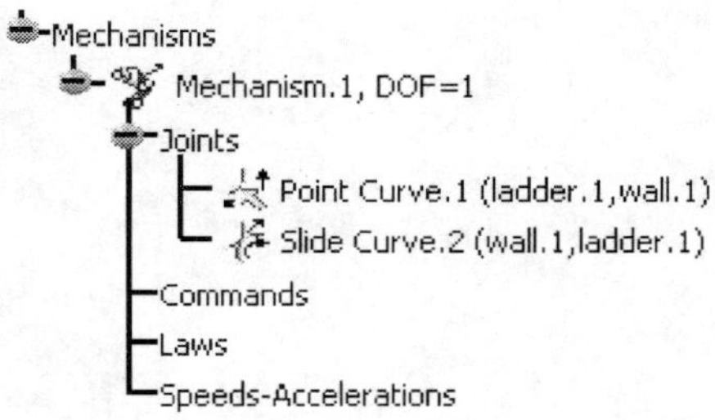

Also note that although the **Anchor** icon was used in the **Assembly Design** workbench, it is not reflected in the mechanism (since we did not convert assembly constraints).
Mechanism simulation requires a fixed part. Of course in this problem we want to fix the wall. To do so, use the **Fixed Part** icon  from the **DMU Kinematics** toolbar

and select the wall from the screen. Upon closing the window, the number of degrees of freedom is reduced to 1. This can be observed from the tree entry **DOF=1**.

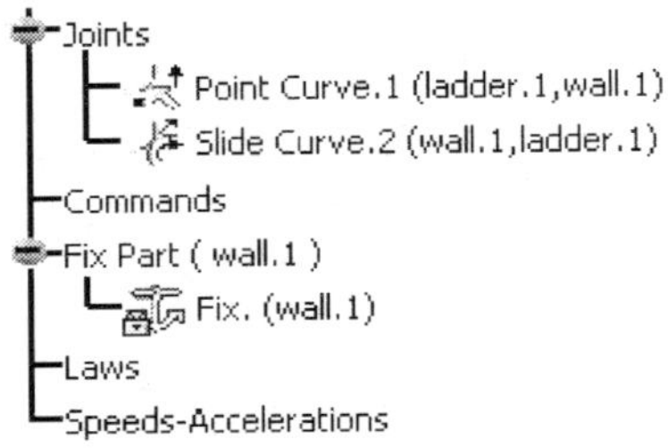

Now, to drive the intended constant velocity motion of the ladder down the wall, we will make the Point Curve joint length driven (alternatively we could have done this when we first created the mechanism). Double click on the Point Curve.1 branch of the joints to open the pop box below. In this box, check the **Length driven** option 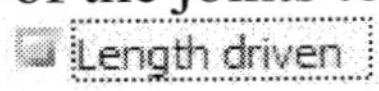

. Note that the joints limits of 5.5 in and 0 in cover the range of motion intended in the problem statement. Note that the position of the elements involved in the joint when the joint is created is the zero point, so in this case the start point will be zero and the upper limit of 5.5 in represents when the ladder hits the ground.

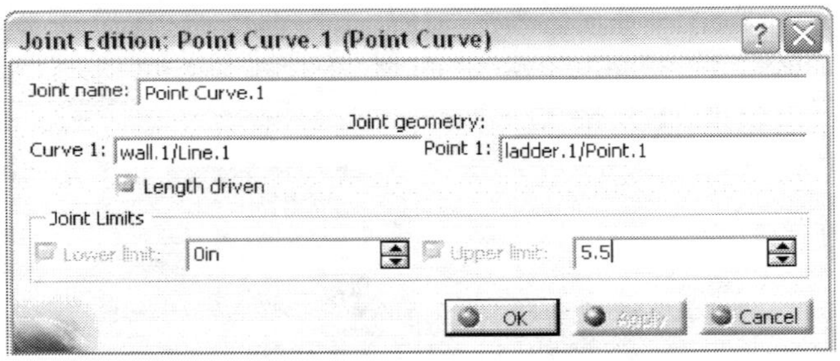

Upon closing the above box and assuming that everything else was done correctly, the following message appears on the screen.

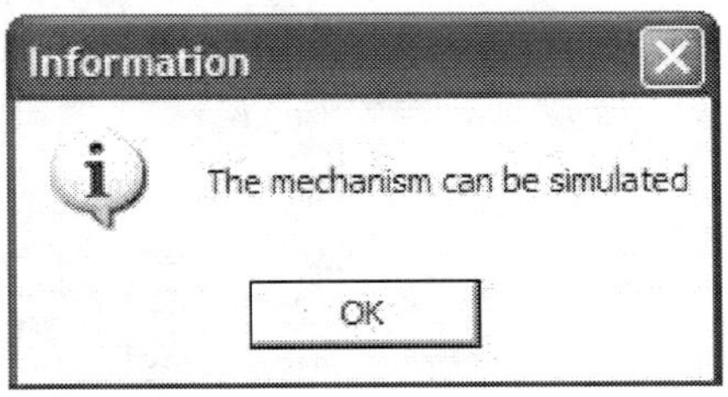

This indeed is good news.

Select the **Simulation** icon  from the **DMU Generic Animation** toolbar

. This enables you to choose the mechanism to be animated if there are several present. In this case, select Mechanism.1 and close the window.

As soon as the window is closed, a Simulation branch is added to the tree.

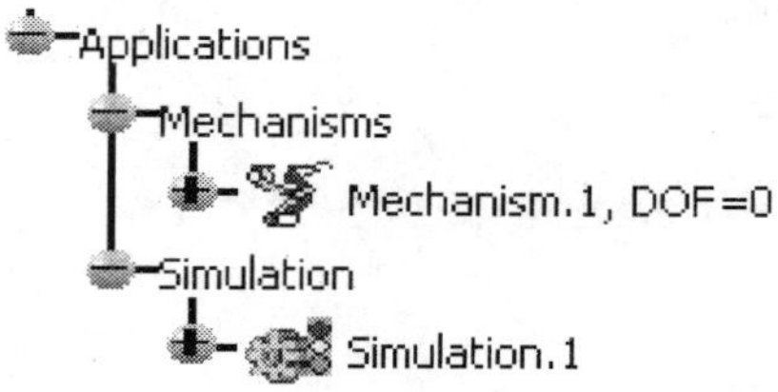

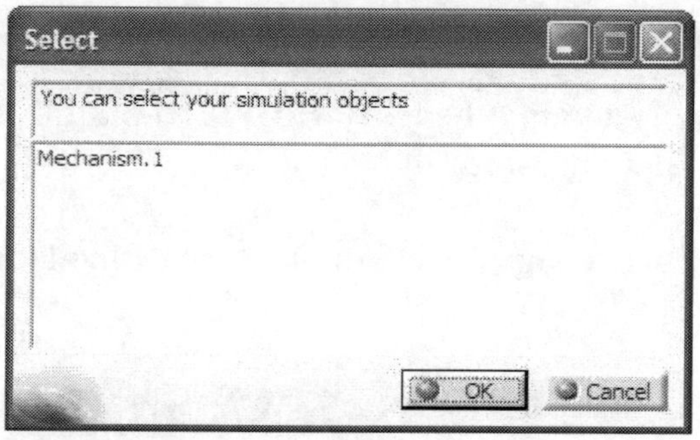

In addition, the two pop up boxes shown below appear.

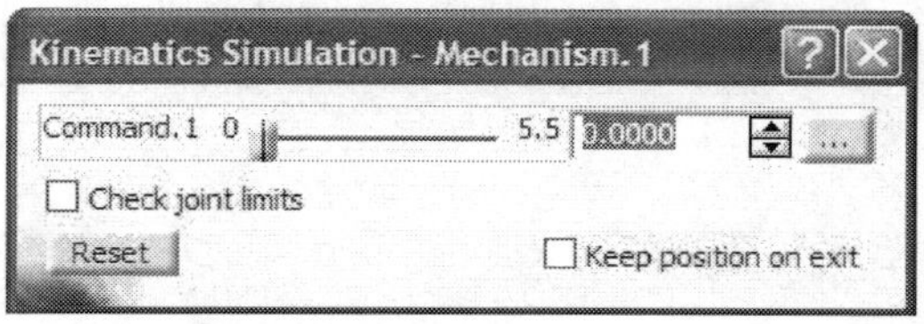

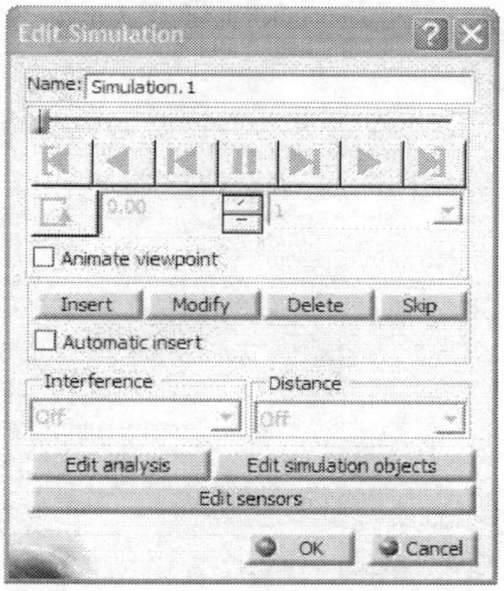

The actual numbers that you may have in this box as the **Command.1,** may vary depending on the ladder's initial configuration.

As you drag the scroll bar from left to right, the ladder begins to slide along the wall. The value of 5.5 represents the length of Line-1.

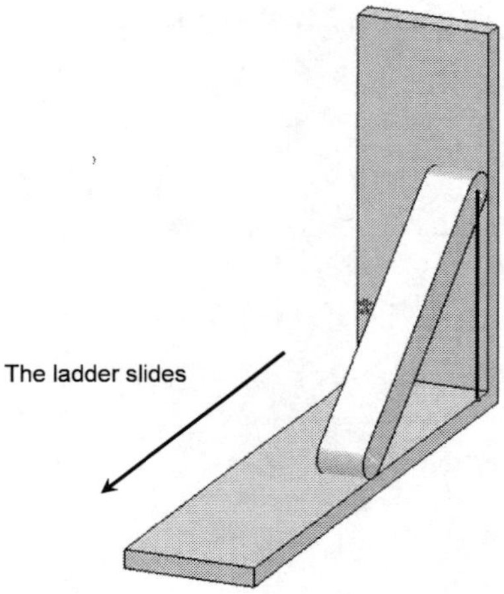

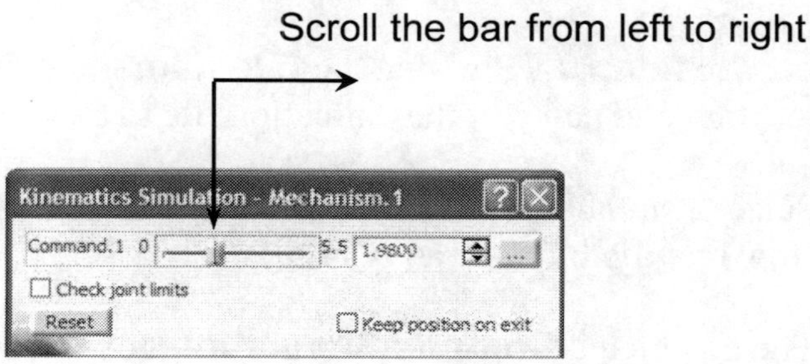

When the scroll bar in the **Kinematics Simulation** pop up box reaches the right extreme end, select the **Insert** button in the **Edit Simulation** pop up box shown above. This activates the video player buttons shown

.

Return the ladder to its original position by picking the **Jump to Start** button .

Note that the **Change Loop Mode** button is also active now.

Upon selecting the **Play Forward** button , the ladder makes fast jump to the original position.

In order to slow down the motion of the ladder, select a different **interpolation step**, such as 0.04.

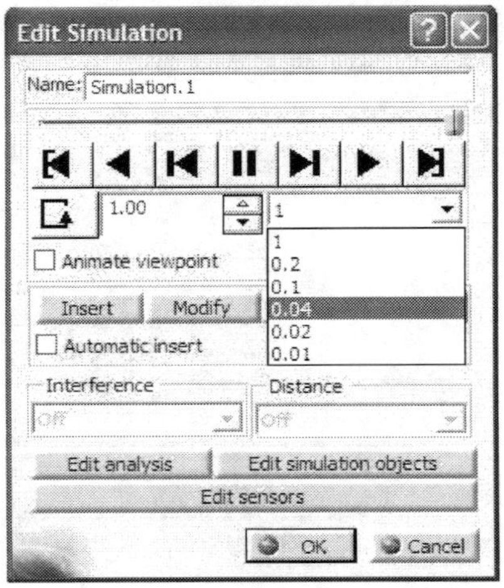

Upon changing the interpolation step to 0 0.04, return the return to its original position by picking the **Jump to Start** button . Apply **Play Forward** button and observe the slow and smooth translation of the ladder.

Select the **Compile Simulation** icon from the **Generic Animation** toolbar

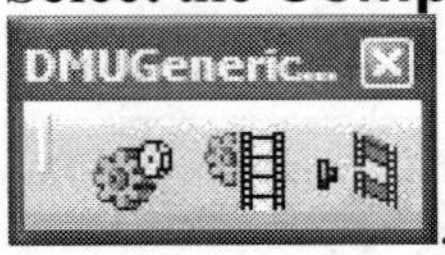

. Pressing the **File name** button | File name ... | allows you to set the location and name of the animation file to be generated as displayed below.

Select a suitable path and file name and change the **Time step** to be 0.04 to produce a slow moving block in an AVI file.

The completed **Compile Simulation** box is shown in the next page.

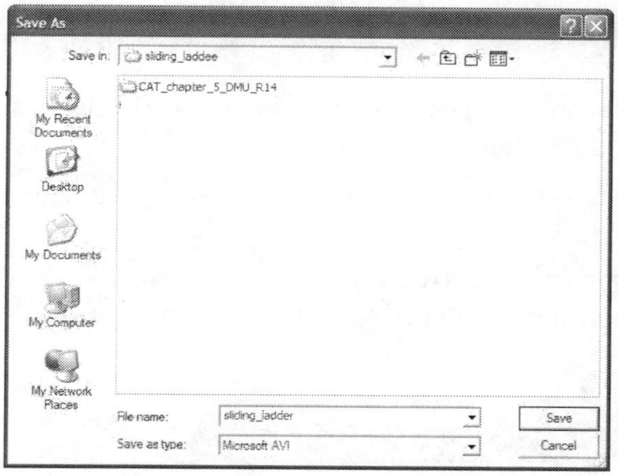

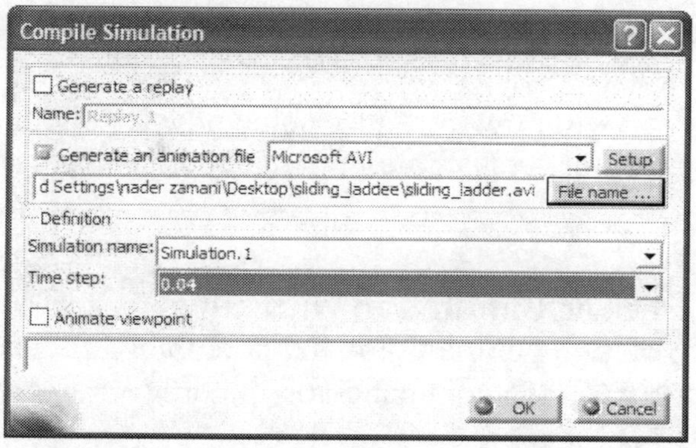

As the file is being generated, the ladder slowly slides. The resulting AVI file can be viewed with the Windows Media Player.

In the event that an AVI file is not needed, but one wishes to play the animation, repeatedly, a **Replay** need be generated. Therefore, in the **Compile Simulation** box, check the **Generate a replay** button.

Note that in this case, most of the previously available options are dimmed out. A **Replay.1** branch has also been added to the tree.

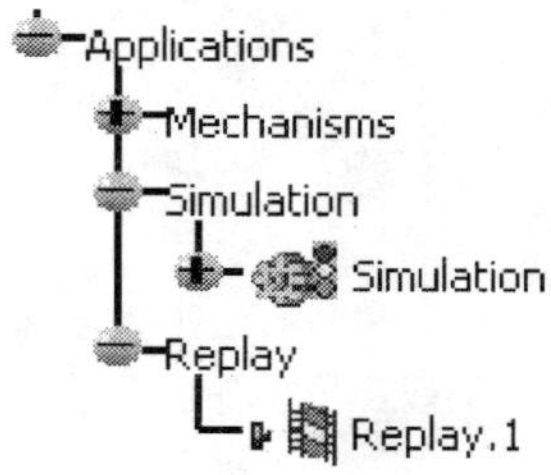

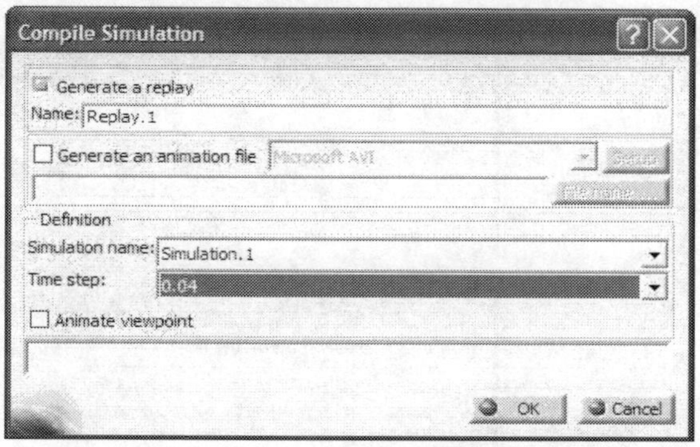

Select the **Replay** icon  from the **Generic Animation** toolbar 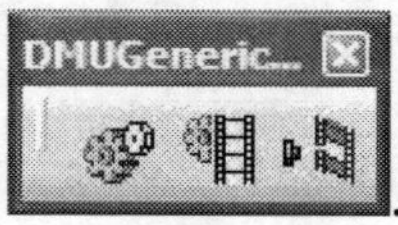.
Double click on **Replay.1** in the tree and the **Replay** pop up box appears.
Experiment with the different choices of the **Change Loop Mode** buttons .
The ladder can be returned to the original position by picking the **Jump to Start** button .

The **skip ratio** (which is chosen to be x1 in the right box) controls the speed of the **Replay**.

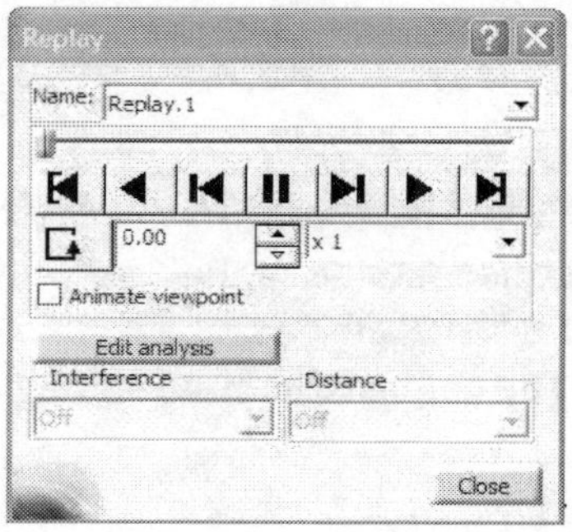

5 Creating Laws in the Motion

You will now introduce some physics into the problem. The objective is to specify the position versus time function and therefore set the velocity and acceleration.

Click on **Simulation with Laws** icon  in the **Simulation** toolbar 

. You will get the following pop up box indication that you need to add at least a relation between the command and the time parameter.

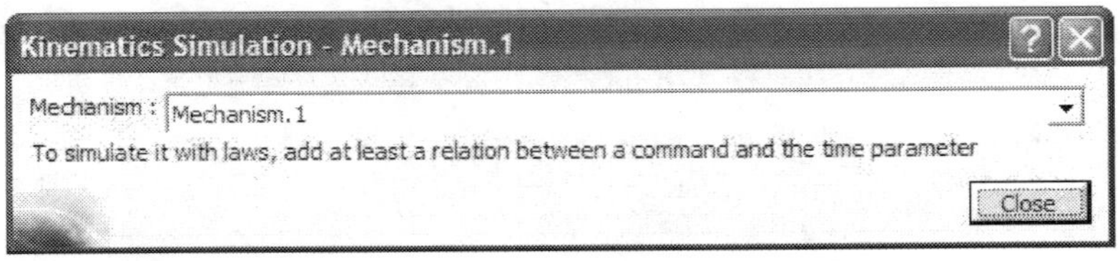

Select the **Formula** icon  from the **Knowledge** toolbar 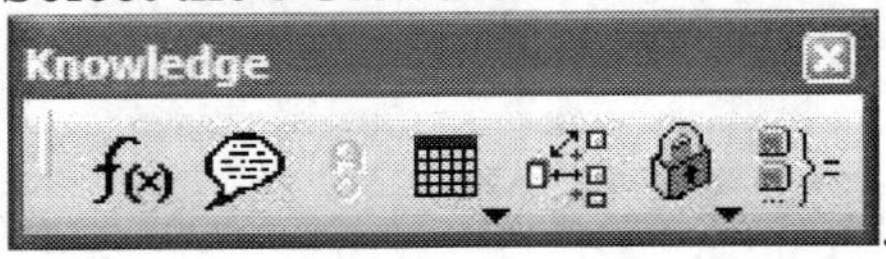

. The pop up box below appears on the screen.

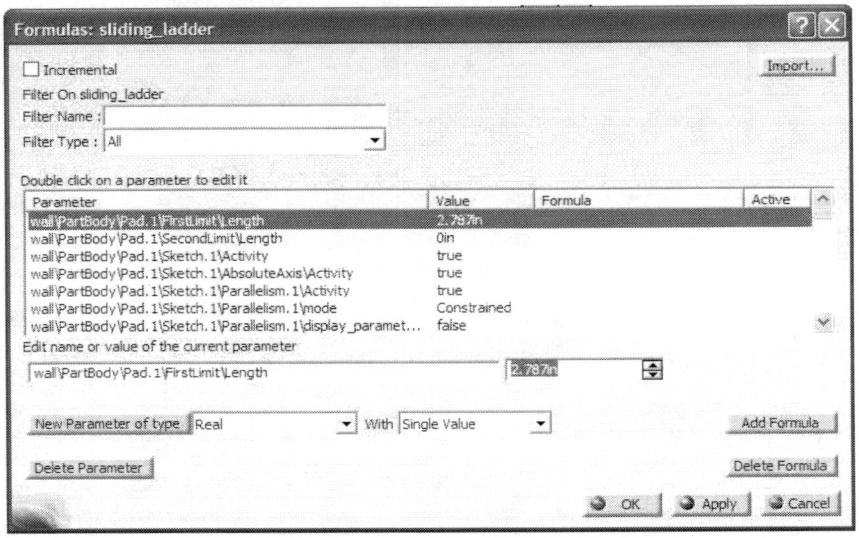

Point the cursor to the **Mechanism.1, DOF=0** branch in the tree and click. The consequence is that only parameters associated with the mechanism are displayed in the **Formulas** box.
The long list is now reduced to two parameters as indicated in the next page.

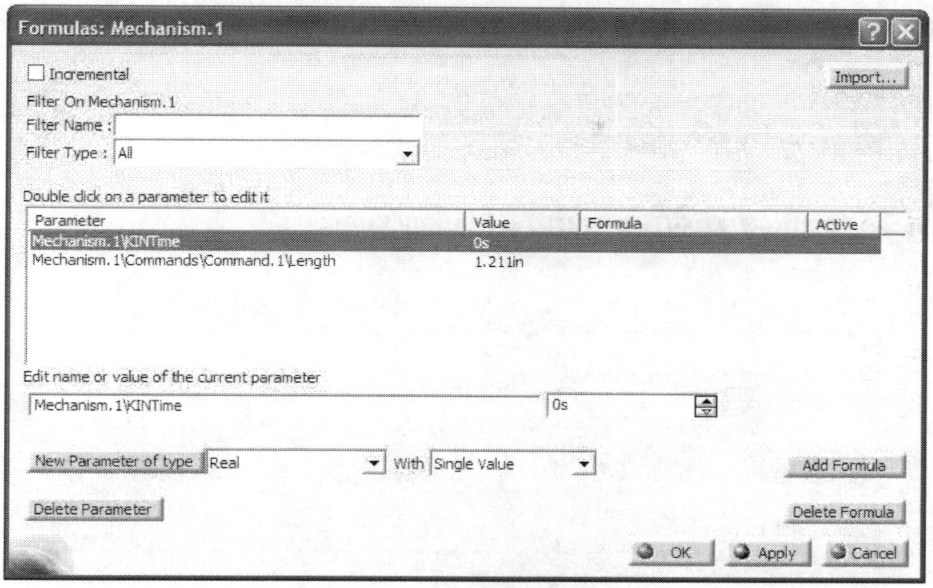

Select the entry **Mechanism.1\Commands\Command.1\Length** and press the **Add Formula** button Add Formula. This action kicks you to the **Formula Editor** box.

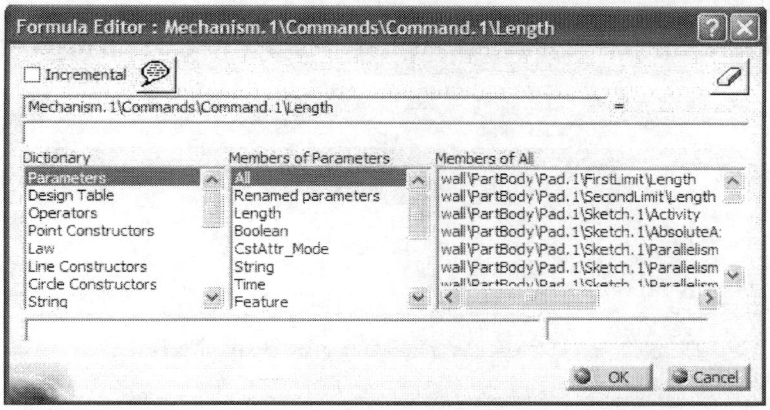

Pick the **Time** entry from the middle column (i.e. **Members of Parameters**).

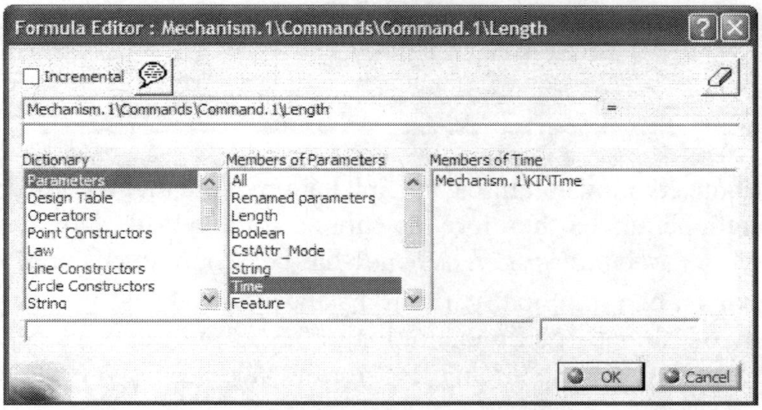

The right hand side of the equality should be such that the formula becomes

$$Mechanism.1 \backslash Commands \backslash Command.1 \backslash Length =$$
$$(10in) * (Mechnism.1 \backslash KINTime) / (1s)$$

Therefore, the completed **Formula Editor** box becomes

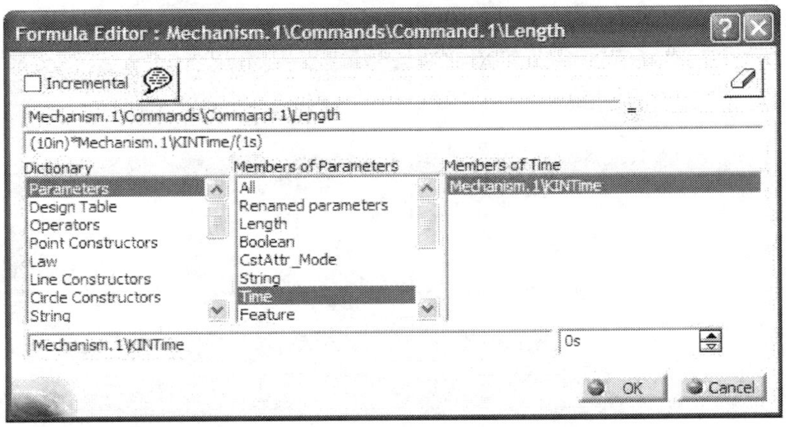

Upon accepting **OK**, the formula is recorded in the **Formulas** pop up box as shown below.

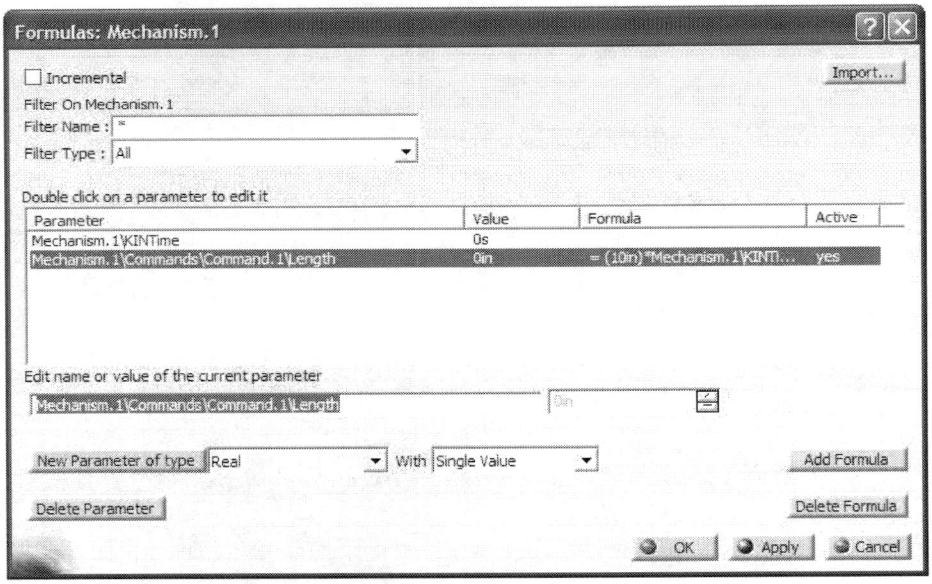

The formula introduced above requires an explanation. Note that the left hand side of the equality is a Length parameter therefore the entire right hand side should be reducing to inches. This is why, $(Mechanism.1 \backslash KINTime)$ has been nondimensionalized by introducing a division by (1s). Finally, (10in) has been introduced since we intend to specify a velocity of 10 in/s. The time duration of 0.5 seconds to produce 5.0 inches of motion down the wall (recall the 0.5 in offset for the ladder radius) is yet to be specified.

In the event that the formula has different units at the different sides of the equality you will get **Warning** messages such as the one shown below.

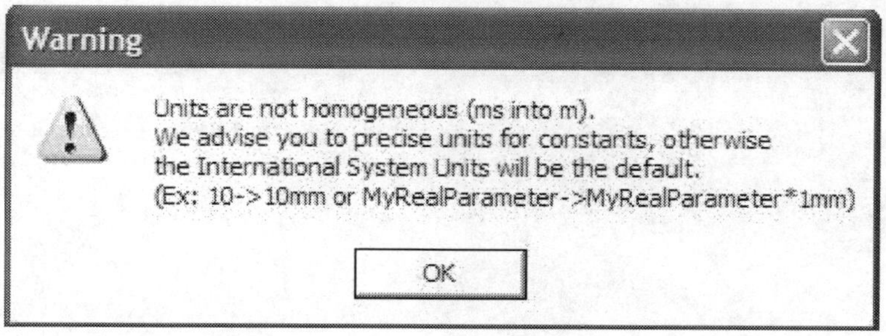

We are spared the warning message because the formula has been properly inputted. Note that the introduced law has appeared in **Law** branch of the tree.

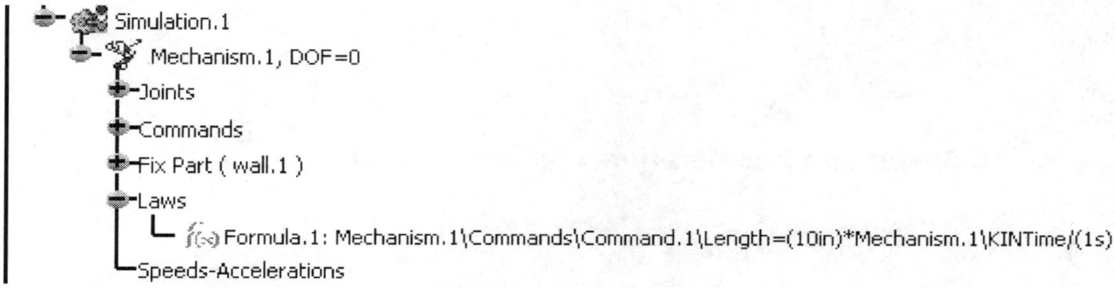

Keep in mind that our interest is to plot the velocity and accelerations at Point-2 generated by this motion.

Select the **Speed and Acceleration** icon  from the **DMU Kinematics** toolbar

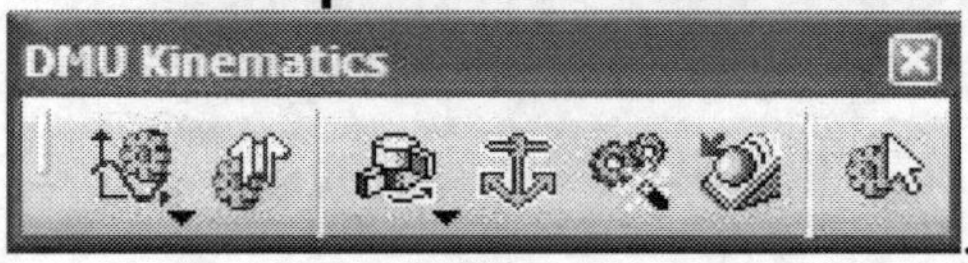

. The pop up box below appears on the Screen.

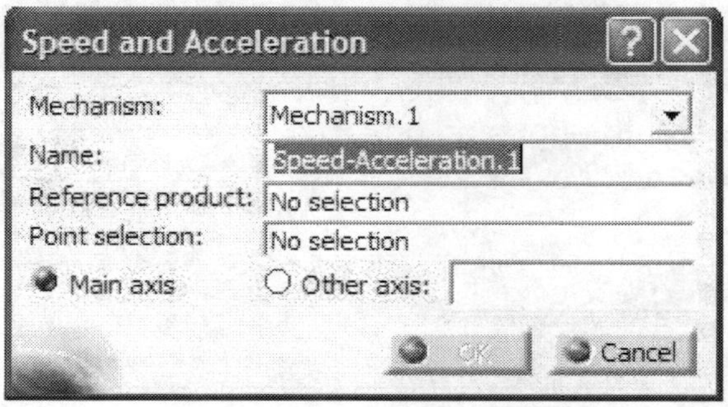

For the **Reference product,** select the wall from the screen or the tree. For the **Point selection**, pick Point.2 as shown in the sketch below.

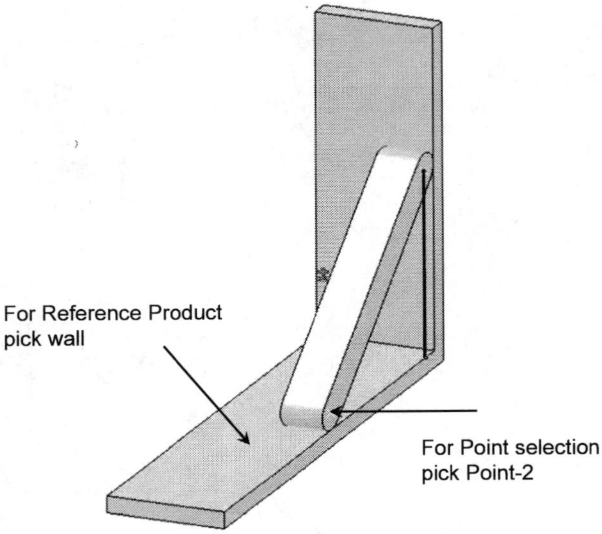

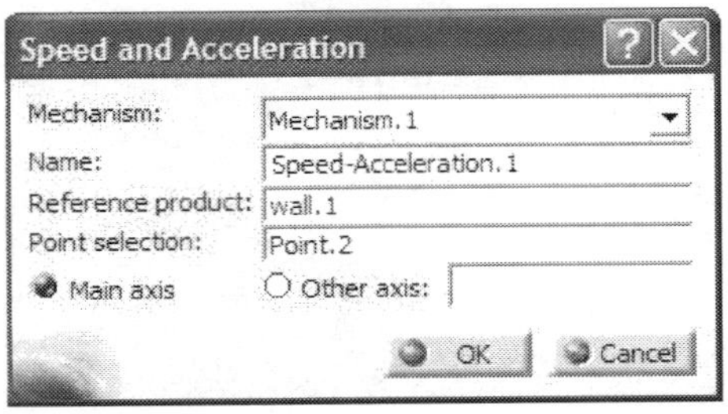

Note that the **Speed and Acceleration.1** has appeared in the tree.

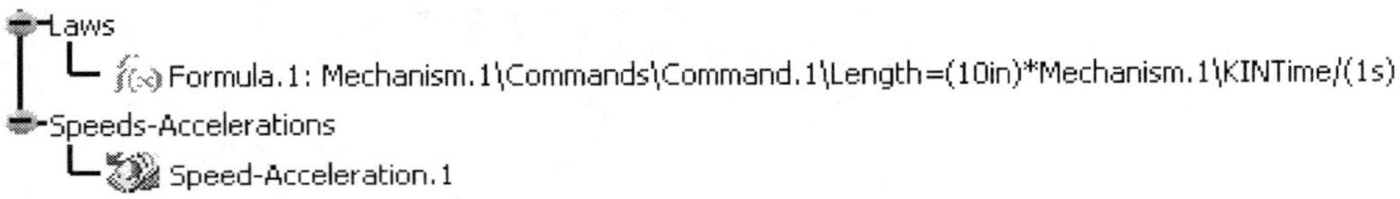

Click on **Simulation with Laws** icon  in the **Simulation** toolbar .
This results in the **Kinematics Simulation** pop up box shown below.

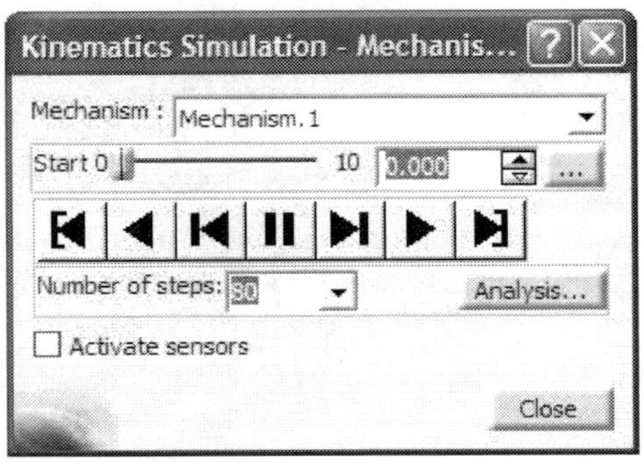

Note that the default time duration is 10 seconds.
To change this value, click on the button 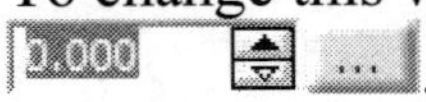. In the resulting pop up box, change the time duration to 0.5 s.

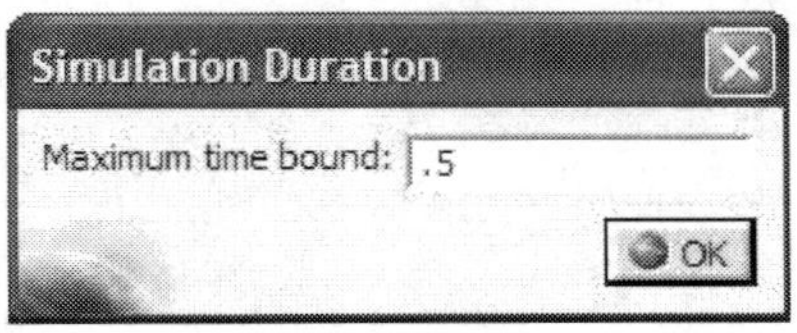

The scroll bar now moves up to 0.5 s.

Check the **Activate sensors** box, at the bottom left corner.

You will next have to make certain selections from the accompanying **Sensors** box.

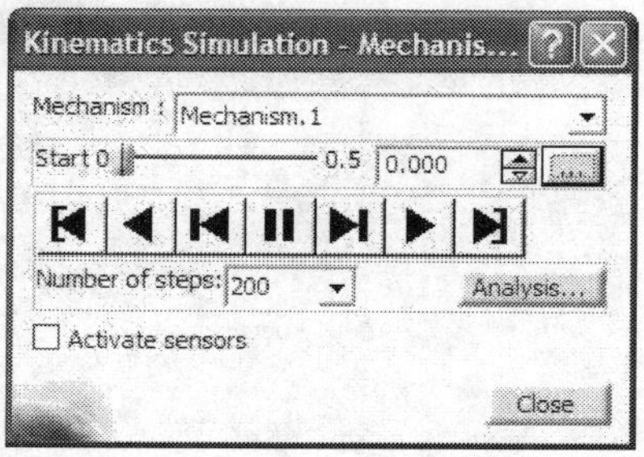

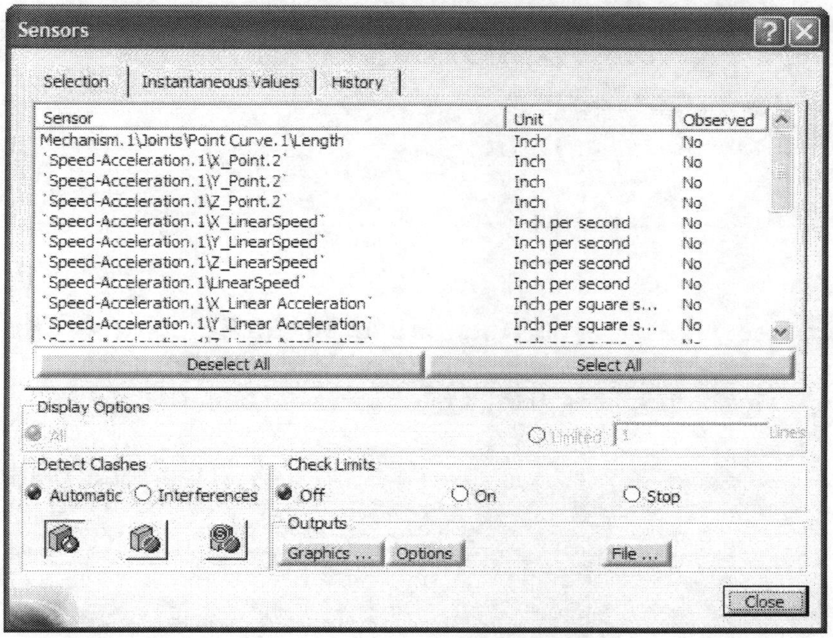

Click on the following item:

Speed-Acceleration.1\LinearSpeed

As you make this selection, the last column in the **Sensors** box, changes to **Yes** for the corresponding items. This is shown in the next page.

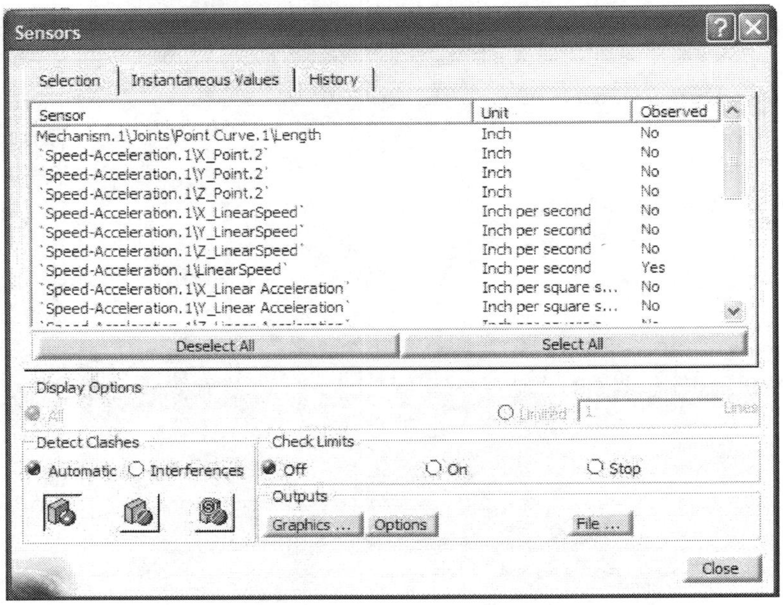

At this point, drag the scroll bar in the **Kinematics Simulation** box. As you do this, the ladder slides along the wall. Once the bar reaches its right extreme point, the ladder also stops sliding. This corresponds to 0.5 s or 5 inches of sliding.

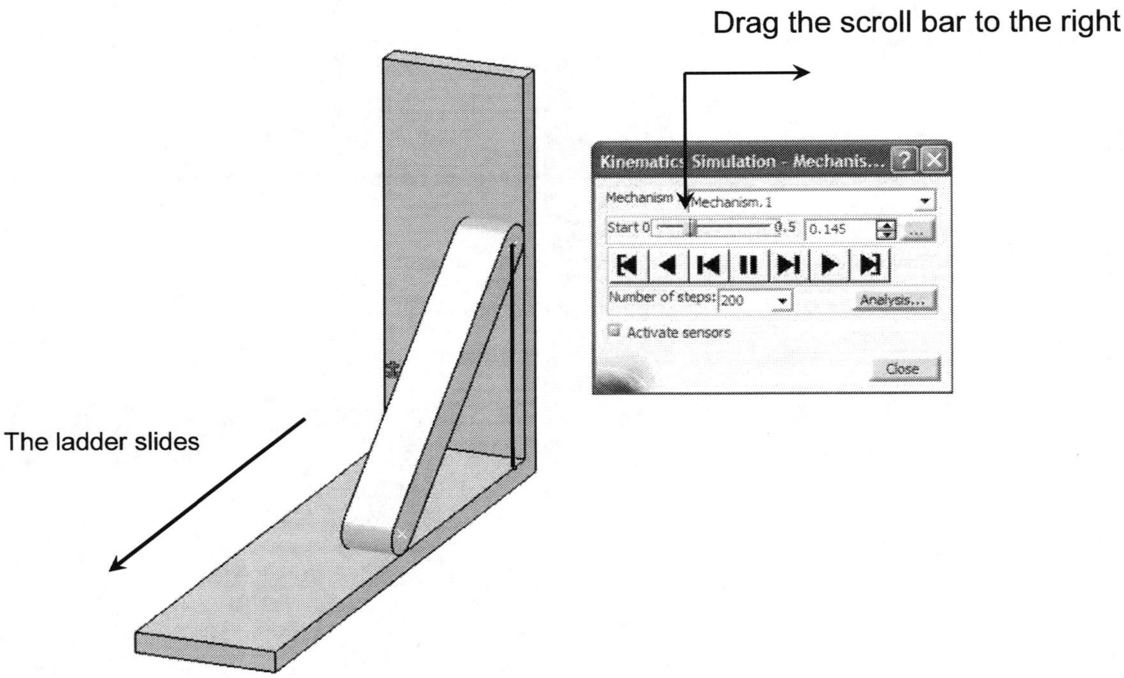

Once the ladder becomes horizontal, click on **Graphics** button in the **Sensor** box. The result is the plot of the velocity as shown in the next page.
The generated graph is in good agreement with the theoretical calculation.

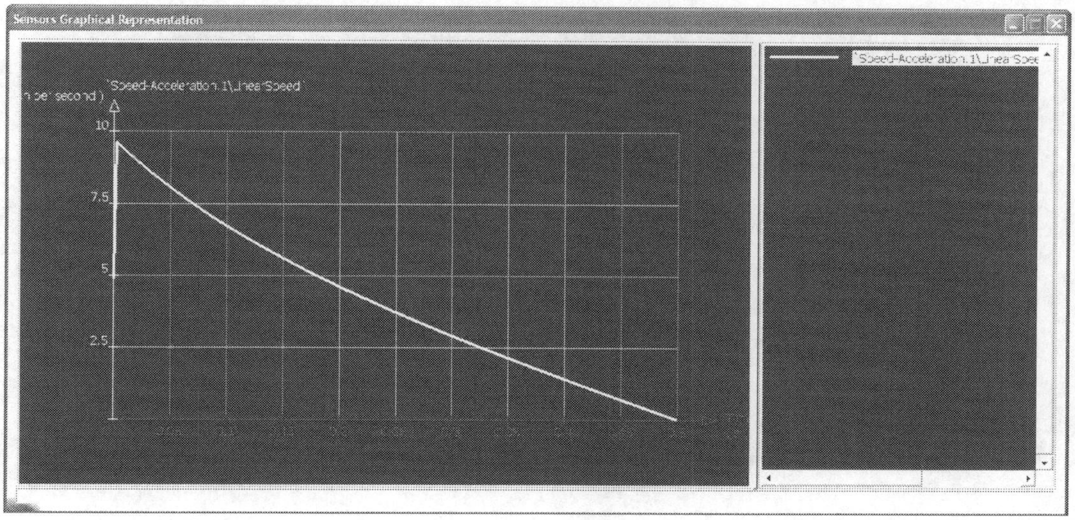

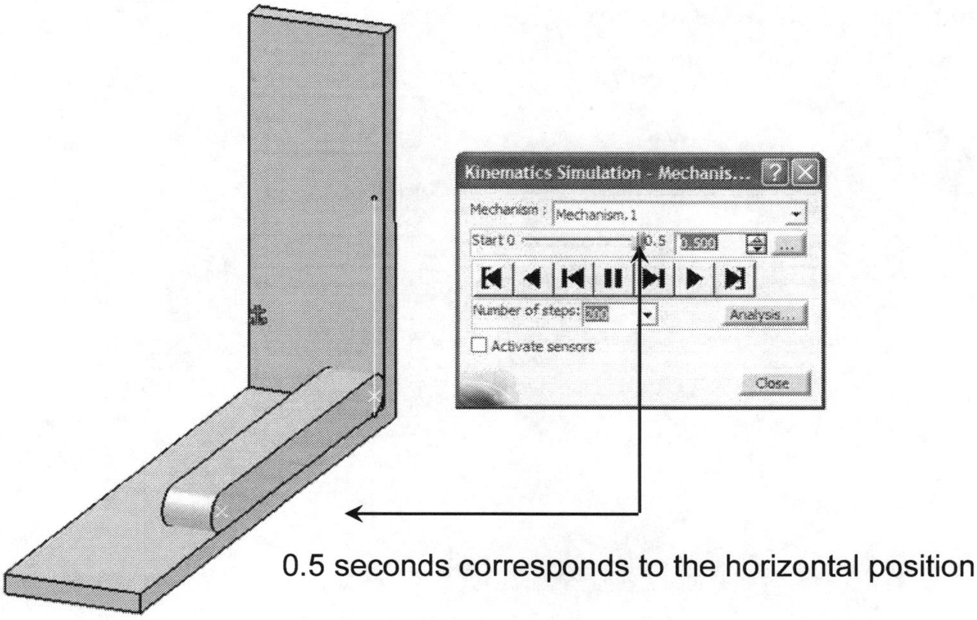

After the velocity data is generated, one can save this velocity/time values by clicking on the **File...** button in the **Sensors** pop up box. The information can be stored as an excel spreadsheet.

The ladder can be returned to the original position by picking the **Jump to Start** button . However, this traces another set of graphs that is not desirable. One can use the **History** tab in the **Sensors** pop up box and **Clear** the data.

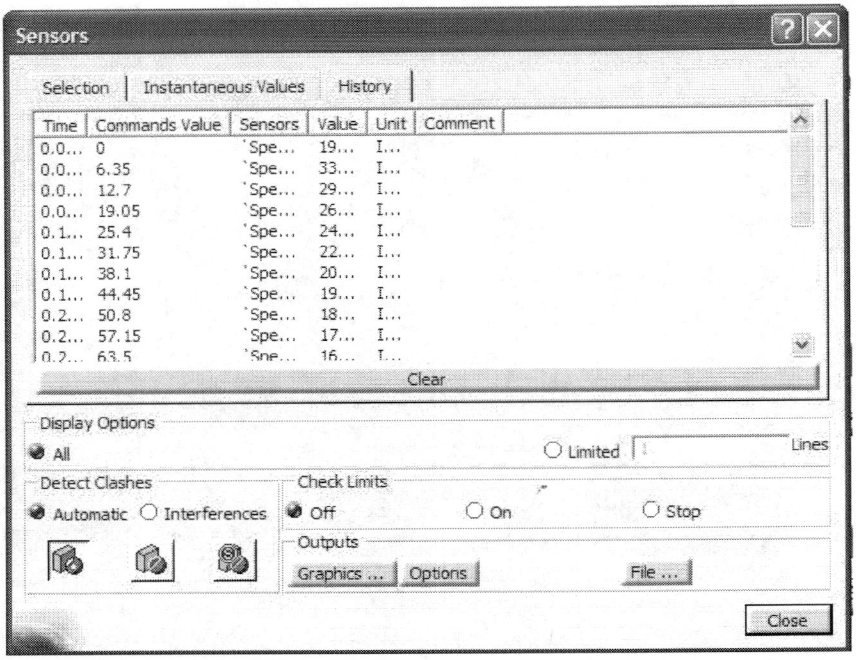

You can now close the **Sensors** box.

You will next generate information on the volume swept by the ladder.

Click on the **Swept Volume** icon  from the **DMU Generic Animation** toolbar

. This opens the **Swept Volume** pop up box. Choose Preview and the swept volume shape is displayed in a separate window.

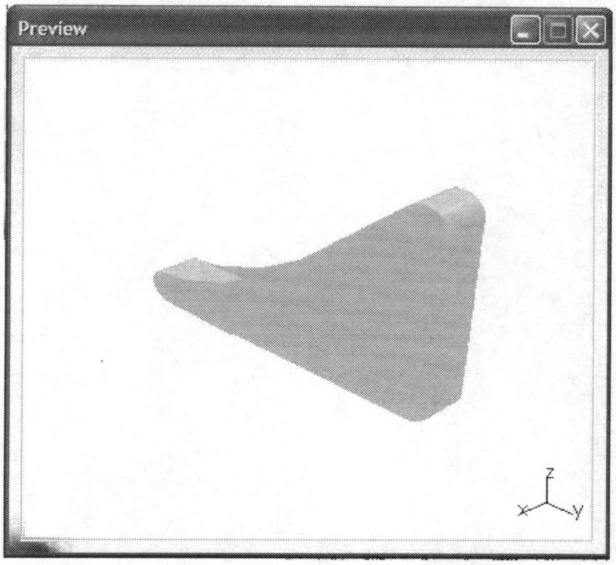

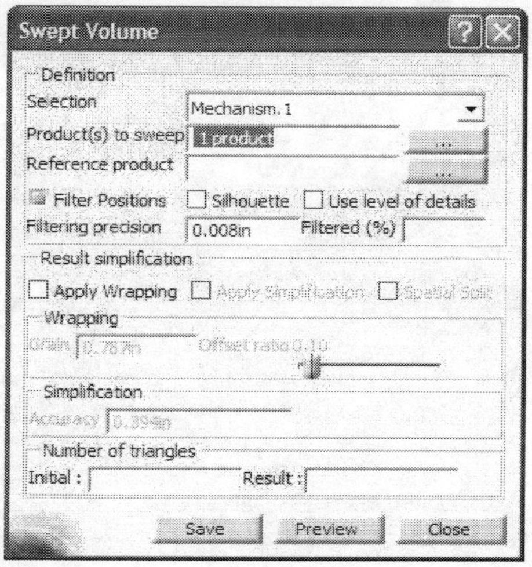

Click on **Save** if you want to save the swept volume as part.

This concludes this tutorial.

NOTES:

Chapter 6

A Geared Mechanism

Introduction

In this tutorial you will create a geared mechanism in which a pinion drives a gear which drives a rack. Both the gear joint and the rack joint have to be created manually in the **Digital Mockup** workbench.

1 Problem Statement

The assembly shown below is made of four parts: gear, pinion, rack and base. While we are not modeling the gear teeth, we are assuming the real-life gear, pinion and rack would have teeth; we simply model the pinion and gear as circular sections having diameters equal to the pitch diameter of the gears they represent. For simplicity, the rack is simply modeled as a rectanguloid. For purposes of this tutorial, the objective is to model the kinematic motion of the system for constant angular velocity of the pinion and to plot the position versus time for the resulting motion of the rack. This will be done using a revolute joint for the pinion, a revolute joint for the gear, a prismatic joint for the rack, and a gear joint between the pinion and the gear.

The constraints imposed in the **Assembly Design** workbench enable you to automatically create two revolute joints and a prismatic joint. However, once the gear joint is created, the revolute joints get consumed and leave you one revolute short for the rack assembly.
The extra revolute joint can be created manually while you are in the **Digital Mockup** workbench.

The pinion is assumed to turn at a constant angular velocity which in turn advances the rack at a constant rate. Therefore, the position of the tip of the rack varies linearly as a function time.

Although the pinion and the gear are assumed to have shafts as indicated in drawing, for the purpose of mechanism creation, they are strictly cosmetic and unnecessary.
The dimensions of the problem are not of importance assuming you enter the appropriate gear ratio for your pinion and gear radii; however, suggested dimensions are proposed within the tutorial.

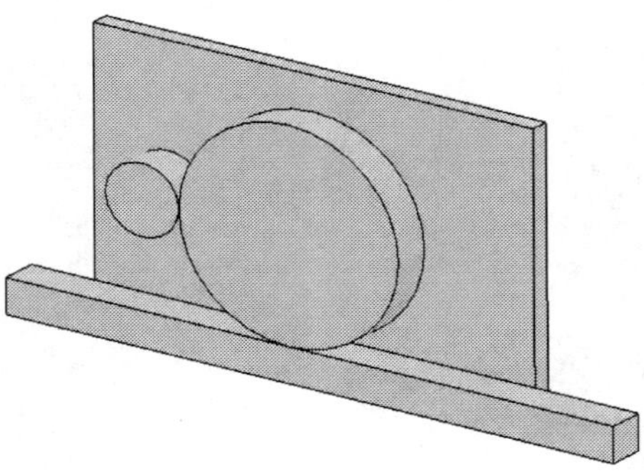

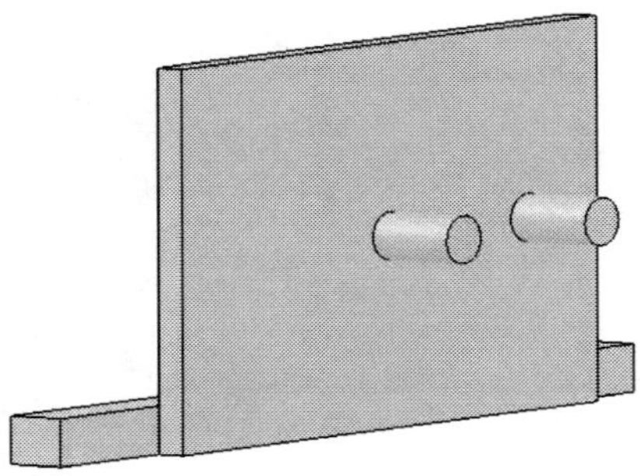

2 Overview of this Tutorial

In this tutorial you will:

1. Model the four CATIA parts required.
2. Create an assembly (CATIA Product) containing the parts.
3. Constrain the assembly in such a way that appropriate degrees of freedom are removed before proceeding to DMU.
4. Enter the **Digital Mockup** workbench and use automatic assembly constraints conversion to create two revolute joints and a prismatic joint.
5. Create a gear joint between the pinion and the gear which consumes or absorbs the two revolute joints created.
6. Create another revolute joint for the gear and use that revolute joint in the creation of a rack joint between the gear and the rack.
7. Simulate the motion of the mechanism without consideration to time (in other words, without implementing the known constant angular velocity given in the problem statement).
8. Add a formula to implement the time based kinematics associated with constant angular velocity of the pinion.
9. Simulate the desired motion and generate a plot of position of the rack vs time.

3 Creation of the Assembly in Mechanical Design Solutions

Model four parts named **base**, **gear, pinion** and **rack** as shown below. It is recommended that you use the indicated dimensions (inches) and in the event that a dimension is missing, estimate it based on the drawing.

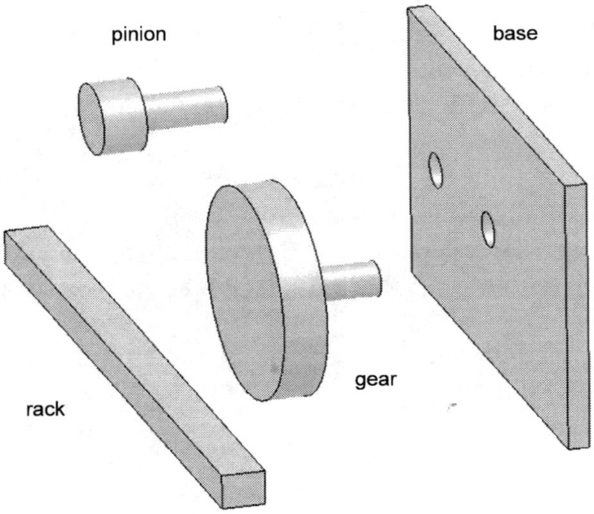

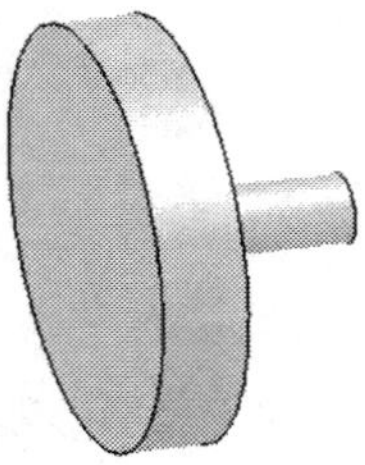

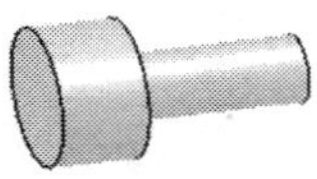

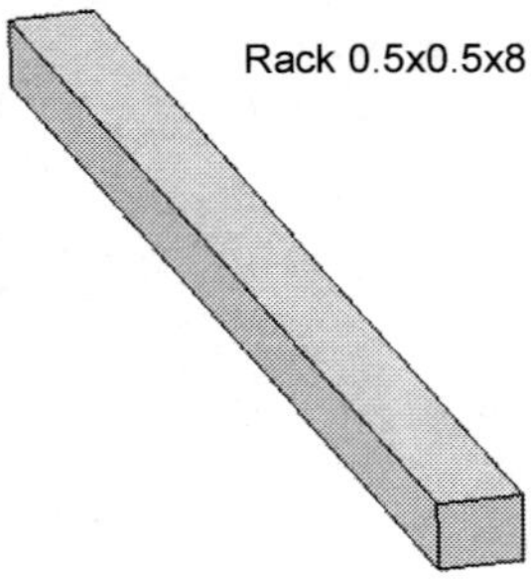

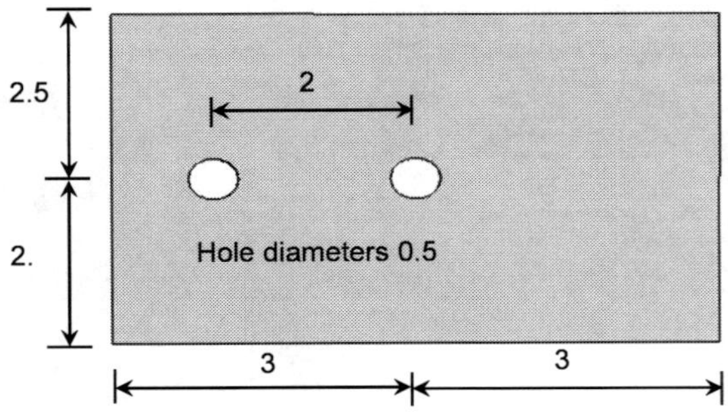

Once the parts are modeled, we will begin the assembly process. Enter the **Assembly Design** workbench which can be achieved by different means depending on your CATIA customization. For example, from the standard Windows toolbar, select **File > New**. From the box shown on the right, select **Product**. This moves you to the **Assembly Design** workbench and creates an assembly with the default name **Product.1**.

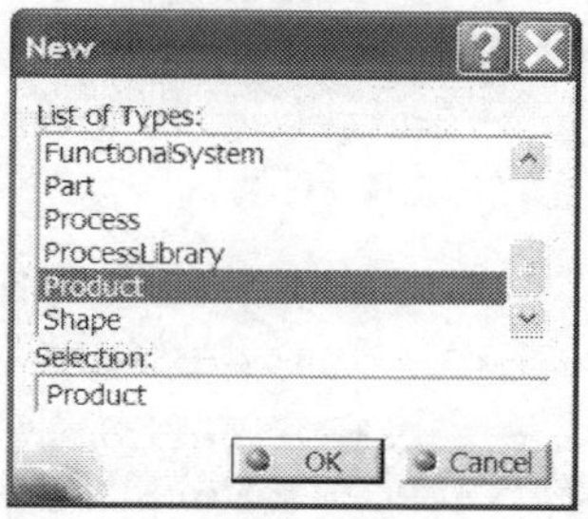

In order to change the default name, move the cursor to **Product.1** in the tree, right click and select **Properties** from the menu list.

From the **Properties** box, select the **Product** tab and in **Part Number** type **gear_mechanism**.

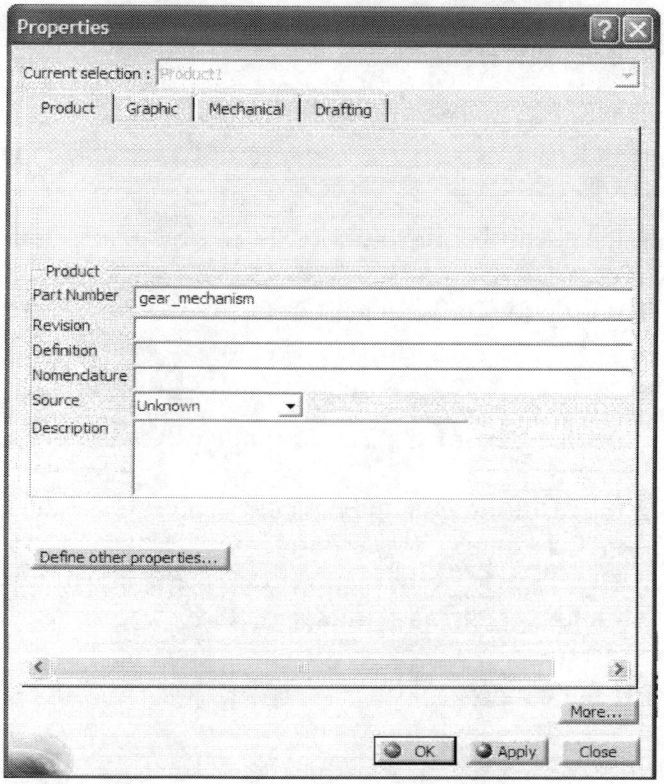

This will be the new product name throughout the chapter. The tree on the top left corner of your computer screen should look as displayed below.

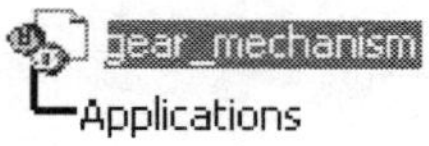

The next step is to insert the existing parts in the assembly just created.

Select the **Existing Component** icon from the **Product Structure Tools** toolbar

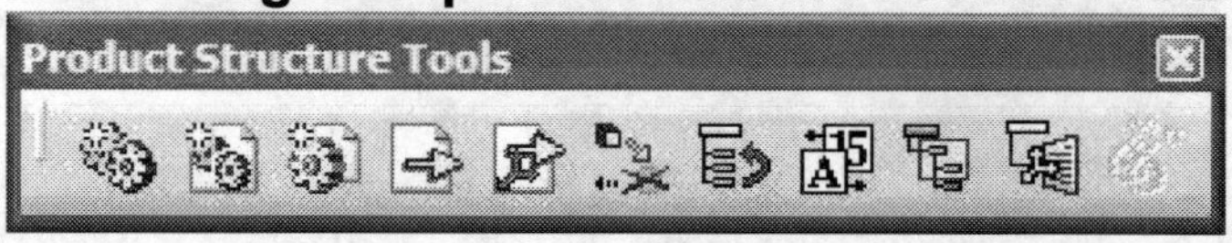

. Point the cursor to the **gear_mechanism** branch of the tree at the very top.

The **File Selection** pop up box opens where you can select all four components simultaneously using the **Ctrl** key.

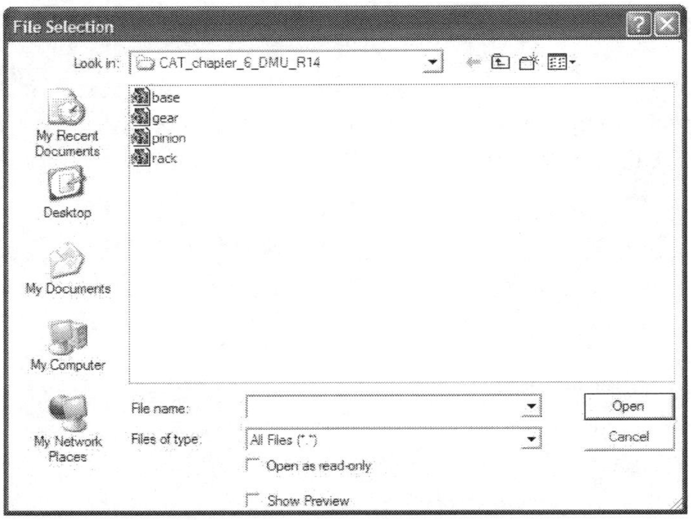

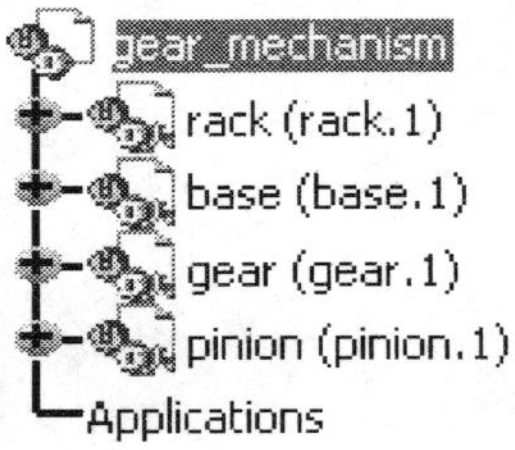

In the event that the order of the appearance of the parts in the tree is to be changed (possibly for convenience), select the **Graph Tree Reordering** icon  from the **Product Structure Tools** toolbar 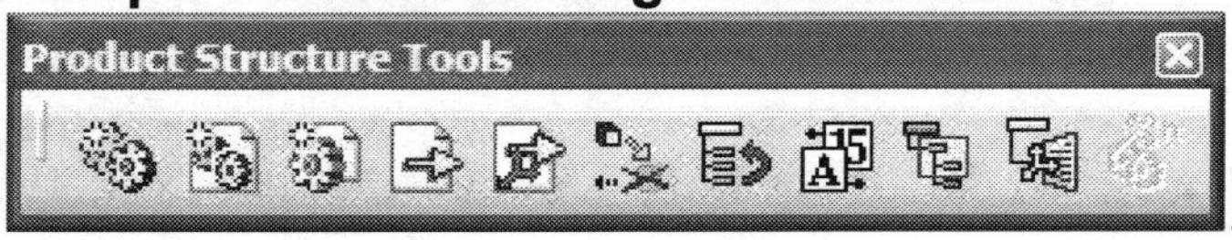.

In the resulting pop up box show, you can use the keys  to rearrange the parts in the desired order. We will keep the order intact.

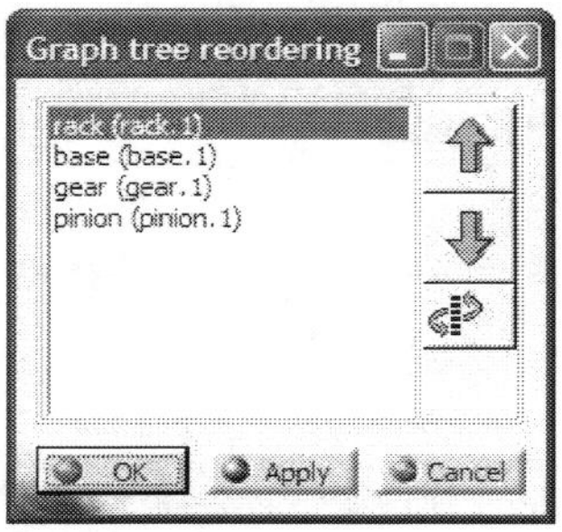

OK the window.

Note that the part names and their instance names were purposely made the same. This practice makes the identifying of the assembly constraint a lot easier down the road. Depending on how your parts were created earlier, on the computer screen you have the four parts scattered as shown below. You may have to use the **Manipulation** icon  in the **Move** toolbar  to rearrange them as desired so they are not overlapping. This will facilitate creation of the assembly constraints.

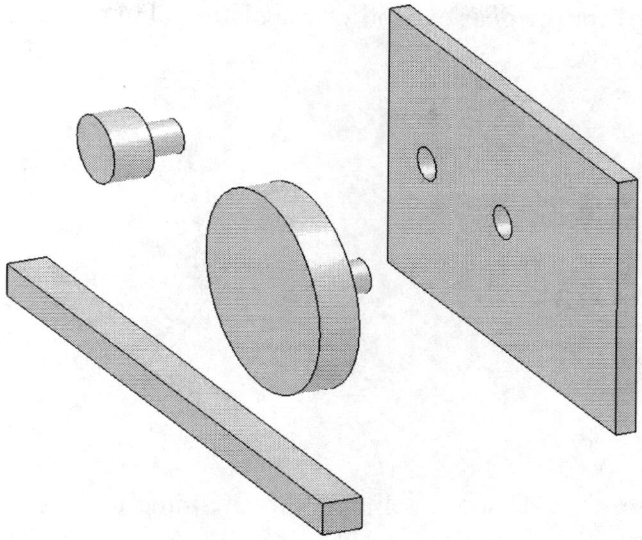

The best way of saving your work is to save the entire assembly.
Double click on the top branch of the tree. This is to ensure that you are in the **Assembly Design** workbench.
Select the **Save** icon . The **Save As** pop up box allows you to rename if desired. The default name is the **gear_mechanism**. Accept that name.

Your next task is to impose assembly constraints. We will begin by anchoring the base thereby removing all six of its degrees of freedom (dof) of motion.

Pick the **Anchor** icon from **Constraints** toolbar and select the **base** from the tree or from the screen.

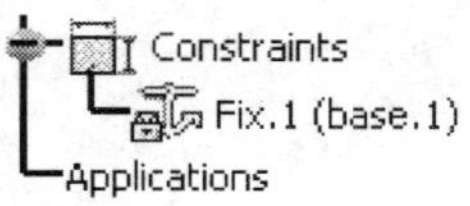

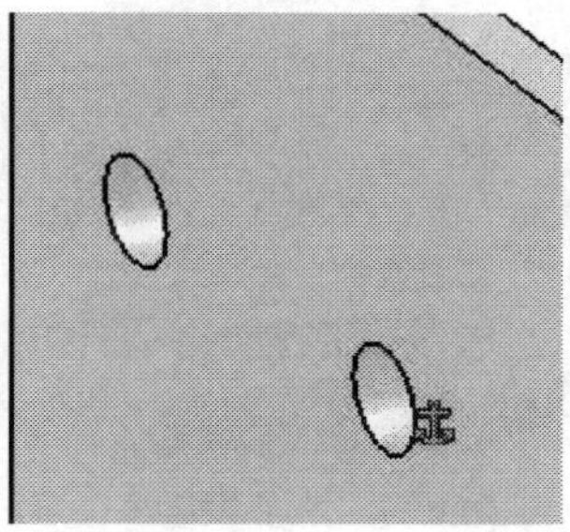

Next we will position the gear to remove all of its dof except for rotation about the axis of the shaft. Pick the **Coincidence** icon from the **Constraints** toolbar

. Select the two axes as shown below.

This removes all dof for the gear except for translation along the axis of the shaft and rotation about that axis.

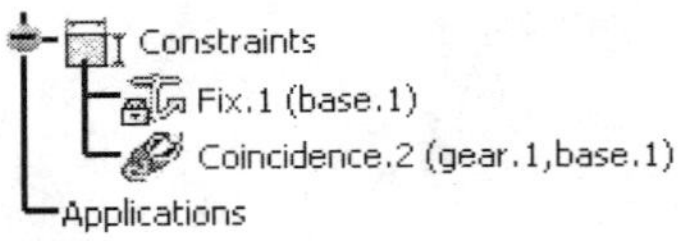

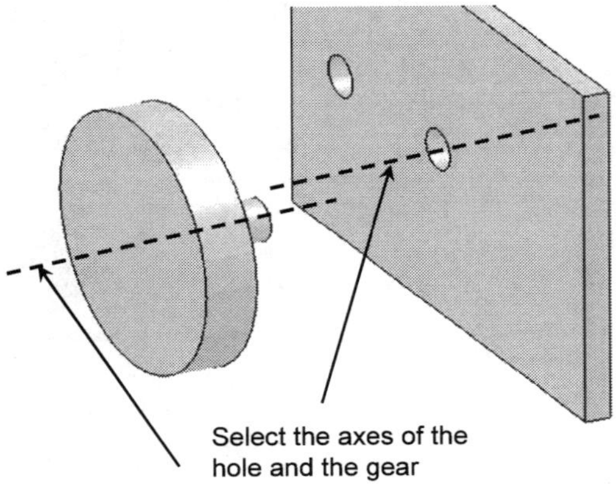

A contact constraint will be used to remove the remaining translational dof. Pick the **Contact** icon from the **Constraints** toolbar and select front face of the **base** and the back face of the **gear** as shown below.

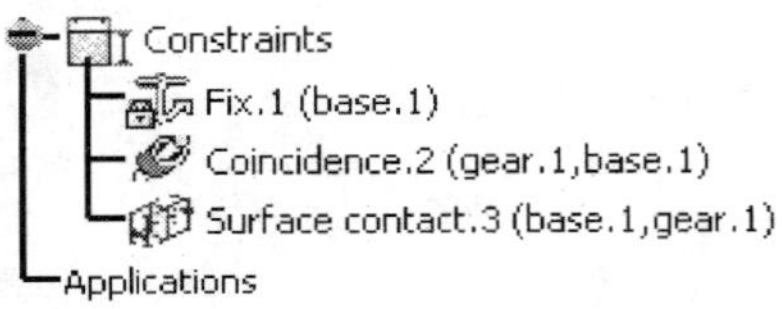

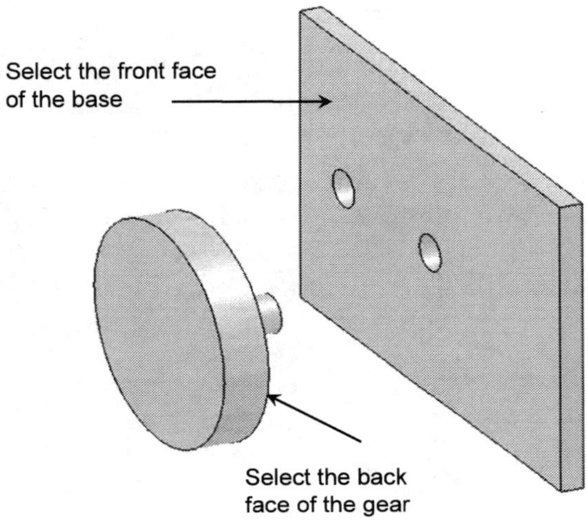

That completes the necessary constraints for the gear. Next, a similar set of constraints will be applied the pinion. Pick the **Coincidence** icon from the **Constraints** toolbar. Select the two axes as shown below.

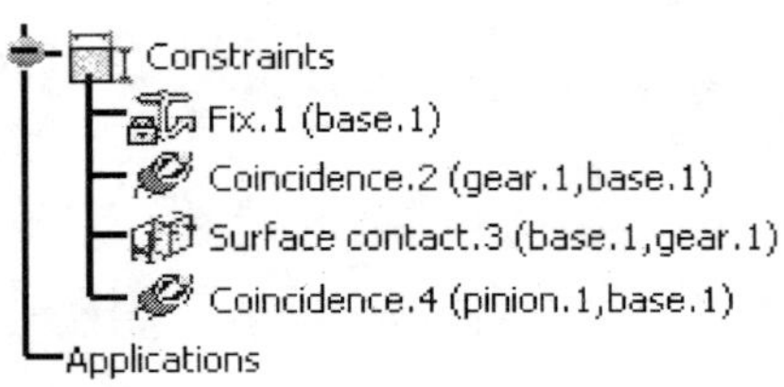

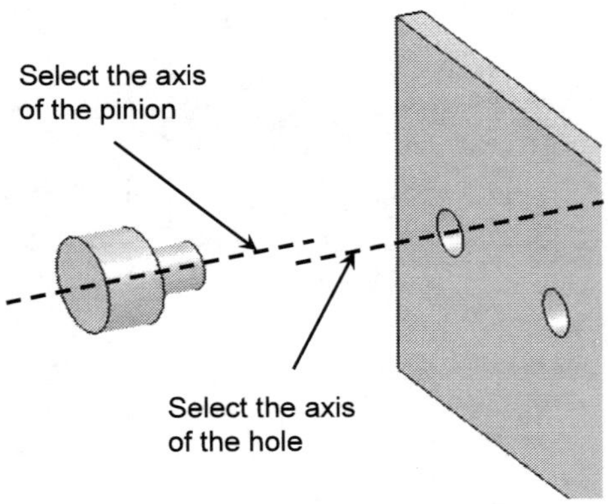

Pick the **Contact** icon  from the **Constraints** toolbar and select front face of the **base** and the back face of the **pinion**.

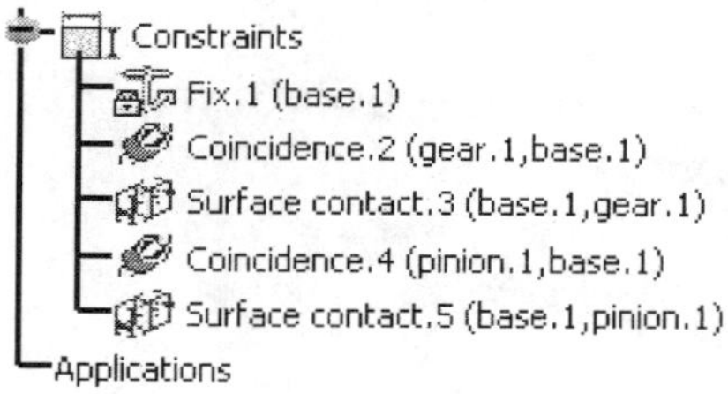

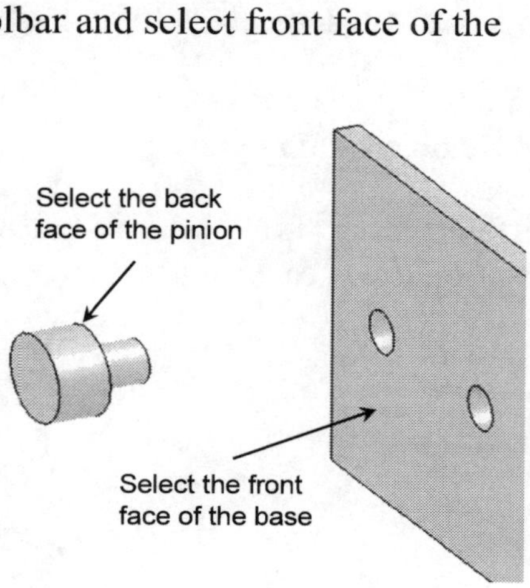

Next you will create the constraints necessary to establish a prismatic joint for the rack. An appropriate set of assembly constraints will remove all dof for the rack except translation in a direction along its length.

Pick the **Coincidence** icon  from **Constraints** toolbar. Select the two edges of the **base** and the **rack** as shown below. This removes all dof except for translation along the coincident edge and rotation about the coincident edge.

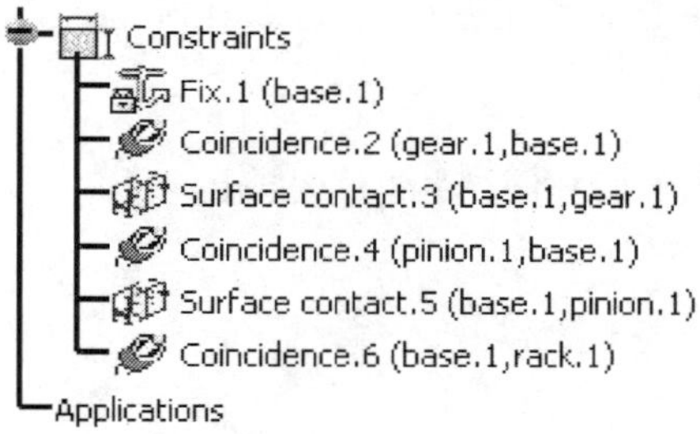

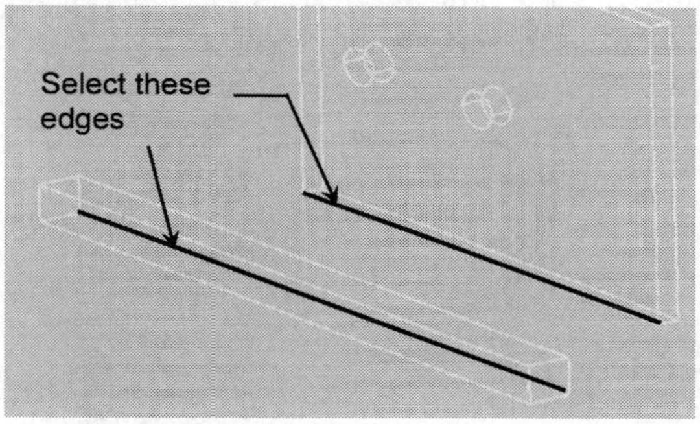

To remove the unwanted rotational dof which remains, pick the **Contact** icon  and select front face of the **base** and the back face of the **rack** which is labeled as ABCD below.

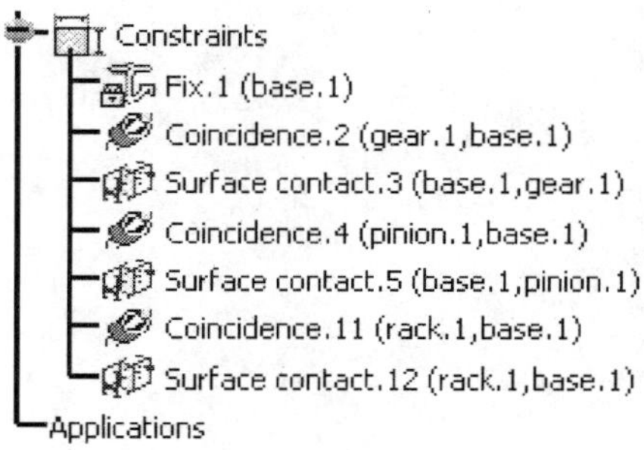

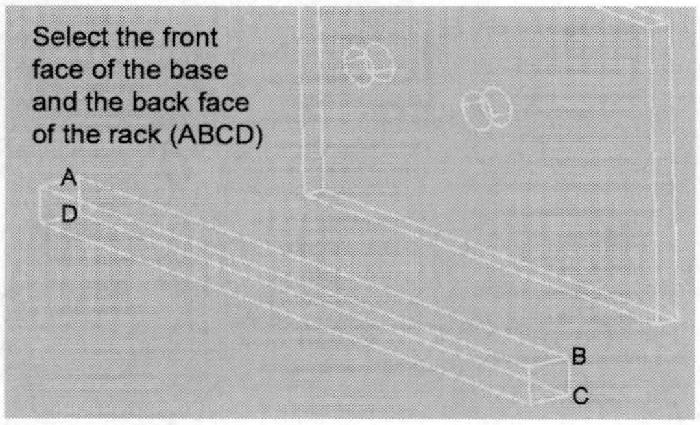

Use **Update** icon  to partially position the parts as shown on the next page.

Note that the **Update** icon  no longer appears on the constraints branches. Depending on how your parts were constructed, the rack may end up in a position quite different from what is shown below. You can always use the **Manipulation** icon  to position it where desired followed by **Update** if necessary.

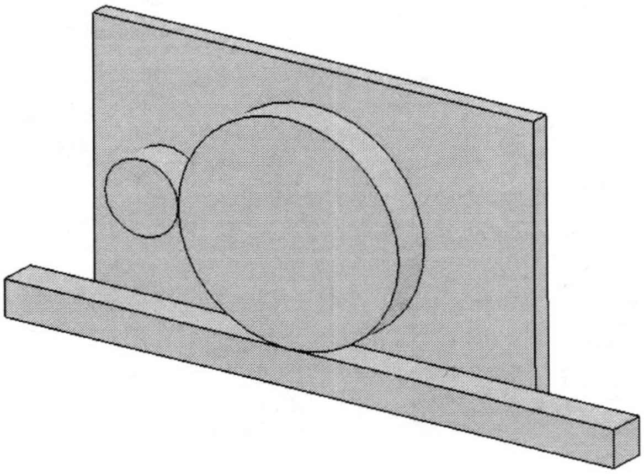

Assuming your hole spacing on the base was consistent with the sum of your pinion and gear radii, your pinion should be in a just-touch condition with the gear as can be seen above.

The assembly is complete and we can proceed to the **Digital Mockup** workbench.

4 Creating Joints in the Digital Mockup Workbench

The **Digital Mockup** workbench is quite extensive but we will only deal with the **DMU Kinematics module**. To get there you can use the standard Windows toolbar as shown below: **Start > Digital Mockup > DMU Kinematics**.

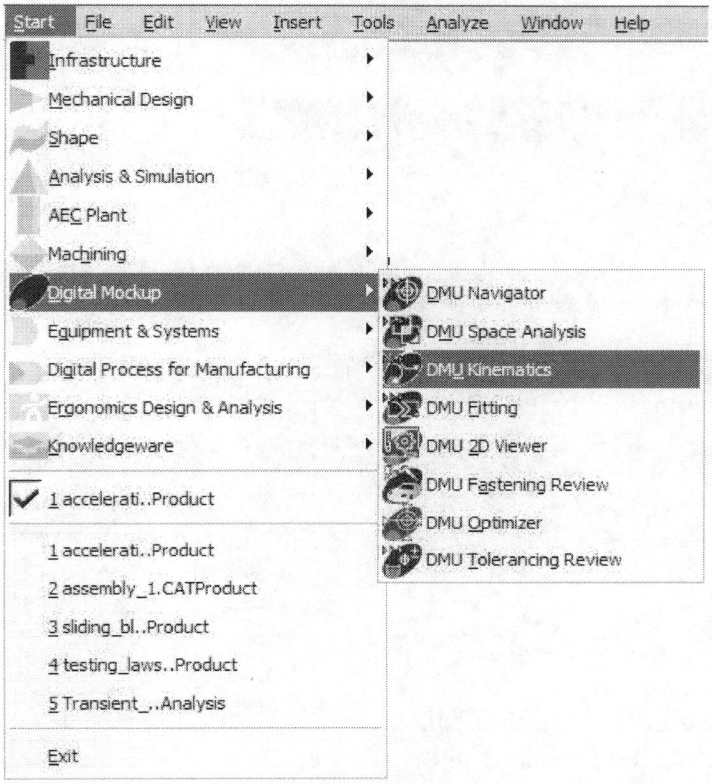

Select the **Assembly Constraints Conversion** icon 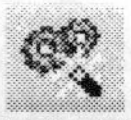 from the **DMU Kinematics** toolbar 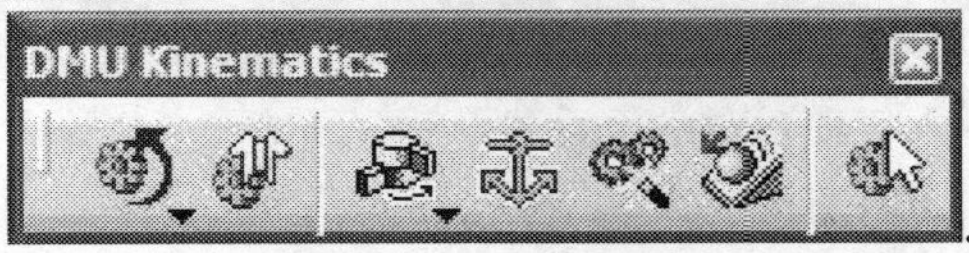

. This icon allows you to create most common joints automatically from the existing assembly constraints.
The pop up box below appears.

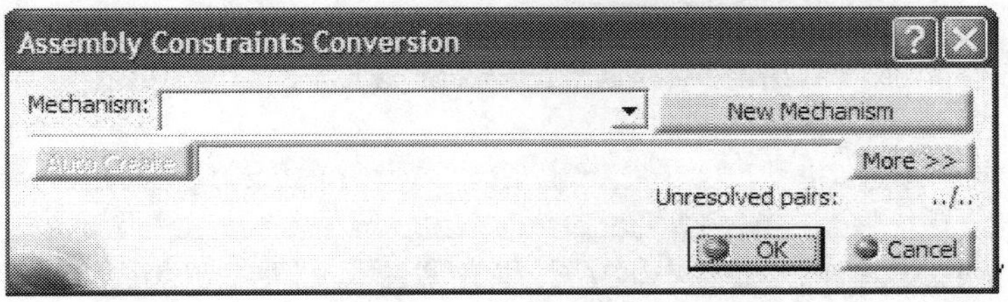

Select the **New Mechanism** button .
This leads to another pop up box which allows you to name your mechanism. The default name is **Mechanism.1**. Accept the default name by pressing **OK**

Note that the box indicates **Unresolved pairs: 3/3**.

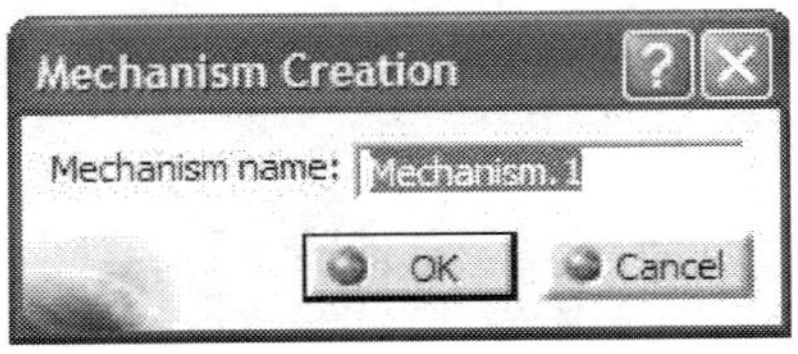

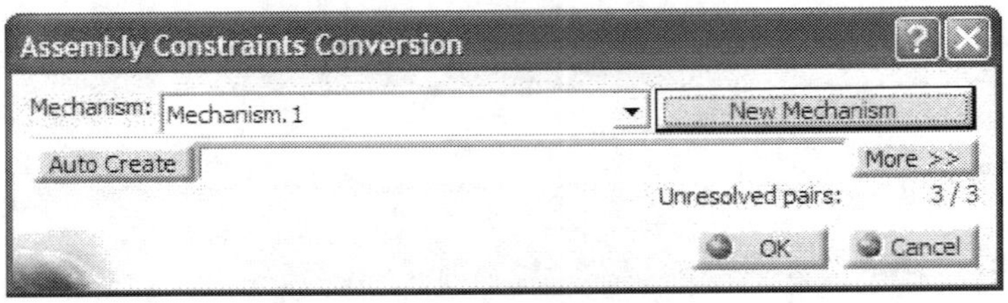

Select the **Auto Create** button . Then if the **Unresolved pairs** becomes **0/3**, things are moving in the right direction.

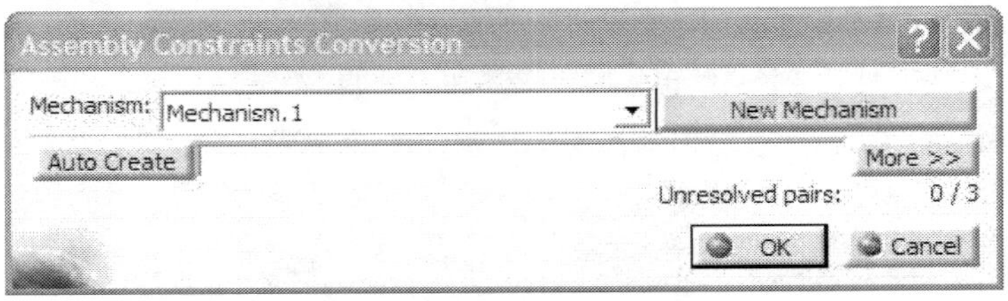

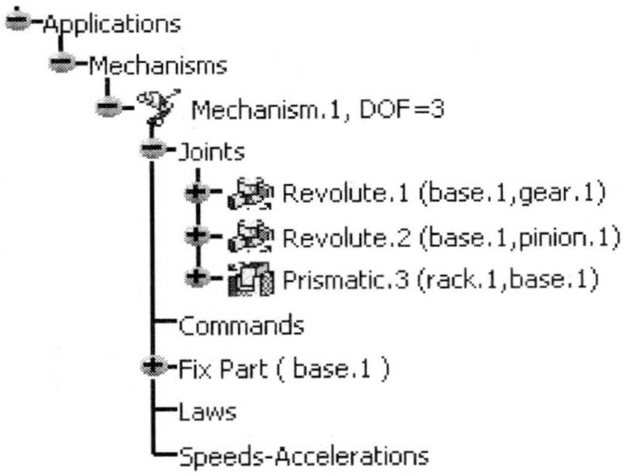

Taking a closer look at the tree, you will note that two revolute joints and a single prismatic joint have been created. The gear joint and the rack joint need to be created manually. The **Assembly Constraint Conversion** icon 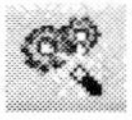 is not capable of creating such joints. The two revolute joints and the prismatic joint which were created are consistent with the dof we removed applying the assembly constraints. In the next page, you are walked through necessary steps to create the gear and rack joints required.

A gear joint requires two revolute joints. However, a rack joint requires a revolute joint and a prismatic joint. *It is much easier to use the* ***Manipulation*** *icon*  *to temporarily separate the gear from the base before proceeding with the next task. Note that this has to be done by first switching to the* Assembly Design *workbench, then returning to DMU Kinematics.*

Select the **Gear Joint** icon  from the **Kinematics Joints** toolbar

The pop up box below appears.

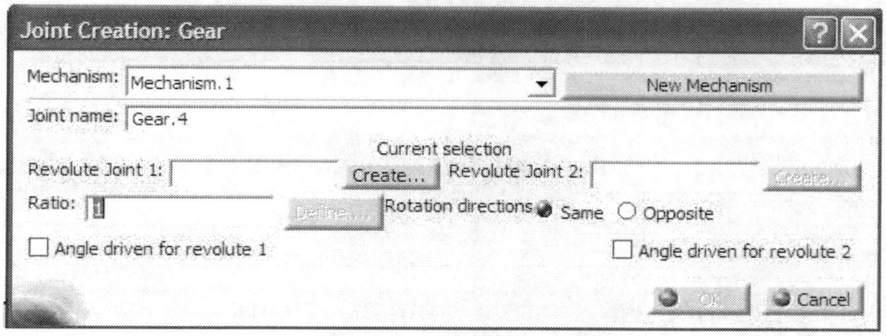

For **Revolute Joint 1**, select **Revolute.1** from the tree.
For **Revolute Joint 2**, select **Revolute.2** from the tree.

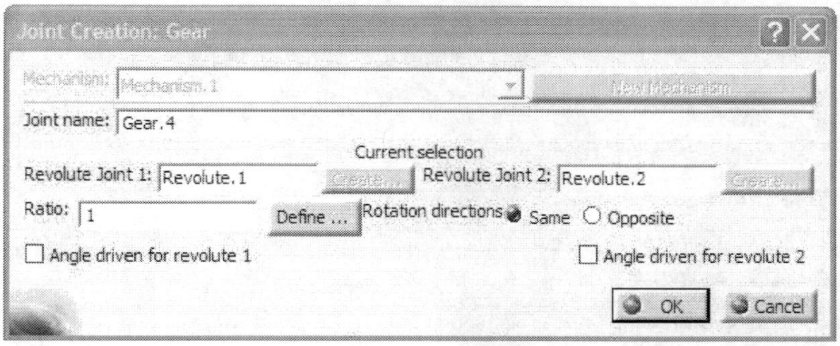

The **Ratio** can be defined arbitrarily defined by picking appropriate radii. Select the **Ratio** 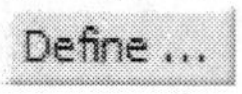 button.

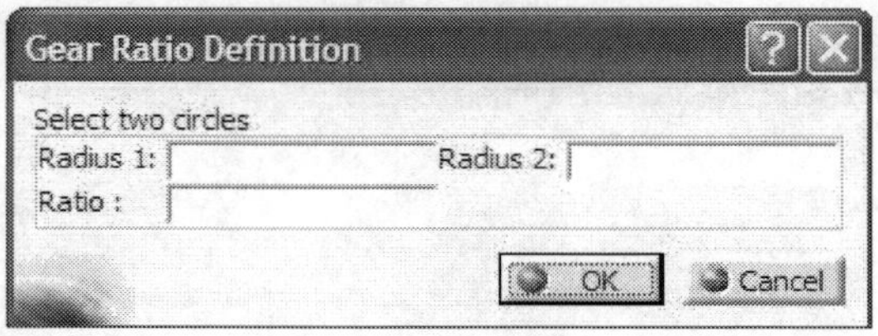

Using the cursor pick the two circles which make the **gear** and **pinion**. The correct gear ratio of 3 is created. Note here that CATIA is working in units of mm regardless of what units you have set.

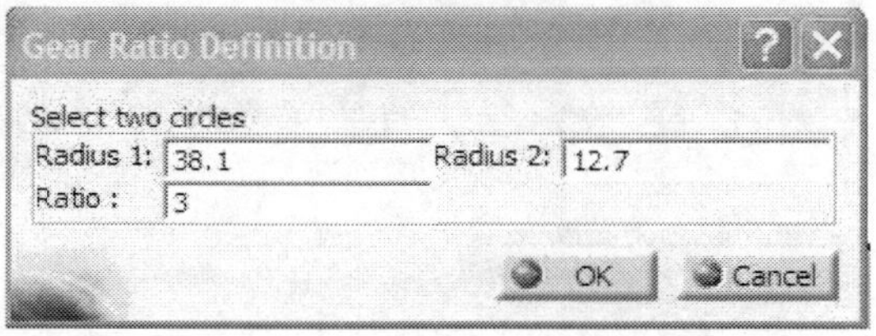

Close the box by pressing **OK**.

Since these are externally engaged gears, the sense of rotation is opposite. Therefore, select the **Opposite** radio button and close the **Joint Creation: Gear** window.

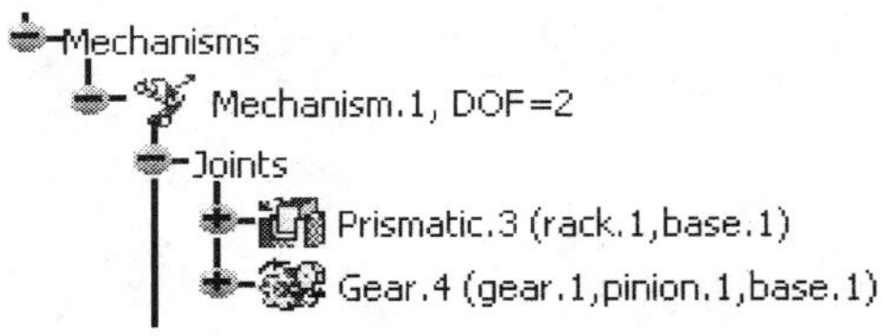

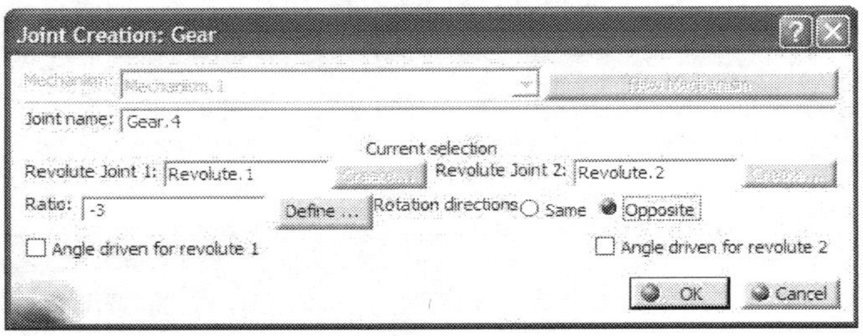

The specification tree indicates that the **Gear.4** joint has been created. However, it has consumed both revolute joints.

Select the **Rack Joint** icon  from the **Kinematics Joints** toolbar

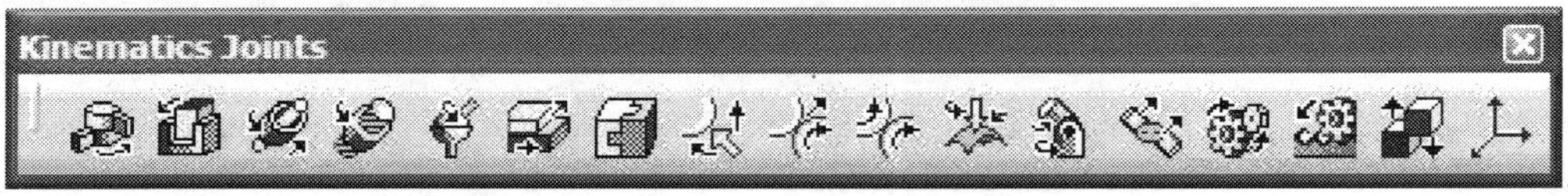

.

The **Joint Creation: Rack** pop up box appears.

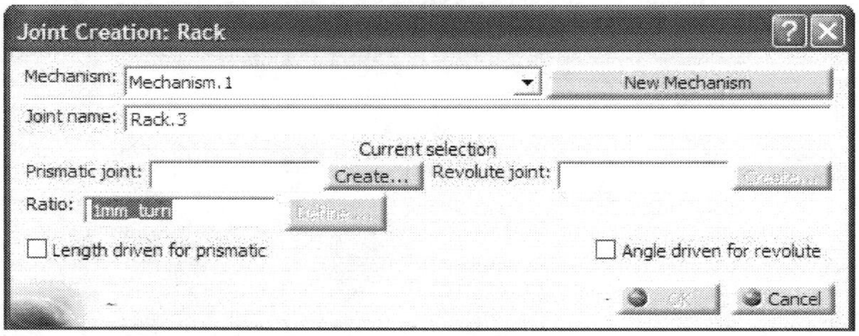

This box requires the selection of a **Prismatic joint** which can be picked as **Prismatic.3** from the tree.

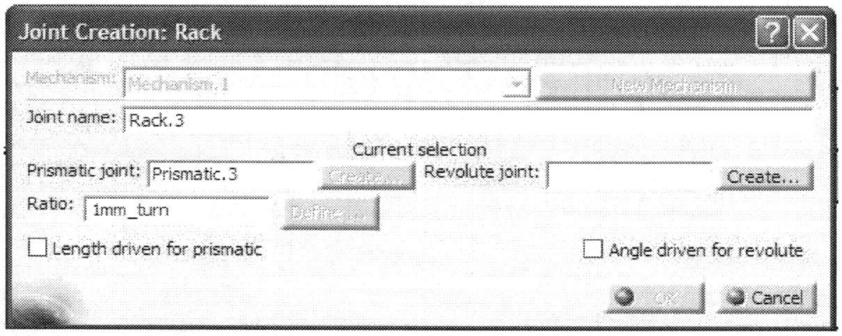

The problem is that no revolute joints are left to be selected. However, this can be created by selecting the **Revolute joint** Create... key.

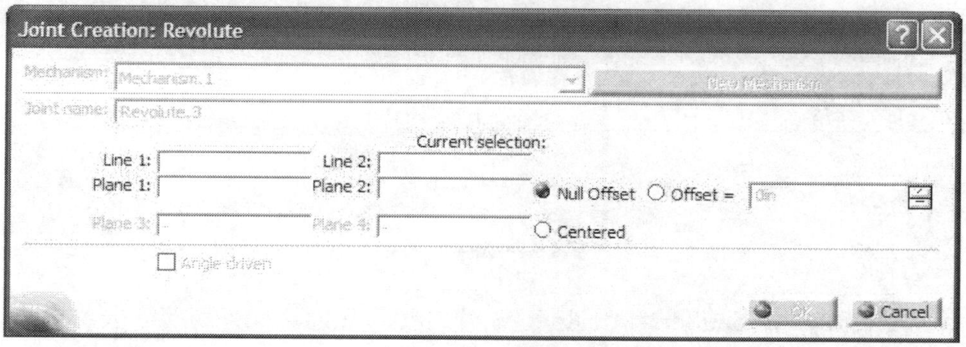

The revolute joint is to be created between the **gear** and the **base** parts.
For, Line 1, Line 2, Plane 1 and Plane 2 make selections as shown below.

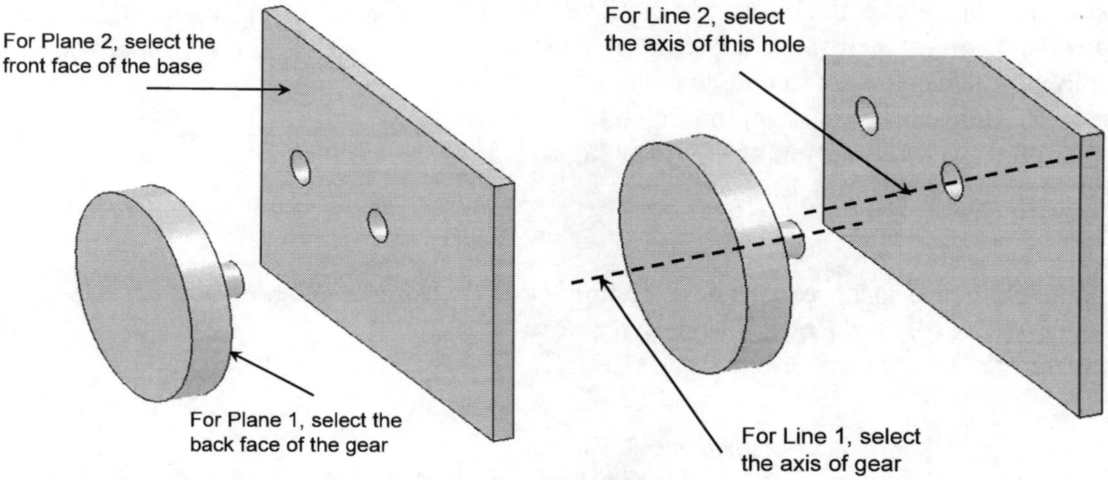

Keep in mind that the selection must be made in a consistent way. **Line 1** and **Plane 1** must belong to the same part and consequently, **Line 2** and **Plane 2** belong to the remaining part. The completed pop up box is shown below which can then be closed by clicking **OK**.

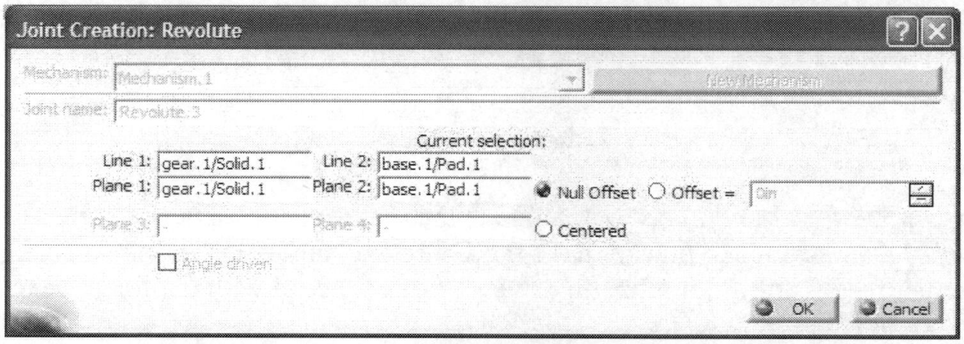

You are then returned automatically to the **Joint Creation: Rack box** which was still on your screen.

Note that a new revolute joint is created in your tree and labeled as **Revolute.3**.

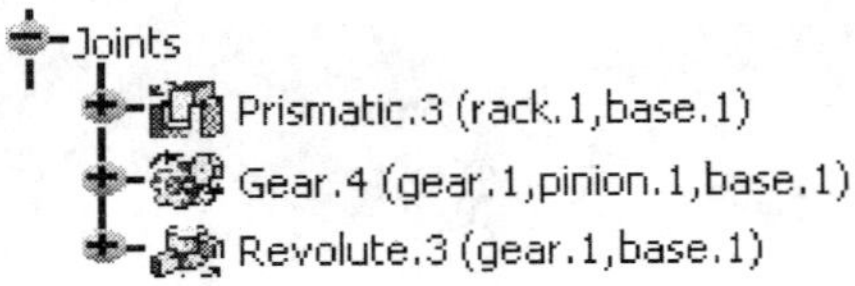

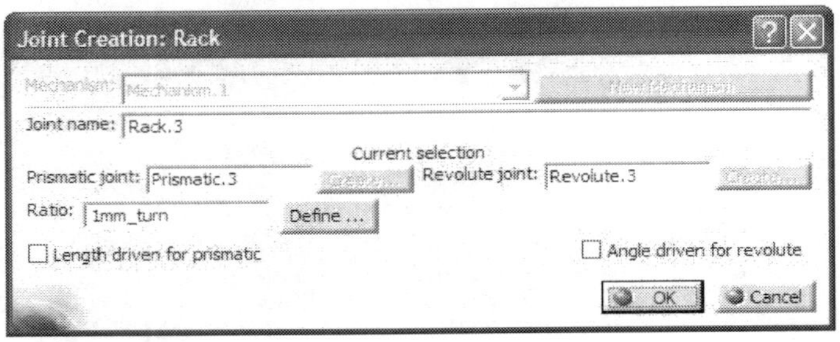

The **Ratio** can now be inputted if desired or, defined consistently as the geometry dictates. Select the **Ratio**  button.

Using the cursor pick the circle which make the **gear**. The correct gear ratio of is created. This number indicates the correct advancement of the **rack** (again in mm even if you modeled in inches) for every revolution of the **gear** (a circumference is computed).

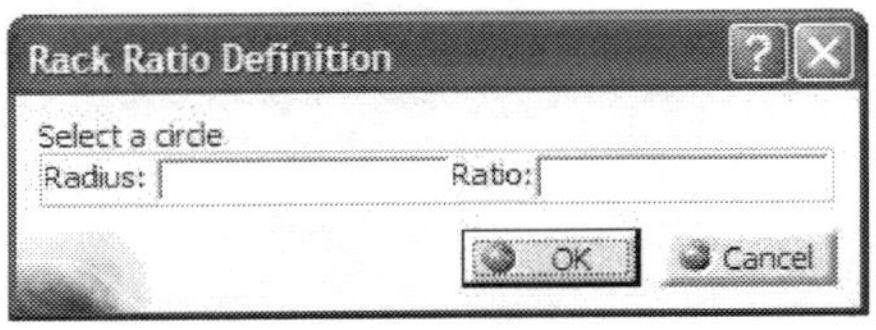

Upon closing this last box, you have completed the **Joint Creation : Rack** box shown below and a **Rack.3** joint is recorded in the tree.

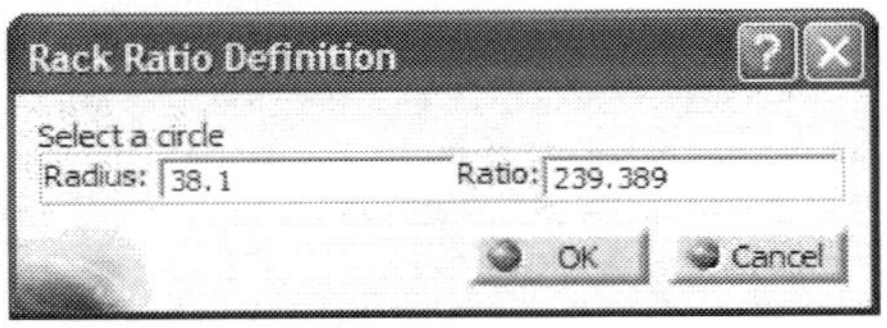

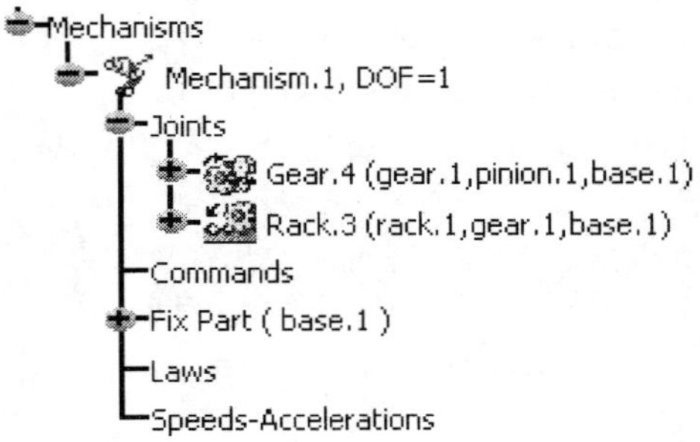

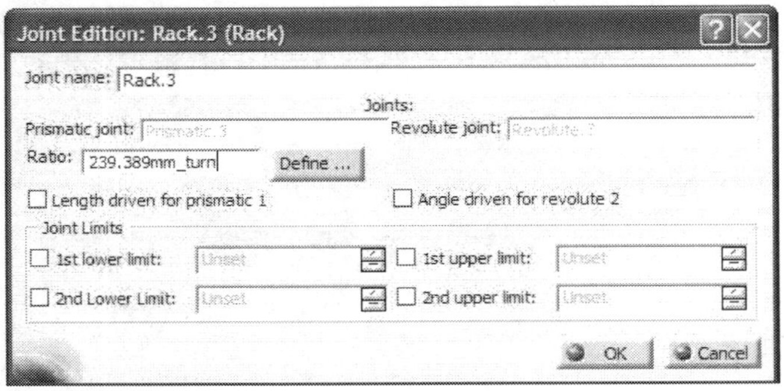

At this point **DOF** is 1 and in order to animate the mechanism, we need to specify one command. As an example, you can make the **Gear.4** an angle driven joint. Alternatively, you can make the **Rack.3** joint length driven. Let us proceed with the former choice.

Double click on **Gear.4** in the tree to open the pop up box shown below.

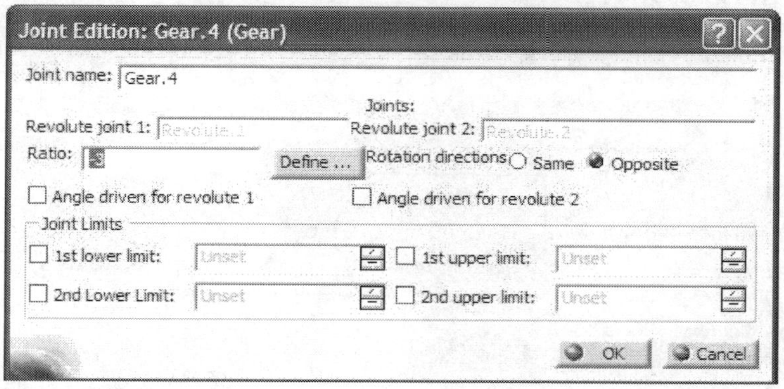

Check the box **Angle driven for revolute 2** as displayed next.

The arrow indicates which revolute is picked and the sense of rotation

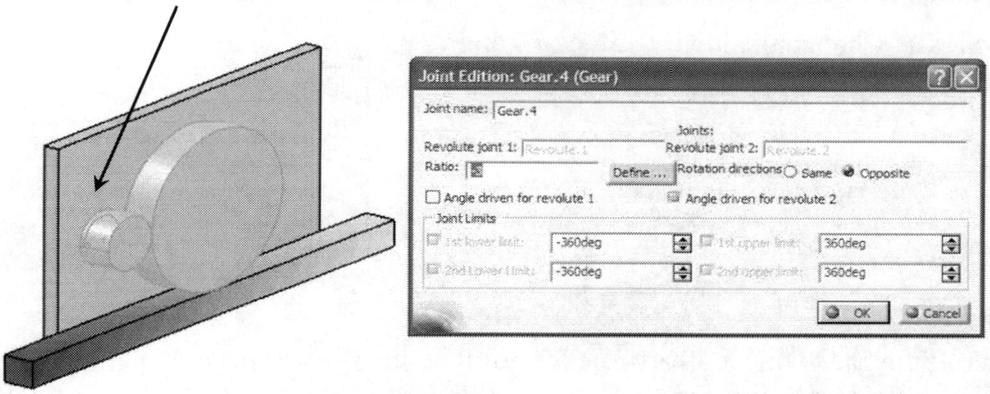

Upon closing the above box and assuming that everything else was done correctly, the following message appears on the screen.

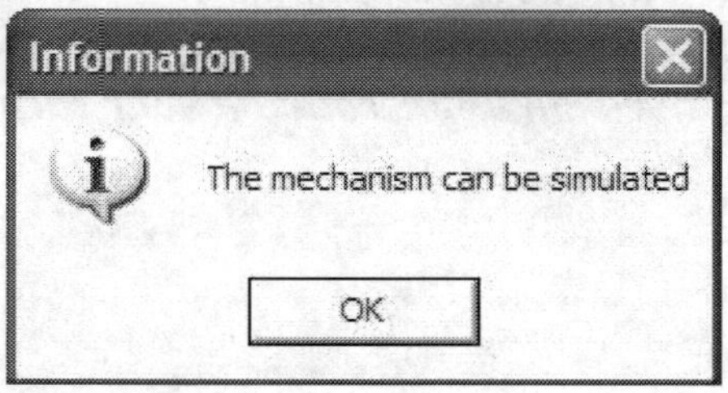

This indeed is good news. We can simulate the motion, initially without regard to the time parameter.

Select the **Simulation** icon  from the **DMU Generic Animation** toolbar

. This enables you to choose the mechanism to be animated if there are several present. In this case, select **Mechanism.1** and close the window by clicking **OK**.

As soon as the window is closed, a Simulation branch is added to the tree.

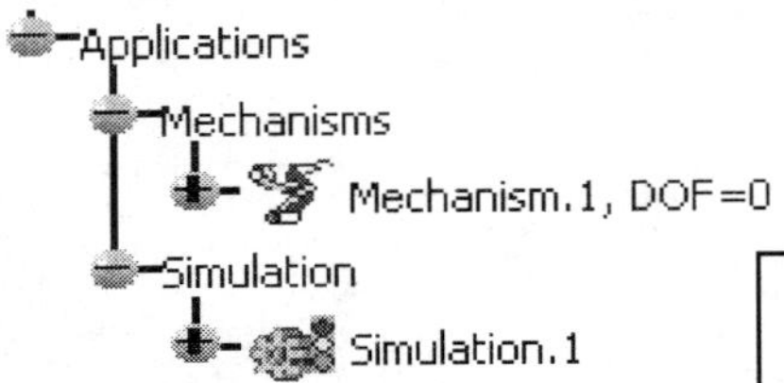

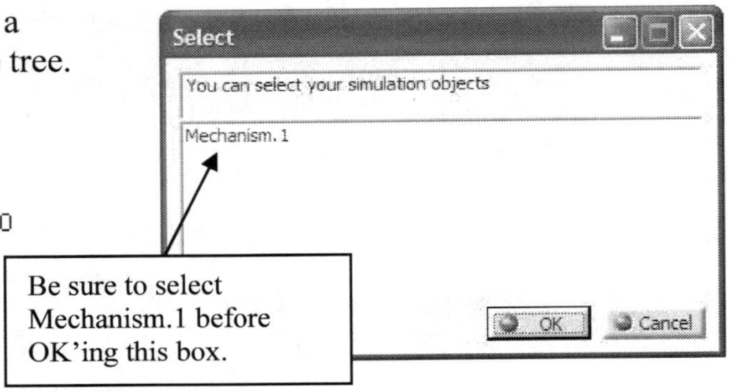

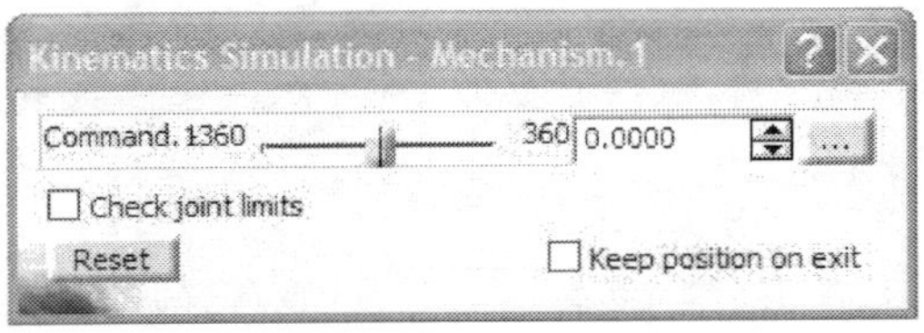

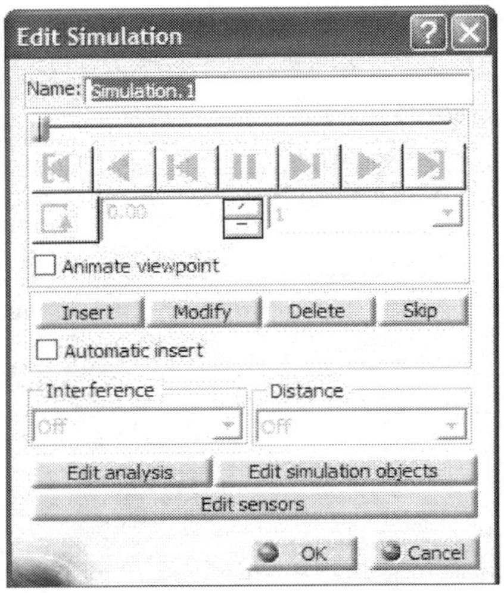

Change the range of rotation of the pinion by clicking on ... . Change the lowest value to 0 and close the pop up box by clicking **OK**.

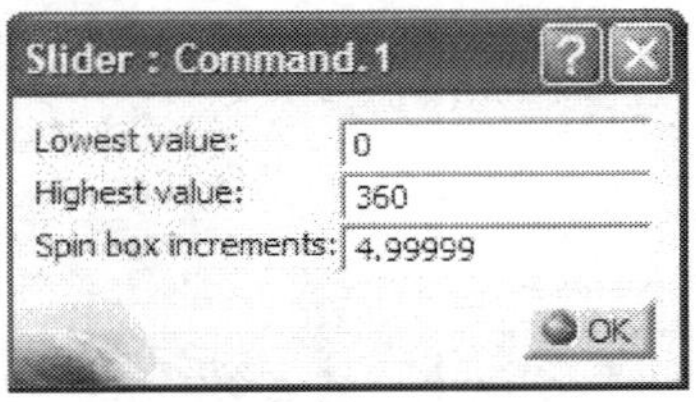

As you scroll the bar in this toolbar from left to right, the **pinion** begins rotating and makes a full 360 degree turn. This in turn causes the **gear** to make a 120 degree rotation and advances the **rack** by 230/3 mm. If you wish to make the rotational motion of the pinion and gear more obvious, you may add a hole to each one to improve the visualization of the rotation. Note: *If your rack moves the wrong direction, try adding a negative sign to the ratio on your rack joint and trying it again!*

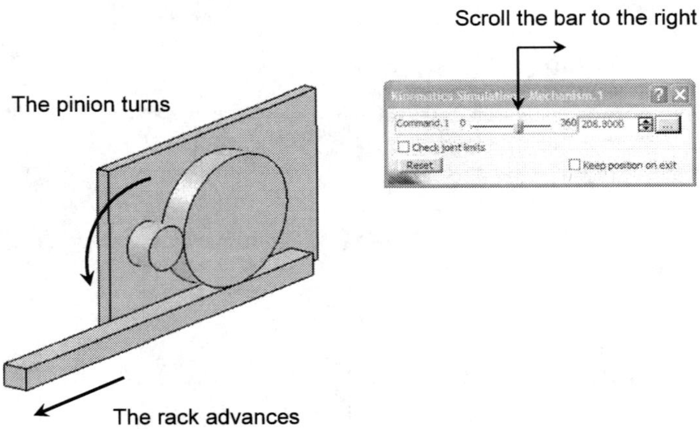

When the scroll bar in the **Kinematics Simulation** pop up box reaches the right extreme end, select the **Insert** button Insert in the **Edit Simulation** pop up box shown above. This activates the video player buttons shown

.

Return the pinion to its original position by picking the **Jump to Start** button.

Note that the **Change Loop Mode** button is also active now.

Upon selecting the **Play Forward** button, the pinion makes fast jump completing its revolution.

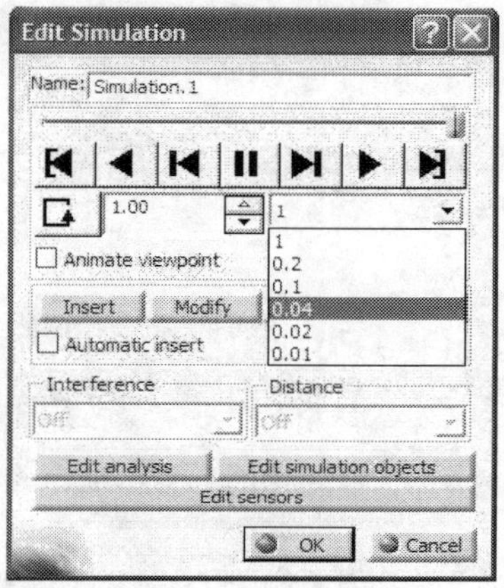

In order to slow down the motion of the pinion, select a different **interpolation step**, such as 0.04.

Upon changing the interpolation step to 0.04, return the pinion to its original position by picking the **Jump to Start** button. Apply **Play Forward** button and observe the slow and smooth rotation of the pinion.

Select the **Compile Simulation** icon from the **Generic Animation** toolbar

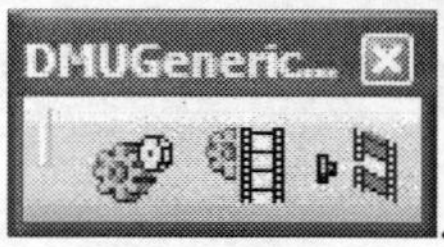

.

Pressing the **File name** button File name ... allows you to set the location and name of the animation file to be generated as displayed below.

Select a suitable path and file name and change the **Time step** to be 0.04 to produce a slow moving rotation in an AVI file.

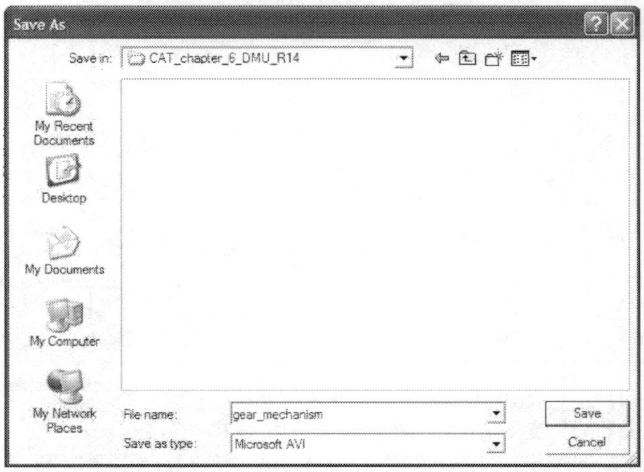

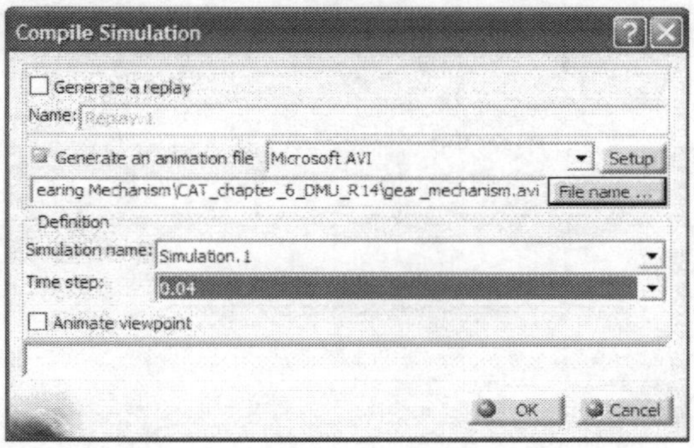

As the file is being generated, the crank slowly rotates. The resulting AVI file can be viewed with the Windows Media Player.

5 Creating Laws in the Motion

You will now introduce some time based physics into the problem. The objective is to specify the angular position versus time function for the driven revolute joint and therefore set the angular velocity and acceleration.

Click on **Simulation with Laws** icon  in the **Simulation** toolbar 

.
You will get the following pop up box indication that you need to add at least a relation between the command and the time parameter.

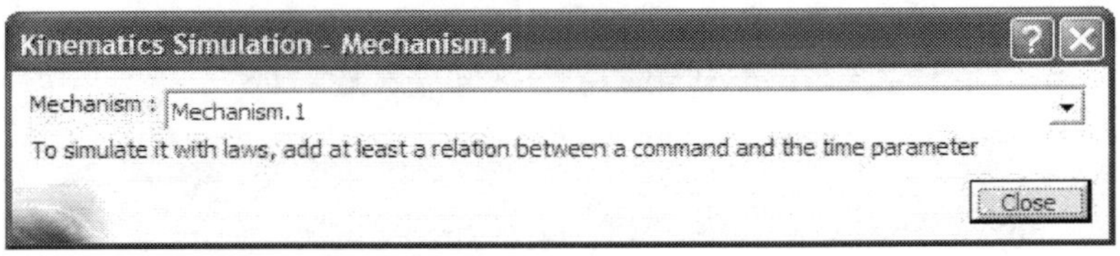

Select the **Formula** icon  from the **Knowledge** toolbar
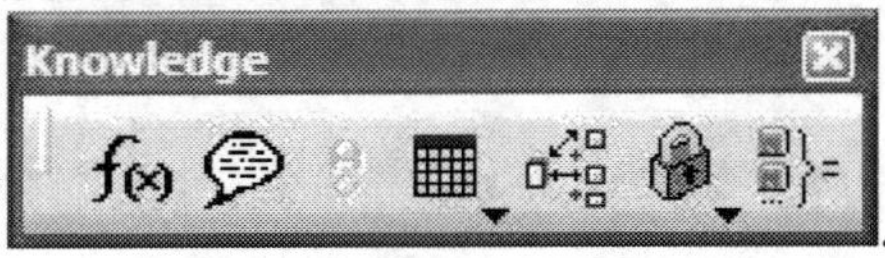

. The pop up box below appears on the screen.

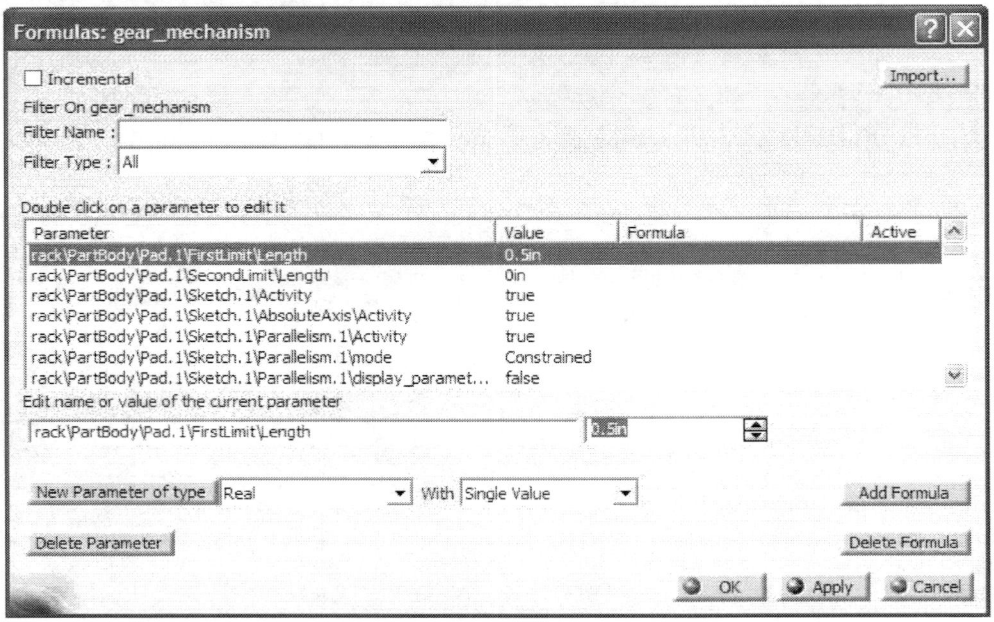

Point the cursor to the **Mechanism.1, DOF=0** branch in the tree and click. The consequence is that only parameters associated with the mechanism are displayed in the **Formulas** box.
The long list is now reduced to two parameters as indicated in the box.

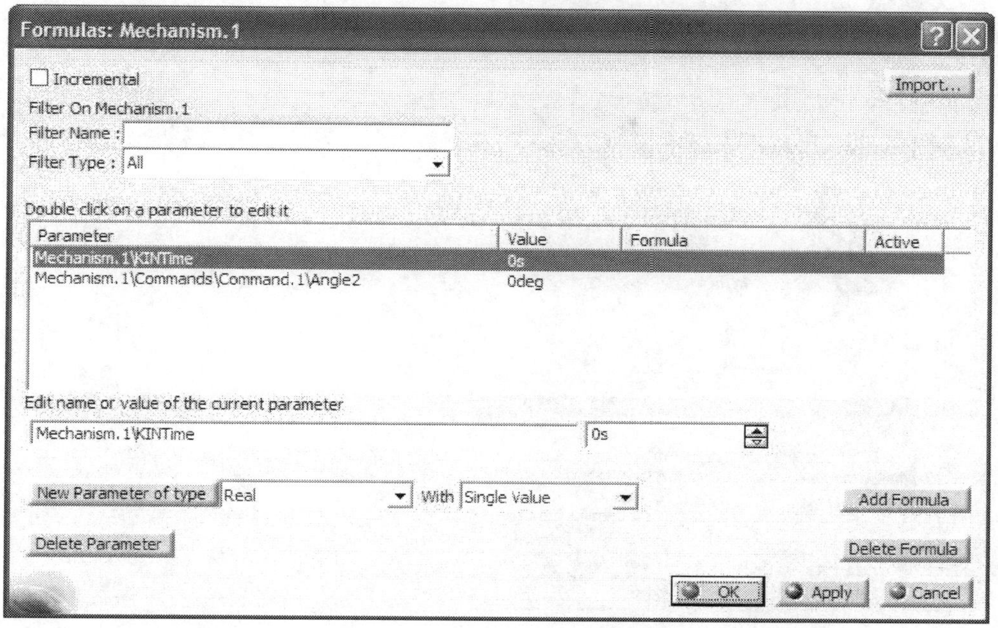

Select the entry **Mechanism.1\Commands\Command.1\Angle2** and press the **Add Formula** button Add Formula. This action kicks you to the **Formula Editor** box.

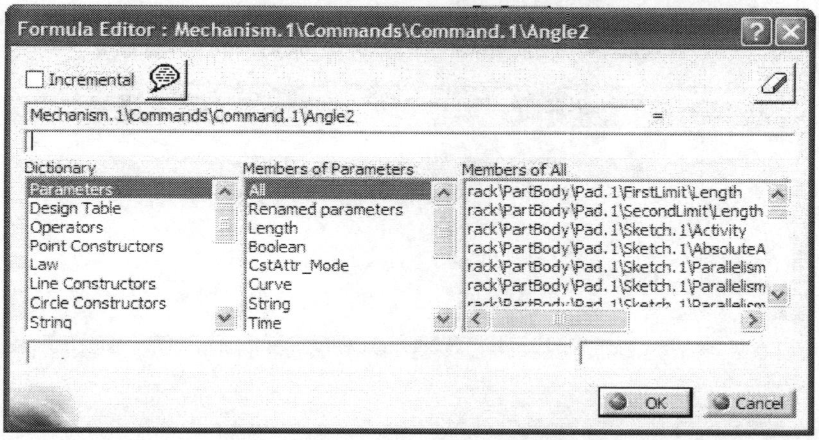

Pick the **Time** entry from the middle column (i.e. **Members of Parameters**).

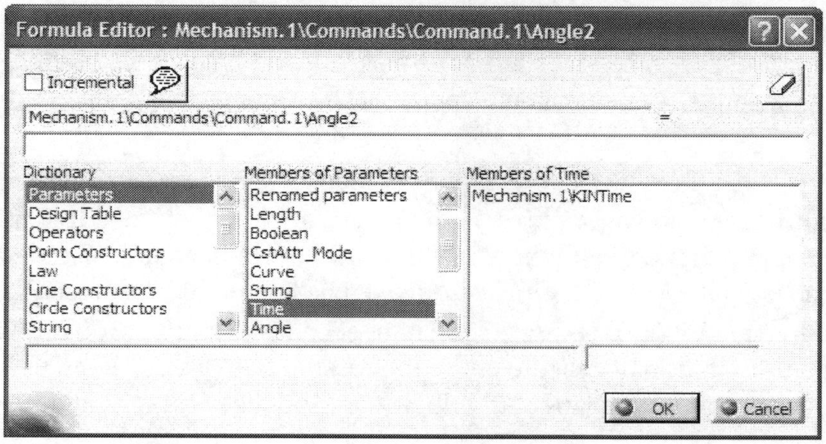

The right hand side of the equality should be such that the formula becomes

$$Mechanism.1 \backslash Commands \backslash Command.1 \backslash Angle2 =$$
$$(360\,\mathrm{deg}) * (Mechanism.1 \backslash KINTime)/(1s)$$

Therefore, the completed **Formula Editor** box becomes

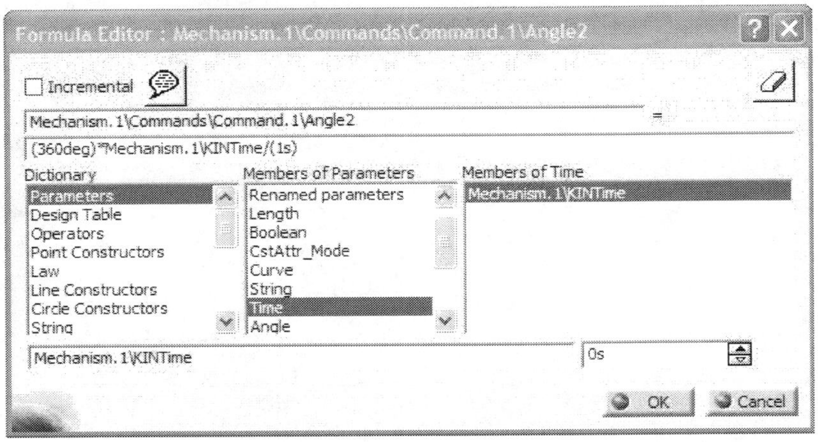

Upon accepting **OK**, the formula is recorded in the **Formulas** pop up box as shown below.

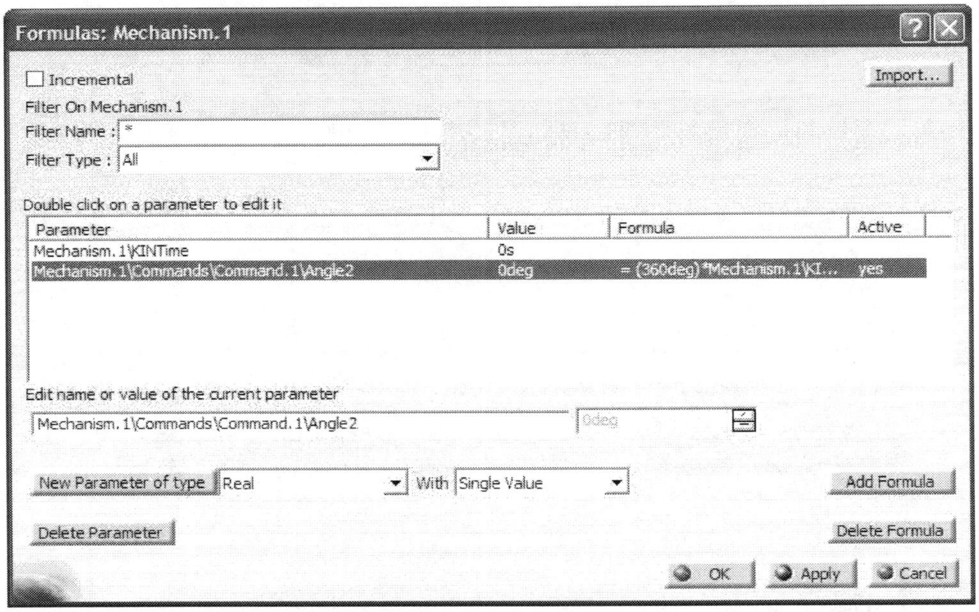

The formula introduced above requires an explanation. Note that the left hand side of the equality is an angle parameter and therefore the entire right hand side should be reducing to degrees. This is why $(Mechanism.1 \backslash KINTime)$ has been nondimensionalized by introducing a division by (1s). Here, "s" refers to seconds. Finally, (360 deg) has been introduced as a term to transforms the entire expression to degrees. Note that the formula is equivalent to multiplying the angular velocity of (360deg)/(1s) by the time parameter.

In the event that the formula has different units at the different sides of the equality you will get **Warning** messages such as the one shown below.

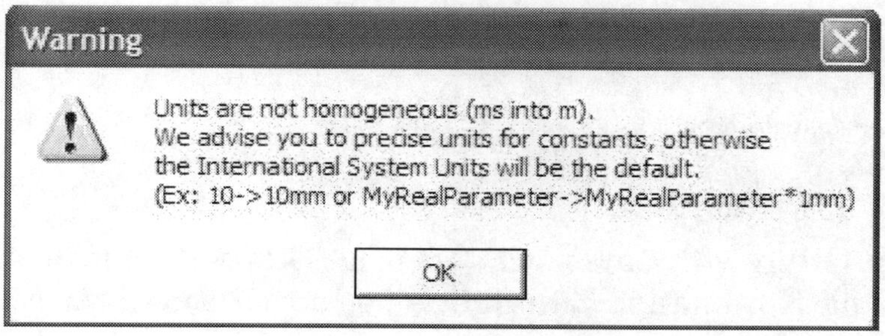

We are spared the warning message because the formula has been properly inputted. Note that the introduced law has appeared in **Law** branch of the tree.

To pick a point on the rack at which to study the kinematics, select the **Speed and Acceleration** icon  from the **DMU Kinematics** toolbar

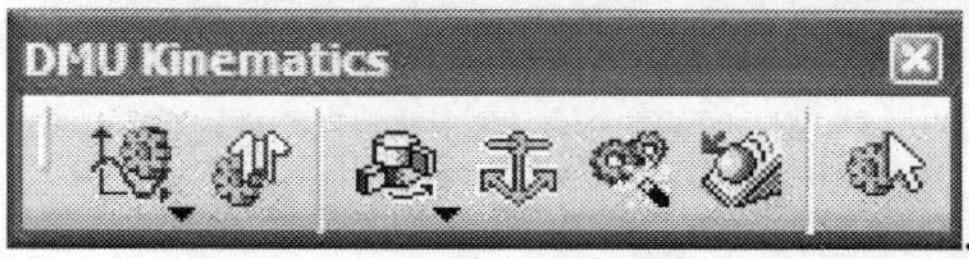

. The pop up box below appears on the Screen.

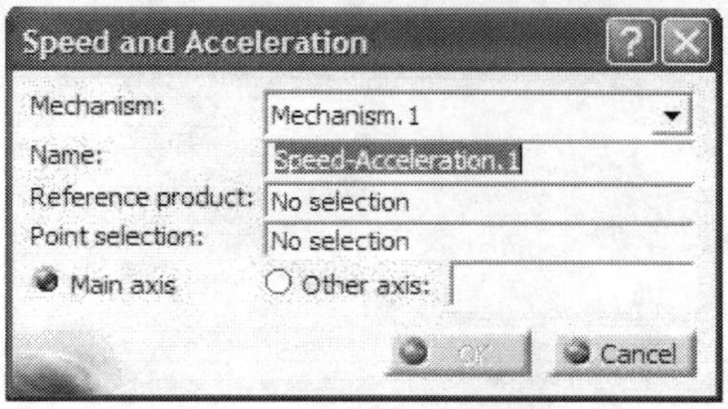

For the **Reference product,** select the **base** from the screen or the tree. For the **Point selection**, pick the vertex of the **rack** as shown in the sketch below.

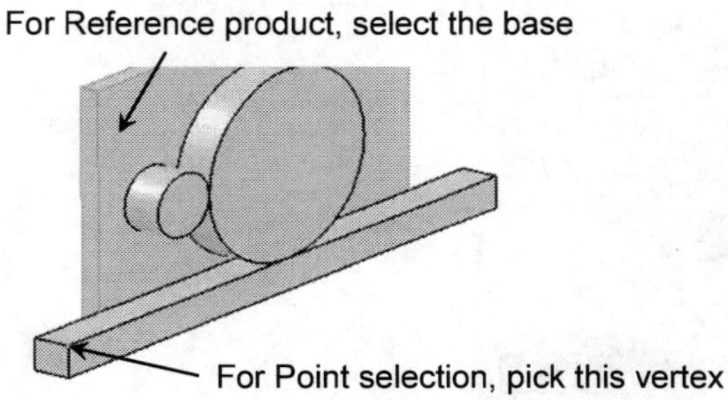

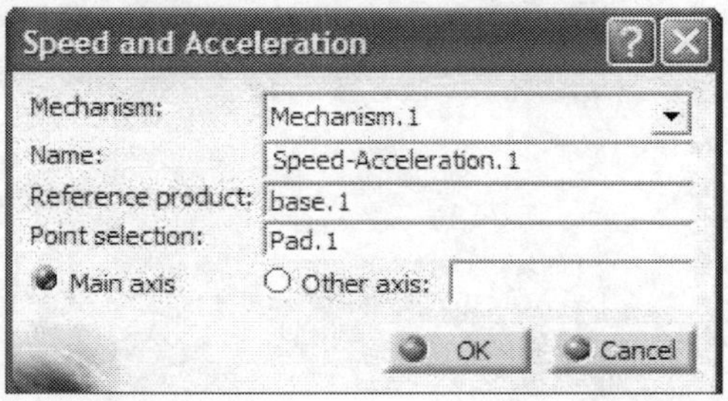

Note that the **Speed and Acceleration.1** has appeared in the tree.

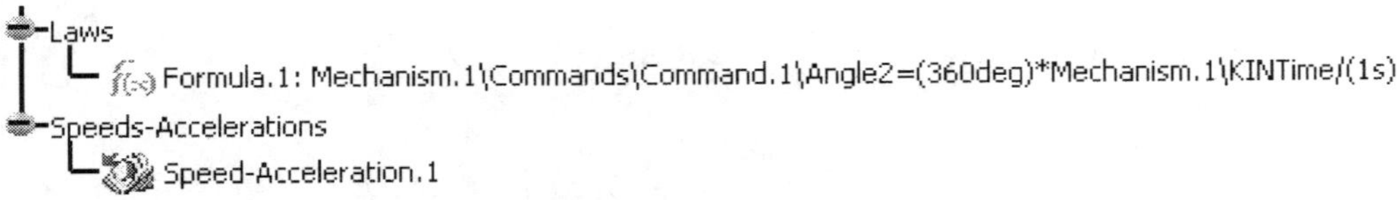

Click on **Simulation with Laws** icon  in the **Simulation** toolbar 

.
This results in the **Kinematics Simulation** pop up box shown below.

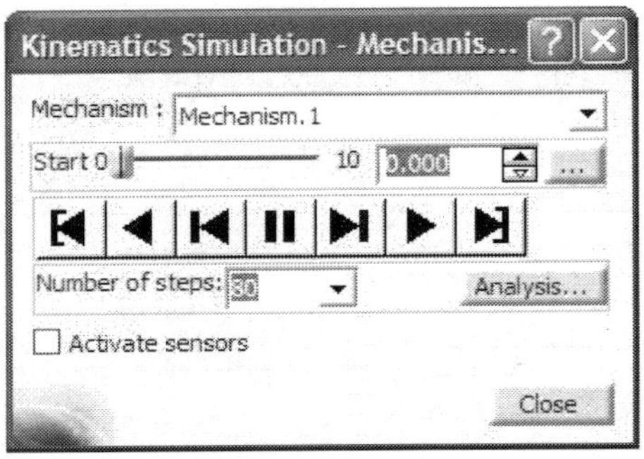

Note that the default time duration is 10 seconds. To change this value, click on the button . In the resulting pop up box, change the time duration to 1s. This is the time duration for the pinion to make one full revolution.

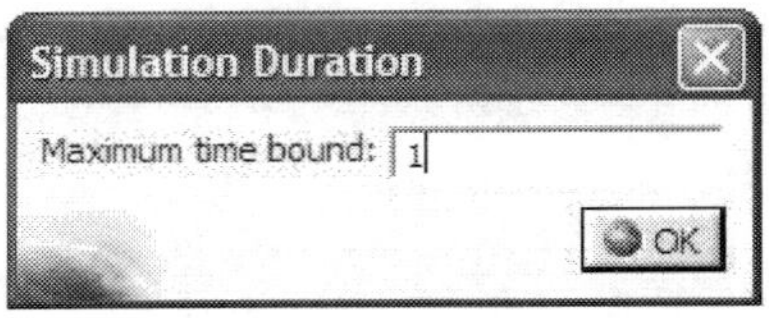

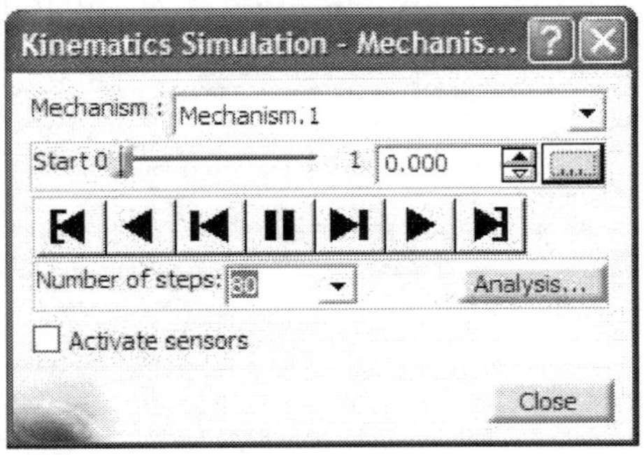

The scroll bar now moves up to 1s.

Check the **Activate sensors** box, at the bottom left corner.

You will next have to make certain selections from the accompanying **Sensors** box.

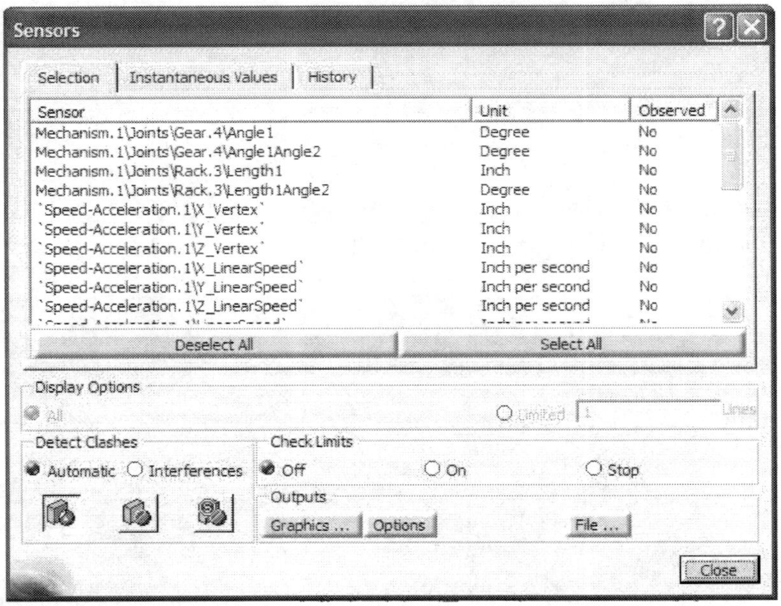

Click on the following items:

Mechanism.1\Joints\Rack.3\Length1

As you make these selections, the last column in the **Sensors** box, changes to **Yes** for the corresponding items. This is shown below. Notice that the vertex we marked earlier could also be picked here by choosing **SpeedAcceleration.1\Y_Vertex** (or the appropriate component based on the orientation your assembly is in), but we will illustrate here that the desired result could be obtained by choosing the joint length. Notice, however, that if we wished to plot velocities or accelerations, we would need to use our sensor vertex since those parameters are not options for the joint length.

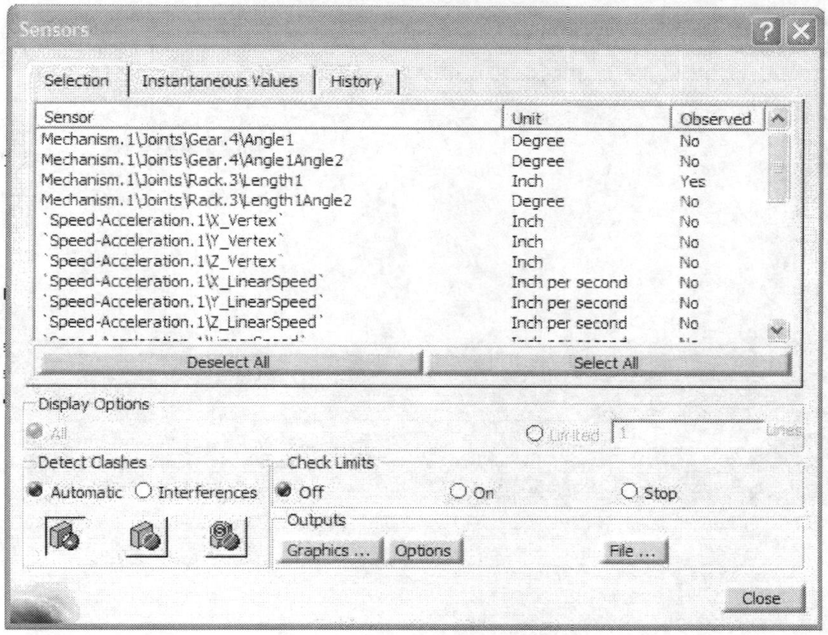

At this point, drag the scroll bar in the **Kinematics Simulation** box. As you do this, the pinion rotates one full turn. Once the bar reaches its right extreme point, the pinion has made one full revolution. This corresponds to 1s.

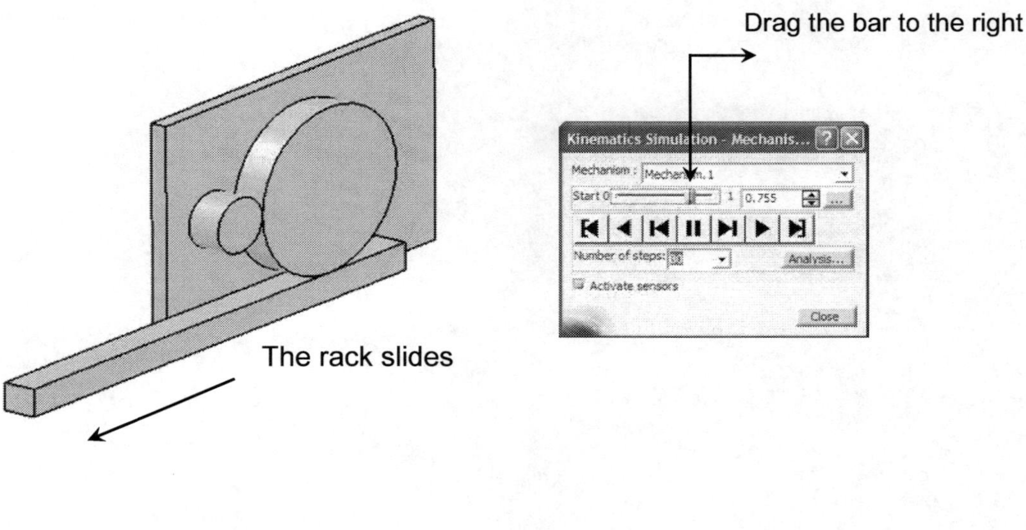

Once the link reaches the end, click on **Graphics** button 

in the **Sensor** box.

The plot that is generated and shown below is the position of the tip of the rack as a function of time. Since the velocity of the pinion is constant, the rack also has a constant velocity and therefore the position varies linearly as shown. The pinion was rotating for 1 second. This corresponded to a full revolution of the pinion and 1/3 of the full turn for the gear. With the radius of the gear being 1.5 inch, the distance traveled by the rack is $1.5 * \frac{2\pi}{3} \approx 3.14$ in. The estimated value is in good agreement with the generated plot.

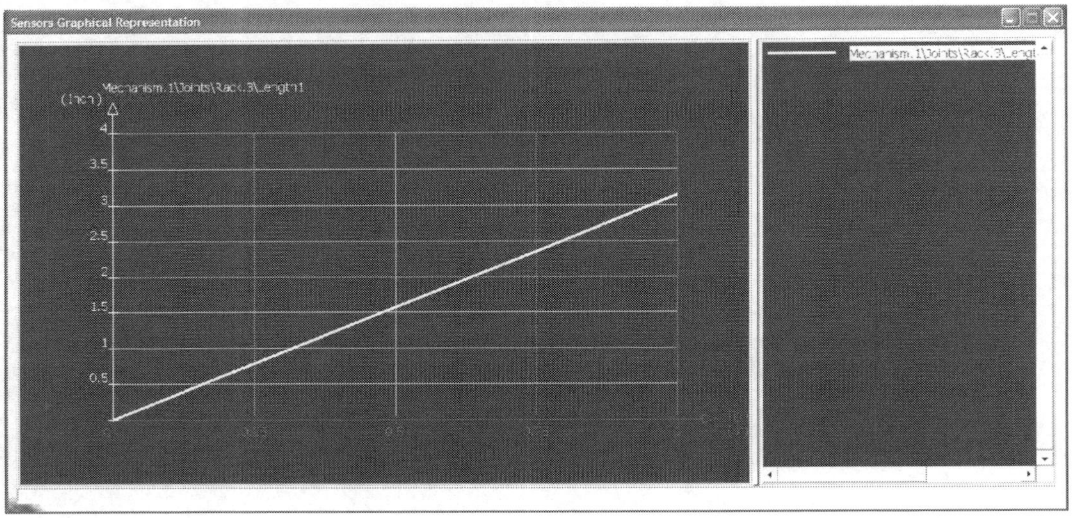

This concludes this tutorial.

Chapter 7

Ellipse Generator Mechanism

Introduction

In this tutorial you will be creating a mechanism which could be used to draw an ellipse. This mechanism involves four parts, three of which are moving. There are two prismatic joints and two revolute joints in this mechanism.

1 Problem Statement

The mechanism shown below consists of a base with two perpendicular grooves. Two identical blocks are allowed to slide feely in these grooves (i.e., prismatic joints). The two blocks are connected together with a link. The link has two pins which are inserted into holes in the blocks; these pin-in-hole connections form the revolute joints in the mechanism.

As one of the revolute joints makes a full 360° turn, the tip of the link traces an ellipse whose major and minor axis are easily related to the length of the link and the distance between the two pins. In order to simulate the present mechanism, you will make one of the revolute joints angle driven. It would be possible to animate the mechanism in this tutorial by making the prismatic joints as length driven. However, the former approach is more straightforward.

The revolute joint used for animation is assumed to rotate at a constant angular velocity of one Hz (i.e., one revolution per second). The linear velocity of the link's tip will be plotted as a function time along with a plot of X vs. Y for the link's tip. The dimensions of the problem are not of importance; however, suggested dimensions are proposed for some of the more important dimensions.

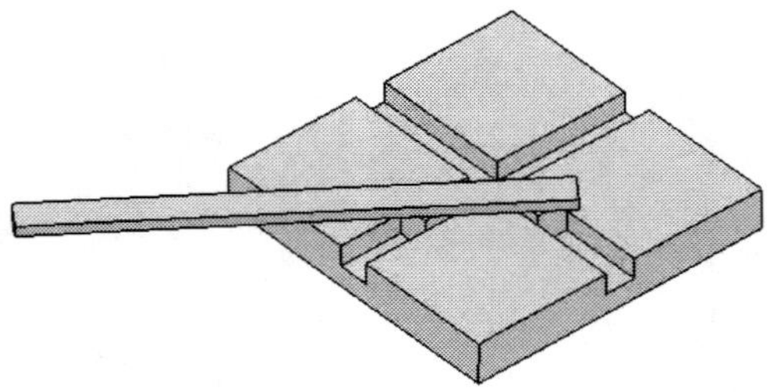

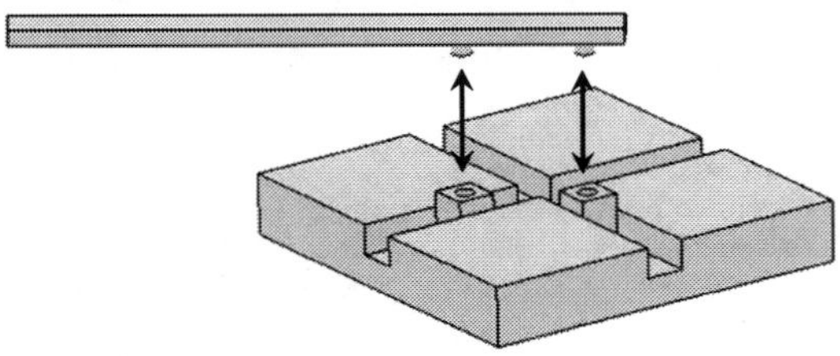

2 Overview of this Tutorial

In this tutorial you will:

1. Model the three CATIA parts required (the block gets used twice in the assembly).
2. Create an assembly (CATIA Product) containing the parts.
3. Constrain the assembly in such a way that appropriate degrees of freedom are removed before proceeding to DMU.
4. Enter the **Digital Mockup** workbench and use automatic assembly constraints conversion to create two revolute joints and two prismatic joints.
5. Simulate the motion of the mechanism without consideration to time (in other words, without implementing the known constant angular velocity given in the problem statement).
6. Add a formula to implement the time based kinematics associated with constant angular velocity of the pinion.
7. Simulate the desired motion and generate a plot of X vs. Y and linear speed vs. time for a point at the end of the link.

3 Creation of the Assembly in Mechanical Design Solutions

Model three CATIA parts named **base, link,** and **block1** as shown below. It is recommended that you use the indicated dimensions (inches) and in the event that a dimension is missing, estimate it based on the drawing. Include a reference point on the link at the location shown below; this will provide a point directly in line with the two pins which we will use in the analysis.

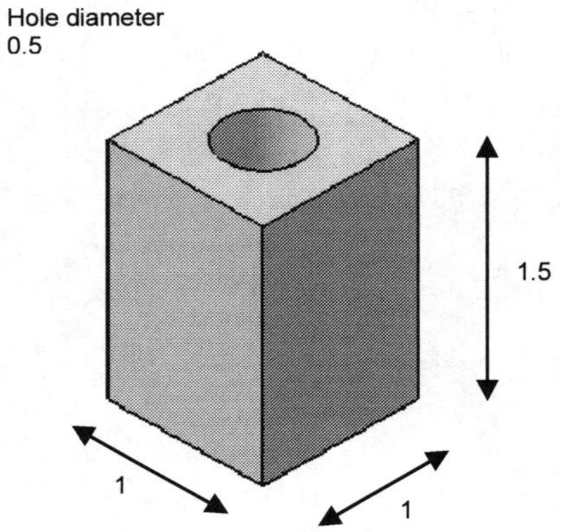

block

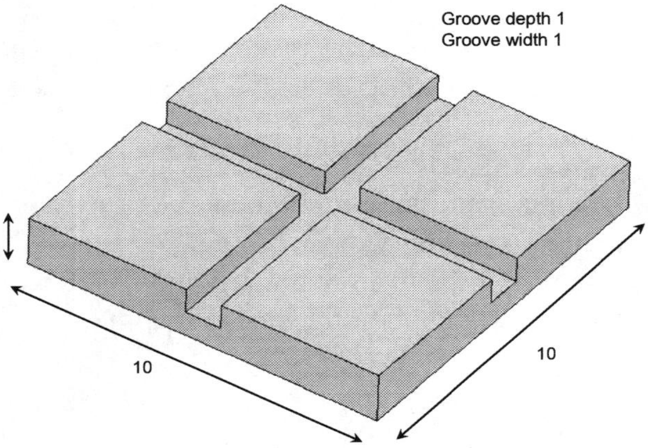

base

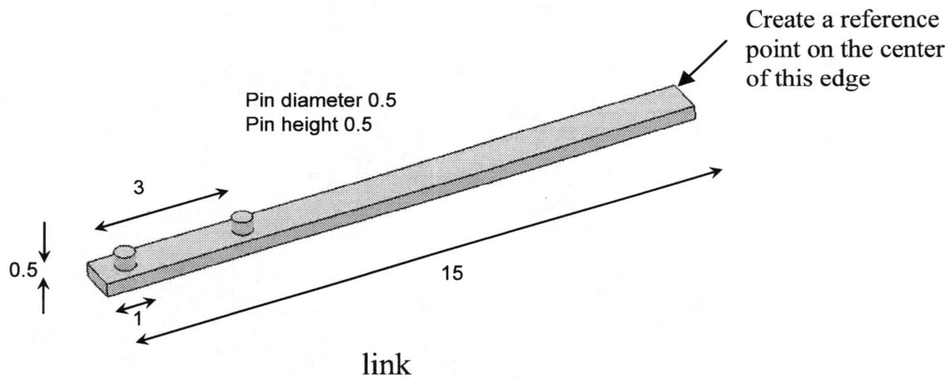

link

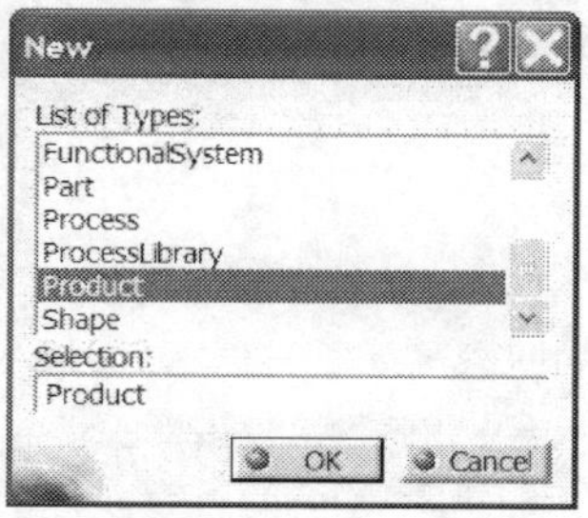

Once your parts are modeled, enter the **Assembly Design** workbench  which can be achieved by different means depending on your CATIA customization. For example, from the standard Windows toolbar, select **File > New** . From the box shown on the right, select **Product**. This moves you to the **Assembly Design** workbench and creates an assembly with the default name **Product.1**.

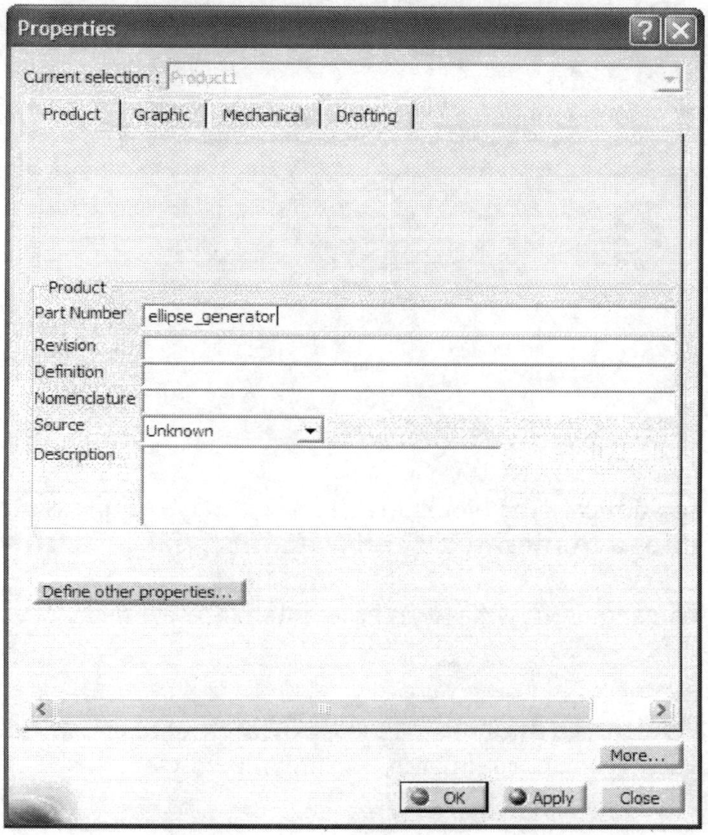

In order to change the default name, move the cursor to **Product.1** in the tree, right click and select **Properties** from the menu list.

From the **Properties** box, select the **Product** tab and in **Part Number** type **ellipse_generator**.

This will be the new product name throughout the chapter. The tree on the top left corner of your computer screen should look as displayed below.

The next step is to insert the existing parts in the assembly just created.

Select the **Existing Component** icon  from the **Product Structure Tools** toolbar 

. Point the cursor to the **ellipse_generator** branch of the tree at the very top.

The **File Selection** pop up box opens where you can select the three components simultaneously using the **Ctrl** key.

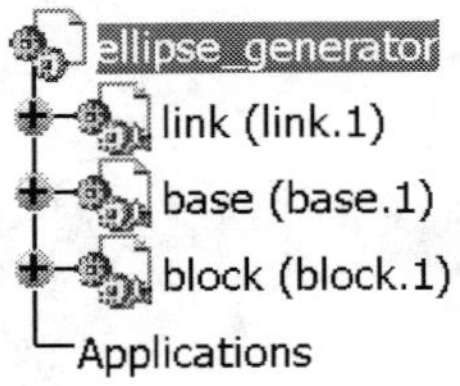

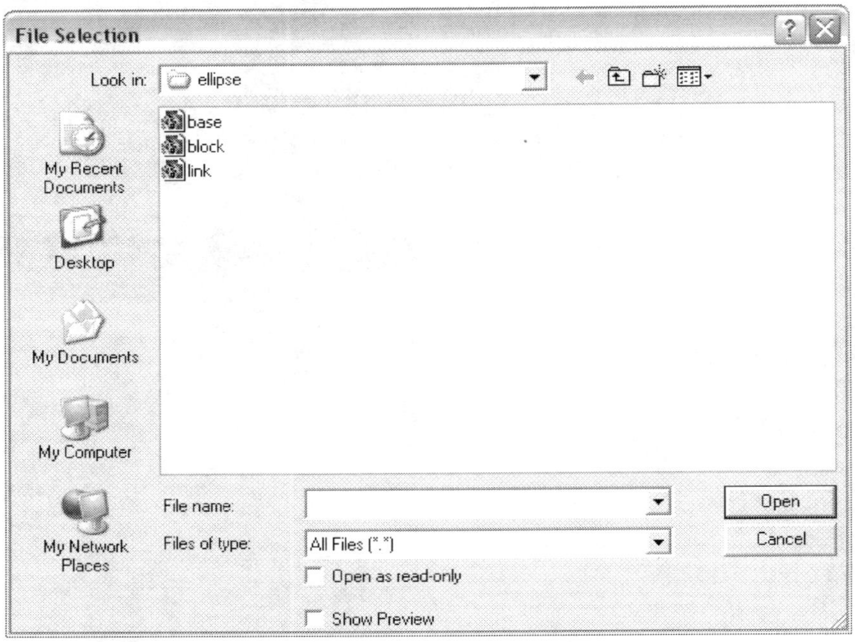

To duplicate the block, highlight it in the tree, press **Ctrl-C** (copy), click on the **ellipse_generator** branch in the tree, and press **Ctrl-V** (paste).

You should now have an assembly with two instances of the block as desired. Use the **Manipulation** icon  in the **Move** toolbar 

to rearrange the parts to be approximately as shown below.

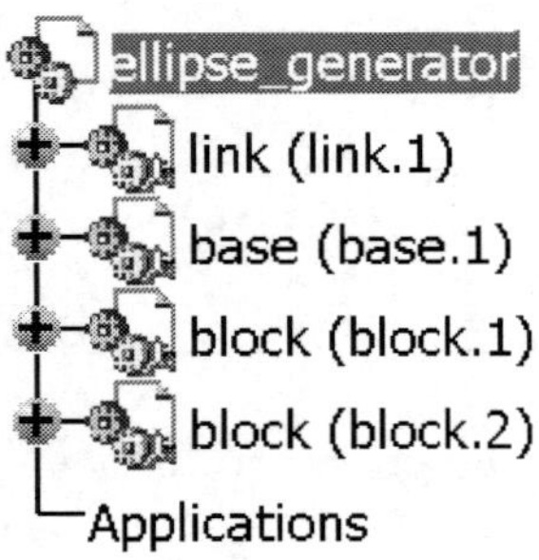

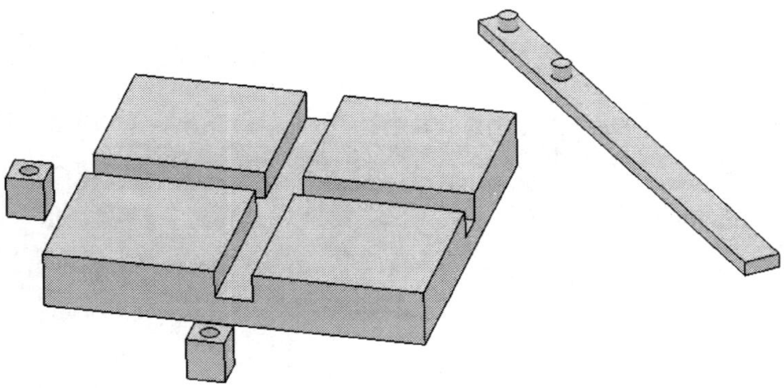

The best way of saving your work is to save the entire assembly.
Double click on the top branch of the tree. This is to ensure that you are in the **Assembly Design** workbench.
Select the **Save** icon . The **Save As** pop up box allows you to rename if desired. The default name is the **ellipse_generator**.

Your next task is to impose assembly constraints. We will begin by anchoring the base.

Pick the **Anchor** icon  from the **Constraints** toolbar and select the **base** from the tree or from the screen.

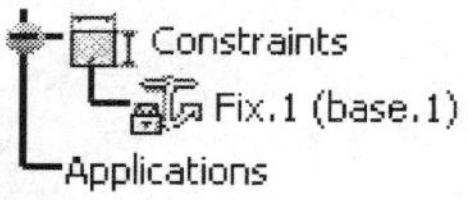

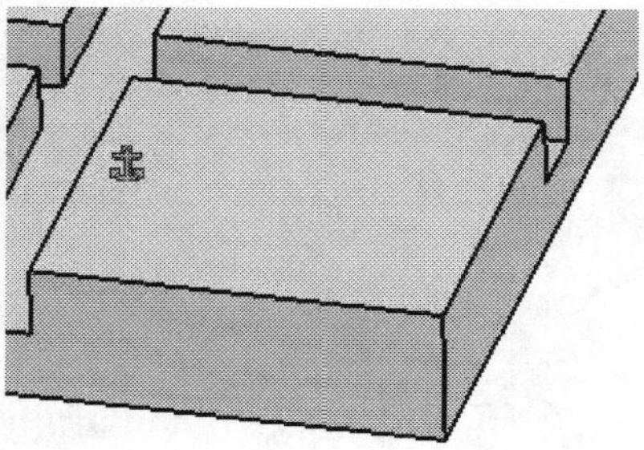

Next, we will constrain one of the two instances of block so that it can only slide along one of the slots in the base. Pick the **Coincidence** icon  from **Constraints** toolbar

. Select the two edges of the **base** and **block.1** as shown below. Since both instances of block look the same in the graphics region, notice that when you move the mouse over a component while in the coincidence command, the instance you are over is highlighted in the tree; this is helpful making sure you are picking the block.1 instance (though it really doesn't matter which one you pick in this case).

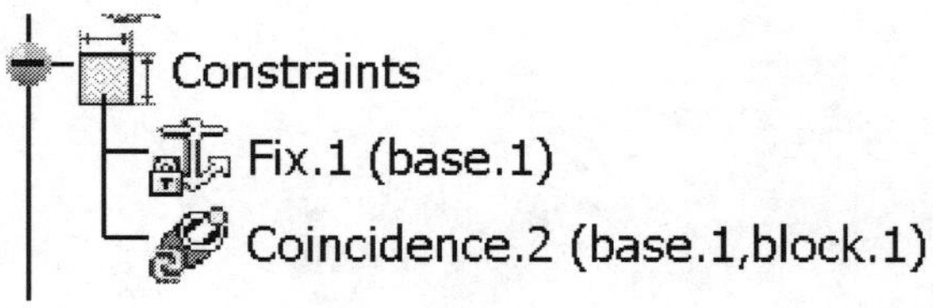

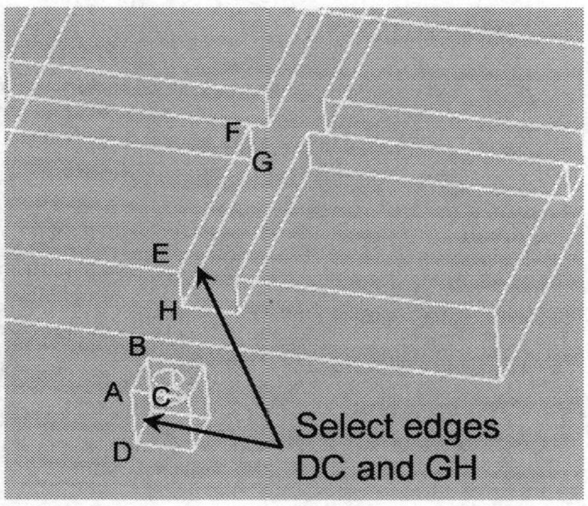

The coincidence constraint just created moves all the dof of block.1 with respect to the base except for translation along the edges of coincidence (a desired dof in the mechanism) and rotation about the edges of coincidence (unwanted in the final mechanism).

To remove the rotational dof, pick the **Contact** icon  from **Constraints** toolbar and select the surfaces ABCD and EFGH.

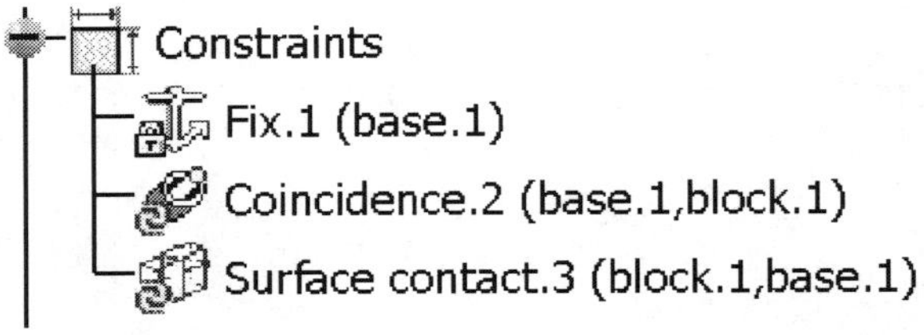

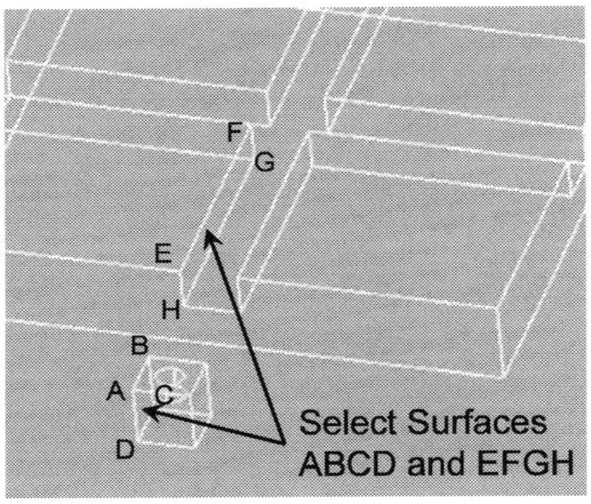

A similar procedure is done to constrain block.2 to the slot which is perpendicular to the slot block.1 is constrained to. Pick the **Coincidence** icon  and select the two edges of the **base** and the **block.2** as shown below.

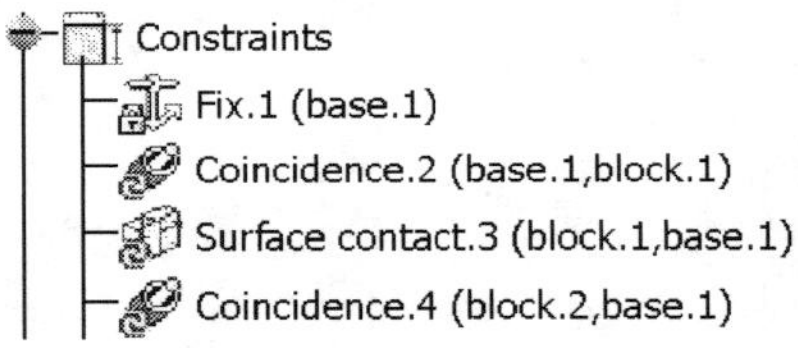

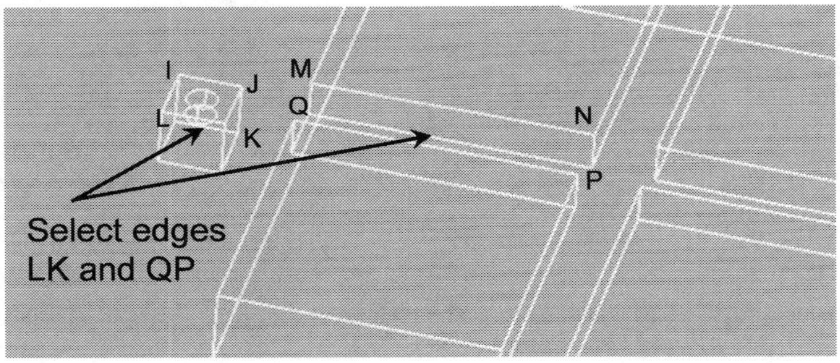

Pick the **Contact** icon  from **Constraints** toolbar and select the surfaces IJKL and MNPQ.

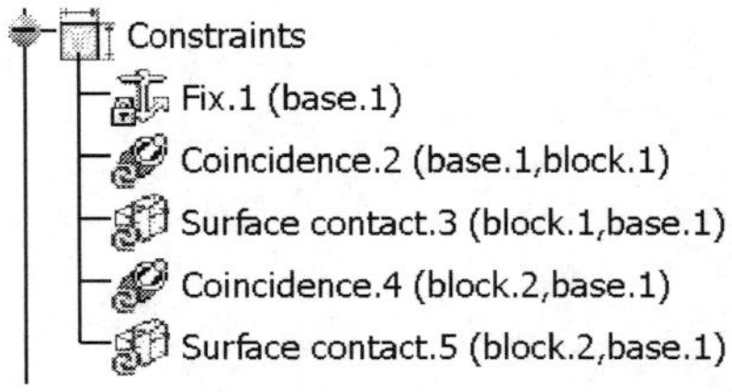

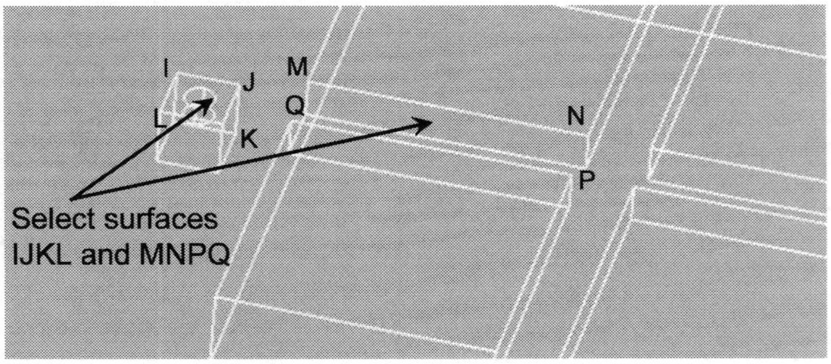

Use **Update** icon  to partially position the parts as shown.

Note that the **Update** icon  no longer appears on the constraints branches.
Your blocks may end up in a position quite different from what is shown below. If so, you can always use the **Manipulation** icon  to position the two blocks approximately as shown followed by **Update** if necessary.

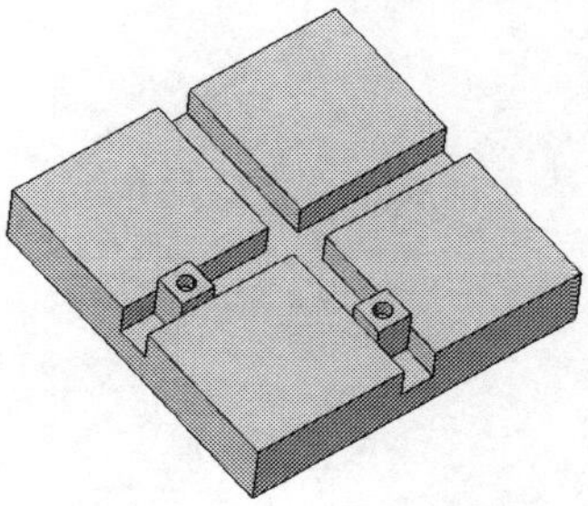

Next, we will constrain the peg near the end of the link to ride in the hole in block.2. We will use a coincidence constraint between the centerline of the pin and the centerline of the hole plus a contact constraint between the two planar surfaces which would be in contact when the parts are assembled as desired. This combination of constraints will leave only the rotational dof between the link and the instance block.2; this is consistent with our desire to create a revolute joint between block.2 and link.

Pick the **Coincidence** icon  and select the axis of **block.2** and the pin of the **link** as shown.

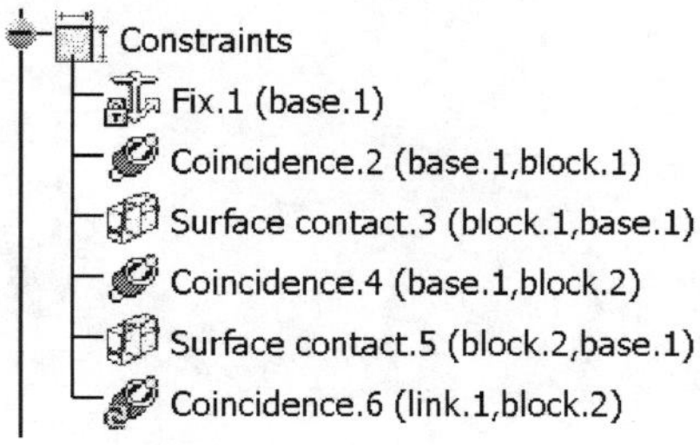

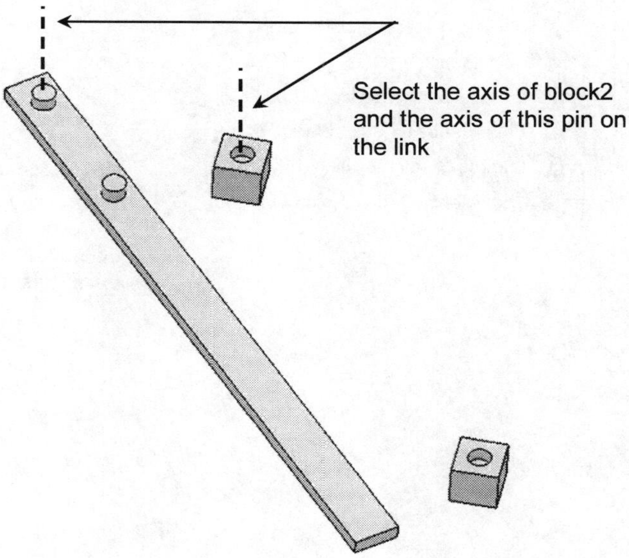

Pick the **Contact** icon from **Constraints** toolbar and select the surfaces WXYZ and RSUT (of **block.2**).

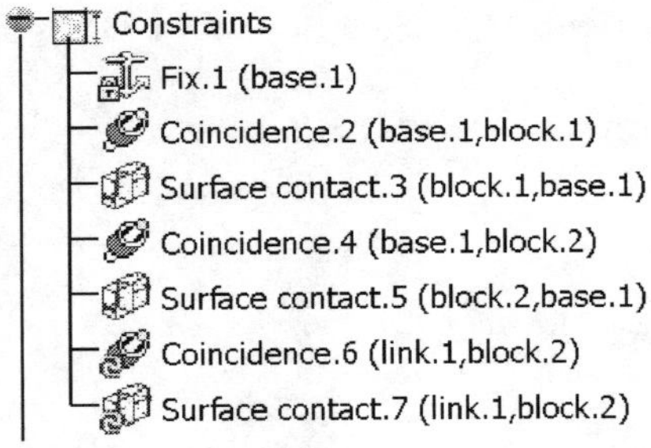

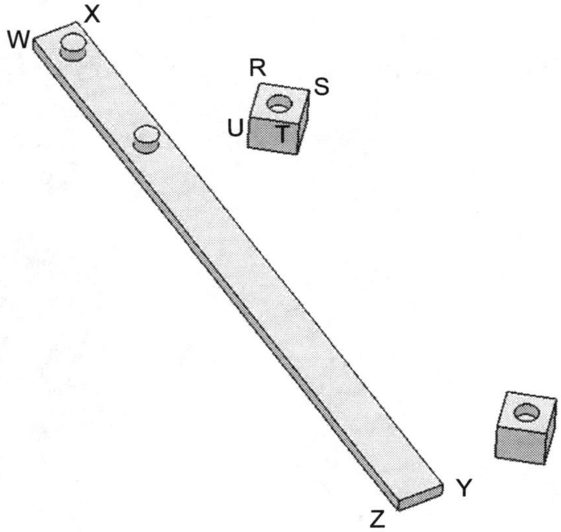

A similar set of constraints is needed between block.1 and the link. Pick the **Coincidence** icon and select the axis of **block1** and the pin of the **link** as shown.

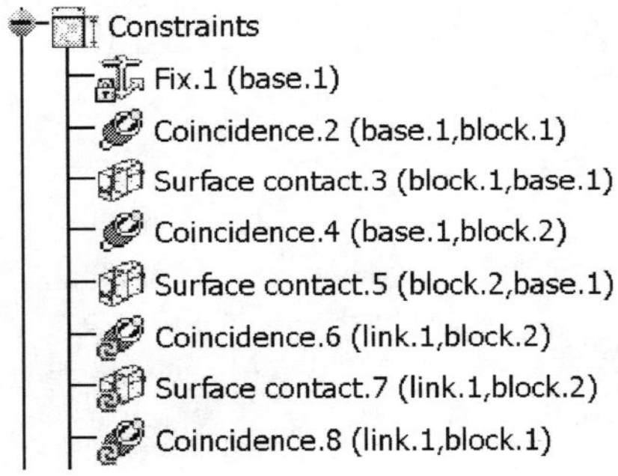

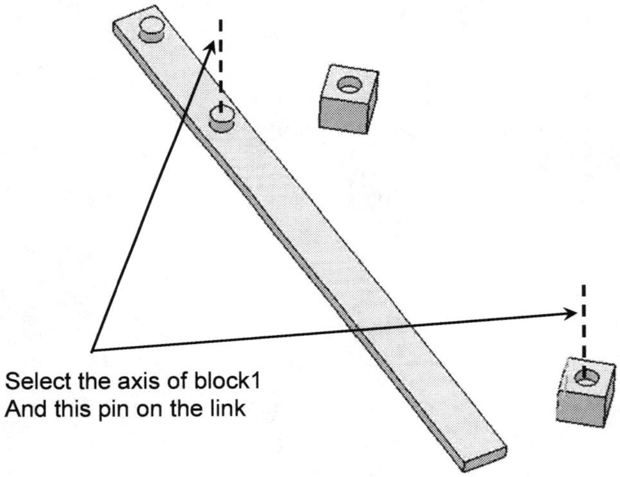

Pick the **Contact** icon  from **Constraints** toolbar and select the surfaces WXYZ and RRSSUUTT (**of block.1**). Note that this constraint is essentially redundant since the link is already constrained against moving in the direction restrained by this contact as a result of the earlier constraints to block.2. Nonetheless, we will leave the redundant constraint in. If you were to skip this constraint, a cylindrical joint would be created instead of a revolute joint at; this would not affect the ability to simulate the mechanism.

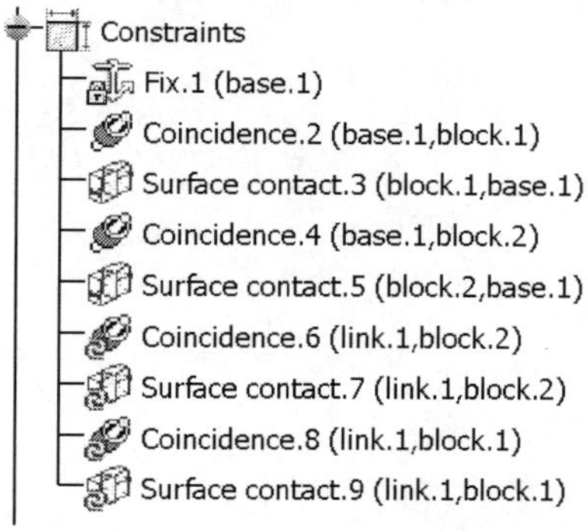

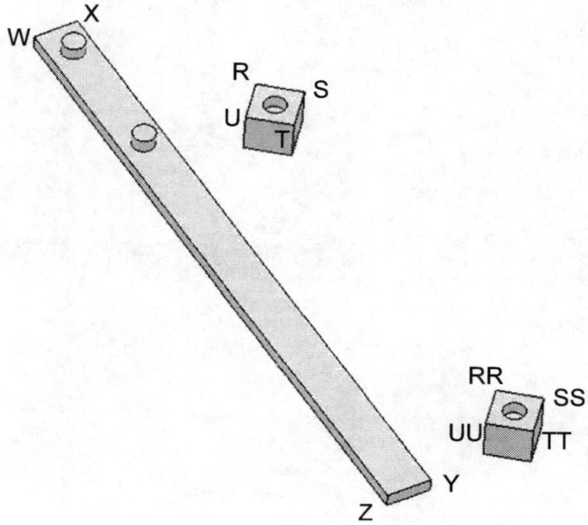

Use **Update** icon  to partially position the parts as shown.

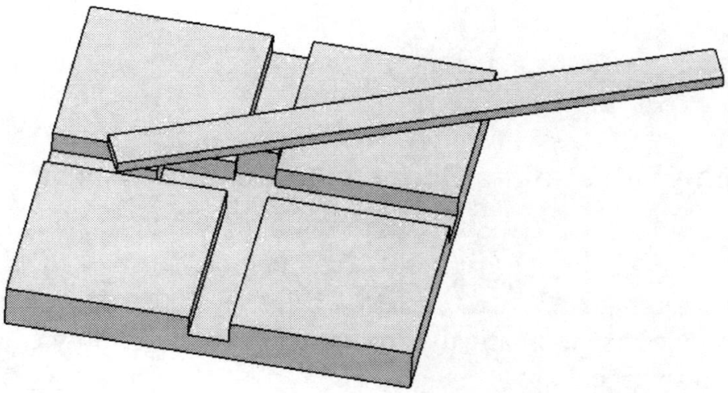

If you wish to prescribe a precise zero position for the kinematic analysis, a temporary constraint can be applied to force the desired zero position. Then this constraint can be deleted. We won't worry about the starting point here. Thus, the assembly is complete and we can proceed to the **Digital Mockup** workbench.

4 Creating Joints in the Digital Mockup Workbench

The **Digital Mockup** workbench is quite extensive but we will only deal with the **DMU Kinematics module**. To get there you can use the standard Windows toolbar as shown below. **Start > Digital Mockup > DMU Kinematics**.

Select the **Assembly Constraints Conversion** icon  from the **DMU Kinematics** toolbar 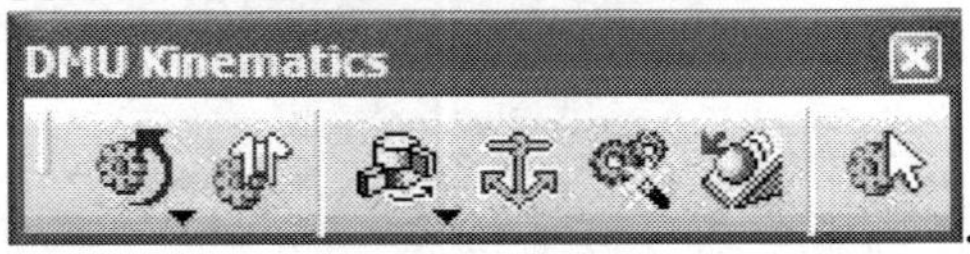

. This icon allows you to create most common joints automatically from the existing assembly constraints. The pop up box below appears.

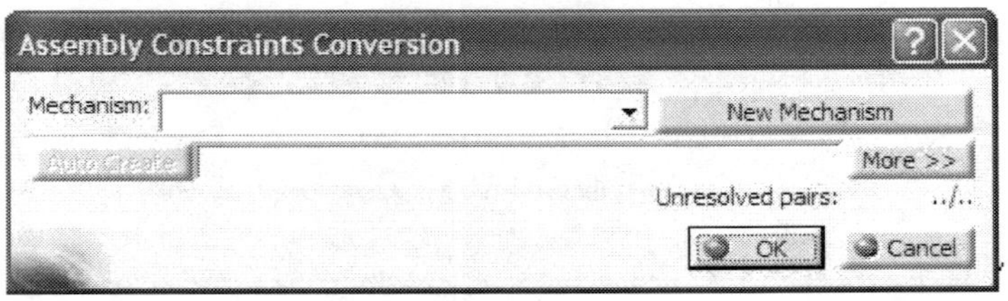

Select the **New Mechanism** button 

.
This leads to another pop up box which allows you to name your mechanism.
The default name is **Mechanism.1**. Accept the default name by pressing **OK**.

Note that the box indicates **Unresolved pairs:4/4**.

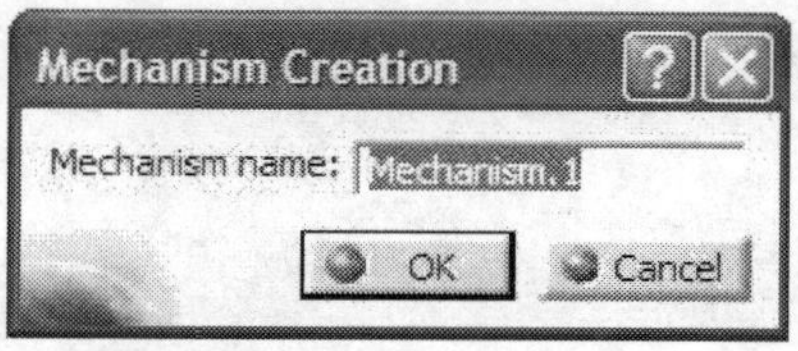

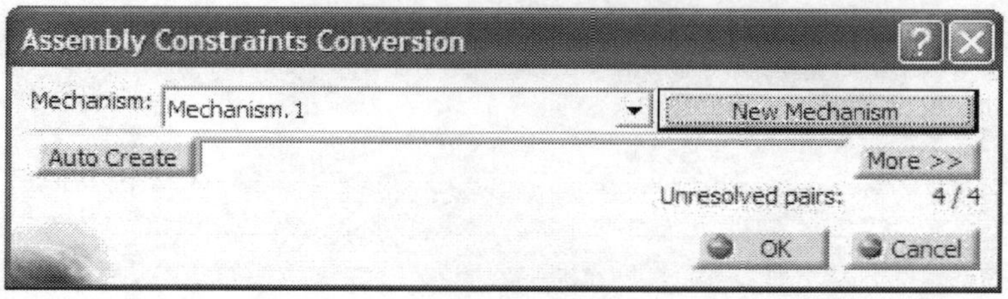

Select the **Auto Create** button 

. Then if the **Unresolved pairs** becomes **0/4**, things are moving in the right direction.

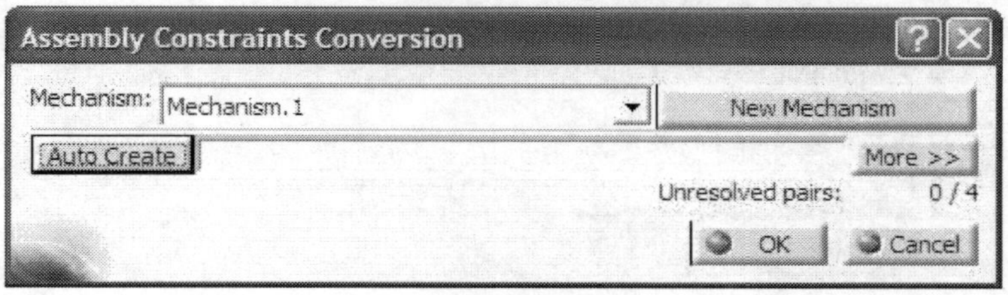

Note that the tree becomes longer by having an **Application** Branch. The expanded tree is displayed below.

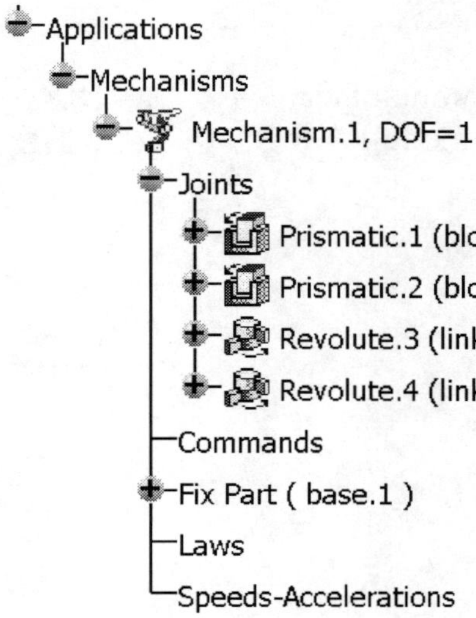

The prismatic joints are due to the motion of block.1 and bock.2 along the grooves. The revolute joints represent the rotation of the link around the pins in the link.

The **DOF** is 1 and in order to animate the mechanism, we need to specify one command. As an example, you can make one of the revolute joints an angle driven joint.

Double click on **Revolute.3** in the tree. The pop up box below appears.

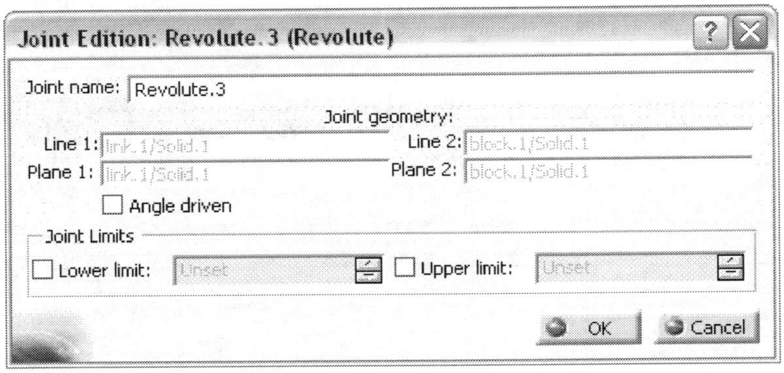

Check the **Angle driven** box. This allows you to change the limits. Change the value of **Lower Limit** to be 0.

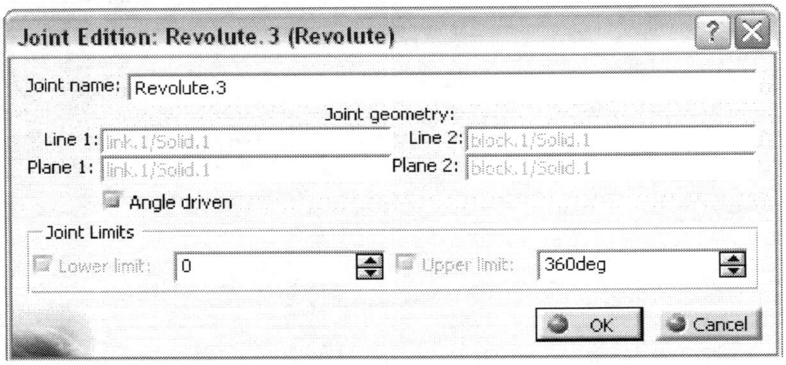

Upon closing the above box and assuming that everything else was done correctly, the following message appears on the screen.

This indeed is good news.

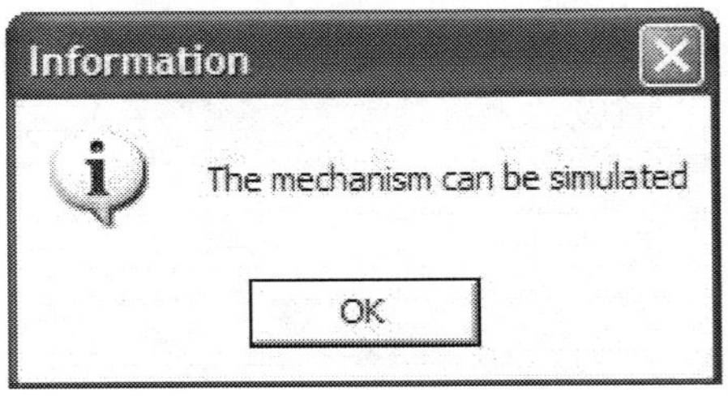

To simulate without regard to time based motion, select the **Simulation** icon  from the **DMU Generic Animation** toolbar 

. This enables you to choose the mechanism to be animated if there are several present. In this case, select **Mechanism.1** and close the window.

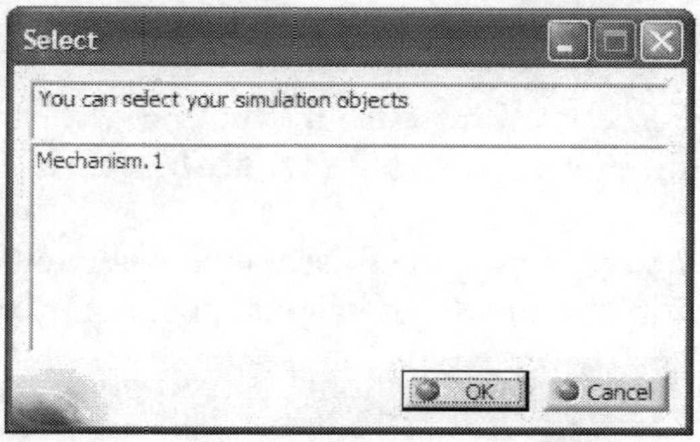

As soon as the window is closed, a Simulation branch is added to the tree.

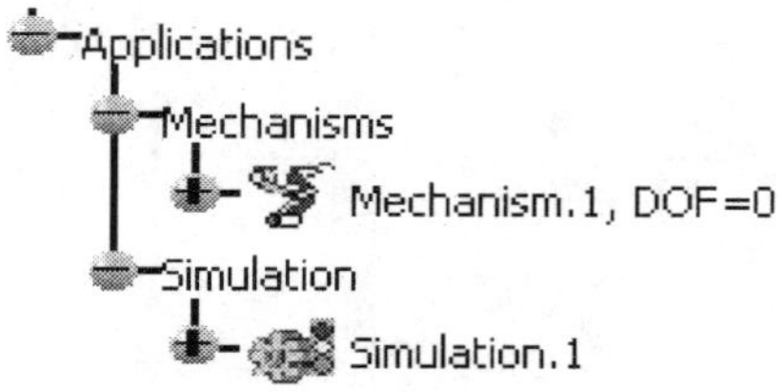

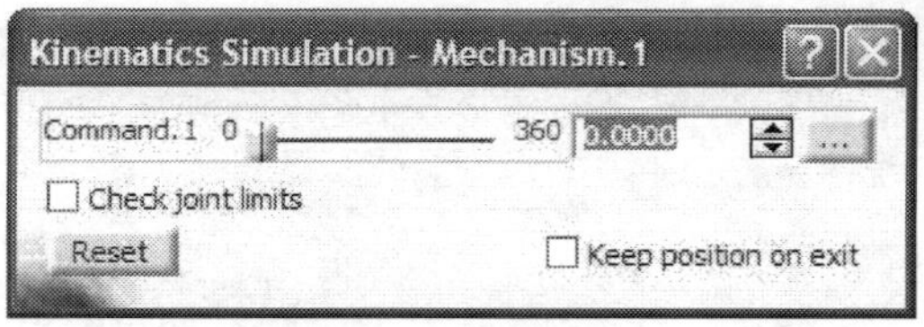

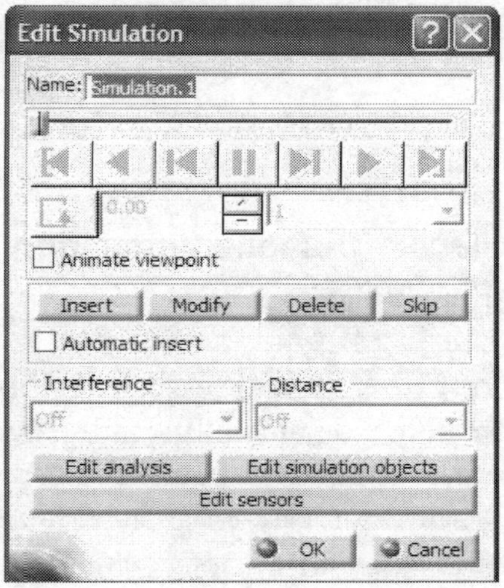

As you scroll the bar in this toolbar from left to right, the link begins rotating and makes a full 360 degree turn.

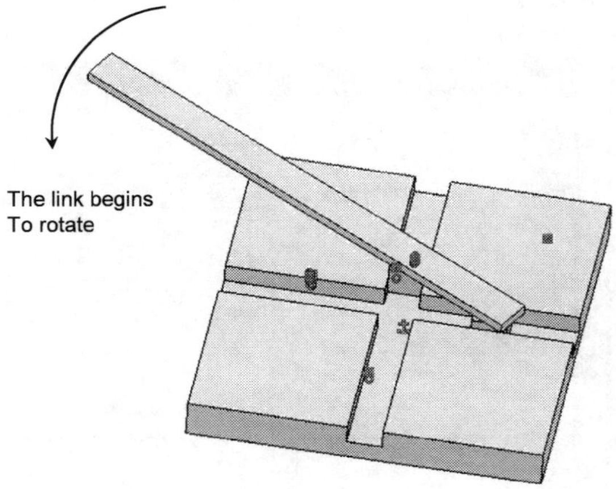

Scroll the bar from left to right

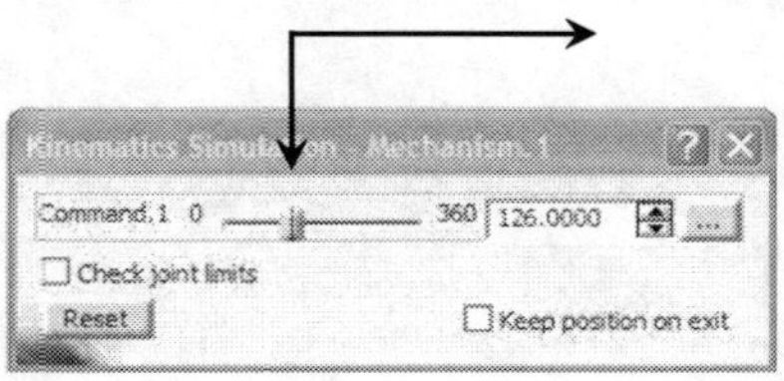

When the scroll bar in the **Kinematics Simulation** pop up box reaches the right extreme end, select the **Insert** button 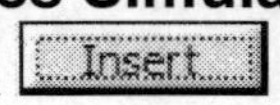

in the **Edit Simulation** pop up box

shown above. This activates the video player buttons shown

.

Return the link to its original position by picking the **Jump to Start** button .

Note that the **Change Loop Mode** button is also active now.

Upon selecting the **Play Forward** button , the link makes fast jump completing its revolution.

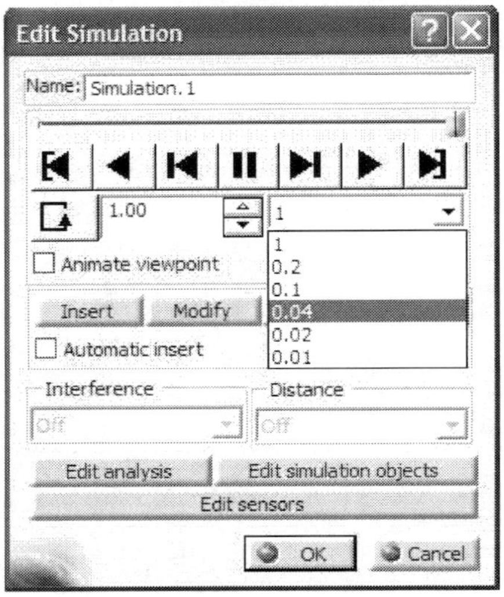

In order to slow down the motion of the link, select a different **interpolation step**, such as 0.04.

Upon changing the interpolation step to 0 0.04, return the link to its original position by picking the **Jump to Start** button . Apply **Play Forward** button and observe the slow and smooth rotation of the link.

Select the **Compile Simulation** icon from the **Generic Animation** toolbar

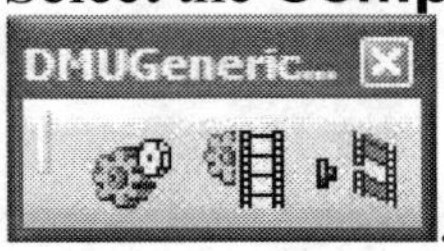

. Pressing the **File name** button File name ... allows you to set the location and name of the animation file to be generated as displayed below.
Select a suitable path and file name and change the **Time step** to be 0.04 to produce a slow moving rotation in an AVI file.

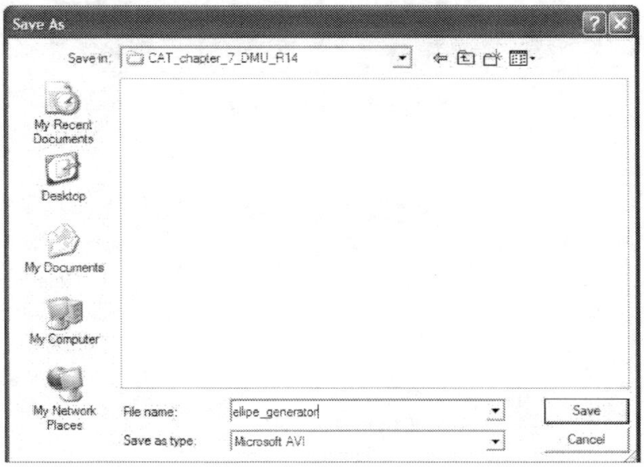

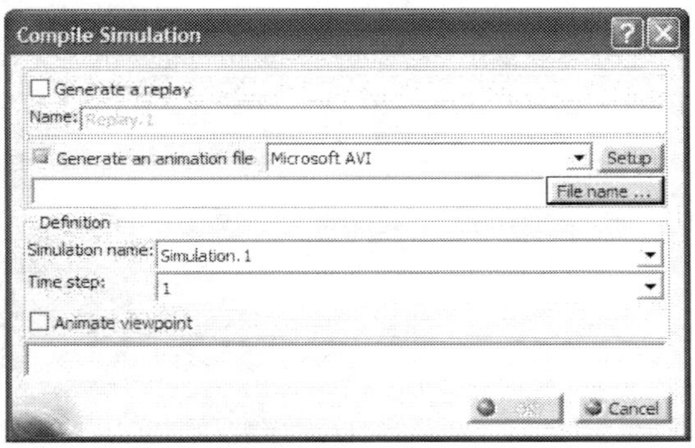

The completed pop up box is displayed for your reference.

As the file is being generated, the crank slowly rotates. The resulting AVI file can be viewed with the Windows Media Player.

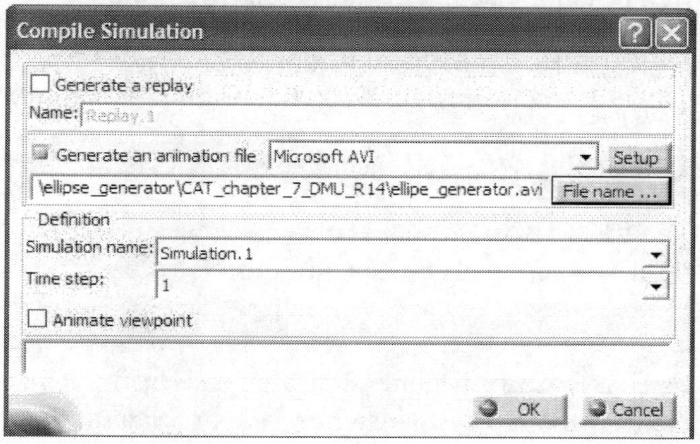

In the event that an AVI file is not needed, but one wishes to play the animation, repeatedly, a **Replay** need be generated. Therefore, in the **Compile Simulation** box, check the **Generate a replay** button.

Note that in this case most of the previously available options are dimmed out.

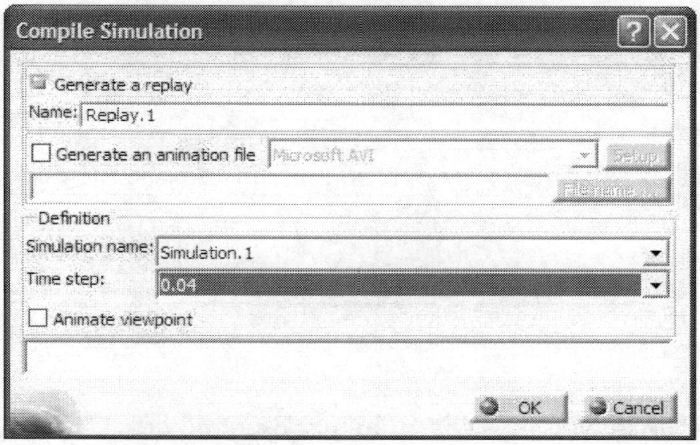

A **Replay.1** branch has also been added to the tree.

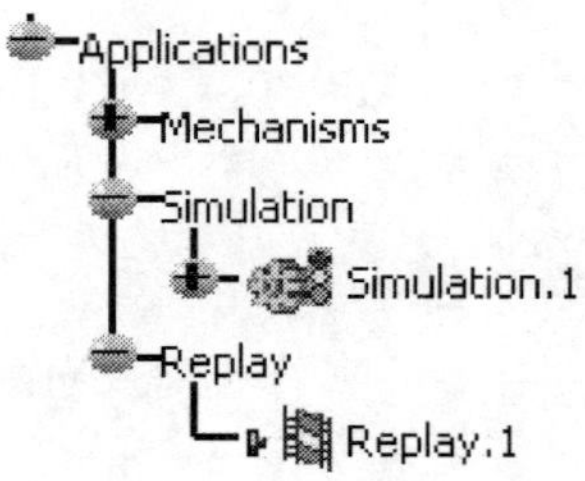

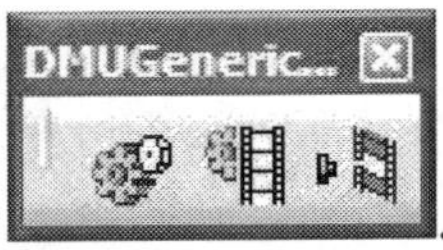

Select the **Replay** icon  from the **Generic Animation** toolbar. Double clock on **Replay.1** in the tree and the **Replay** pop up box appears.

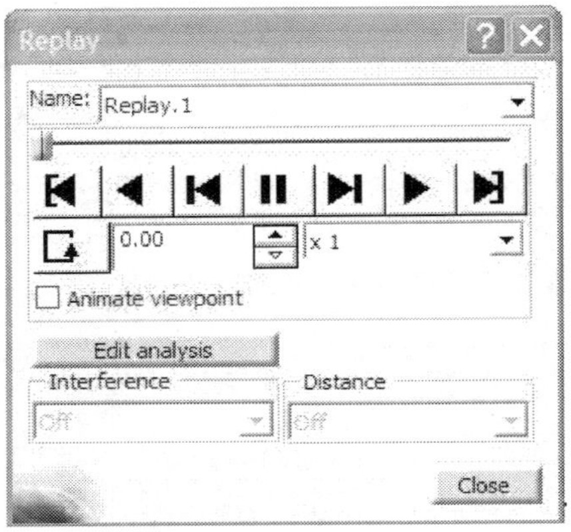

Experiment with the different choices of the **Change Loop Mode** buttons , , . The block can be returned to the original position by picking the **Jump to Start** button .

The **skip ratio** (which is chosen to be x1 in the right box) controls the speed of the **Replay**.

Once a **Replay** is generated such as **Replay.1** in the tree above, it can also be played with a different icon.

Select the **Simulation Player** icon  from the **DMUPlayer** toolbar.

The outcome is the pop up box above. Use the cursor to pick **Replay.1** from the tree.

The player keys are no longer dimmed out. Use the **Play Forward (Right)** button  to being the replay.

You will next generate the path that the tip of the link generates as it rotates 360 degrees.

Select the **Trace** icon  from the **DMU Generic Animation** toolbar

.

In the resulting pop up box, for **Elements to trace out**, select the reference point at the center of the lead edge of the link as shown below. Note that multiple selections can be made for tracing purposes.

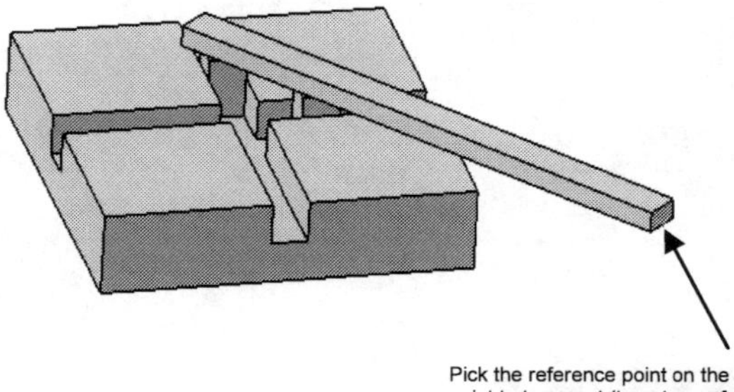

Pick the reference point on the center of this edge as the point to trace out (to get a perfect ellipse, you need a point in line with the two pin centerlines)

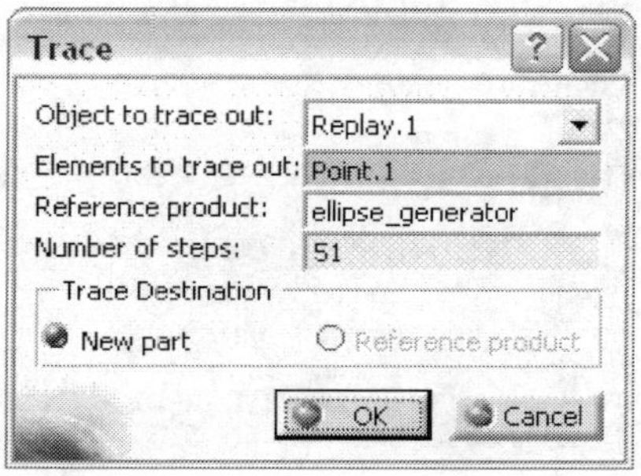

A part by the default name of **Trace1** is generated in a separate window on your screen. This part involves 26 points and a spline which interpolates the points. The spline represents the path of the reference point on the link. The number of the traced point could have been specified in the **Trace** box shown above.

The size of the major and minor axes of the ellipse can easily be related to the size of the length of the link and the relative positioning of the pins on it.

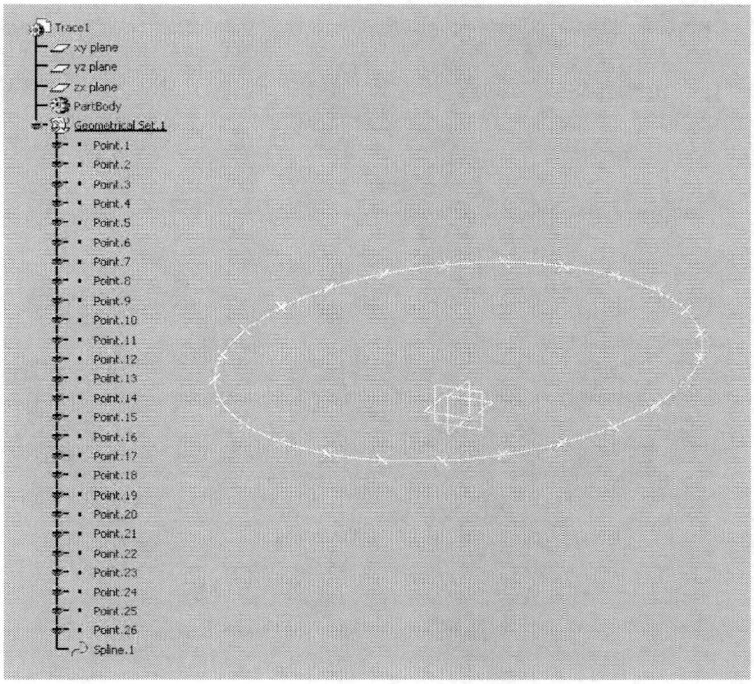

You can save this trace part in the usual way. To add the part to the assembly, return to **Assembly Design** and select the **Existing Component** icon  from the **Product Structure Tools** toolbar 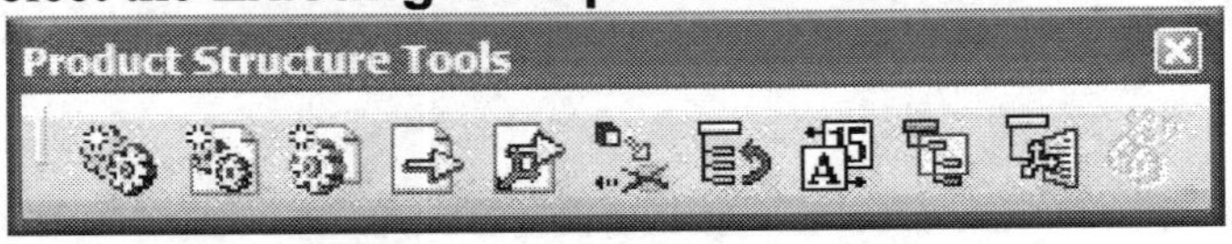

. Point the cursor to the **ellipse_generator** branch of the tree at the very top and click.
The **File Selection** pop up box opens where you can select **Trace1**. The ellipse is now displayed in reference to the assembly. Clearly if you animate the mechanism, the reference point stays on this ellipse.

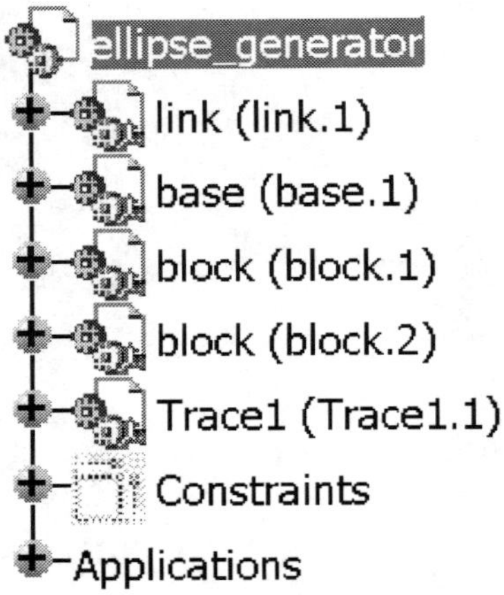

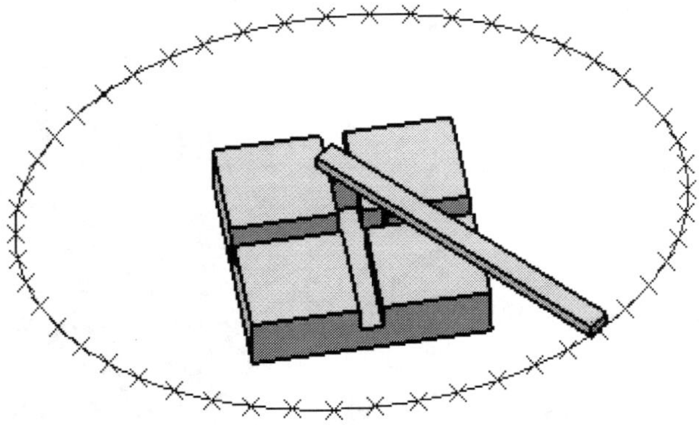

5 Creating Laws in the Motion

You will now introduce some time based analysis into the problem. The objective is to specify the angular position versus time function for one of the revolute joints and therefore set the angular velocity and angular acceleration. Recall from the problem statement that we wish to set the angular velocity of one of the revolute joints to 1 Hz.

Click on **Simulation with Laws** icon  in the **Simulation** toolbar 

. You will get the following pop up box indication that you need to add at least a relation between the command and the time parameter.

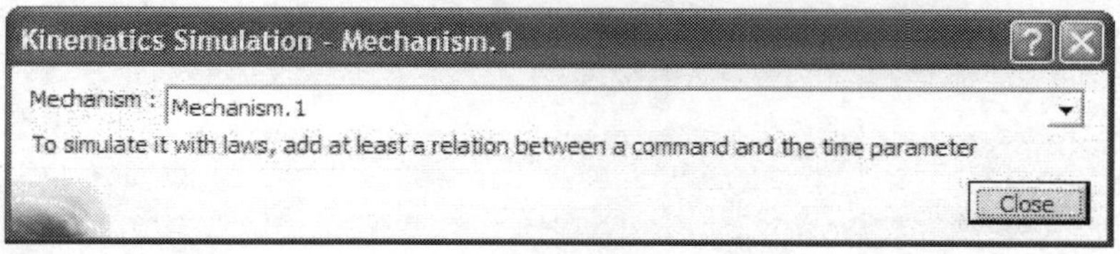

Select the **Formula** icon  from the **Knowledge** toolbar 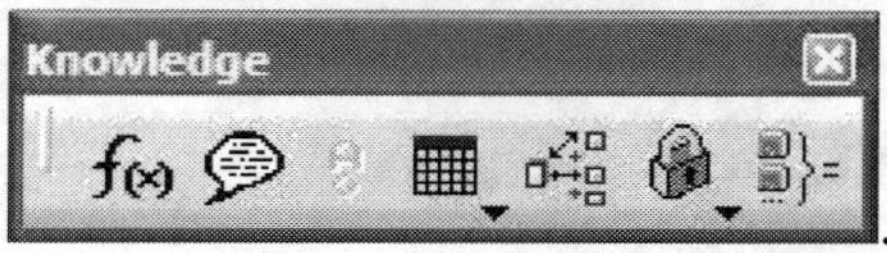

. The pop up box below appears on the screen.

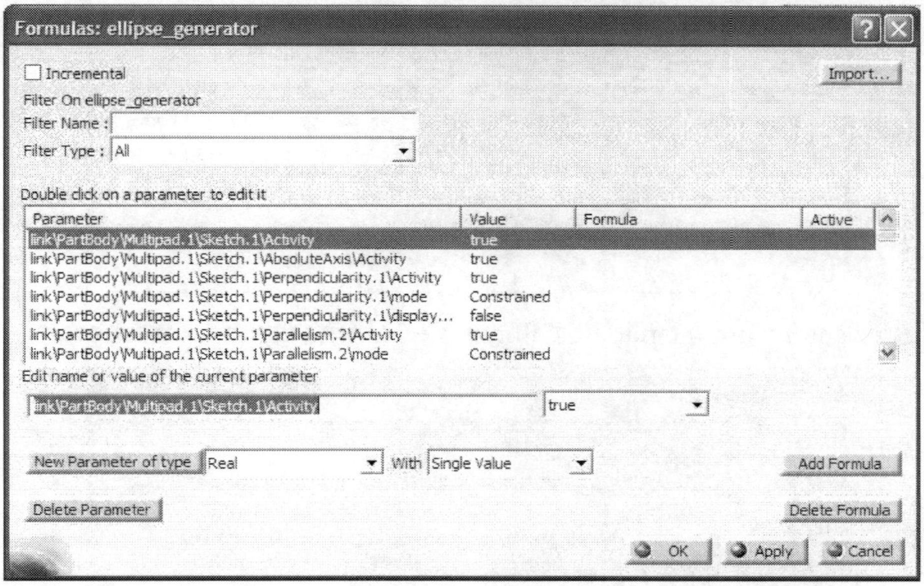

Point the cursor to the **Mechanism.1, DOF=0** branch in the tree and click. The consequence is that only parameters associated with the mechanism are displayed in the **Formulas** box.

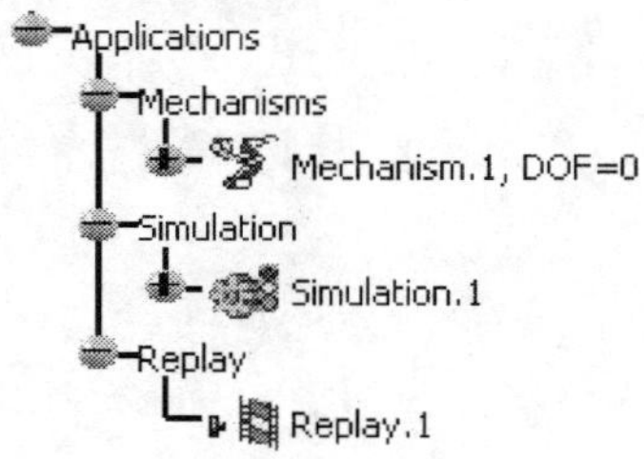

The long list is now reduced to two parameters as indicated in the box.

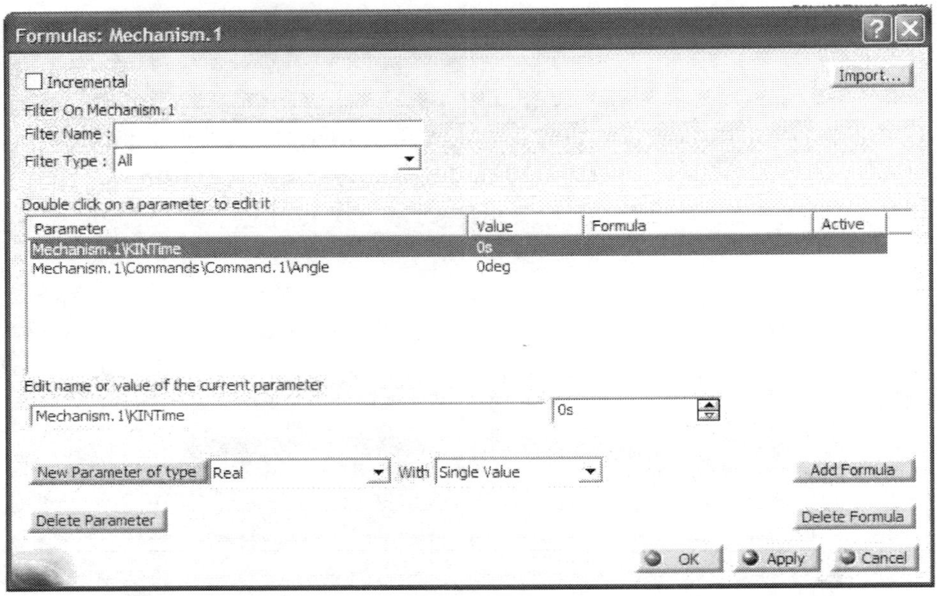

Select the entry **Mechanism.1\Commands\Command.1\Angle** and press the **Add Formula** button Add Formula. This action kicks you to the **Formula Editor** box.

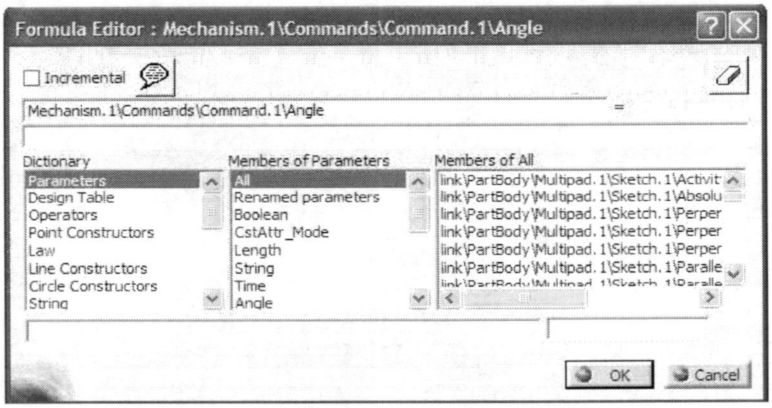

Pick the **Time** entry from the middle column (i.e., **Members of Parameters**).

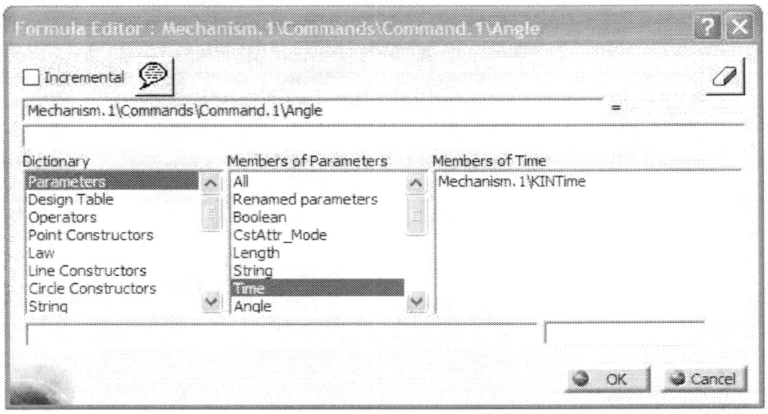

The right hand side of the equality should be such that the formula becomes

$$Mechanism.1 \backslash Commands \backslash Command.1 \backslash Angle =$$
$$(360\,\text{deg}) * (Mechanism.1 \backslash KINTime) / (1s)$$

Therefore, the completed **Formula Editor** box becomes

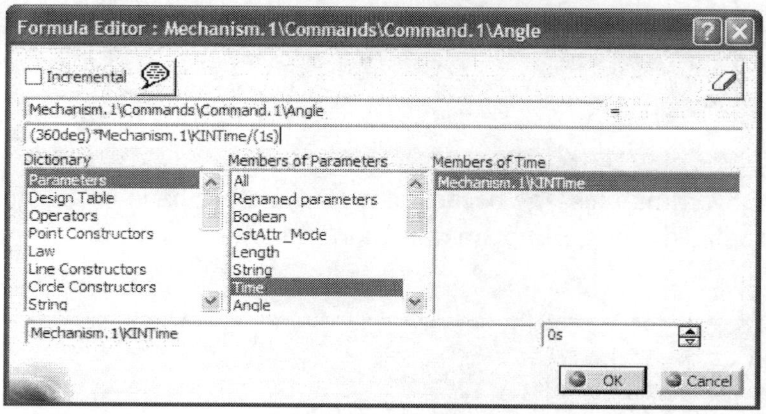

Upon accepting **OK**, the formula is recorded in the **Formulas** pop up box as shown below.

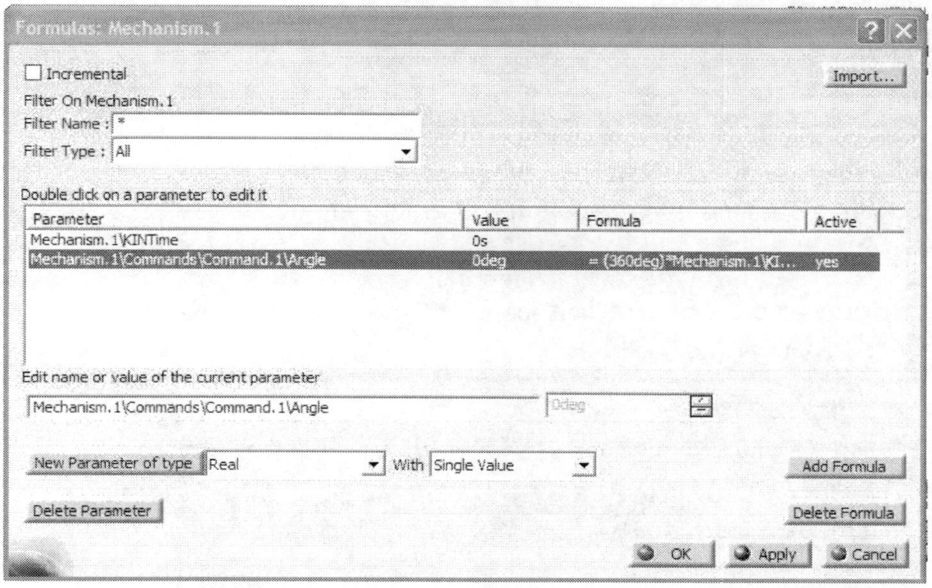

The formula introduced above requires an explanation. Note that the left hand side of the equality is an angle parameter; therefore, the entire right hand side should be reducing to degrees. Since an angular velocity of 1 Hz is equivalent to 360 deg/s, you can see that the right side of the equation is such that when this angular velocity is multiplied by time $(Mechanism.1 \backslash KINTime)$, the angle in degrees is computed.

In the event that the formula has different units at the different sides of the equality you will get **Warning** messages such as the one shown below.

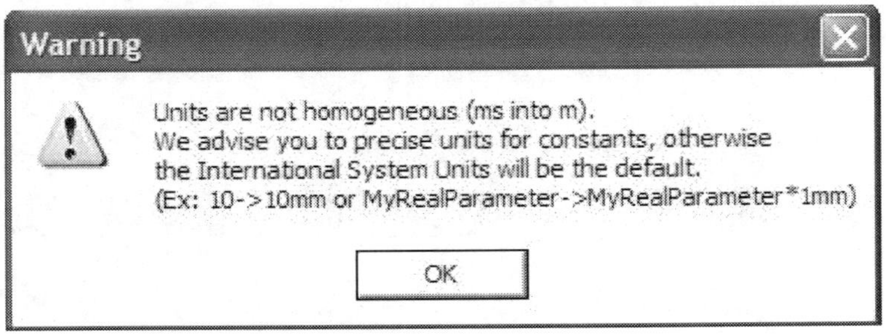

We are spared the warning message because the formula has been properly inputted. Note that the introduced law has appeared in **Law** branch of the tree.

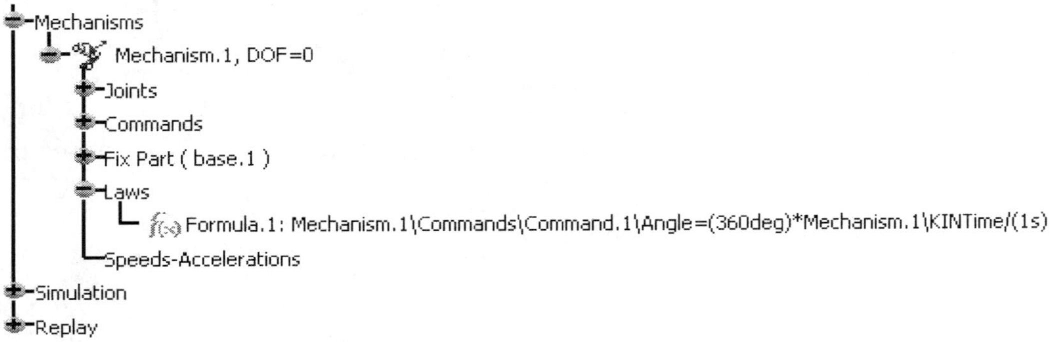

Keep in mind that our interest is to plot the linear speed and X vs. Y for the reference point on the link generated by this motion.

Select the **Speed and Acceleration** icon  from the **DMU Kinematics** toolbar

. The pop up box below appears on the Screen.

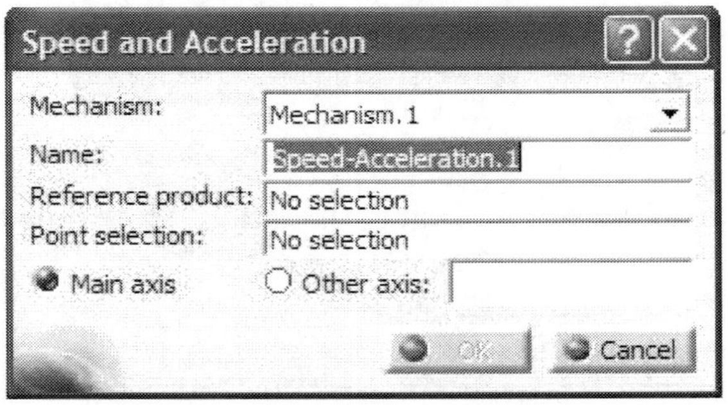

For the **Reference product,** select the **base** from the screen or the tree. For the **Point selection**, pick the reference point on the **link** as shown in the sketch below. You may find it helpful to hide the **Trace1** part to avoid accidentally picking one of the points on that part. This can be done as a right-clink option in the tree.

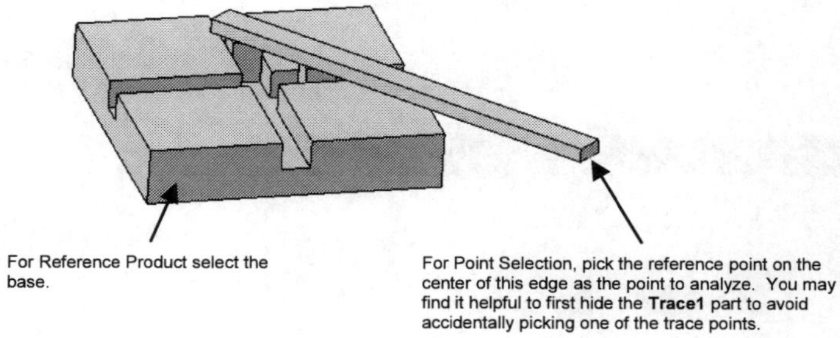

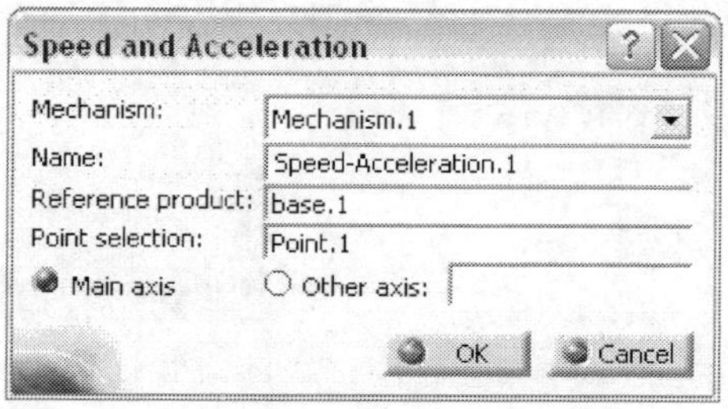

Note that the **Speed and Acceleration.1** has appeared in the tree.

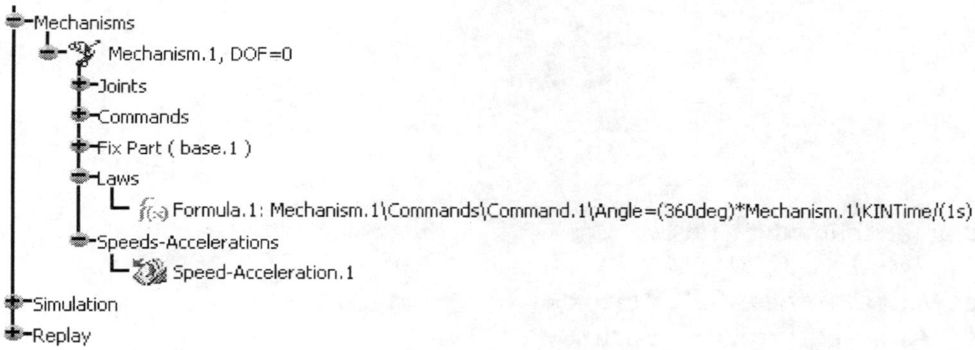

Click on **Simulation with Laws** icon  in the **Simulation** toolbar 

. This results in the **Kinematics Simulation** pop up box shown below.

Note that the default time duration is 10 seconds. To change this value, click on the button ... . In the resulting pop up box, change the time duration to 1s. This is the time duration for the link to make one full revolution.

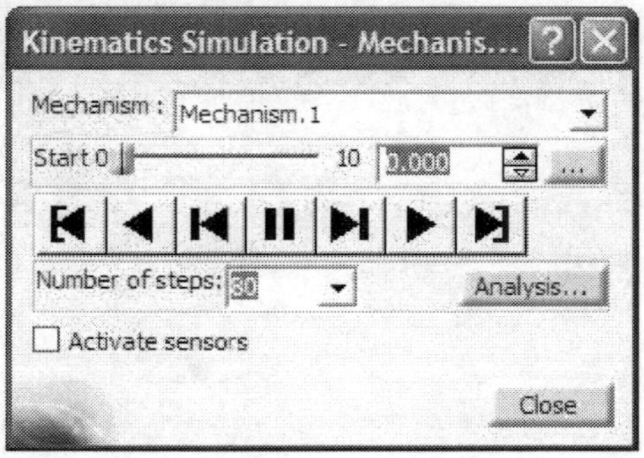

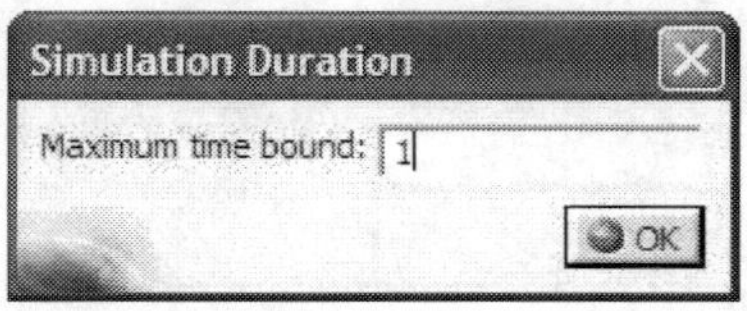

The scroll bar now moves up to 1s.

Check the **Activate sensors** box, at the bottom left corner.

You will next have to make certain selections from the accompanying **Sensors** box to support the desired plots of linear speed vs time and X vs Y for the reference point.

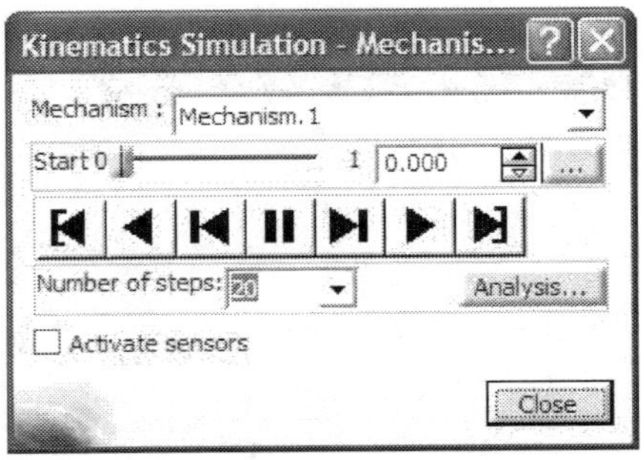

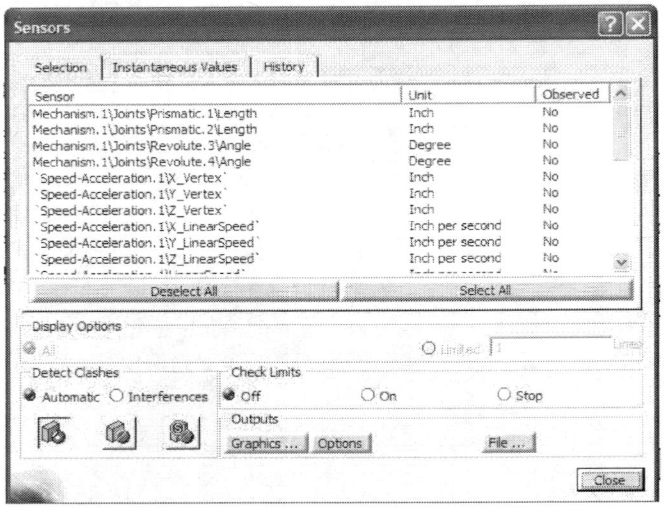

Click on the following items:

Speed-Acceleration.1\X_Vertex
Speed-Acceleration.1\Y_Vertex
Speed-Acceleration.1\LinearSpeed

As you make these selections, the last column in the **Sensors** box, changes to **Yes** for the corresponding items. This is shown below.

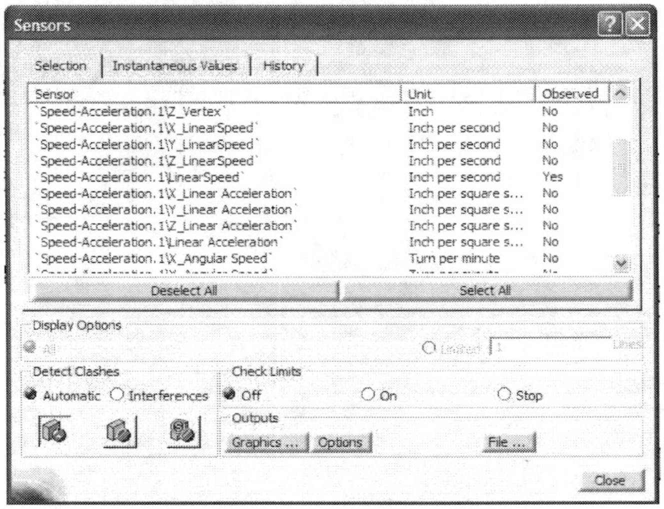

Since the default plots are vs. time, but we desire a plot of X vs. Y, click on the **Options** button in the **Sensors** box. This will open the **Graphical Representations** box shown below.

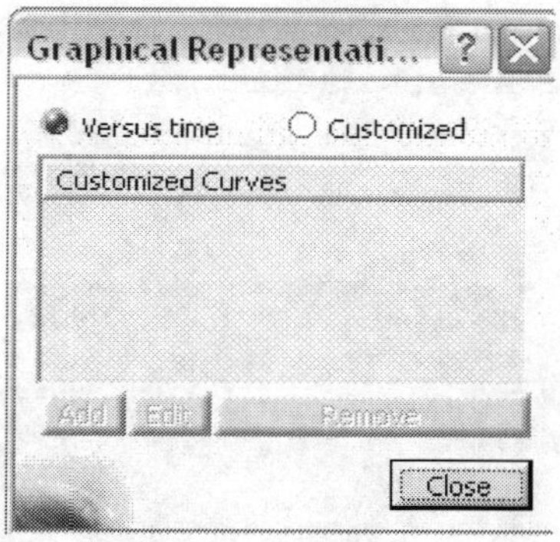

In the **Graphical Representations** box, click on **Customized**, then click on **Add**, and complete the **Curve Creation** box which appears to specify the Abscissa and Ordinate values as shown below.

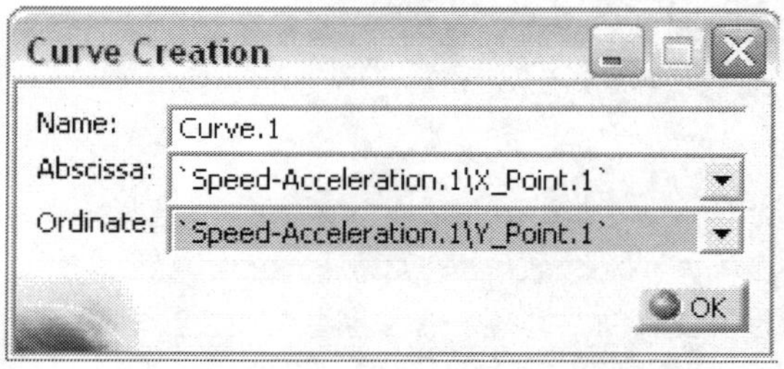

OK the **Curve Creation** box and **Close** the **Graphical Representations** box.

Finally, change the **Number of steps to 80**. The larger this number, the smoother the velocity plot will be.

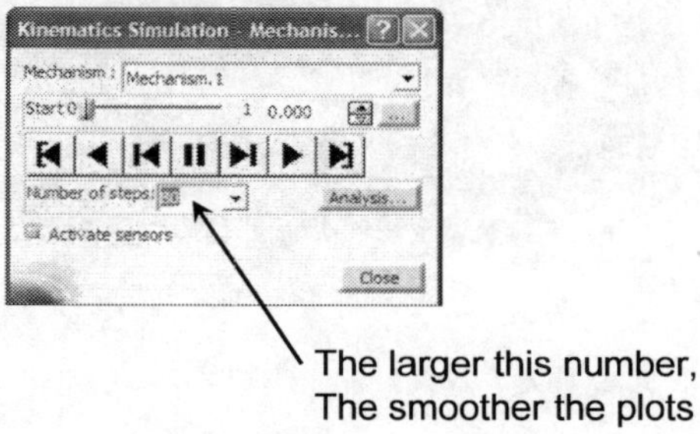

At this point, drag the scroll bar in the **Kinematics Simulation** box. As you do this, the link rotates about the base. Once the bar reaches its right extreme point, the link has made one full revolution. This corresponds to 1s.

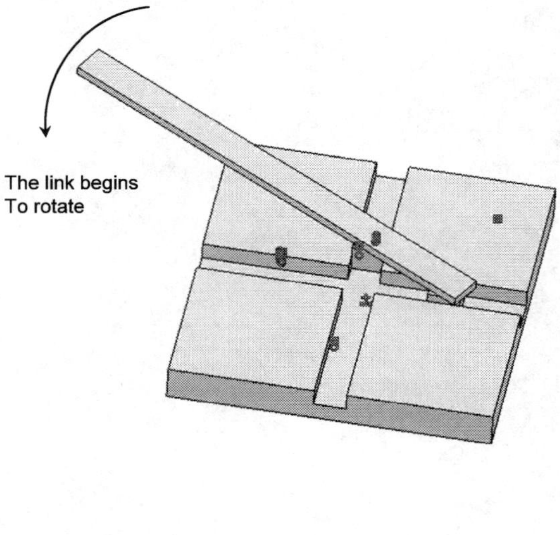

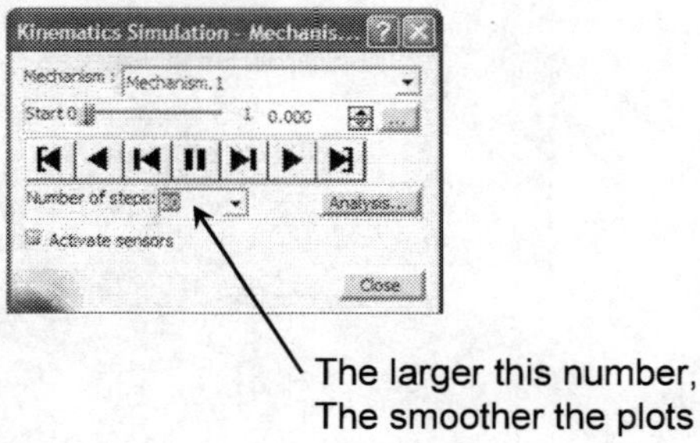

Once the link reaches the end, click on **Graphics** button 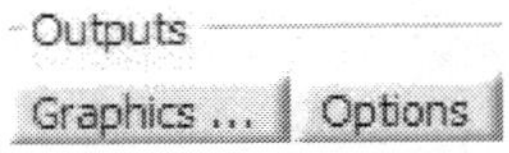

in the **Sensor** box. The curve of X vs Y which you setup appears similar to the one shown below. This shows the elliptical trace generated at the reference point analogous to the trace generated earlier.

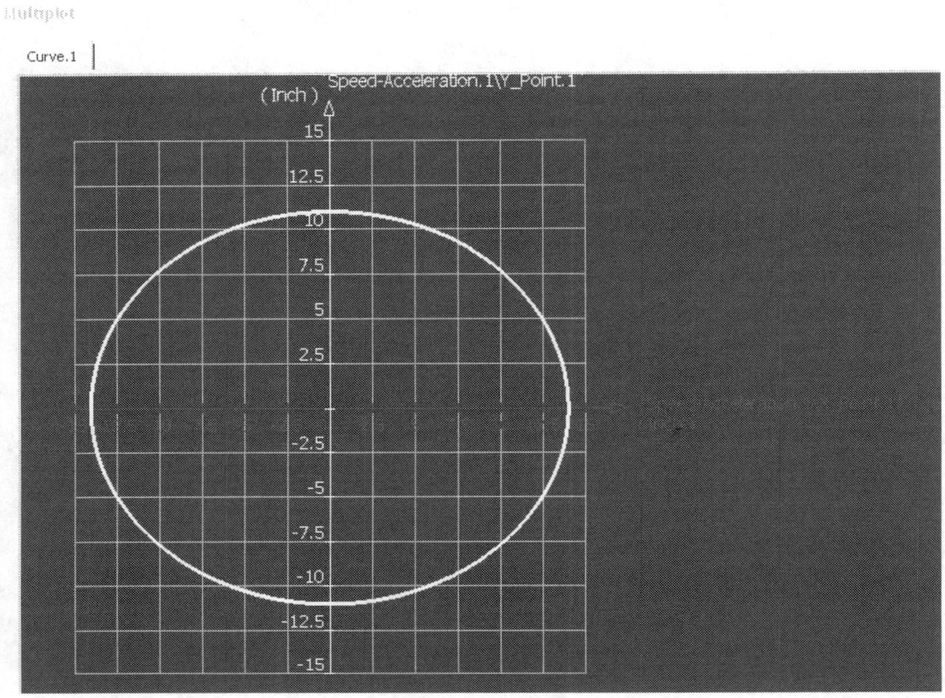

To see the plot of linear speed vs. time, first close the window containing the X-Y plot.

Next, click on the **Graphics** button 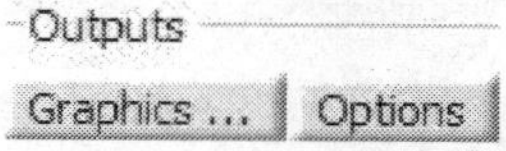

in the **Sensor** box. In the **Graphical Representations** box which appears, change it from **Customized** to **Versus time**. **Close** the **Graphical Representations** box.

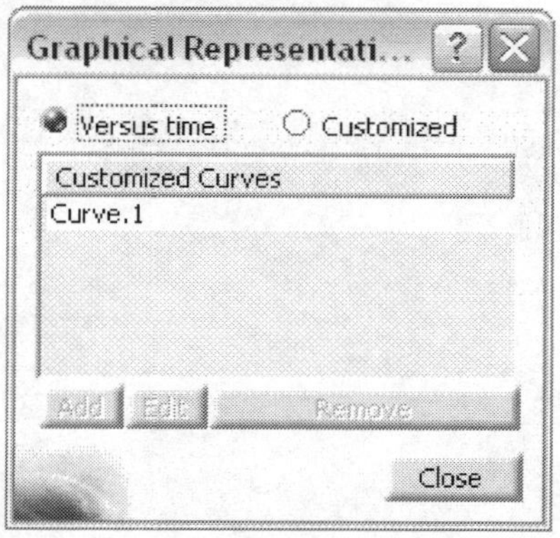

Now, if you click on the **Graphics** button in the **Sensors** box again, you will get plots of the linear speed vs. time (along with X vs. time and Y vs. time since we had active sensors for those parameters too). Your plot should look similar to the one shown below.

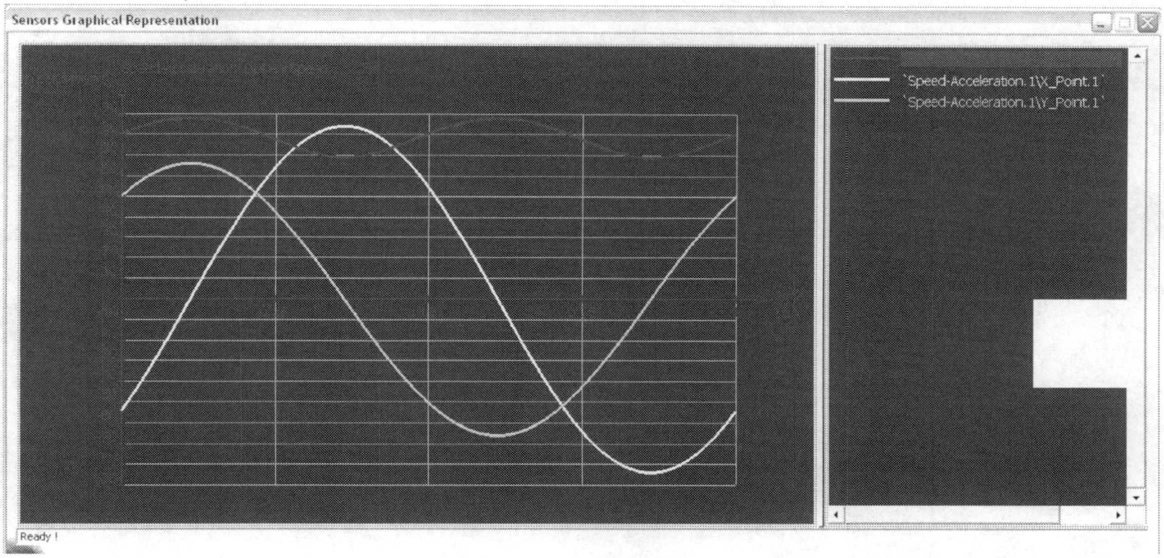

As a final note, remember that sensor values get stored until cleared. Hence, if you ever need to re-run a simulation and want a fresh start on your data, you need to go to the **History** tab in the **Sensors** box and choose **Clear**.

This concludes this tutorial.

NOTES:

Chapter 8

Cam-Follower Mechanism

Introduction

In this tutorial you will model a cam-follower mechanism consisting of one revolute, one prismatic and one point-surface joint. The revolute and prismatic joints are created through automatic assembly constraints conversion. The point-surface joint has to be created manually in the **Digital Mockup** workbench. For a given constant rotational speed of the cam, the displacement and acceleration of the follower are plotted versus angular displacement of the cam.

1 Problem Statement

Three different views of a cam-follower assembly are displayed below. The assembly consists of three parts: base, pin and cam. The mechanism consists of a revolute joint about which the cam rotates, a prismatic joint along which the pin slides, and a point-surface joint maintaining contact between the cam and the pin (follower). The goal is to create and animate the assembly, impose a constant angular velocity for the cam of one revolution per second (360° per second) and generate plots of the linear velocity and linear acceleration of the pin vs. cam angle. At the end of the tutorial, you are also exposed to the **Distance Analysis and the Ban Analysis** in CATIA.

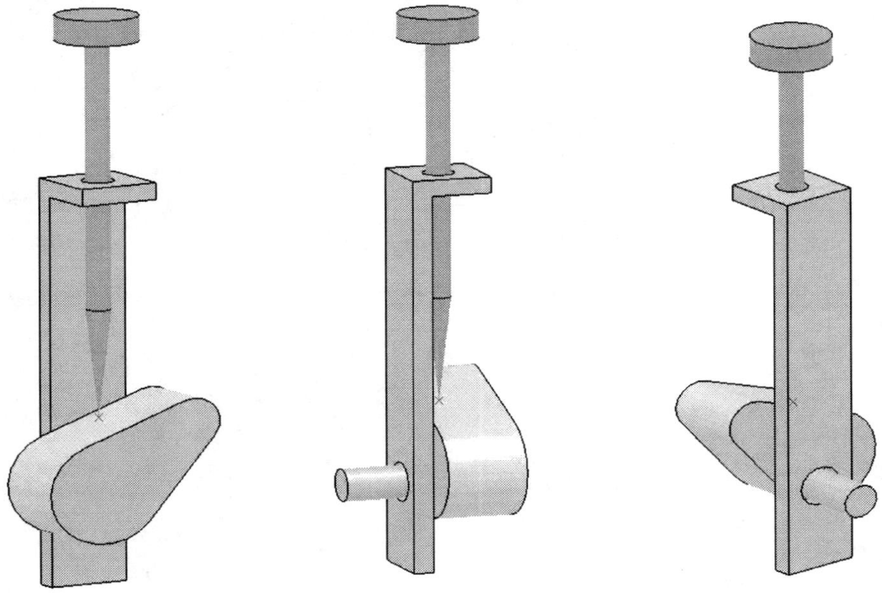

2 Overview of this Tutorial

This tutorial will involve the following steps:

1. Model the three CATIA parts required.
2. Create an assembly (CATIA Product) containing the parts.
3. Constrain the assembly in such a way that the only unconstrained degree of freedom is the rotation of the cam about the axis of the base.
4. Enter the **Digital Mockup** workbench and convert the assembly constraints into a revolute joint and a prismatic joint representing the desired rotation of the cam and the motion of the follower (pin).
5. Create a Point Surface joint representing the motion of the pin tip on the cam.
6. Simulate the relative motion of the assembly without consideration to time (in other words, without implementing the time based angular velocity given in the problem statement).
7. Adding a formula to implement the time based kinematics.
8. Simulating the desired constant angular velocity motion and generating plots of the results.

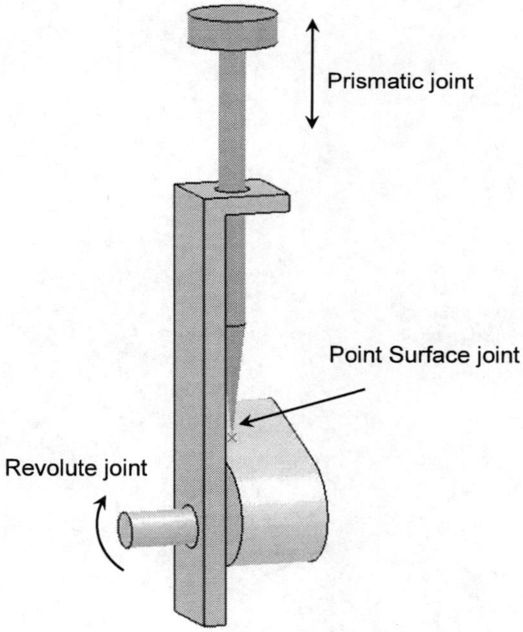

3 Creation of the Assembly in Mechanical Design Solutions

Model three parts named **pin**, **cam** and **base** as shown below with the suggested dimensions. If certain dimensions are missing, use the overall figure to estimate the missing dimensions. While it is assumed that you are sufficiently familiar with CATIA to model these parts fairly quickly, it is important to have a pickable point at the tip of the pin. In addition, some of the required aspects of modeling the **cam** the may be unfamiliar to the reader. Therefore, detailed instructions are presented regarding how to model those two parts.

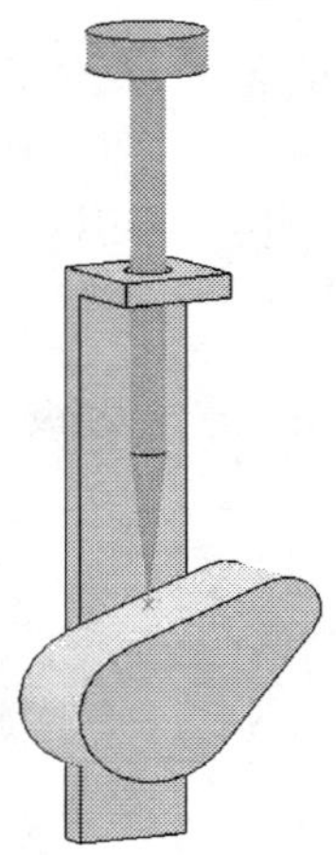

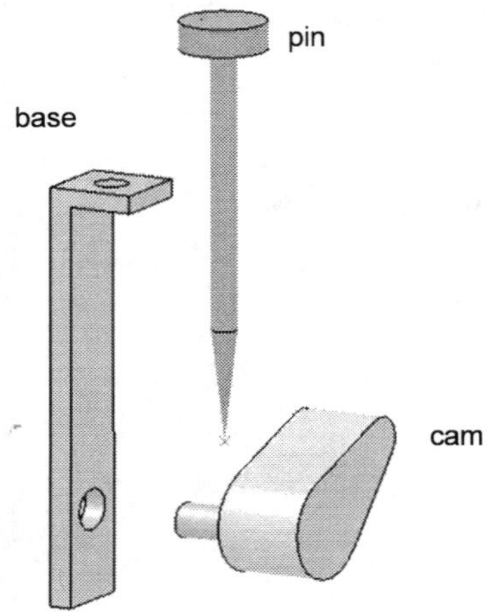

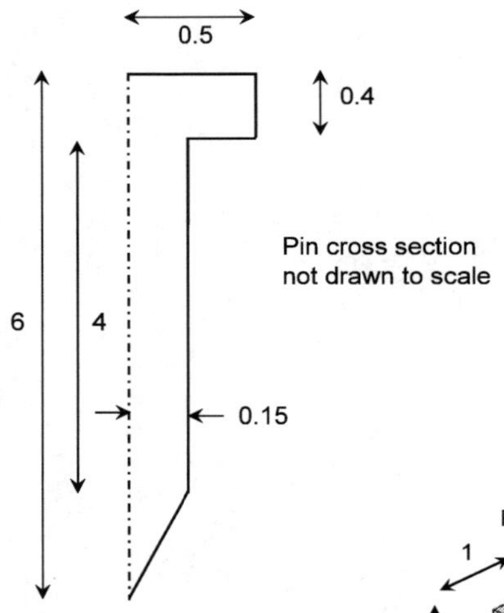

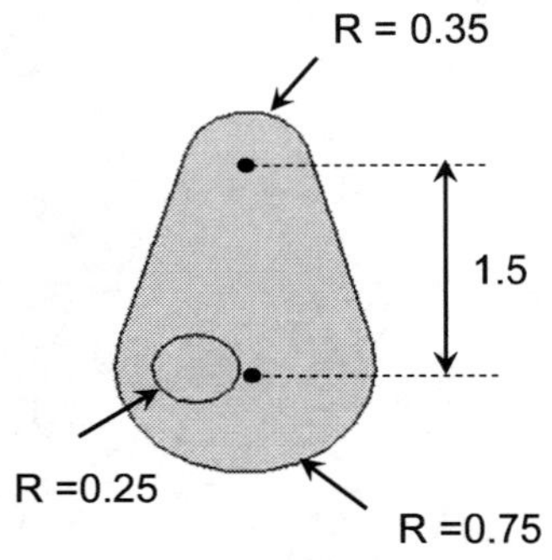

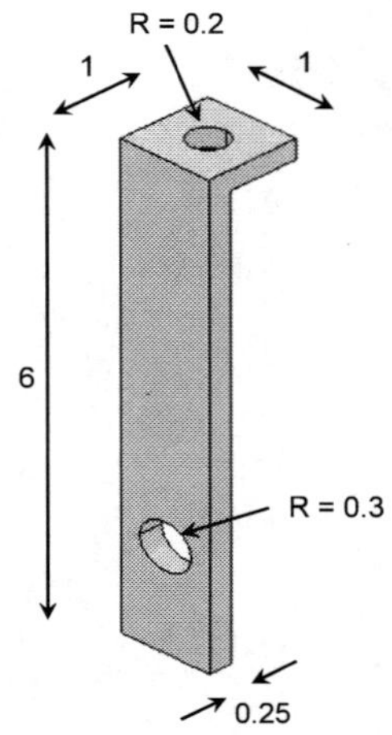

Outline of creating the pin:

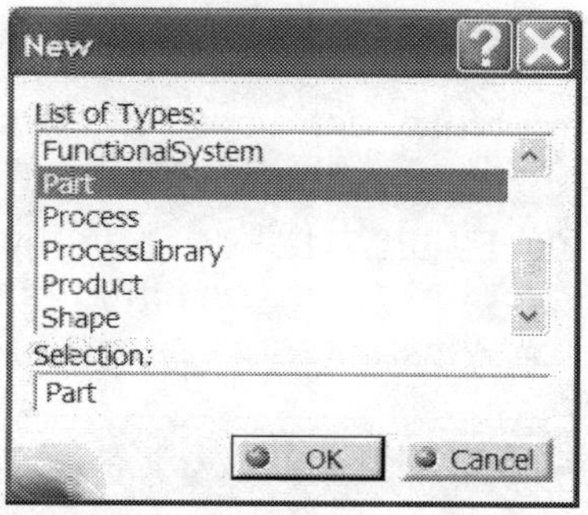

Enter the **Part Design** workbench which can be achieved by different means depending on your CATIA customization. For example, from the standard Windows toolbar, select **File > New** . From the box shown on the right, select **Part**. This moves you to the **Part Design** workbench and creates a part with the default name **Part.1**.
In order to change the default name, move the cursor to **Part.1** in the tree, right click and select **Properties** from the menu list.

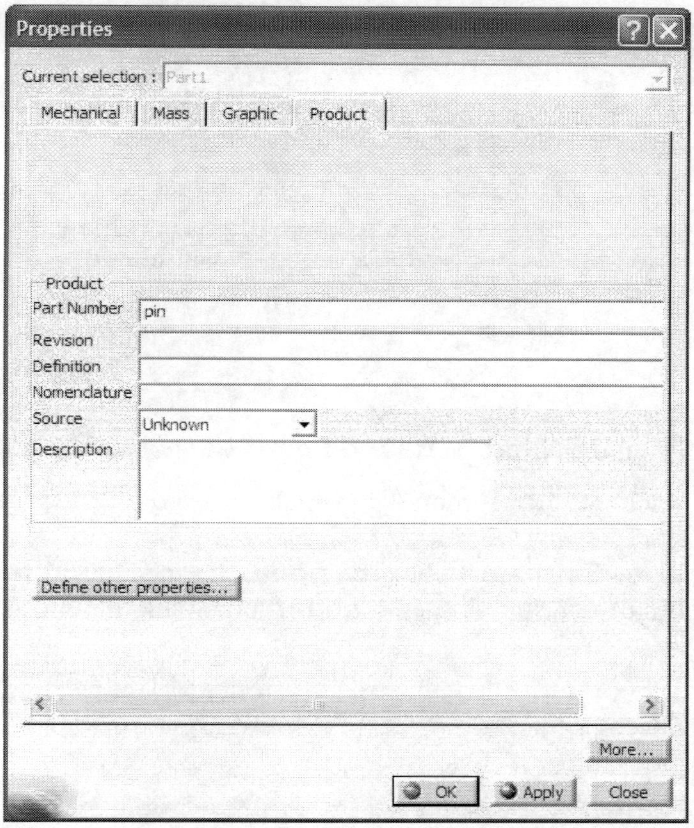

From the **Properties** box, select the **Product** tab and in **Part Number** type **pin**. This will be the new part name throughout the chapter. The tree on the top left corner of the screen should look as displayed below.

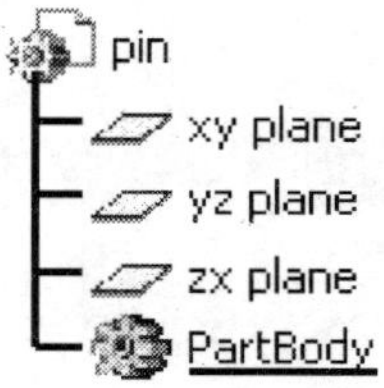

From the tree, select the **yz** plane and enter the **Sketcher**. In the **Sketcher**, use the **Profile** icon from the **Profile** toolbar

to draw the pin cross section and dimension it. <u>Make certain to pick the origin as the bottom tip of your profile; later we will need to have a pickable point at the tip, and the origin meets this requirement</u>. An alternative approach would be to create a reference point at any locations where one might be needed for assembly constraint or mechanism joint creation purposes.

Note that the drawing on the right is not to scale.

Leave the **Sketcher**.

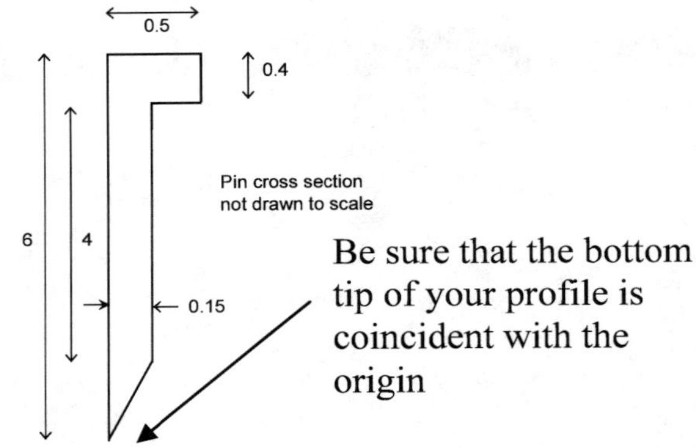

From the **Sketch- Based Features** toolbar

, select the **Shaft** icon, which causes the **Shaft Definition** box to open.

In the **First angle** box, type **360**. For the **Selection** box, pick **Sketch.1** from the tree. Finally, for the **Axis Selection** box, pick the line as shown below.

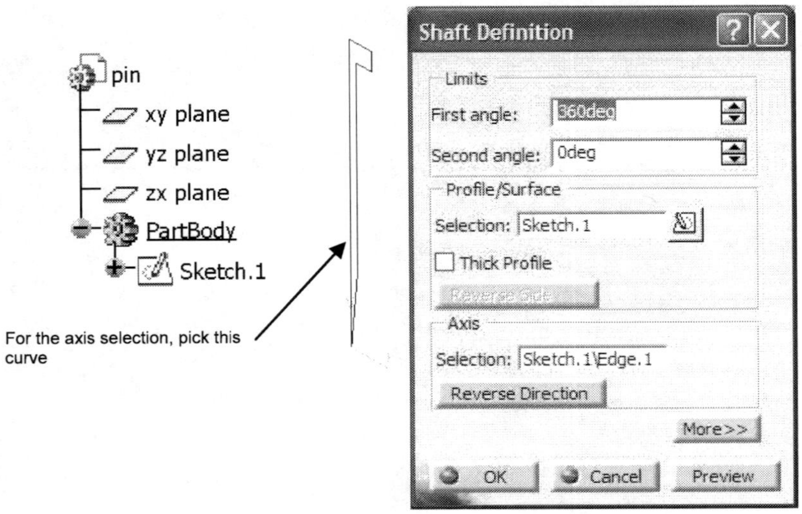

The pin is now created. We will use the fact that the tip is coincident with the part origin when we assemble the parts and create the point-surface joint in the mechanism.

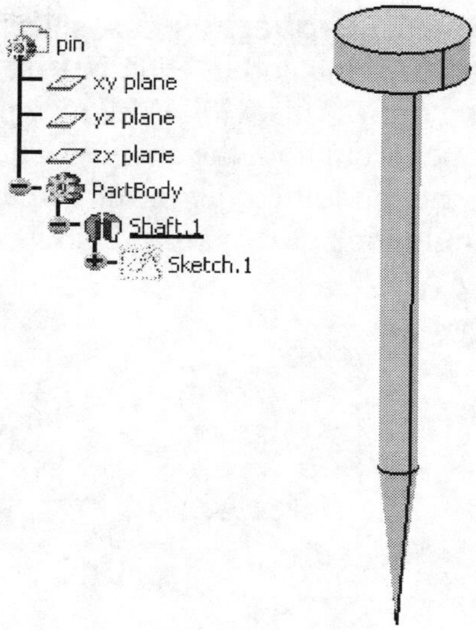

<u>Outline of creating the cam and the needed surface</u>:

The complication in creating the cam is that we need a single surface around the follower contact region of the cam such that we can create a point-surface joint which will track a complete revolution. The instructions which follow step you through how to model the cam and create the required surface.

Enter the **Part Design** workbench  which can be achieved by different means depending on your CATIA customization. For example, from the standard Windows toolbar, select **File > New** . From the box shown on the right, select **Part**. This moves you to the **Part Design** workbench and creates a part with the default name **Part.2**.
In order to change the default name, move the cursor to **Part.2** in the tree, right click and select **Properties** from the menu list.

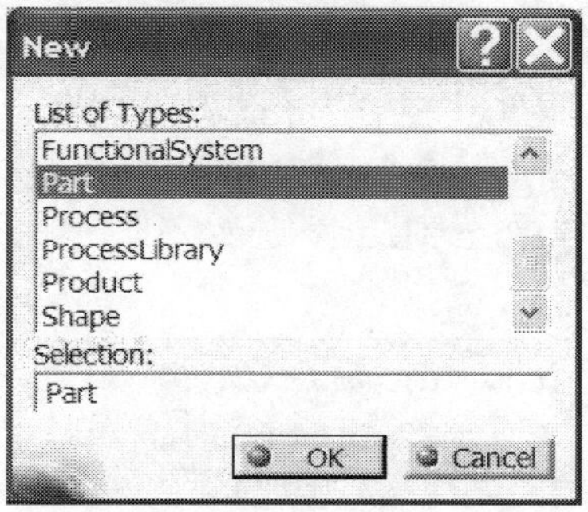

From the **Properties** box, select the **Product** tab and in **Part Number** type **cam**. This will be the new part name throughout the chapter. The tree on the top left corner of the screen should look as displayed below.

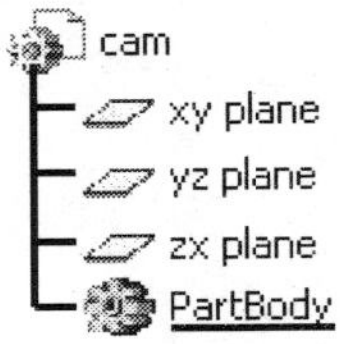

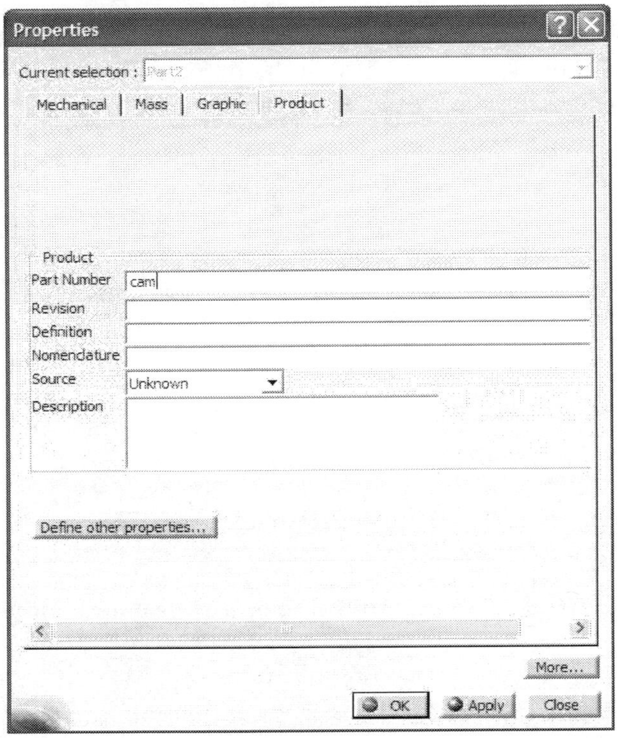

From the tree, select the **yz** plane and enter the **Sketcher** . In the **Sketcher**, use the **Profile** icon  from the **Profile** toolbar 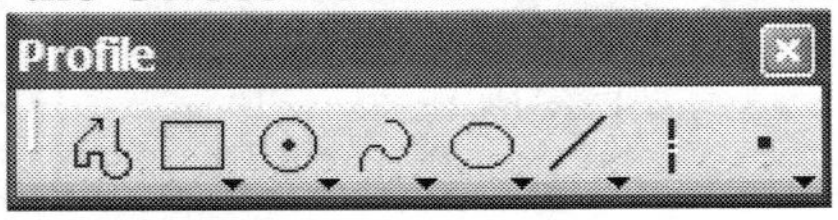

to draw the cam cross section and dimension it 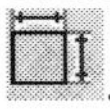. Add any necessary tangency constraints not automatically created.

Leave the **Sketcher** .

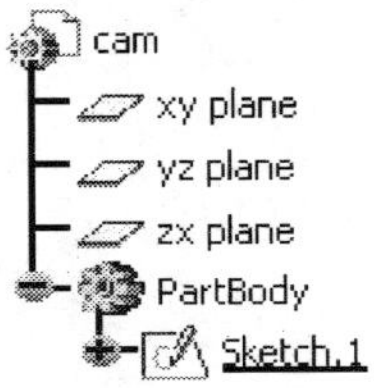

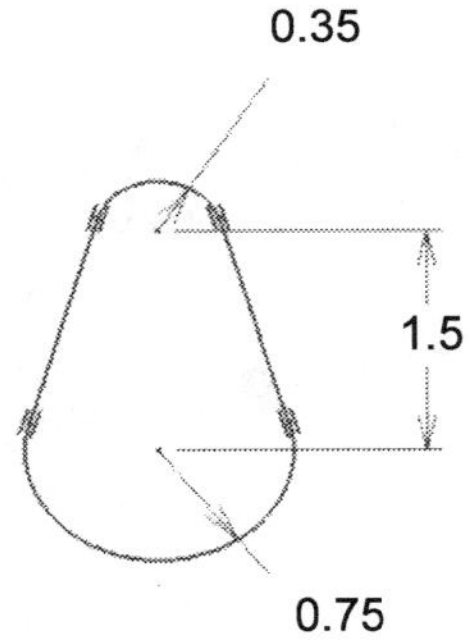

Using the icon , pad the **Sketch.1** by 1 in.

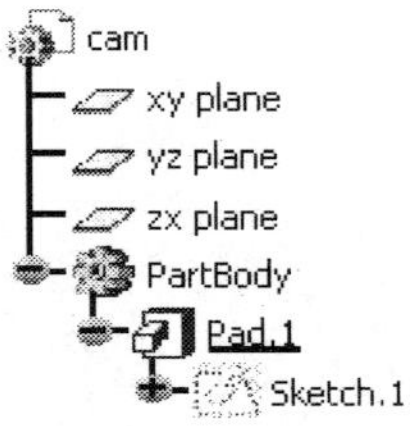

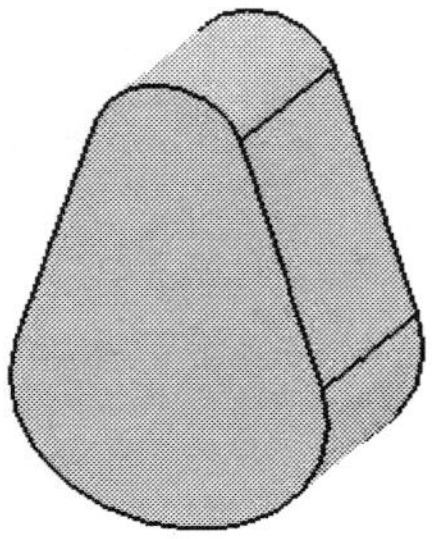

Select the front face of the cam, and enter the **Sketcher** .

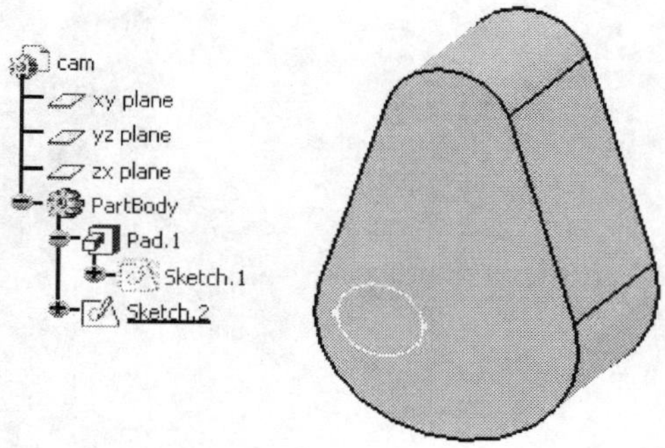

Draw a **Circle** of radius 0.25 making sure that it is not concentric with the existing arcs.
Although the kinematics of the mechanism depends on the location of the center of this circle, we leave it as unspecified here for simplicity.

Using the icon , pad the **Sketch.2** by 1 in.
The final shape of the cam is displayed on the right.

Your next task is to generate the surface required to create the **Point Surface** joint.

Surfaces are dealt with in the Wireframe and **Surface Design** workbench.
Therefore, select **Start > Mechanical Design > Wireframe and Surface Design**.

Click on the **Extract** icon in the **Operations** toolbar 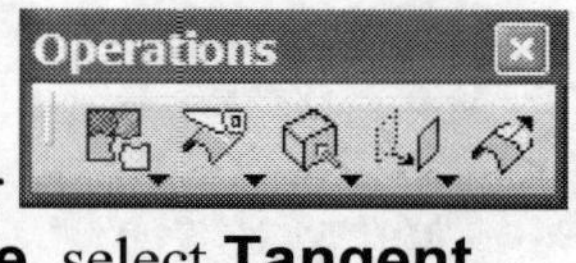 which leads to the box shown below. For the **Propagation Type**, select **Tangent Continuity.** For the **Element(s) to Extract**, select one of the lateral surfaces on the cam. This selects the entire tangent continuous surface as shown on the next page.

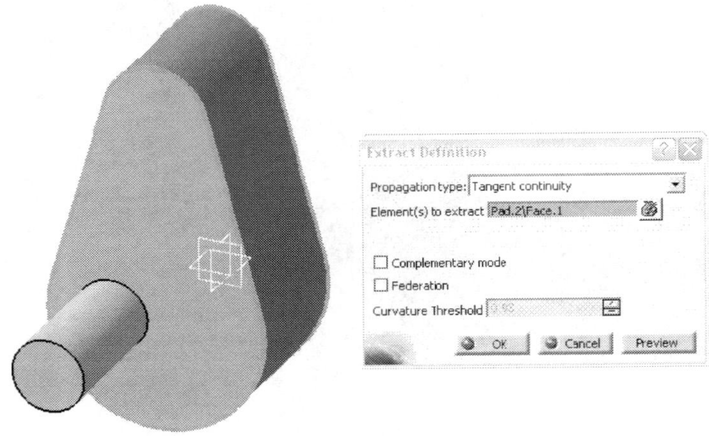

The task of creating the **base** is left to you. You are now in the position to assemble the three parts and to impose the constraints.

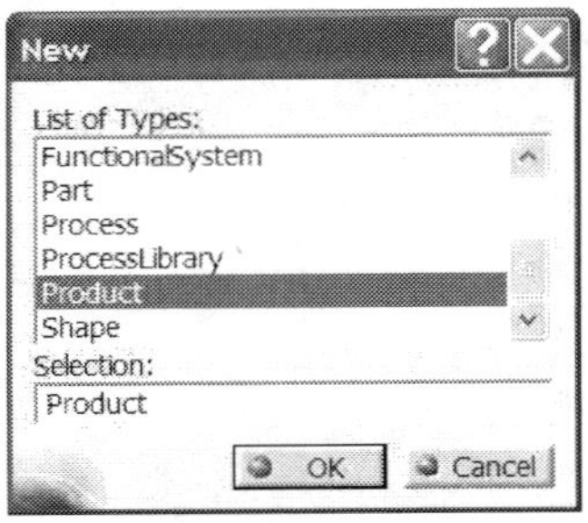

Enter the **Assembly Design** workbench which can be achieved by different means depending on your CATIA customization. For example, from the standard Windows toolbar, select **File > New**. From the box shown on the right, select **Product**. This moves you to the **Assembly Design** workbench and creates an assembly with the default name **Product.1**.

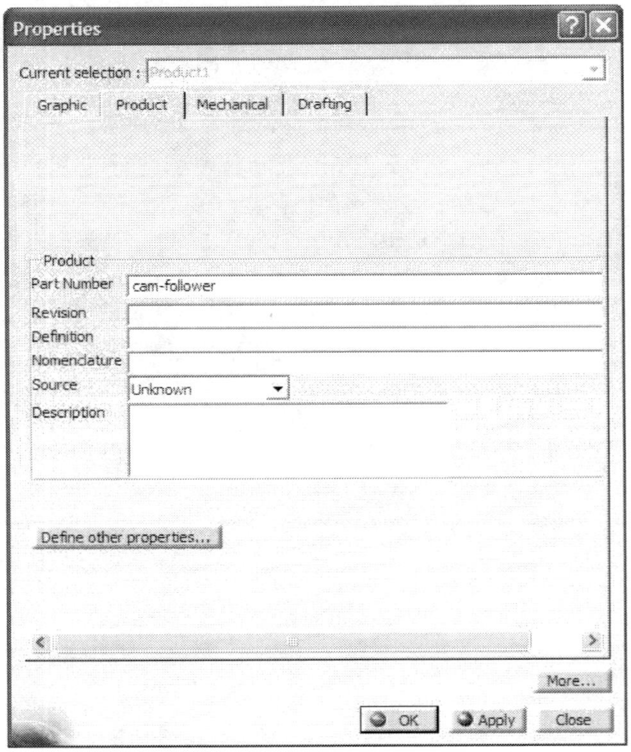

In order to change the default name, move the cursor to **Product.1** in the tree, right click and select **Properties** from the menu list.

From the **Properties** box, select the **Product** tab and in **Part Number** type **cam-follower**.

This will be the new product name throughout the chapter. The tree on the top left corner of your computer screen should look as displayed below.

The next step is to insert the existing parts into the assembly just created.

From the standard Windows toolbar, select **Insert > Existing Component**.
From the **File Selection** pop up box choose **pin**, **cam**, and **base**. Remember that in CATIA multiple selections are made with the **Ctrl** key.
The tree is modified to indicate that the parts have been inserted.

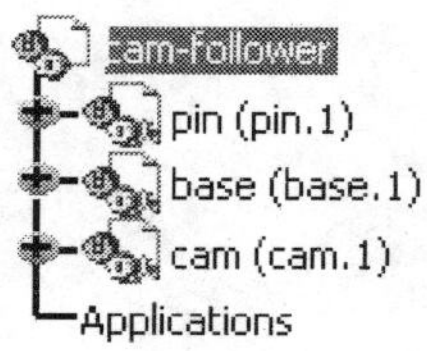

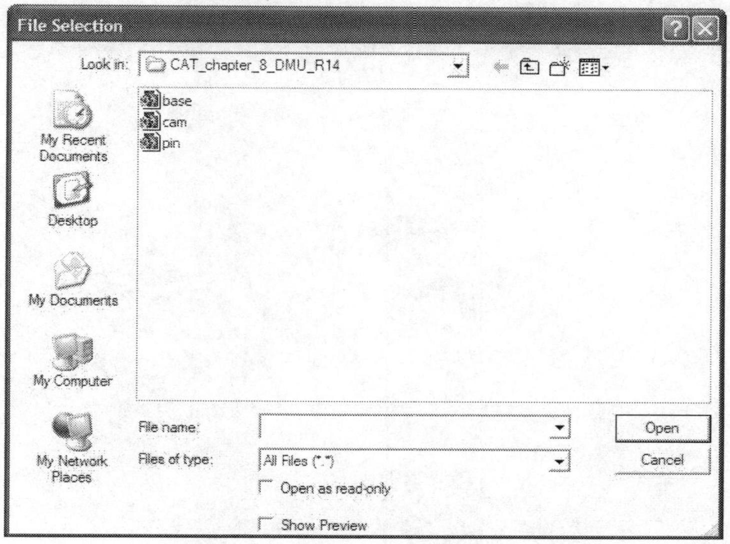

The best way of saving your work is to save the entire assembly.
Double click on the top branch of the tree. This is to ensure that you are in the **Assembly Design** workbench.
Select the **Save** icon . The **Save As** pop up box allows you to rename if desired. The default name is the **cam-follower**.

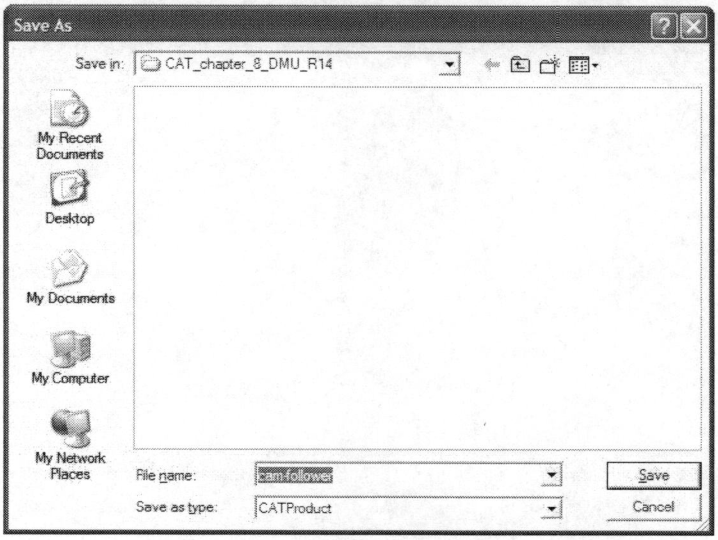

Note that the part names and their instance names were purposely made the same. This practice makes the identifying of the assembly constraint a lot easier down the road.

Depending on how your parts were created earlier, on the computer screen you have the three parts scattered as shown below. You may have to use the **Manipulation** icon  in the **Move** toolbar 

to rearrange them as desired.

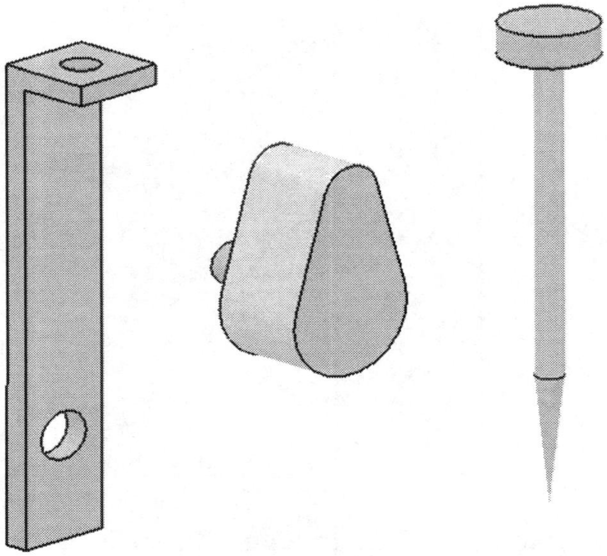

Although not necessary, you may have to manipulate the parts to achieve this formation

Your next task is to impose assembly constraints. We will begin this process by anchoring the base.

Pick the **Anchor** icon  from **Constraints** toolbar and select the **base** from the tree or from the screen.

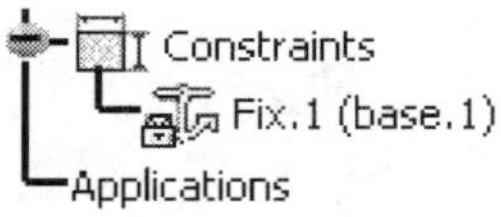

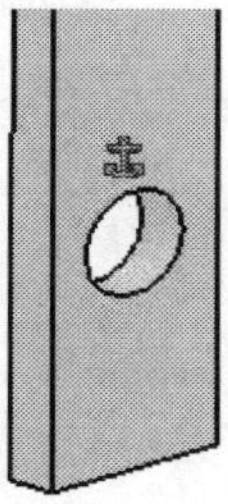

Recall that we ultimately wish to create a revolute joint between the cam and the base. This will be done with a coincidence constraint and a surface contact constraint. We will start with a coincidence constraint between the axis of the cam-shaft and the axis of the hole in the base. To do so, pick the **Coincidence** icon  from the **Constraints** toolbar 

. Select the axis of the **base** and the **cam-shaft** as shown below.

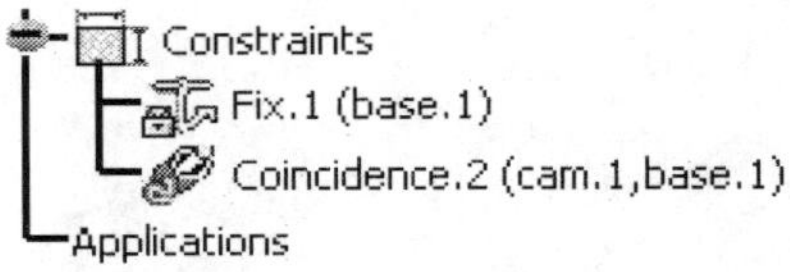

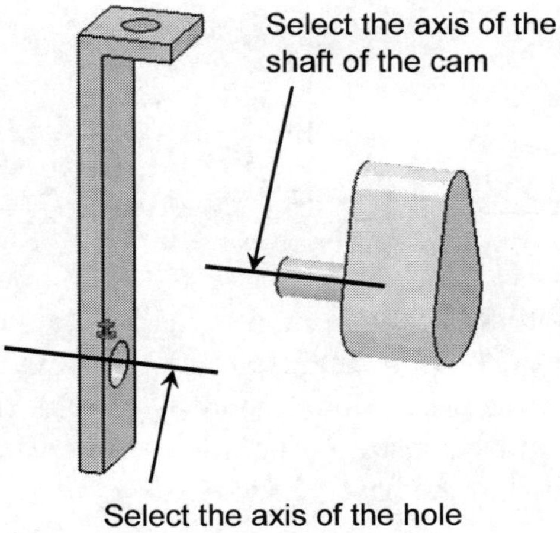

The coincidence constraint we just created removes all of the degrees of freedom of the cam with respect to the base except for rotation about the axis of coincidence (a desired rotation) and translation along that axis (an undesired translation).

A contact constraint between the surface of the cam and side surface of the base will remove the undesired translation. To create this constraint, pick the **Contact** icon from **Constraints** toolbar and select the surfaces shown below. The tree is modified to reflect this constraint.

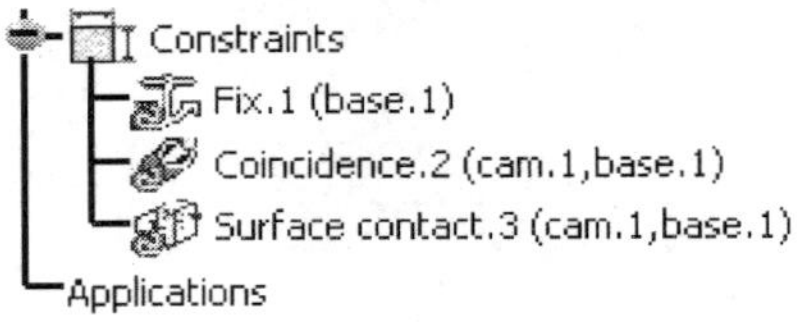

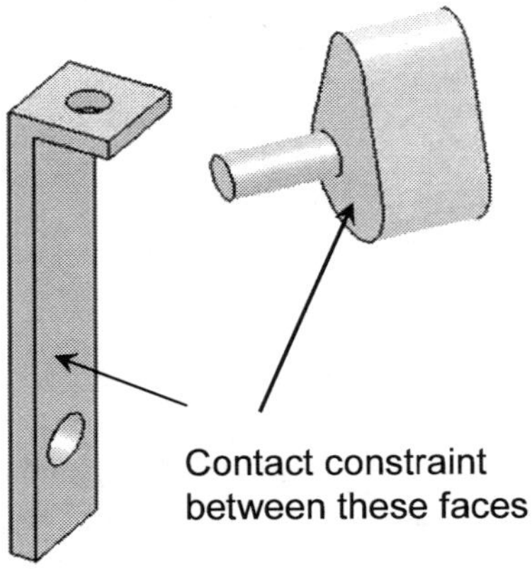

The next step is to insert the pin in the top hole and create assembly constraints consistent with the ultimate intention of creating a prismatic joint between the two. We will begin with a coincidence constraint between the axis of the pin and the axis of the hole in the upper part of the base. Pick the **Coincidence** icon from **Constraints** toolbar. Select the axis of the pin and the axis of the top hole as shown.

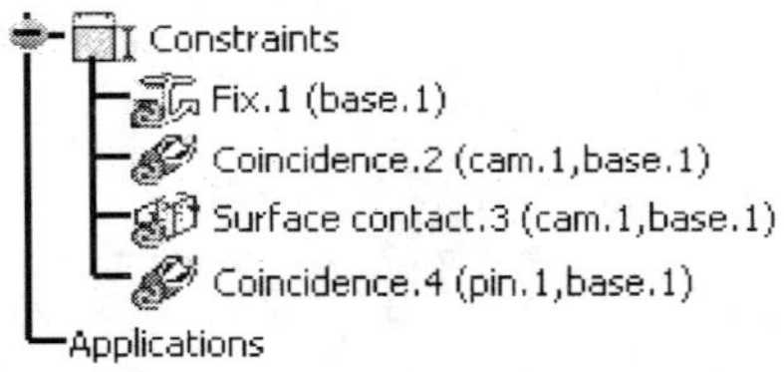

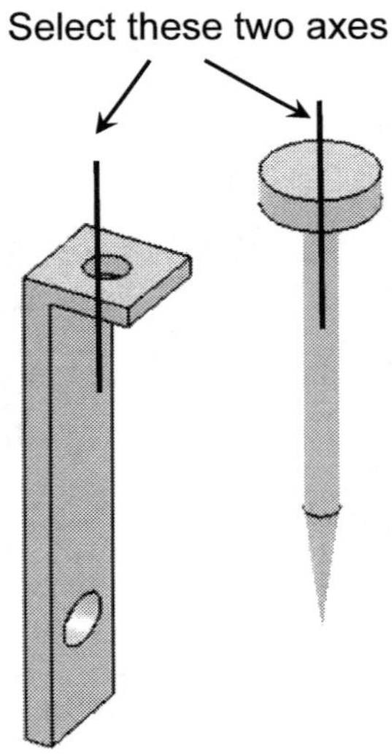

With this constraint, although the pin can travel along the axis of the hole, it can also rotate. You will eliminate the rotational degree of freedom. One way to achieve this is to impose and angular constraint (parallelism) between the **zx** planes of the pin and the base.

Pick the **Angle Constraint** icon  from the **Constraints** toolbar. Select the **zx** planes of the pin and the base. You may find it easiest to pick these planes from the tree by drilling down into each part until the planes are listed. In the **Constraint Properties** box which appears, choose **Parallelism** as shown below.

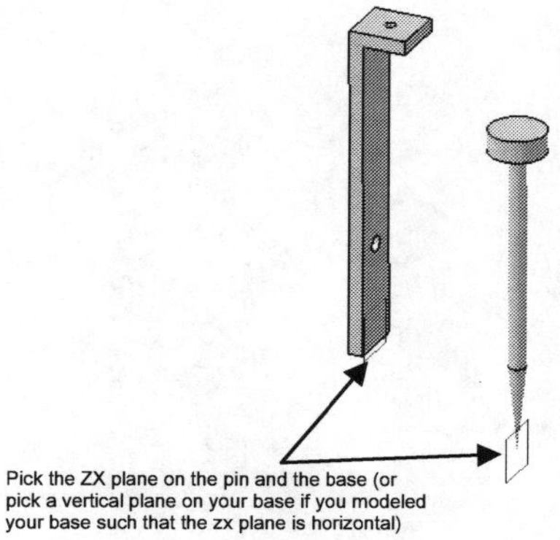

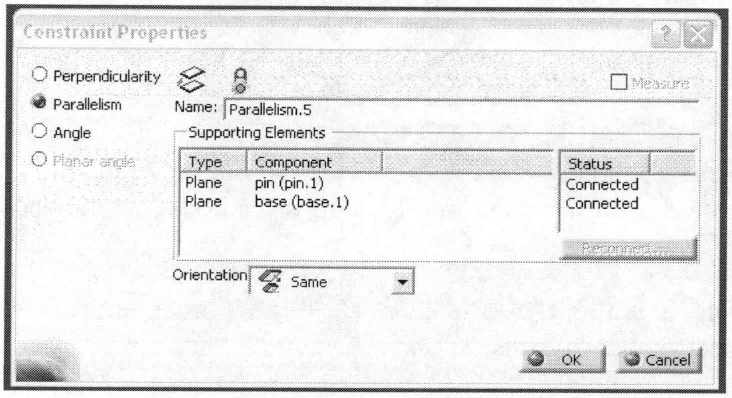

This constraint maintains parallelism of the selected planes and therefore prevents the pin from spinning about its own axis.

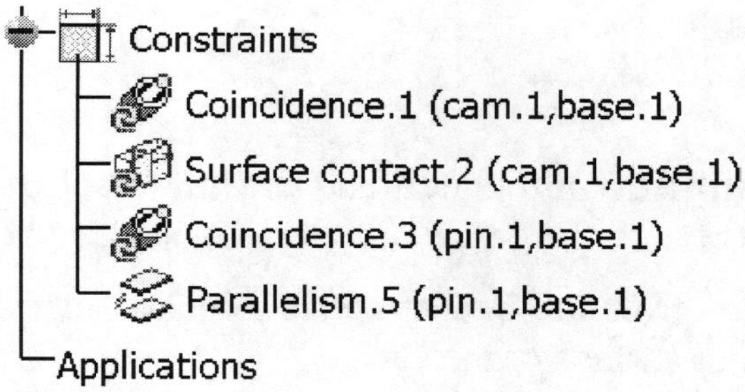

Use **Update** icon  to enforce constraints just created resulting in relative position the parts similar to as shown below.

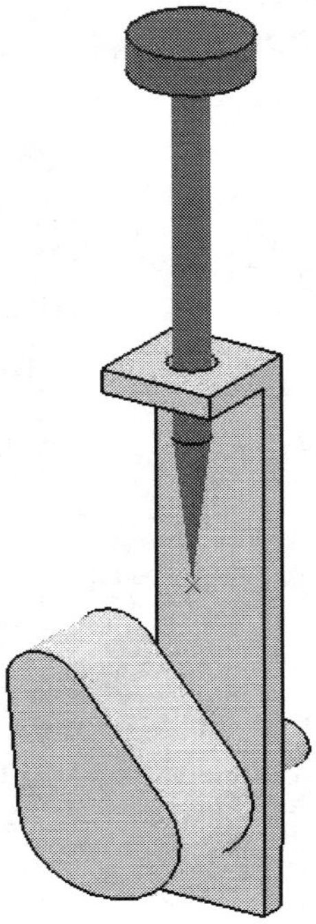

Your updated position may be completely different from the configuration shown (though consistent with the applied constraints). If so, use the **Manipulation** icon  in the **Move** toolbar 

to rearrange them as desired bringing them into the approximate formation shown.

Note that the **Update** icon  no longer appears on the constraints branches.

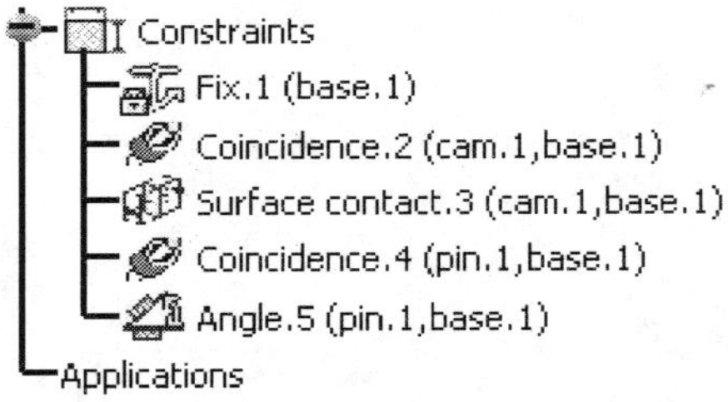

In order to create the **Point Surface** joint in the **Digital Mockup**, the point of the pin (which we made coincident with the origin of that part) needs to be on the surface. Pick the **Coincidence** icon  from the **Constraints** toolbar. Select the origin of the pin <u>from the tree</u> and the planar surface of the cam.

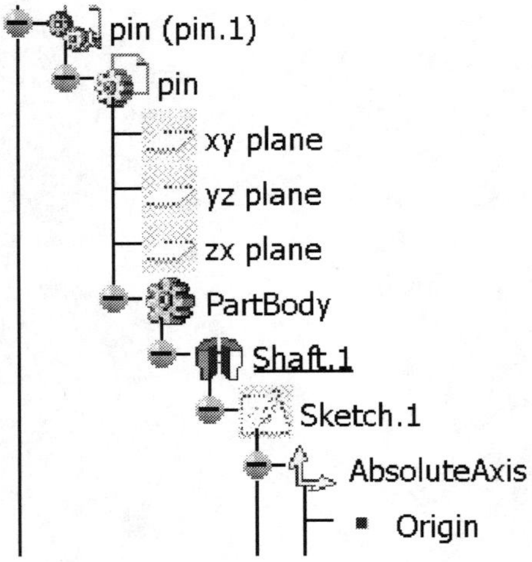

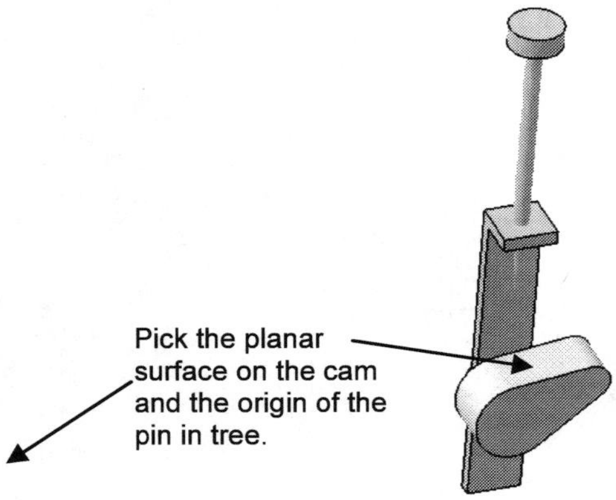

After update , the point should end up directly on the planar section. However, since the planar section is treated as an infinite plane, it is possible you will need to manually rotate the cam using the manipulate command such that, upon update, the tip of the cam lies on the actual cam surface.

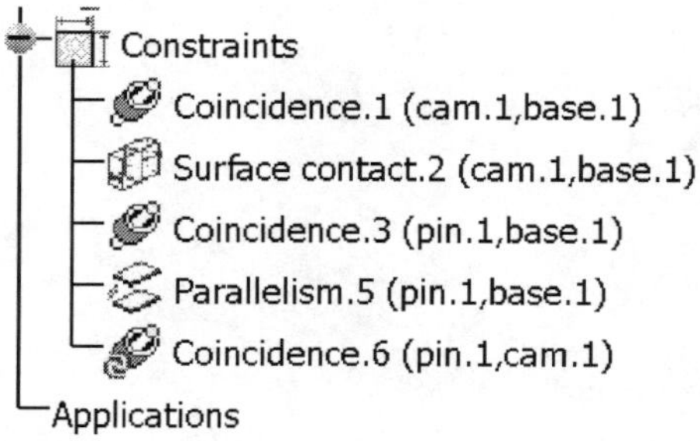

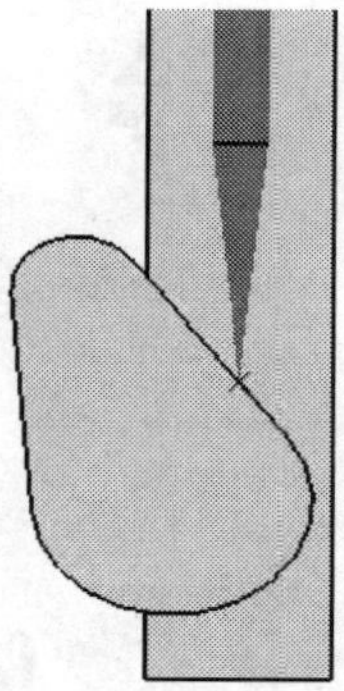

The assembly is complete and we can proceed to the **Digital Mockup** workbench.

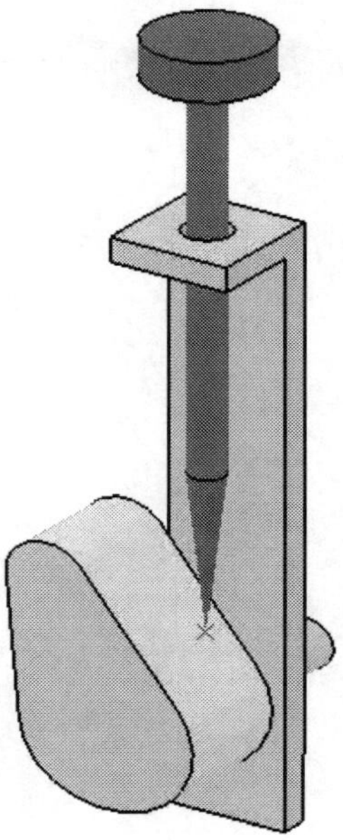

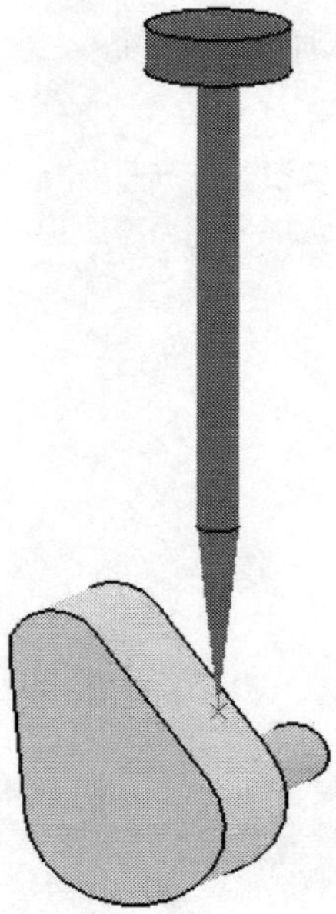

4 Creating Joints in the Digital Mockup Workbench

The **Digital Mockup** workbench is quite extensive but we will only deal with the **DMU Kinematics module**. To get there you can use the standard Windows toolbar as shown below: **Start > Digital Mockup > DMU Kinematics**.

Select the **Assembly Constraints Conversion** icon 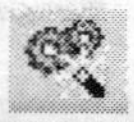 from the **DMU Kinematics** toolbar 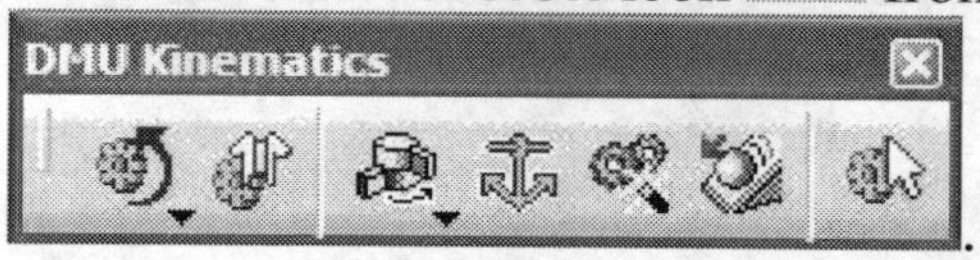

. This icon allows you to create most common joints automatically from the existing assembly constraints. The pop up box below appears.

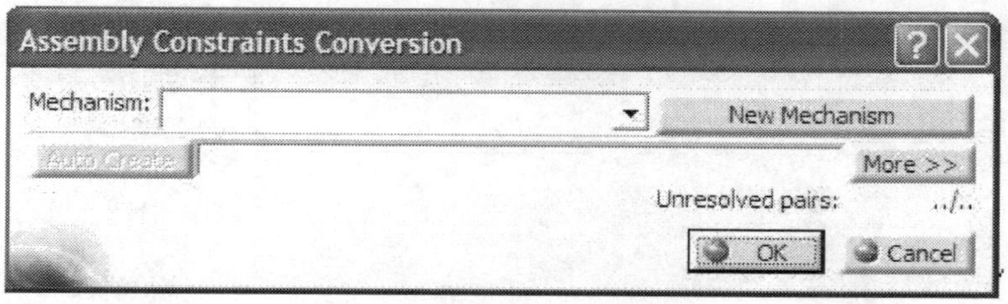

Select the **New Mechanism** button 

.
This leads to another pop up box which allows you to name your mechanism. The default name is **Mechanism.1**. Accept the default name by pressing **OK**.

Note that the box indicates **Unresolved pairs: 3/3**.

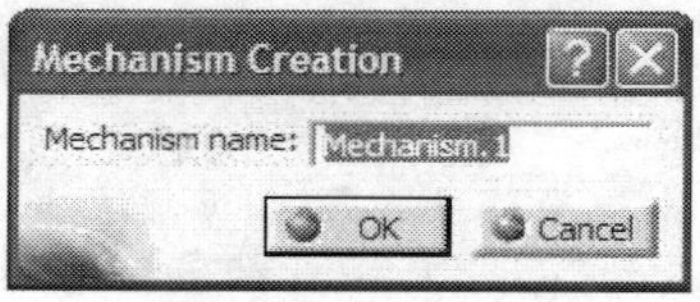

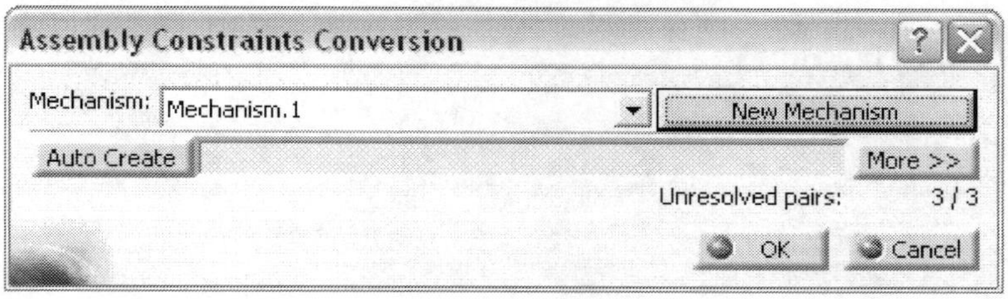

Select the **Auto Create** button 

. Then if the **Unresolved pairs** becomes **1/3**, things are moving in the right direction. It may at first seem like an issue that one of the three pairs remains unresolved, but as we shall see shortly, the point-surface constraint we made was ignored; we will create the corresponding mechanism joint manually shortly.

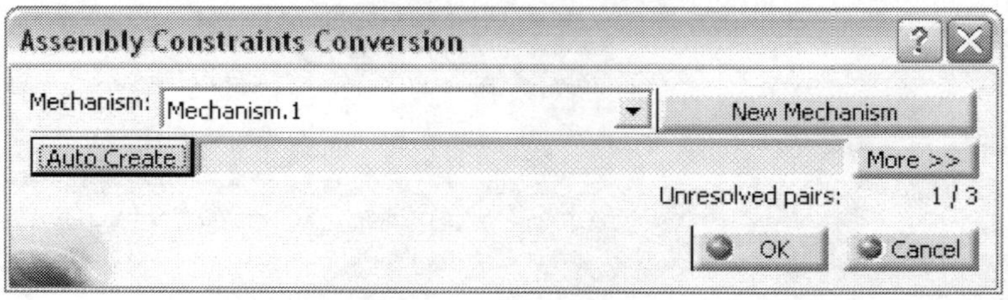

Note that the tree becomes longer by having an **Application** Branch. The expanded tree is displayed below. It clearly indicates the existence of a **Revolute.1** joint, and a **Prismatic.2** joint. These correspond to the rotation of the cam and the translation of the pin. Initially there are two degrees of freedom since the pin can move independently of the cam rotation at this point.

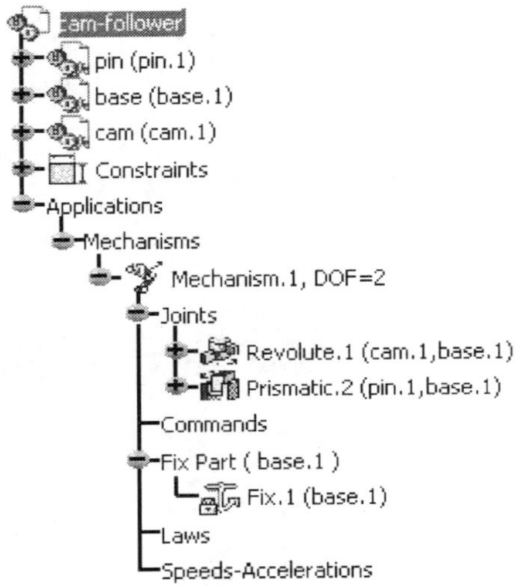

Next we will manually create the **Point Surface Joint**.

Select the **Point Surface Joint** icon 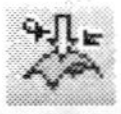 from the **Kinematics Joints** toolbar

.

In the resulting pop up box, for **Surface 1**, select the extracted surface of the cam, or **cam.1/Extract.1** from the tree. For **Point 1**, select the origin of the pin from the tree.

Close the box by clicking on **OK**.

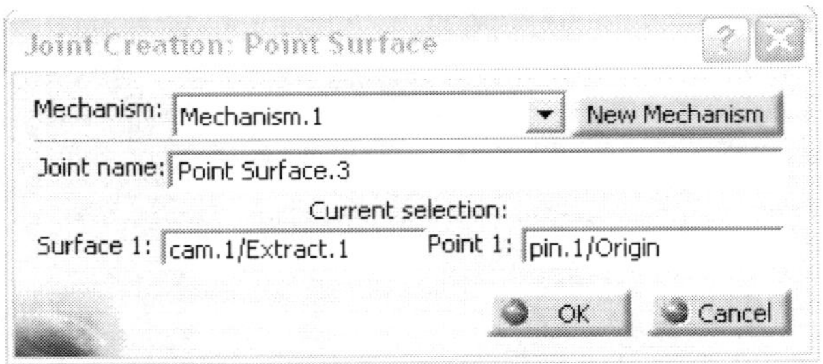

Note that the **Point Surface.3** joint has been created and recorded in the tree. Furthermore, **DOF** has been reduced to **1**.

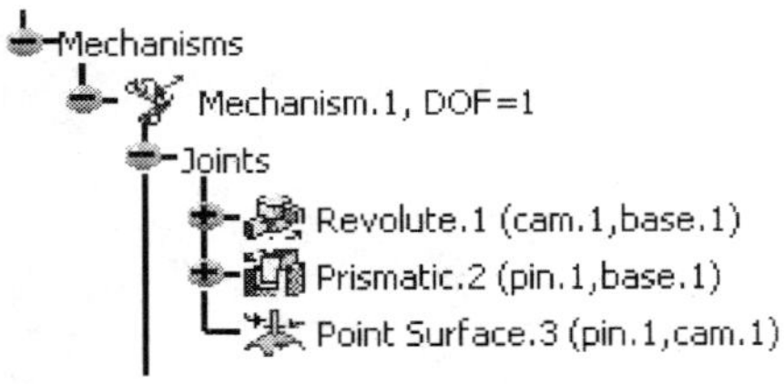

In order to animate the mechanism, you need to remove the one degree of freedom present. This will be achieved by turning **Revolute.1** into an **Angle driven** joint. Double click on **Revolute.1** in the tree. The pop up box below appears.

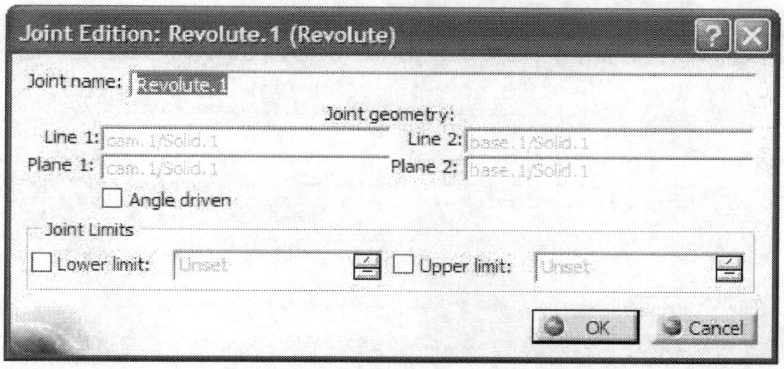

Check the **Angle driven** box and change the **Lower limit** and **Upper limit** to read as indicated below. Keep in mind that these limits can also be changed elsewhere.

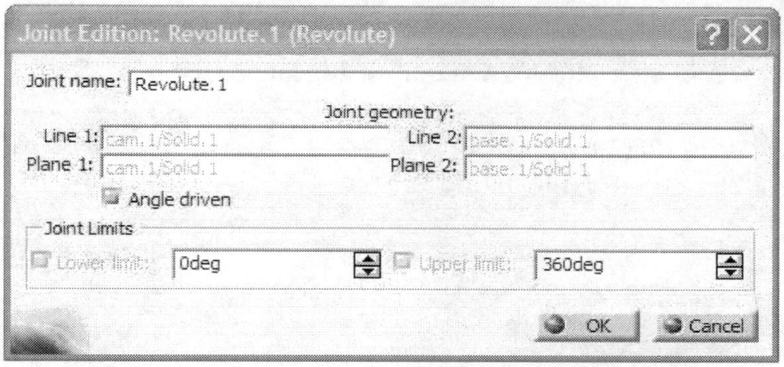

Upon closing the above box and assuming that everything else was done correctly, the following message appears on the screen.

This indeed is good news.

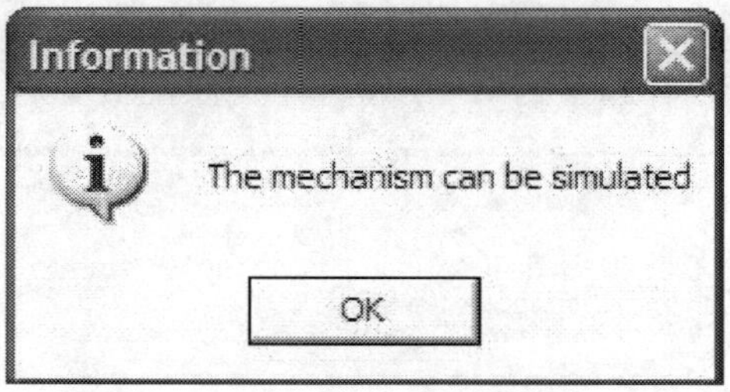

To simulate the motion without regard to time based angular velocity, select the **Simulation** icon  from the **DMU Generic Animation** toolbar 

. This enables you to choose the mechanism to be animated if there are several present. In this case, select Mechanism.1 and close the window.

As soon as the window is closed, a Simulation branch is added to the tree.

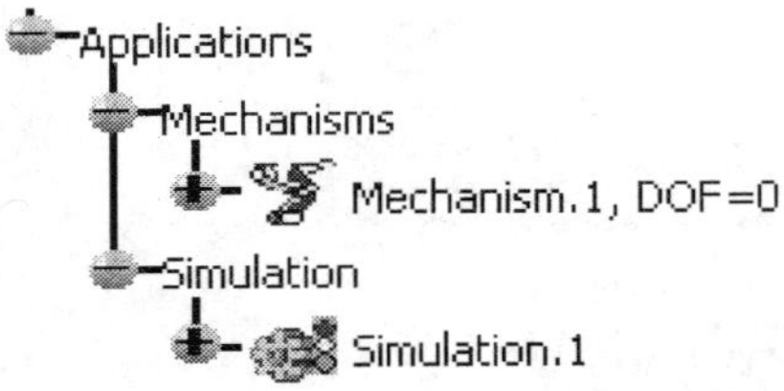

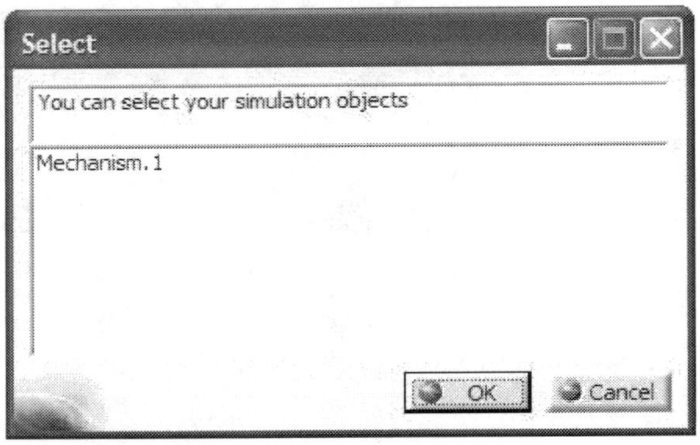

In addition, the two pop up boxes shown below appear.

As you scroll the bar in this toolbar from left to right, the cam begins to rotate, translating the pin along its axis.

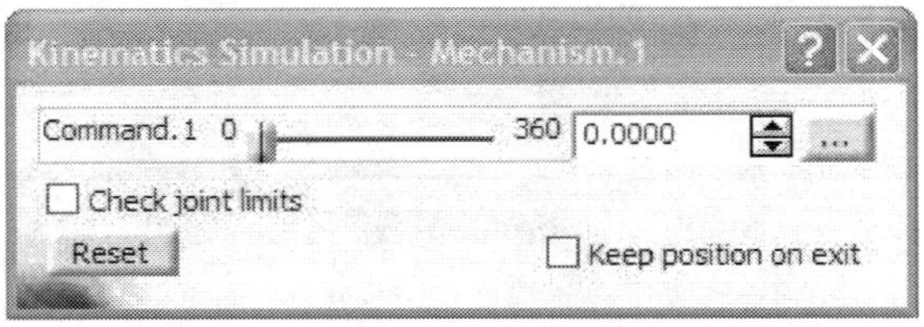

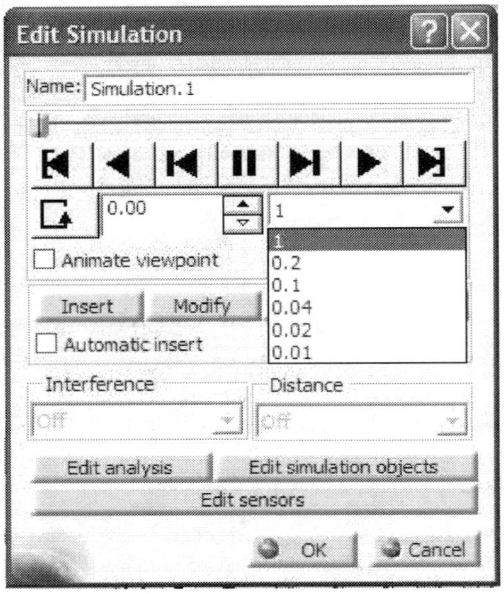

When the scroll bar in the **Kinematics Simulation** pop up box reaches the right extreme end, select the **Insert** button  in the **Edit Simulation** pop up box shown above. This activates the video player buttons shown .

Return the cam to its original position by picking the **Jump to Start** button .

Note that the **Change Loop Mode** button  is also active now.

Apply **Play Forward** button and observe the slow and smooth rotation of the cam. If nothing seems to be moving, change the default value of 1, to a smaller value such as 0.04 or 0.02.

Next, we will introduce the time based angular velocity of the cam given in the problem statement.

5 Creating Laws in the Motion and Simulating the Desired Kinematics

The motion animated this far was not tied to the time parameter or the angular velocity given in the problem statement. You will now introduce some time based physics into the problem. The objective is to specify a constant cam angular velocity of 360 deg/s.

Click on **Simulation with Laws** icon  in the **Simulation** toolbar 

.
You will get the following pop up box indication that you need to add at least a relation between the command and the time parameter.

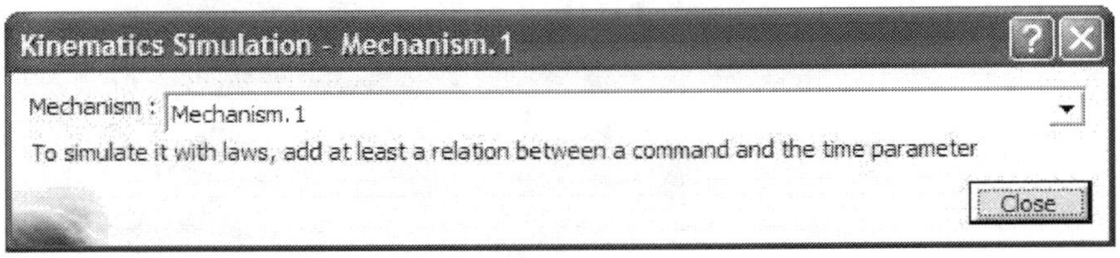

Select the **Formula** icon  from the **Knowledge** toolbar

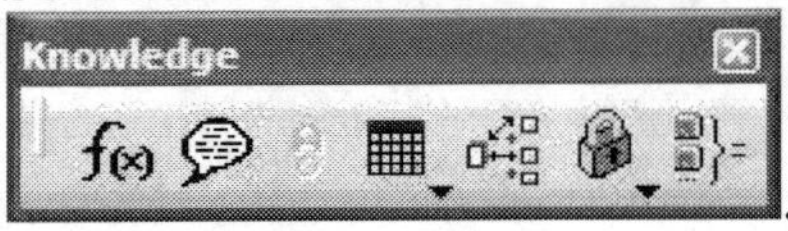

. The pop up box below appears on the screen.

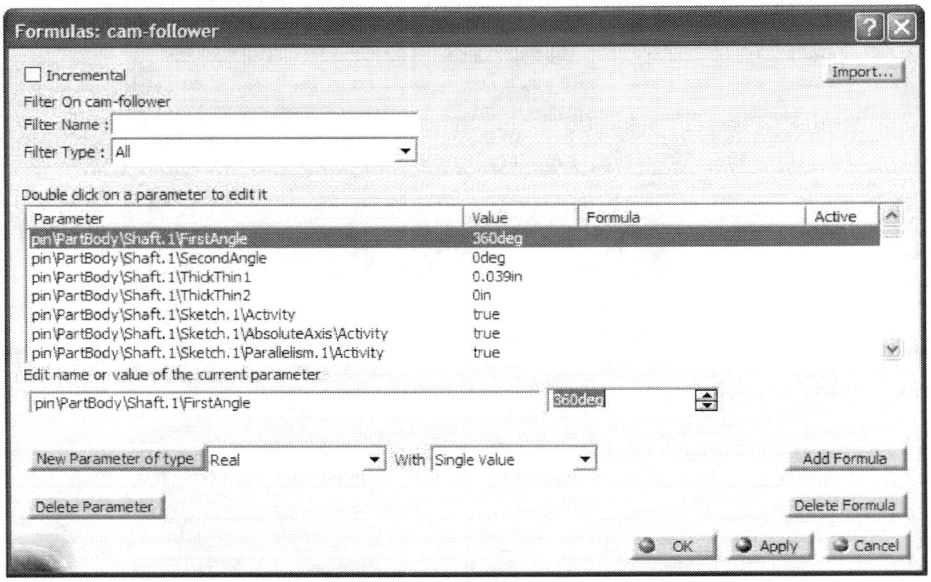

Point the cursor to the **Mechanism.1, DOF=0** branch in the tree and click. The consequence is that only parameters associated with the mechanism are displayed in the **Formulas** box.
The long list is now reduced to two parameters as indicated in the box.

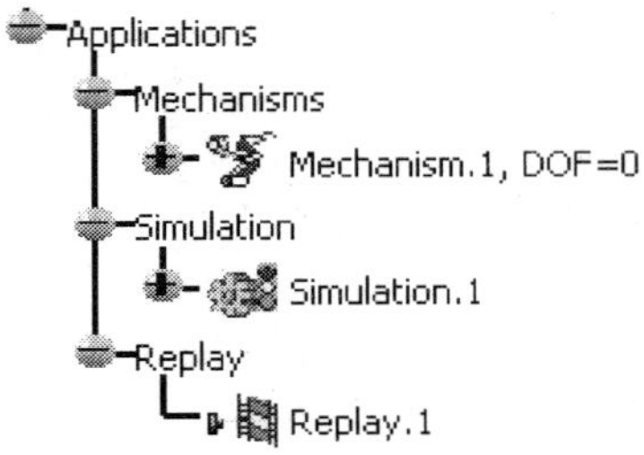

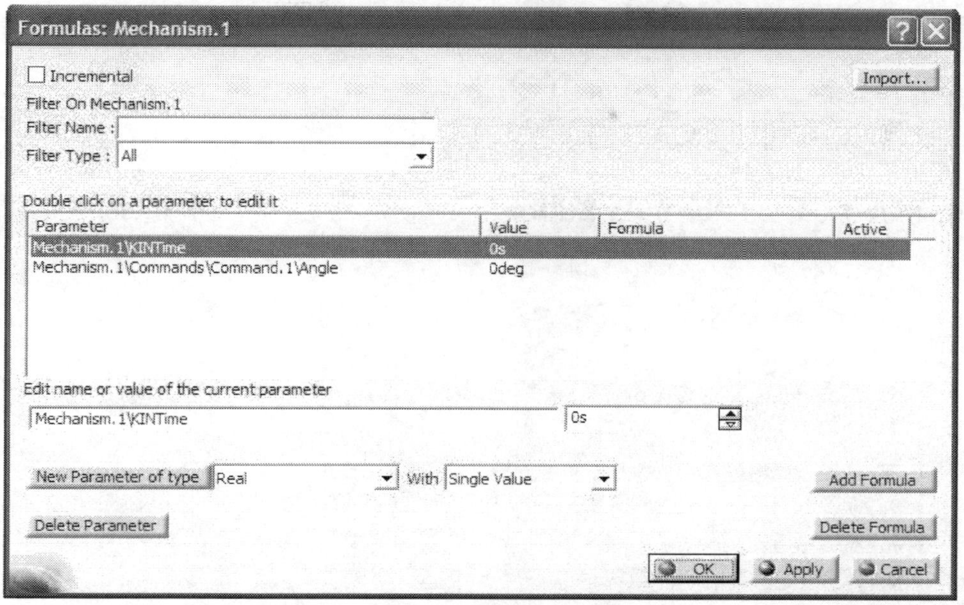

Select the entry **Mechanism.1\Commands\Command.1\Angle** and press the **Add Formula** button . This action kicks you to the **Formula Editor** box.

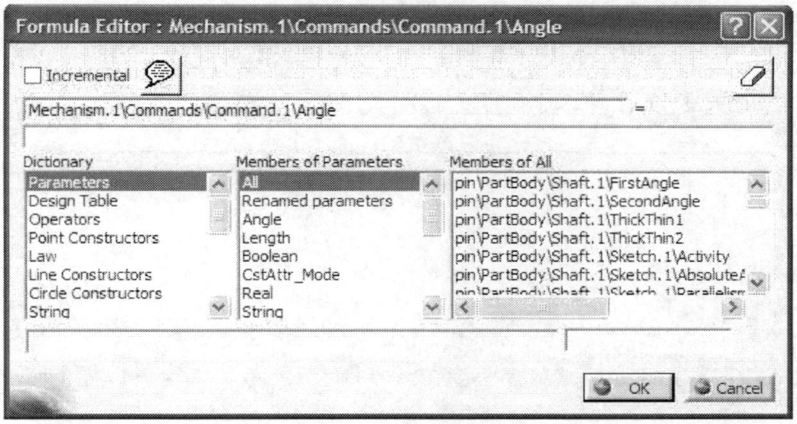

Pick the **Time** entry from the middle column (i.e. **Members of Parameters**).

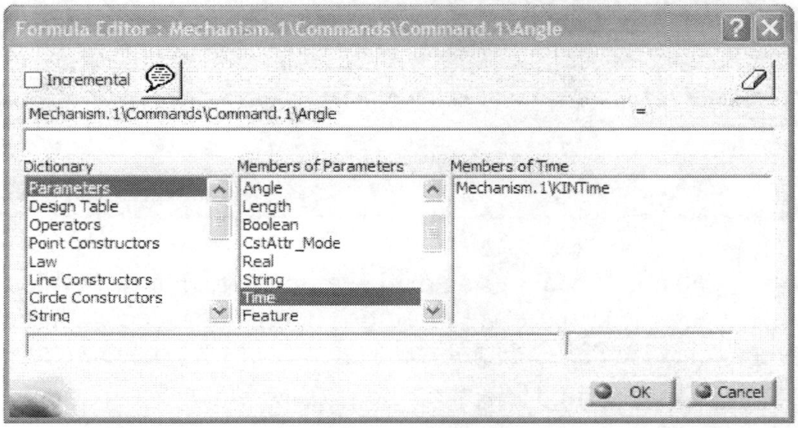

The right hand side of the equality should be such that the formula becomes

$$Mechanism.1 \backslash Commands \backslash Command.1 \backslash Angle = (360\,\text{deg}/1s) * Mechnism.1 \backslash KINTime$$

Therefore, the completed **Formula Editor** box becomes

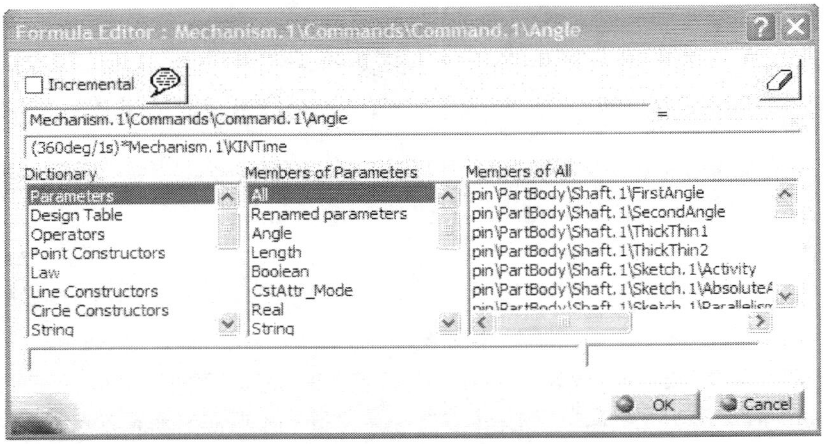

Upon accepting **OK**, the formula is recorded in the **Formulas** pop up box as shown below.

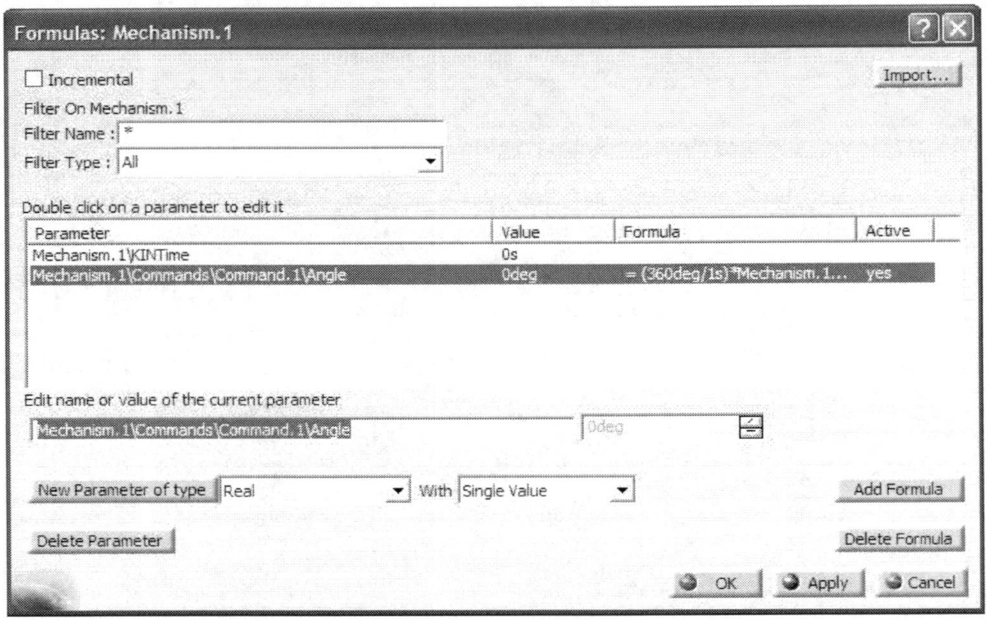

The formula introduced above requires an explanation. Note that the left hand side of the equality is an Angle parameter therefore the entire right hand side should be reducing to an angle in degrees. This is why $(Mechanism.1 \backslash KINTime)$ has been nondimensionalized by introducing a division by (1s). Here, "s" refers to seconds.

In the event that the formula has different units on the different sides of the equality you will get **Warning** messages such as the one shown below.

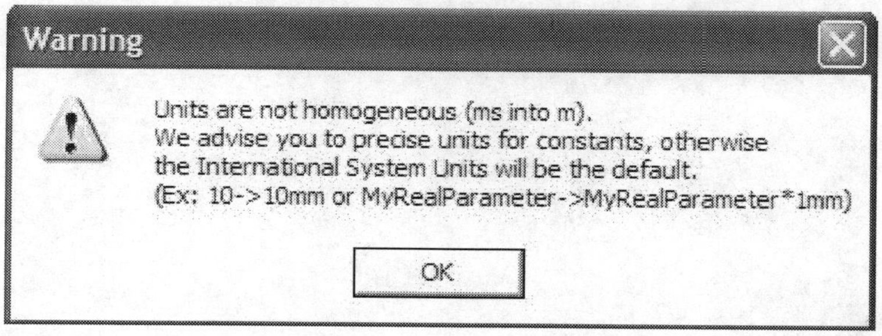

We are spared the warning message because the formula has been properly inputted. Note that the introduced law has appeared in the **Law** branch of the tree.

Keep in mind that our interest is to plot the velocity and accelerations of the follower (pin) tip generated by this motion.

Select the **Speed and Acceleration** icon  from the **DMU Kinematics** toolbar

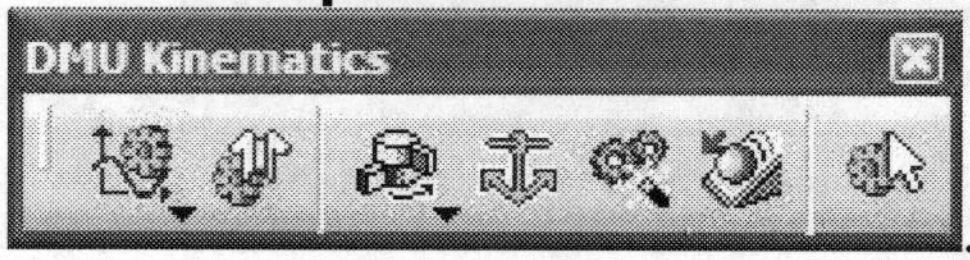

. The pop up box below appears on the Screen.

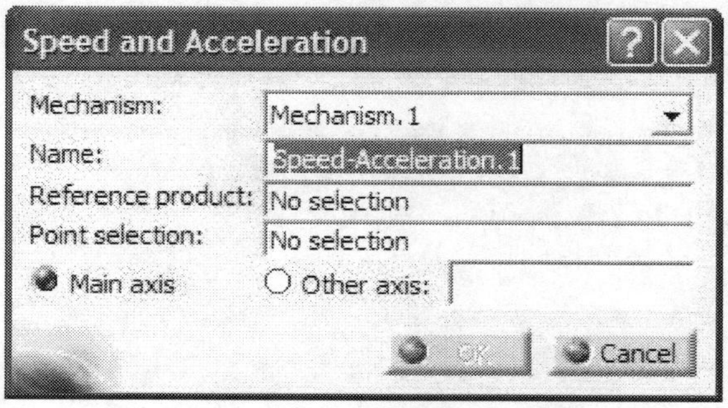

For the **Reference product**, select the **base** from the screen or the tree. For the **Point selection**, pick the tip of the origin of the **pin** from the tree.

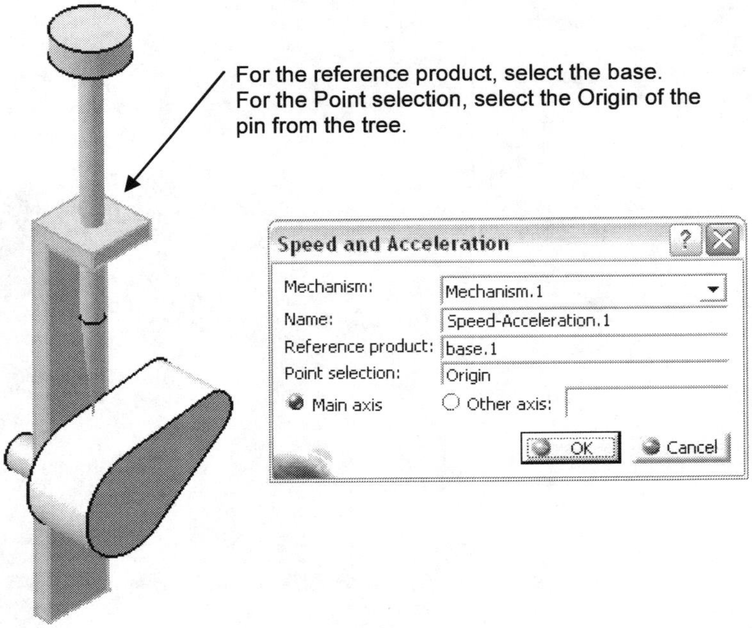

Note that **Speed and Acceleration.1** has appeared in the tree.

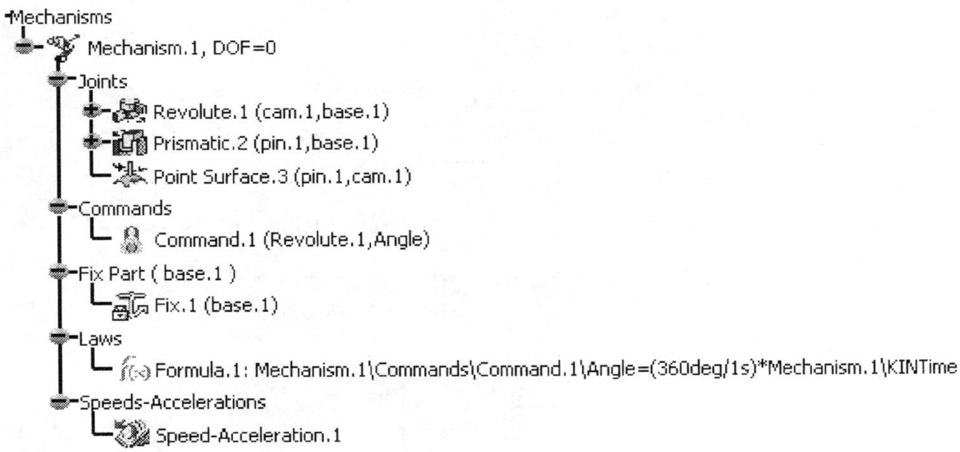

Next we will set things up to simulate the time based motion. Click on **Simulation with Laws** icon  in the **Simulation** toolbar .

This results in the **Kinematics Simulation** pop up box shown below.

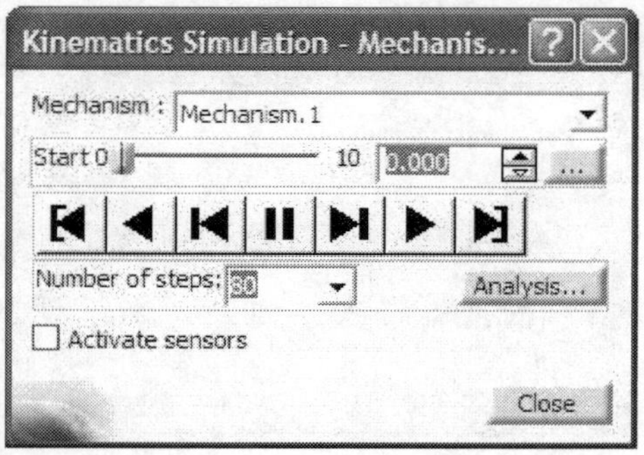

Note that the default time duration is 10 seconds.
To change this value, click on the button 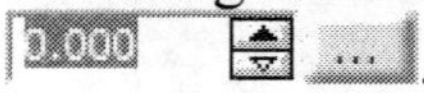. In the resulting pop up box, change the time duration to 1s (this will give one rotation at our angular velocity of 360 deg/s).

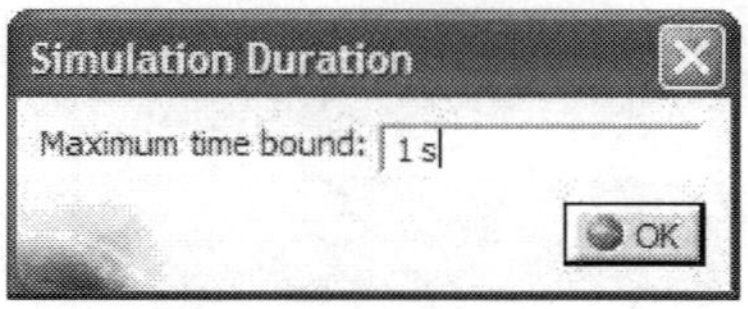

The scroll bar now moves up to 1s.

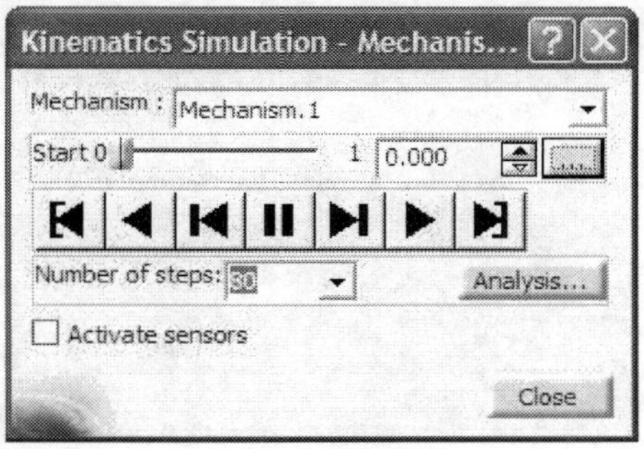

Check the **Activate sensors** box, at the bottom left corner.

You will next have to make certain selections from the accompanying **Sensors** box to indicate the kinematics parameters you would like to compute and store results on.

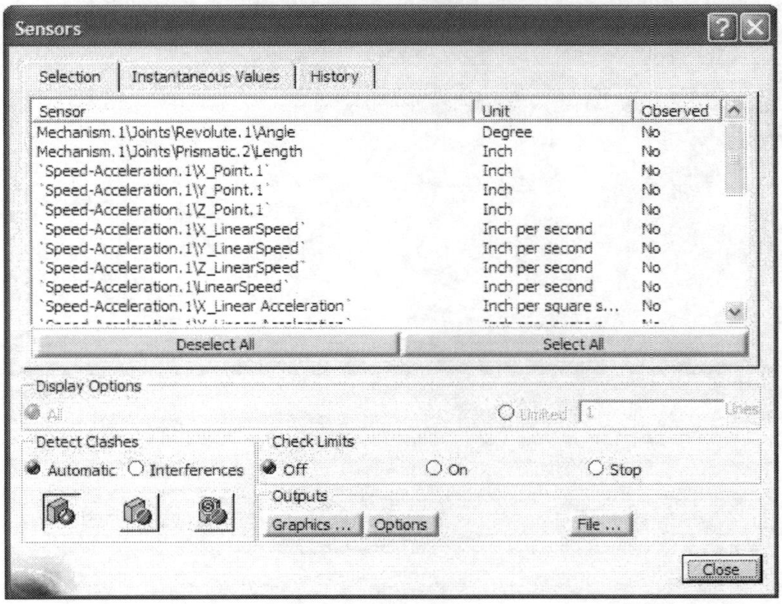

Since we want to plot the pin's velocity and acceleration in the Z direction vs. angle of the cam, click on the following items:

Mechanism.1\Joints\Revolute.1\Angle
Speed-Acceleration.1\Z_LinearSpeed
Speed-Acceleration.1\Z_LinearAcceleration

As you make these selections, the last column in the **Sensors** box, changes to **Yes** for the corresponding items. This is shown below.

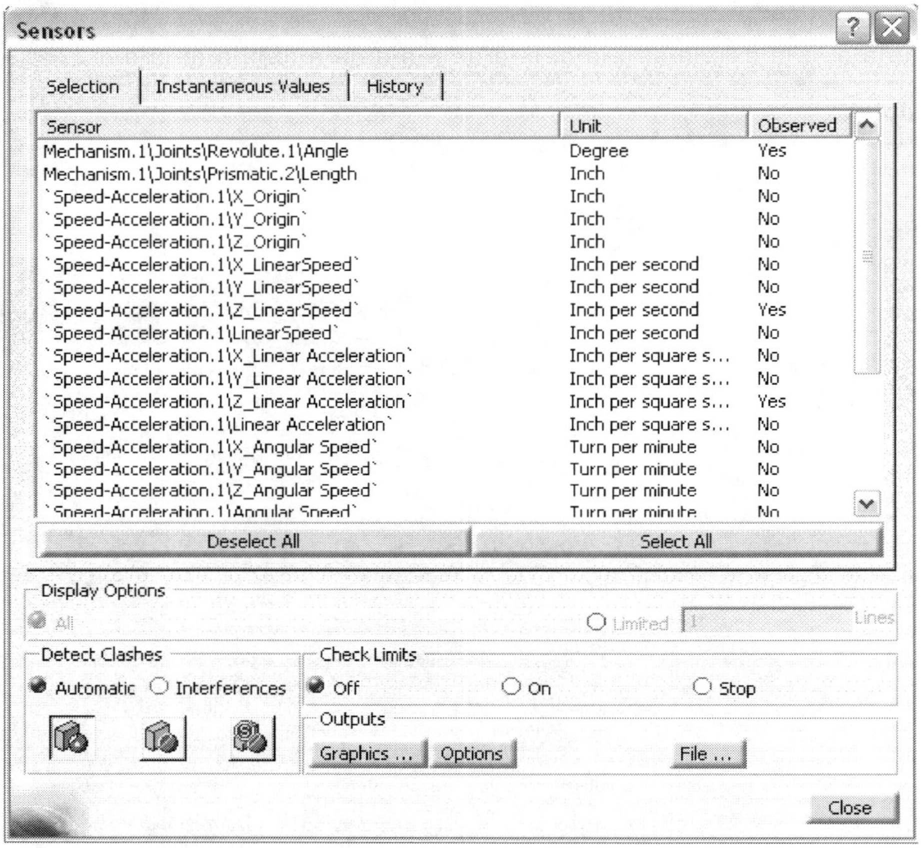

Plots versus anything other than time need to be setup. Since we intend to plot velocity and acceleration vs. angle, click on **Options** in the **Sensors** box. In the **Graphical Representations** box which appears, choose **Customized**, then **Add**. In the **Curve Creation** popup, make the selections for a plot of velocity vs. angle as shown below.

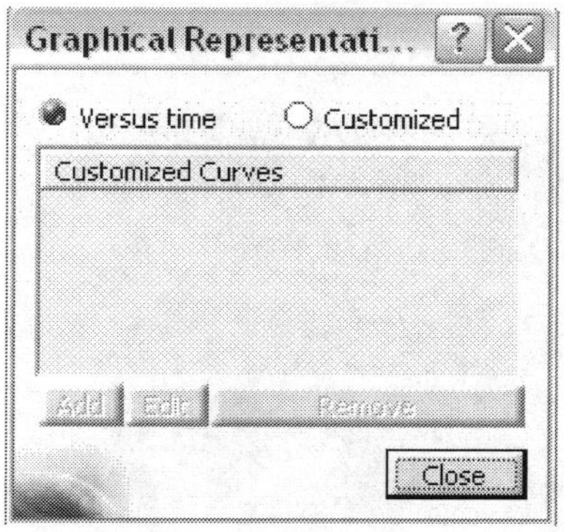

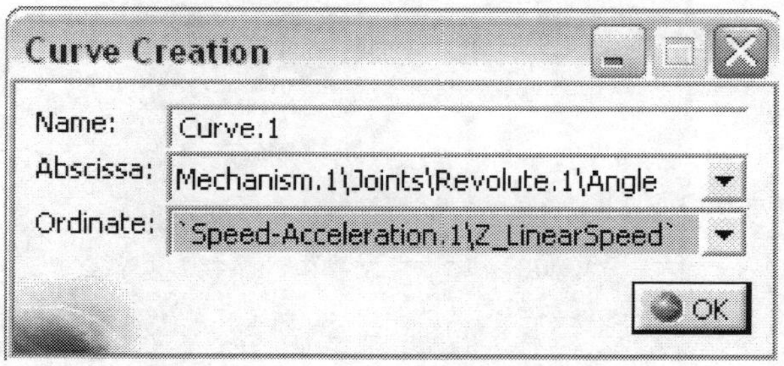

After you **OK** the **Curve Creation** box, click **Add** again and setup the plot for acceleration vs. angle as shown below then **OK** the **Curve Creation** box and **Close** the **Graphical Representations** box.

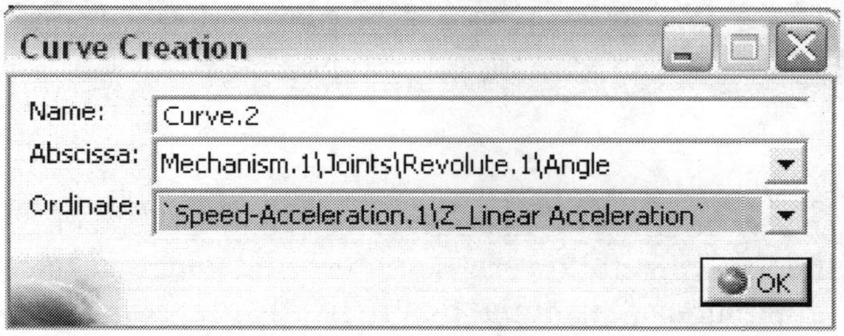

At this point, drag the scroll bar in the **Kinematics Simulation** box. As you do this, the cam rotates about the base hole. Once the bar reaches its right extreme point, the cam has made one full revolution. This corresponds to 1s and a rotation of 360°.

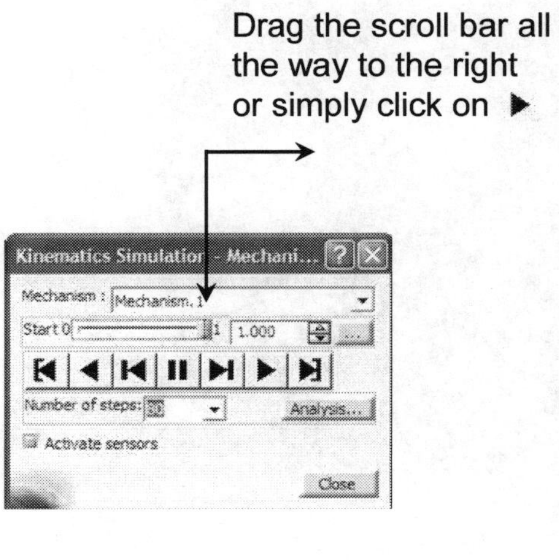

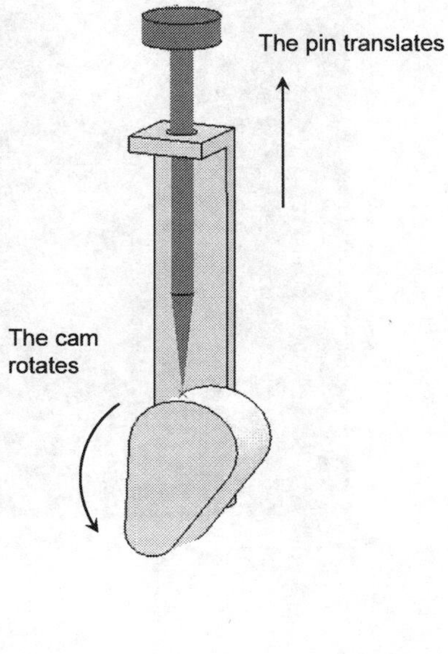

Once the cam makes a full revolution, click on **Graphics** button 

in the **Sensor** box. The result is a window showing the first curve we set up (Curve.1) as shown below. This is the velocity of the pin versus the angle of the cam.

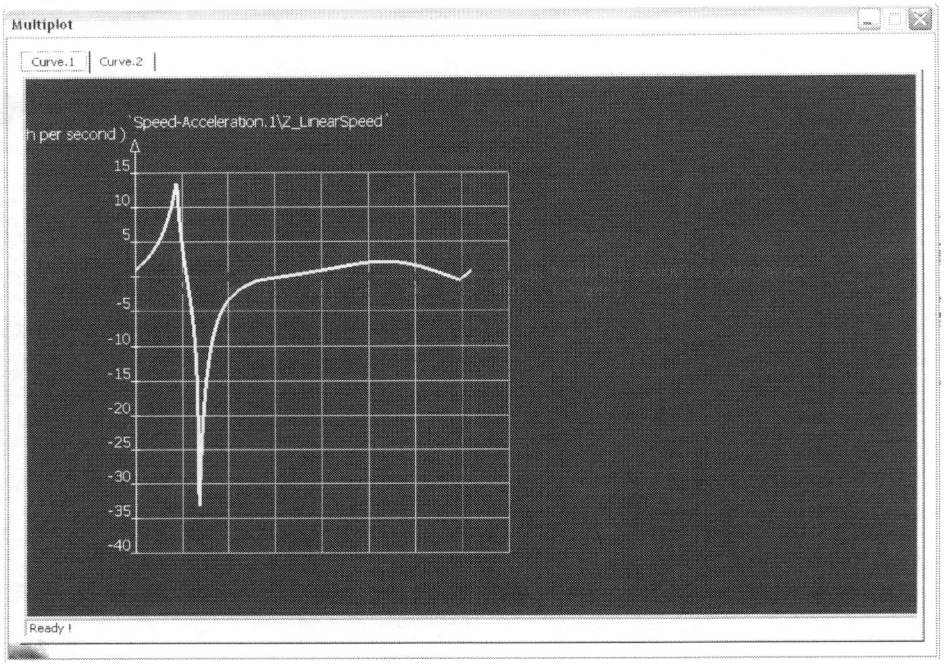

In the **Multiplot** window, toggle to **Curve.2** to see the plot of acceleration versus angle as shown below. Of course this follower was in for some tough accelerations since the profile was tangent continuous only at the first derivative level.

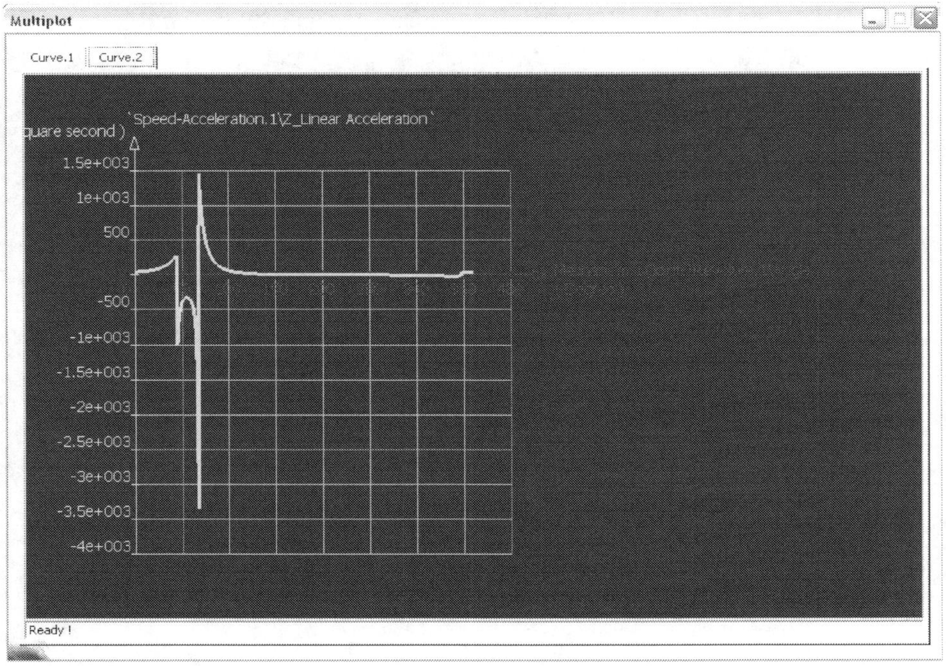

Remember that if you want to create any new plots, you first need to clear the numbers generated already. To do so, click on the **History** tab  of the **Sensors** box and choose **Clear**.

You will next use the **Simultation.1** to create a **Replay** model.

Select the **Compile Simulation** icon  from the **Generic Animation** toolbar 

.

Therefore, in the **Compile Simulation** box, check the **Generate a replay** button. A **Replay.1** branch has also been added to the tree.

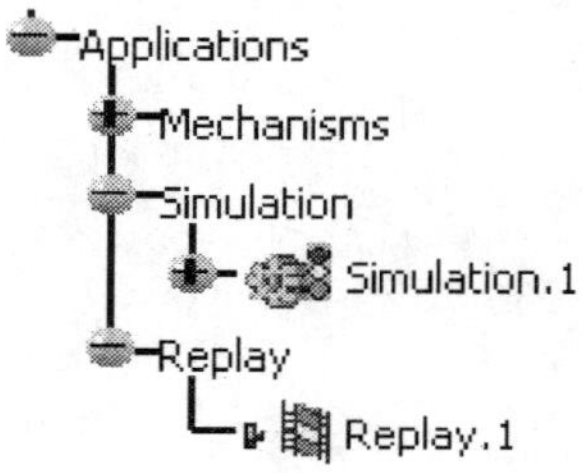

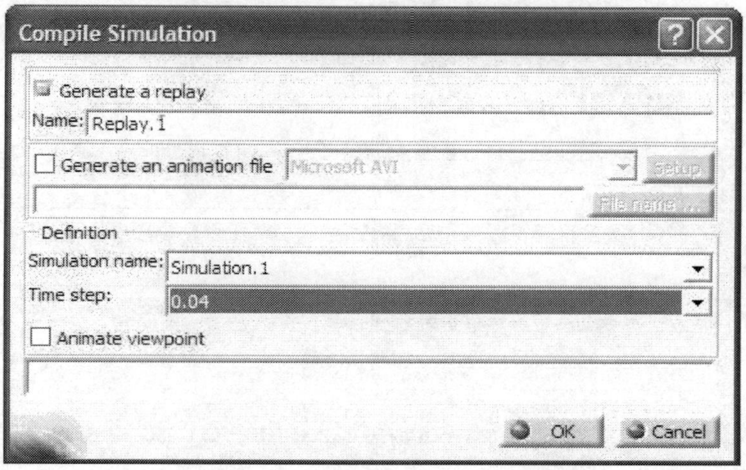

Double click on the **Replay.1** branch of the tree to open the **Replay** pop up box below.

By clicking on the **Step Forward** key  repeatedly, you can move the cam in steps and the therefore the pin translates in discrete steps. For example several steps forward, creates the following formation of the assembly.

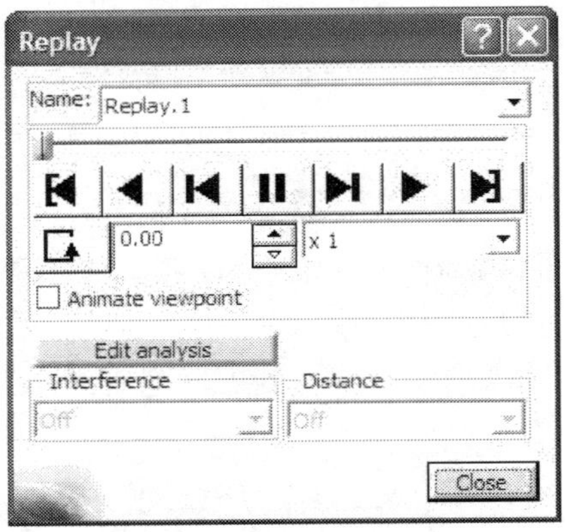

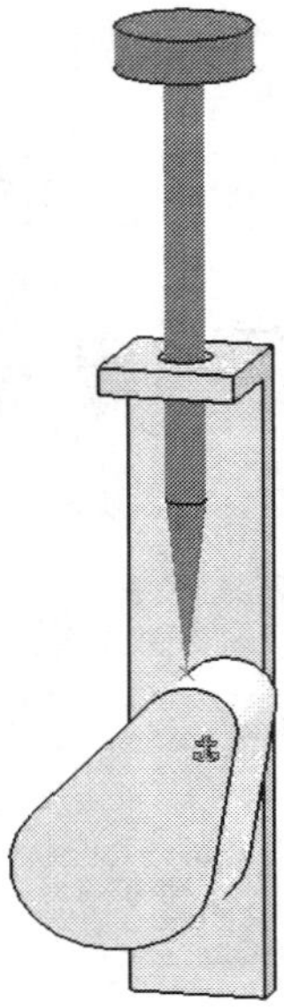

The formation of the assembly shown on the left corresponds to current position of the scroll bar

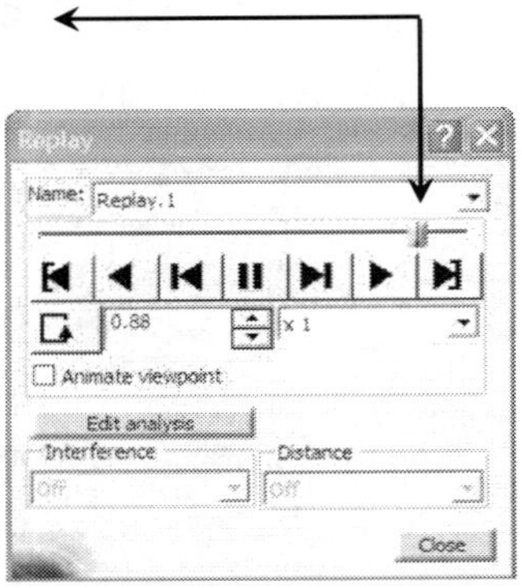

In the next few steps you will find the vertical distance (the z distance) between the pin and the base.

Select the **Distance and Band Analysis** icon  from the **DMU Sp** toolbar 

.

The pop up box below opens.

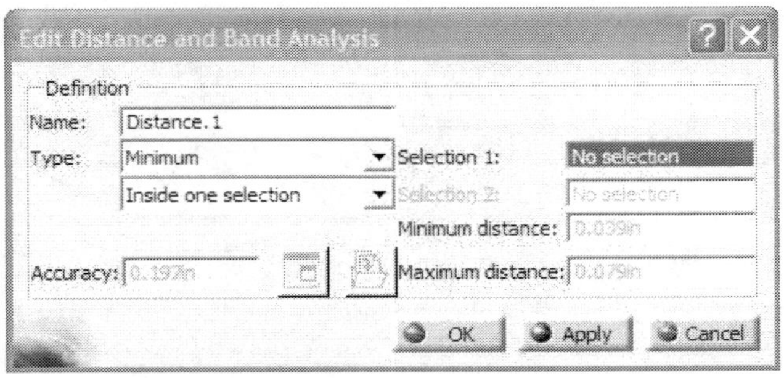

For the **Type** box, select **Along z** from the pull down menu. Also for the third box from the top, choose **Between two selections** in the pull down menu.

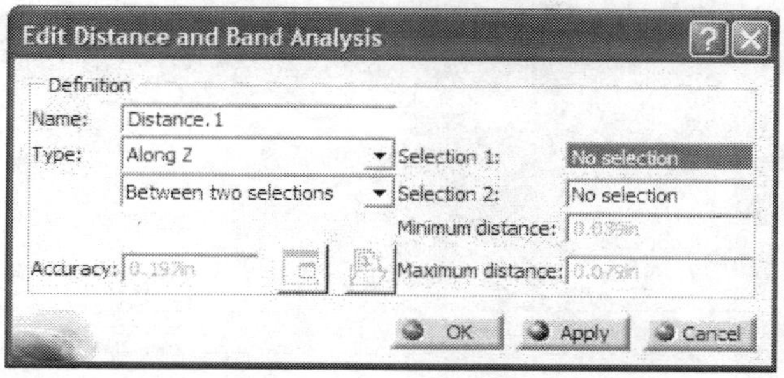

For **Selection 1**, choose the pin from the screen, and for **Selection 2**, pick the base from the screen.

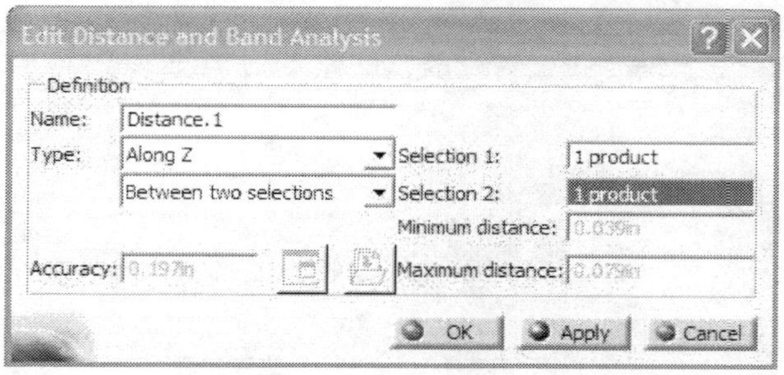

Click on the **Apply** button . In the resulting **Preview** window, the minimum z-distance between the two parts is shown. Detailed information is also supplied in the accompanied **Edit Distance and Band Analysis** pop up box.

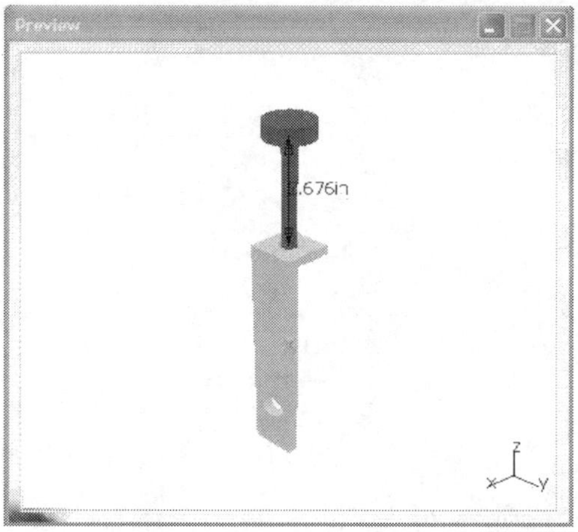

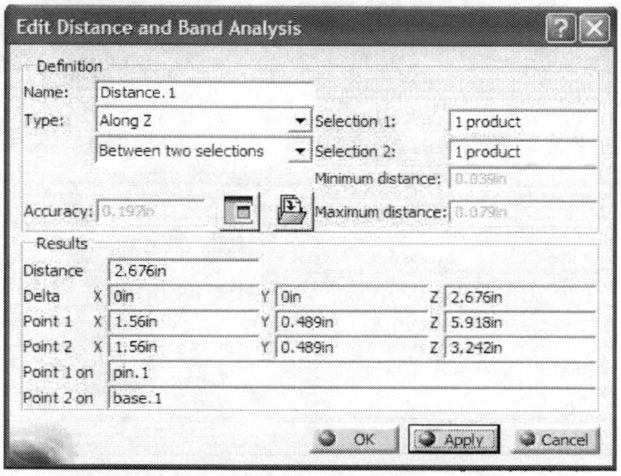

While all these windows are open, the position of the cam can be modified using the **Step Forward** key  in the **Replay** box. Once the desired position is obtained, pressing the **Apply** button  leads to the new distance information. If you get a zero distance, make sure you have a clearance condition between your pin and the base.

A typical new configuration and the minimum z-distance are shown next.

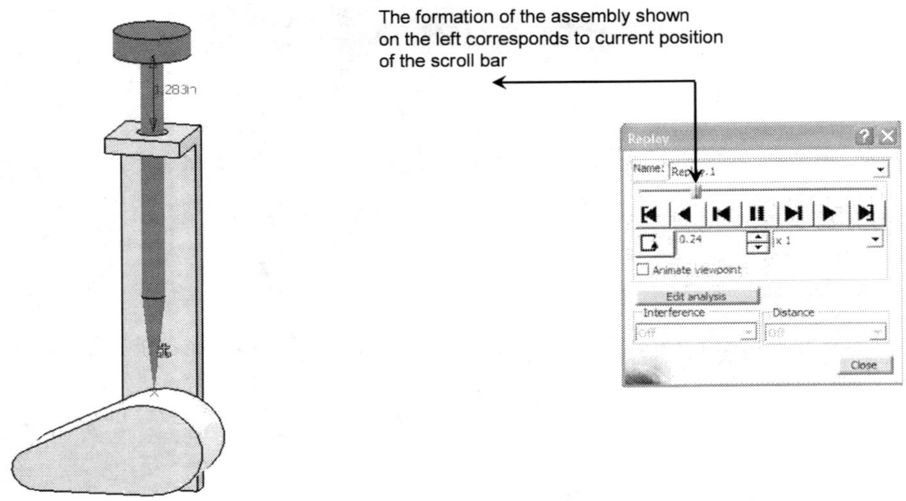

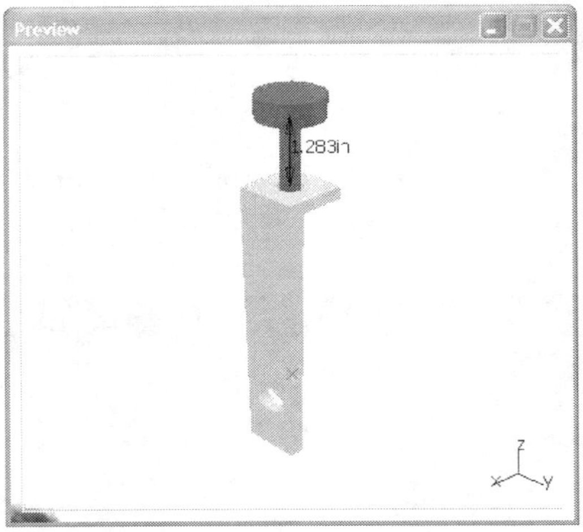

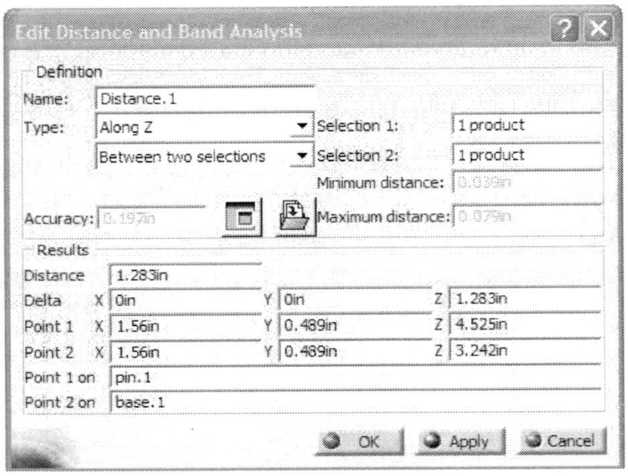

Note that a Distance.1 branch has appeared in the tree.

This concludes the tutorial.

Chapter 9

Planetary Gear Mechanism

Introduction

In this tutorial you will create a planetary gear mechanism similar to those used in a typical automatic transmission of an automobile. Roll-Curve joints are used to emulate the gear interaction. The mechanism is simulated by first fixing the ring gear, and then fixing the arm carrier (analogous to different gear selections in the transmission analogy).

1 Problem Statement

Typical automatic transmissions found in cars and trucks use a planetary gear mechanism to provide the various forward gear ratios and reverse. A simplified model of such a mechanism is displayed below.
The planet and the sun are tied together with the arm carrier (not labeled in the figure).

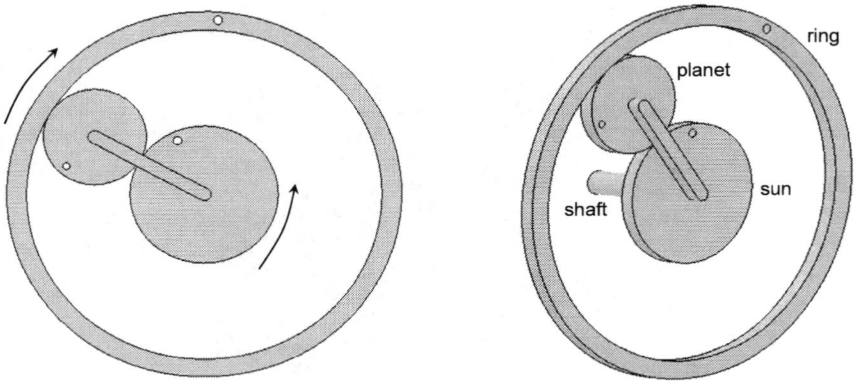

In the present tutorial it is assumed that the sun and the ring have N_S=30 and N_R=72 teeth respectively. Using the basics of the gear theory, this assumption determines the relative dimensions of the part.

With the sun, carrier, and ring all allowed to rotate about their axes independently (constrained only by any gear engagements), this arrangement would be a two degree of freedom system. As we will discuss below, in a typical transmission, different gear ratios can be obtained by fixing the sun, the carrier, or the ring and using two other as the input and output components. Partial results are described in the following table.

Input	Output	Fix	Formula	Gear Ratio
sun	carrier	ring	$1+N_R/N_S$	3.4:1
carrier	ring	sun	$1/(1+ N_S/N_R)$	0.71:1
sun	ring	carrier	$- N_R/N_S$	-2.4:1

Clearly, the first gear ratio in the table is a reduction in speed, while the second is an overdrive. Furthermore, the last scenario is a reduction of speed in the reverse direction. The objective of this tutorial is to simulate this system for the ring fixed and again for the carrier fixed and to verify the above gear ratios result.

2 Overview of this Tutorial

In this tutorial you will:

1. Model the five CATIA parts required (shaft, sun, planet, carrier, and ring).
2. Create an assembly (CATIA Product) containing the parts.
3. Constrain the assembly in such a way that the assembly constraints are equivalent from a degrees of freedom standpoint to four revolute joints (one between the ring and the shaft, one between the sun and the shaft, one between the carrier and the sun, and one between the carrier and the planet).
4. Enter the **Digital Mockup** workbench and convert the assembly constraints into four revolute joints.
5. Manually create two roll-curve joints which emulate the interaction between the sun, ring and planet parts.
6. Simulate the relative motion of the mechanism by fixing the ring and driving the sun.
7. Add a formula to implement the time based kinematics associated with constant angular velocity of the sun.
8. Simulate the desired constant angular velocity motion and generate plots of the kinematic results illustrating the achieved gear ratio.
9. As a separate simulation, release the ring, and fix the carrier and repeat the Steps 7 and 8.

3 Creation of the Assembly in Mechanical Design Solutions

In CATIA, model five parts named **sun, ring, planet, carrier, and the shaft** as shown below. The critical dimensions of these parts are also displayed. The padded length of these pars is irrelevant however we have used a pad distance of 0.5 in for this purpose. Clearly, the shaft has a larger pad value. The purpose of the holes present in the ring, sun and planet is to be able to visually observe the motion of the mechanism. Because of the relative dimensions of the ring and the sun, one can assume that the ring poses 72 teeth whereas the sun has 30 teeth.

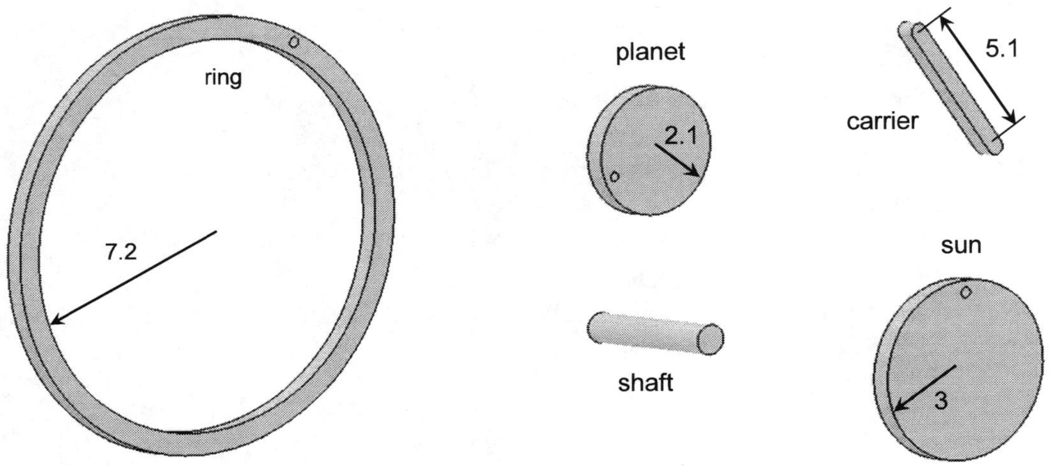

In order to generate angular velocity plots, you need to create sensors at desired points. Therefore, you need to create three points at the centers of the small holes. This is a straightforward process, however; we suggest the following approach to create the point for the sun.

Load the part named **sun** into the **Part Design** workbench 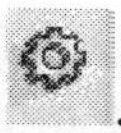.

Select the **Point** icon  from the **Reference Element** toolbar 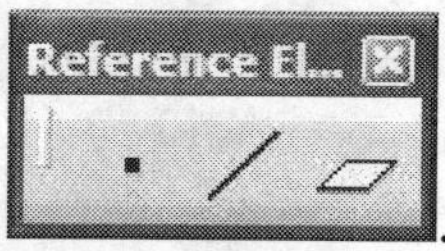.

In the resulting pop up box, for the **Point type**, choose **Circle/Sphere center**.

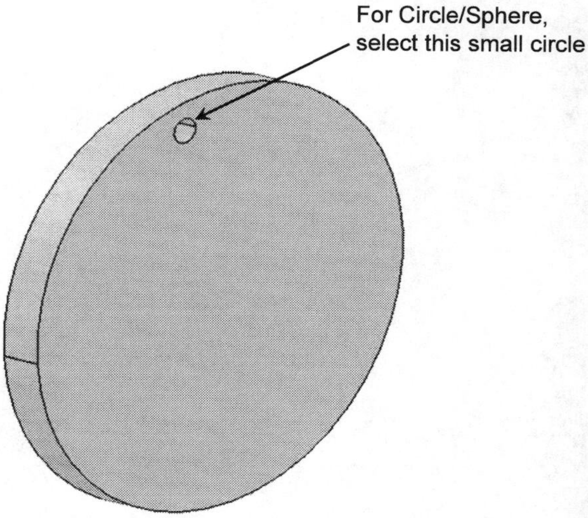

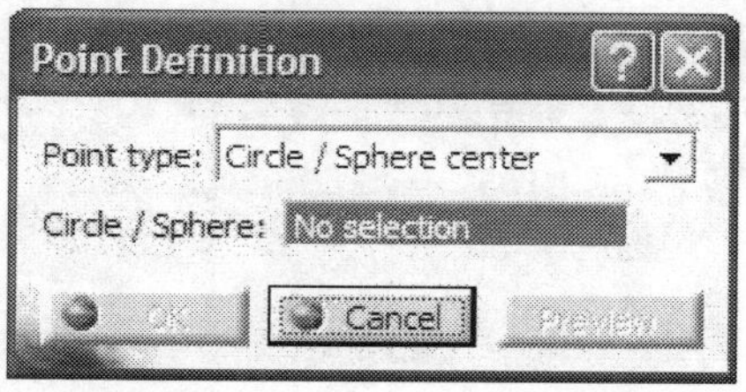

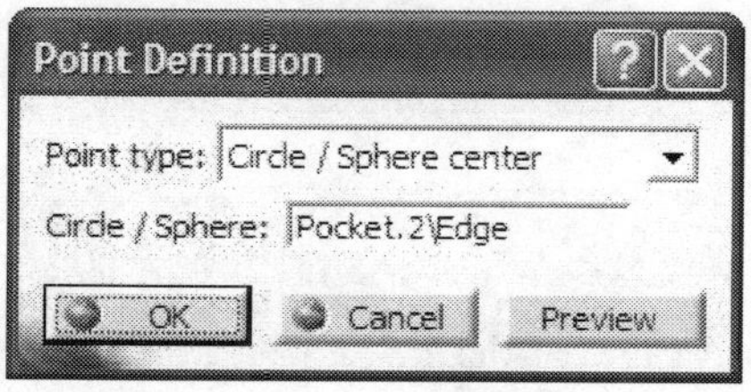

This process creates a point at the desired location. Repeat the procedure to create two other points on the ring and planet.

Next, we will assemble the parts. Enter the **Assembly Design** workbench  which can be achieved by different means depending on your CATIA customization. For example, from the standard Windows toolbar, select **File > New** .
From the box shown on the right, select **Product**. This moves you to the **Assembly Design** workbench and creates an assembly with the default name **Product.1**.

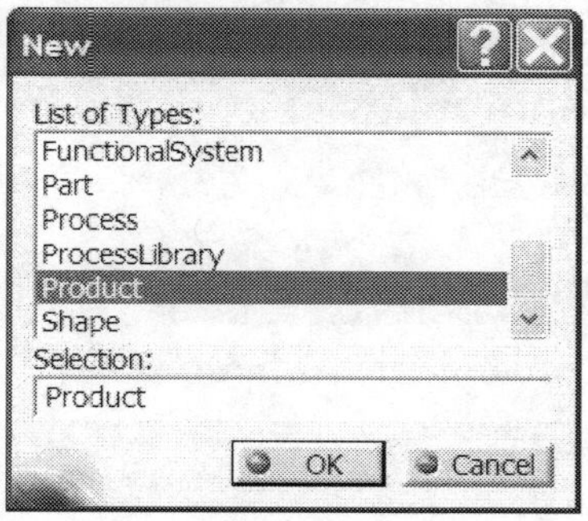

In order to change the default name, move the cursor to **Product.1** in the tree, right click and select **Properties** from the menu list.

From the **Properties** box, select the **Product** tab and in **Part Number** type **planetary_gear**.

This will be the new product name throughout the chapter. The tree on the top left corner of your computer screen should look as displayed on the right.

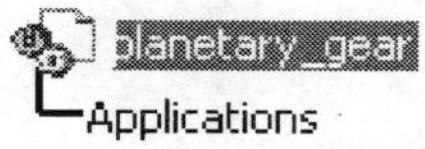

The next step is to insert the existing parts block and base into the assembly just created.

From the standard Windows toolbar, select **Insert > Existing Component**.
From the **File Selection** pop up box choose **carrier**, **planet**, **ring**, **shaft**, and **sun**.
Remember that in CATIA multiple selections are made with the **Ctrl** key.
The tree is modified to indicate that the parts have been inserted.

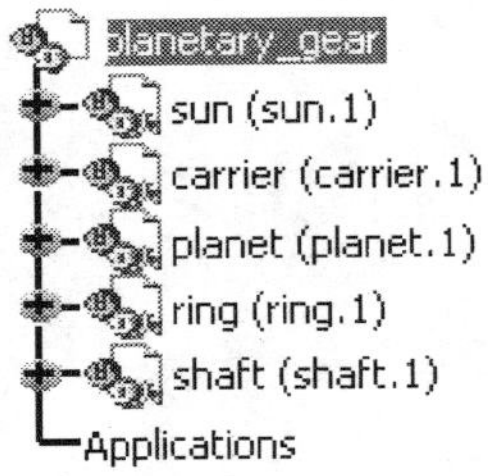

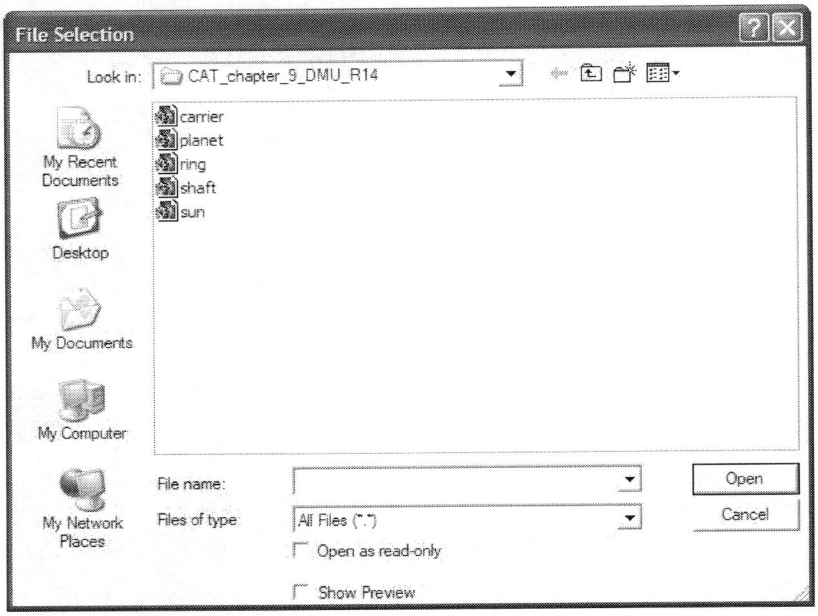

Depending on how the parts were created, they may appear tangled up on your screen such as the configuration below.

To make the tasks easier, you can use the

Manipulation icon  from the **Move** toolbar

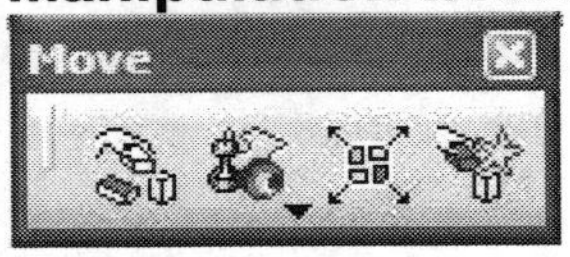

to rearrange them in more convenient configuration.

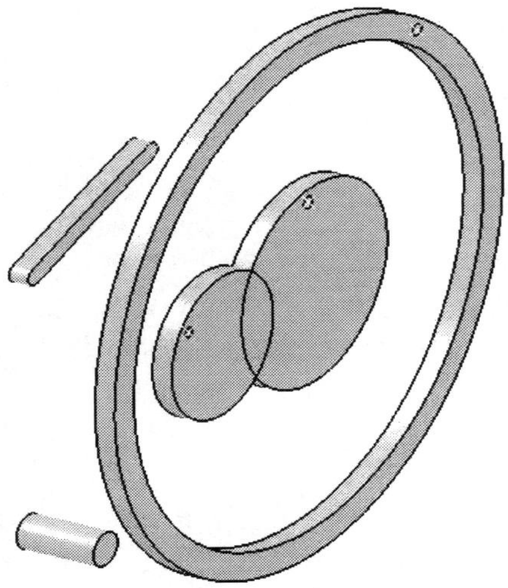

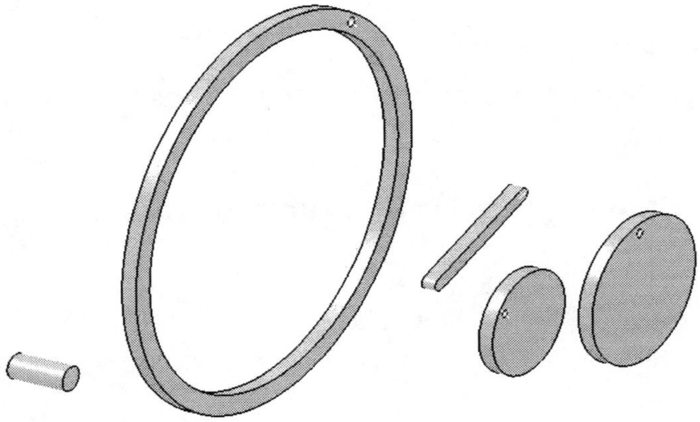

The best way of saving your work is to save the entire assembly.
Double click on the top branch of the tree. This is to ensure that you are in the **Assembly Design** workbench.
Select the **Save** icon . The **Save As** pop up box allows you to rename if desired. The default name is the **planetary_gear**. CATIA also informs you that this action causes other save operations which you will accept.

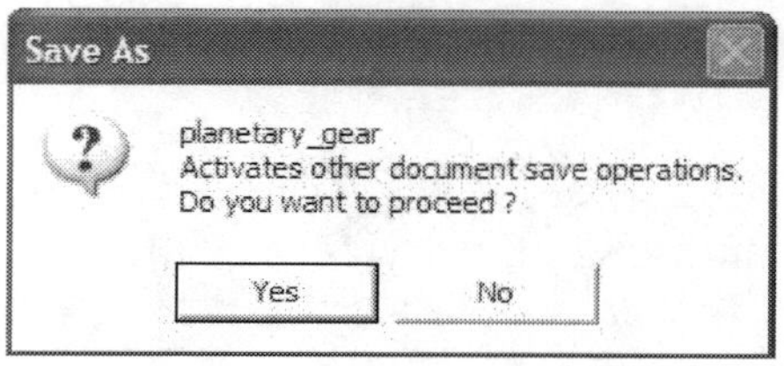

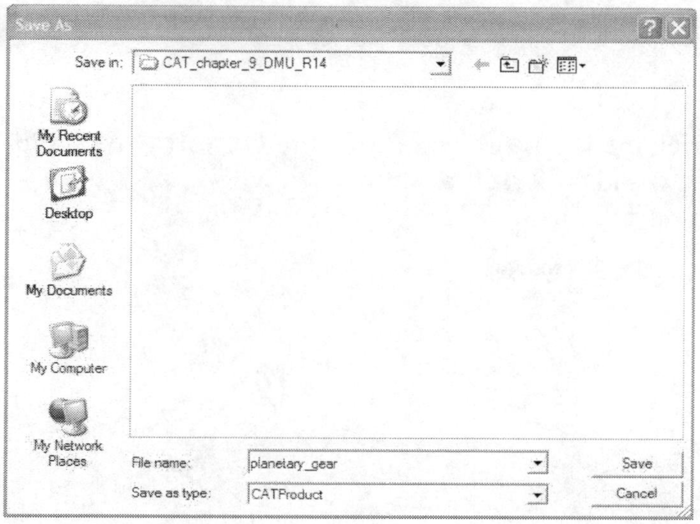

Your next task is to impose assembly constraints. We'll begin by anchoring the shaft. This part will serve as our inertial reference. A part consisting only of an axis system could also have been used for this purpose.

Select the **Fix Component** icon  from the **Constraints** toolbar 

. Pick the **shaft** from the screen or from the tree.

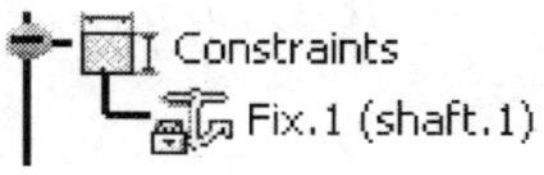

We would like to remove all of the degrees of freedom of the sun with respect to the shaft except for rotation about the axes of the parts. This will be done by constraining the two axes to be coincident and then adding a surface contact constraint to remove translation along the axes.

Pick the **Coincidence** icon from **Constraints** toolbar and select the axes of the **sun** and the **shaft** as shown.

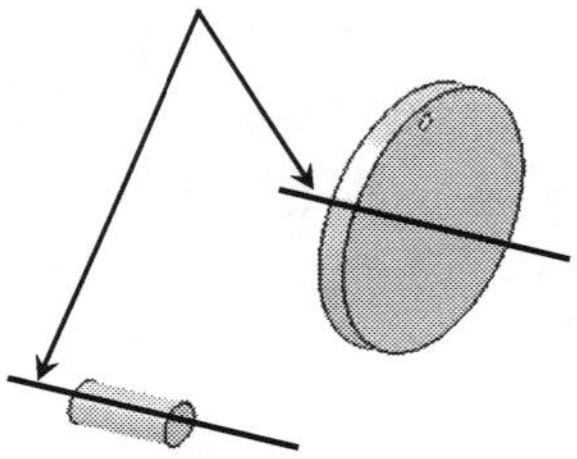

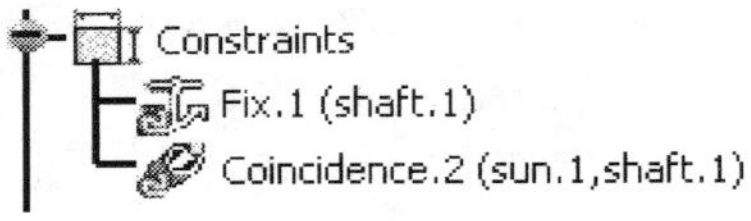

Pick the **Contact** icon from **Constraints** toolbar and select the surfaces of the **sun** and the **shaft** as shown below.

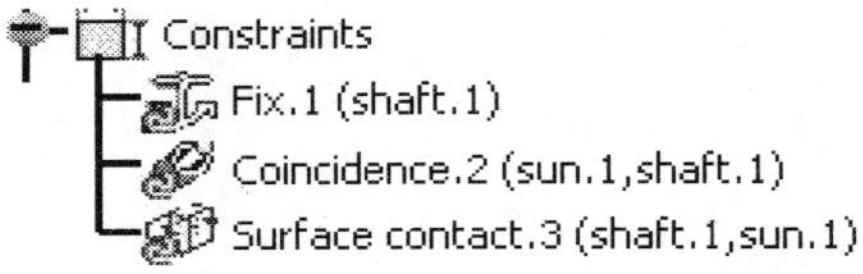

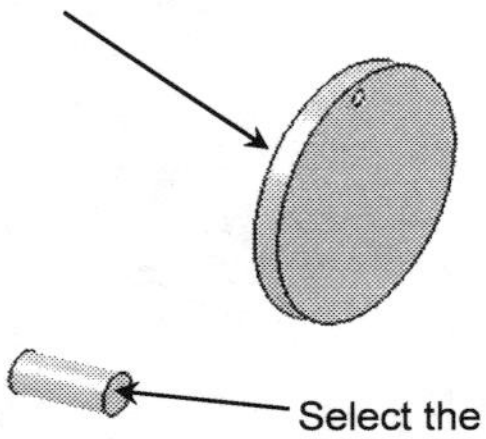

If the **Update** icon is used, the shaft and the sun are reoriented to impose the assembly constraints as shown. However, if you chose to do so, use the **Manipulation** icon to separate the parts to facilitate imposing the next constraint. At this point, you have created sufficient assembly constraints for a revolute joint to be automatically created later in DMU.

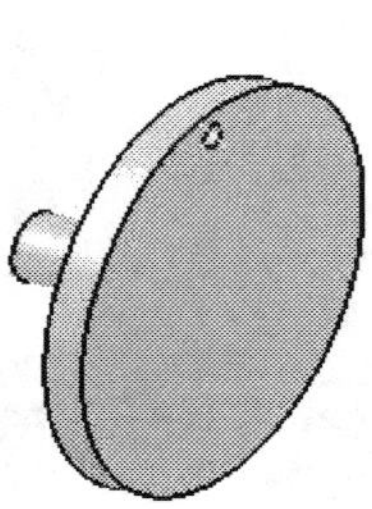

A similar sequence will be followed to constrain the ring to the shaft. Pick the **Coincidence** icon from the **Constraints** toolbar and select the axes of the **shaft** and the **ring** as shown. Note that for selecting the axis of the ring, you can point the cursor to the curved surface of the ring. This makes the selection process much easier.

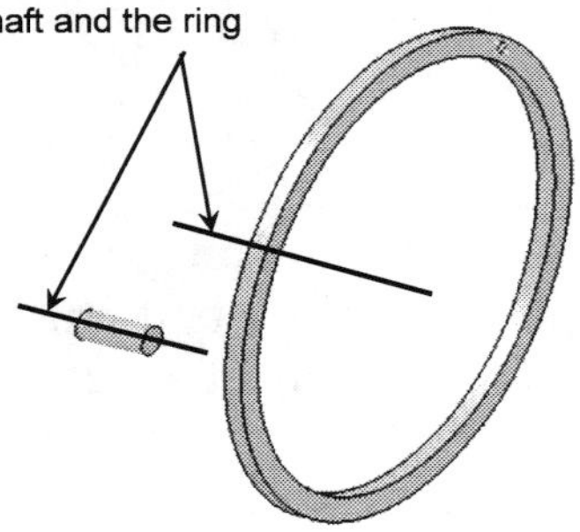

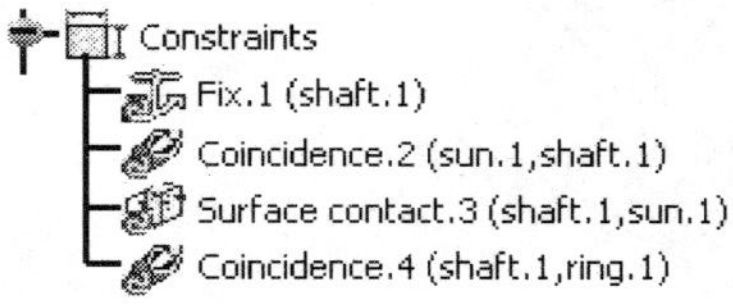

Pick the **Contact** icon  from **Constraints** toolbar and select the surfaces of the **ring** and the **shaft** as shown below.

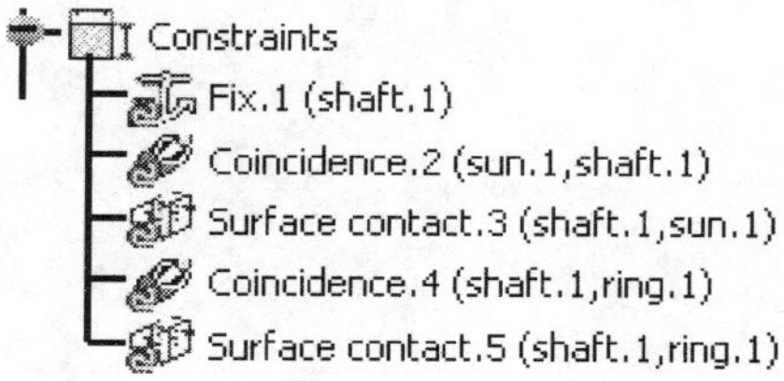

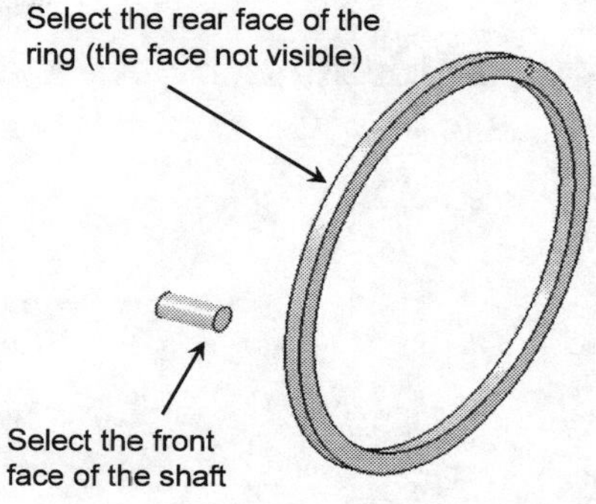

If the **Update** icon  is used, the shaft and the sun are reoriented to impose the assembly constraints as shown. However, if you chose to do so, use the **Manipulation** icon  to separate the parts to facilitate imposing the next constraint.

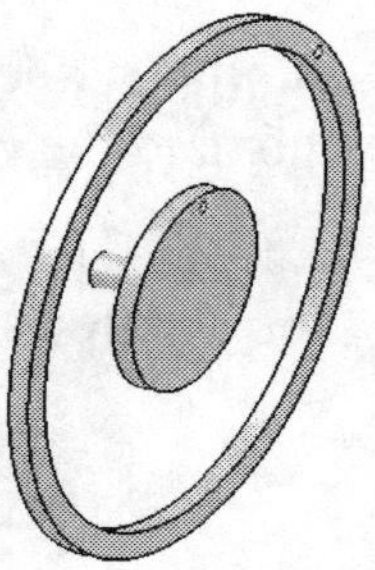

You will next create the needed assembly constraints between the **sun** and the **carrier** for a revolute joint.

Pick the **Coincidence** icon  from **Constraints** toolbar and select the axes of the **sun** and the **carrier** as shown. (The system could also be modeled by connecting the carrier to the shaft, but we'll stick with connecting the carrier to the sun herein).

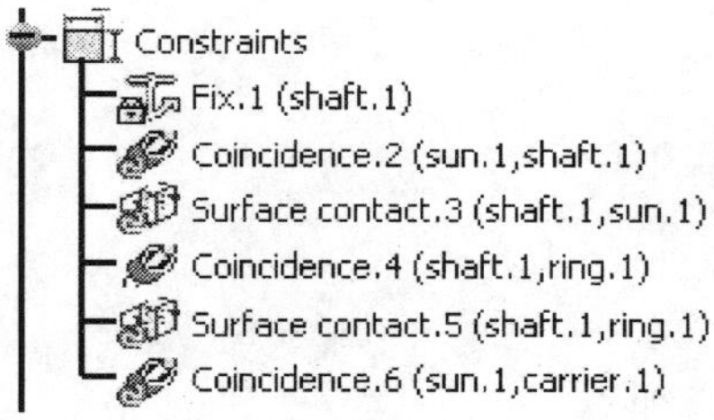

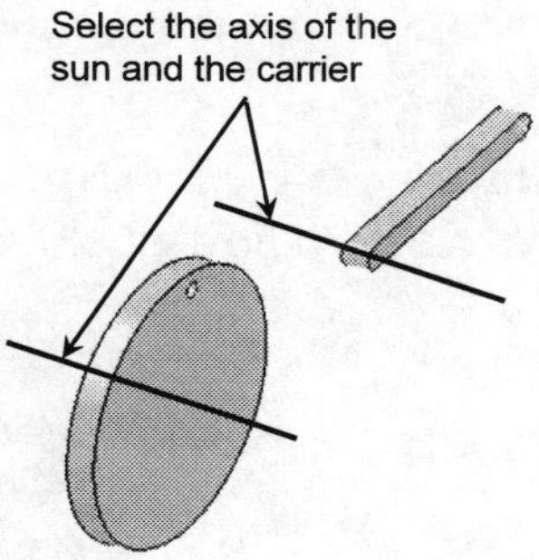

Pick the **Contact** icon  from **Constraints** toolbar and select the surfaces of the **sun** and the **carrier** as shown below.

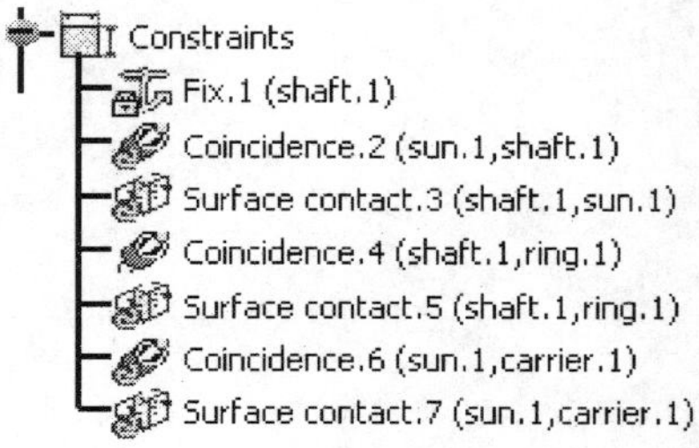

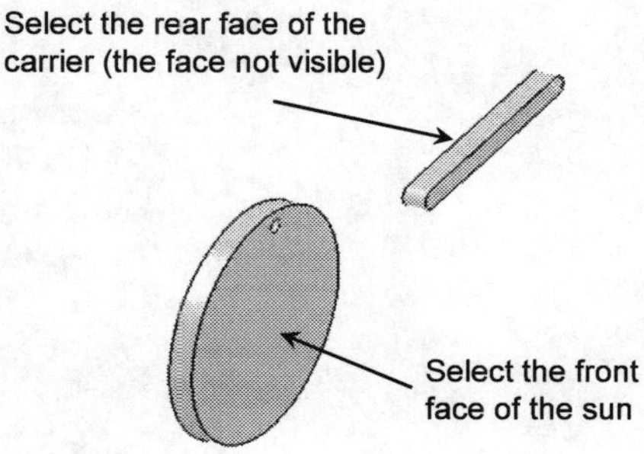

Use the **Update** icon to check your constraints.

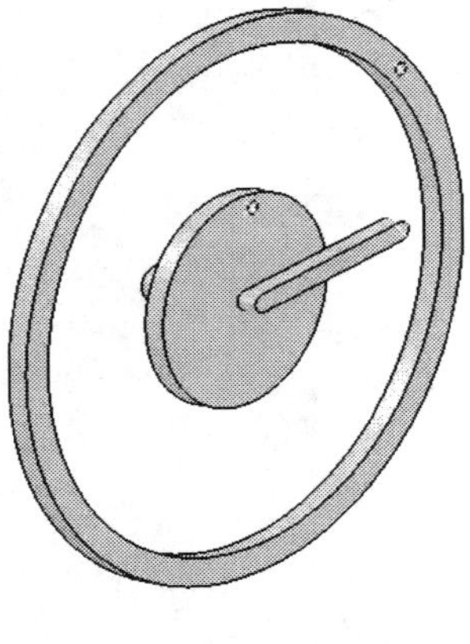

A similar sequence will be used to constrain the planet and the carrier. Pick the **Coincidence** icon from **Constraints** toolbar and select the axes of the **planet** and the **carrier** as shown.

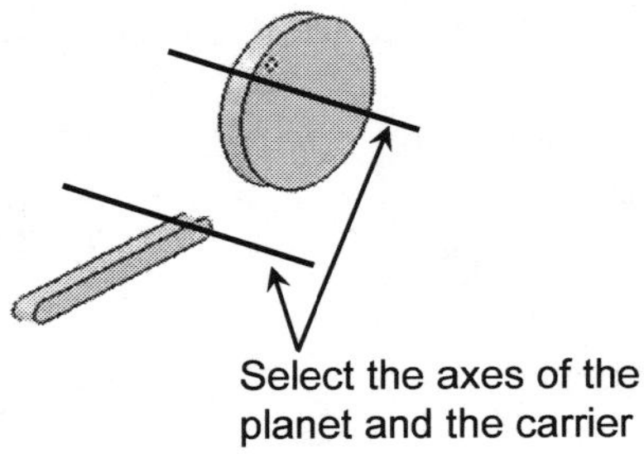

- Constraints
  - Fix.1 (shaft.1)
  - Coincidence.2 (sun.1,shaft.1)
  - Surface contact.3 (shaft.1,sun.1)
  - Coincidence.4 (shaft.1,ring.1)
  - Surface contact.5 (shaft.1,ring.1)
  - Coincidence.6 (sun.1,carrier.1)
  - Surface contact.7 (sun.1,carrier.1)
  - Coincidence.8 (planet.1,carrier.1)

Pick the **Contact** icon from **Constraints** toolbar and select the surfaces of the **planet** and the **carrier** as shown below.

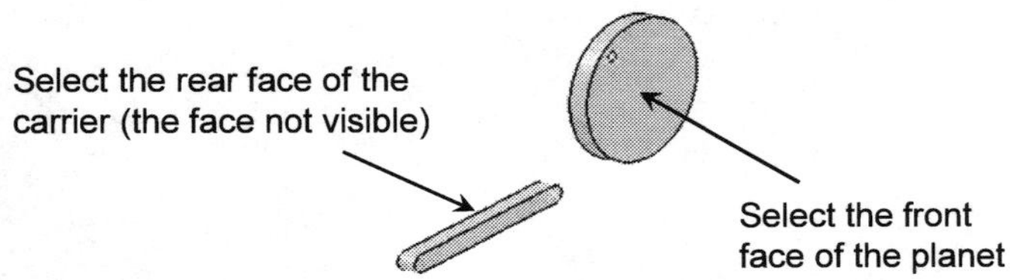

- Constraints
  - Fix.1 (shaft.1)
  - Coincidence.2 (sun.1,shaft.1)
  - Surface contact.3 (shaft.1,sun.1)
  - Coincidence.4 (shaft.1,ring.1)
  - Surface contact.5 (shaft.1,ring.1)
  - Coincidence.6 (sun.1,carrier.1)
  - Surface contact.7 (sun.1,carrier.1)
  - Coincidence.8 (planet.1,carrier.1)
  - Surface contact.9 (carrier.1,planet.1)

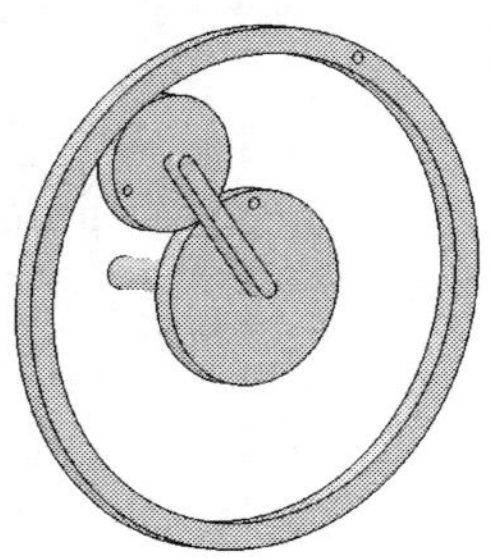

Use the **Update** icon  to check your constraints. Your assembly should be properly assembled similar to what is shown below.

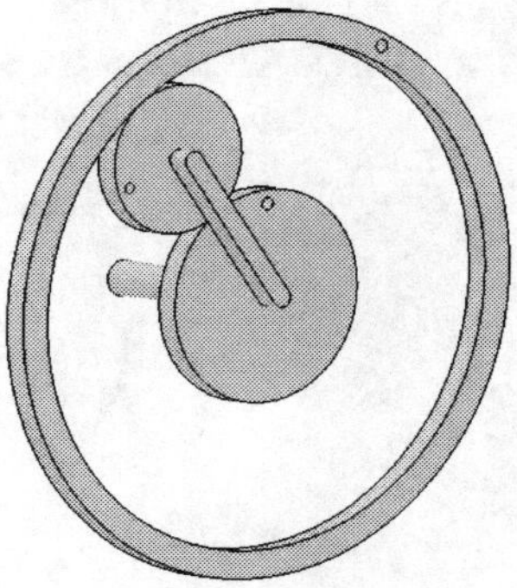

If properly applied, the assembly constraints made above should be consistent from a degrees of freedom standpoint with creating the desired four revolute joints in DMU.

The assembly is complete and we can proceed to the **Digital Mockup** workbench.

4 Creating Joints in the Digital Mockup Workbench

The **Digital Mockup** workbench is quite extensive but we will only deal with the **DMU Kinematics module**. To get there you can use the standard Windows toolbar as shown below: **Start > Digital Mockup > DMU Kinematics**.

The first step will involve using automatic assembly constraints conversion to convert the assembly constraints we have implemented into mechanism joints. If we have properly constrained the assembly thus far, this should result in four revolute joints being created. Proceed to see the steps involved.

Select the **Assembly Constraints Conversion** icon 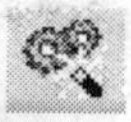 from the **DMU Kinematics** toolbar 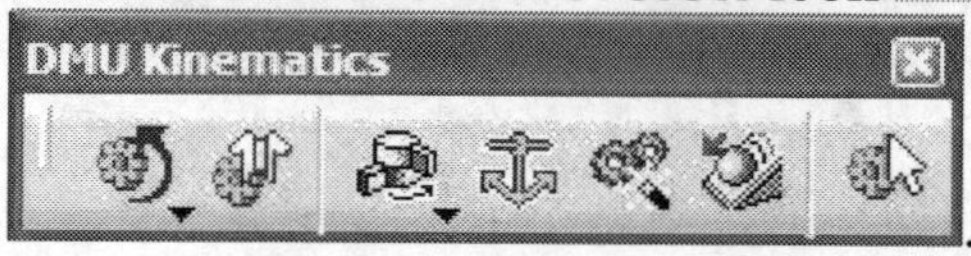

. This icon allows you to create most common joints automatically from the existing assembly constraints. The pop up box below appears.

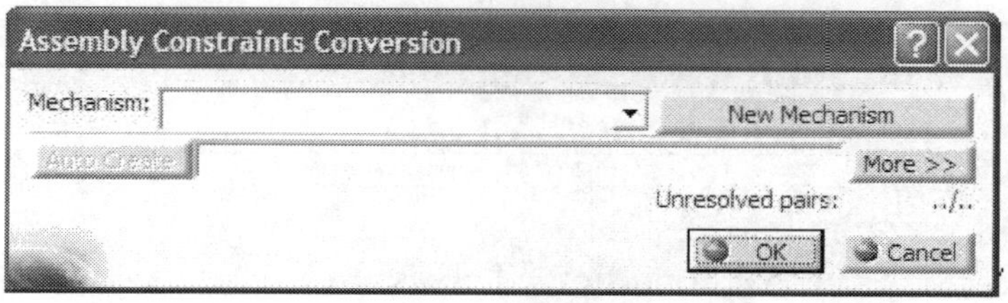

Select the **New Mechanism** button 

.
This leads to another pop up box which allows you to name your mechanism.
The default name is **Mechanism.1**. Accept the default name by pressing **OK**.

Note that the box indicates **Unresolved pairs: 4/4**.

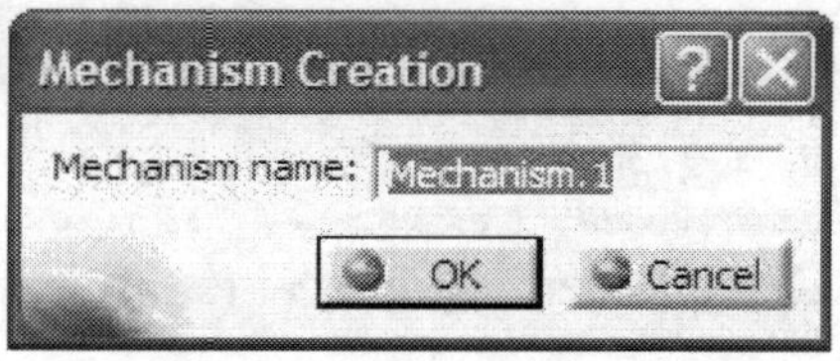

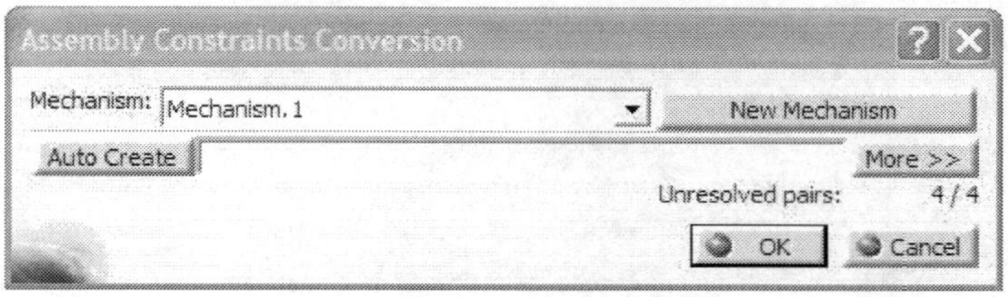

Select the **Auto Create** button 

. Then if the **Unresolved pairs** becomes **0/4**, things are moving in the right direction.

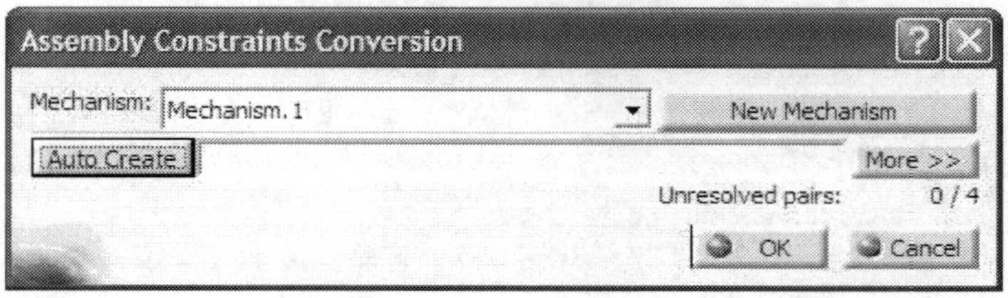

Note that the tree becomes longer by having an **Application** Branch. The expanded tree is displayed below. It clearly indicates the existence of four revolute joints and a Fixed Part **Fix.1**. The **DOF** is 4 which represent each revolute joint being independent.

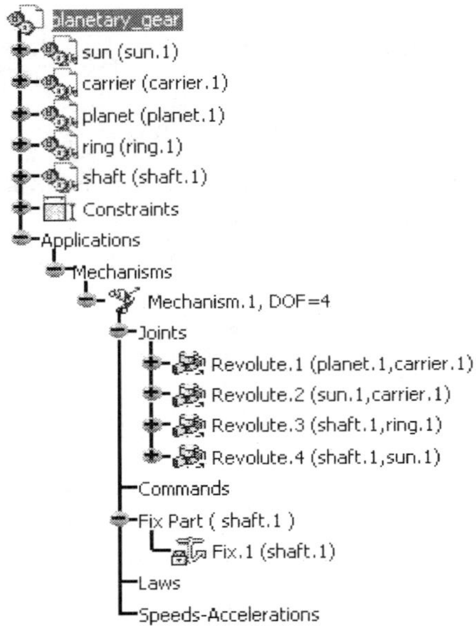

The next task in to create the gearing mechanisms. It is ironic that you will not use the gear joint feature in the **Digital Mockup** but the roll curve instead. A gear joint requires that each of the two revolute joints involved in the joint be attached to a single common part; this mechanism does not meet that condition. This is why we will use roll curve joints.

Select the **Roll Curve Joint** icon 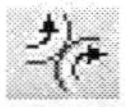 from the **Kinematics Joint** toolbar

.

The following pop up box appears on your screen.

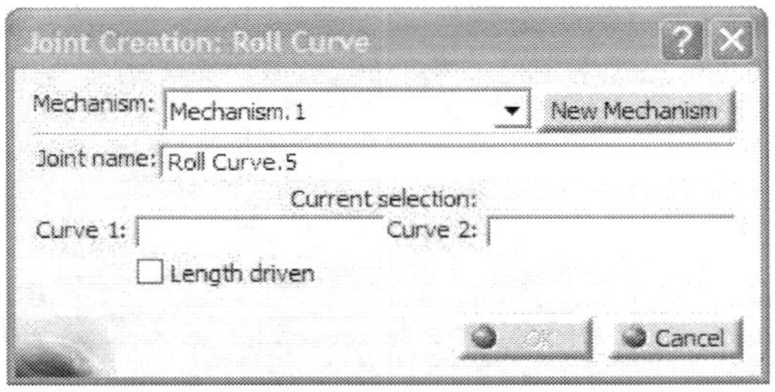

For **Curve.1** and **Curve.2**, make selections shown below from the **ring** and the **planet**.

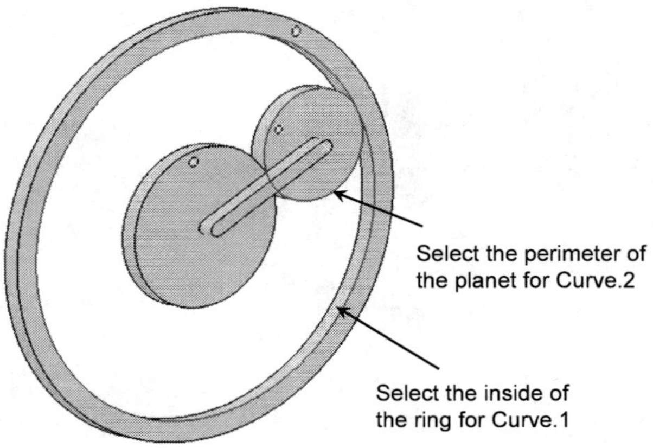

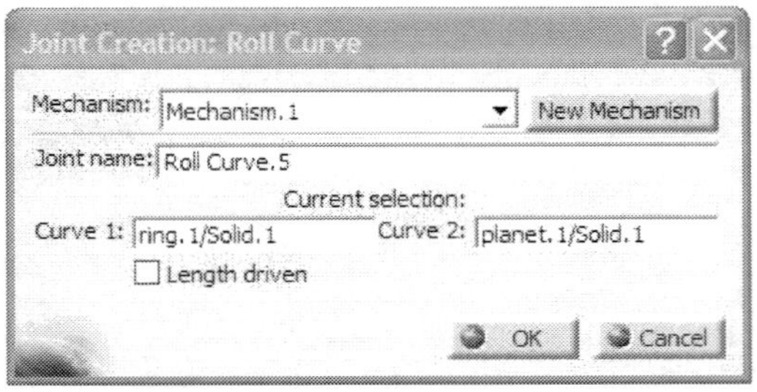

The created joint is reflected in the tree. Note that the degrees of freedom is reduced by one.

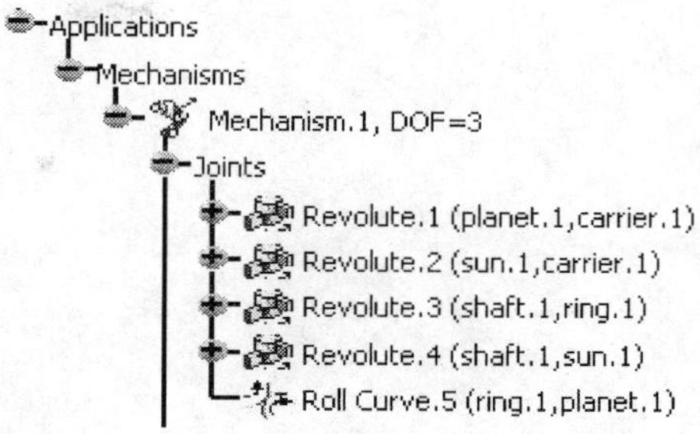

Once again select the **Roll Curve Joint** icon .
In the resulting pop up box, make the following selections for **Curve.1** and **Curve.2**, from the **planet** and the **sun**.

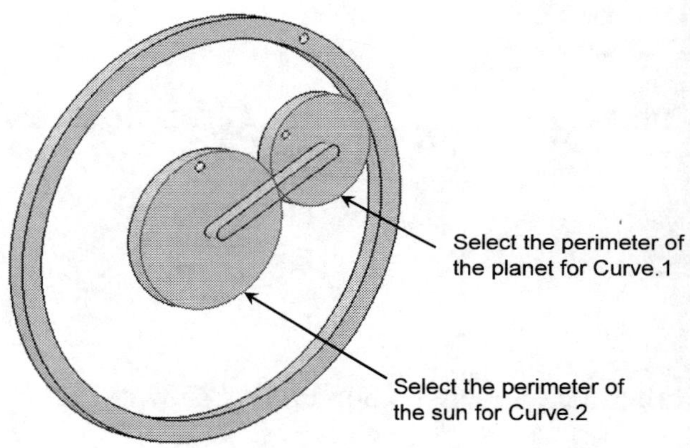

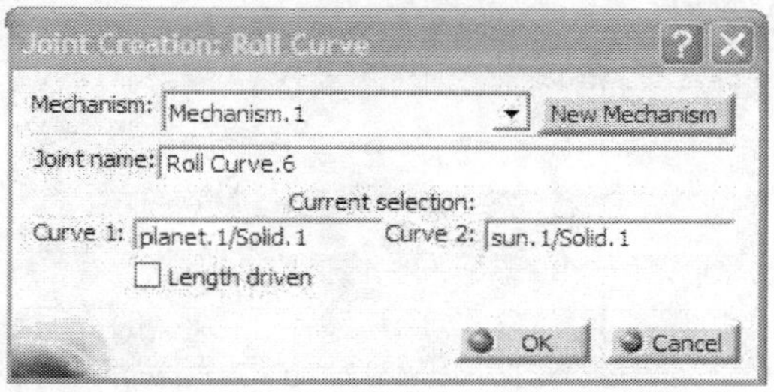

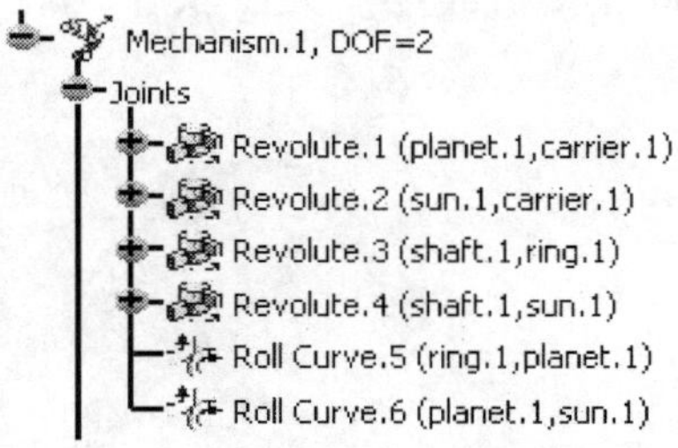

The created joint is reflected in the tree. Note that the degree of freedom is again reduced by one.

It is well known that, barring the fixing of any of the members, the planetary gear constructed has two degrees of freedom.

These two degrees of freedom can be removed by specifying appropriate commands for this purpose. For example, **Revolute.3** and **Revolute.4** can be declared to be angle driven joints.

Double click on the **Revolute.3** branch of the tree to open the pop up box shown. Pick the **Angle driven** selection box.

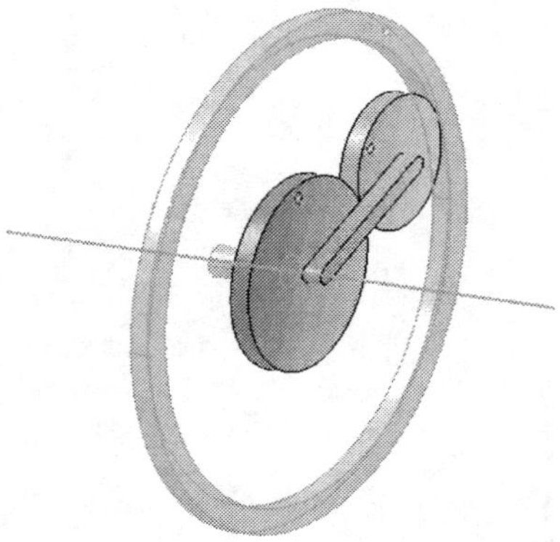

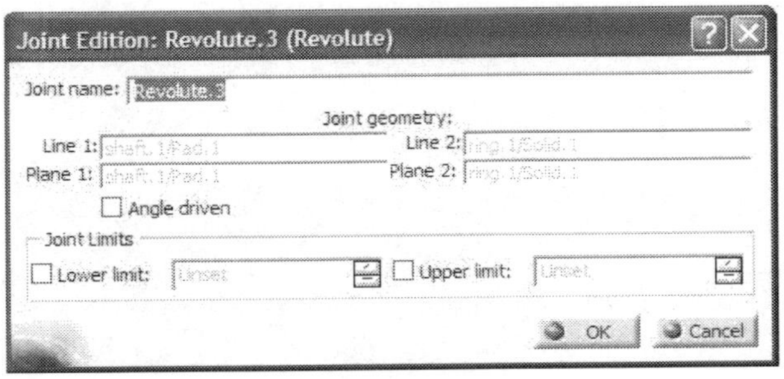

Check the Angle driven box

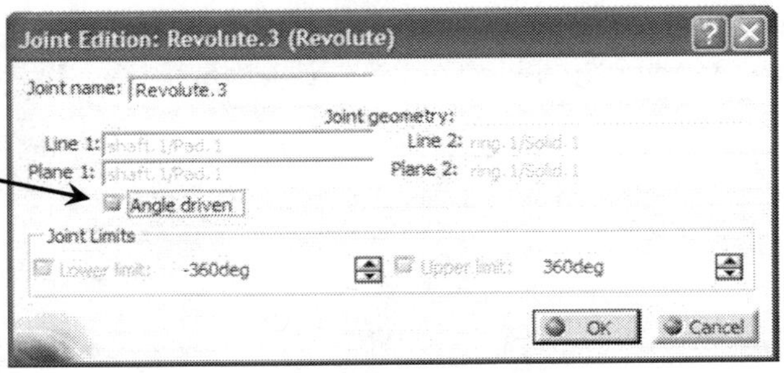

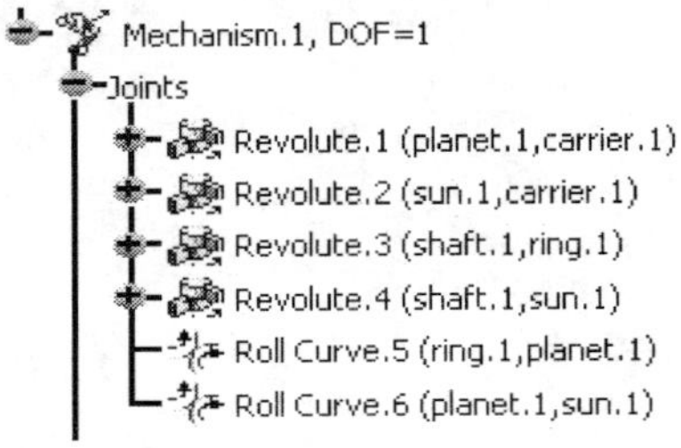

Repeat the same process for Revolute.4.
Double click on the **Revolute.4** branch of the tree to open the pop up box shown. Pick the **Angle driven** selection box.

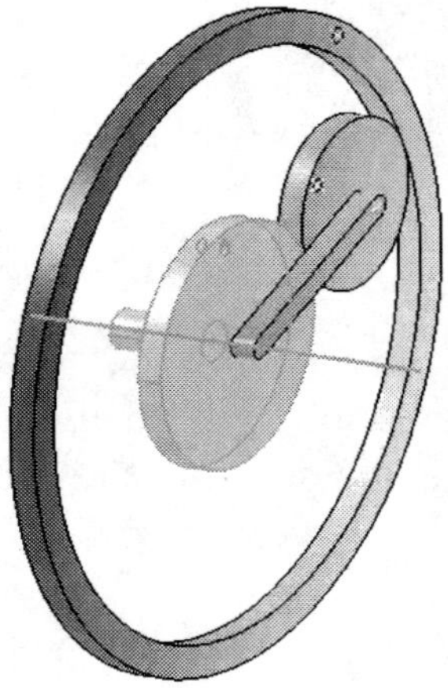

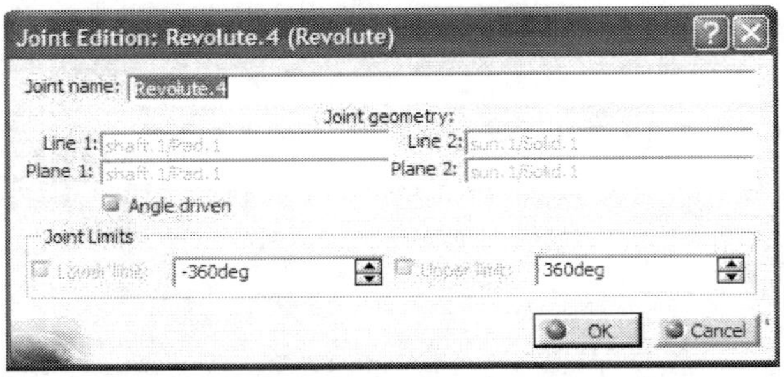

This reduces the degree of freedom to zero as show by the tree on the right.

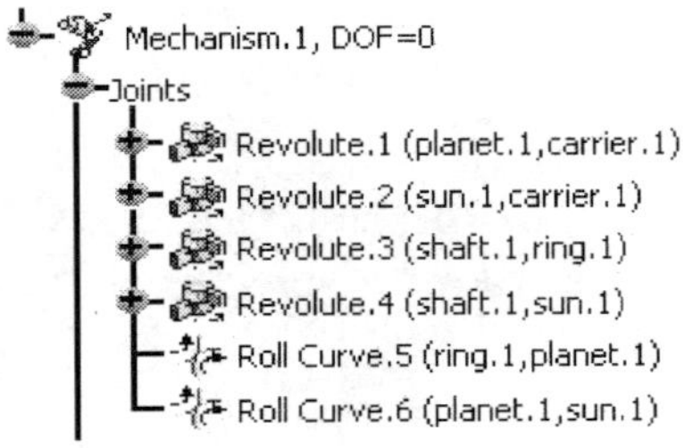

As soon as the last pop up box is closed, the message "**The mechanism can be simulated**" appears on the screen.

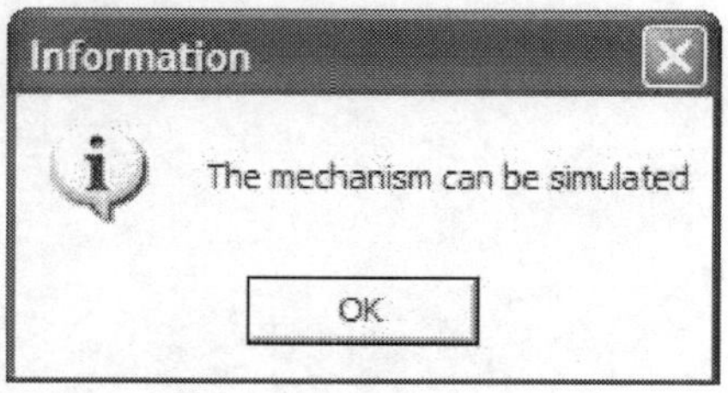

To simulate the motion with separate slider control of the two angle driven joints, select the **Simulation with Commands** icon  from the **Simulation** toolbar 

. The **Kinematics Simulation** pop up box below appears.

Note that by pressing the **Less** 

button, the compact version of this box is displayed.

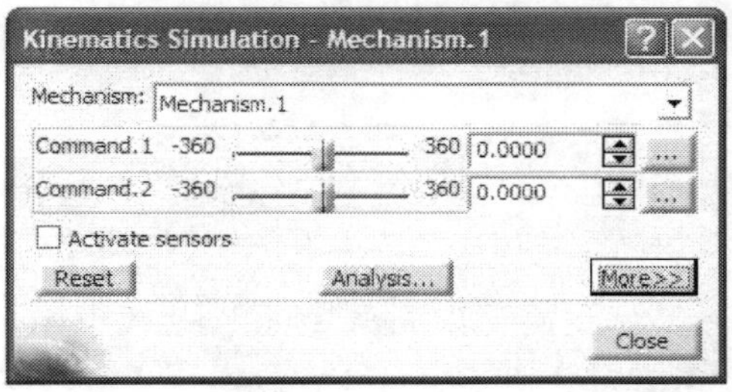

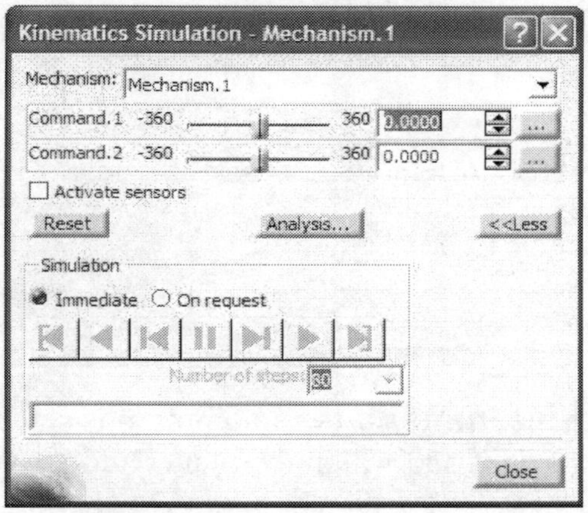

Note that there are two scroll bars present. This reflects the fact that ordinarily, the planetary gear under study has two degrees of freedom.

The number of steps represents resolution for capturing the motion. There are two radio buttons present, **Immediate** and **On Request**. If **Immediate** is selected, as the scroll bar is being dragged from the left to right, the motion can be observed on the screen. This is displayed in the next page. Upon reaching the end, use the **Reset** 

button to return the planet to the starting position. This can also be achieved by dragging the scroll bar to the position -360.

Note that the range for the revolute joint can be set by pressing on the button .
In the resulting pop up box, the new range can be imposed.

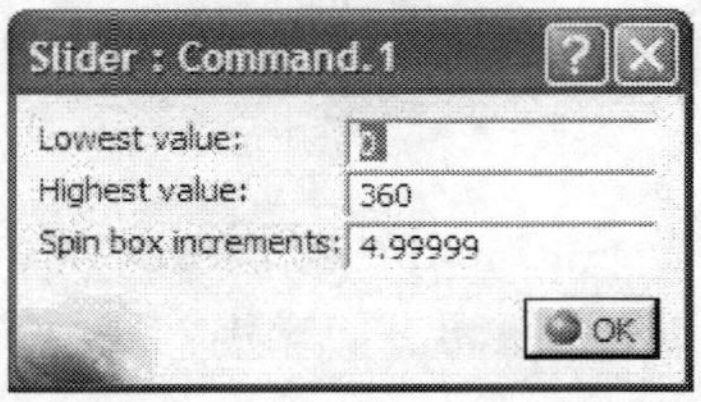

Set the range for both **Command.1** and **Command.2** to (0,360) as shown below.

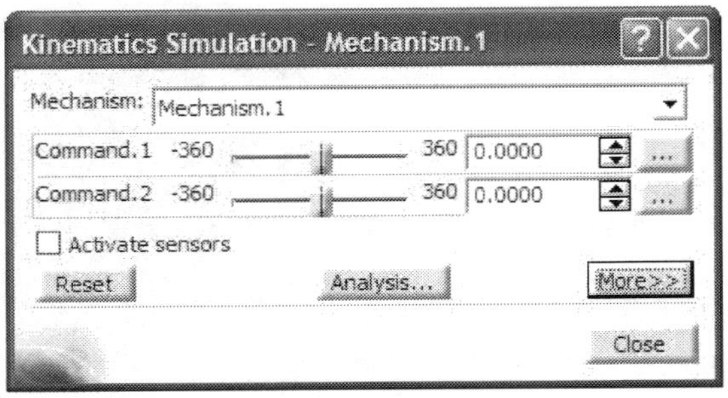

Click the **More** button to expand the box to its full view.

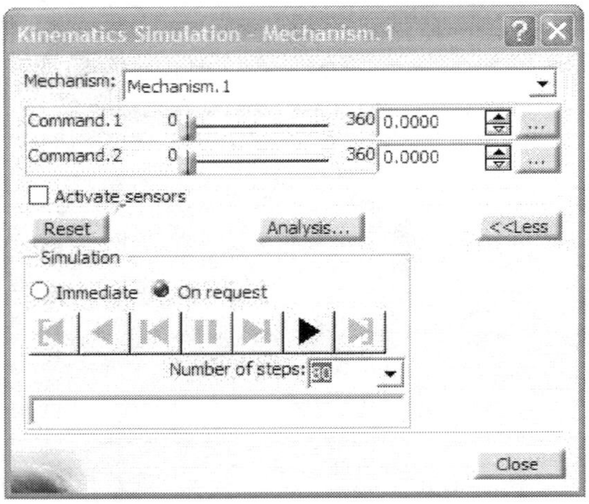

With the **Immediate** radio button is selected, move the scroll bar **Command.1** from left to right and watch the planet and the ring rotating while the sun remains stationary.

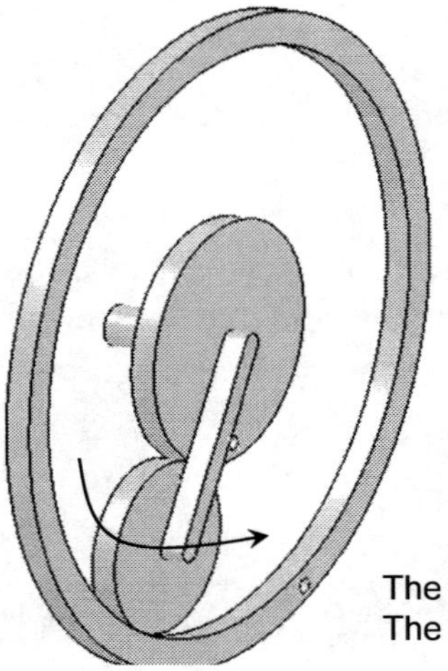

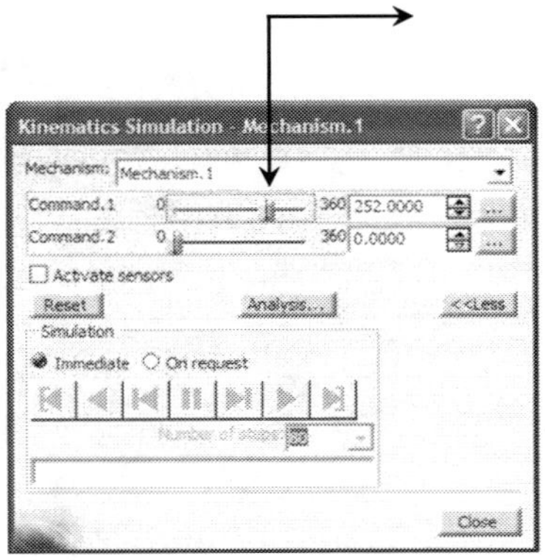

Now move the scroll bar **Command.2** from left to right and watch the planet and the sun rotating while the ring remaining stationary.

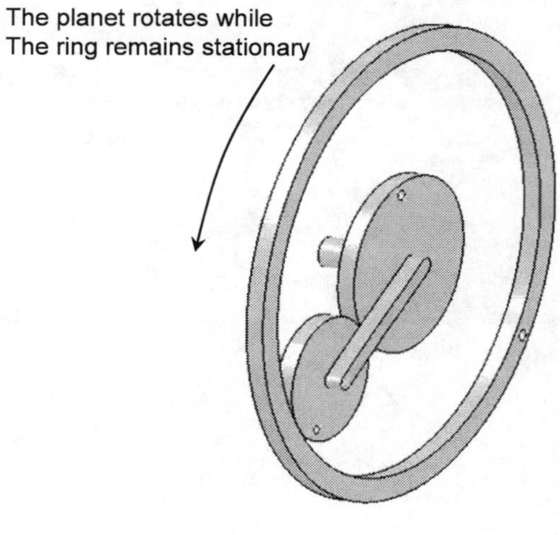

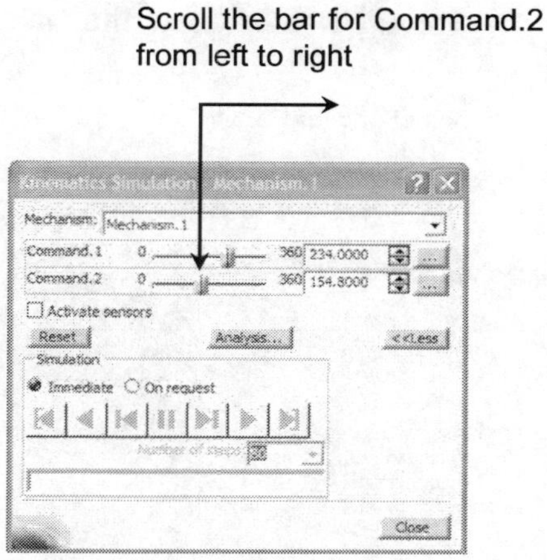

You will next delete one of the commands, namely the one that controls the revolute joint between the ring and the shaft.

Point the cursor to the **Command.2** branch, right click and **Delete**.

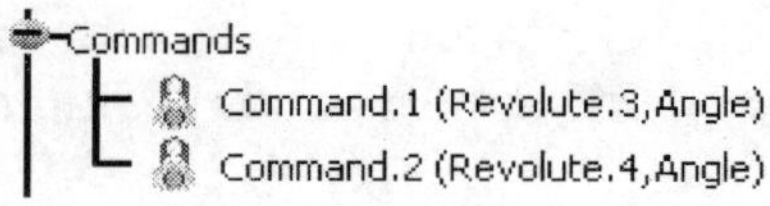

The resulting pop up box informs you that the mechanism can no longer be simulated.

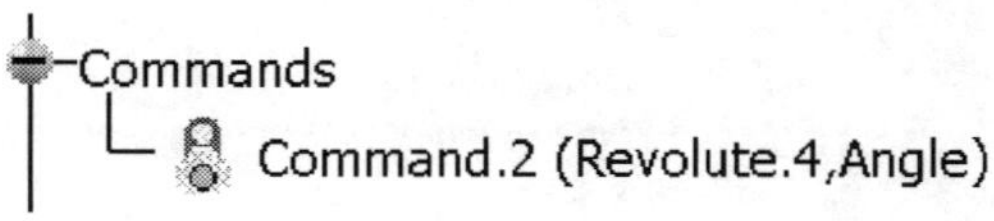

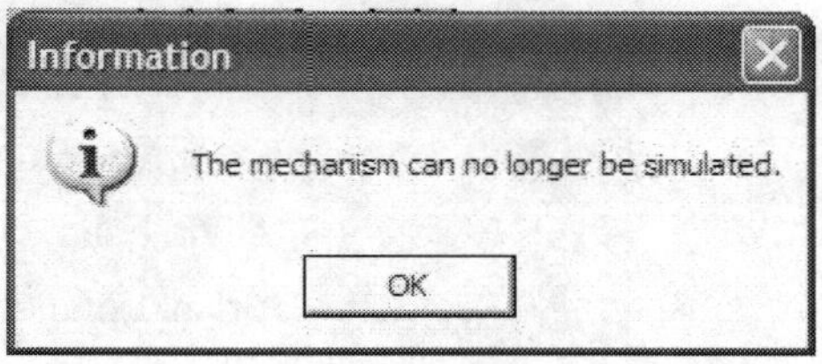

In order to simulate the mechanism, you will next fix the ring. Notice the DOF has returned to 1 upon deletion of this command.

To fix the ring, click on the **Rigid Joint** icon  from the **Constraints** toolbar. This results in the following pop up box.

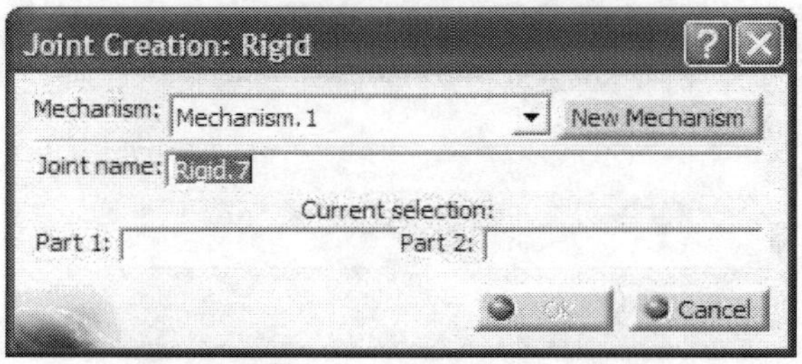

For **Part.1** and **Part.2**, select the **ring** and the **shaft** respectively from the tree.

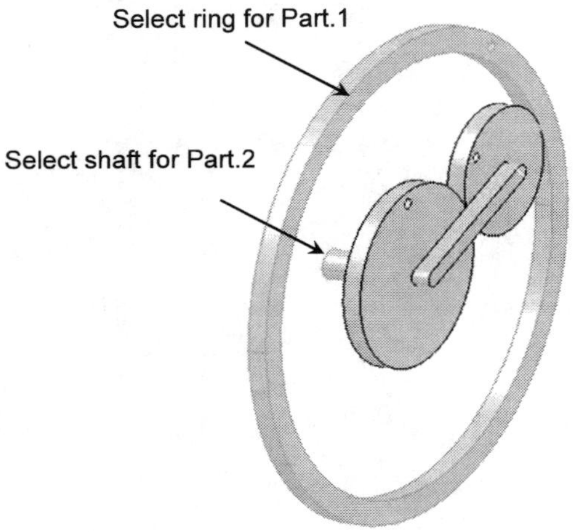

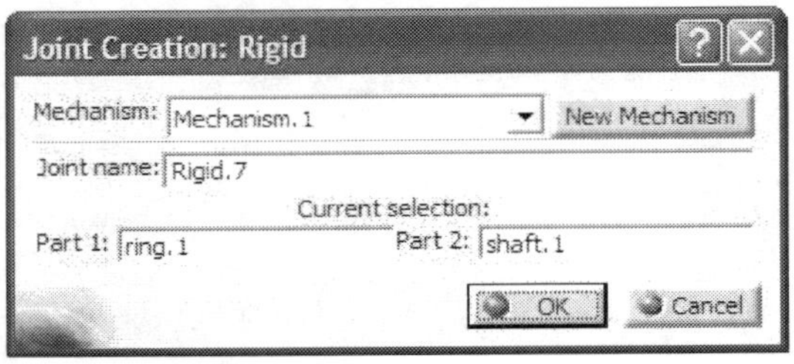

This rigid joint removes the 1 dof and the message "**The Mechanism can be simulated**" appears and the number of degrees of freedom reverts back to zero.

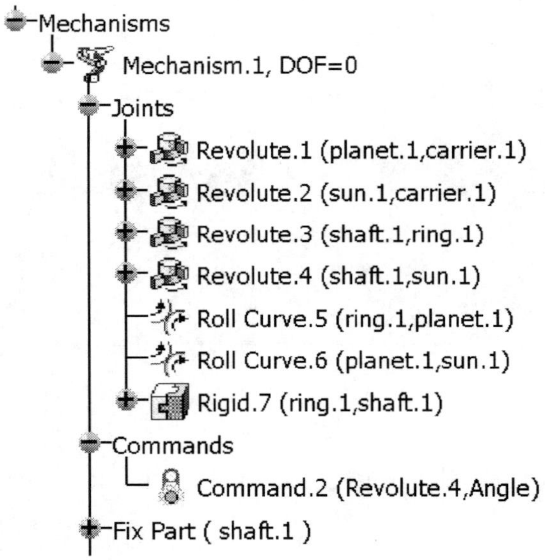

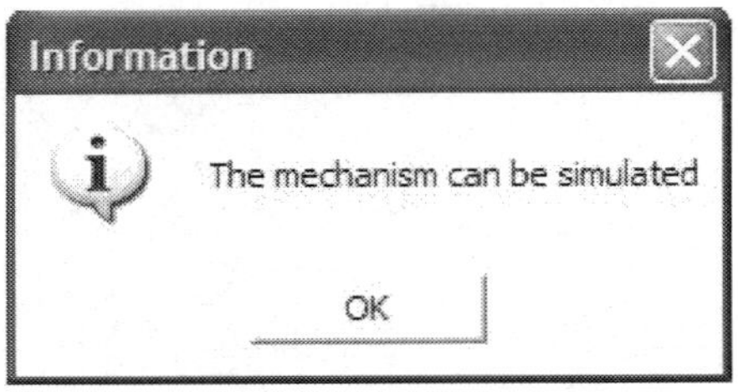

To simulate the fixed ring motion, select the **Simulation** icon  from the **DMU Generic Animation** toolbar 

. This enables you to choose the mechanism to be animated if there are several present. In this case, select Mechanism.1 and close the window.

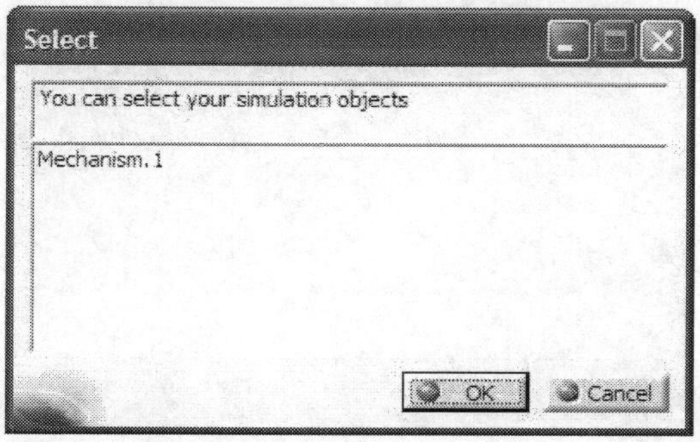

As soon as the window is closed, a Simulation branch is added to the tree.

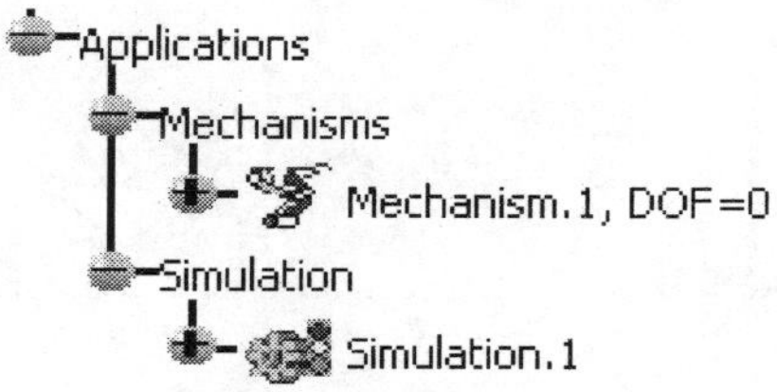

In addition, the two pop up boxes shown below appear.

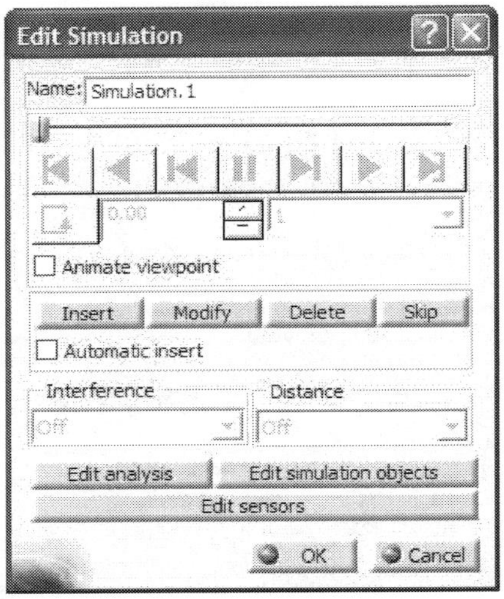

As you scroll the bar in the **Kinematics Simulation** pop up box, from left to right, the planet begins to rotate while the ring is stationary. The range (0,360) can be made larger say (0,1800) to observe at least a full revolution of the carrier.

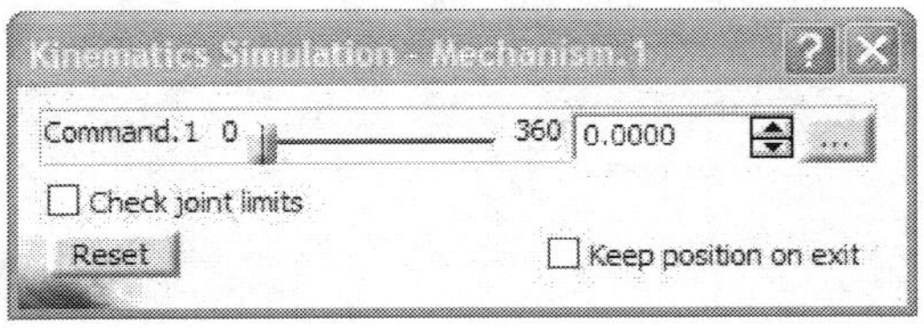

When the scroll bar in the **Kinematics Simulation** pop up box reaches the right extreme end, select the **Insert** button  in the **Edit Simulation** pop up box shown above. This activates the video player buttons shown .

Return the planet to its original position by picking the **Jump to Start** button .

Note that the **Change Loop Mode** button  is also active now.

Upon selecting the **Play Forward** button , the planet makes such a fast jump to the end that there does not seem to be any motion.

In order to slow down the motion of the planet, select a different **interpolation step**, such as 0.04.

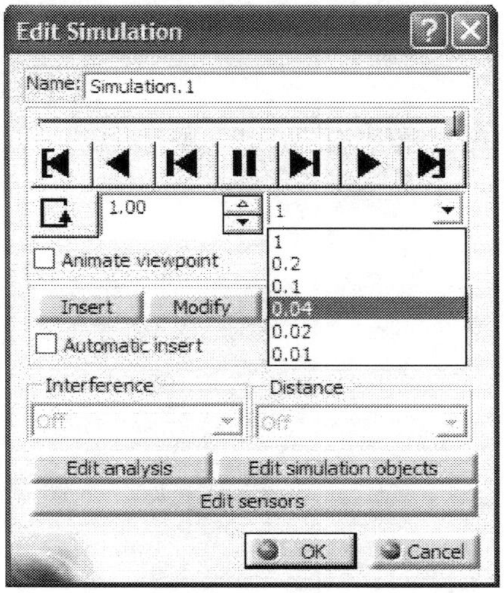

In the event that an AVI file is not needed, but one wishes to play the animation, repeatedly, a **Replay** needs to be generated. Therefore, in the **Compile Simulation** box, check the **Generate a replay** button.

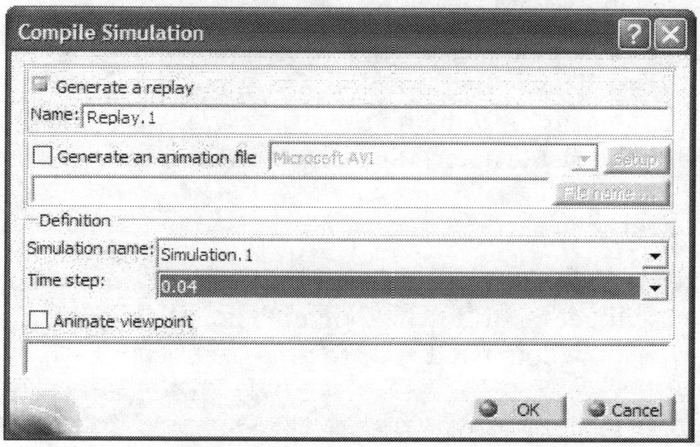

Note that in this case most of the previously available options are dimmed out.
A **Replay.1** branch has also been added to the tree.

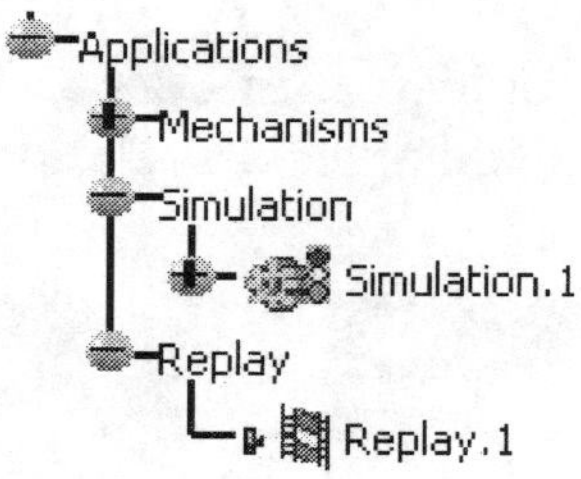

Select the **Replay** icon  from the **Generic Animation** toolbar.
Double clock on **Replay.1** in the tree and the **Replay** pop up box appears.
Experiment with the different choices of the **Change Loop Mode** buttons , , .
The block can be returned to the original position by picking the **Jump to Start** button .

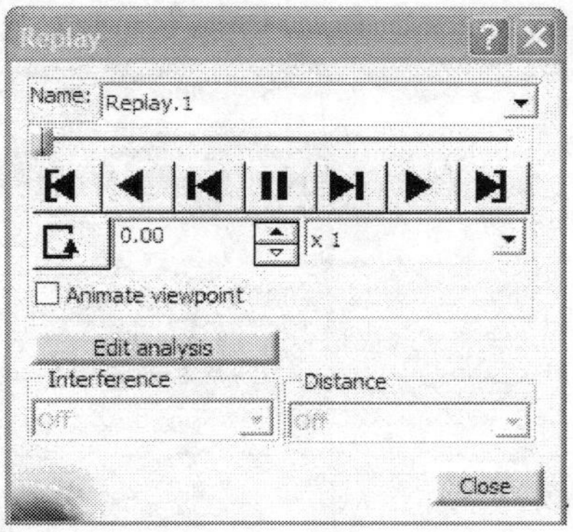

The **skip ratio** (which is chosen to be x1 in the right box) controls the speed of the **Replay**.

5 Creating Laws in the Motion and Simulating the Desired Kinematics

The motion animated this far was not tied to the time parameter or the angular velocity given in the problem statement. You will now introduce some time based physics into the problem. The objective is to specify a constant angular velocity of $\omega = 360$ deg/s on the **sun**. This will allow plots of various relative angular velocities to illustrate the effective gear ratios being achieved. We will begin with the ring fixed (as it was at the end of the last chapter), the sun considered to be the input, and the carrier the output.

Click on **Simulation with Laws** icon  in the **Simulation** toolbar 

.
You will get the following pop up box indication that you need to add at least a relation between the command and the time parameter.

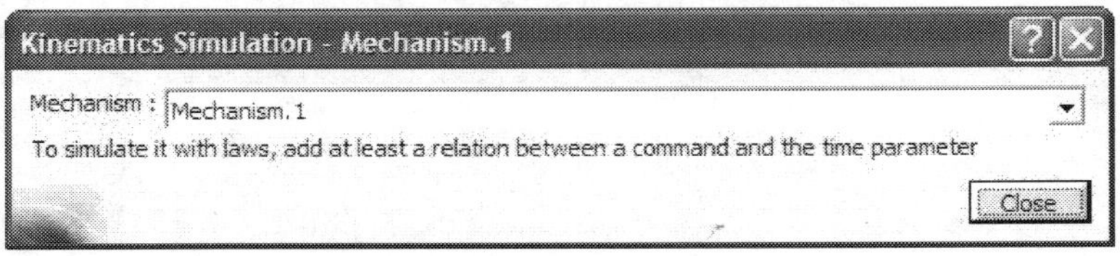

Select the **Formula** icon  from the **Knowledge** toolbar
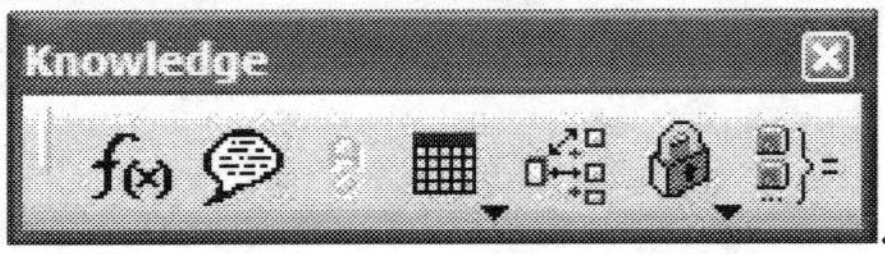

. The pop up box below appears on the screen.

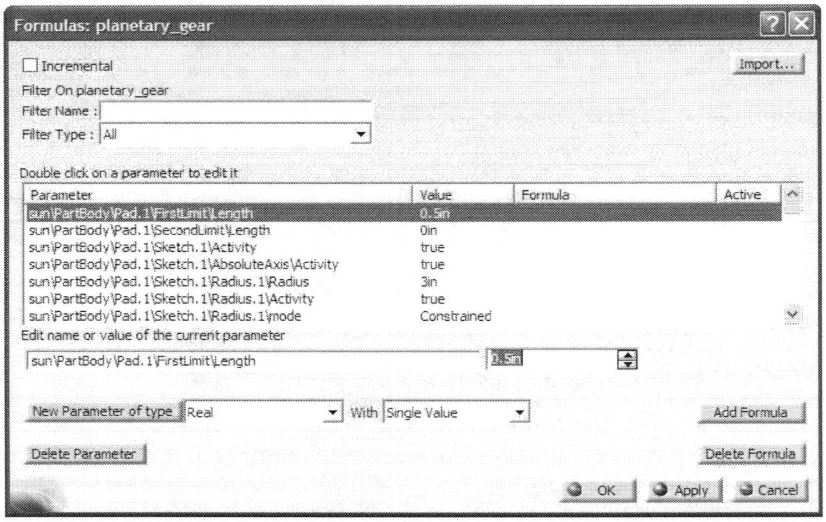

Point the cursor to the **Mechanism.1, DOF=0** branch in the tree and click. The consequence is that only parameters associated with the mechanism are displayed in the **Formulas** box.
The long list is now reduced to two parameters as indicated in the box shown on the next page.

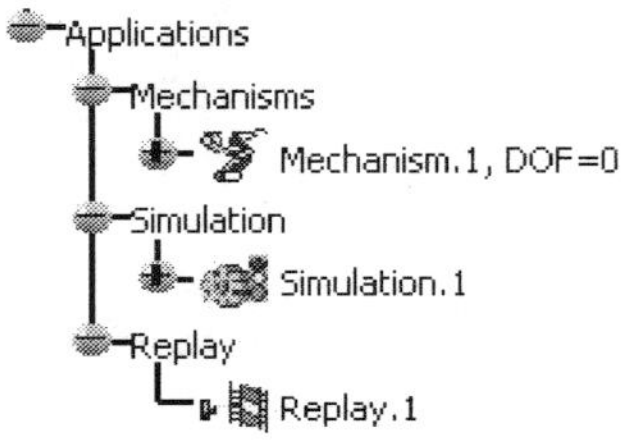

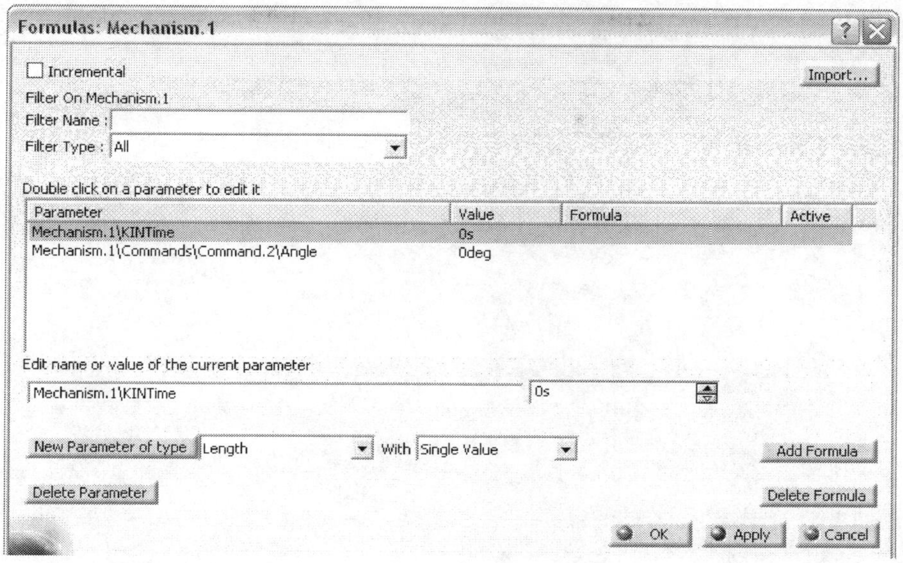

Select the entry **Mechanism.1\Commands\Command.2\Angle** and press the **Add Formula** button Add Formula. This action kicks you to the **Formula Editor** box.

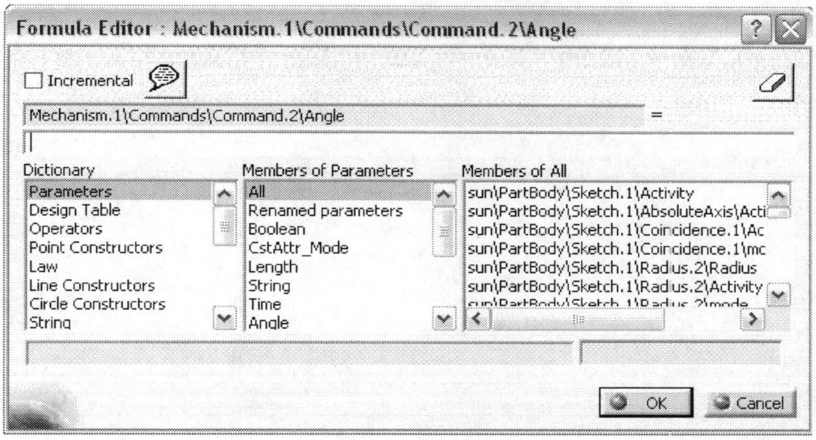

Pick the **Time** entry from the middle column (i.e. **Members of Parameters**).

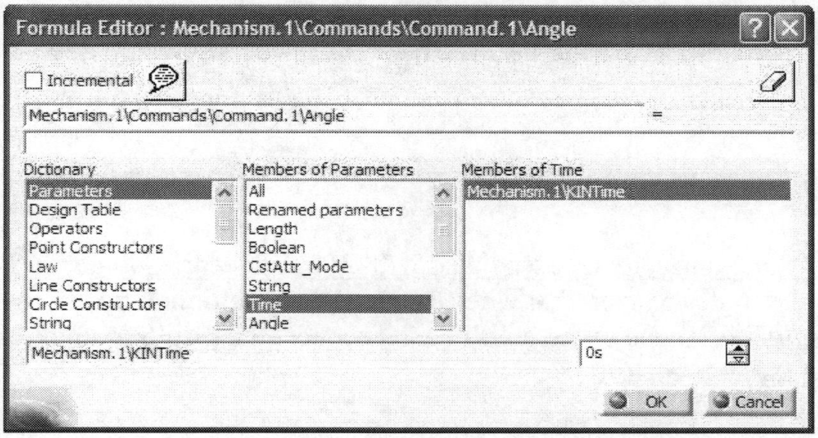

The right hand side of the equality should be such that the formula becomes

$$Mechanism.1 \backslash Commands \backslash Command.2 \backslash Angle =$$
$$(360\deg)/(1s)*(Mechnism.1 \backslash KINTime)$$

Therefore, the completed **Formula Editor** box becomes

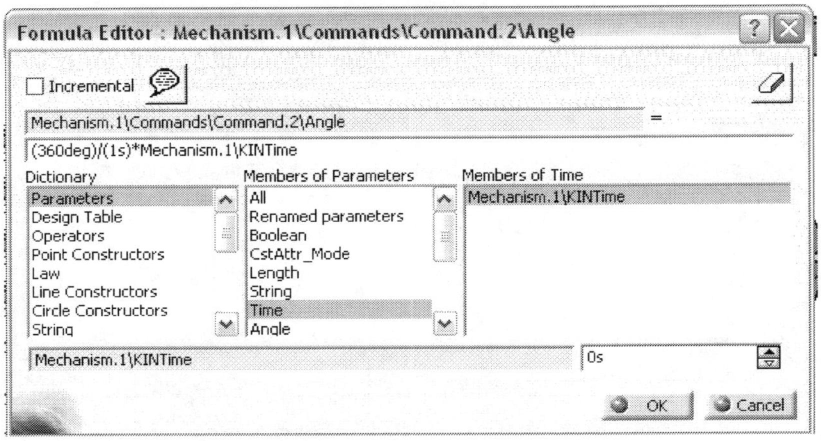

Upon accepting **OK**, the formula is recorded in the **Formulas** pop up box as shown below.

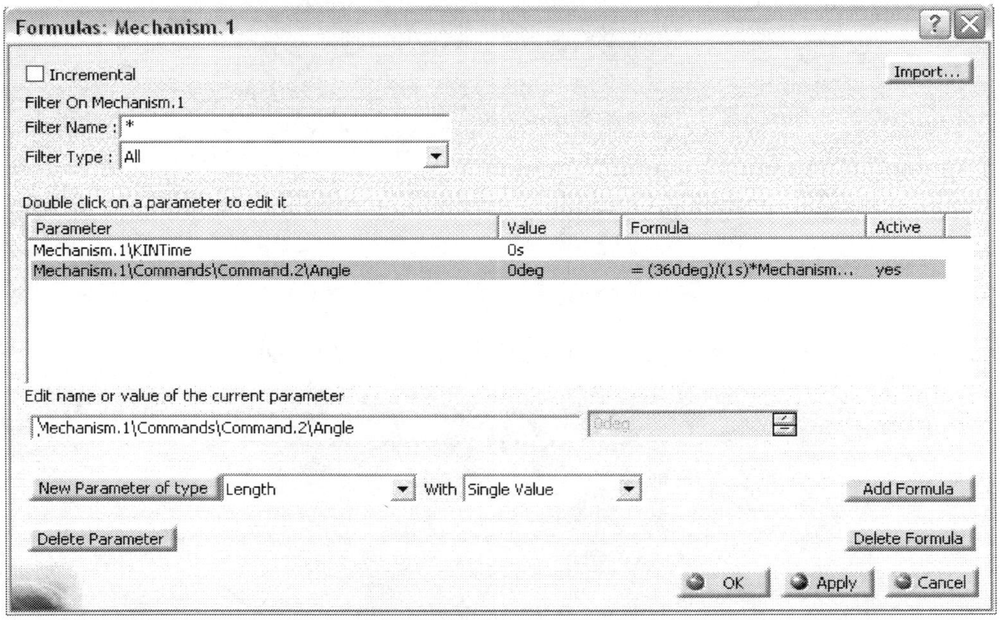

Note that the angular velocity associated with 360 deg/s corresponds to 60 rpm. Also notice that the units are such that when 360deg/s are multiplied by $(Mechanism.1 \backslash KINTime)$ which will be in seconds, the resulting units are degrees as they should be.

In the event that the formula has different units on the different sides of the equality you will get **Warning** messages such as the one shown below.

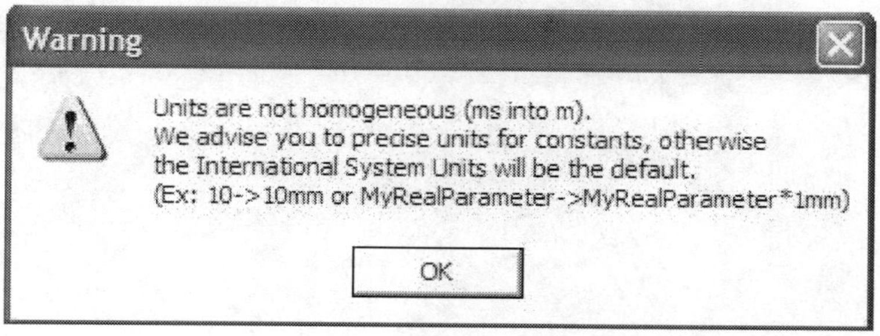

We are spared the warning message because the formula has been properly inputted. Note that the introduced law has appeared in the **Law** branch of the tree.

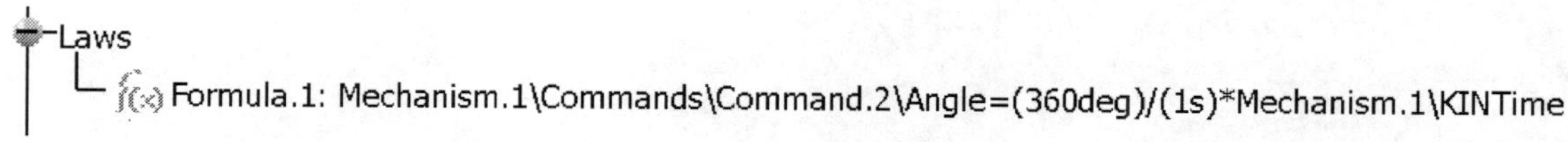

Keep in mind that our interest is to plot the angular velocity of the carrier generated by this motion. This can be achieved by plotting the angular velocity of the point already created at the tip of the carrier. Of course a point theoretically has no orientation and thus no angular velocity; this theoretical restriction will not affect the functionality in DMU, and we will get the angular velocity of the solid containing the point.

Select the **Speed and Acceleration** icon  from the **DMU Kinematics** toolbar

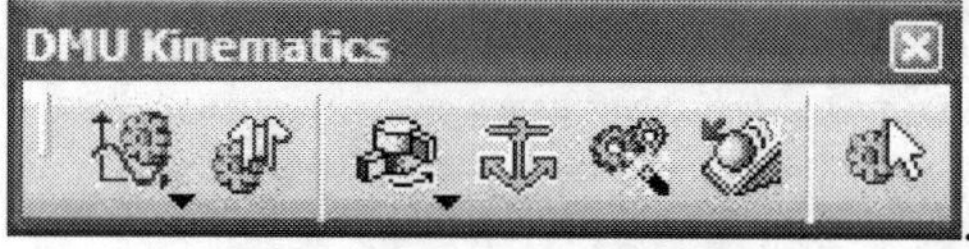

. The pop up box below appears on the Screen.

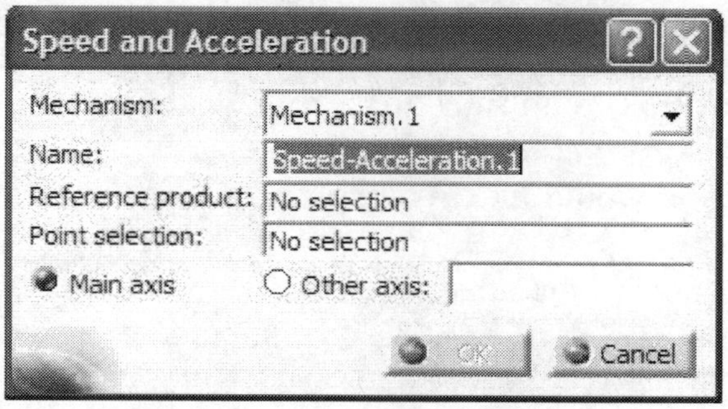

For the **Reference product,** select the **shaft** from the screen or the tree. For the **Point selection**, pick any point on the **carrier** such as a vertex along one of the edges as shown in the sketch below.

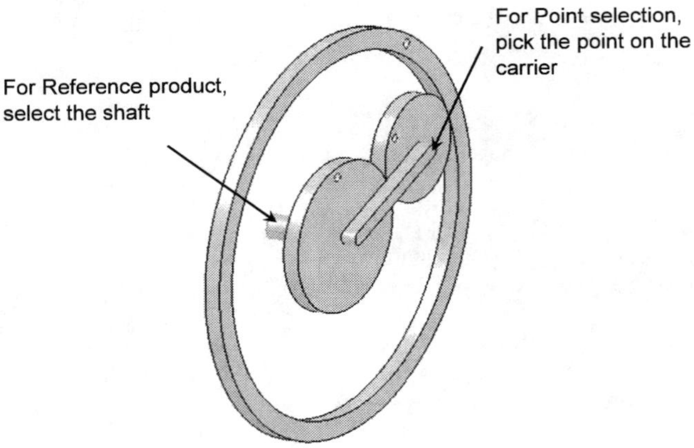

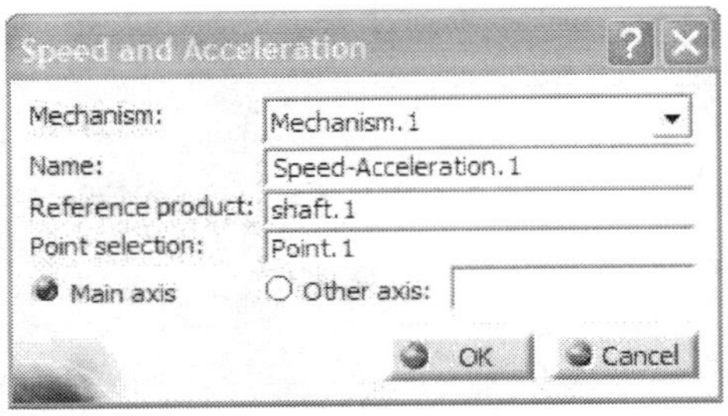

Note that the **Speed and Acceleration.1** has appeared in the tree.

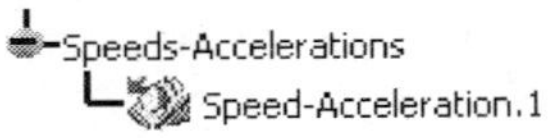

Next, click on **Simulation with Laws** icon  in the **Simulation** toolbar

.

This results in the **Kinematics Simulation** pop up box shown below.

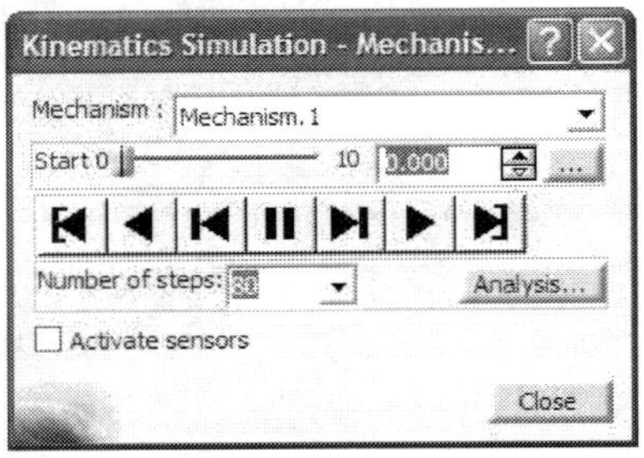

Note that the default time duration is 10 seconds.

Check the **Activate sensors** box, at the bottom left corner.

You will next have to make certain selections from the accompanying **Sensors** box to indicate the kinematics parameters you would like to compute and store results on.
The **Sensors** box is shown in the next page.

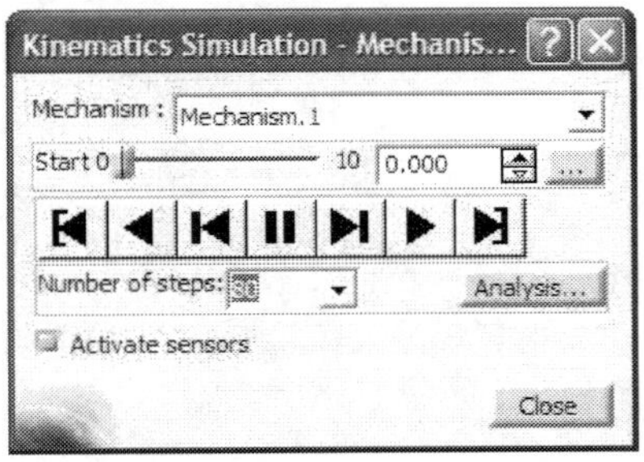

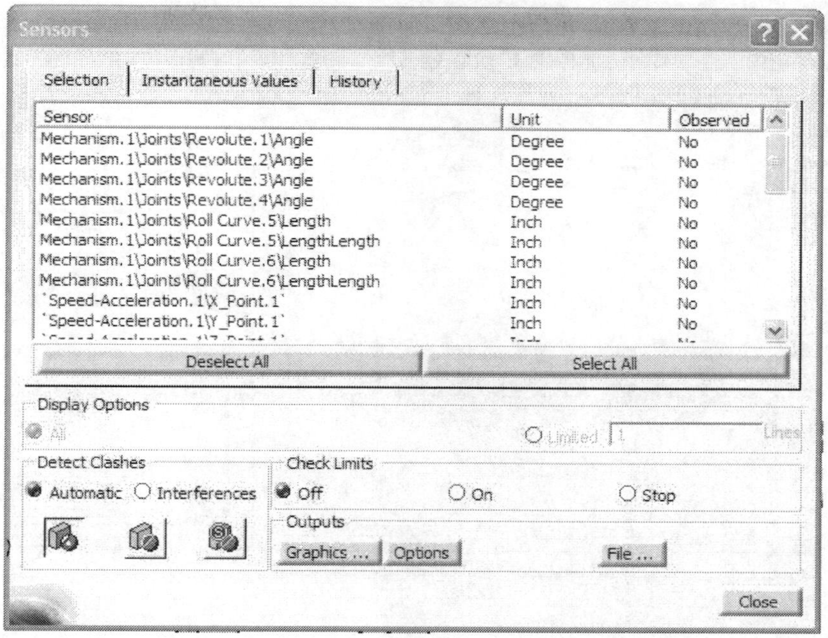

In the Sensors pop up box, click on the following item:

Speed-Acceleration.1\X_Angular Speed

As you make these selections, the last column in the **Sensors** box, changes to **Yes** for the corresponding items.

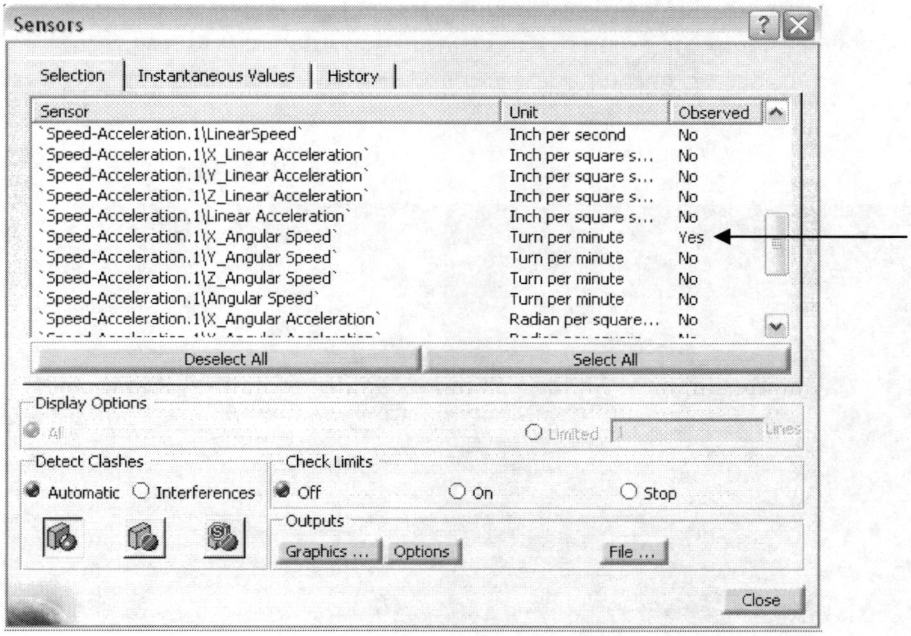

Note: If your axes of the joints does not lie along the world x direction, choose the component of angular velocity which is appropriate for the orientation of your parts.

At this point, drag the scroll bar in the **Kinematics Simulation** box. As you do this, the planet rotates about the shaft. Once the bar reaches its right extreme point, ten seconds has elapsed and the sun has made several rotations.

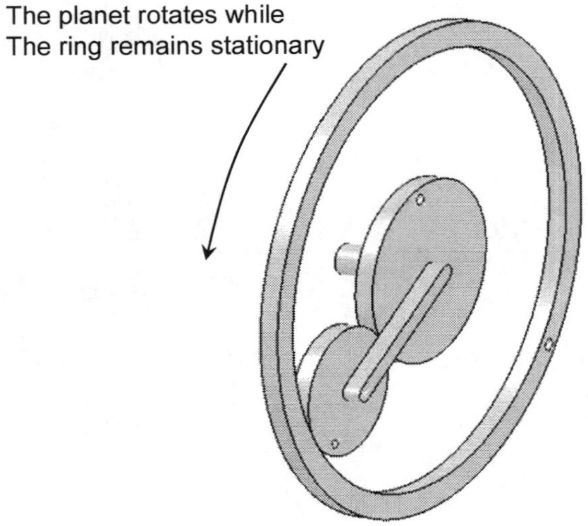

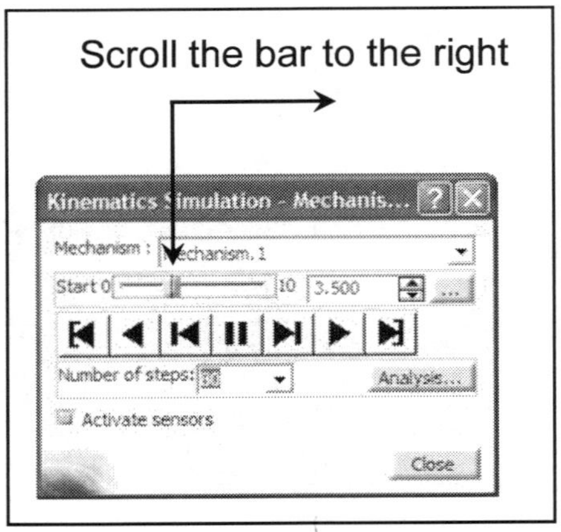

Once the sun completes its motion, click on **Graphics** button 

in the **Sensor** box. The result is the plot of the angular velocity of the carrier. The numerical value is 17.5 rpm which agrees with the theoretical value presented in the problem statement. **<u>This value corresponds to a speed reduction of 60:17.5 or 3.4:1</u>**.

Note: Depending upon the positive orientation of your driven revolute joint, you may have to either drag the slider in reverse or put a negative sign in your law in order to get the sun to be driven in the positive direction in accordance with the right hand rule. If your sun is being driven in the negative direction, you will get a negative result for this speed.

In the final phase of this tutorial, you will create a second mechanism which is identical to the first one with the only exception. In this new mechanism, the carrier will be stationary and the sun is acting as an input gear. This is included to provide additional practice with DMU; a more elegant approach to driving the various desired combinations of motion would be to have left both revolute joints angle driven and to have written a law for each angle. Then, the law corresponding to the fixed member would simply be set to zero. This approach is left to the reader as an exercise.

6 Creating a Second Mechanism

More than one mechanism model may be associated with an assembly. To create a second mechanism for this assembly, select the **Assembly Constraints Conversion** icon  from the **DMU Kinematics** toolbar 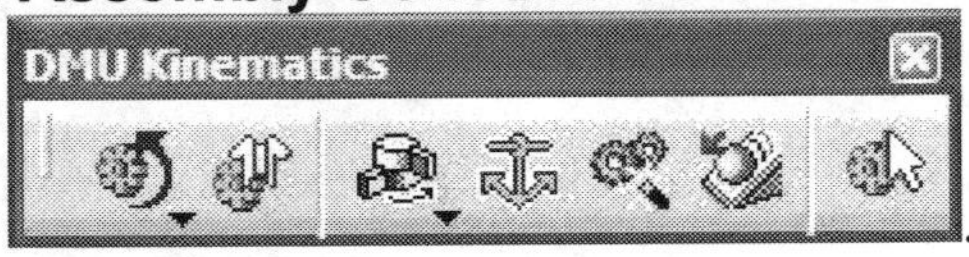

.
This icon allows you to create most common joints automatically from the existing assembly constraints.
The pop up box below appears.

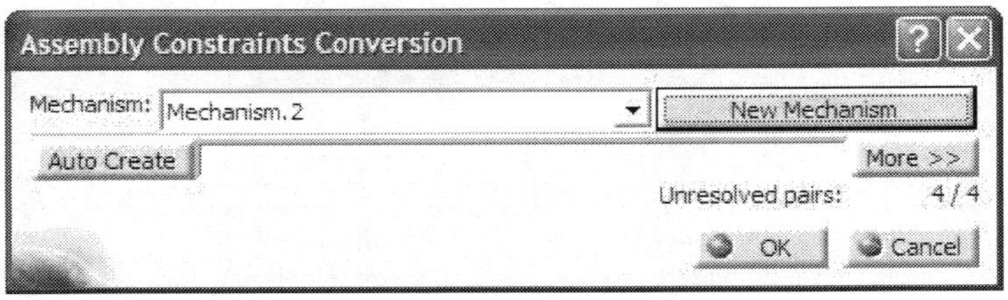

Click on the **New Mechanism** button 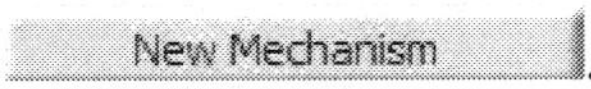

. In the resulting pop up box, a default name **Mechanism.2** is given.

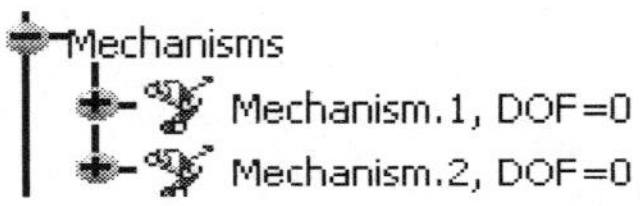

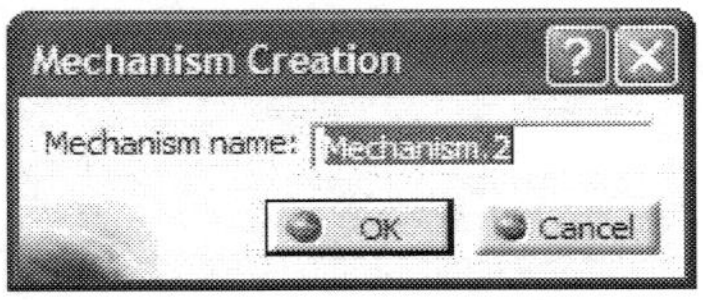

Note that the box indicates **Unresolved pairs: 4/4**.

Select the **Auto Create** button 

. Then if the **Unresolved pairs** becomes **0/4**, things are moving in the right direction.

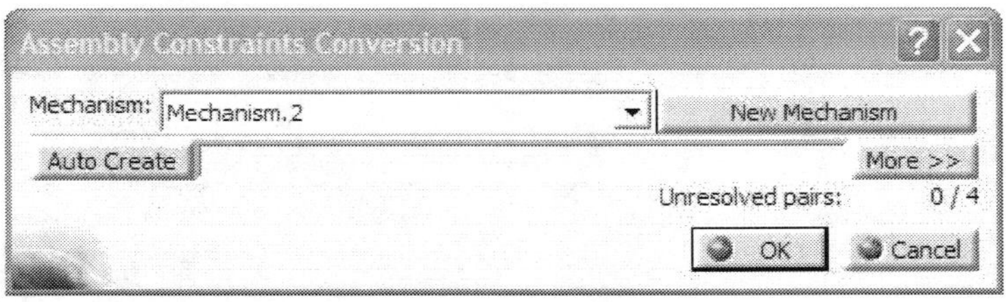

The tree indicates that the rigid joint **Rigid.3** from the previous mechanism was inherited. Delete **Rigid.3** from the tree. In the next few steps, you will create a revolute joint between the **ring** and the **shaft**.

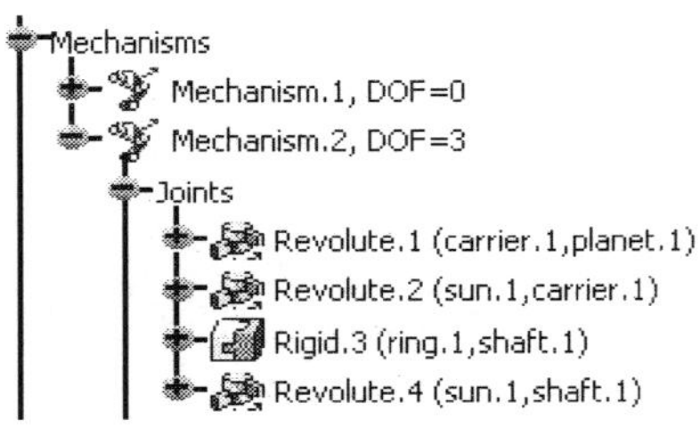

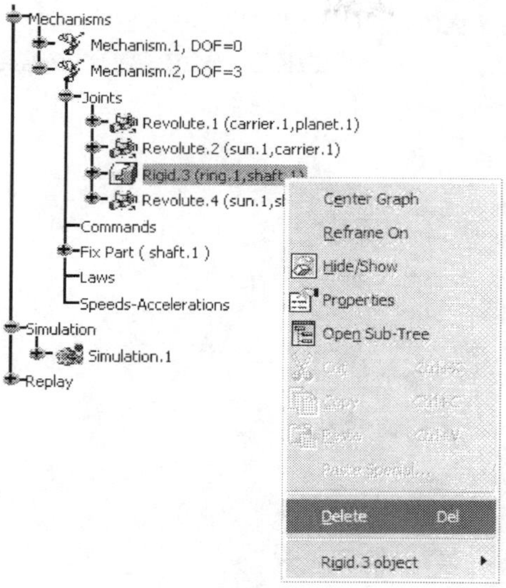

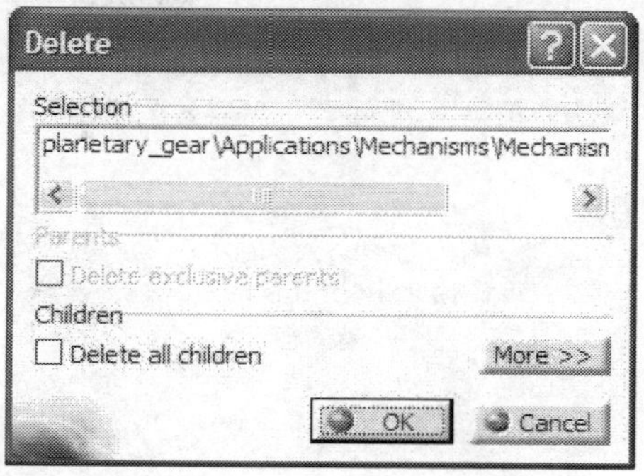

The tree is modified to reflect the deletion of the **Rigid.3** joint.

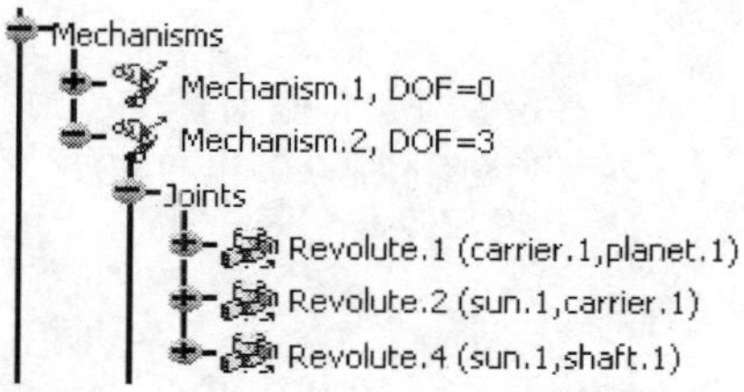

Click on the **Revolute Joint** icon  from the **Kinematics Joint** toolbar

.

The pop up box below appears. Use the pull-down menu to choose **Mechanism.2**.

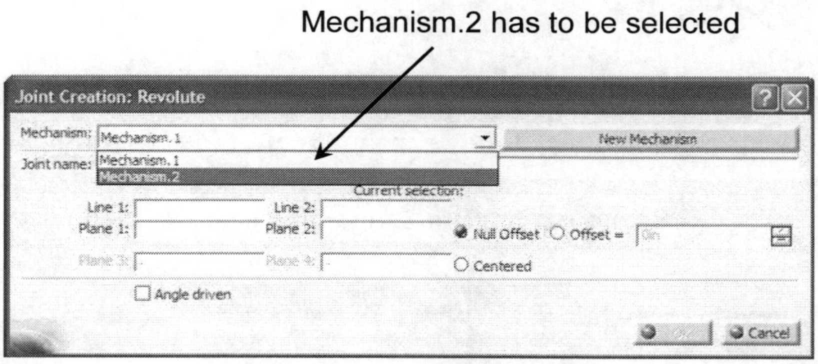

Make the selections between the **ring** and the **shaft** shown in the next figure. Keep in mind that although the order of picking the ring and the shaft is irrelevant, the **Line** and **Plane** must be picked consistently.

Note that the instructions below assume that the two parts **ring** and **shaft** were not manipulated in space and maintained their position in the assembly. Appropriate changes have to be made if these parts were moved around.

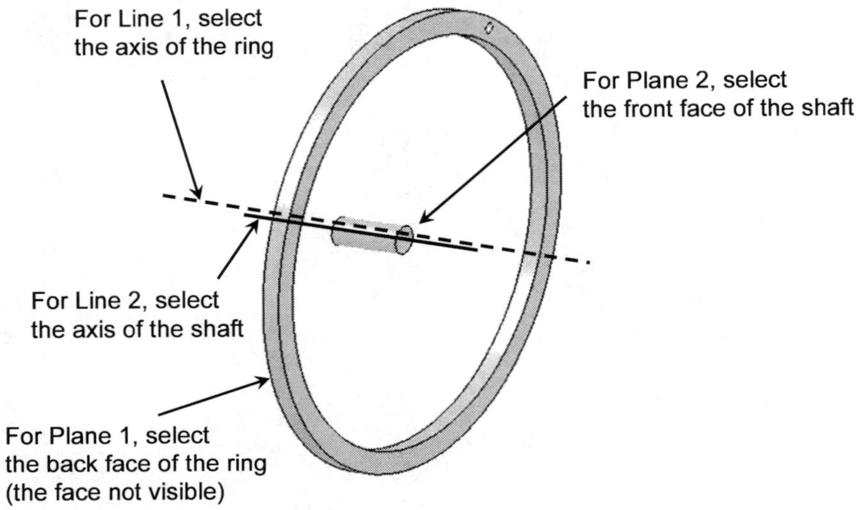

The completed pop up box is shown below. Upon closing box, the new revolute joint is reflected in the tree.

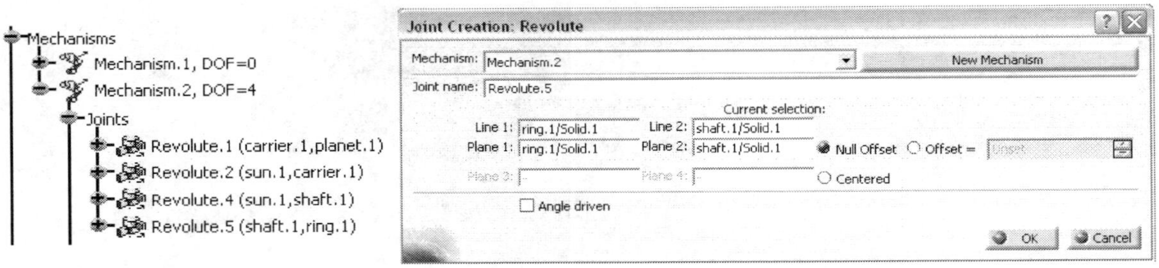

We need to once again create the roll curve joints. Select the **Roll Curve Joint** icon . In the pop up box, use the pull-down menu to select **Mechanism.2**.

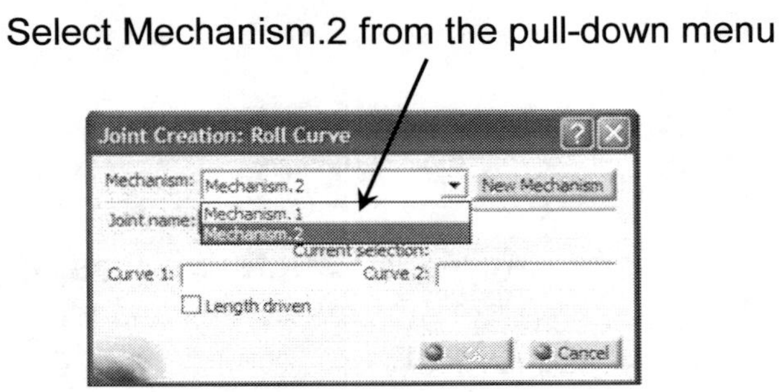

Make the selections between the **ring** and the **planet** shown in the next figure.
<u>Note that the instructions below assume that the two parts **ring** and **planet** were not manipulated in space and maintained their position in the assembly. Appropriate changes have to be made if these parts were moved around. Roll Curve joints cannot be created if the two curves are not tangent to each other</u>.

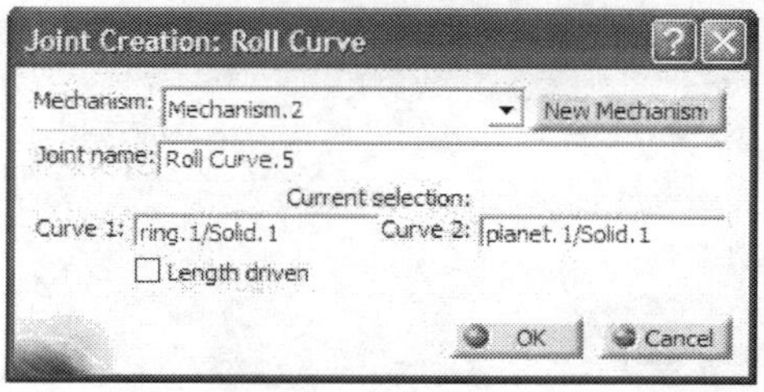

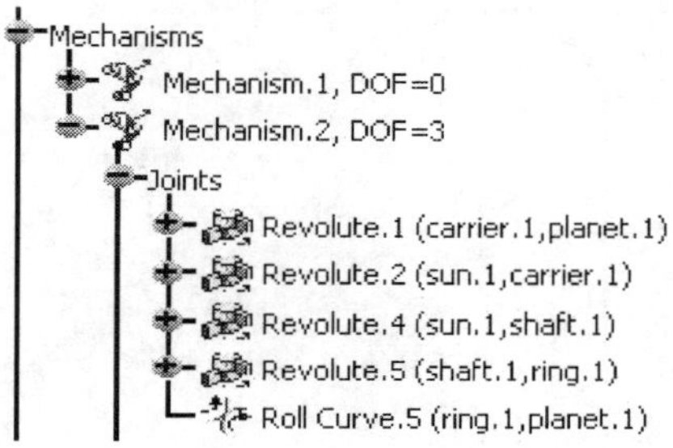

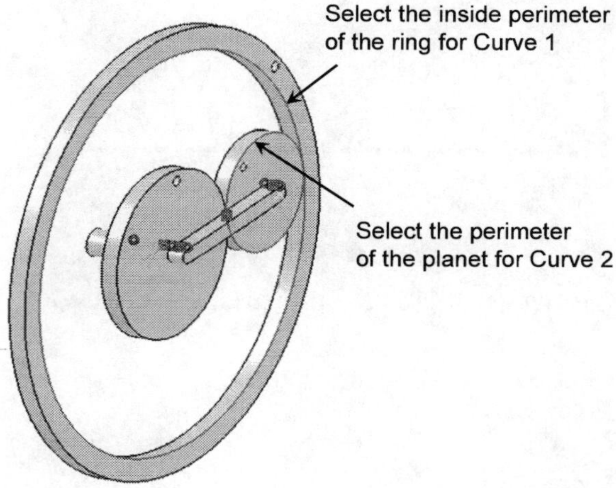

Select the **Roll Curve Joint** icon 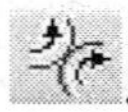. In the pop up box, use the pull-down menu to select **Mechanism.2**.

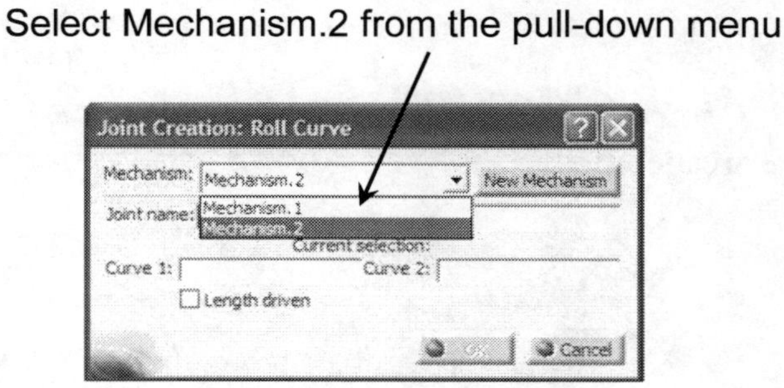

Make the selections between the **sun** and the **planet** shown in the next figure.

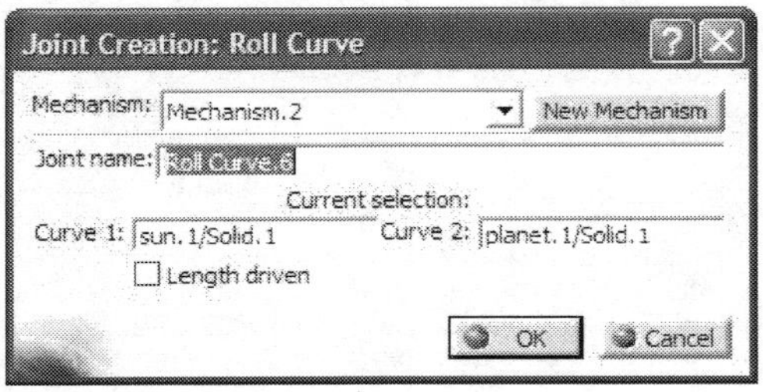

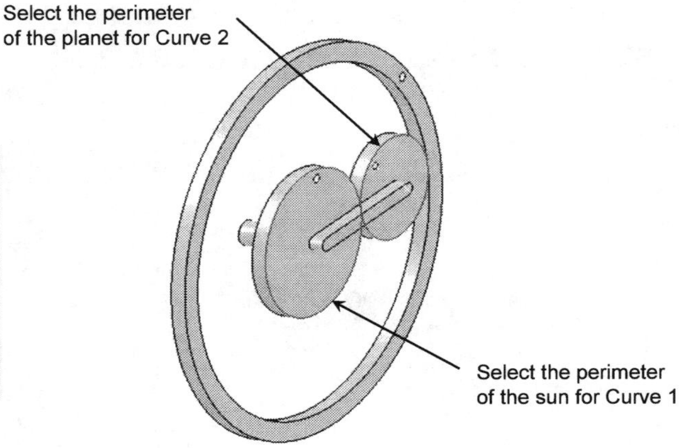

The two Roll curve joints are now created.

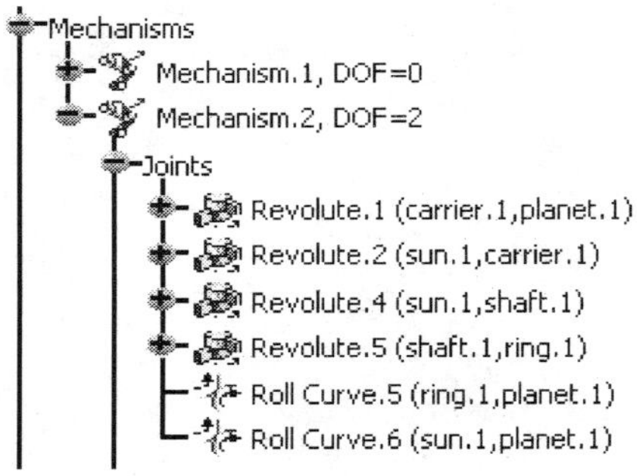

Click on the **Rigid Joint** icon  from the **Constraints** toolbar. This results in the following pop up box. Use the pull-down menu to select **Mechanism.2**.

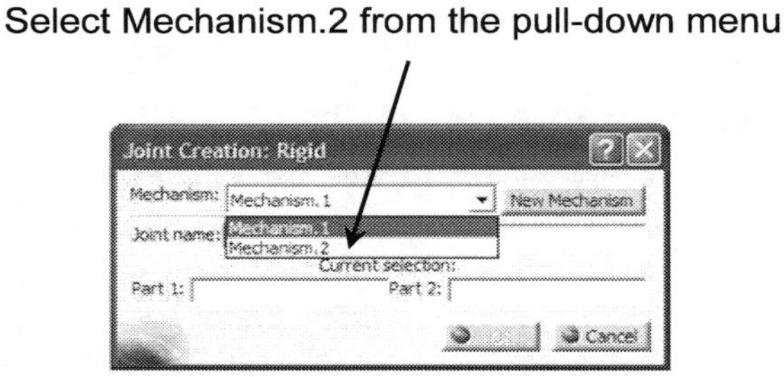

For **Part 1** and **Part 2**, select the **shaft** and the **carrier** respectively.

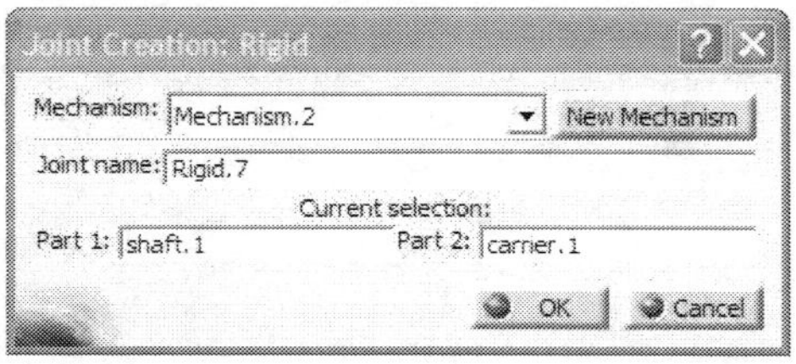

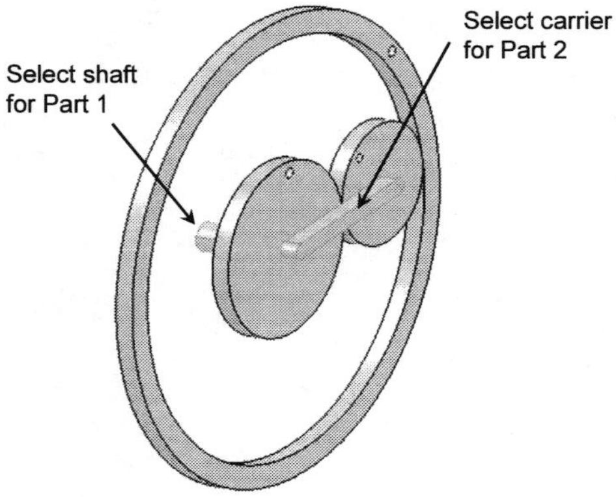

The degree of freedom for **Mechanism.2** is now reduced to 1.

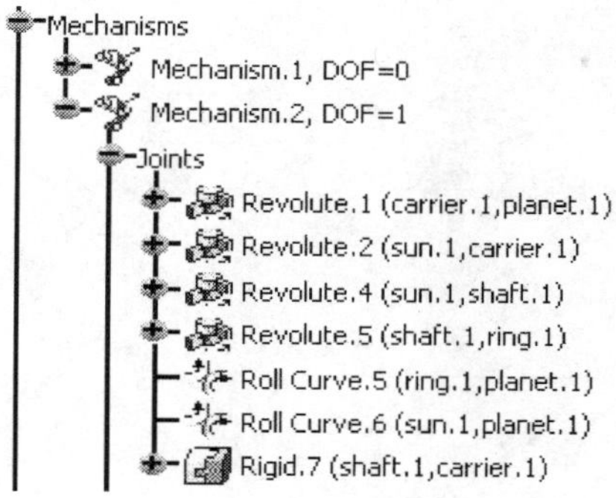

Double click on **Revolute.4** and declare it as **Angle driven** by checking the box at the bottom left corner.

Check this box

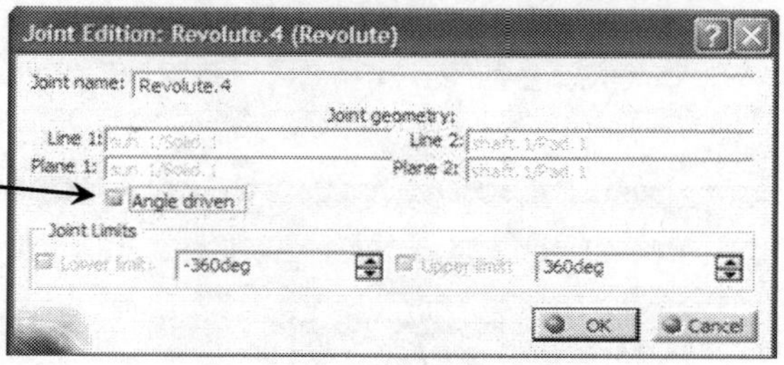

The message "**The Mechanism can be simulated**" appears and the number of degrees of freedom changed to zero.

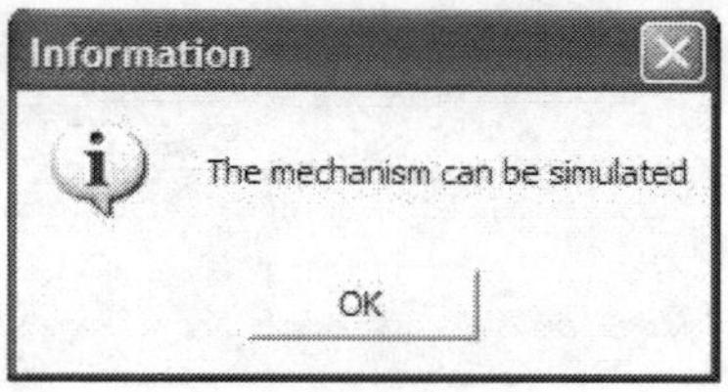

Select the **Formula** icon  from the **Knowledge** toolbar

. The pop up box below appears on the screen.

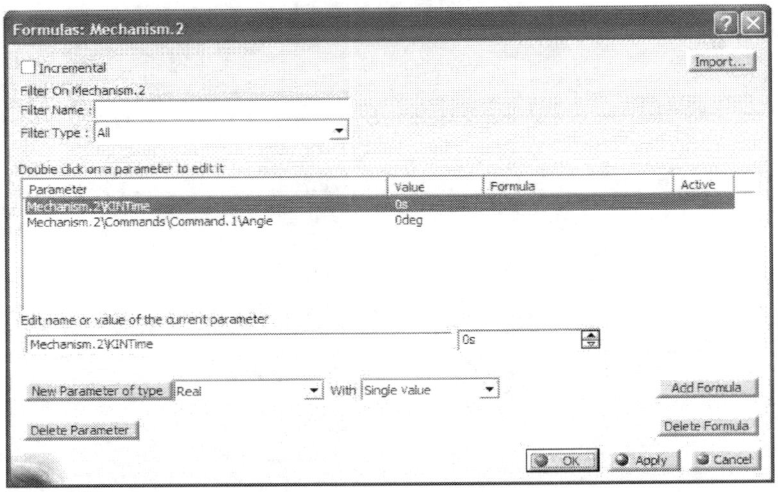

Point the cursor to the **Mechanism.2, DOF=0** branch in the tree and click. The consequence is that only parameters associated with the mechanism are displayed in the **Formulas** box.

The long list is now reduced to two parameters as indicated in the box.

Select the entry **Mechanism.2\Commands\Command.1\Angle** and press the **Add Formula** button Add Formula. This action kicks you to the **Formula Editor** box.

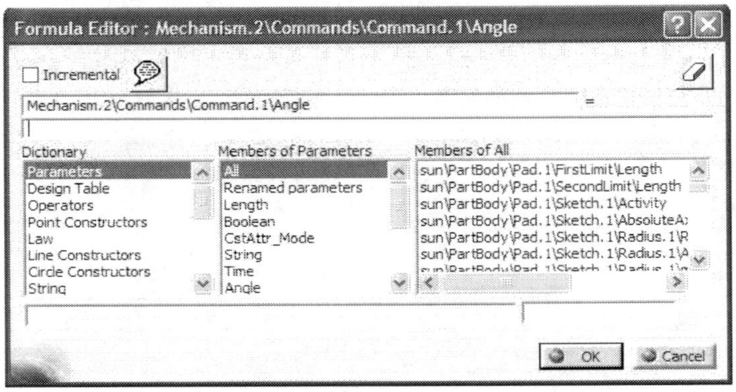

Pick the **Time** entry from the middle column (i.e. **Members of Parameters**).

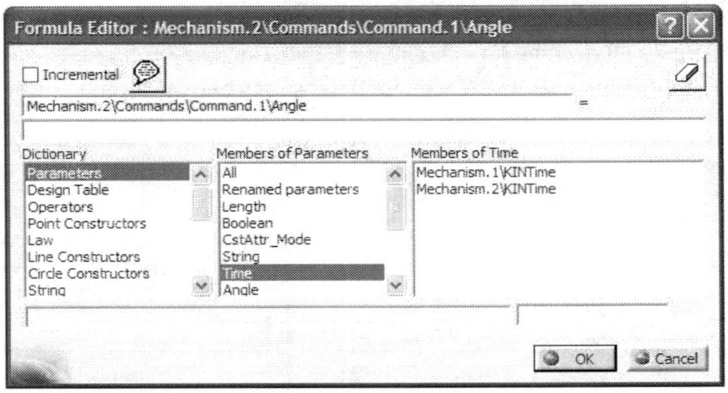

The right hand side of the equality should be such that the formula becomes

$$Mechanism.2 \setminus Commands \setminus Command.1 \setminus Angle =$$
$$(360\,\text{deg})/(1s)*(Mechnism.2 \setminus KINTime)$$

Therefore, the completed **Formula Editor** box becomes

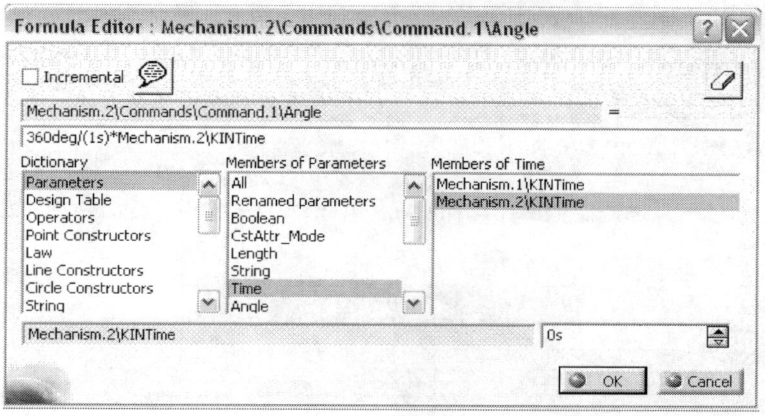

Upon accepting **OK**, the formula is recorded in the **Formulas** pop up box as shown below.

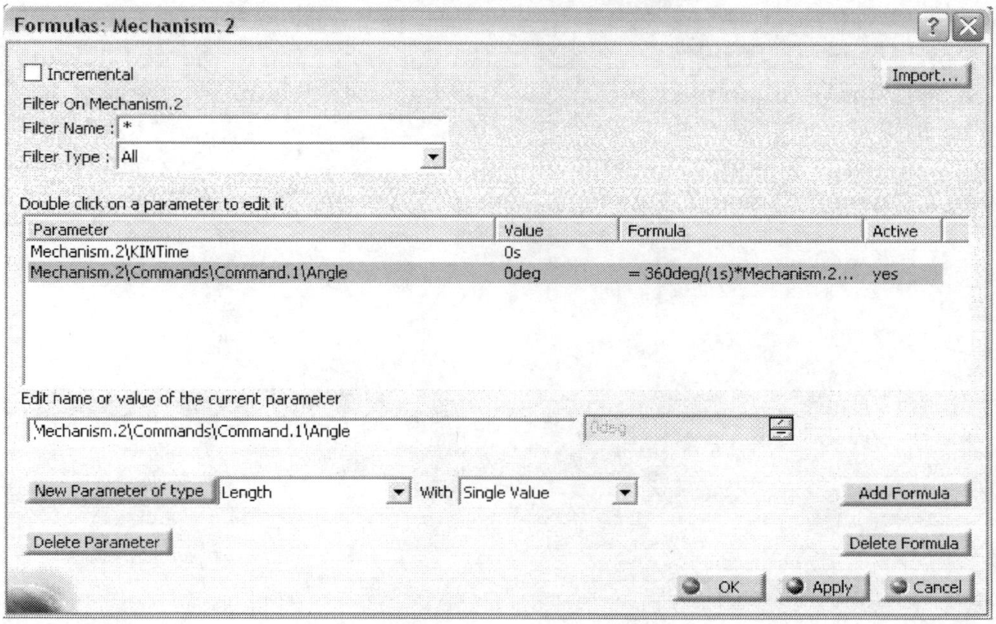

Note that the angular velocity associated with 360 deg/s corresponds to 60 rpm.

Select the **Speed and Acceleration** icon  from the **DMU Kinematics** toolbar 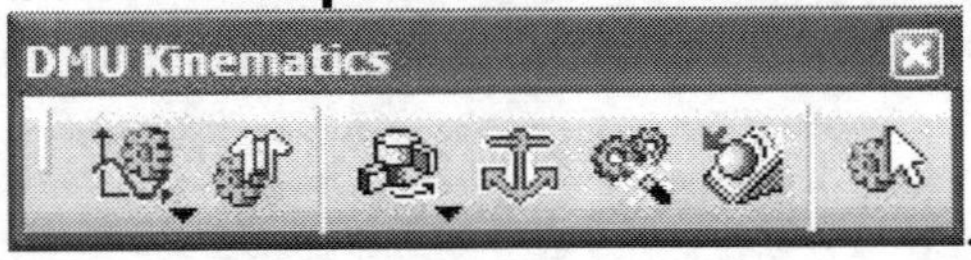

. The pop up box below appears on the Screen. Select **Mechanism.2** from the pull-down menu.

Select Mechanism.2 from the pull-down menu

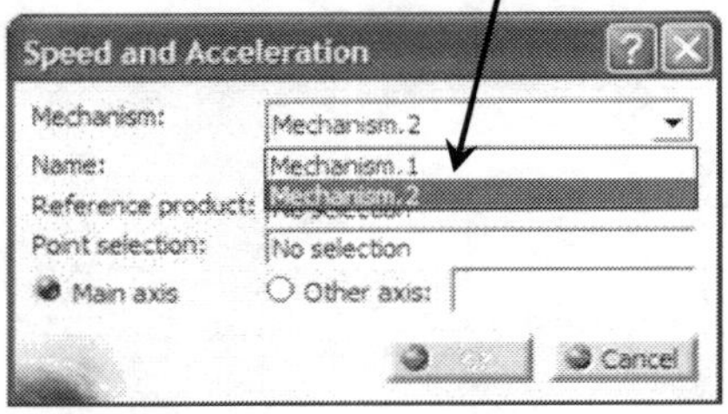

For the **Reference product,** select the **shaft** from the screen or the tree. For the **Point election**, pick the point on the **ring** as shown in the sketch below.

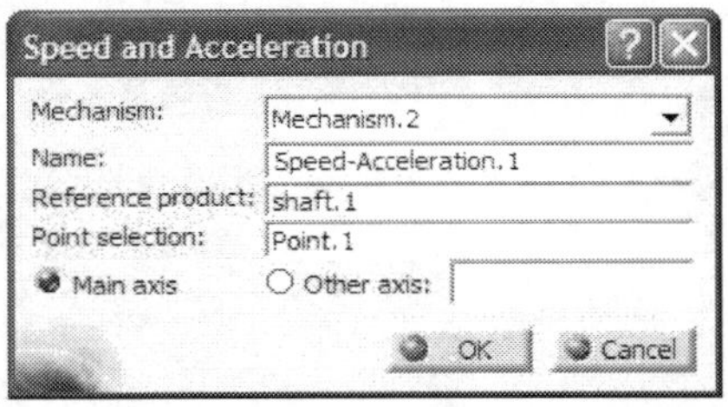

For Point selection, select The point on the ring

For Reference product select the shaft

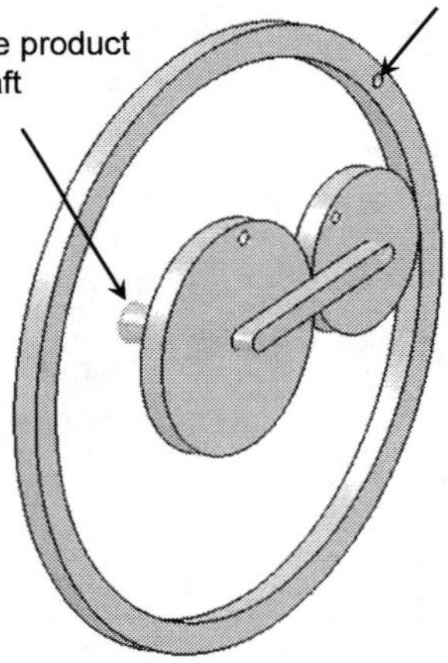

Click on **Simulation with Laws** icon  in the **Simulation** toolbar. This results in the **Kinematics Simulation** pop up box shown below. Select **Mechanism.2** from the pull-down menu.

Select Mechanism.2 from the pull-down menu

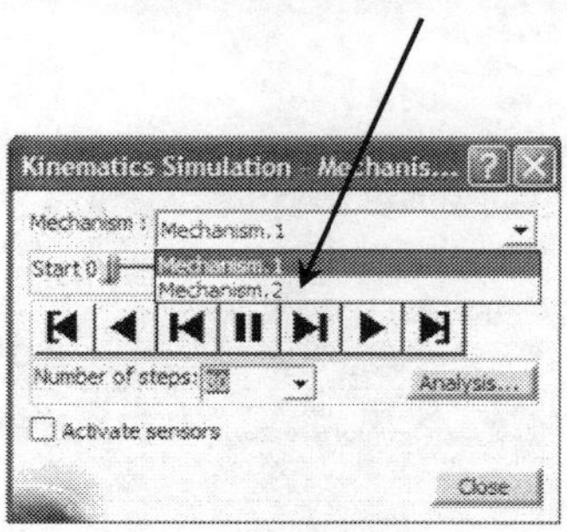

Check the **Activate sensors** box, at the bottom left corner.

You will next have to make certain selections from the accompanying **Sensors** box to indicate the kinematics parameters you would like to compute and store results on.

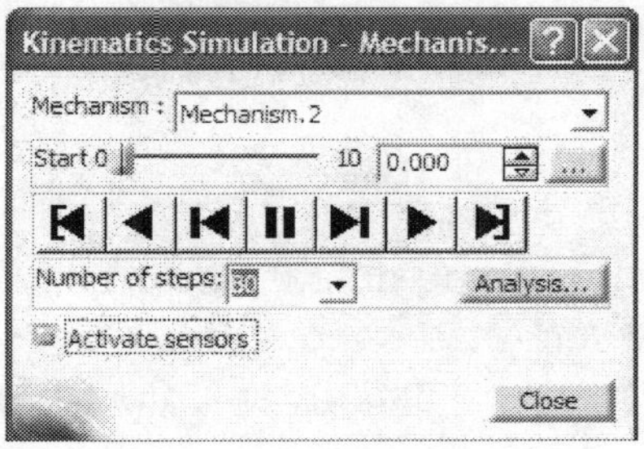

The **Sensors** box is shown below.

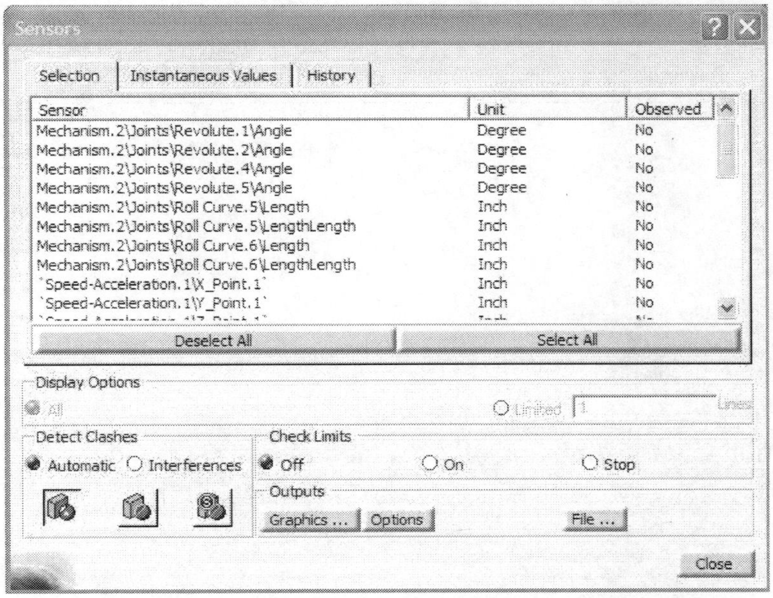

In the Sensors pop up box, click on the following item:

Speed-Acceleration.2\X_Angular Speed

As you make these selections, the last column in the **Sensors** box, changes to **Yes** for the corresponding items. Once again, choose an alternate component of angular speed if your parts are oriented such that the x axis is not aligned with your joint axes.

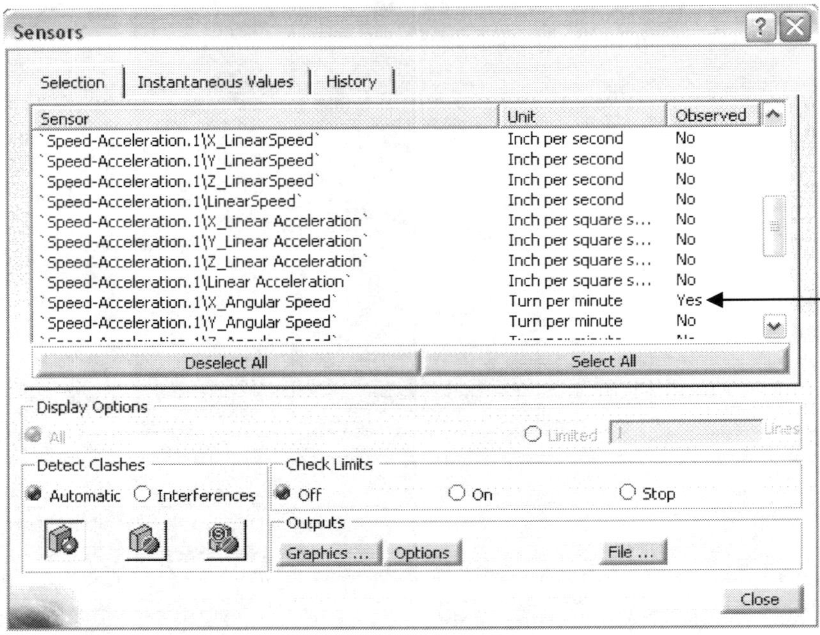

At this point, drag the scroll bar in the **Kinematics Simulation** box. As you do this, the sun rotates about the base. Once the bar reaches its right extreme point, ten seconds has elapsed and the sun has made several rotations.

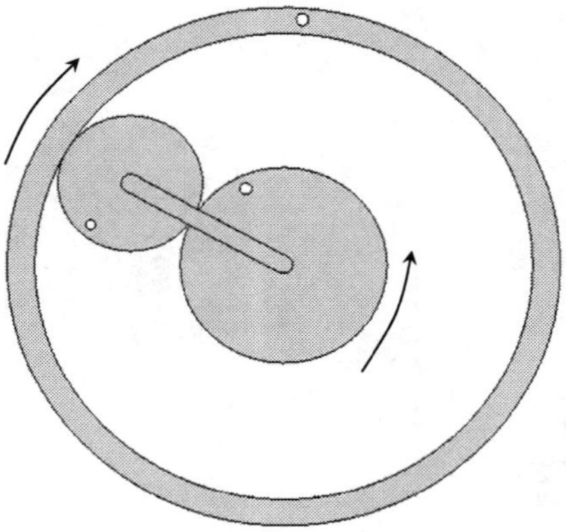

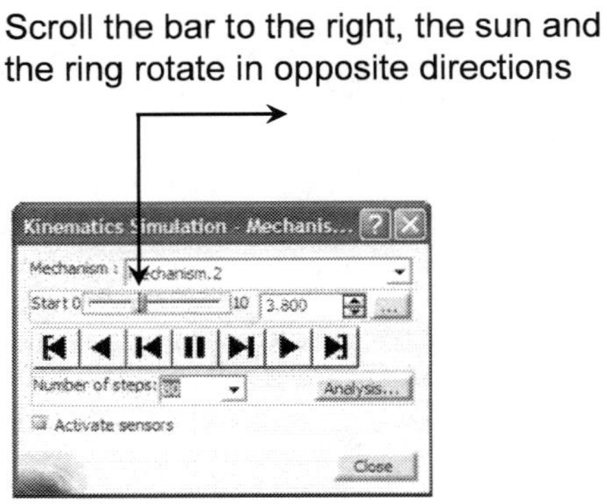

It should be clear from the motion that the direction of the rotation for the sun and the ring are opposite to one another.

Once the sun completes its motion, click on **Graphics** button 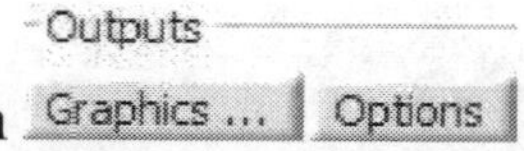

in the **Sensor** box. The result is the plot of the angular velocity of the carrier. The signed numerical value is -25 rpm which agrees with the theoretical value presented in the problem statement. **This value corresponds to a speed reduction of -60:25 or -2.4:1**. Note: Depending upon the positive orientation of your driven revolute joint, you may have to either drag the slider in reverse or put a negative sign in your law in order to get the sun to be driven in the positive direction in accordance with the right hand rule (and hence get the negative output speed as you should).

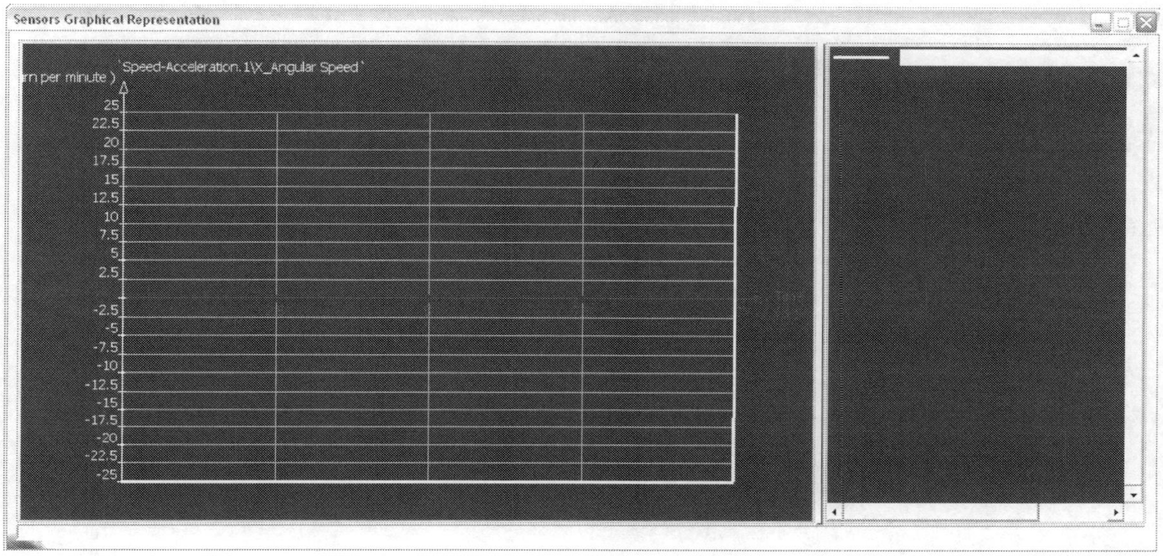

This completes the tutorial.

NOTES:

Chapter 10

Telescoping Mechanism

Introduction

This tutorial deals with a telescopic mechanism having one end connected to the ground by a ball and socket type of connection with the other end traversing a desired path represented by a curve. The combination of spherical, point-curve, point-surface and prismatic joints are used to simulate the mechanism. This mechanism illustrates how an unwanted degree of freedom, namely rotation of the telescopic mechanism about its own axis, can be constrained away to enable the simulation to be performed.

1 Problem Statement

A telescopic mechanism consisting of a pair of tubular parts is shown below. The bottom end is constrained to a point with a spherical joint whereas the top of the telescope is constrained to move along a path at a constant linear velocity of 1 in/s. The total length of the path is 12.45 in and therefore the travel time for one revolution is 12.45 s. The objective of this tutorial is to simulate this mechanism and to generate a plot of the linear acceleration versus time for the point on the telescopic mechanism which is following the curve. Of course, since the curve is being traversed at constant speed, the tangential acceleration is always zero and thus the net linear acceleration will represent the normal component of acceleration. Velocity will also be plotted just to confirm it is 1 in/s as desired.

The initial attempt to simulate the mechanism with a spherical joint at the base, a prismatic joint between the tubular parts, and a point curve joint between the tip of the upper tube and the desired path curve runs into a problem where the degree of freedom is persisting to be one even when driving the length of the point curve joint. This degree of freedom is representative of the fact that the arm can freely spin about its own axis. This degree of freedom is removed by creating a point-surface joint eliminating the rotation.

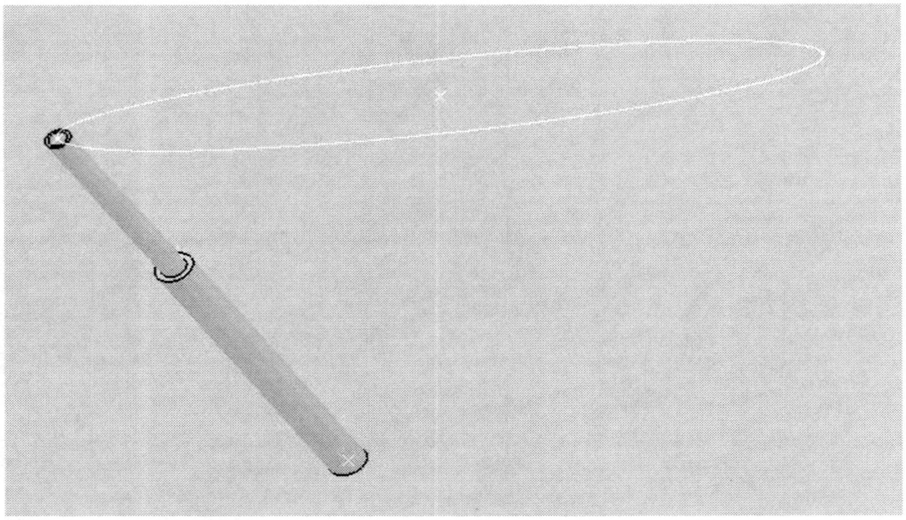

2 Overview of this Tutorial

This tutorial will involve the following steps:

1. Modeling the three CATIA parts required.
2. Creating an assembly (CATIA Product) containing the parts.
3. Constraining the assembly in such a manner which locates the parts at their start position for the mechanism simulation and which is consistent with the desired spherical joint and a prismatic joint.
4. Entering the **Digital Mockup** workbench and converting the assembly constraints into a spherical joint and a prismatic joint.
5. Creating the required Point Curve joint and Point Surface joint.
6. Simulating the relative motion of the assembly without consideration to time (in other words, without implementing the time based linear velocity given in the problem statement).
7. Adding a formula to implement the time based kinematics.
8. Simulating the desired constant linear velocity motion and generating plot of the resulting acceleration of the point following the path curve.

3 Creation of the Assembly in Mechanical Design Solutions

Model three parts named **outer**, **inner** and **dummy** as shown below with the suggested dimensions. It is assumed that you are sufficiently familiar with CATIA to model these parts fairly quickly. However in this section, we will assist you to create the part named **dummy** since it actually contains no solid geometry, but rather a point at which the telescopic arm will be attached, a point at the center of the desired path, and a curve representing the intended path of a point at the tip of the mechanism.

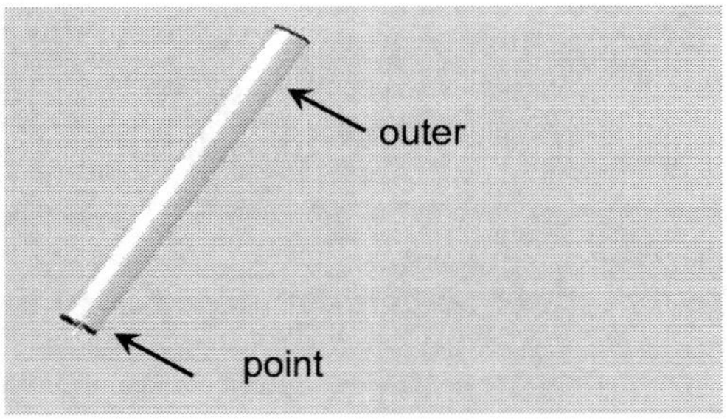

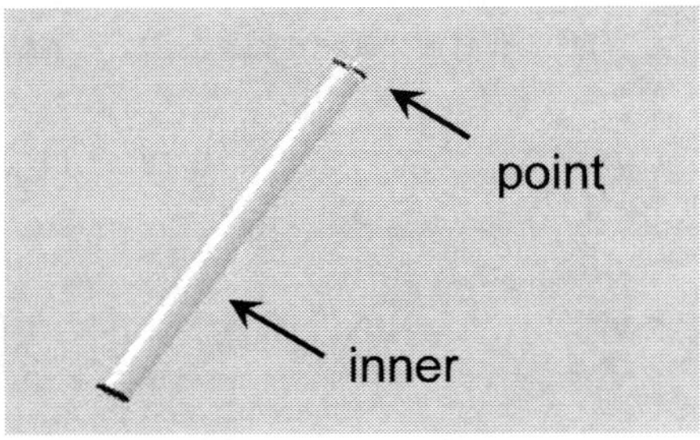

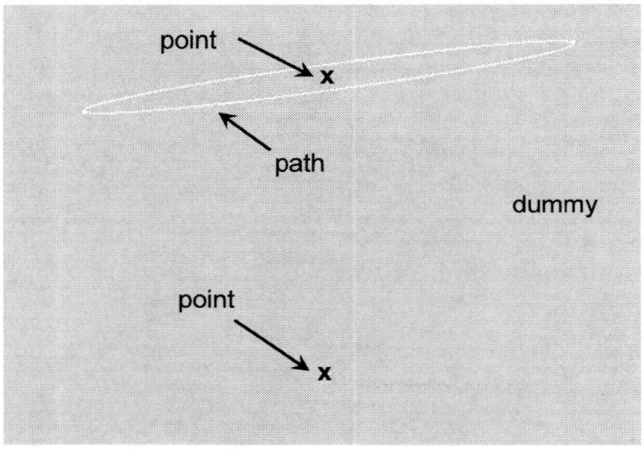

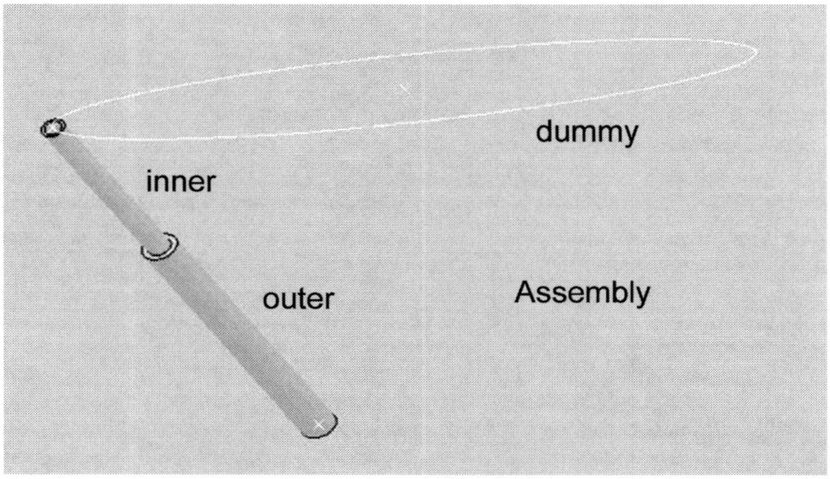

Outline of creating the part named **dummy**:

Enter the **Part Design** workbench which can be achieved by different means depending on your CATIA customization. For example, from the standard Windows toolbar, select **File > New** . From the box shown on the right, select **Part**. This moves you to the **Part Design** workbench and creates a part with the default name **Part.1**.

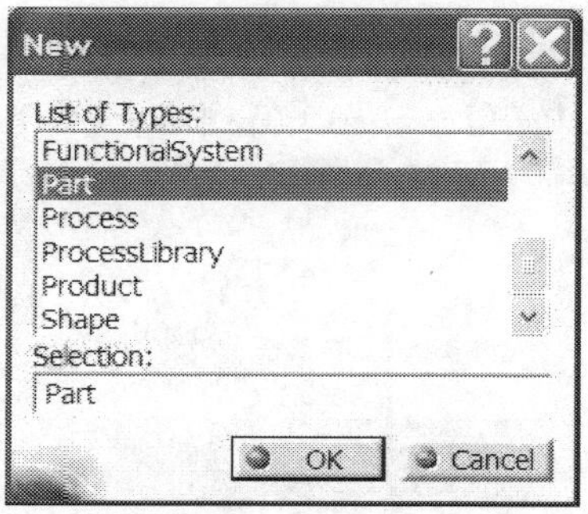

In order to change the default name, move the cursor to **Part.1** in the tree, right click and select **Properties** from the menu list.

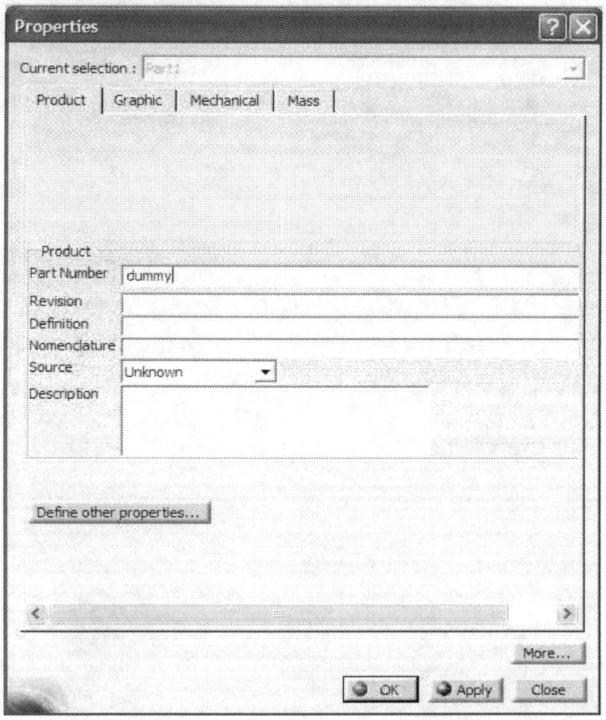

From the **Properties** box, select the **Product** tab and in **Part Number** type **dummy**. This will be the new part name throughout the chapter. The tree on the top left corner of the screen should look as displayed below.

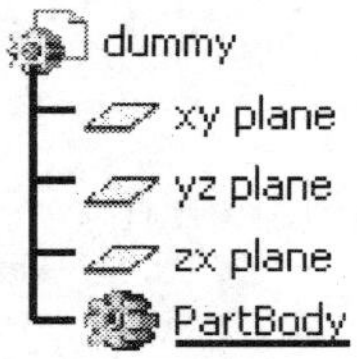

Change workbenches by selecting **Start > Wireframe and Surface Design**.

Select the **Point** icon from the **Wireframe** toolbar. Create a point with coordinates (0,0,0) by selecting the default values in the pop up box.

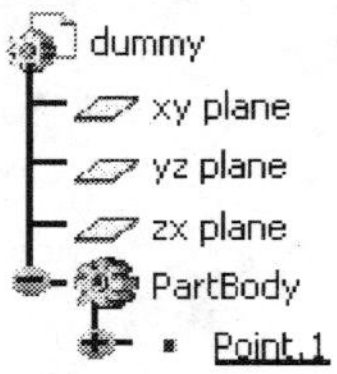

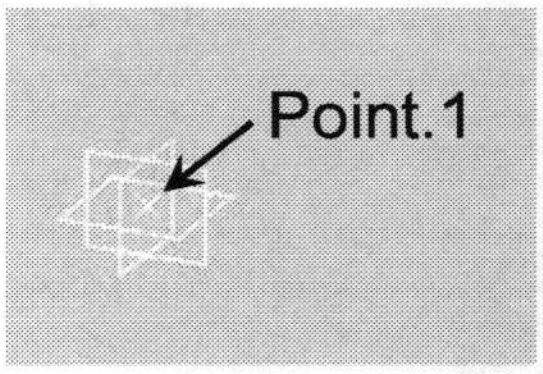

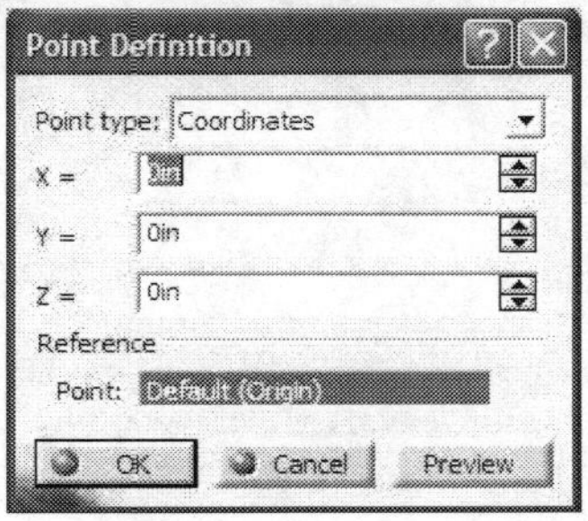

Next we will create a plane which will ultimately contain the path curve. Select the **Plane** icon  from the **Wireframe** toolbar 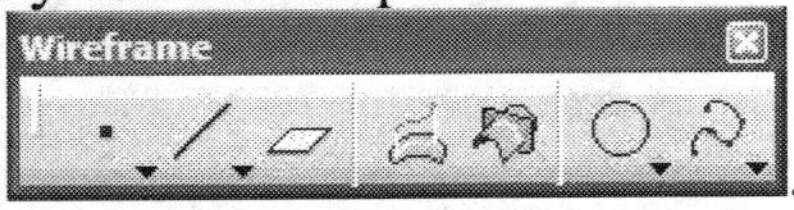

.
In the resulting pop up box, for **Plane type**, choose **Offset from plane**. For **Reference**, choose **xy plane** from the screen or the tree. Finally for **Offset**, use 4.

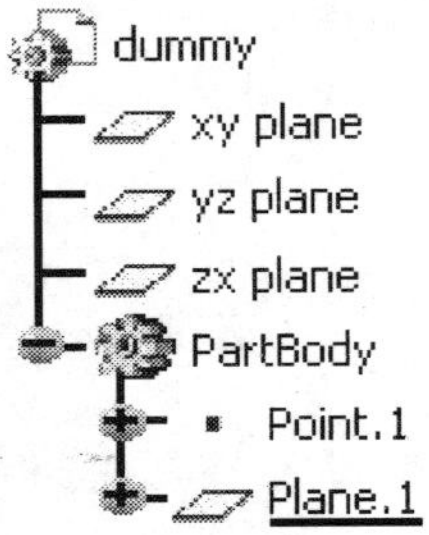

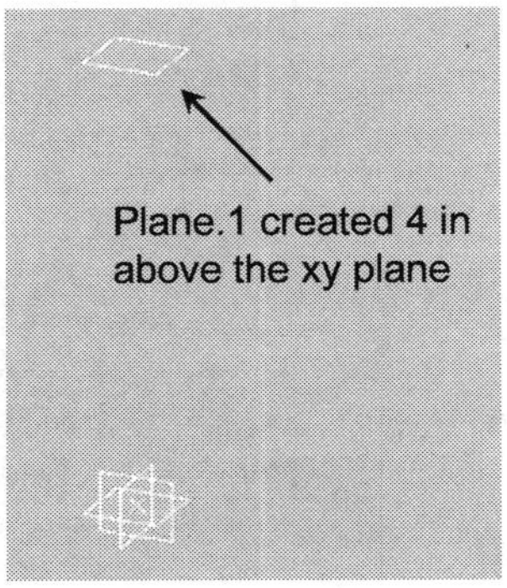

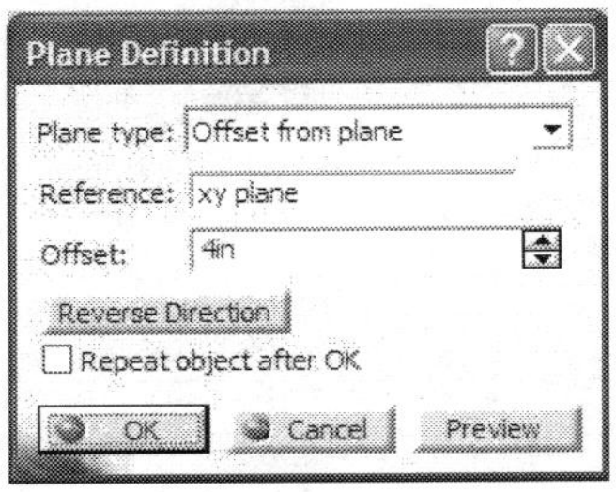

With the cursor, select the plane just created and click on the **Sketcher** icon .

Select the **Ellipse** icon  from the **Conic** toolbar 

. Draw an ellipse centered at the sketcher origin and aligned with the horizontal and vertical directions as shown below.

Use the **Constraint** icon 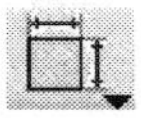 to make the major axis 3 in and the minor axis 0.5 in.

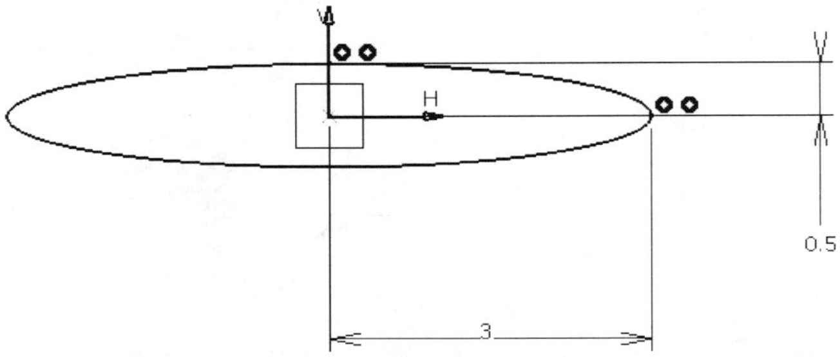

Exit the **Sketcher** 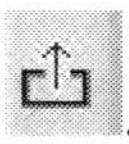.

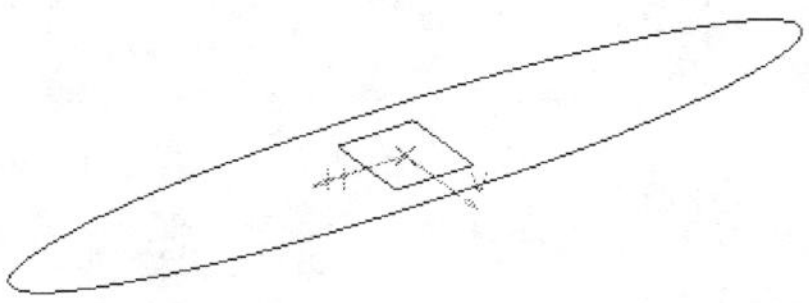

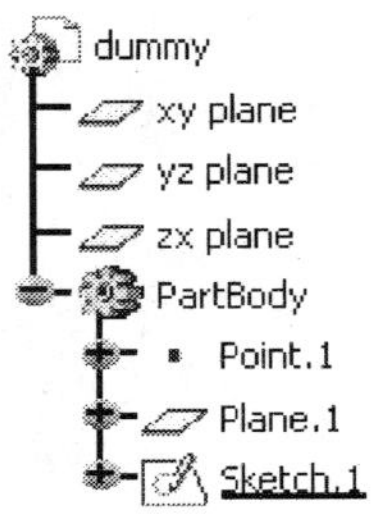

This completes the construction of the part named **dummy**. The point at the origin will be used to connect the outer tube, and the ellipse represents the desired path curve for the tip of the inner tube to follow.
The construction of the parts **inner** and **outer** is straightforward. However, you should create a point at the bottom of the tubular geometry **outer**. You should also create a point at the top of the tubular geometry **inner**. This is easily done by selecting **Circle/Sphere center** option in the **Point Definition** box as displayed below. The lengths and diameters are not critical to the simulation except for aesthetics purposes; lengths of 3 inches for each part works well here with the inside diameter of the part **outer** set to match the outside diameter of the part **inner**.

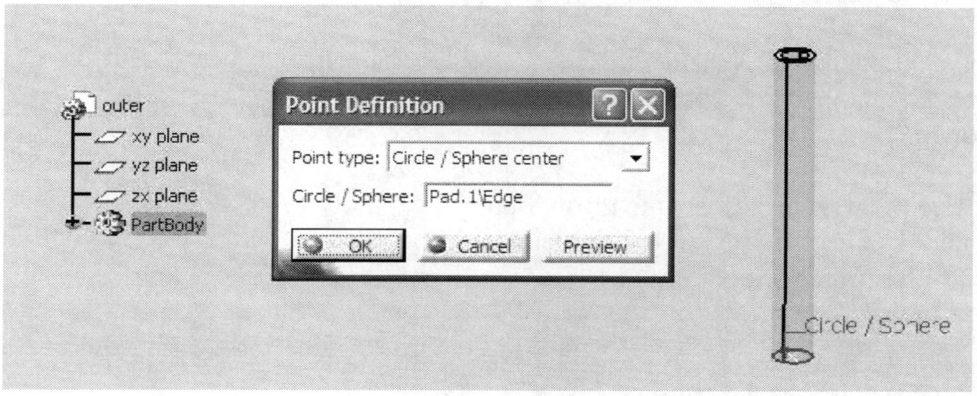

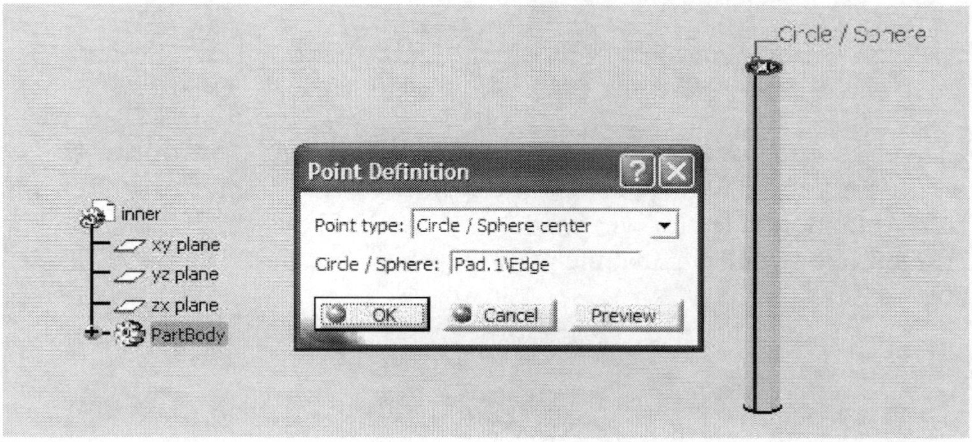

You will next assemble the three parts and impose constraints.

Enter the **Assembly Design** workbench  which can be achieved by different means depending on your CATIA customization. For example, from the standard Windows toolbar, select **File > New** .
From the box shown on the right, select **Product**. This moves you to the **Assembly Design** workbench and creates an assembly with the default name **Product.1**.

In order to change the default name, move the cursor to **Product.1** in the tree, right click and select **Properties** from the menu list.

From the **Properties** box, select the **Product** tab and in **Part Number** type **telescopic**.

This will be the new product name throughout the chapter. The tree on the top left corner of your computer screen should look as displayed below.

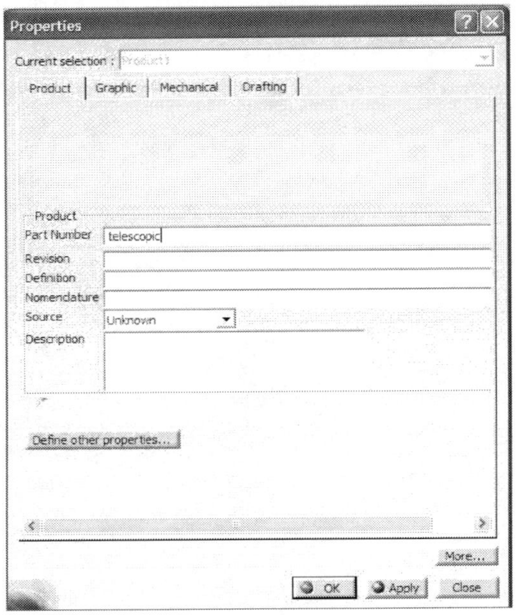

The next step is to insert the existing parts into the assembly just created.

From the standard Windows toolbar, select **Insert > Existing Component**.
From the **File Selection** pop up box choose **dummy**, **inner**, and **outer**. Remember that in CATIA multiple selections are made with the **Ctrl** key.
The tree is modified to indicate that the parts have been inserted.

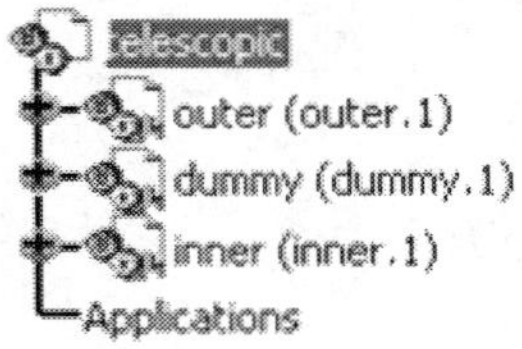

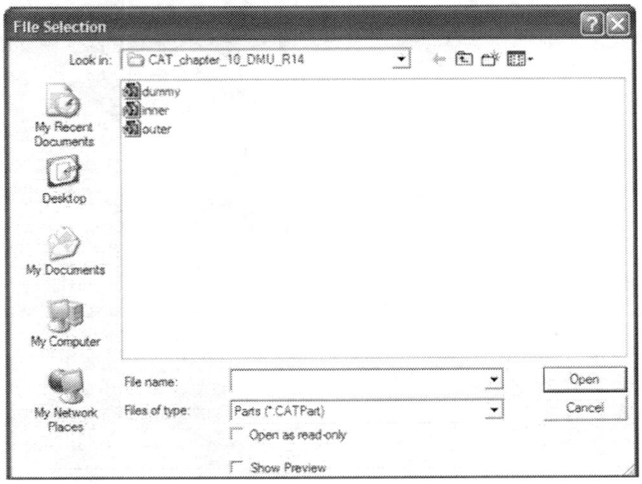

The best way of saving your work is to save the entire assembly.
Double click on the top branch of the tree. This is to ensure that you are in the **Assembly Design** workbench.
Select the **Save** icon . The **Save As** pop up box allows you to rename if desired. The default name is the **telescopic**.

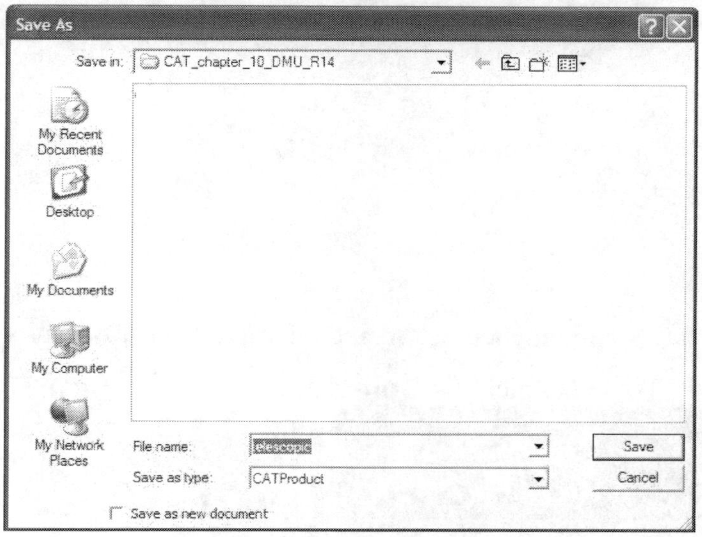

Note that the part names and their instance names were purposely made the same. This practice makes later identification of the assembly constraint a lot easier.
Depending on how your parts were created earlier, on the computer screen you have the four parts scattered as shown below. You may have to use the **Manipulation** icon  in the **Move** toolbar 

to rearrange them as desired so they are not overlapping.

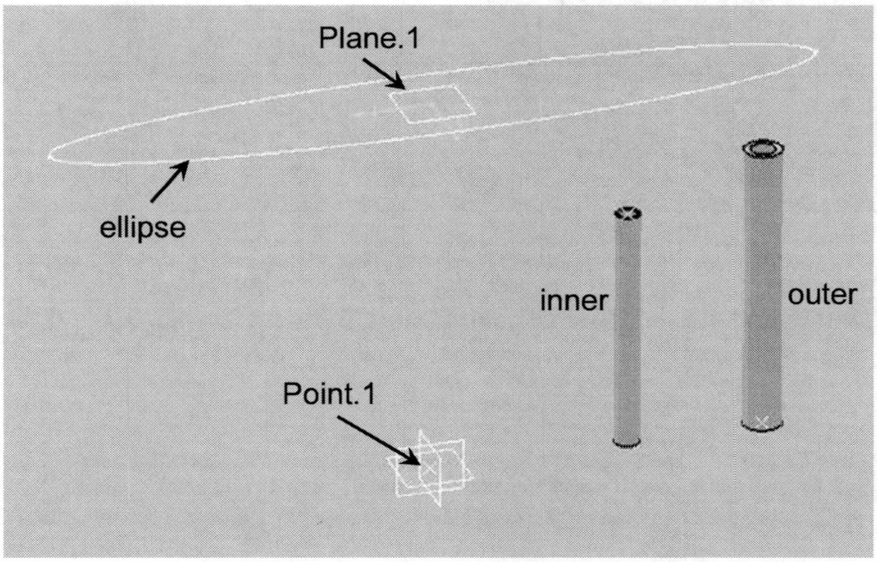

Pick the **Anchor** icon  from **Constraints** toolbar and select the **dummy** part from the tree or from the screen.

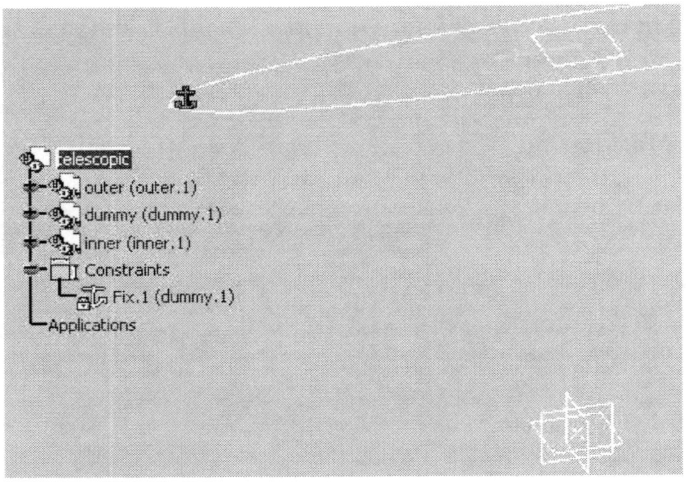

We will next create a coincidence between the **Point.1** on **dummy** and the point at the bottom of **outer**. To do so, pick the **Coincidence** icon  from **Constraints** toolbar 

. Select the points as shown in the figure below (next to the coincident constraint symbols).

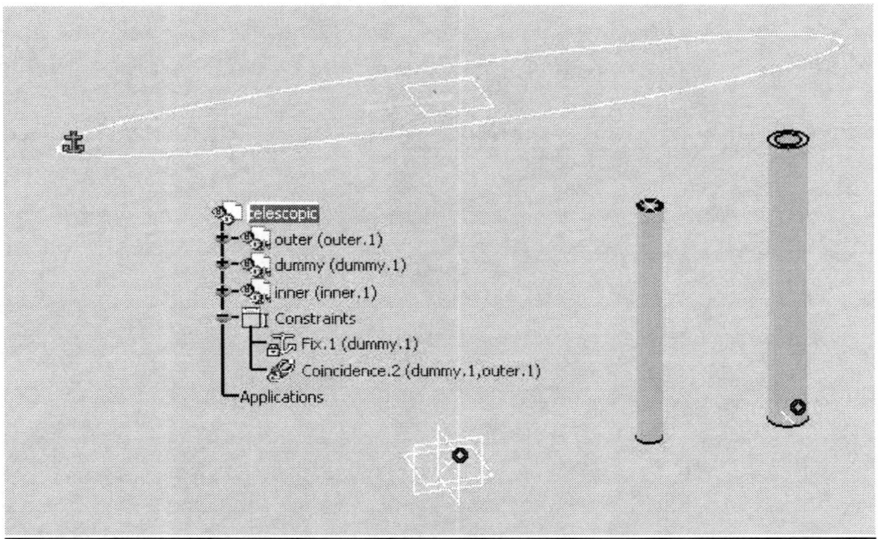

This constraint removes all the translational degrees of freedom (dof) at that point on the **dummy** and will eventually become a spherical joint between the **outer** and the **dummy**.

You will next create the constraints necessary for a prismatic joint between the inner and outer parts. This requires removing all relative dof except for translation of one of the part's axis along the axis of the other part.

Pick the **Coincidence** icon from **Constraints** toolbar and select the axes of the parts shown.

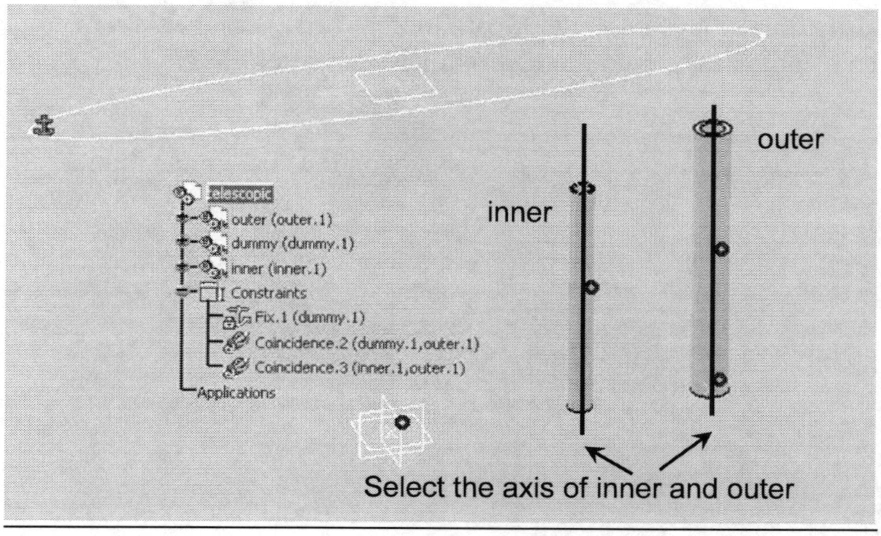

The constraint just imposed is sufficient for a cylindrical joint between the tubular parts, however one must prevent the relative rotation about the axis in order to create a prismatic joint. To achieve this, it suffices to impose and angular constrain between any of the two vertical planes in inner and outer parts.

Select the **Angle constraint** icon from the **Constraints** toolbar. Accept the default angle of zero degrees (assuming you picked two initially parallel planes).

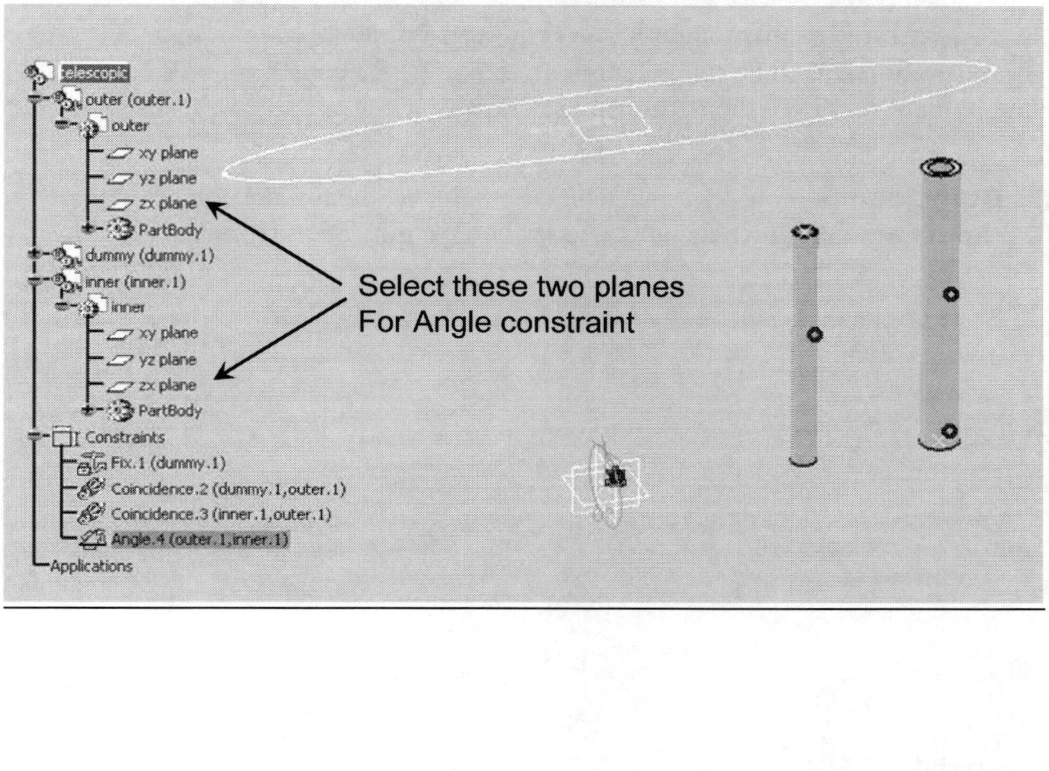

Use **Update** icon  to enforce constraints just created resulting in relative position the parts similar to as shown below.
Your updated position may be completely different from the configuration shown. If so, use the **Manipulation** icon  in the **Move** toolbar 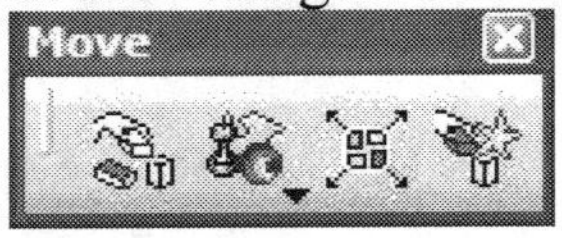

to rearrange them as desired bringing them into the approximate formation shown.

Note that the **Update** icon  no longer appears on the constraints branches.

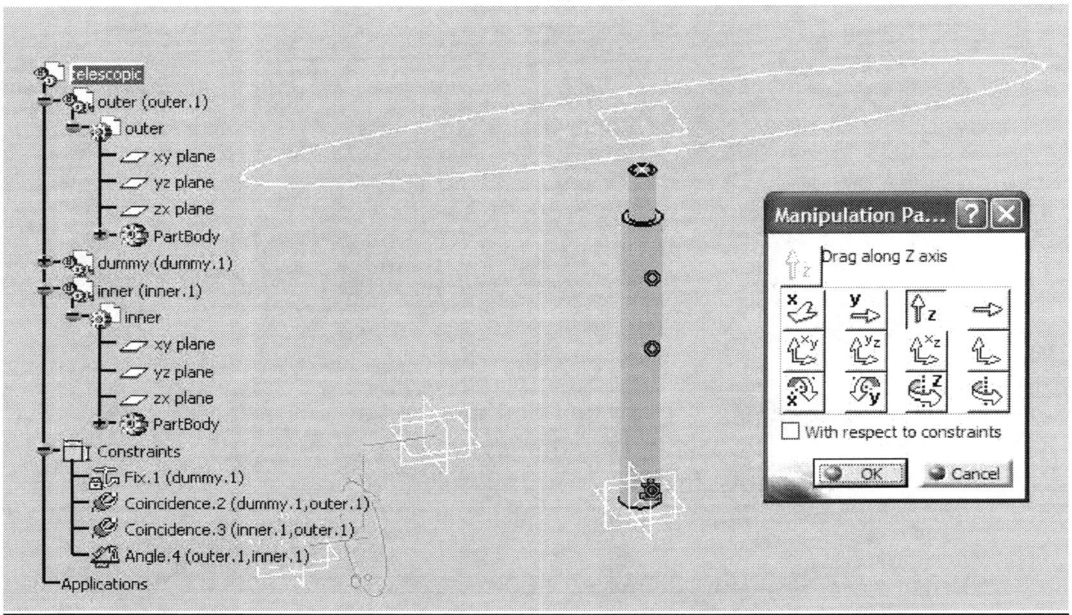

Later in the **Digital Mockup**, you will be creating a Point Curve joint manually. In order to do so, the point needs to be on the ellipse. A coincidence constraint will be applied to locate the point at the tip of the **inner** on the ellipse.

Pick the **Coincidence** icon , and select the point on the top portion of the inner part, and the ellipse from the screen as indicated in the figure on the next page.

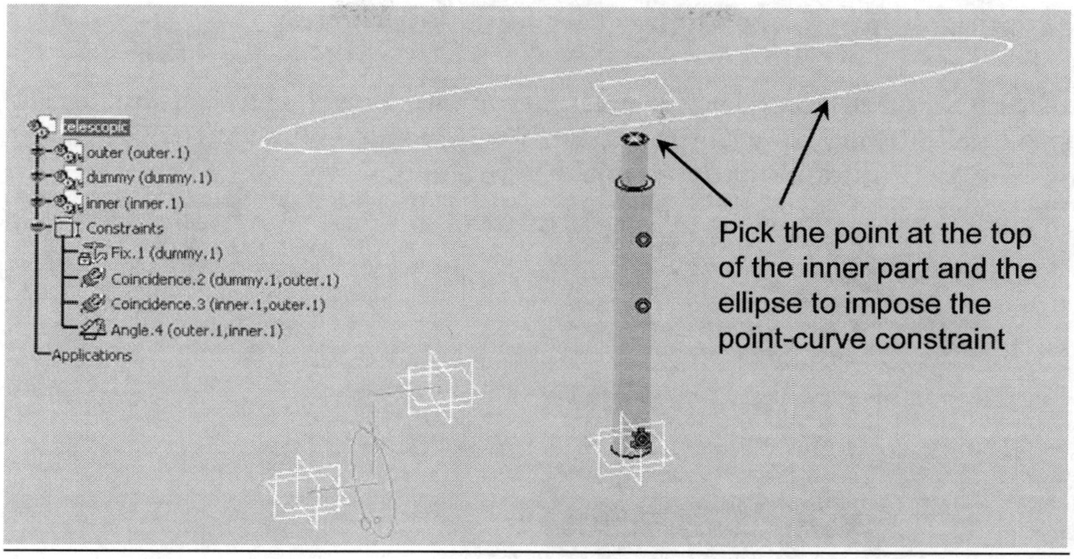

Use **Update** icon  to enforce the constraint just created.

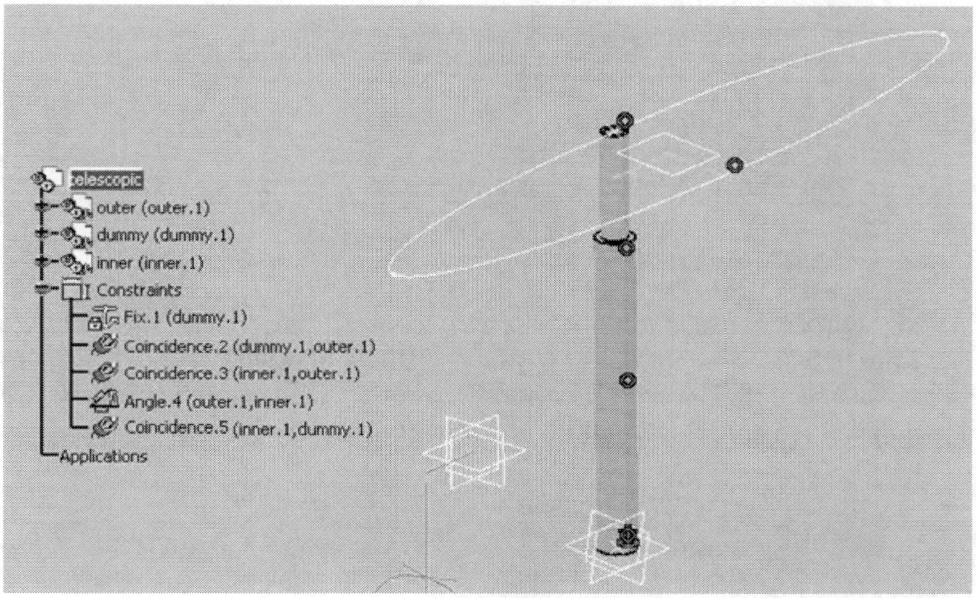

The assembly is complete and we can proceed to the **Digital Mockup** workbench.

4 Creating Joints in the Digital Mockup Workbench

The **Digital Mockup** workbench is quite extensive but we will only deal with the **DMU Kinematics module**. To get there you can use the standard Windows toolbar as shown below: **Start > Digital Mockup > DMU Kinematics**.

Our first step will be to use automatic assembly constraints conversion to create a spherical joint between the bottom of **outer** and the point at the origin of **dummy**. Since we constrained the upper point on **inner** to be on the curve of **dummy**, we will also get an unwanted spherical joint there; we will delete that joint.

Select the **Assembly Constraints Conversion** icon from the **DMU Kinematics** toolbar

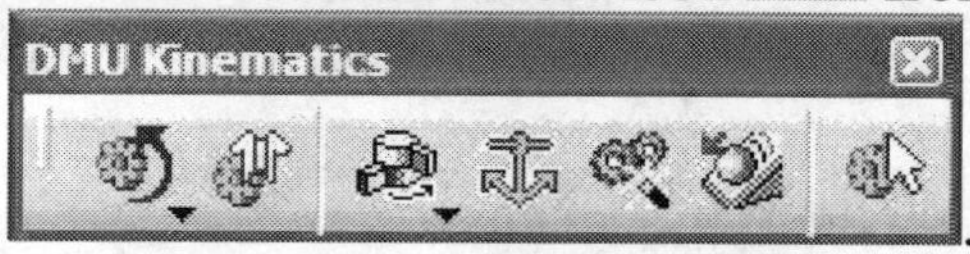

. This icon allows you to create most common joints automatically from the existing assembly constraints. The pop up box below appears.

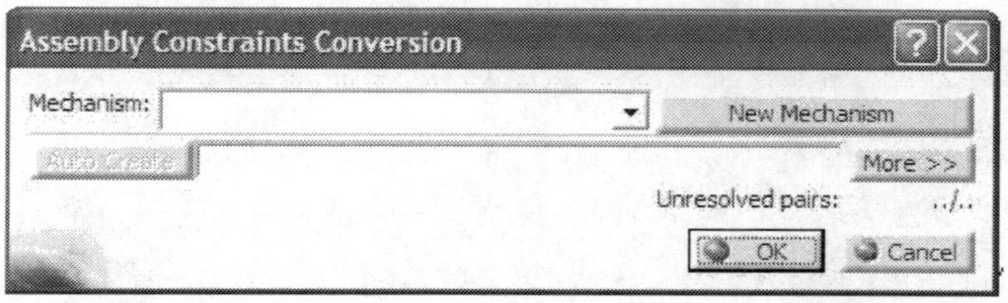

Select the **New Mechanism** button New Mechanism.
This leads to another pop up box which allows you to name your mechanism.
The default name is **Mechanism.1**. Accept the default name by pressing **OK**.

Note that the box indicates **Unresolved pairs: 3/3**.

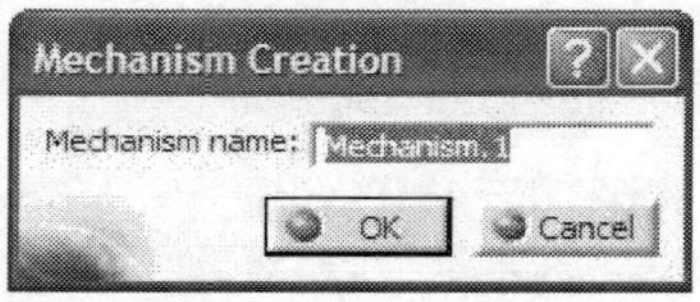

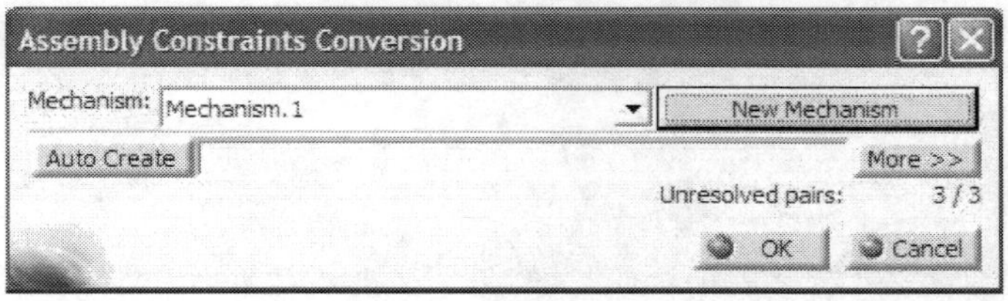

Select the **Auto Create** button Auto Create. Then if the **Unresolved pairs** becomes **0/3**, things are moving in the right direction.

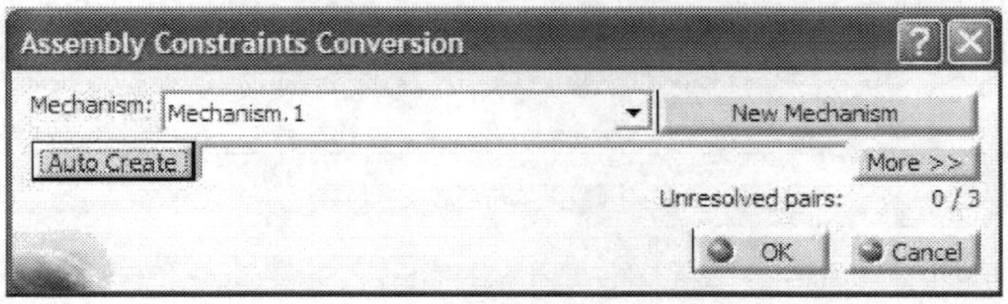

The **Spherical.1** joint between **inner** and **dummy** needs to be deleted; otherwise the inner part is rigidly attached to the ellipse and will be unable to move.

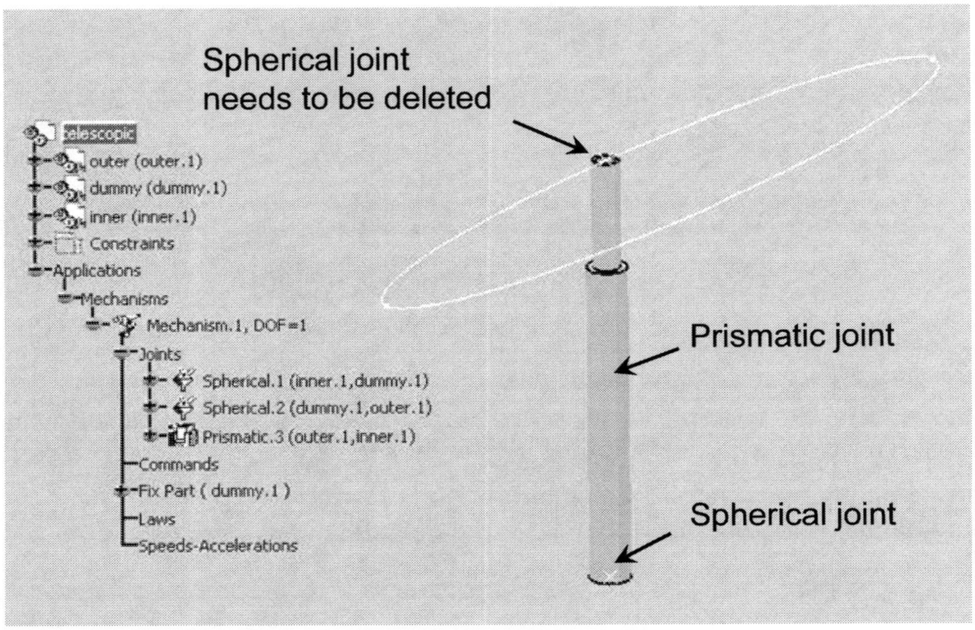

After deleting this joint, the number of degrees of freedom is changed to 4, **DOF = 4**.

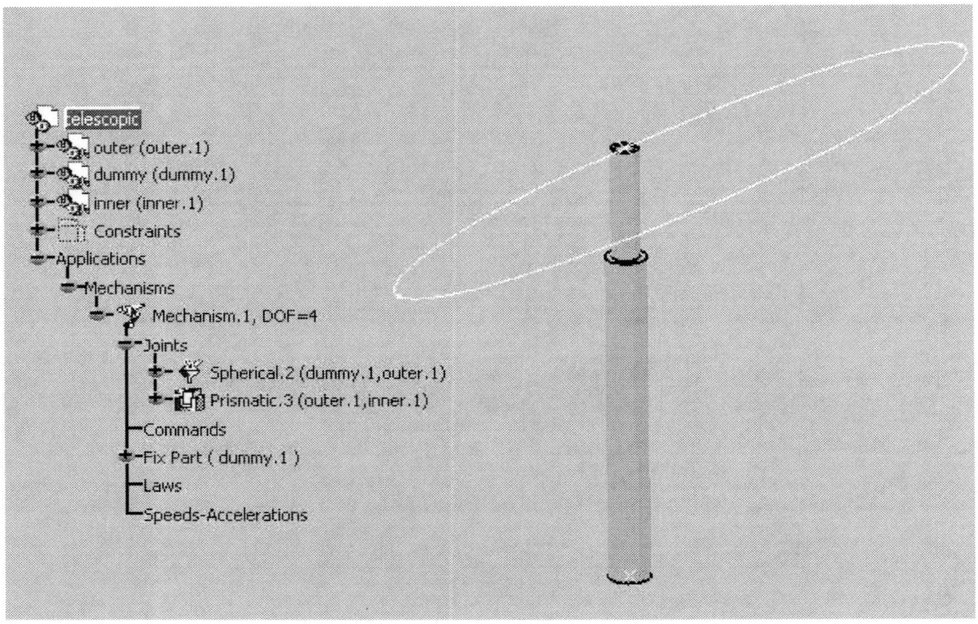

You are now in the position to create the Point Curve joint to hold the upper point on **inner** on the curve on **dummy**.

Pick the **Point Curve Joint** icon  from the **Kinematics Joint** toolbar

In the resulting pop up box, make selection as indicated in the following figure.

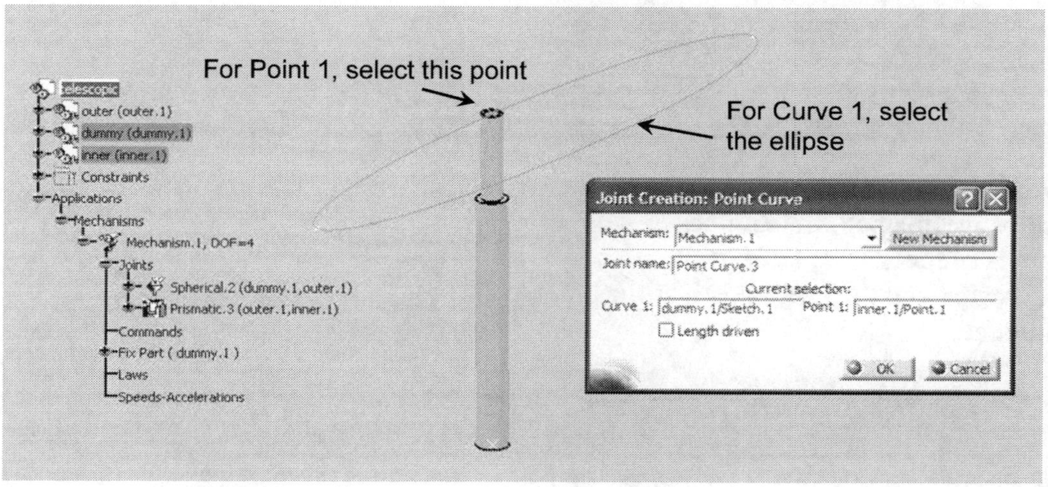

Upon closing the box, the degrees of freedom is changed to 2, **DOF = 2**.

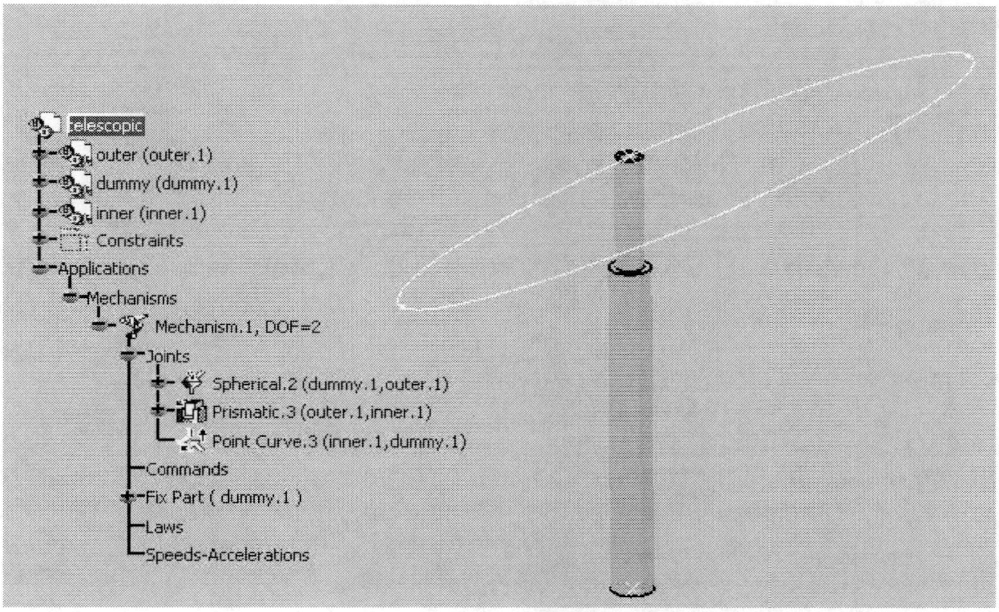

Next, you will be making the **Point Curve.3** joint, length driven.
Double click on the **Point Curve.3** branch in the tree and choose the **Length driven** option.

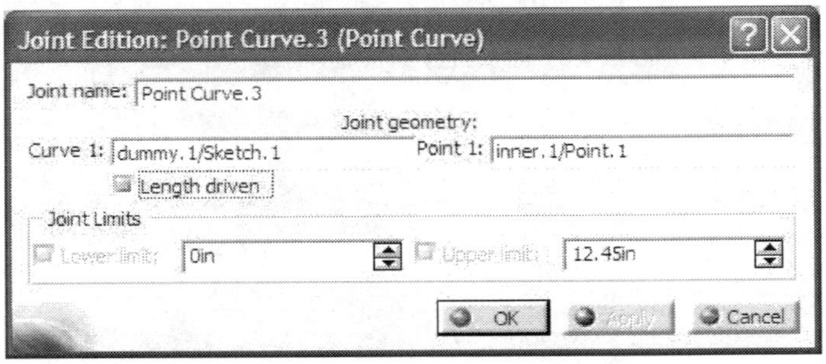

Upon closing this box, the number of degrees of freedom is reduced to 1, **DOF = 1**.
This indicates that the mechanism still cannot be simulated.

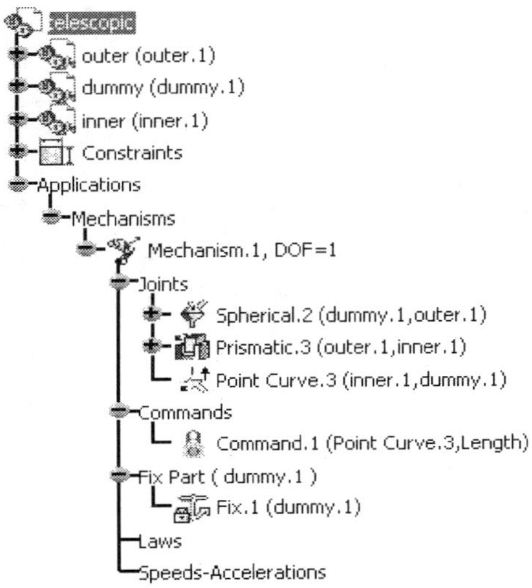

So, what is the problem?

The reason behind the remaining degree of freedom is that the combination of the inner/outer tube can freely spin about its tubular axis. This rotation has to be eliminated in order to simulate the mechanism.

There are different methods for achieving this objective. In order to save time on the previous steps taken, we propose the following strategy (a summary of the strategy is given below with detailed instructions for each step given on subsequent pages).

Step 1) In **Part Design** workbench, create a point in the **dummy** part (say the center of the path).
Step 2) In the **Assembly Design** workbench, create an assembly constraint to make the point coincident with the yz plane of the **outer** part.

Step 3) In the **Digital Mockup** workbench, create a **Point Surface Joint**  between the **Point** and the yz plane of **outer**. Note that the purpose of step (2) is to make sure that the point lies on the plane otherwise the desired joint cannot be created.

This joint prevents the free rotation of the inner/outer part and reduced the degree of freedom by one. Consequently, the mechanism can be simulated.

Outline of Step 1: Creating a Point in Dummy

Load the **dummy** part into the **Part Design** workbench.

Pick the **Point** icon  from the **Reference Element** toolbar 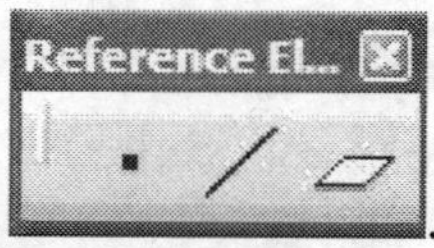

. In the **Point Definition** box, use the pull down menu and select **Circle/Sphere center**.

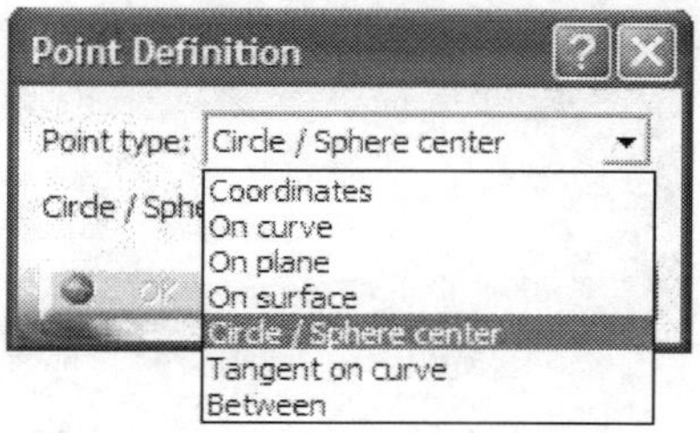

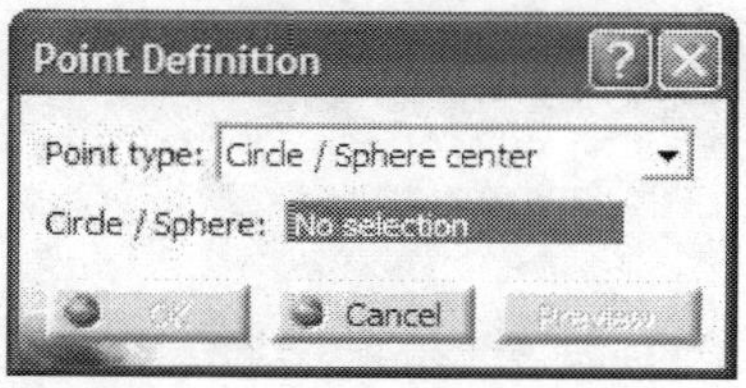

For **Circle/Sphere**, select the path in the dummy. A point is created at the center of the path. This is the point that will remain on the yz plane of **outer**.

Save your part.

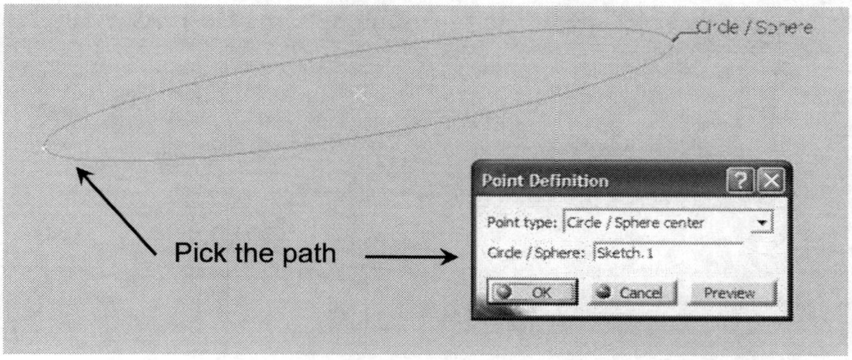

Outline of Step 2:

With the above changes, enter the **Assembly Design** workbench. Pick the **Coincidence** icon , from the **Constraints** toolbar, and select the yz plane of outer from the tree and the point created in Step 1.

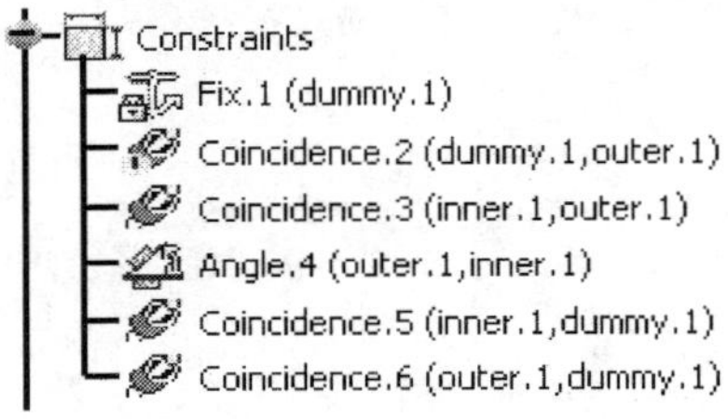

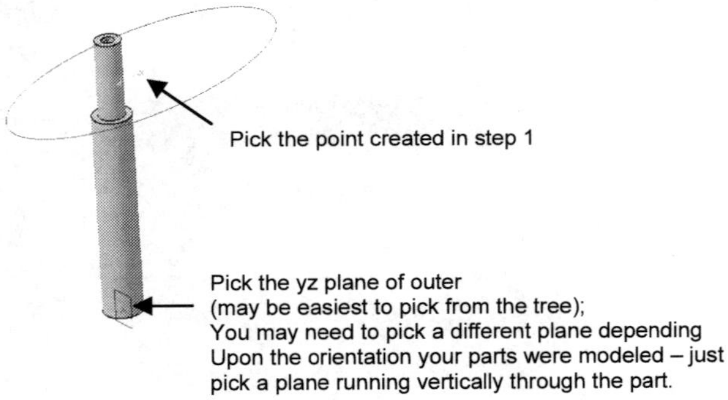

Use **Update** icon  to enforce the constraint just created. If by chance, the constraint was already met by the current position, the **Update** icon would be dimmed and there is no need for updating.

Outline of Step 3:

With the above changes, enter the **Digital Mockup** workbench.

Pick the **Point Surface Joint** icon  from the **Kinematics Joints** toolbar.
For **Surface 1** select the yz plane (or whichever plane was vertical in your part) of **dummy**. For **Point 1**, select the point generated in Step 1. Note that despite the image size illustrating the plane, the plane is treated as infinite.

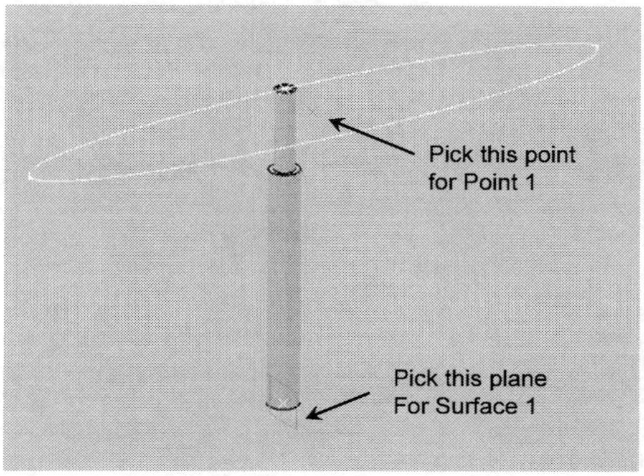

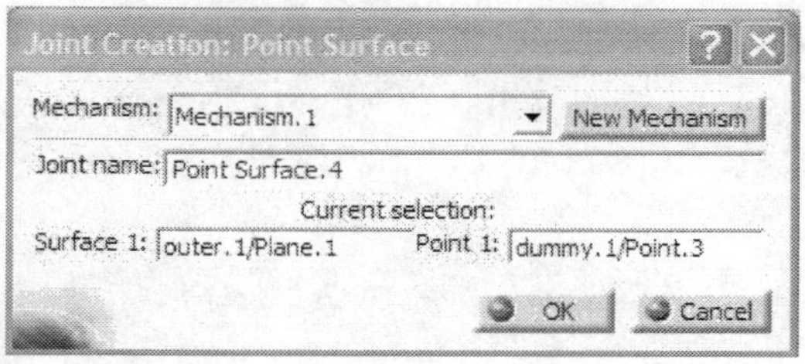

The **Point Surface.4** Joint is generated and reflected in the tree.
Upon closing the box, the message "**Mechanism can be Simulated**" appears.

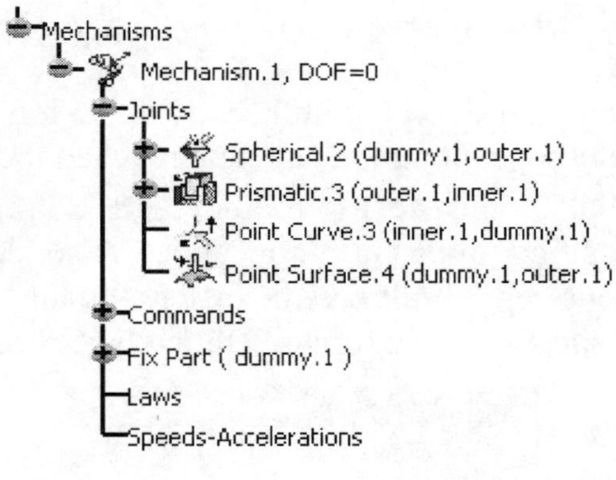

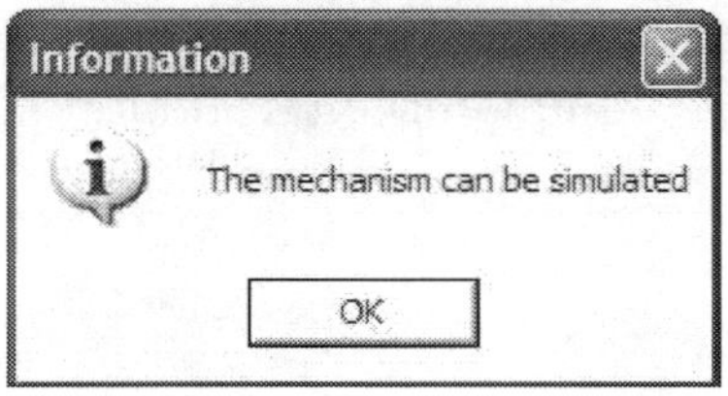

Select the **Simulation** icon  from the **DMU Generic Animation** toolbar 

. This enables you to choose the mechanism to be animated if there are several present. In this case, select Mechanism.1 and close the window.

As soon as the window is closed, a Simulation branch is added to the tree.

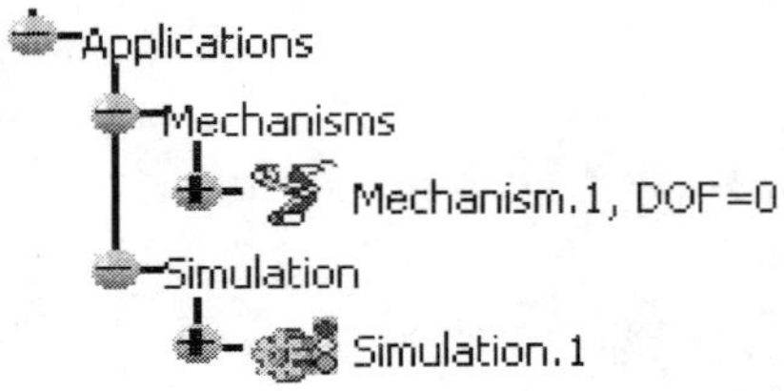

In addition, the two pop up boxes shown below appear.

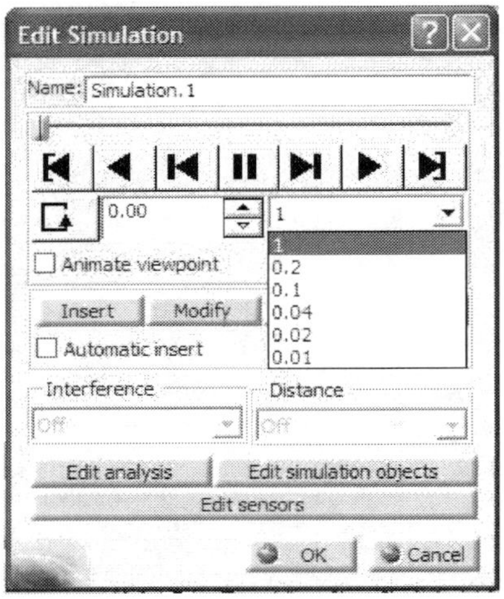

As you scroll the bar in this toolbar from left to right, the telescopic part begins traveling along the path.

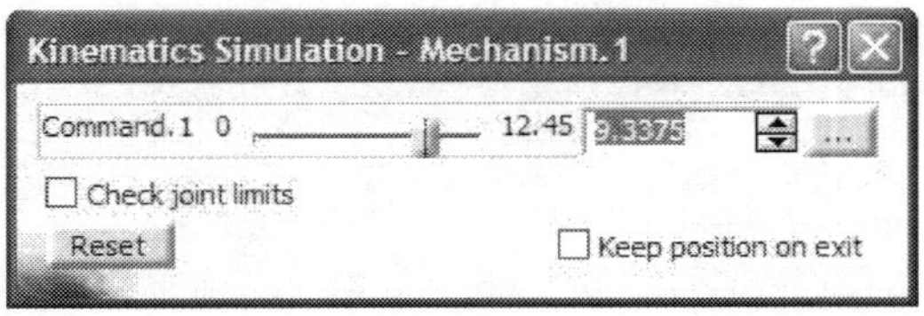

Your **Command.1** limits most probably do not match the one above. Note that the position of the telescope is not at the point 0. If you simulate the mechanism from the current location, you will observe only part of the motion. First we will return the telescope to the "0" location.

Drag the scroll bar all he way to the left to bring it to position "0". As you do this, the telescope along the path and reached the point "0". Once the position "0" is reached, click on the **Modify** button 

. <u>This resets the position to the current location</u>. Also, depending upon how your ellipse was modeled, your upper limit may be different than 12.45. If so, simply use your limit which is respective of your path length elsewhere in this tutorial where we use 12.45.

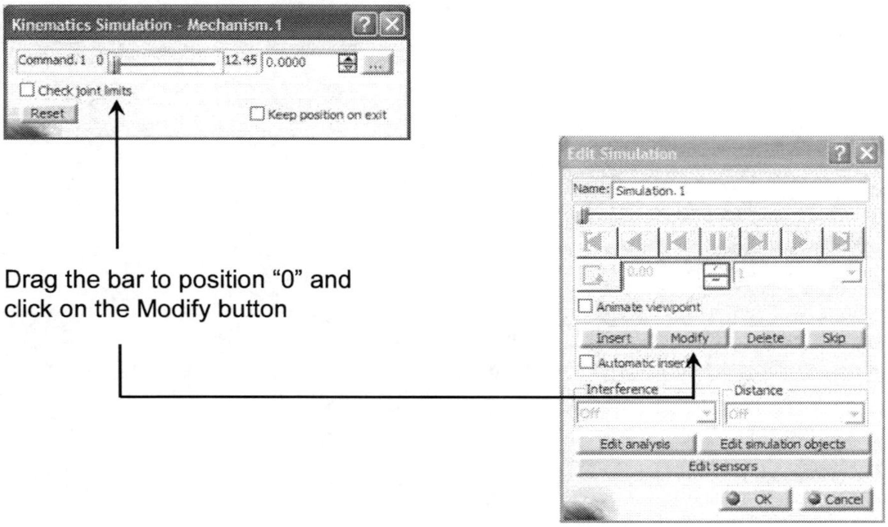

As you scroll the bar in this toolbar from left to right, the telescope begins to travel along the path, starting from the "0" position.

When the scroll bar in the **Kinematics Simulation** pop up box reaches the right extreme end, select the **Insert** button [Insert] in the **Edit Simulation** pop up box shown above. This activates the video player buttons shown

.

Return the cam to its original position by picking the **Jump to Start** button.

Note that the **Change Loop Mode** button is also active now.

Upon selecting the **Play Forward** button, the telescope makes such a fast jump to the end that there does not seem to be any motion.

In order to slow down the motion of the mechanism, select a different **interpolation step**, such as 0.04.

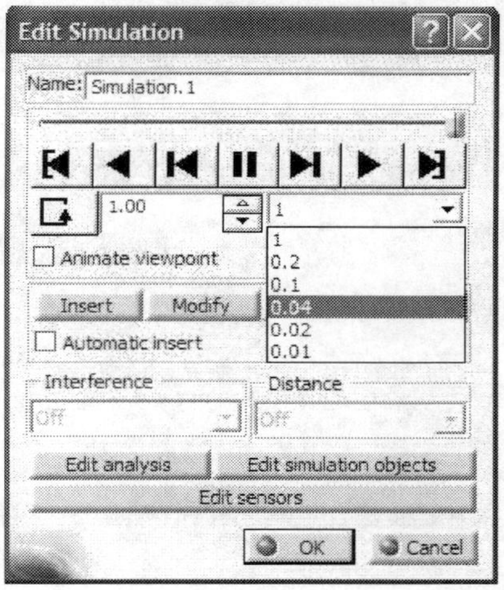

Upon changing the interpolation step to 0.04, return the telescope to its original position by picking the **Jump to Start** button. Apply **Play Forward** button and observe the slow and smooth motion of the mechanism.

We are now confident in our ability to generate the proper motion without regard to time based kinematics. The time based constant velocity along the path will be implemented in the next chapter.

5 Creating Laws in the Motion and Simulating the Desired Kinematics

The motion animated this far was not tied to the time parameter or the translational velocity given in the problem statement. You will now introduce some time based physics into the problem. The objective is to specify a constant linear velocity of 1 in/s.

Click on **Simulation with Laws** icon  in the **Simulation** toolbar .

You will get the following pop up box indication that you need to add at least a relation between the command and the time parameter.

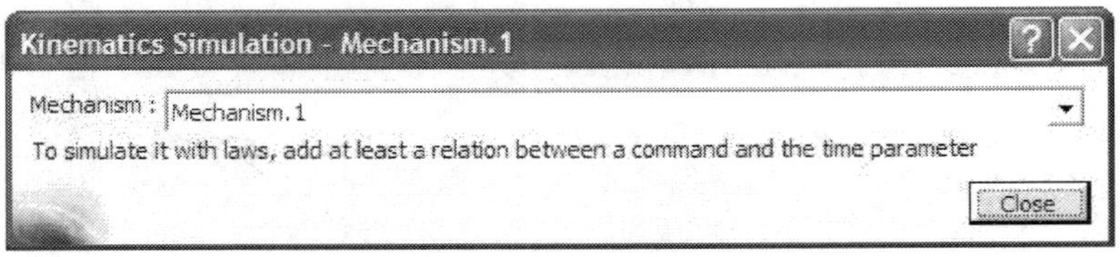

Select the **Formula** icon  from the **Knowledge** toolbar 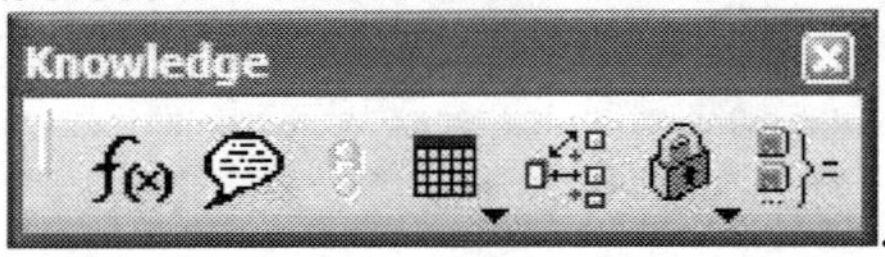

. The pop up box below appears on the screen.

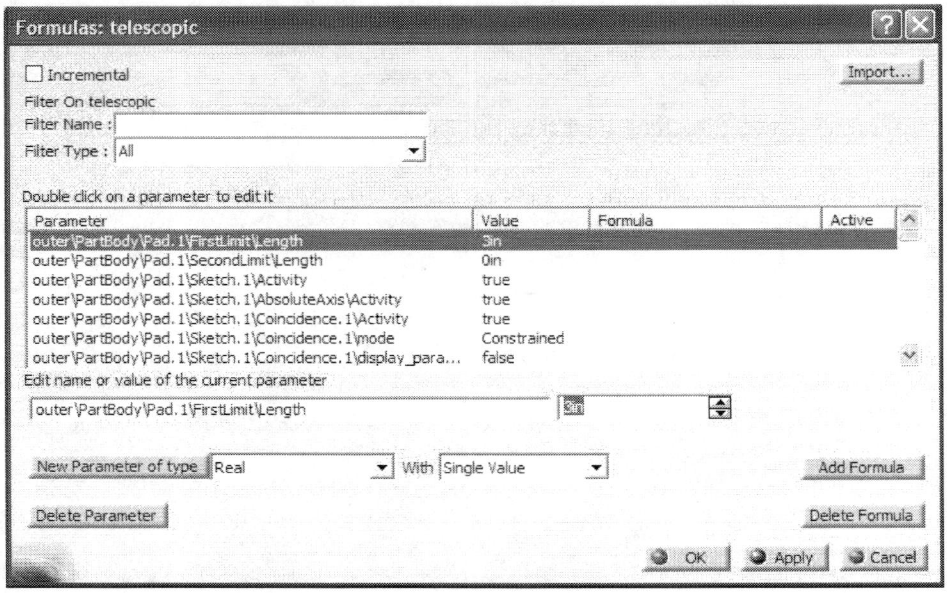

Point the cursor to the **Mechanism.1, DOF=0** branch in the tree and click. The consequence is that only parameters associated with the mechanism are displayed in the **Formulas** box.
The long list is now reduced to two parameters as indicated in the box.

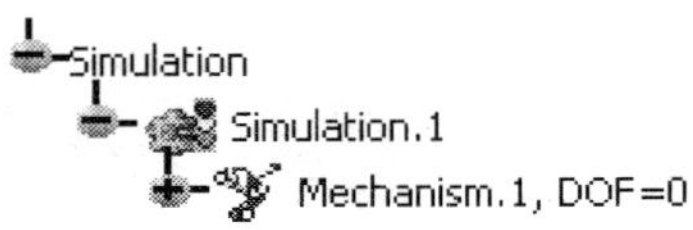

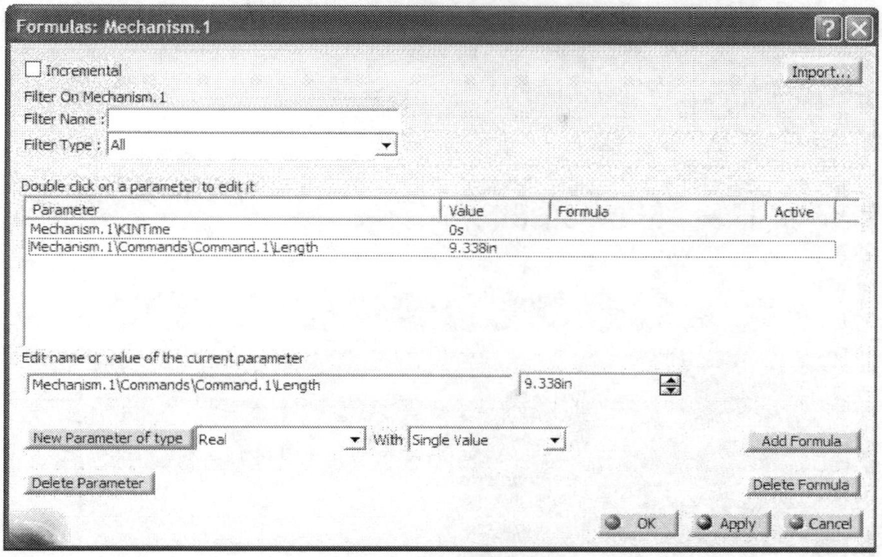

Select the entry **Mechanism.1\Commands\Command.1\Length** and press the **Add Formula** button . This action kicks you to the **Formula Editor** box.

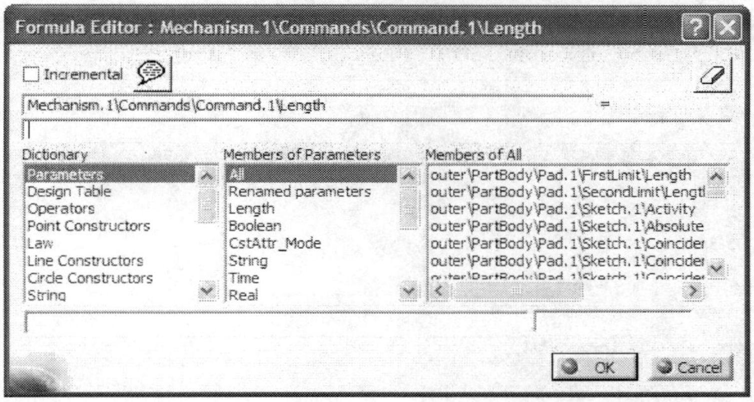

Pick the **Time** entry from the middle column (i.e. **Members of Parameters**).

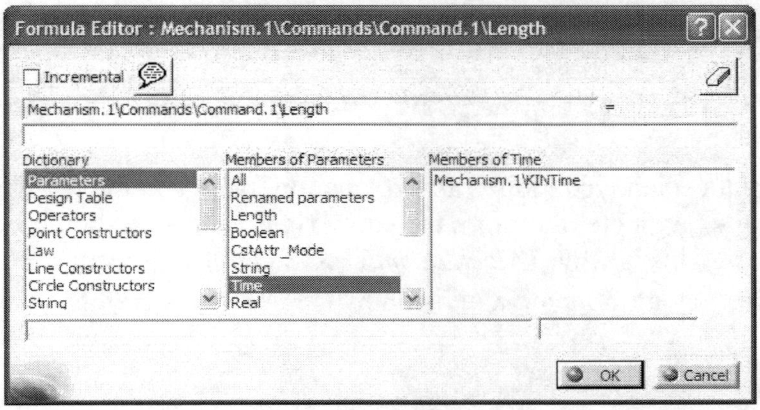

The right hand side of the equality should be such that the formula becomes

$$Mechanism.1 \setminus Commands \setminus Command.1 \setminus Length =$$
$$(1in) * Mechnism.1 \setminus KINTime/(1s)$$

Therefore, the completed **Formula Editor** box becomes

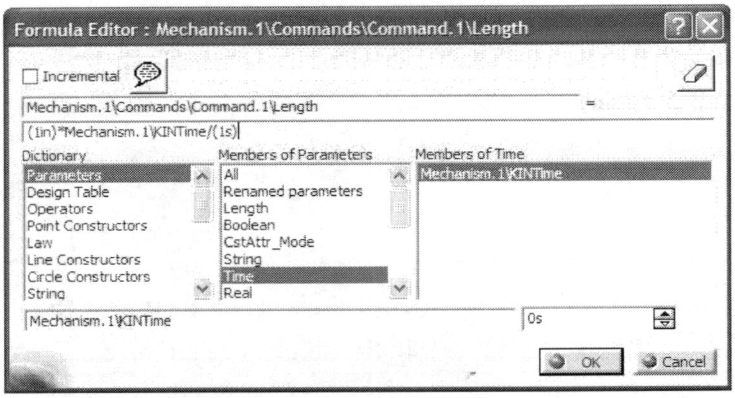

Upon accepting **OK**, the formula is recorded in the **Formulas** pop up box as shown below.

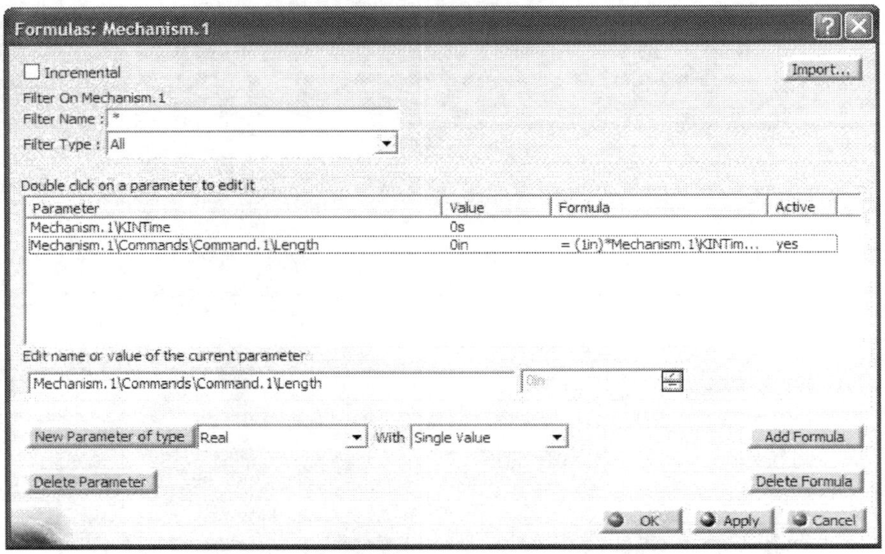

The formula introduced above requires an explanation. Note that the left hand side of the equality is an Angle parameter therefore the entire right hand side should be reducing to an angle in degrees. This is why, $(Mechanism.1 \setminus KINTime)$ has been nondimensionalized by introducing a division by (1s). Here, "s" refers to seconds.

In the event that the formula has different units on the different sides of the equality you will get **Warning** messages such as the one shown below.

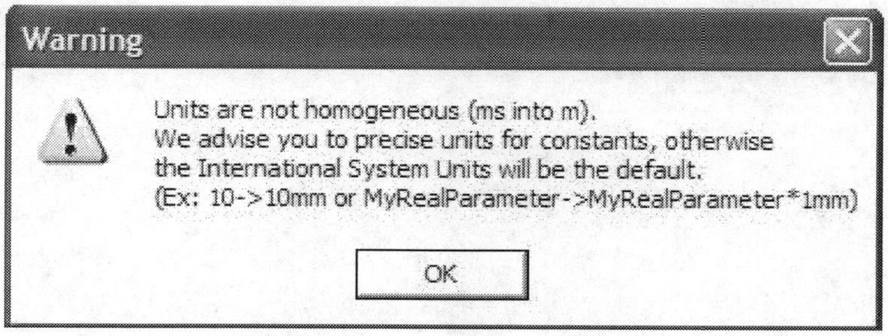

We are spared the warning message because the formula has been properly inputted. Note that the introduced law has appeared in the **Law** branch of the tree.

Keep in mind that our interest is to plot the velocity and accelerations of the arm tip generated by this motion. This requires setting up a speed and acceleration sensor. To do so, select the **Speed and Acceleration** icon  from the **DMU Kinematics** toolbar 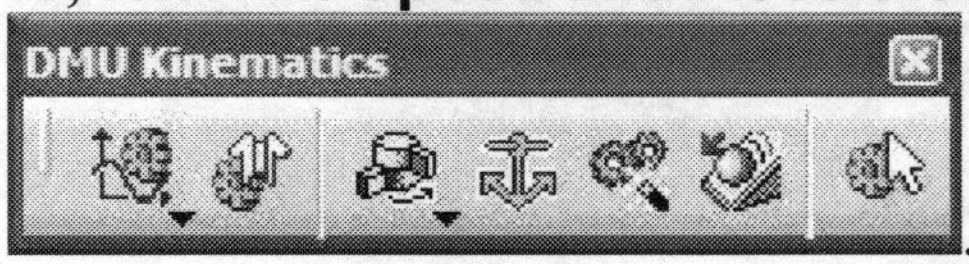

. The pop up box below appears on the Screen.

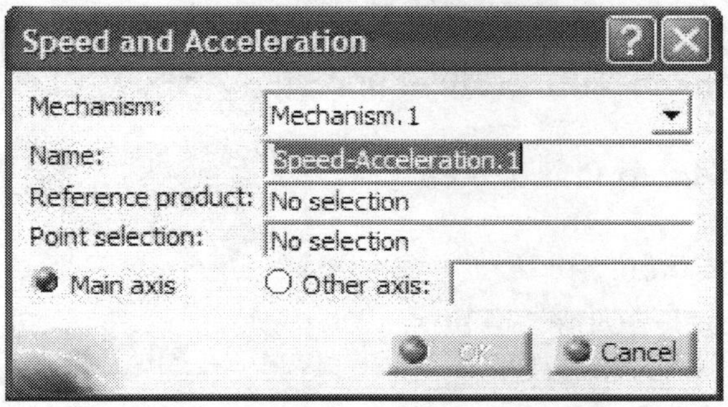

For the **Reference product**, select the **dummy** from the screen or the tree. For the **Point selection**, pick the point at the top of the **inner** part which is on the path as shown in the sketch below.

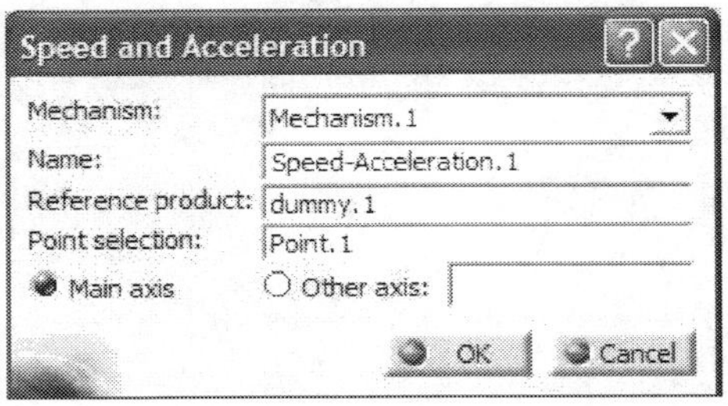

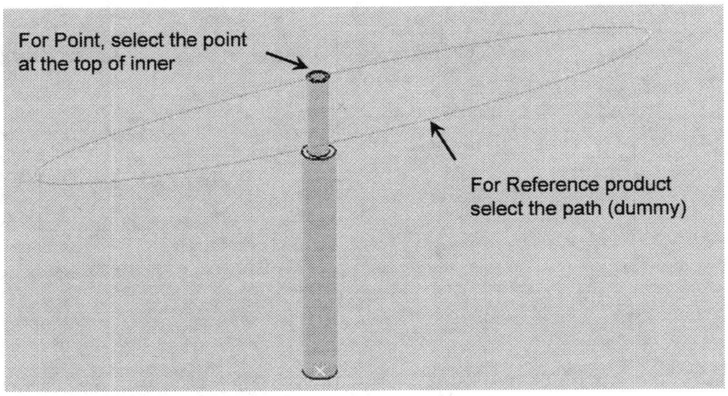

Note that the **Speed and Acceleration.1** has appeared in the tree.

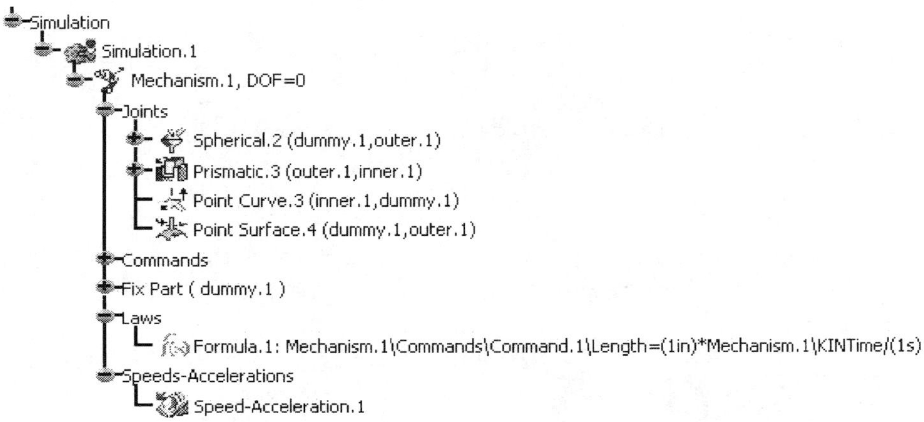

Click on **Simulation with Laws** icon  in the **Simulation** toolbar 

.
This results in the **Kinematics Simulation** pop up box shown below.

Note that the default time duration is 10 seconds.
To change this value, click on the button 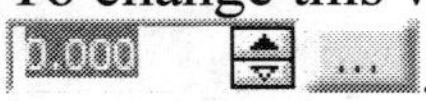

. In the resulting pop up box, change the time duration to 12.45s. (Or whatever your path length was in inches as time in seconds).

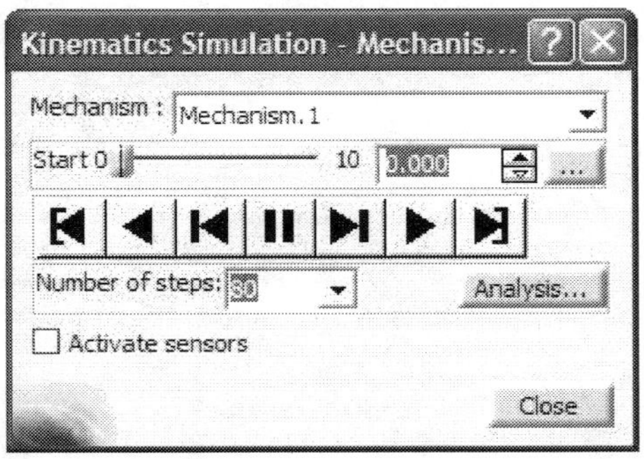

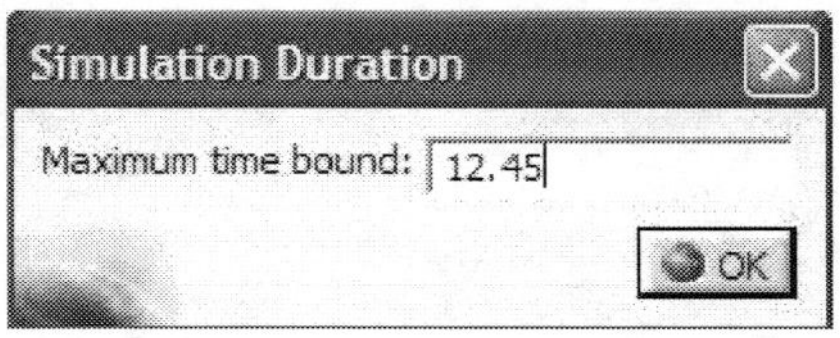

The scroll bar now moves up to 12.45s.

Check the **Activate sensors** box, at the bottom left corner.

You will next have to make certain selections from the accompanying **Sensors** box to indicate the kinematics parameters you would like to compute and store results on.

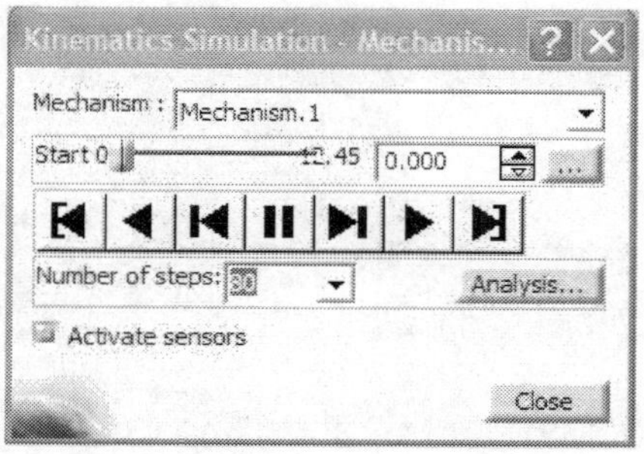

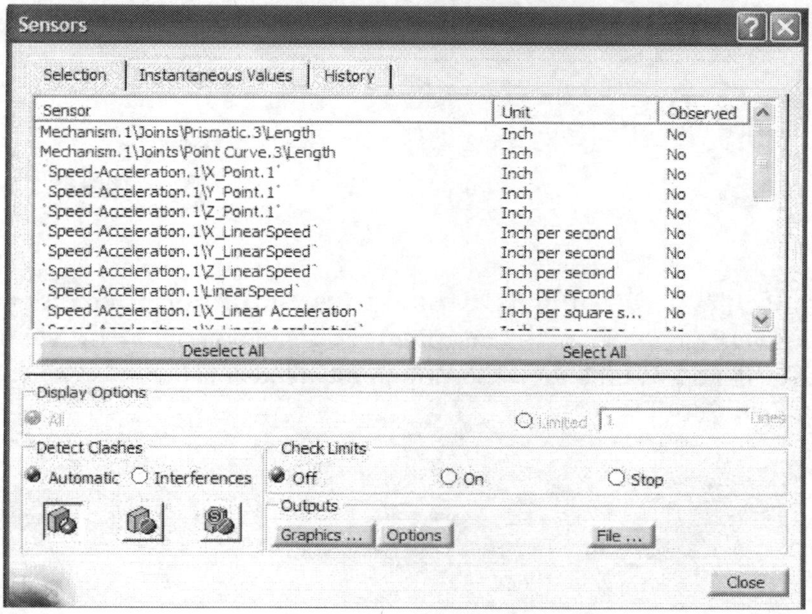

Click on the following items

Speed-Acceleration.1\LinearSpeed
Speed-Acceleration.1\LinearAcceleration

As you make these selections, the last column in the **Sensors** box, changes to **Yes** for the corresponding items. This is shown in the next page.

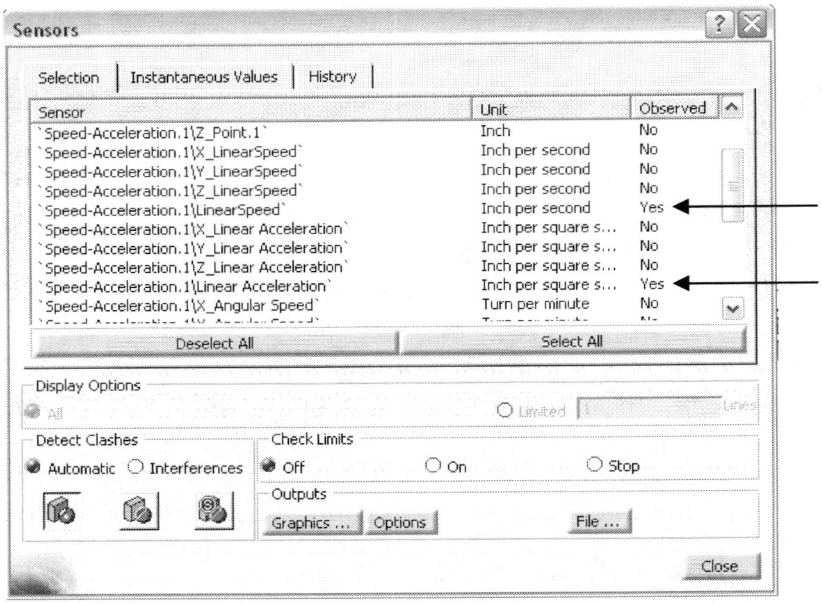

At this point, drag the scroll bar in the **Kinematics Simulation** box. As you do this, the telescope travels along the path. Once the bar reaches its right extreme point, the part has made a full trip and returns to its starting point. This corresponds to 12.45 s or 12.45 in which is the length of the path.

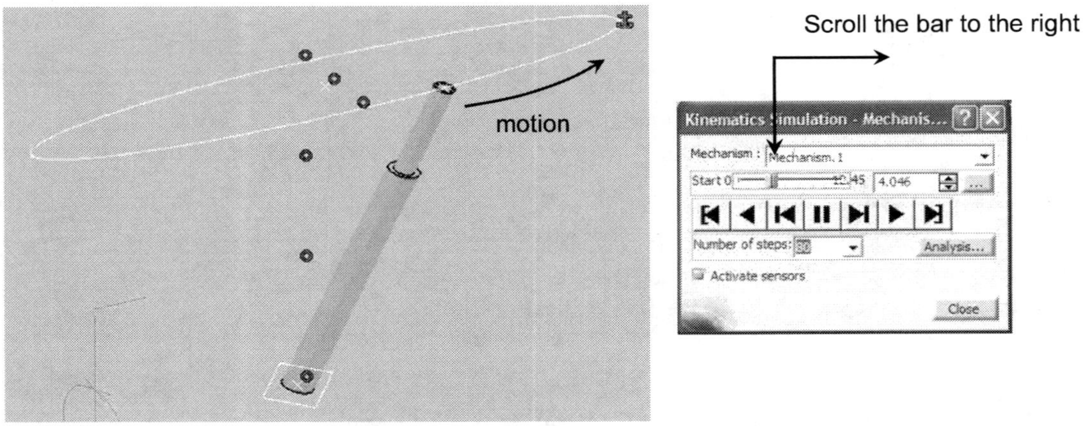

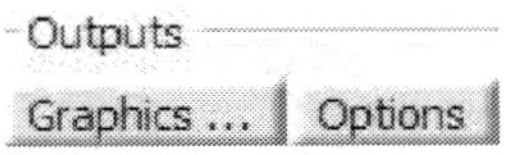

Once the part makes a full trip, click on **Graphics** button in the **Sensor** box. The result is the plot of the velocity and acceleration as shown on the next page. You need to toggle on each curve in the right portion of the dialog box to have the y axis scale appropriately for each plot.

The plot scaled for units of velocity is as follows. Of course it shows constant speed of 1 in/s since we were driving the length at that rate.

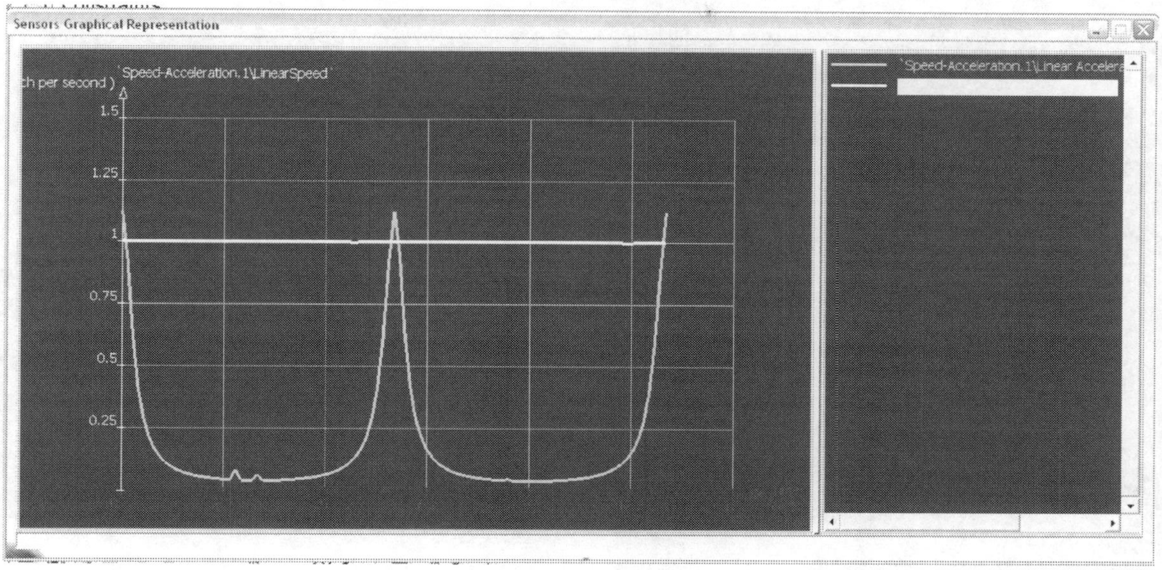

The plot scaled for units of acceleration is as follows. Notice that since this represents the normal acceleration, it peaks at about 3 inches per second squared in the two regions with the highest radius of curvature, and is lowest (about 0.2 inches per second squared) in the two regions of the ellipse with minimum radius of curvature.

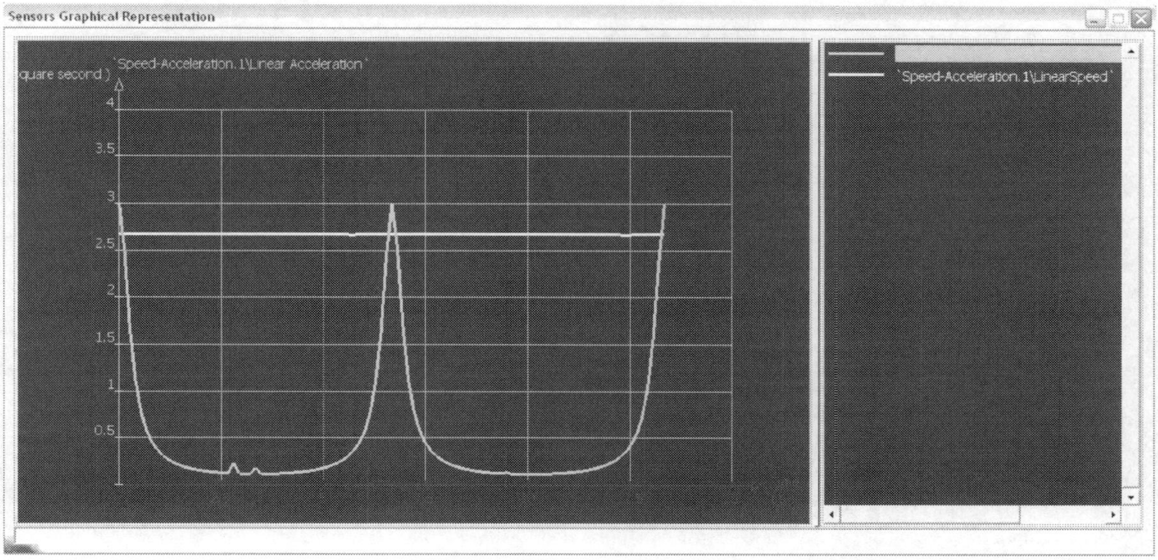

This concludes this tutorial.

NOTES:

Chapter 11

Robotic Arm

Introduction

In this tutorial, a model is developed of a three degree of freedom robot consisting of two revolute joints and a prismatic joint. This robot configuration is often referred to as a SCARA (selective compliance assembly robot arm) type of robot. This tutorial involves simulating the motion of the robot as its end effector (a point at the tip of the last link for our purposes) tracks a curve at constant speed. This is representative of a number of typical robotic assembly tasks such as dispensing adhesives, hemming sheet metal, etc.

1 Problem Statement

A three degree of freedom robot consisting of two revolute joints and a prismatic joint is shown below. The objective is to have the bottom tip of the prismatic joint (where an end effector would typically be located in a real application) track a curve in space. In a real application, this curve might represent the path to be followed while the robot dispenses an adhesive. For a constant speed of 1 in/s along the path, we would like to plot the angles of each of the two revolute joints versus time. In a real application, the robot's controller would take these angles and figure out the joint torques (i.e., motor power levels) to apply to attain the desired motion.

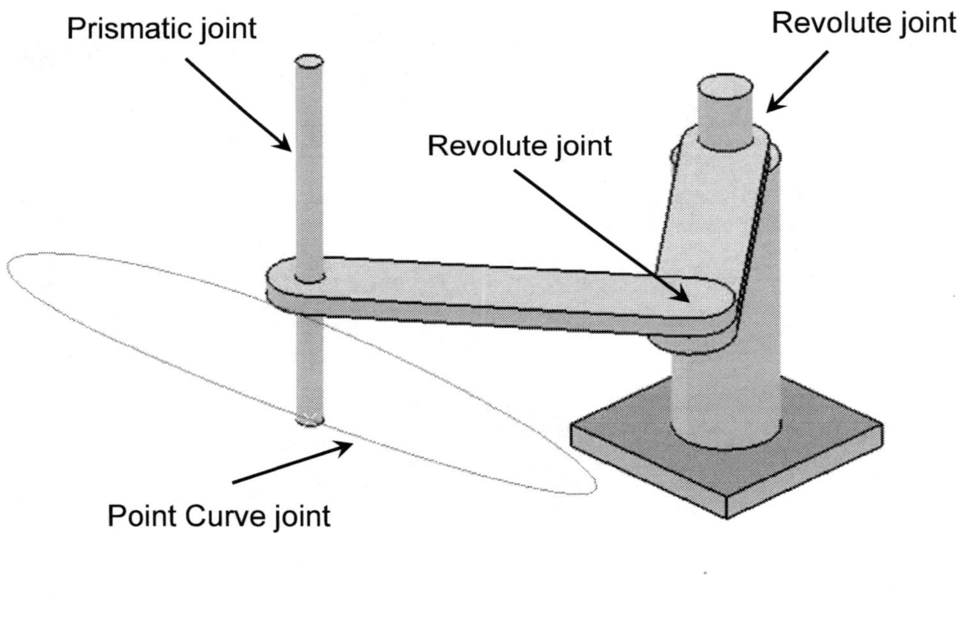

2 Overview of this Tutorial

This tutorial will involve the following steps:

1. Model the four CATIA parts required.
2. Create an assembly (CATIA Product) containing the parts.
3. Constrain the assembly in such a way that the tip of the last link is on the curve and automatic assembly constraints conversion will produce the desired joints.
4. Enter the **Digital Mockup** workbench and convert the assembly constraints into two revolute joints and a prismatic joint.
5. Create the Point Curve joint.
6. Simulate the relative motion of the assembly without consideration to time (in other words, without implementing the time based linear velocity along the path).
7. Adding a formula to implement the time based kinematics.
8. Simulating the desired constant speed motion and generating plots of the two revolute joint angles versus time.

3 Creation of the Assembly in Mechanical Design Solutions

Model four parts named **base**, **link_1**, **link_2** and **link_3** as shown below with the suggested dimensions. It is assumed that you are sufficiently familiar with CATIA to model these parts fairly quickly. Use pad lengths of 0.25 in for the main portion of each link. Recall that **link_3** has to track a path defined by a curve in space. This path can be created as a separate part or it can be made as part of the **base**. We propose the latter approach and provide you with an outline of the steps needed to add the curve to the base.

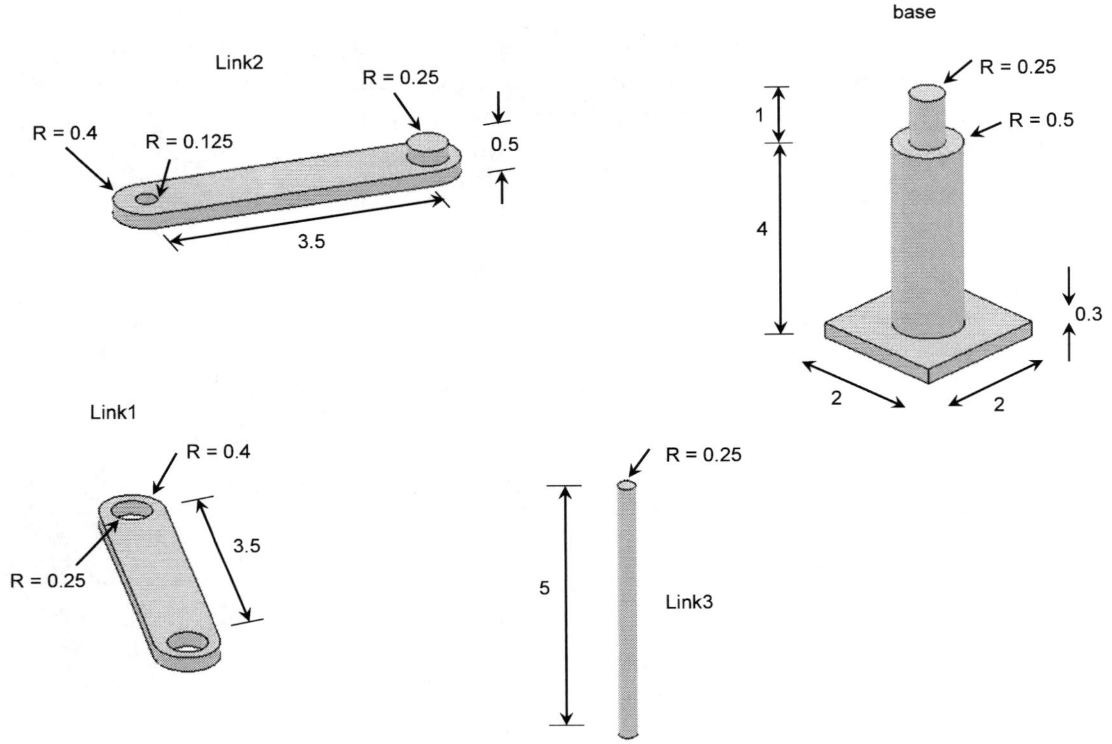

To model the path curve as part of the **base**, begin by loading the part named **base** into CATIA and enter the **Part Design** workbench.

Pick the **Plane** icon  from the **Reference Element** toolbar 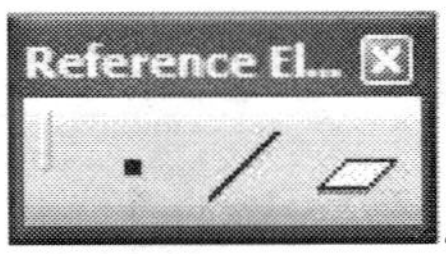

.

In the resulting **Plane Definition** pop up box, for **Plane type**, select the **Angle/Normal to plane**. This choice modifies the look of the pop up box as displayed on the next page.

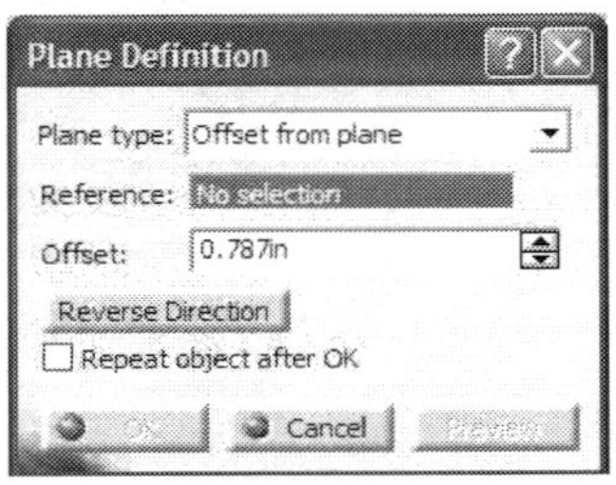

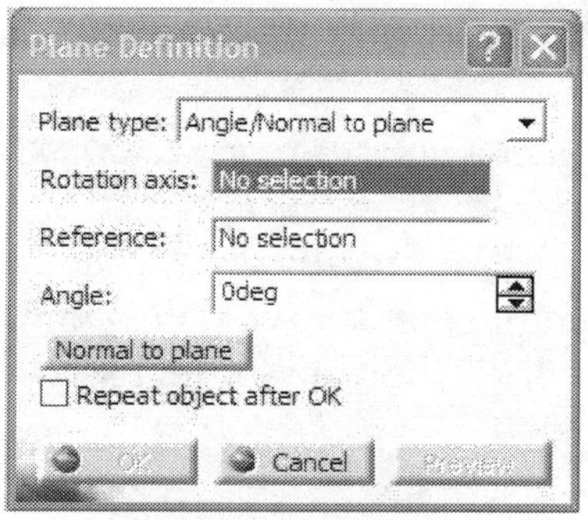

For the **Rotation** axis and **Reference**, refer to the following sketch and use a 70deg **Angle**.

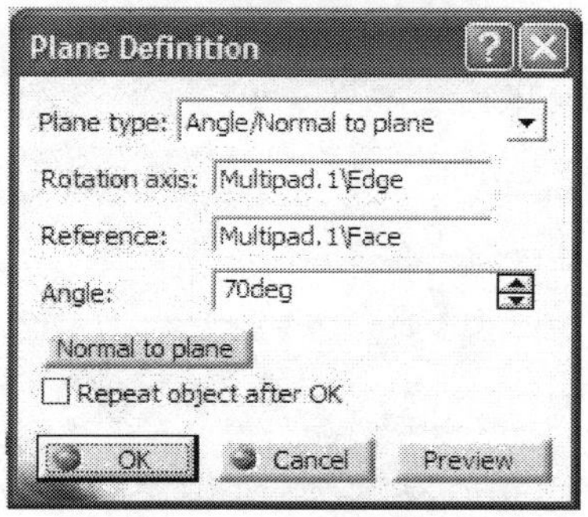

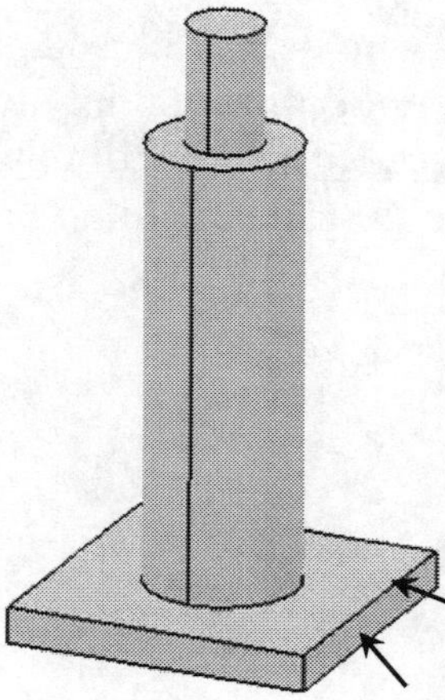

Note: If your plane tilts the opposite way, try an angle of -70 deg.
This procedure creates a tilted plane on which the path can be drawn.

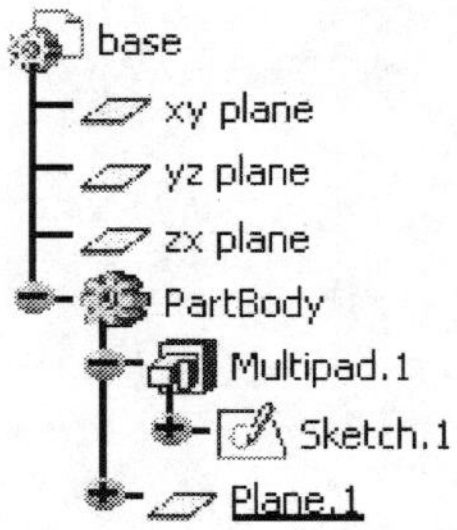

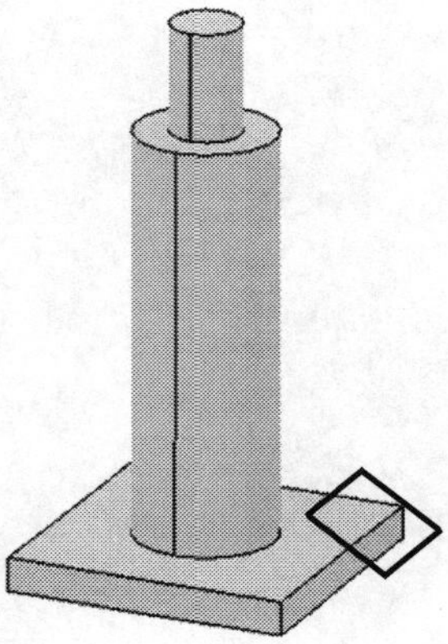

To draw the curve representing the desired path for the robot to trace, pick the **Sketcher** icon and select the plane that was just constructed. This lands you in the **Sketcher**. Use the **Spline** icon to draw a closed path and then exit the **Sketcher**. The specifics of the path are not critical; simply try to make it resemble that shown below and make sure it doesn't exceed 7 inches from the axis of the cylindrical portion of the base. The robot will be unable to reach anything beyond this dimension.

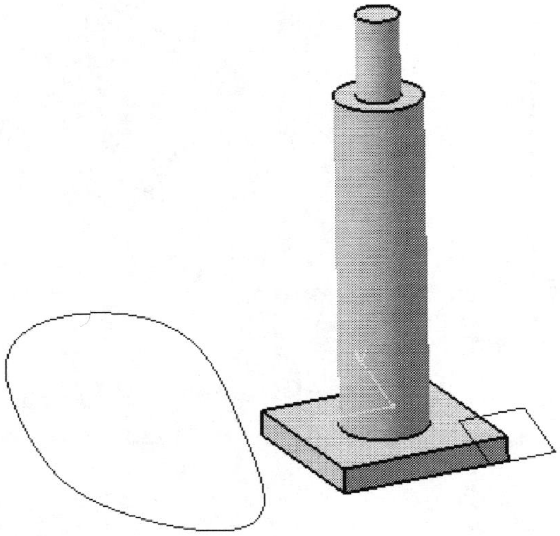

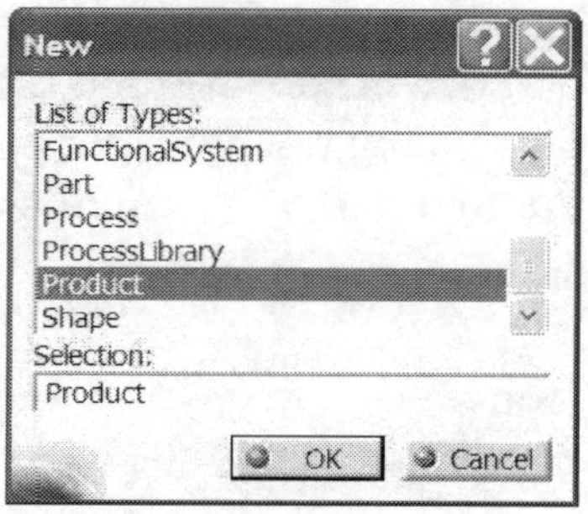

Once all parts are modeled, it is time to create the assembly. Enter the **Assembly Design** workbench  which can be achieved by different means depending on your CATIA customization. For example, from the standard Windows toolbar, select **File > New** . From the box shown on the right, select **Product**. This moves you to the **Assembly Design** workbench and creates an assembly with the default name **Product.1**.

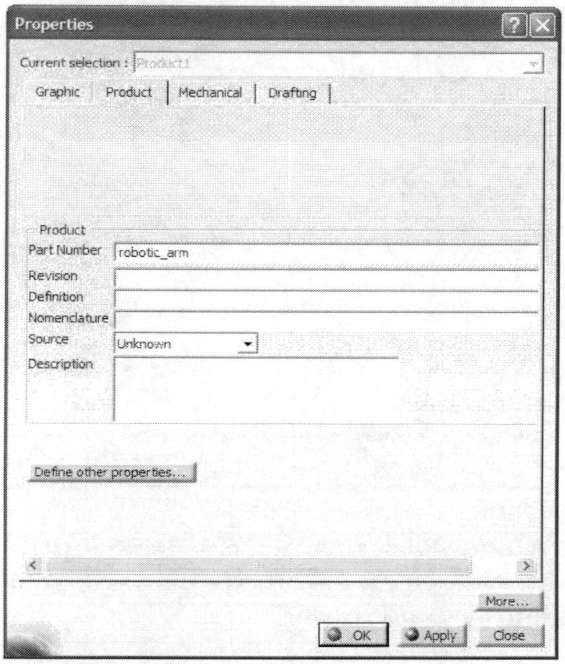

In order to change the default name, move the cursor to **Product.1** in the tree, right click and select **Properties** from the menu list.

From the **Properties** box, select the **Product** tab and in **Part Number** type **robotic_arm**.

This will be the new product name throughout the chapter. The tree on the top left corner of your computer screen should look as displayed below.

The next step is to insert the existing parts in the assembly just created. From the standard Windows toolbar, select **Insert > Existing Component**.
From the **File Selection** pop up box choose all four parts. Remember that in CATIA multiple selections are made with the **Ctrl** key. The tree is modified to indicate that the parts have been inserted.

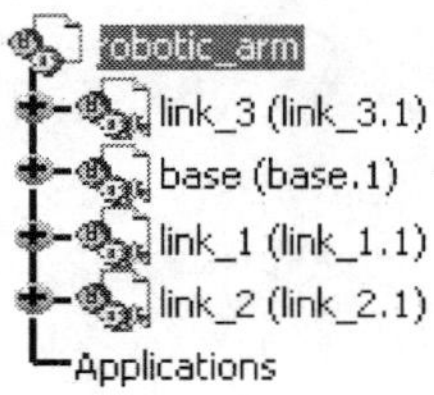

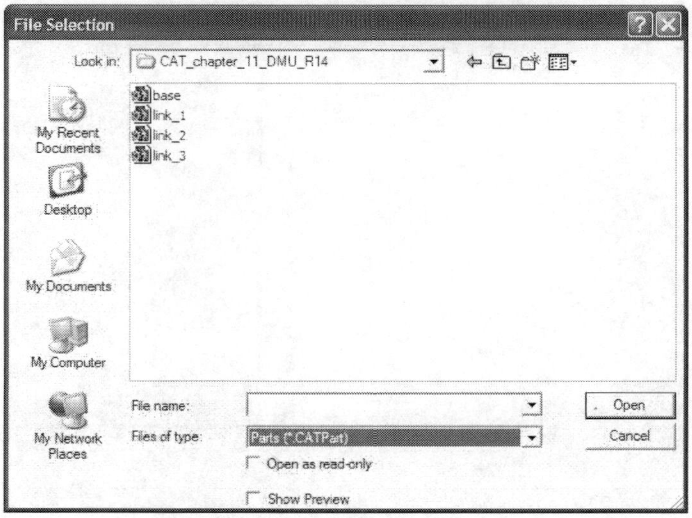

Note that the part names and their instance names were purposely made the same. This practice makes the identification of the assembly constraints a lot easier down the road. Depending on how your parts were created earlier, on the computer screen may you have the four parts all clustered around the origin. You may have to use the **Manipulation** icon  in the **Move** toolbar 

to rearrange them so they are not overlapping and thus will be easier to pick in the constraint creation process.

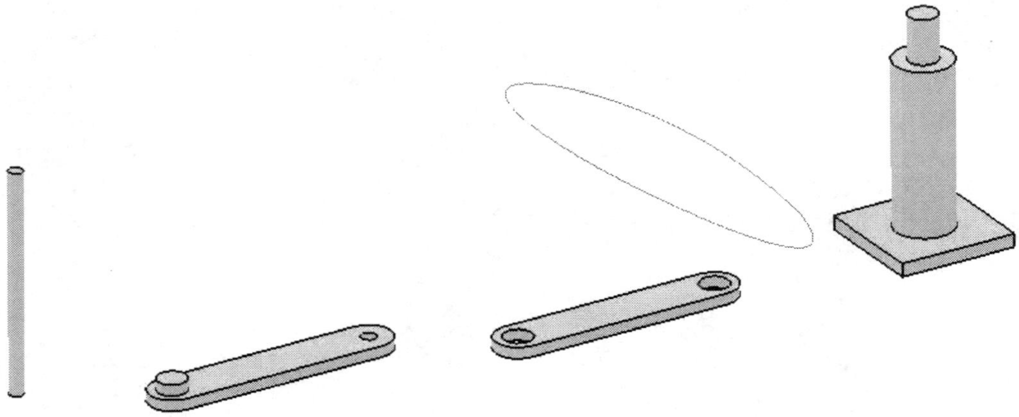

The best way of saving your work is to save the entire assembly.
Double click on the top branch of the tree. This is to ensure that you are in the **Assembly Design** workbench.

Select the **Save** icon . The **Save As** pop up box allows you to rename if desired. The default name is the **robotic_arm**.

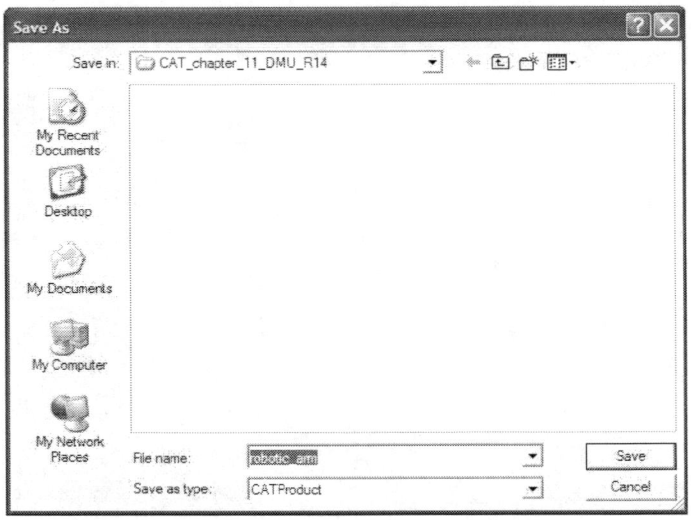

Your next task is to impose assembly constraints.

Pick the **Anchor** icon from the **Constraints** toolbar and select the **base** from the tree or from the screen. This removes all six degrees of freedom for the base.

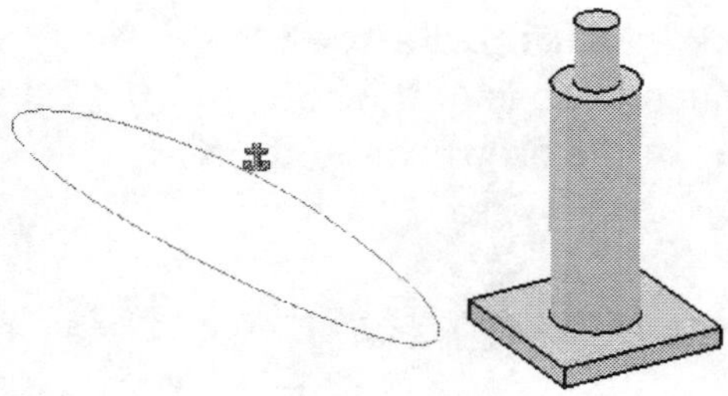

The next step is to impose the constraints on the base and link_1. Ultimately we want to remove all relative degrees of freedom (dof) except for rotation about the common axis. This is consistent with a revolute joint between the two parts. A combination of a coincident constraint and a surface contact constraint will achieve the objective.

Pick the **Coincidence** icon from **Constraints** toolbar. Select the axis of the **base** and the axis of the hole in **link_1**.

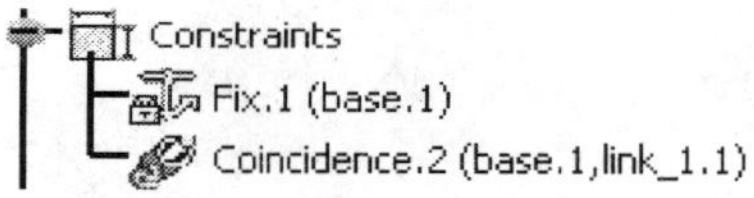

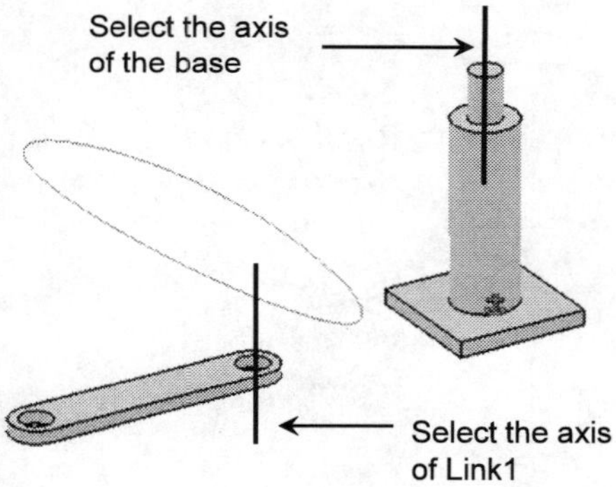

Pick the **Contact** icon, and make the surface selection as shown below.

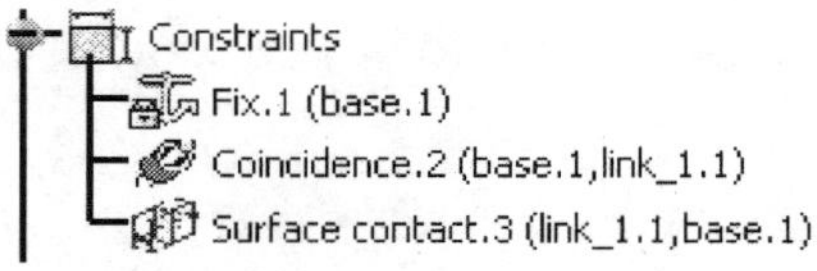

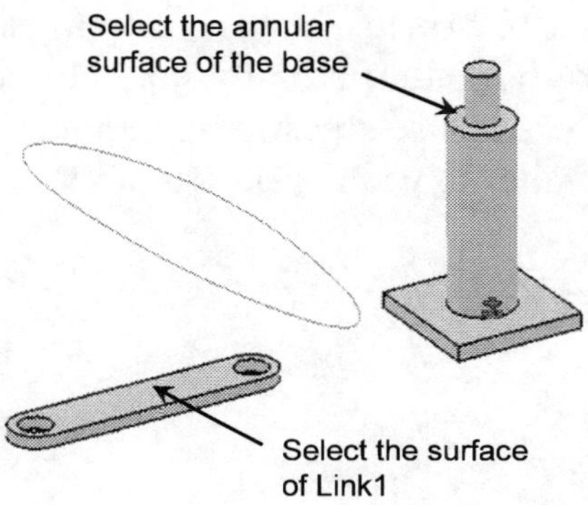

Use **Update** icon to partially position the two parts as shown on the next page.

The next step is to impose the constraints between **link_1** and **link_2**. A similar combination of constraints will be made here as was done between the **base** and **link_1**.

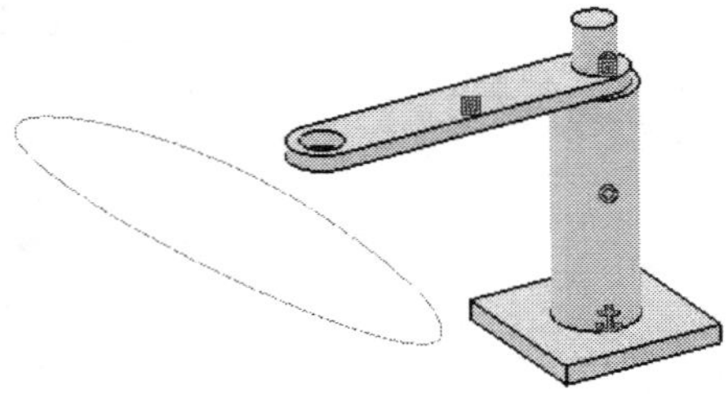

Pick the **Coincidence** icon.
Select the axis of the hole in **link_1** and the axis of the protrusion in **link_2**.

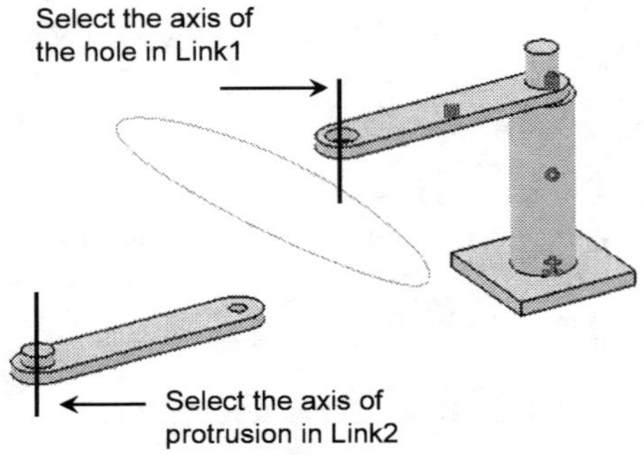

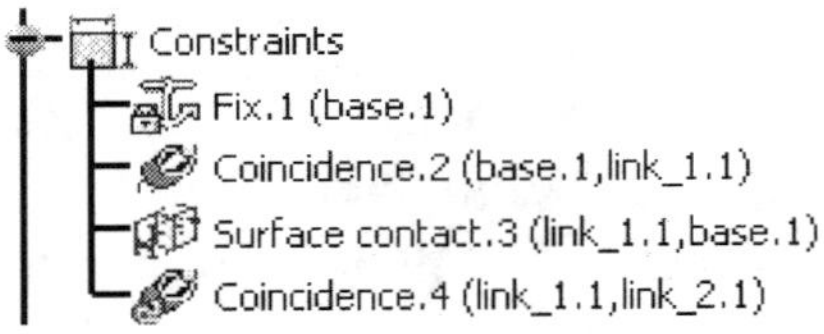

Pick the **Contact** icon, and make the surface selection as shown below.

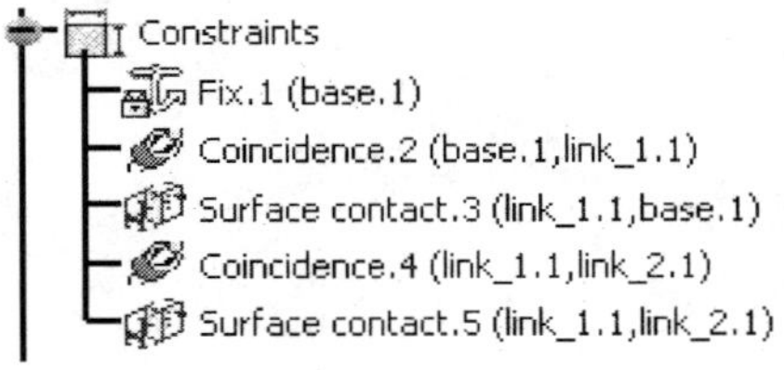

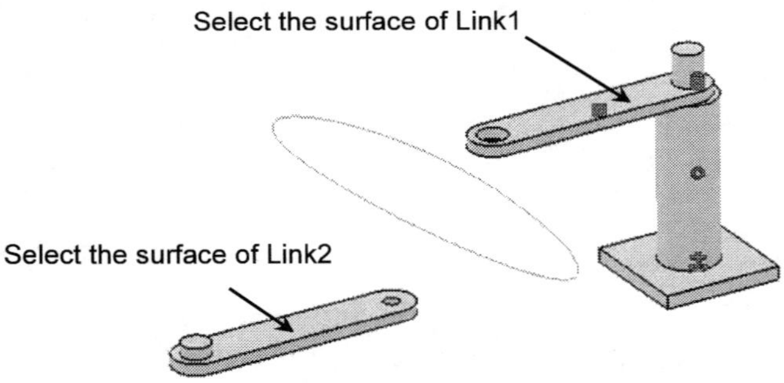

Use **Update** icon to partially position the two parts as shown. The updated configuration initially may not be very desirable such as what is shown below. You will need to use the Manipulation icon to move the parts around to a convenient position similar to what is shown on the right below.

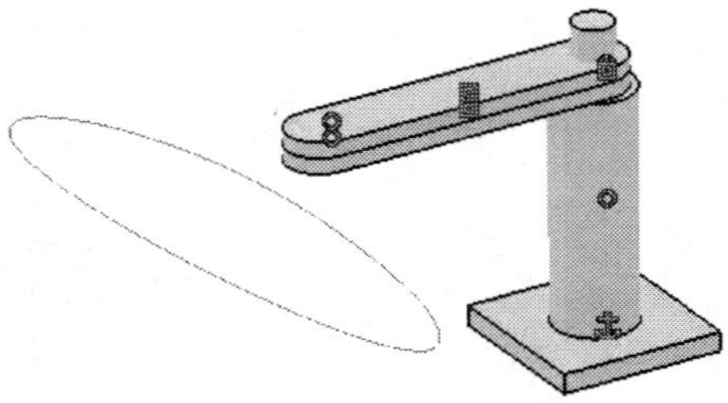

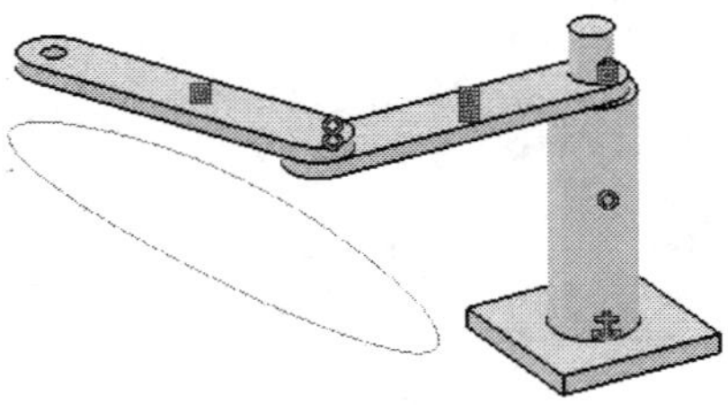

The next step is to impose the constraints between **link_2** and **link_3**. From a dof standpoint, we ultimately want a prismatic mechanism joint between these two components, so we need to remove all the relative dof except for translation along the vertical axis. We will begin with a coincident constraint between an axis on each part; this removes all but translation and rotation about that axis. Then we will remove the unwanted rotation with an angular constraint.

Pick the **Coincidence** icon .
Select the axis of the hole in **link_2** and the axis **link_3**.

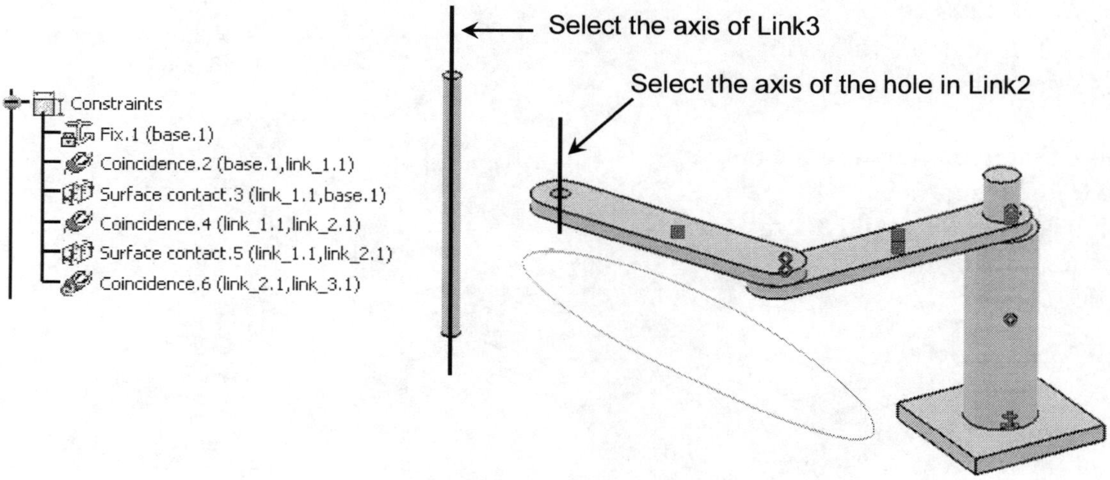

Use **Update** icon  to partially position the parts as shown.

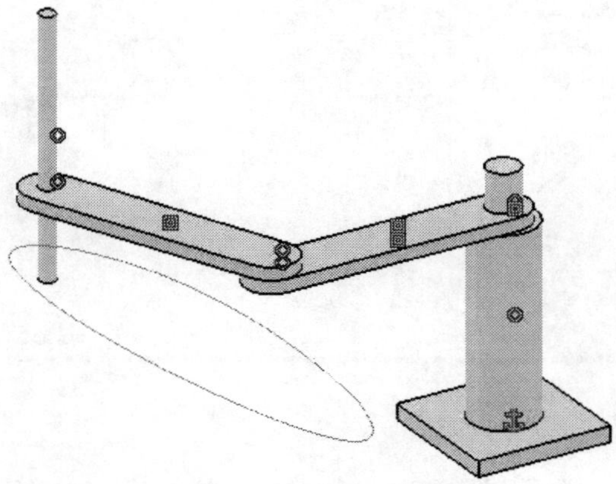

Note that the current constraint between **link_3** and **link_2** would lead to a **Cylindrical Joint** in the mechanism since **link_3** can freely spin about its own axis. We will remove this dof by imposing an angular dimension between a vertical plane of **link_3** and a vertical plane of **link_2**.

Pick the **Angle Constraint** icon  from the **Constraints** toolbar

. Select the **zx plane** of **link_3** and **link_2** as shown.

Accept the default values in the resulting pop up box and close it.

Note that your values in the pop up box are most probably different. The value of the angle doesn't matter (and could be keyed in as 0 deg if desired).

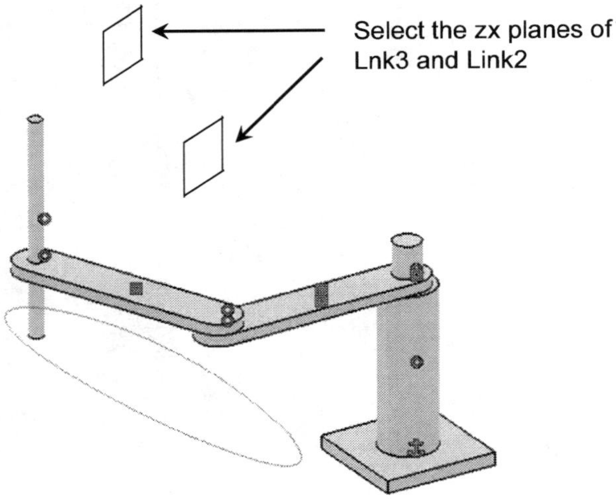

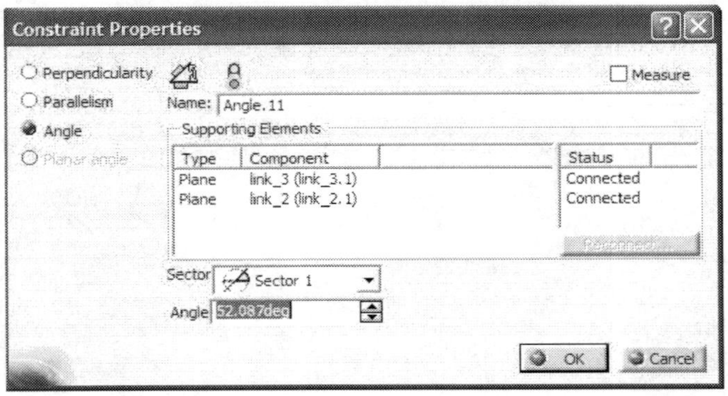

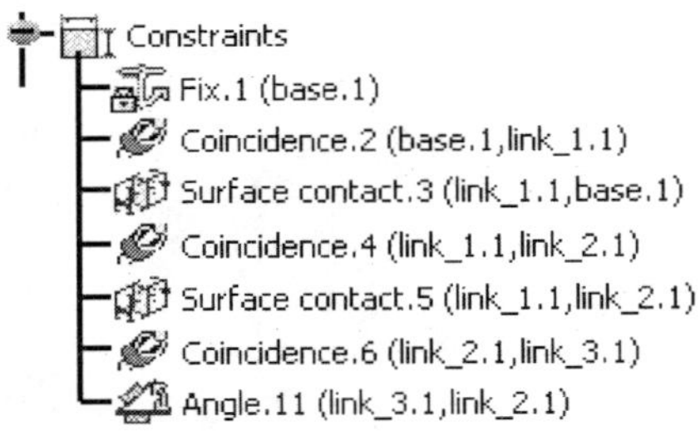

Use **Update** icon  to update the positions.

Next, you have to put **link_3** in physical contact with the path. This is required before one can create a **Point Curve Joint** in the **Digital Mockup** workbench.

One way to achieve this is to create two points. One of the points should be on the curve and the second point being at the bottom of **link_3**. You then make the two points coincident. Just keep in mind that after the point on link_3 lands on the curve, the responsible coincidence constraint must deleted. Otherwise it will lead to a **Spherical Joint** in the assembly and the entire assembly will remain fixed (unless that joint is deleted).

Load the part **base** into CATIA.

Select the **Point** icon 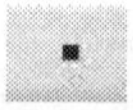 from the **Reference Elements** toolbar 

.
Using the pull down menu, change the **Point type** to **On curve**.
Use the cursor to pick any arbitrary point on the path and close the pop up box by pressing **OK**. Save your results .

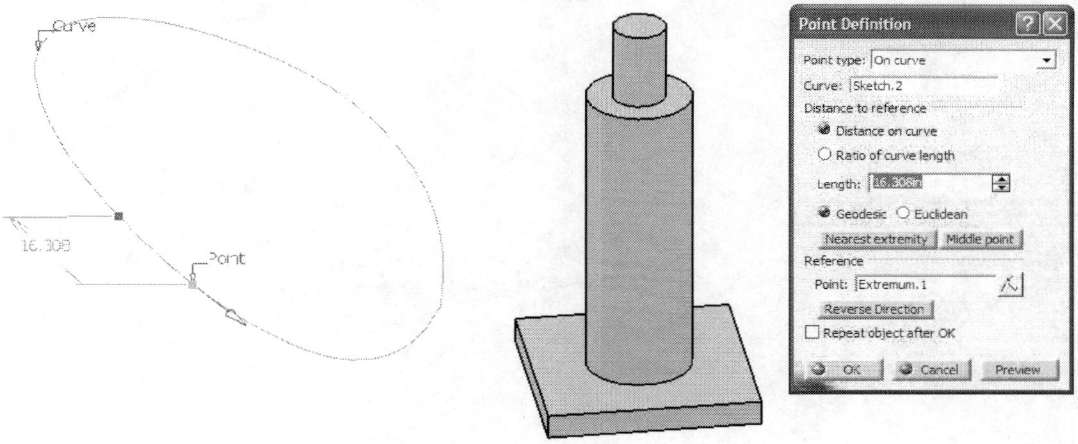

Next load the part **Link3** into CATIA.

Select the **Point** icon .

Using the pull down menu, change the **Point type** to **Circle/Sphere center.**
Use the cursor to pick the bottom circle of **link_3**.

Save your results .

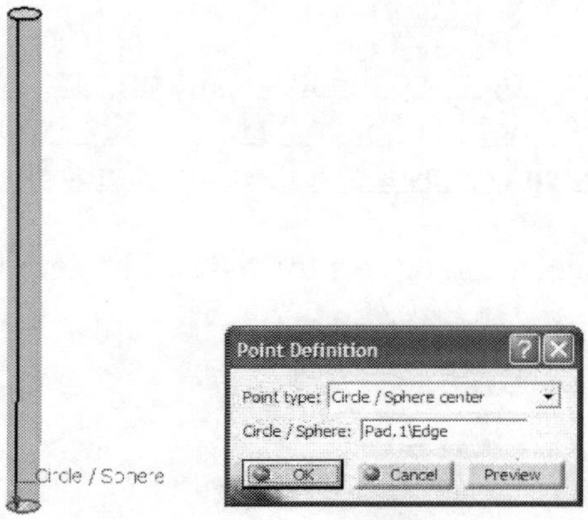

Pick the **Coincidence** icon and select the two points just created.

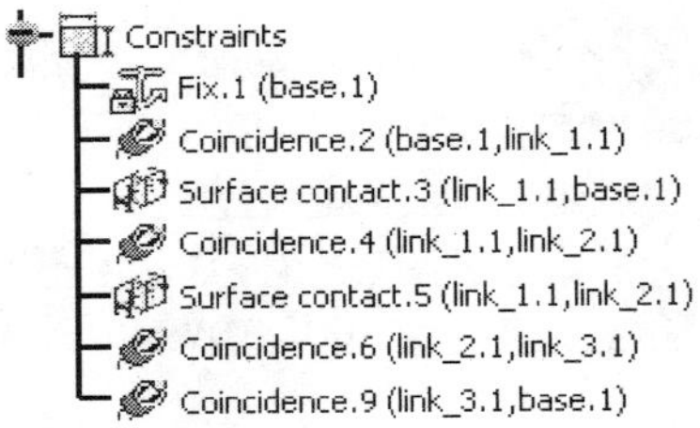

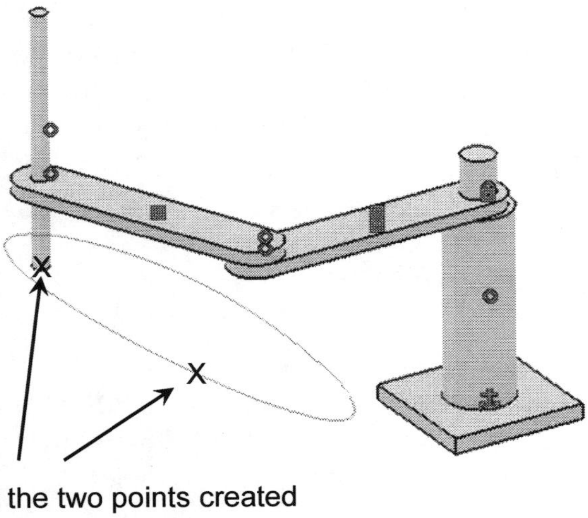

Use **Update** icon to partially position the parts as shown.

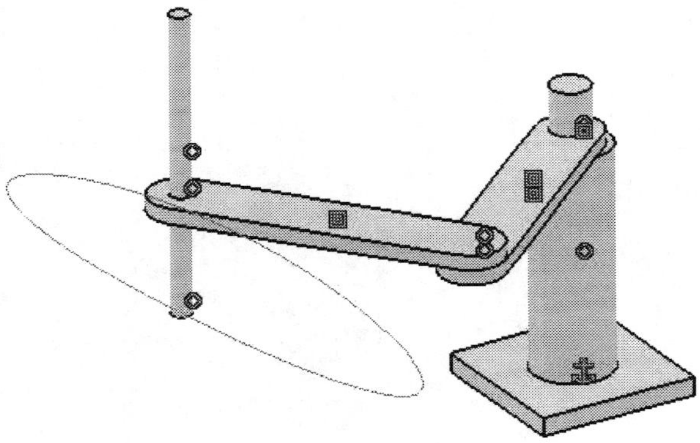

Once you have the tip of the arm in contact with the path curve, delete the coincident constraint just made. This ensures we will not end up with a spherical joint in the mechanism as a result of that constraint.

Proceed to convert the assembly into a mechanism and animate its motion along the path.

3 Creating Joints in the Digital Mockup Workbench

The **Digital Mockup** workbench is quite extensive but we will only deal with the **DMU Kinematics module**. To get there you can use the standard Windows toolbar as shown below: **Start > Digital Mockup > DMU Kinematics**.

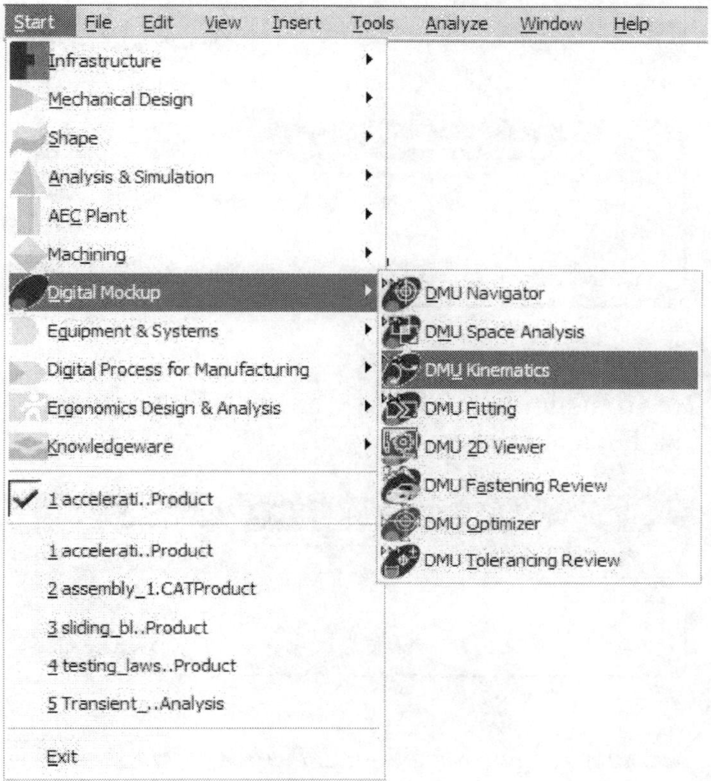

Select the **Assembly Constraints Conversion** icon 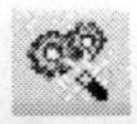 from the **DMU Kinematics** toolbar 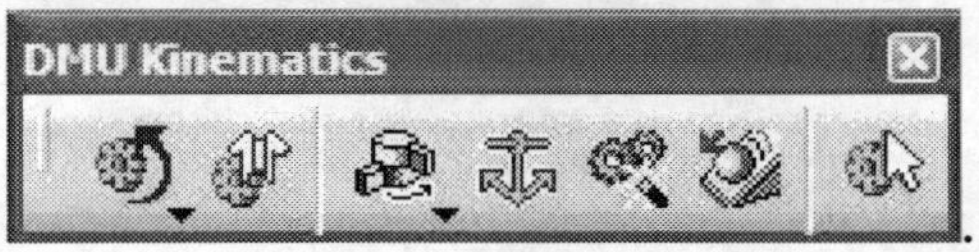

. This icon allows you to create most common joints automatically from the existing assembly constraints.
The pop up box below appears.

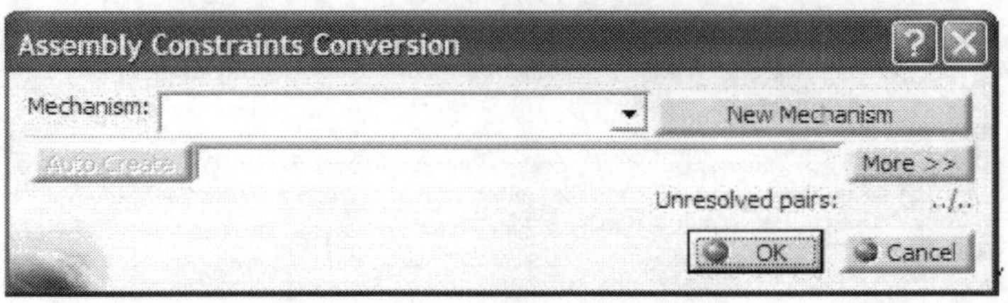

Select the **New Mechanism** button 

.
This leads to another pop up box which allows you to name your mechanism.
The default name is **Mechanism.1**. Accept the default name by pressing **OK**.

Note that the box indicates **Unresolved pairs: 3/3**

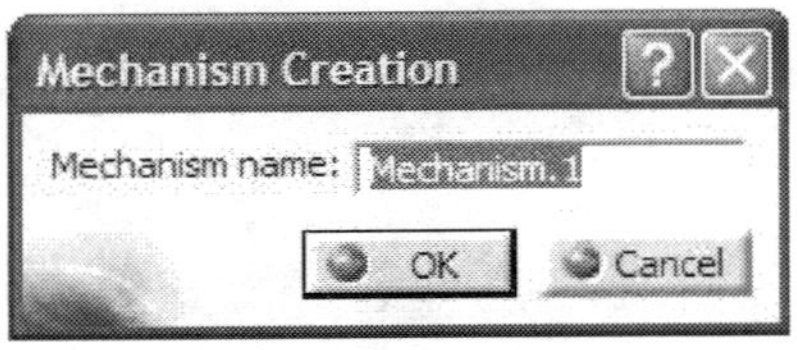

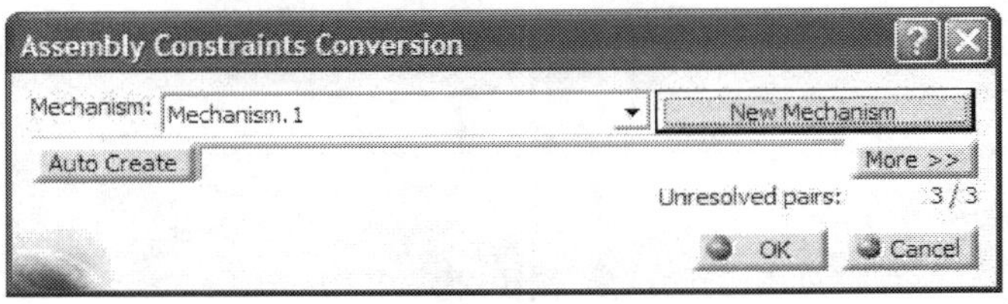

Select the **Auto Create** button 

. Then the **Unresolved pairs** become **0/3**, things are moving in the right direction.

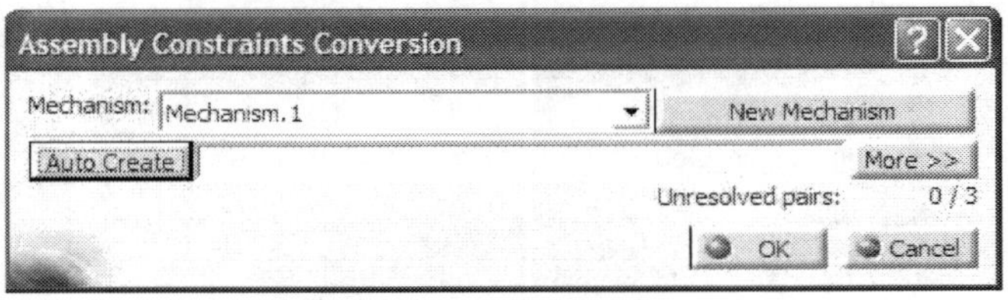

Note that the tree becomes longer by having an **Application** Branch. The expanded tree is displayed below. The dof is currently three representing the three independent motions of the joints (since we have yet to impose the path constraint yet).

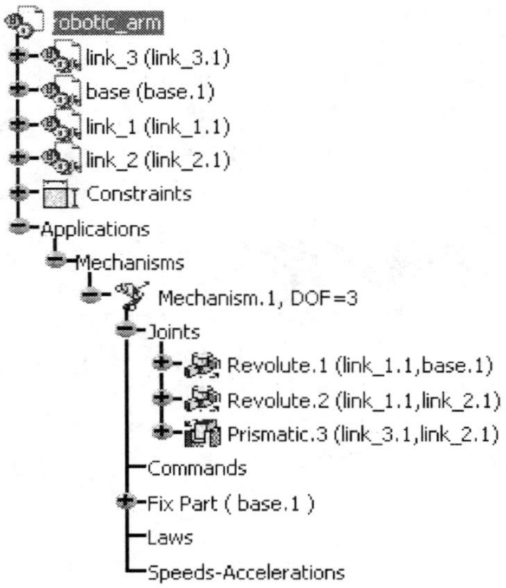

The **Point Curve Joint** needs to be created manually. To do so, pick the **Point Curve Joint** icon  and in resulting pop up box, make selections shown below.

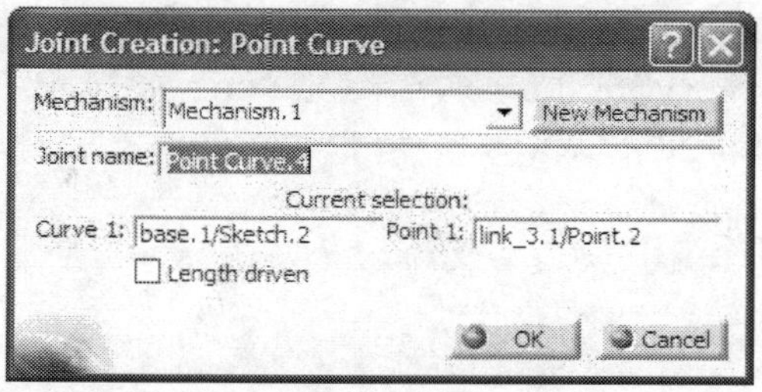

Note: <u>If you are having difficulties picking the point at the bottom of **link_3**, hide the curve and the point on the curve first</u>.

For Curve 1, pick the path

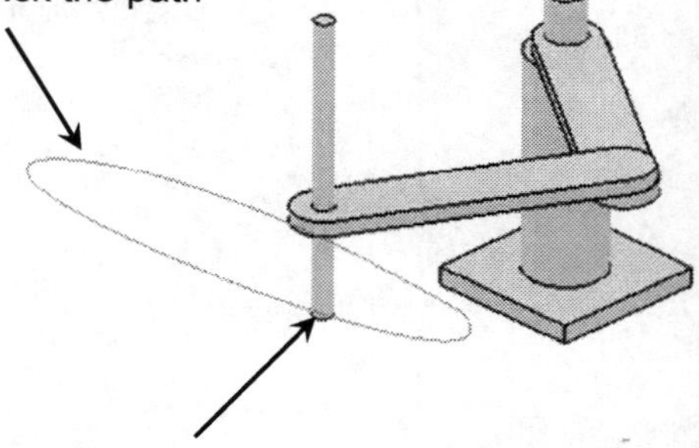

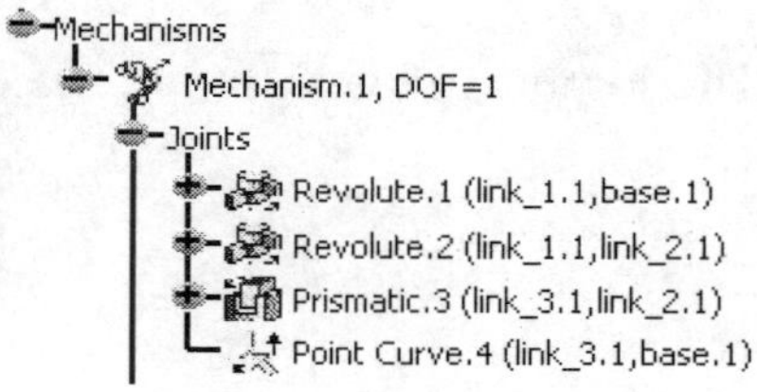

For Point 1, select the point at the bottom of Link3

The fact that the degree of freedom has been reduced to one implies that the mechanism can be simulated as soon as a **Command** is specified.
Double click on the Point Curve.4 branch to open the corresponding definition box.

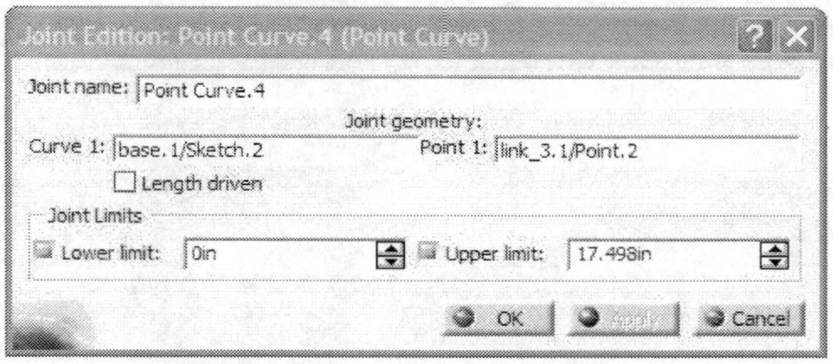

Make this a **Length driven** joint by checking the appropriate box.

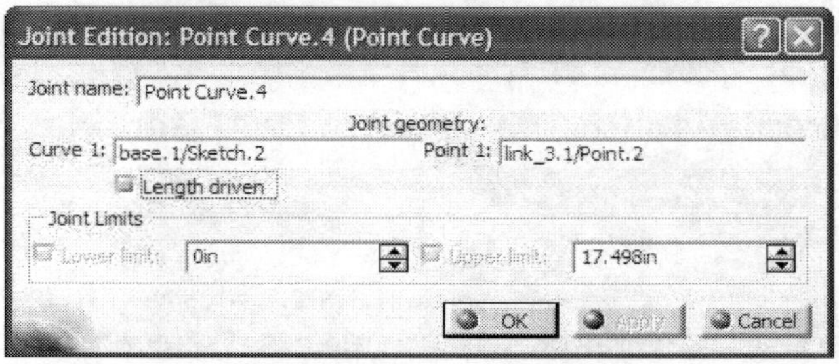

Upon closing the above box and assuming that everything else was done correctly, the following message appears on the screen.

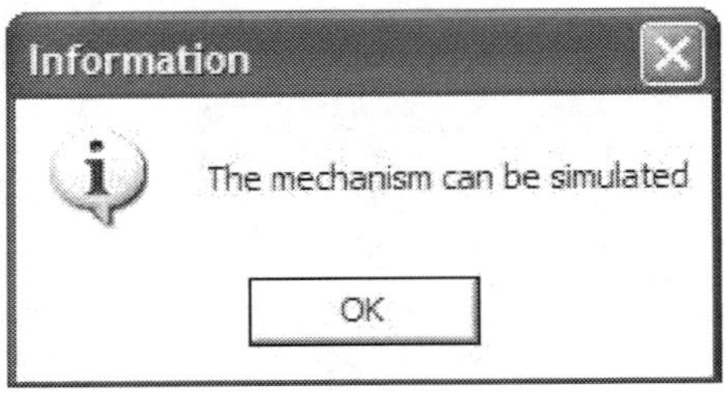

This indeed is good news.

The degree of freedom is reduced to zero. And the **Command.1** appears as a branch of the tree.

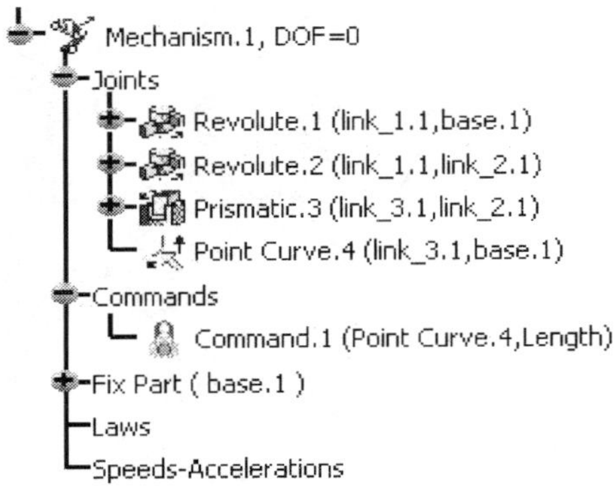

The joints are identified in the figure below.

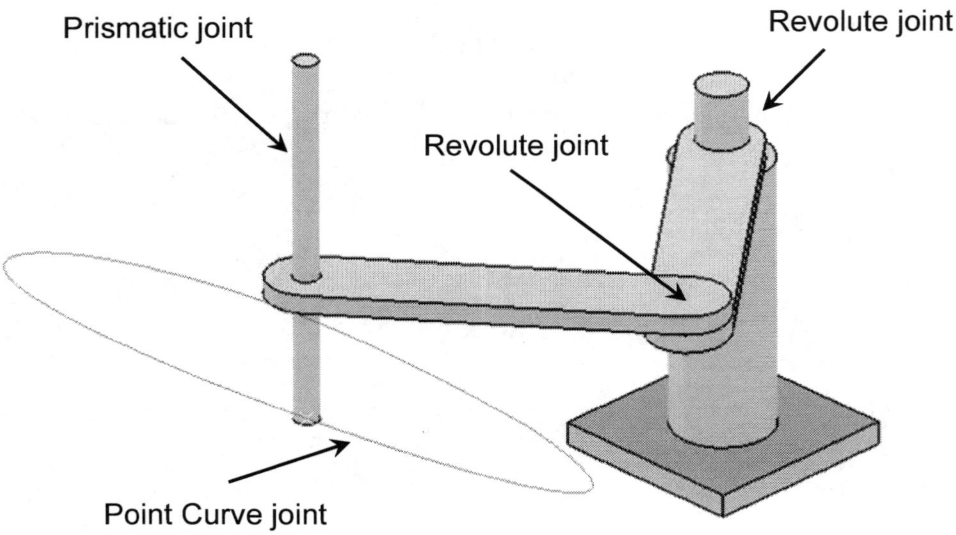

We will now simulate the motion without regard to time based motion. Select the **Simulation** icon  from the **DMU Generic Animation** toolbar 

. This enables you to choose the mechanism to be animated if there are several present. In this case, select **Mechanism.1** and close the window.

As soon as the window is closed, a Simulation branch is added to the tree.

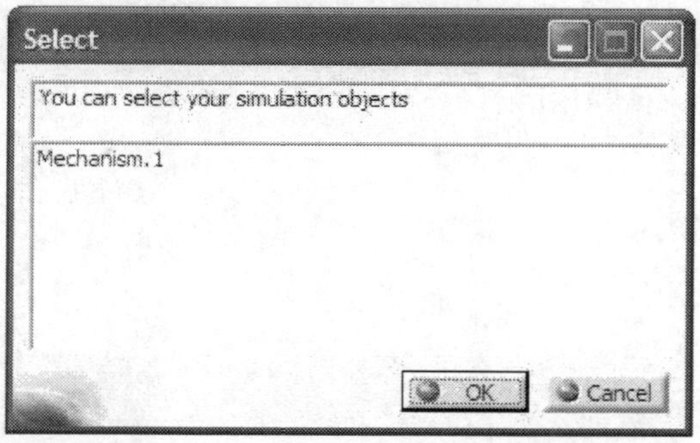

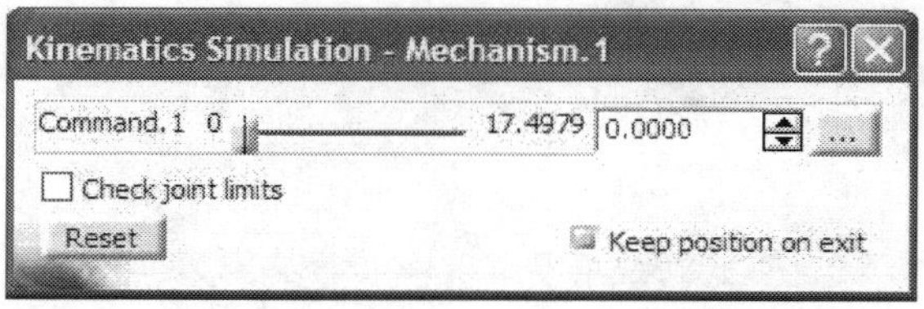

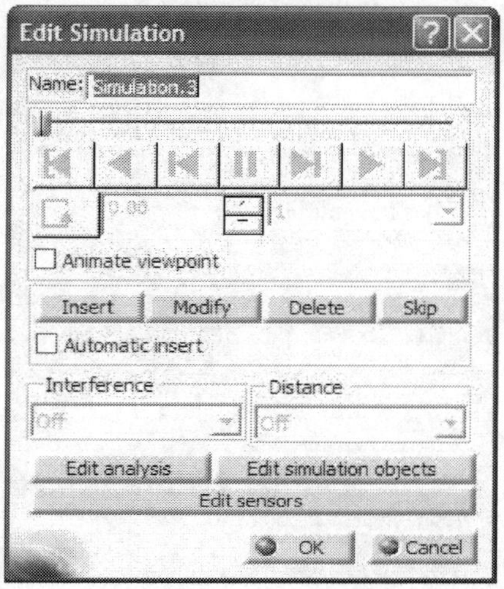

As you scroll the bar in this toolbar from left to right, **link_3** begins to travel along the path. Notice that the zero position is simply the initial position of the assembly when the joint was created. Thus, if a particular zero position had been desired, a temporary assembly constraint could have been created earlier to locate the mechanism to the desired zero position. This temporary constraint would need to be deleted before conversion to mechanism joints (or the resulting joint could be deleted).

When the scroll bar in the **Kinematics Simulation** pop up box reaches the right extreme end, select the **Insert** button 

in the **Edit Simulation** pop up box shown above. This activates the video player buttons shown

.

Return the robot to its original position by picking the **Jump to Start** button .

Note that the **Change Loop Mode** button  is also active now.

Upon selecting the **Play Forward** button , the robot makes a fast jump completing its revolution.

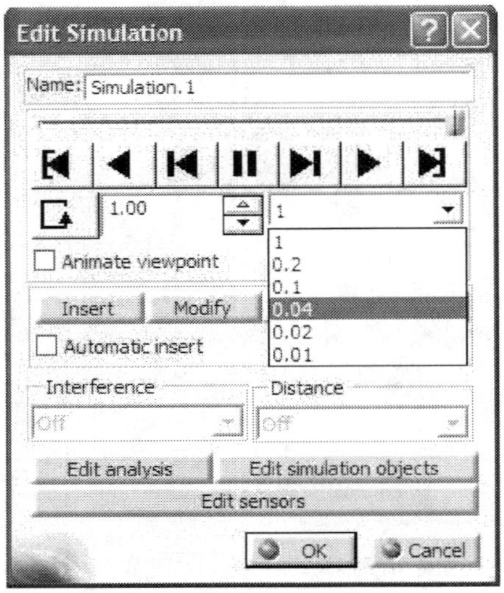

Select the **Compile Simulation** icon  from the **Generic Animation** toolbar 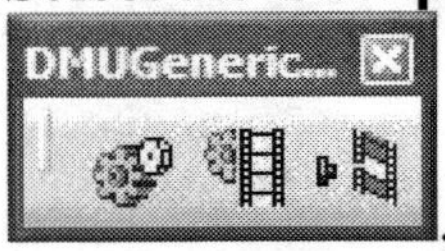

. Pressing the **File name** button 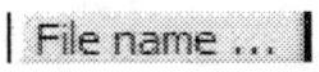

allows you to set the location and name of the animation file to be generated as displayed below.
Select a suitable path and file name and change the **Time step** to be 0.04 to produce a slow moving robot in an AVI file.

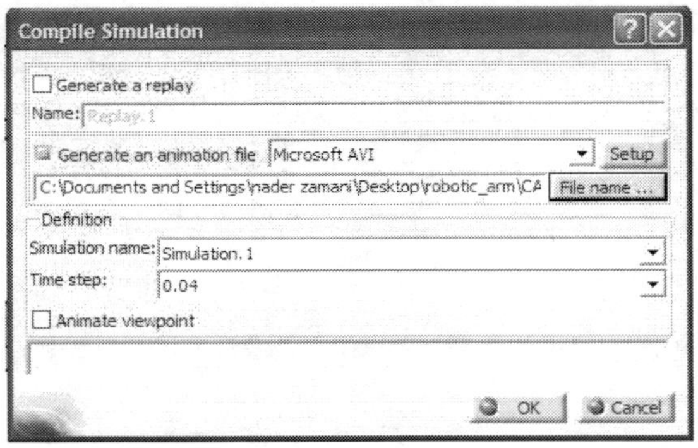

In the event that an AVI file is not needed, but one wishes to play the animation, repeatedly, a **Replay** need be generated. Therefore, in the **Compile Simulation** box, check the **Generate a replay** button.

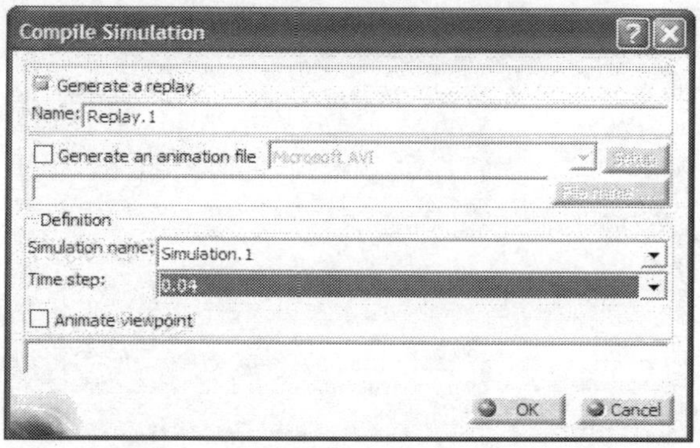

Note that in this case most of the previously available options are dimmed out.

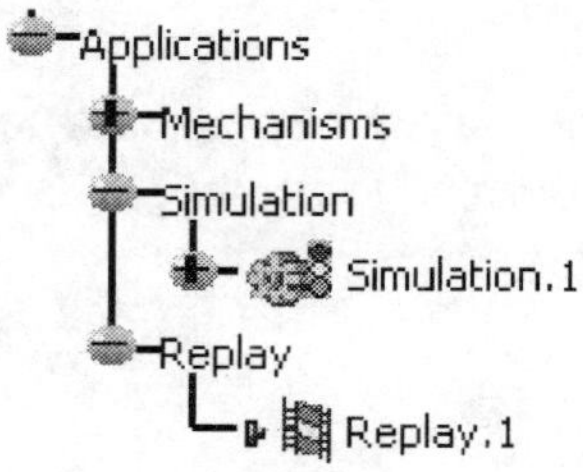

A **Replay.1** branch has also been added to the tree.

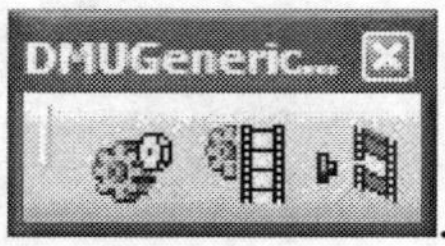

Select the **Replay** icon  from the **Generic Animation** toolbar. Double clock on **Replay.1** in the tree and the **Replay** pop up box appears. Experiment with the different choices of the **Change Loop Mode** buttons .
The crank can be returned to the original position by picking the **Jump to Start** button .

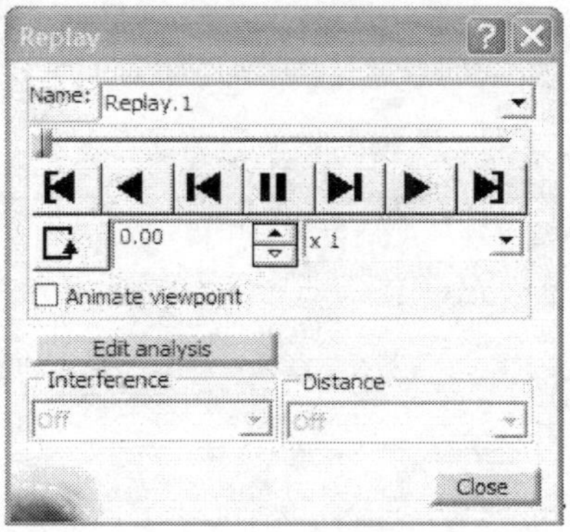

The **skip ratio** (which is chosen to be x1 in the right box) controls the speed of the **Replay**.

Once a **Replay** is generated such as **Replay.1** in the tree above, it can also be played with a different icon.

Select the **Simulation Player** icon  from the **DMUPlayer** toolbar 

.

The outcome is the pop up box above. Use the cursor to pick **Replay.1** from the tree.

The player keys are no longer dimmed out. Use the **Play Forward (Right)** button  to begin the replay.

4 Creating Laws in the Motion

You will now introduce some time based physics into the problem by specifying the linear velocity of **link_3** along the path. Recall the desired speed of 1 in/s was given in the problem statement.

Click on **Simulation with Laws** icon  in the **Simulation** toolbar 

.
You will get the following pop up box indication that you need to add at least a relation between a command and the time parameter.

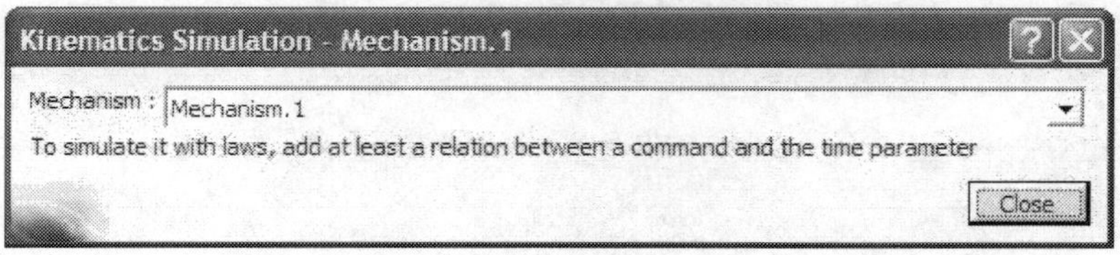

To create the required relation, select the **Formula** icon  from the **Knowledge** toolbar 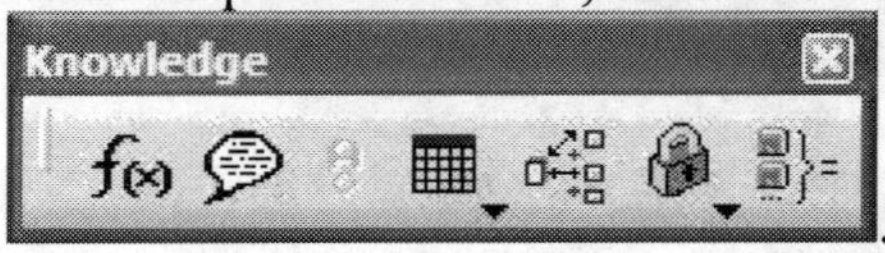

. The pop up box below appears on the screen.

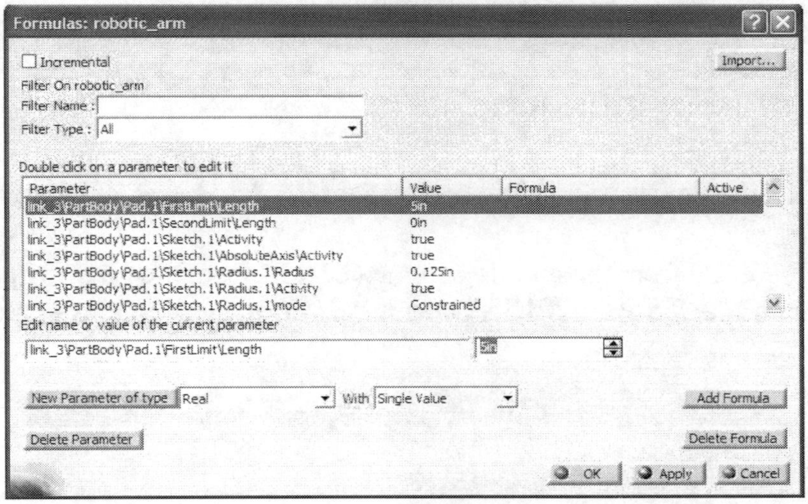

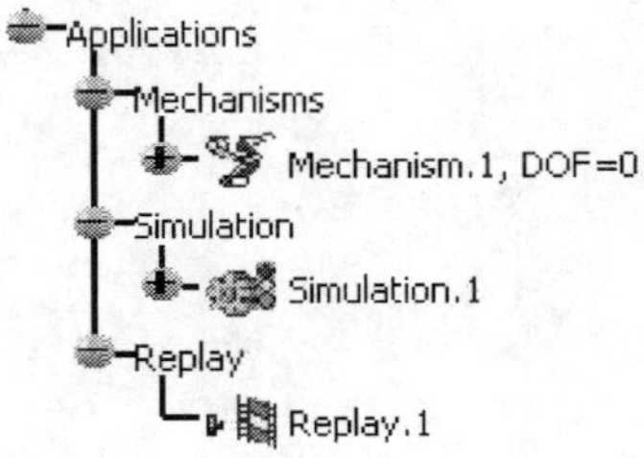

Point the cursor to the **Mechanism.1, DOF=0** branch in the tree and click. The consequence is that only parameters associated with the mechanism are displayed in the **Formulas** box.
The long list is now reduced to two parameters as indicated in the box shown on the next page.

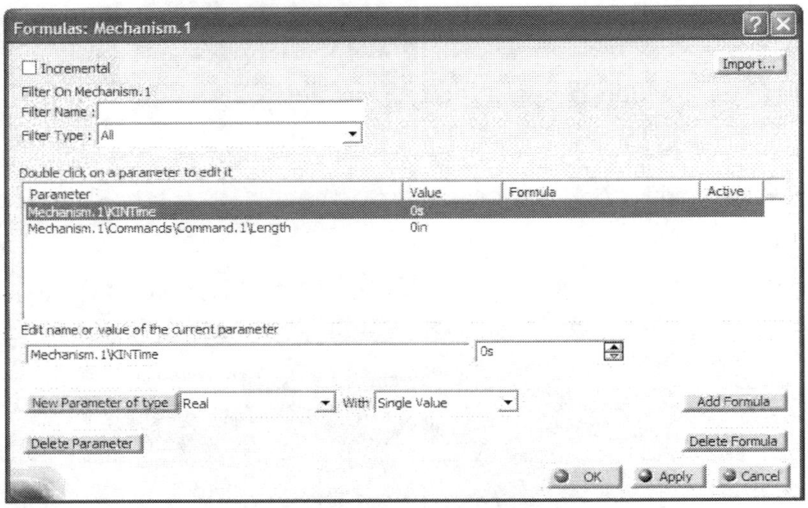

Select the entry **Mechanism.1\Commands\Command.1\Length** and press the **Add Formula** button Add Formula. This action kicks you to the **Formula Editor** box.

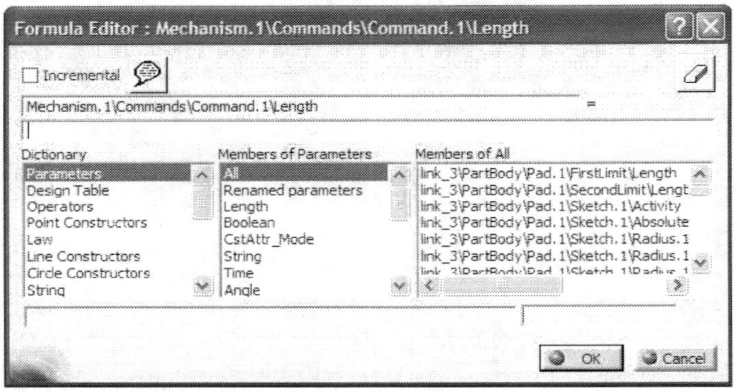

Pick the **Time** entry from the middle column (i.e. **Members of Parameters**) then double click on **Mechanism.1\KINTime** in the **Members of Time** column.

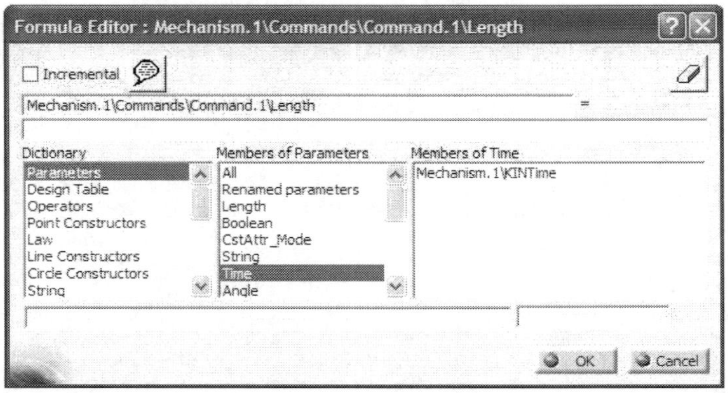

Since length can be computed as the product of linear velocity (1in/1s) in our case and time, edit the box containing the right hand side of the equality such that the formula becomes:

$$Mechanism.1 \backslash Commands \backslash Command.1 \backslash Length =$$
$$(1in/1s) * Mechnism.1 \backslash KINTime$$

The completed **Formula Editor** box should look as shown below.

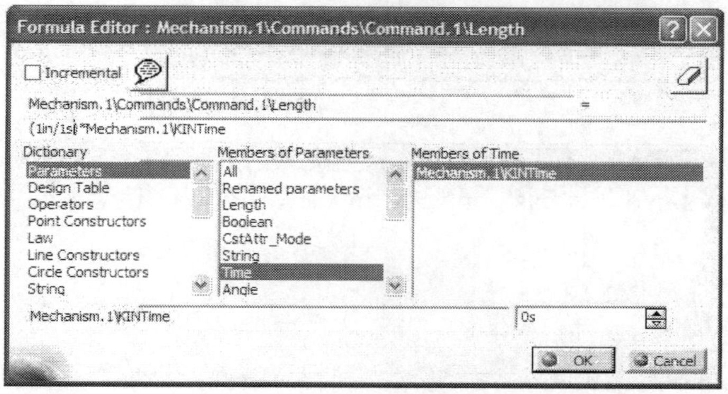

Upon accepting **OK**, the formula is recorded in the **Formulas** pop up box as shown below.

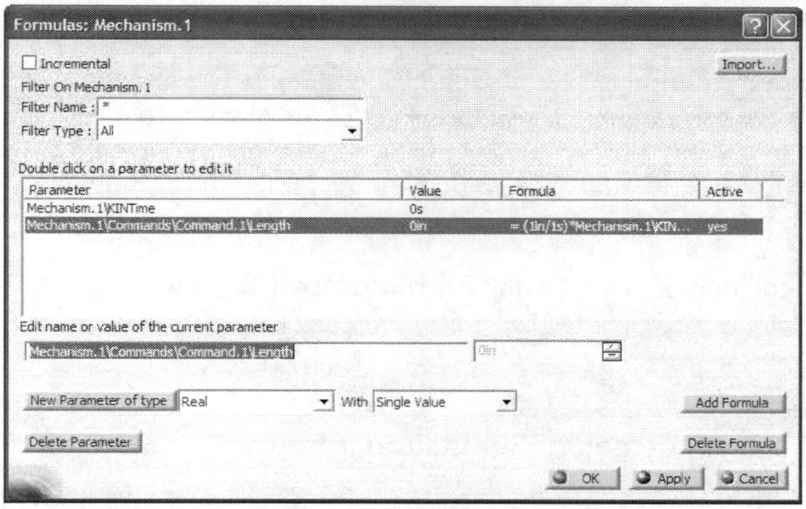

Careful attention must be given to the units when writing formulas involving the kinematic parameters. In the event that the formula has different units at the different sides of the equality you will get **Warning** messages such as the one shown below.

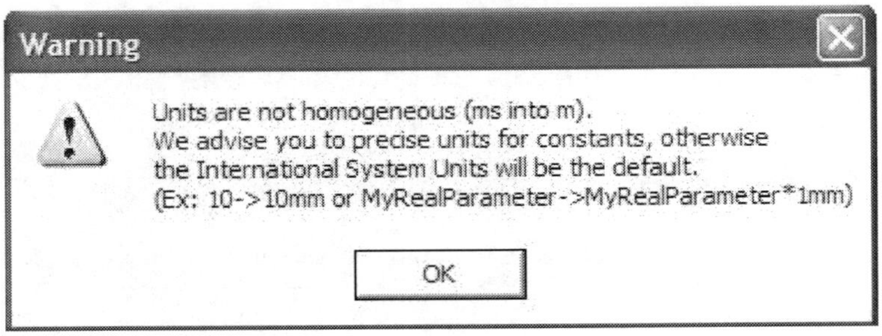

We are spared the warning message because the formula has been properly inputted. Note that the introduced law has appeared in **Law** branch of the tree.

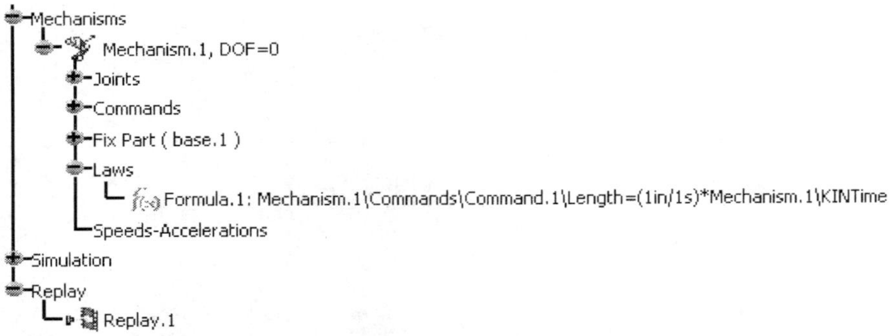

Keep in mind that our interest is to plot the angular positions required at the two revolute joints to achieve this motion. Since these angles are already created with the joints, we do not need to add any sensors to make the desired plots. We would require sensors if we wished to plot velocities and accelerations (even for the joint angles).

To simulate the motion, click on the **Simulation with Laws** icon  in the **Simulation** toolbar 

.
This results in the **Kinematics Simulation** pop up box shown below.

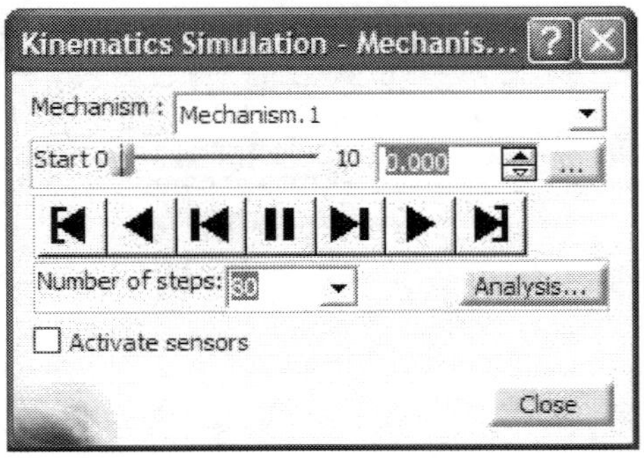

Note that the default time duration is 10 seconds.
To change this value, click on the button 0.000. In the resulting pop up box, change the time duration so that after that duration the robot will have traversed once around the path. You can use the **Measure item** in the **DMU Measure** toolbar to measure you path length in inches, and since the speed along the path is 1 in/s, enter this number of seconds for your time.

The scroll bar now moves up to your max time (shown here as 10.398s).

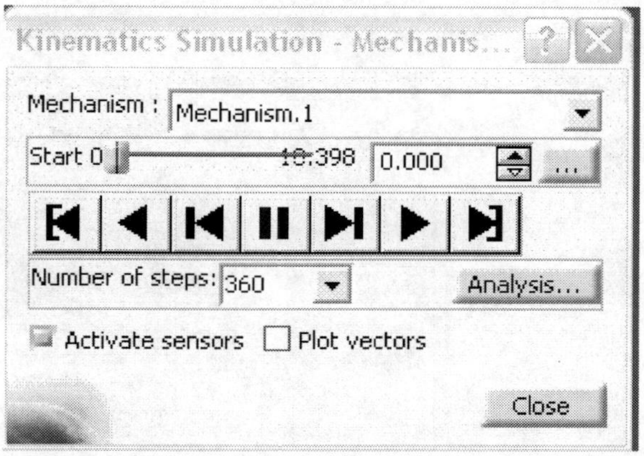

Check the **Activate sensors** box, at the bottom left corner. (Note: CATIA V5R15 users will also see a **Plot vectors** box in this window).

You will next have to make certain selections from the accompanying **Sensors** box.

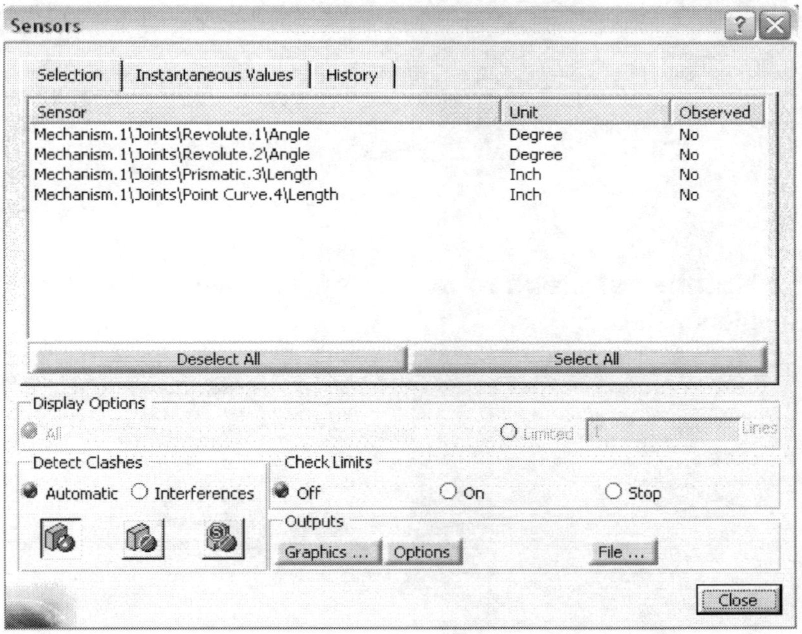

Click on the following item to record the angles of each of the two revolute joints:

Mechanism.1\Joints\Revolute.1\Angle
Mechanism.1\Joints\Revolute.1\Angle

As you make selections in this window, the last column in the **Sensors** box, changes to **Yes** for the corresponding items. This is shown below. Do not close the **Sensors** box after you have made your selection (leave it open to generate results).

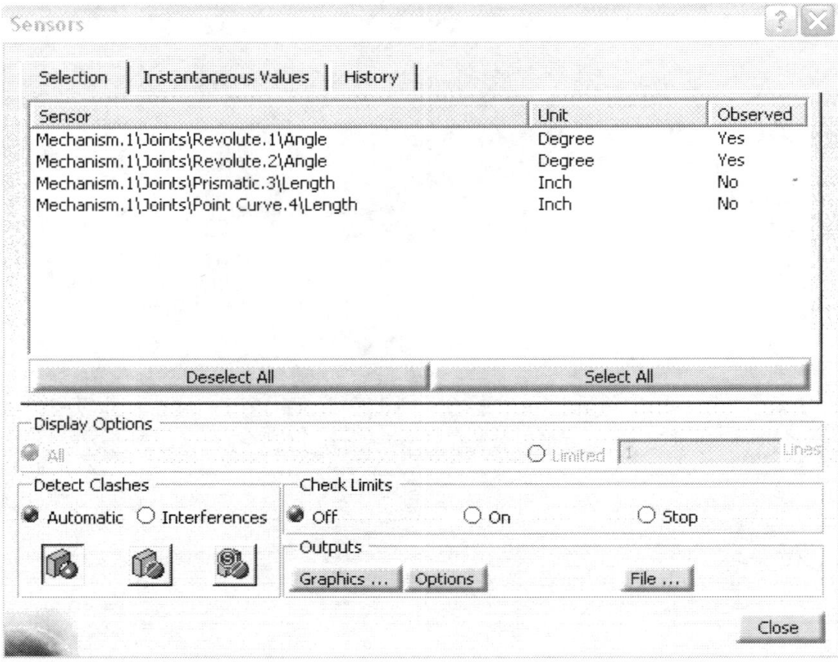

Also, change the **Number of steps to 80** if it is not already so. The larger this number, the smoother the plots will be.

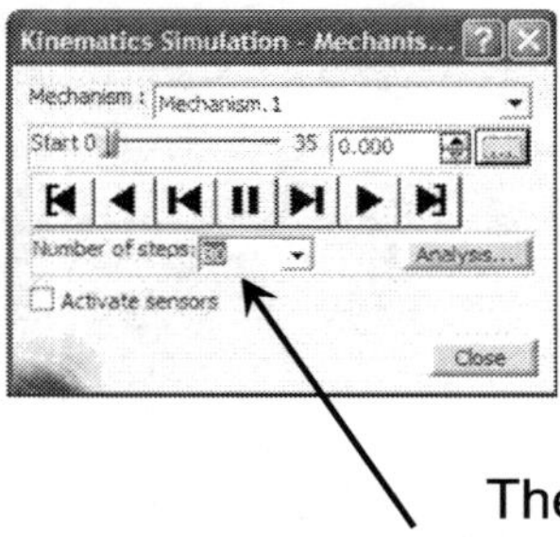

The larger this number the smoother the plot

Finally, drag the scroll bar in the **Kinematics Simulation** box. As you do this, the tip of **link_3** travels along the path. Once the bar reaches its right extreme point, **link_3** has made one complete traversal of the path.

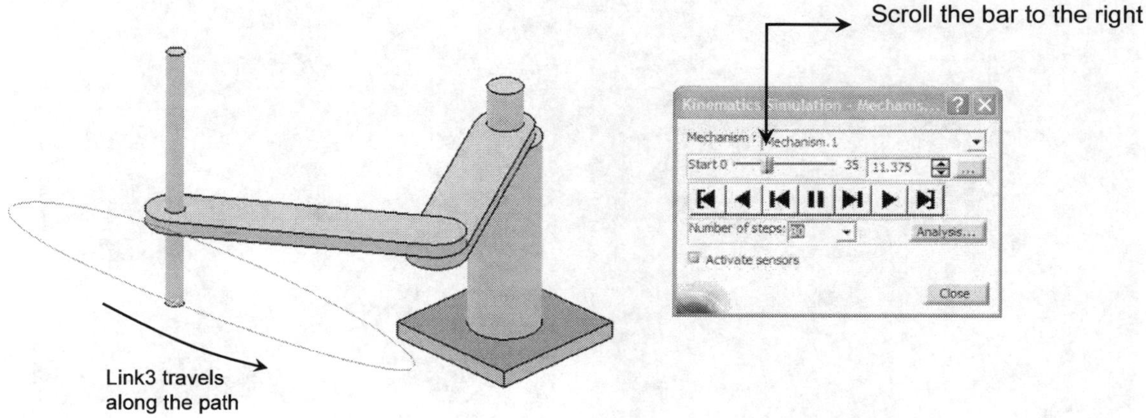

Once Link3 reaches the end of its trip, click on the **Graphics** button 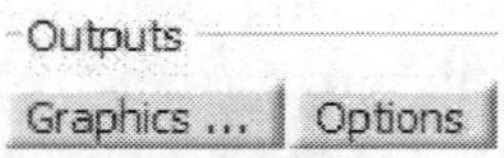

in the **Sensor** box. The result is the plot of the two revolute joint angles versus time. Recall that Revolute.1 is the joint between the base and link_1, and Revolute.2 is the joint between link_1 and link_2. The y axis of the plot is scaled based on whichever plot is selected in the right portion of the window. The two plots are shown below, first scaled for the first joint, then for the second.

Scaled for the first joint:

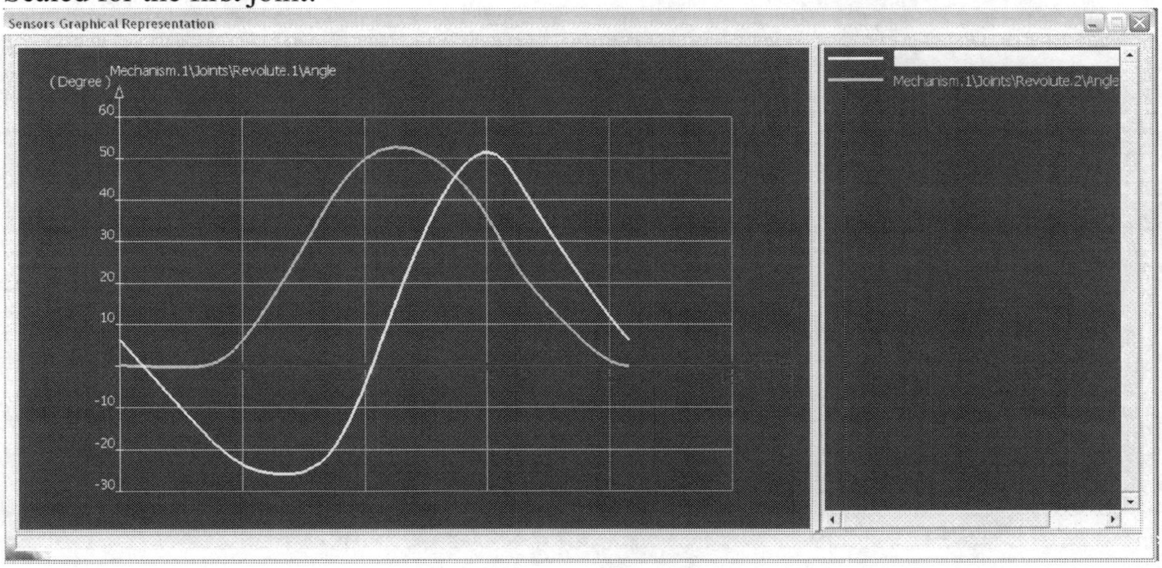

Scaled for the second joint:

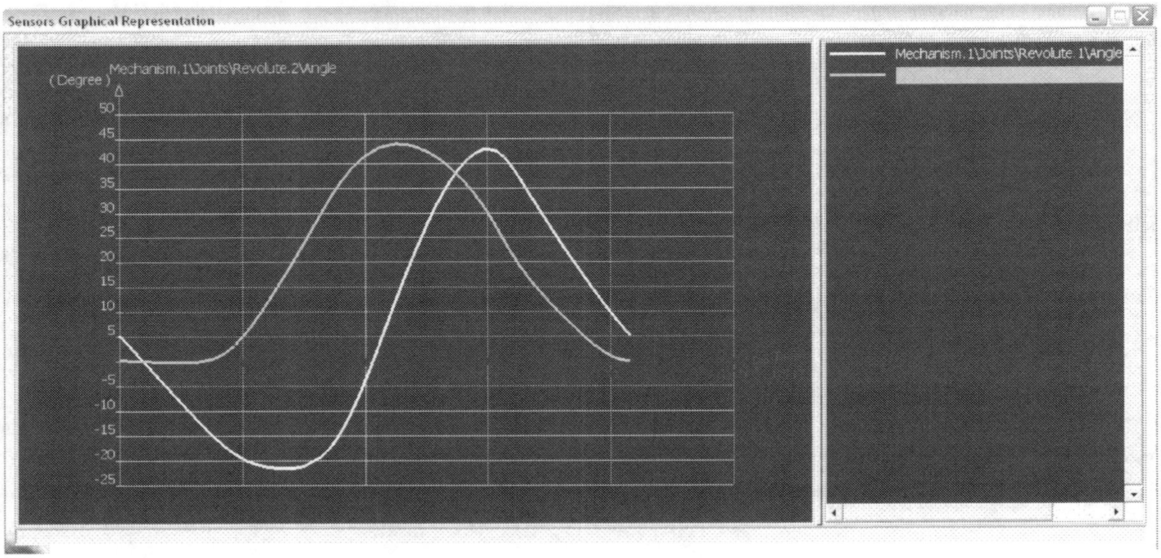

It is not uncommon that you may develop a variety of simulation results before determining exactly how to achieve the desired results. In this case, prior results stored need to be erased. To do this, click on the **History** tab History of the **Sensors** box.

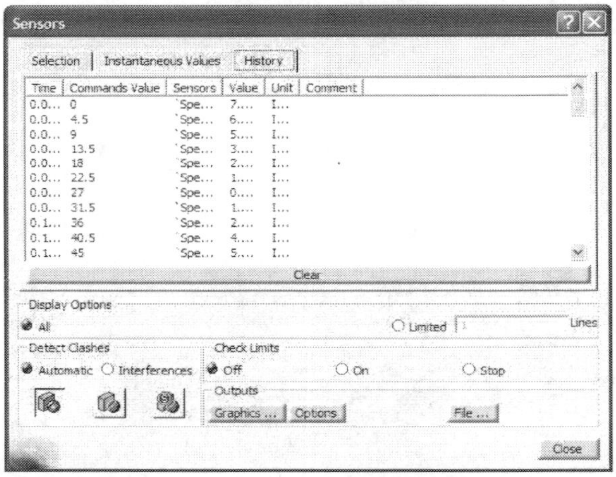

Use the **Clear** key Clear to erase the values generated.

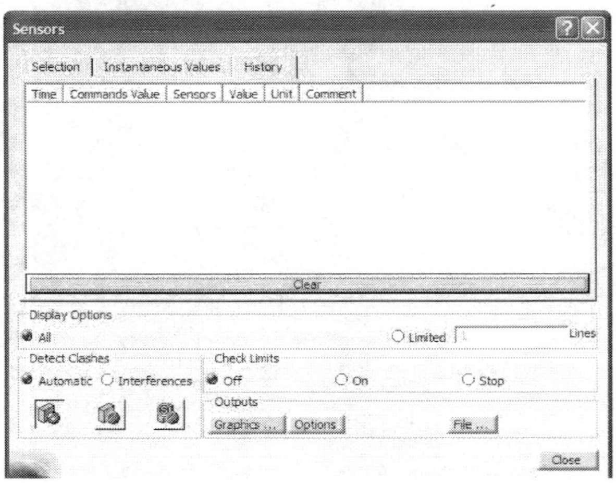

The instantaneous angles can also be displayed. Select the **Instantaneous Values** Instantaneous Values tab from the **Sensors** box.

Click on the **Step forward** button . The instantaneous values are displayed in the Sensors box as **link_3** moves.

Instantaneous values are shown as you step through the motion.

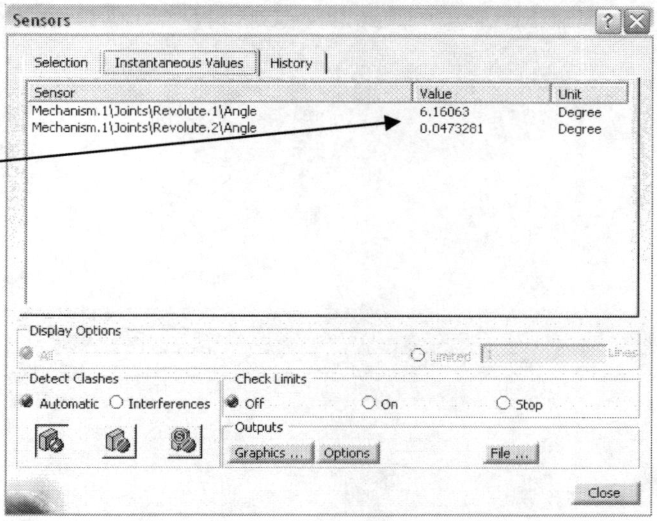

This concludes the tutorial.

NOTES:

Chapter 12

Single Cylinder Engine

Introduction

This tutorial is very similar to the slider crank mechanism tutorial presented earlier. The main difference is that it involves modeling a single cylinder engine similar to those found in lawnmowers, single cylinder motorcycles, and various other applications.

1 Problem Statement

The assembly discussed in this chapter consists of several engine components (for the labeling of these parts see page 12-5). The piston is driven along a block (cylinder block) through the rotation of a crank (crankshaft). The angular velocity of the crank is assumed to be 600 rpm (3600°/s). The five mechanism joints required will be created automatically by imposing the appropriate assembly constraints and converting them into mechanism joints. The piston/block joint is cylindrical (or prismatic), the crank/conrod, crank/block, and conrod/pin joints will be revolute, and finally the pin/piston joint will be rigid. The rigid joint is to prevent the free spinning of the pin in the piston hole. The objective is to plot the position, velocity and acceleration of the piston as a function of time for ten crankshaft revolutions.

In spite of its rather complicated look, the assembly is fundamentally identical to the slider crank mechanism, except that in the former case the crank was offset (i.e., the axis of motion of the upper conrod connection did not intersect the axis of rotation of the crank, whereas in this engine example it does).

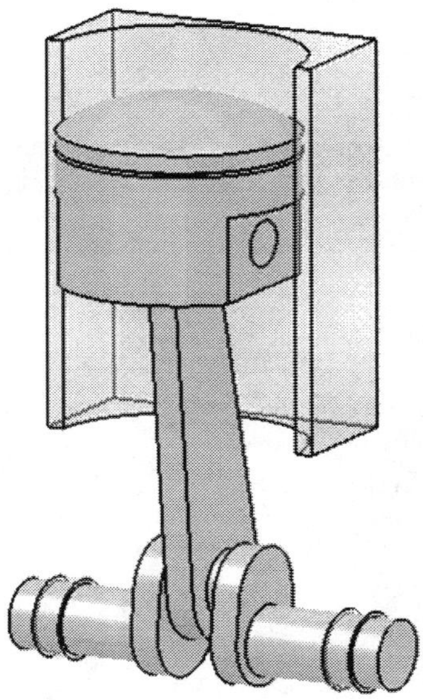

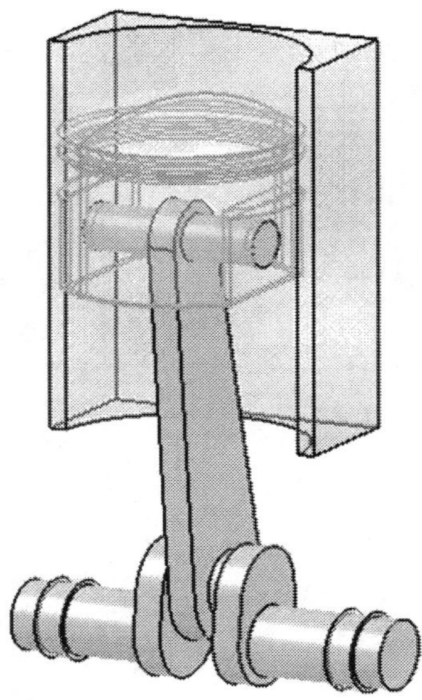

2 Overview of this Tutorial

In this tutorial you will:

1. Model the five CATIA parts required.
2. Create an assembly (CATIA Product) containing the parts.
3. Constrain the assembly in such a way that only one degree of freedom is unconstrained. This remaining degree of freedom can be thought of as rotation of the crank.
4. Enter the **Digital Mockup** workbench and convert the assembly constraints into one cylindrical joint, three revolute joints, and a rigid joint.
5. Simulate the motion of the engine as the crankshaft spins without consideration to time (in other words, without implementing the time based angular velocity given in the problem statement).
6. Add a formula to implement the time based kinematics associated with constant angular velocity of the crank.
7. Simulate the desired constant angular velocity motion and generate plots of the kinematic results for the piston.

3 Creation of the Assembly in Mechanical Design Solutions

In this tutorial you need to create five parts **cylinder, conrod, crank, pin, and block** as shown below. It is recommended that you use the dimensions (inches) given herein, and in the event that a dimension is missing, estimate it based on the drawing.
Since these parts are more involved than the parts in the earlier tutorials we will walk you through the steps necessary to create these parts even though we assume you are familiar with the basics of part modeling in CATIA.

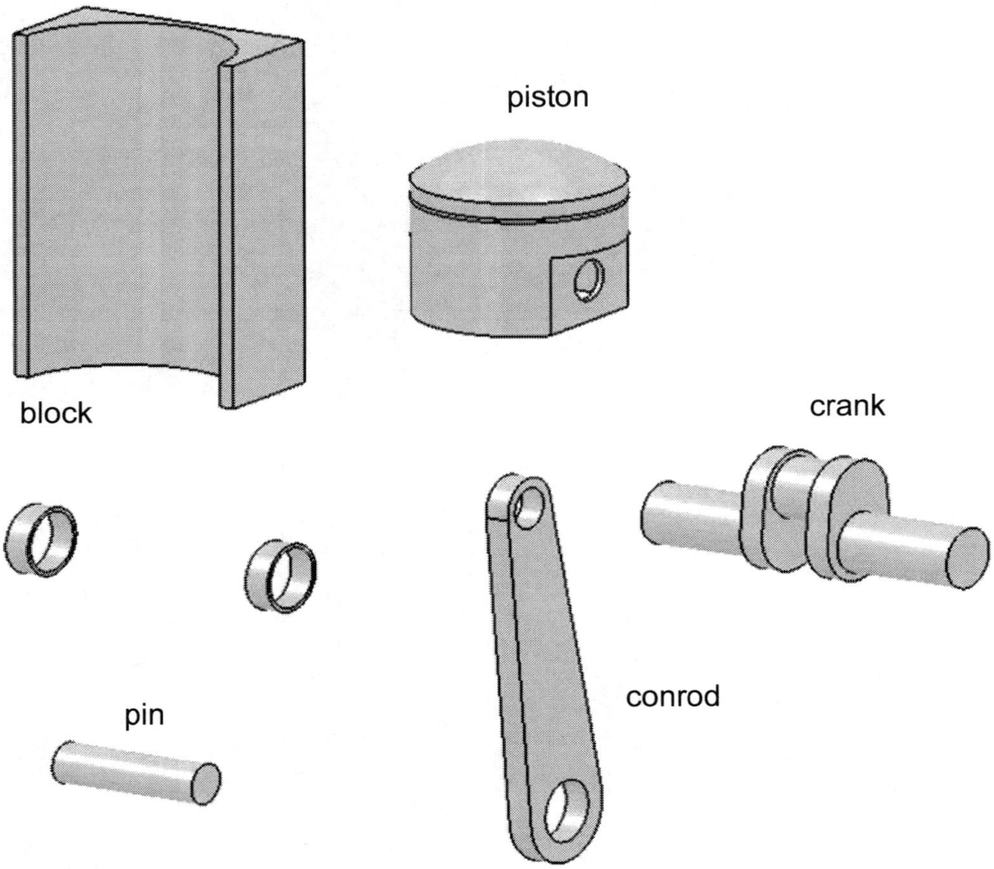

Note that the two rings shown below the block are the bearings which hold the crank. These are part of the block, though for simplicity they are not connected by material to the block.

Outline of creating the piston:

Enter the **Part Design** workbench. Begin creating a part named **piston**.

Select the **yz** plane and enter the **Sketcher**. In the **Sketcher**, use the **Profile** icon from the **Profile** toolbar

, to draw the piston cross section and dimension it as shown.

Make a note of the following points.

The bottom left corner of the sketch should be at the origin of the sketch plane.
The center of the top arc lies on the V axis of the Sketcher.

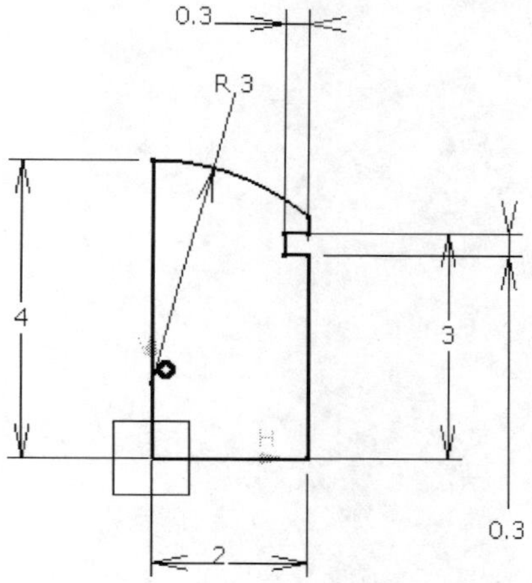

Exit the **Sketcher**.

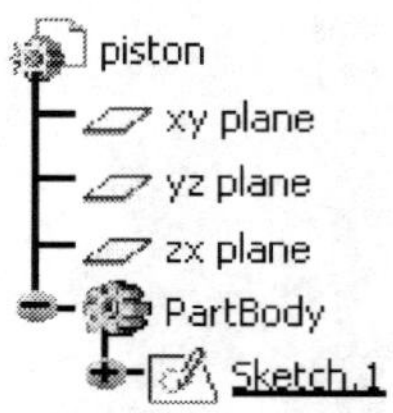

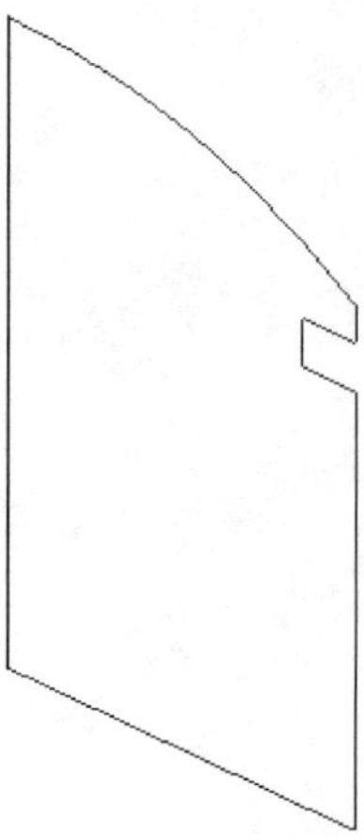

Use the **Shaft** icon  to open the pop up box shown on the right.

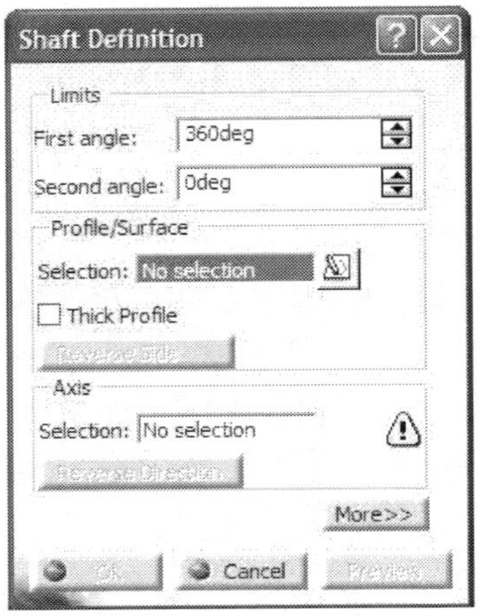

For **Profile/Surface Selection**, pick **Sketch.1**. For **Axis Selection**, pick the edge shown.

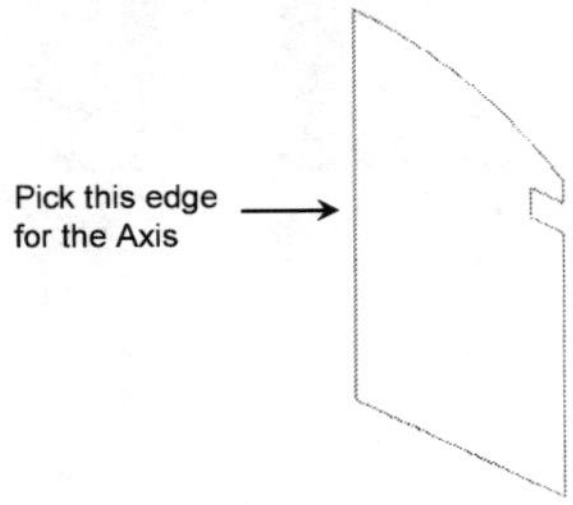

As soon as the Axis is selected, wireframe shape of the resulting object is displayed.

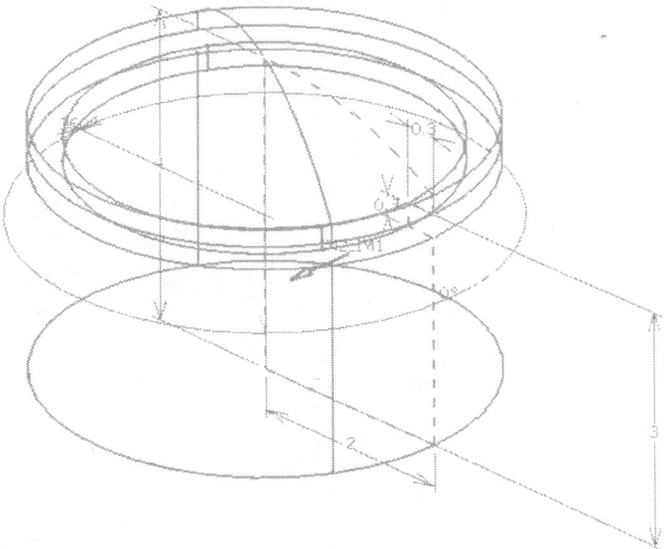

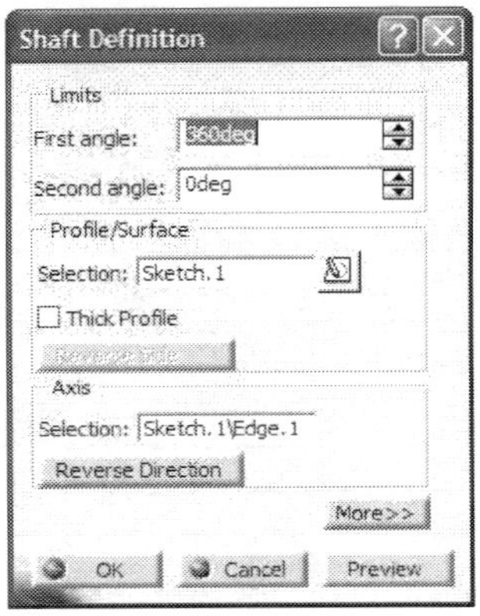

Close the pop up box by pressing **OK**.

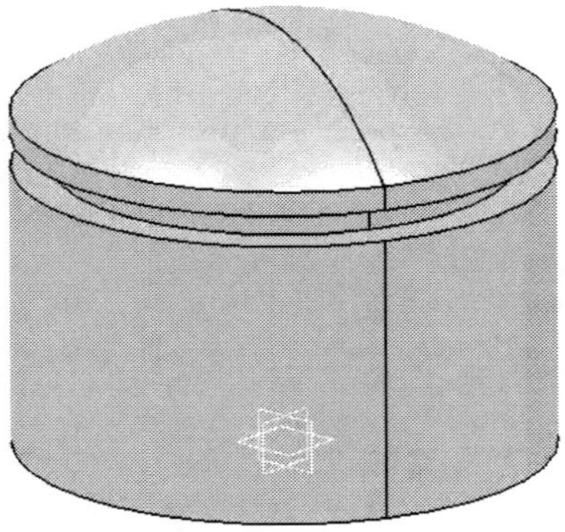

Select the **zx** plane and enter the **Sketcher** .

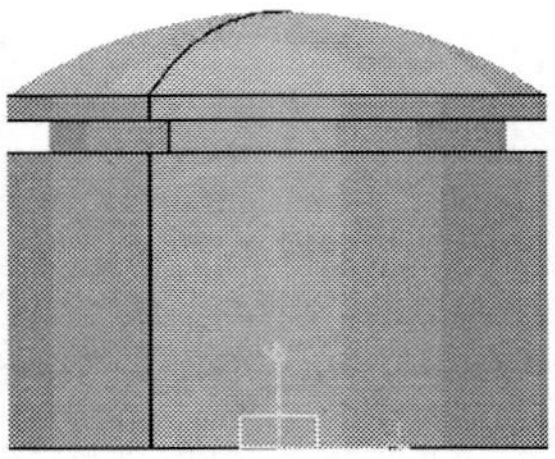

In the **Sketcher**, use the **Rectangle** icon to draw the rectangle below and dimension it as indicated.

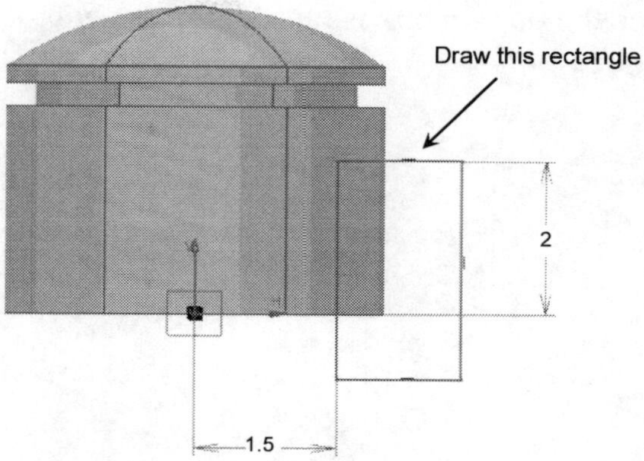

Exit the **Sketcher** .

Select the **Pocket** icon .
For **Profile/Surface Selection**, pick **Sketch.2**.
Make sure you have the Mirror extent box checked ☐ Mirrored extent .
Enter a large enough number (the default of 4in is adequate) for **Depth** so that the pocket completely encompasses the cylinder.

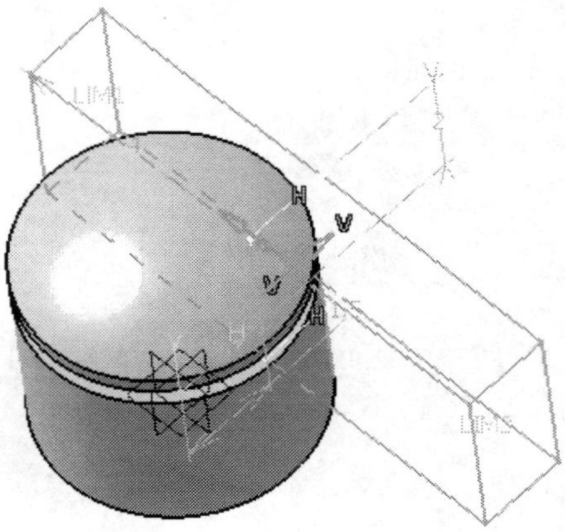

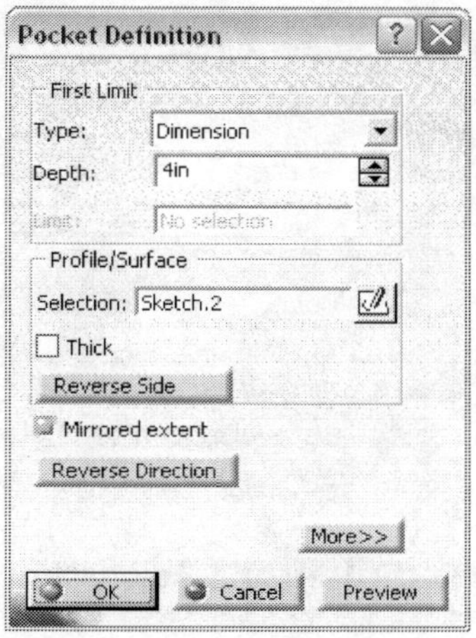

Once the pop up box is closed, the cylinder is cut on the side with a flat plane as shown below.

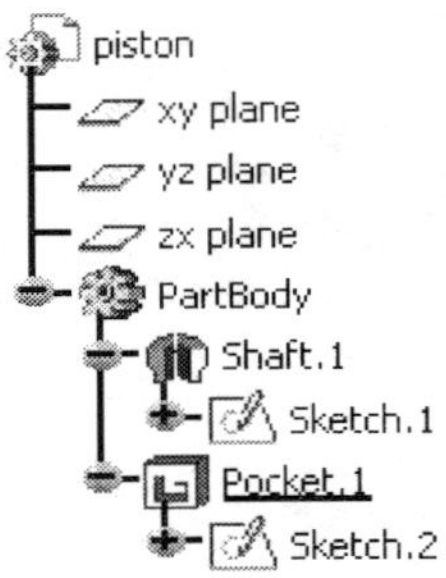

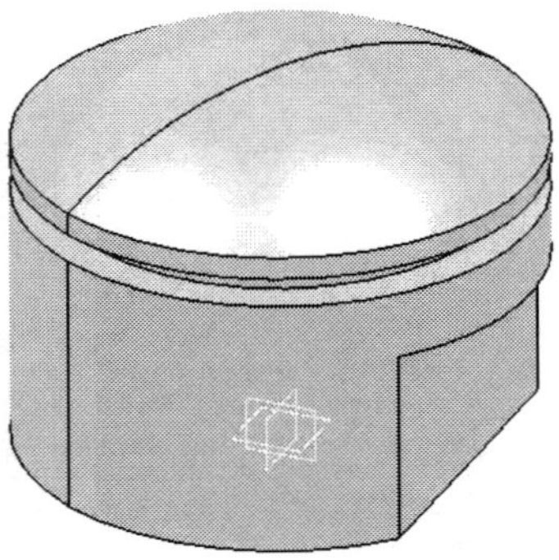

To mirror the pocket to the other side, select the **Pocket.1** feature just created and pick the **Mirror** icon  from the **Transformation Features** toolbar 

. The resulting pop up box is shown in the next page.

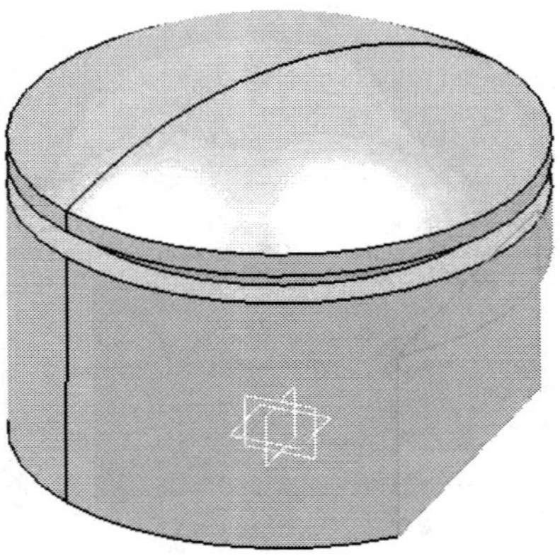

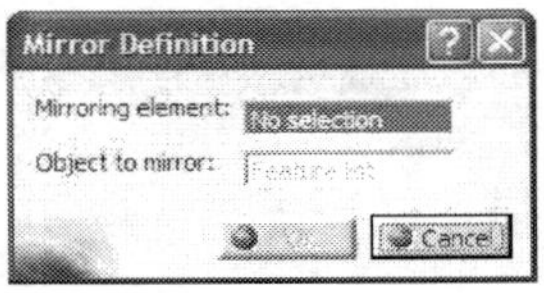

For **Mirroring element**, select the **yz** plane.

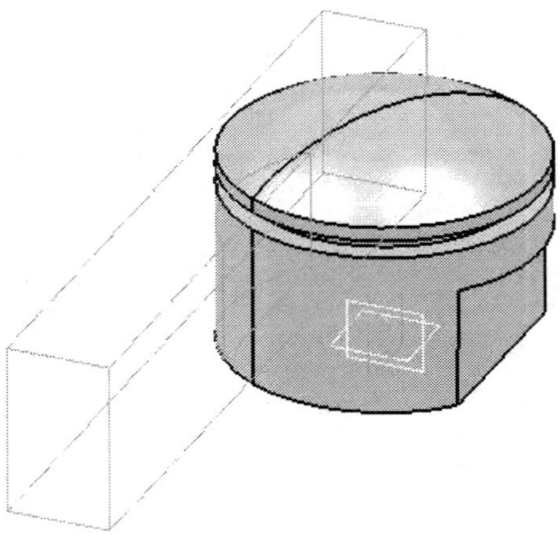

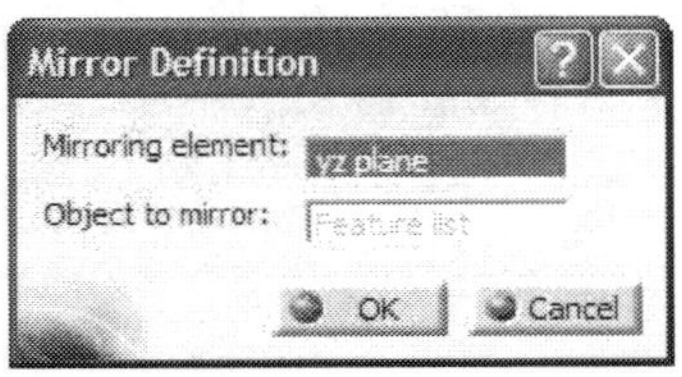

After pressing **OK**, the pocket feature is mirrored.

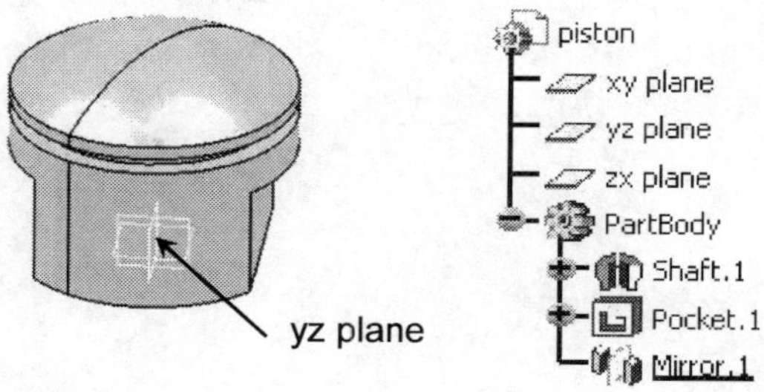

Next we will make the hole for the pin. Select the flat surface shown and enter the **Sketcher**.

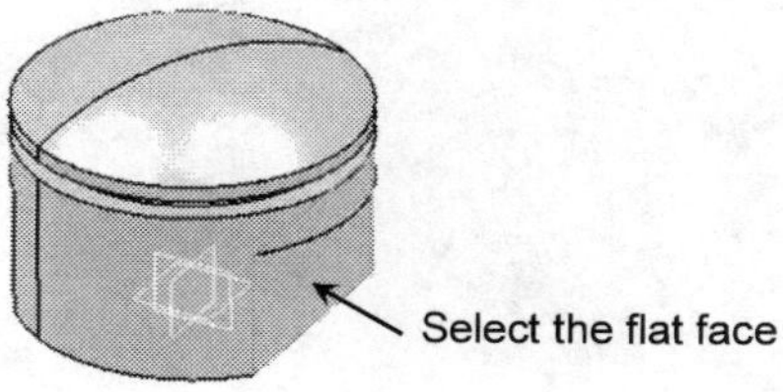

On this face, draw a circle 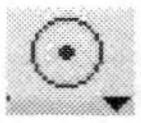 of radius 0.5, centered in the middle of the rectangle.

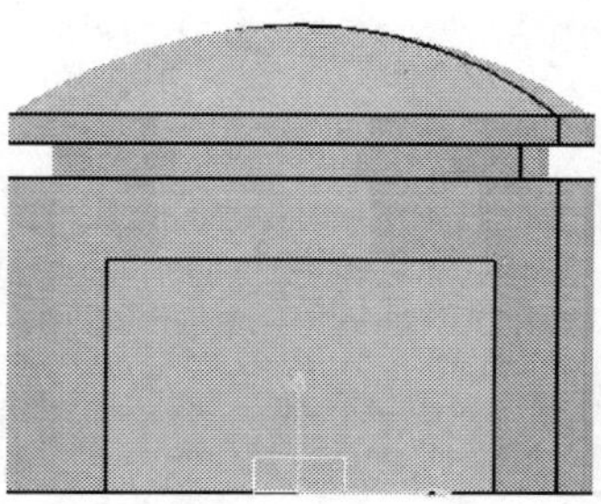

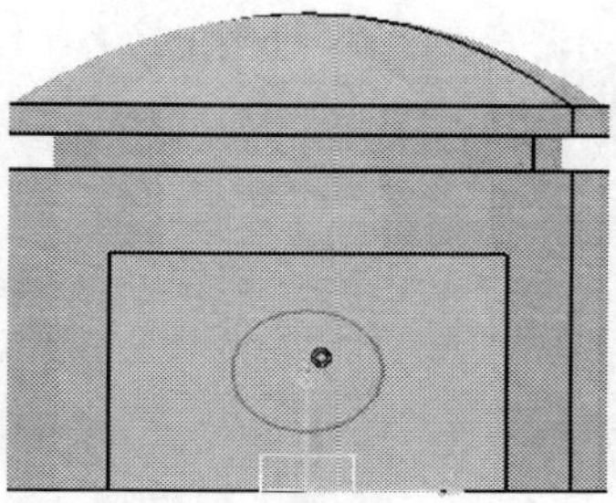

Exit the **Sketcher** 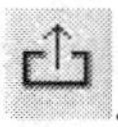.

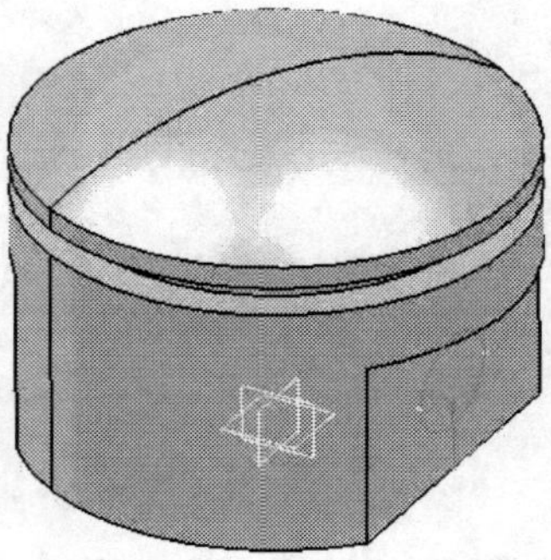

Pick the **Pocket** icon . For **Type**, choose **Up to Last** and click on **Reverse Direction** if necessary to get a through hole.

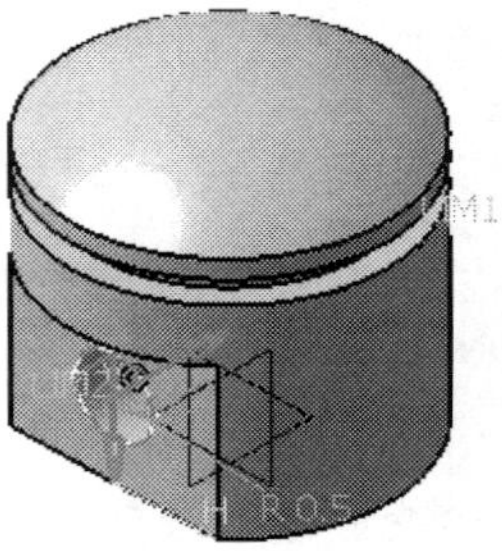

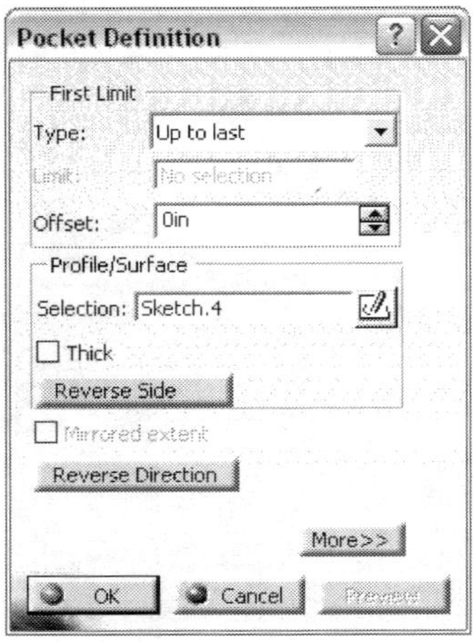

Click **OK** in the **Pocket Definition** box. Your piston and tree should now look as shown below.

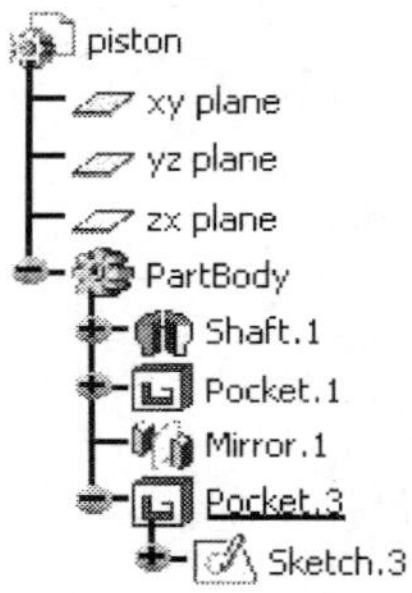

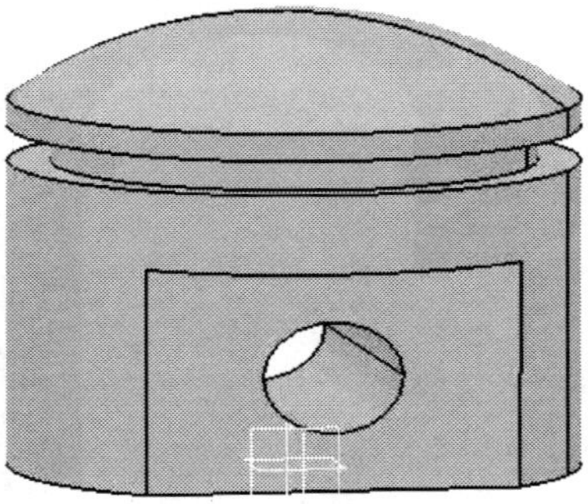

To hollow out the piston, select the **Shell** icon  from the **Dress-Up Features** toolbar 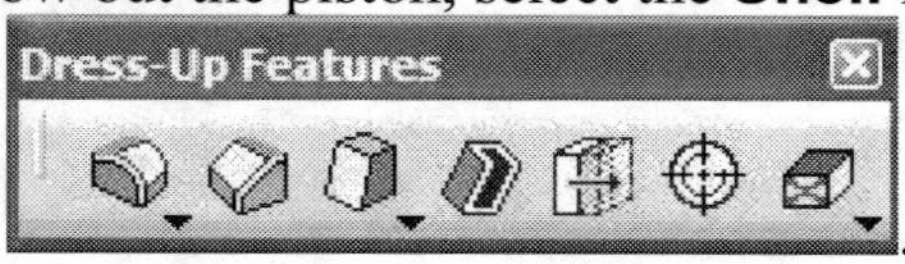.

This selection results in the pop up box shown on the right hand side.

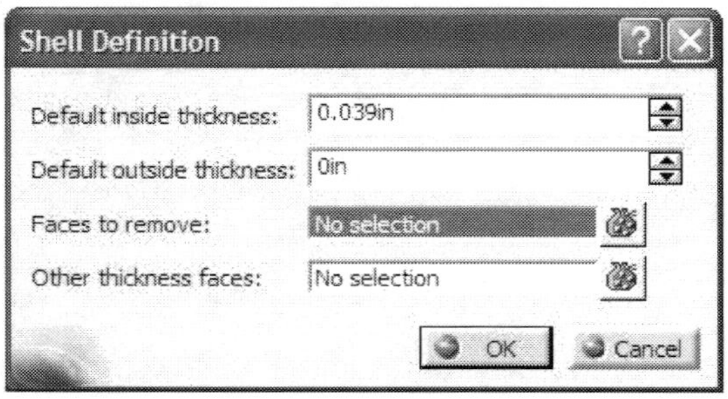

Remove the two faces shown in the figure and use a **Default inside thickness** of **0in** and a **Default outside thickness** of **0.1in**. This will result in a piston diameter of 3.2 inches.

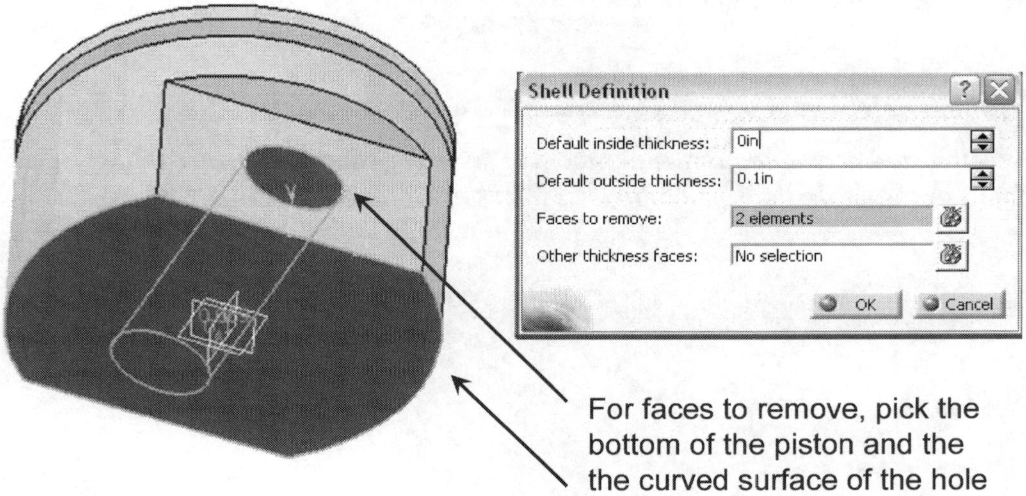

Upon completing the shelling operation, a hollow piston is created.

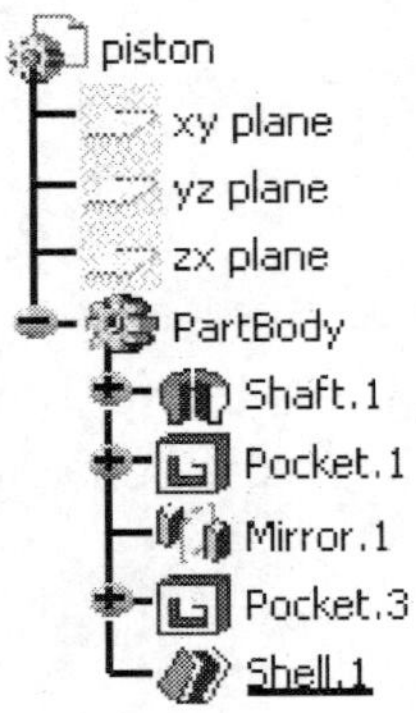

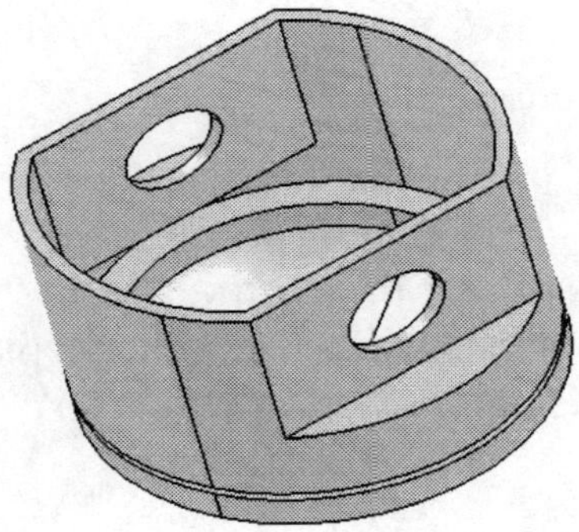

This step completes the creation of the part named **piston**.

Save your part .

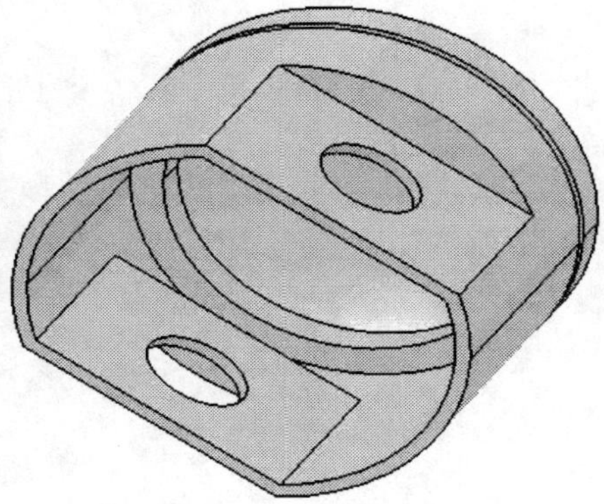

Outline of creating the conrod:

Enter the **Part Design** workbench. Begin creating a part named **conrod**.

Select the **yz** plane and enter the **Sketcher**. In the **Sketcher**, use the **Profile** icon from the **Profile** toolbar

, to draw the conrod (connecting rod) cross section and dimension it as shown. *Ensure that the centers of all four curves lie on the vertical axis of the sketch plane.*

Exit the **Sketcher**.

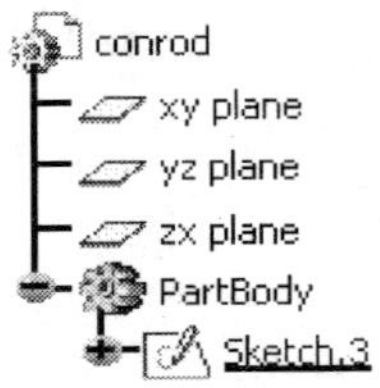

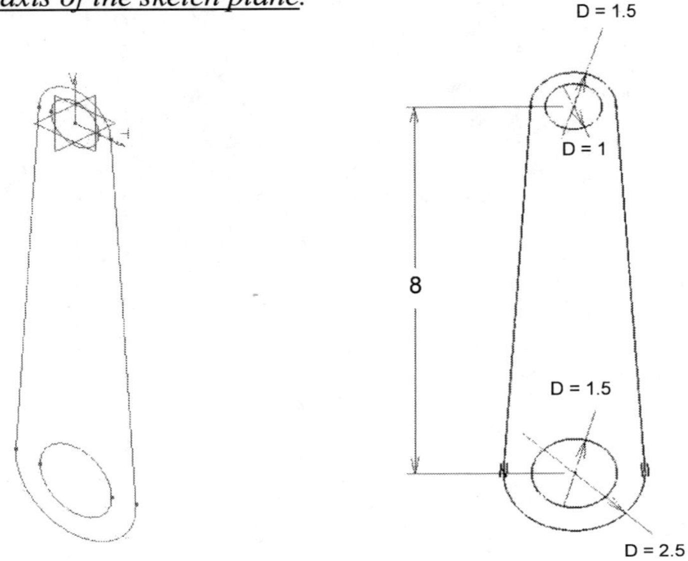

Pick the **Pad** icon. In the resulting pop up box, select Sketch conrod profile. Make sure to check, **Mirrored extent** and use a **Length** of 0.25. Mirrored extent is chosen so that the yz plane will remain down the center of the part; this facilitates applying constraints later.

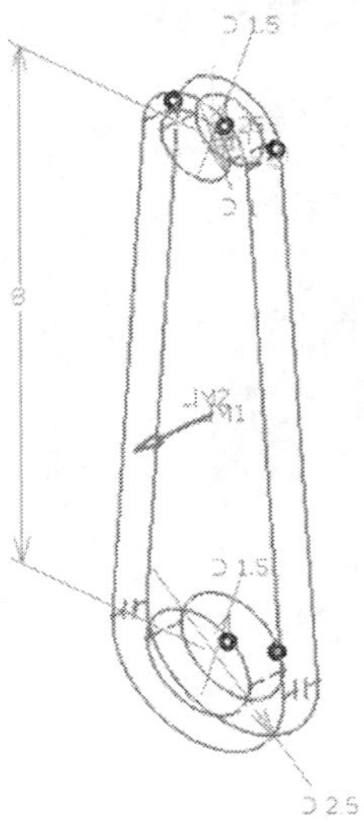

Make sure to select Mirror extent

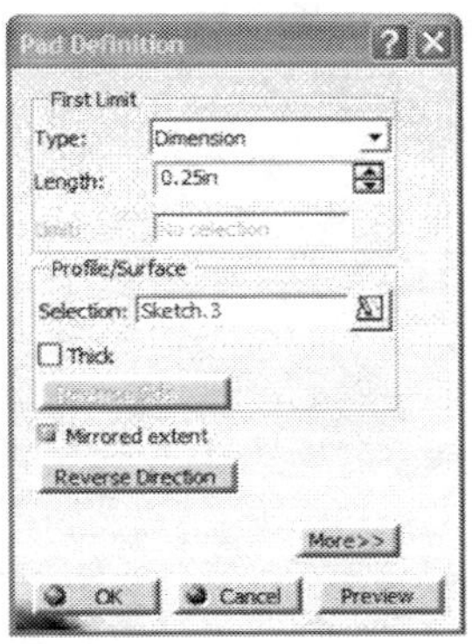

Upon closing the **Pad Definition** box, the part conrod is created.

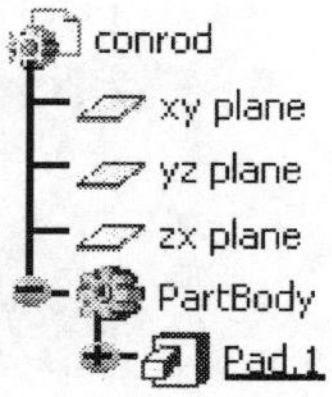

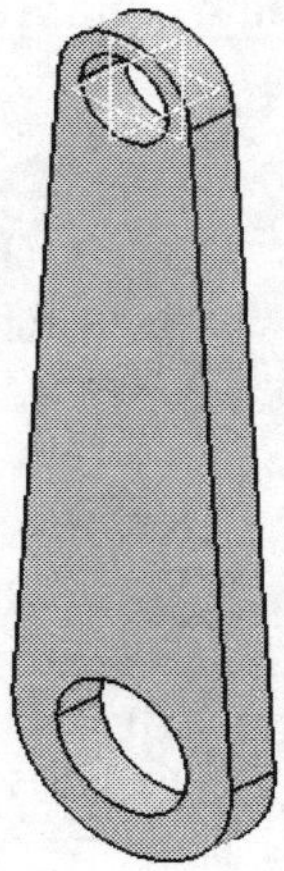

This concludes the creation of conrod.

Outline of creating the pin:

This is an easy task since we will not model any of the details of a real piston pin. To model the pin, draw a circle of radius R = 0.5 in the **yz** plane and pad it with a length of 1.6 while **Mirrored extent** Mirrored extent box is checked. This leads to a pin of total length 3.2 whose axis is in the x-direction as shown. Mirrored extent is chosen so that the yz plane will remain down the center of the part; this facilitates applying constraints later.

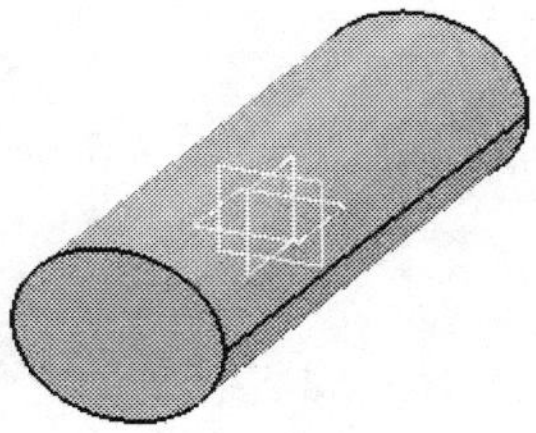

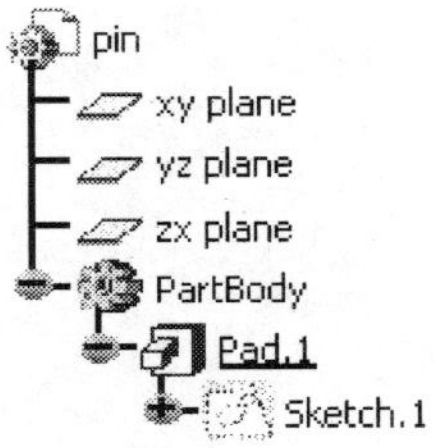

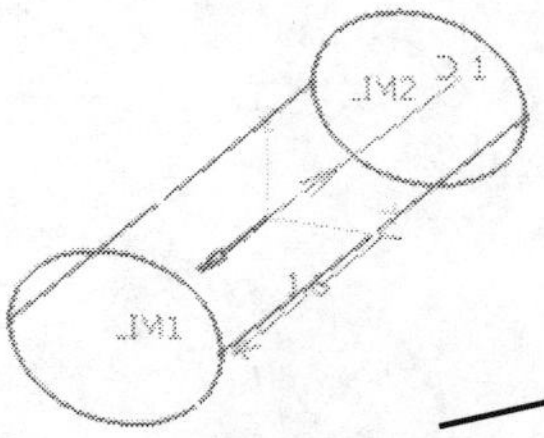

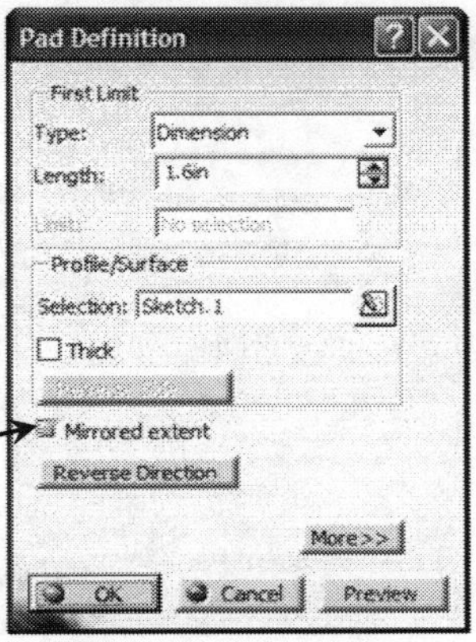

Make sure that the Mirrored extent box is checked

Outline of creating the crank:

Enter the **Part Design** workbench. Begin creating a part named **crank**.

Select the **yz** plane and enter the **Sketcher**. In the **Sketcher**, draw a circle of diameter 1.5in centered on the origin.

Exit the Sketcher.

Pick the **Pad** icon and pad the circle by 0.5.
This time DO NOT USE **Mirrored extent** Mirrored extent while padding.

Select the face shown and enter the **Sketcher** again.

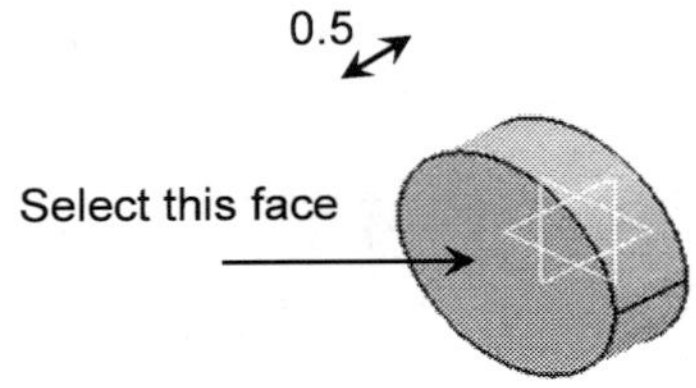

In the Sketcher, draw the profile shown and dimension it. Center the upper arc on the origin. The center to center dimension will ultimately define the stroke of the engine (stroke will be twice the 1 in dimension shown).

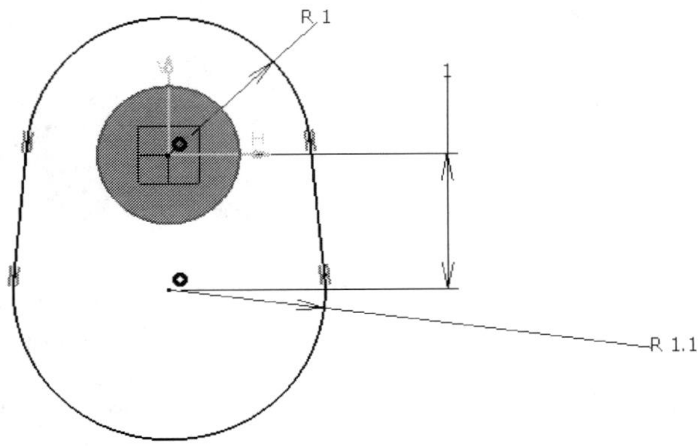

Exit the **Sketcher** and **Pad** the sketch by 1 in.

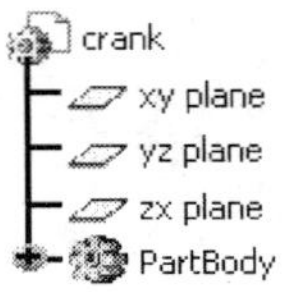

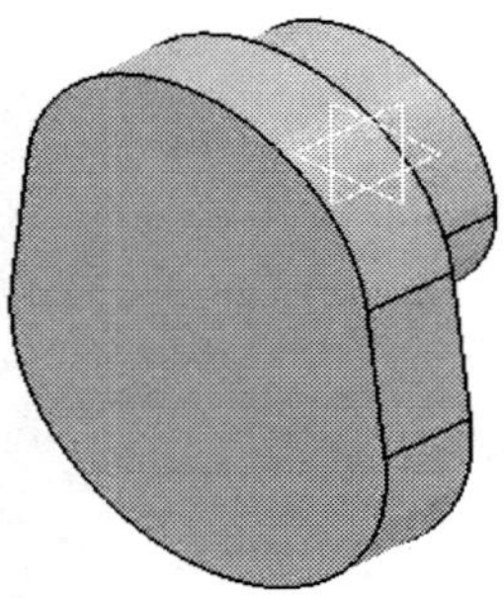

Select the face shown and enter the **Sketcher** again.

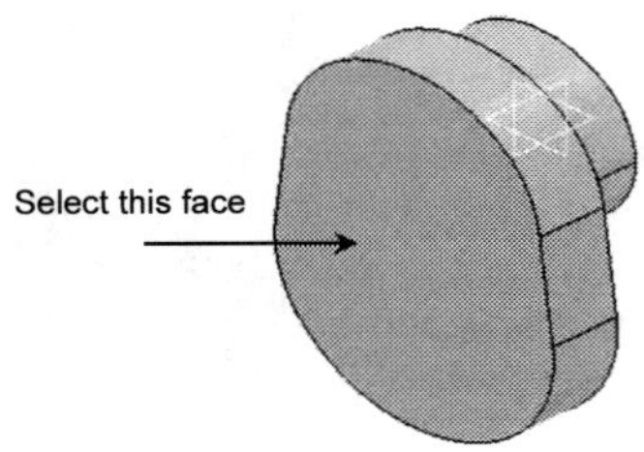

In the **Sketcher**, draw a circle  of diameter 1.5 in centered at the center of the lower arc from the previous step. One way to locate the center is to constrain it to be on the V axis and to be 1in below the H axis as shown.

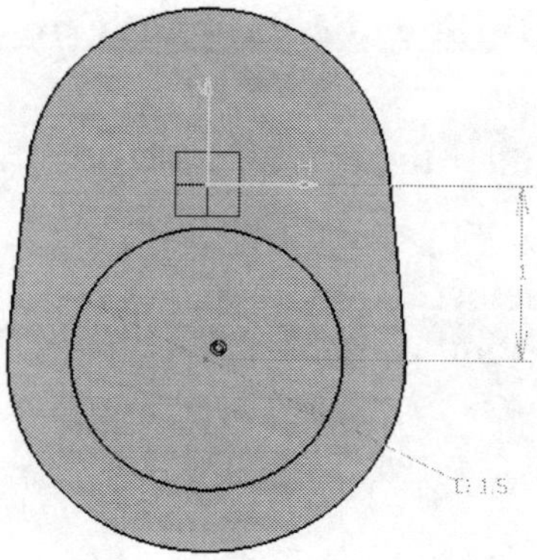

Exit the **Sketcher** 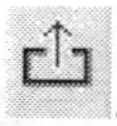.

Pick the **Pad** icon  and pad the circle by 2.5.

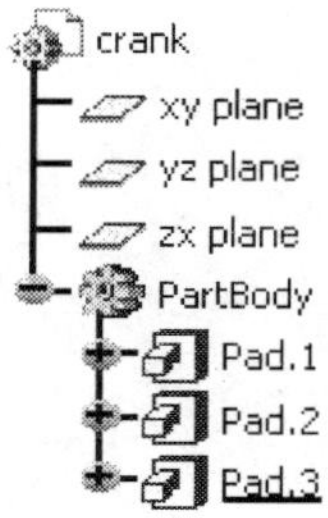

Select the **Mirror** icon  from the **Transformation Features** toolbar 

. In the resulting pop up box, for **Mirroring element**, select the end surface of the first pad as indicated below.

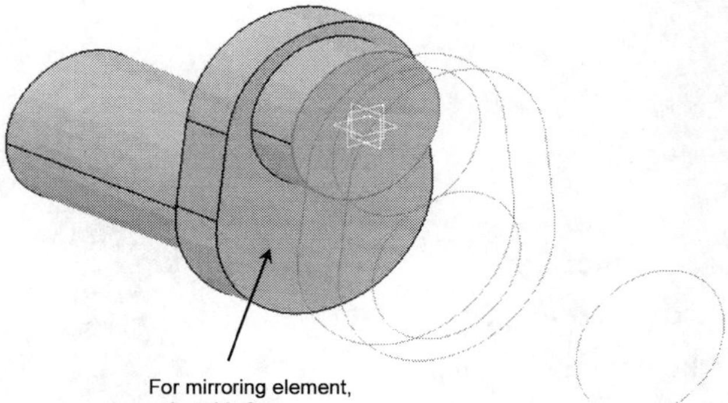

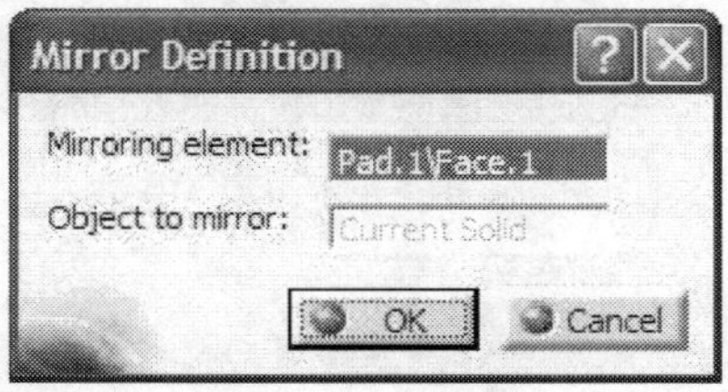

The generated crank (crankshaft) is displayed next.

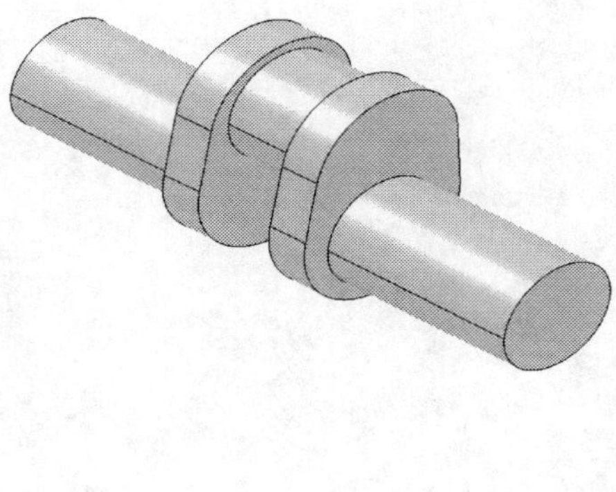

Outline of creating the block:

Enter the **Part Design** workbench. Begin creating a part named **block**.

Select the **xy** plane and enter the **Sketcher**. Draw the sketch shown and dimension as indicated.

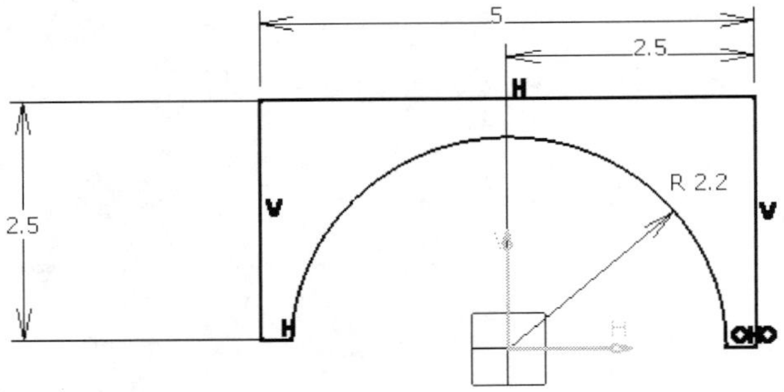

Exit the Sketcher.

Pick the **Pad** icon. Pad the sketch by 8.5 in.

Select the face of the above padded part and enter the **Sketcher**. Draw two concentric circles with the given diameters and the indicated position. Make sure the circles are centered on the V axis of the sketch.

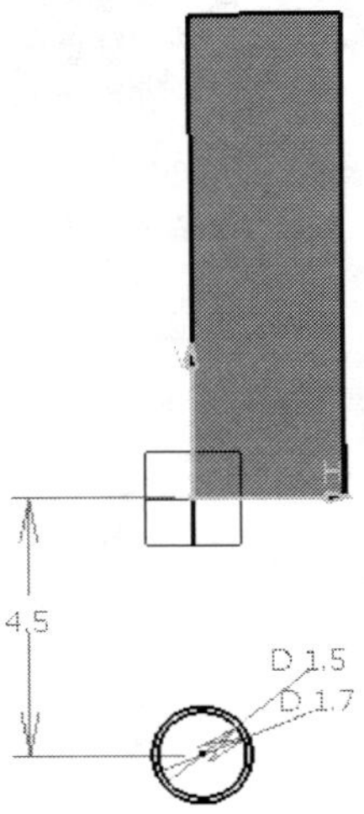

Exit the Sketcher and pad the sketch by 0.5 in.

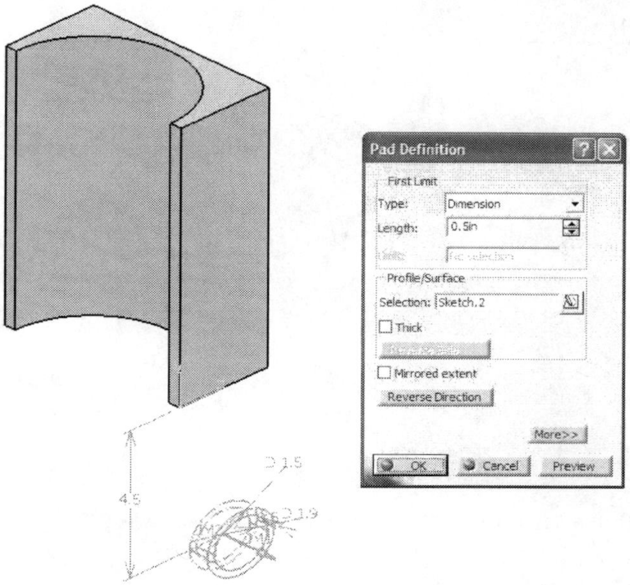

With the just created pad pre-selected in the tree, select the **Mirror** icon  from the **Transformation Features** toolbar 

. In the resulting pop up box, for **Mirroring element**, select the **yz** plane as indicated below.

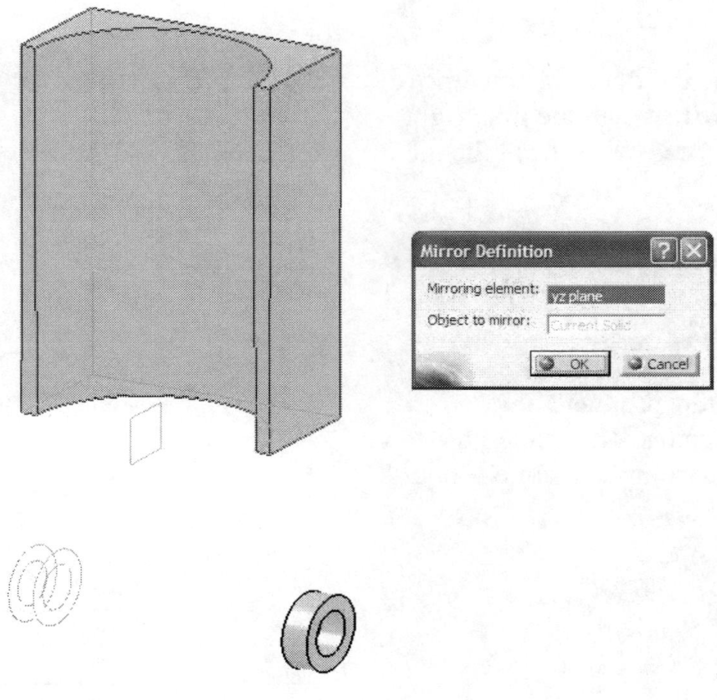

The two rings just constructed belong to the part named **block** and act as the bearing surfaces which will support the **crank**.

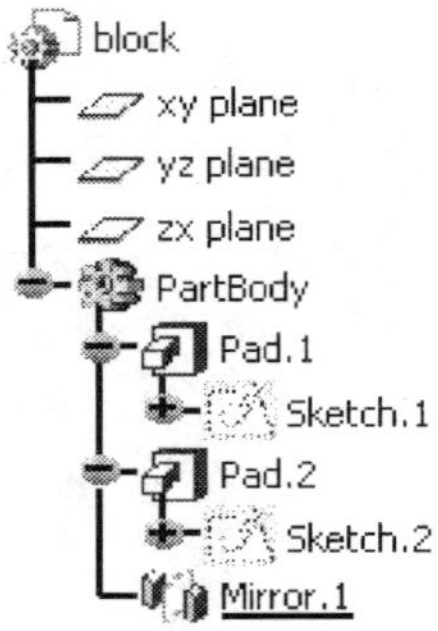

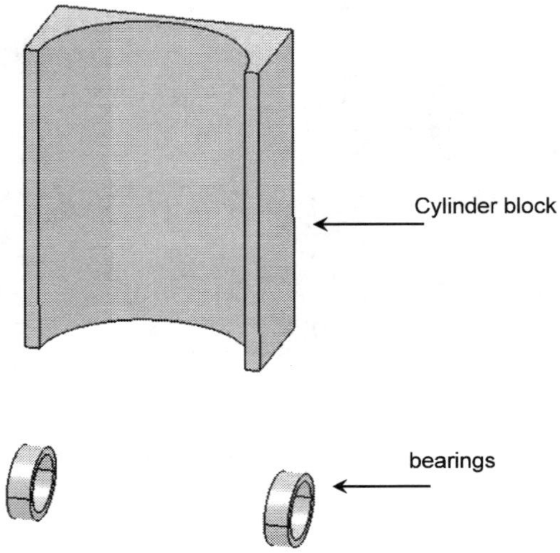

You have now constructed all five parts and are prepared to initiate the assembly process.

Outline of creating the Assembly:

Enter the **Assembly Design** workbench 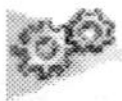 which can be achieved by different means depending on your CATIA customization. For example, from the standard Windows toolbar, select **File > New** 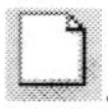.
From the box shown on the right, select **Product**. This moves you to the **Assembly Design** workbench and creates an assembly with the default name **Product.1**.

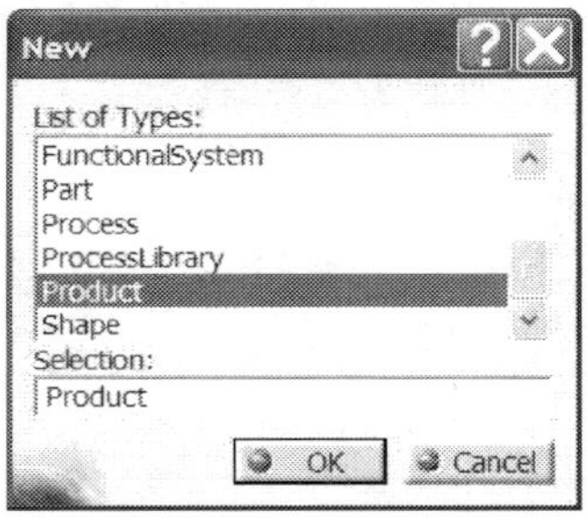

In order to change the default name, move the cursor to **Product.1** in the tree, right click and select **Properties** from the menu list.

From the **Properties** box, select the **Product** tab and in **Part Number** type **single_cylinder**.

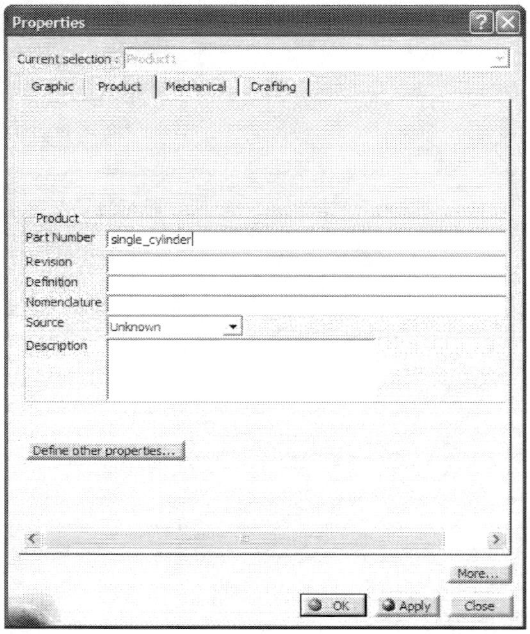

This will be the new product name throughout the chapter. The tree on the top left corner of your computer screen should look as displayed below.

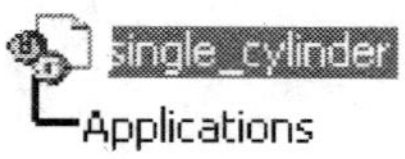

The next step is to insert the five parts into the assembly just created. From the standard Windows toolbar, select **Insert > Existing Component**. From the **File Selection** pop up box choose **cylinder**, **pin**, **conrod**, **crank**, and **block**. Remember that in CATIA multiple selections are made with the **Ctrl** key.
The tree is modified to indicate that the parts have been inserted.

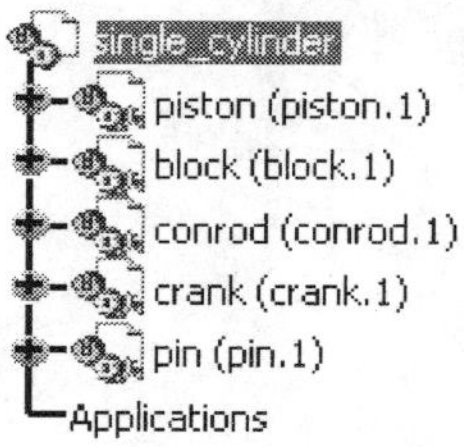

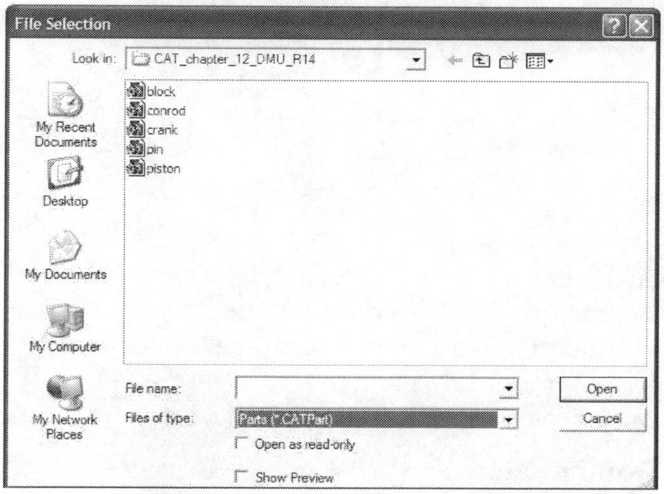

The five parts will appear on your screen.
Keep in mind that the relative positioning of the parts on your screen depends on how they were generated. Most probably your parts overlap as is the case on the right.

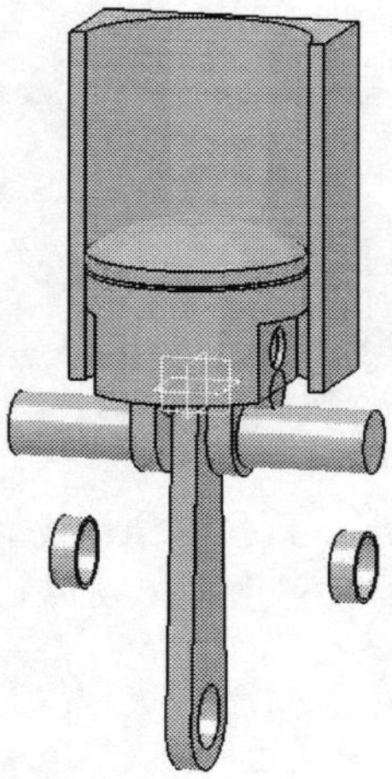

You can use the **Manipulation** icon  to separate the parts to make it easier to apply assembly constraints.

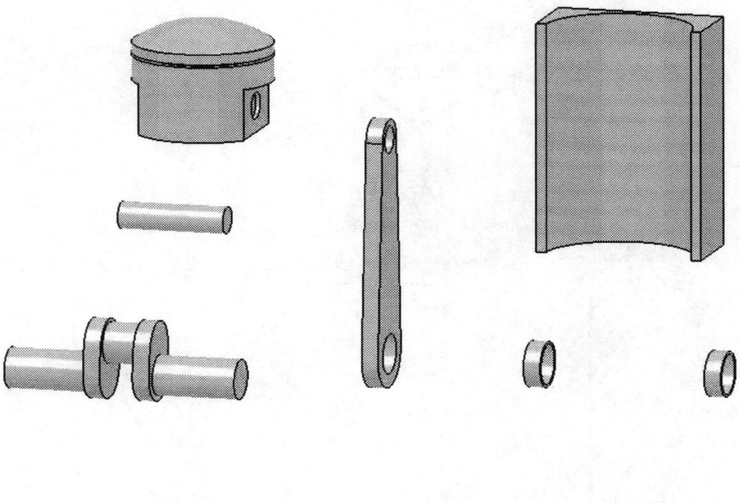

We will begin by anchoring the block so it cannot move as we apply the remaining constraints. Pick the **Anchor** icon from **Constraints** toolbar and select the **block**.

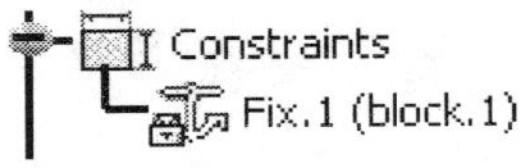

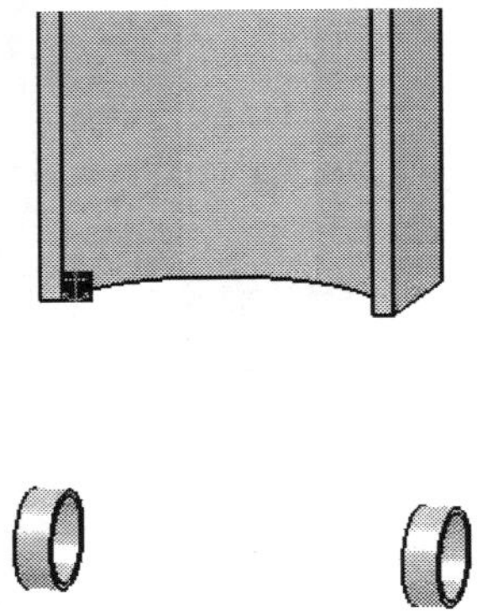

Next, we will create two coincident constraints between the crank and the block consistent with removing all the relative degrees of freedom (dof) except for rotation of the crank. Pick the **Coincidence** icon from **Constraints** toolbar and select the axes of the **crank** and the **block** as shown.

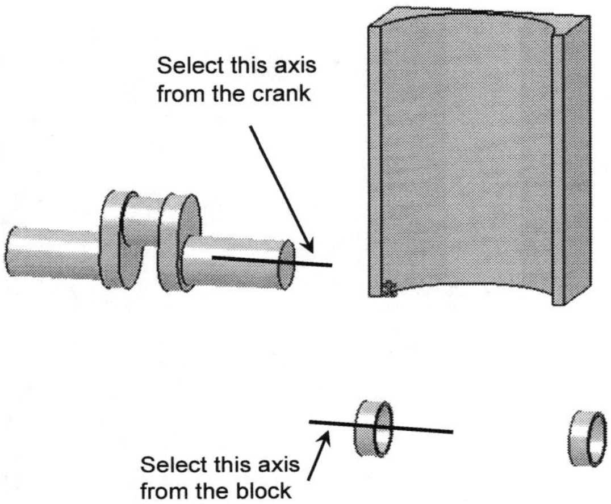

Pick the **Coincidence** icon and select the symmetry planes from the **crank** and the **block** as shown and close the pop up box.

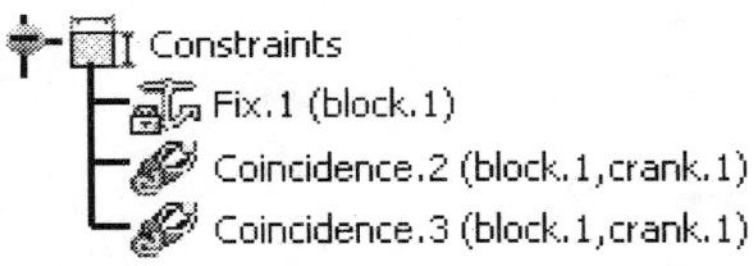

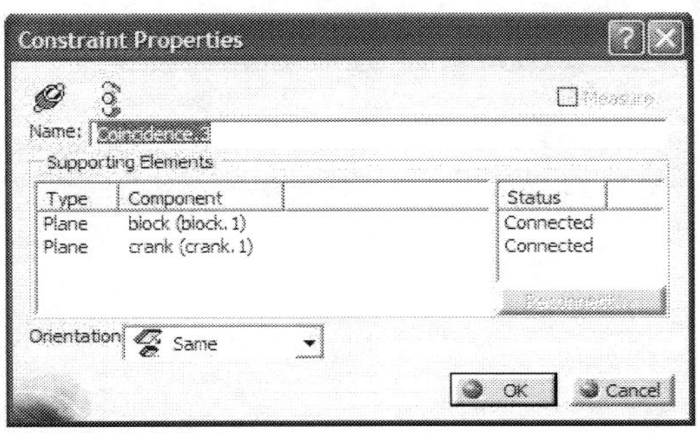

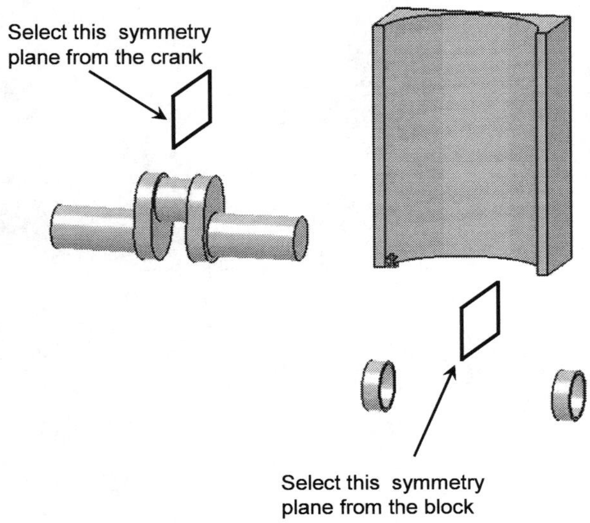

Use the **Update** icon  to enforce the two constraints just created resulting in relative position of the two parts similar to as shown below.

The next step is to apply the constraints between the **crank** and the **conrod**. We would like to remove all relative dof except for rotation. Once again this will be done with two coincidence constraints. You may simplify the task by using the **Manipulation** icon  to separate the parts first.

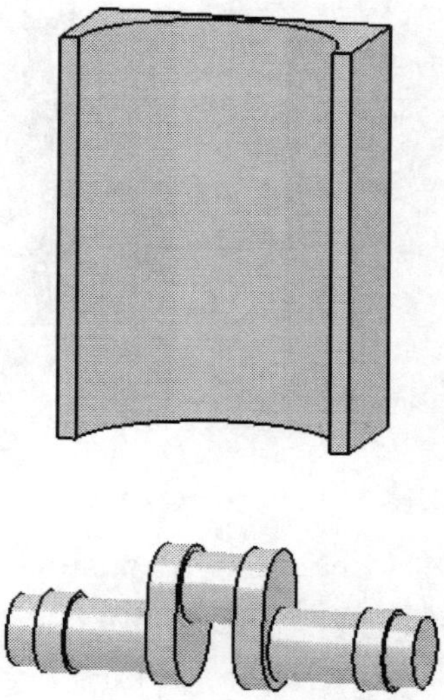

Pick the **Coincidence** icon  from **Constraints** toolbar and select the axes of the **crank** and the **conrod** as shown.

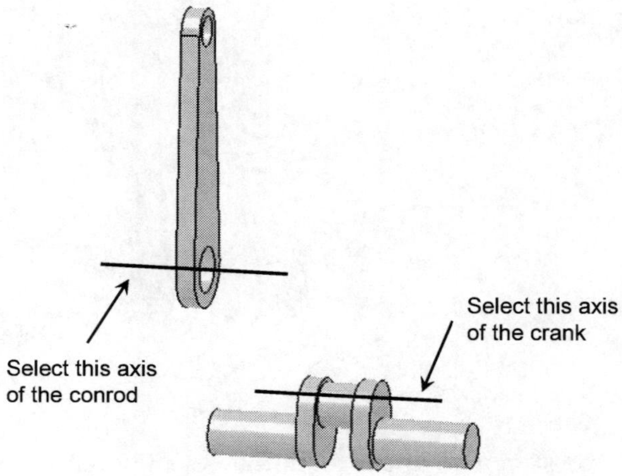

Pick the **Coincidence** icon  and select the symmetry planes from the **crank** and the **conrod** as shown and close the pop up box.

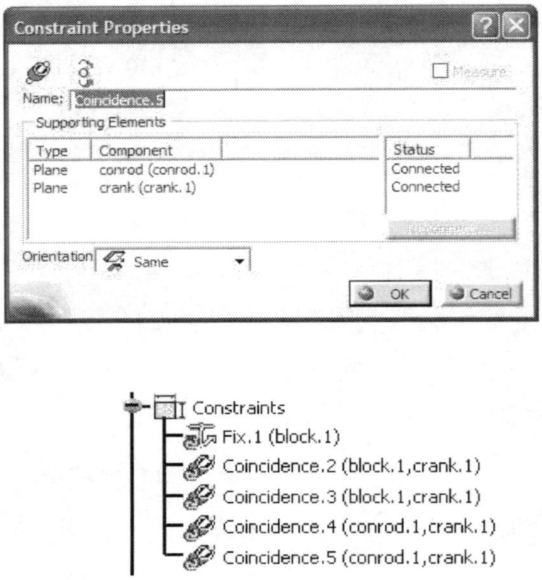

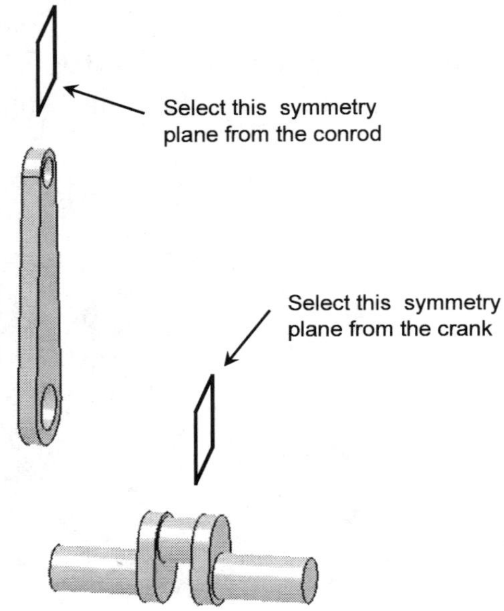

Use the **Update** icon  to enforce the two constraints just created resulting in relative position of the two parts similar to as shown below.

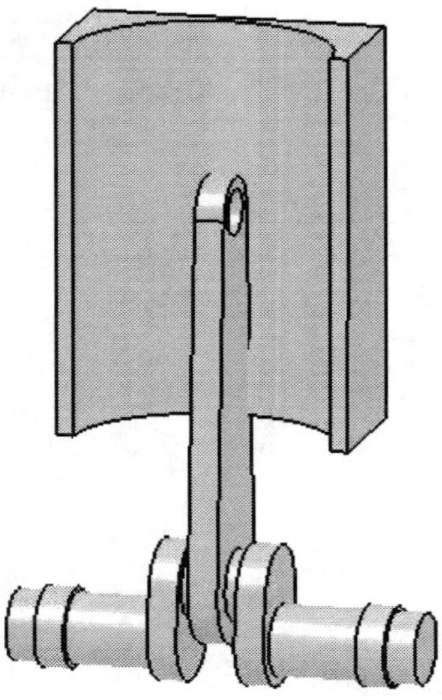

The next step is to apply a similar set of constraints between the **pin** and the **conrod**.

You may simplify the task by using the **Manipulation** icon  to separate the parts first.

Pick the **Coincidence** icon from **Constraints** toolbar and select the axes of the **pin** and the **conrod** as shown.

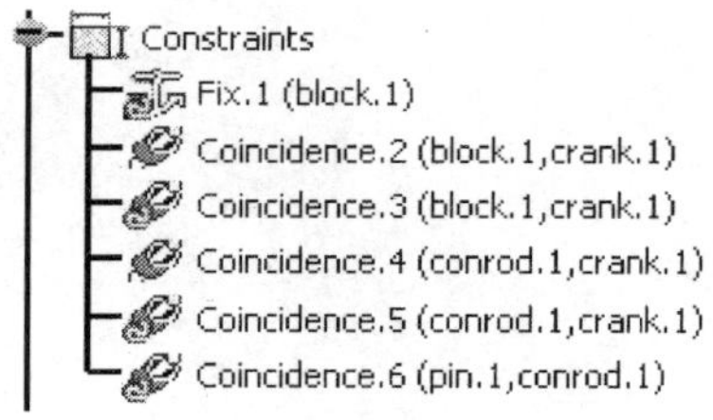

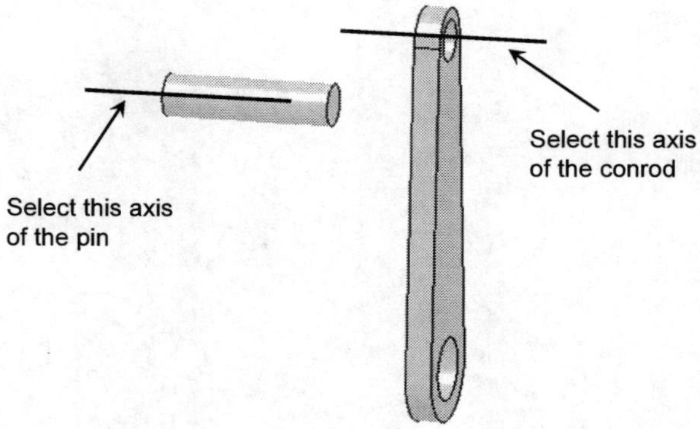

Pick the **Coincidence** icon and select the symmetry planes from the **pin** and the **conrod** as shown and close the pop up box.

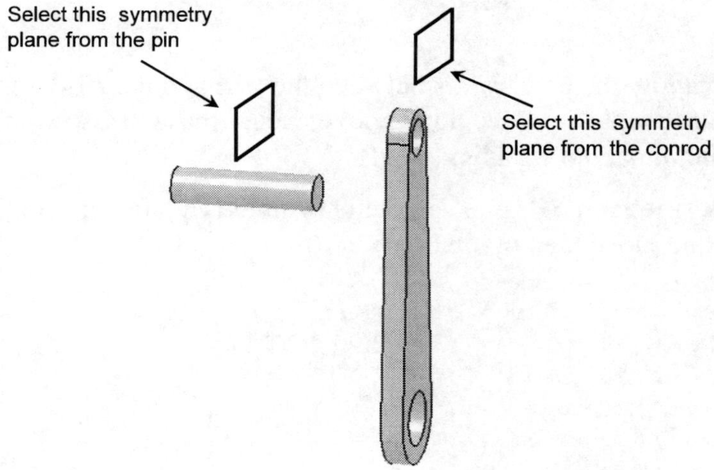

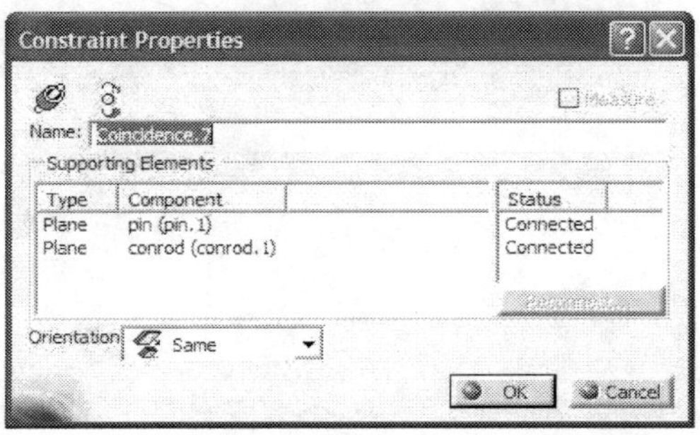

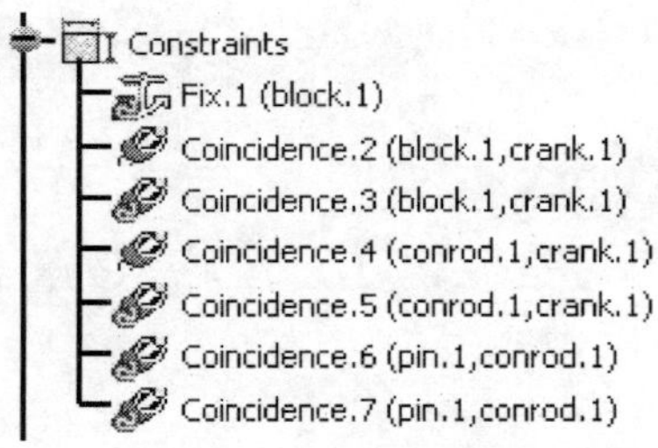

Use the **Update** icon to enforce the two constraints just created resulting in relative position of the two parts similar to as shown below.

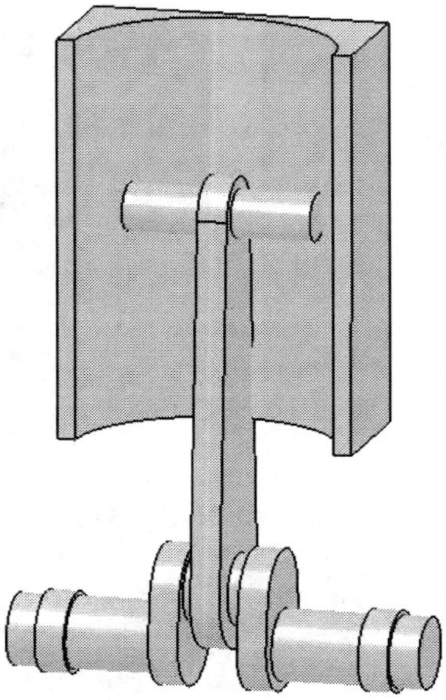

The next step is to apply the constraints between the **pin** and the **piston**. The constraints used will be similar to what we have done above except that we also want to remove the rotational dof of the pin about its axis.

Pick the **Coincidence** icon and select the symmetry planes from the **pin** and the **piston** as shown and close the pop up box.

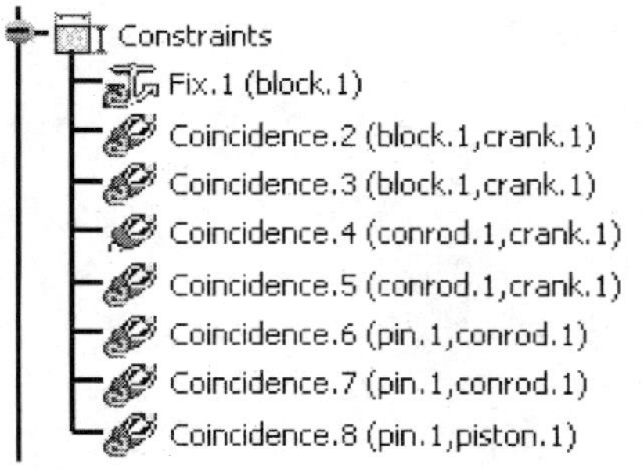

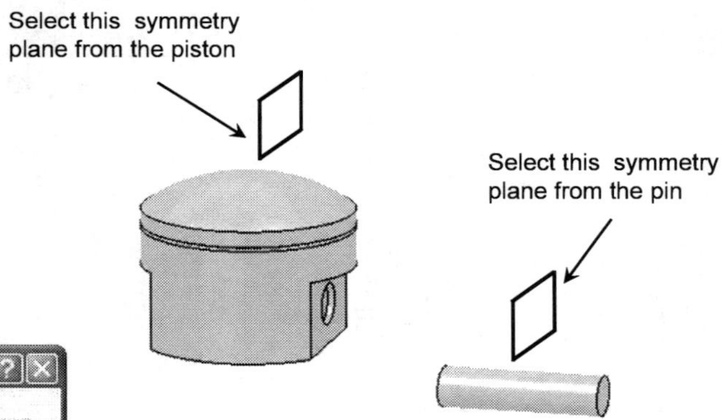

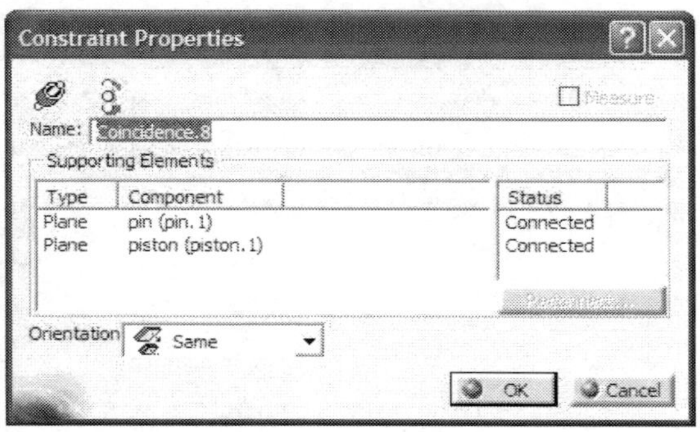

Pick the **Coincidence** icon from **Constraints** toolbar and select the axes of the **pin** and the **piston** (piston hole) as shown.

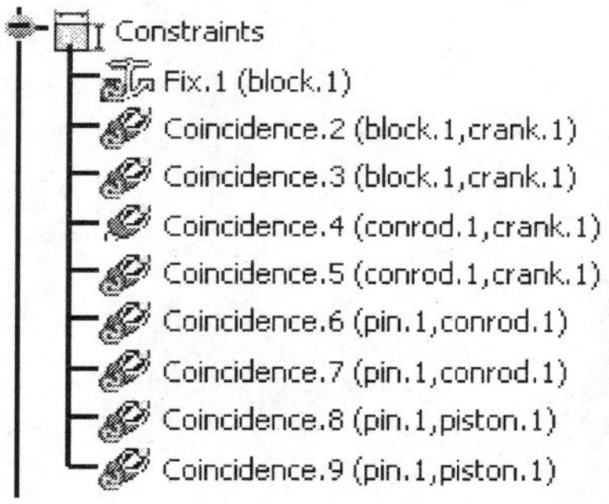

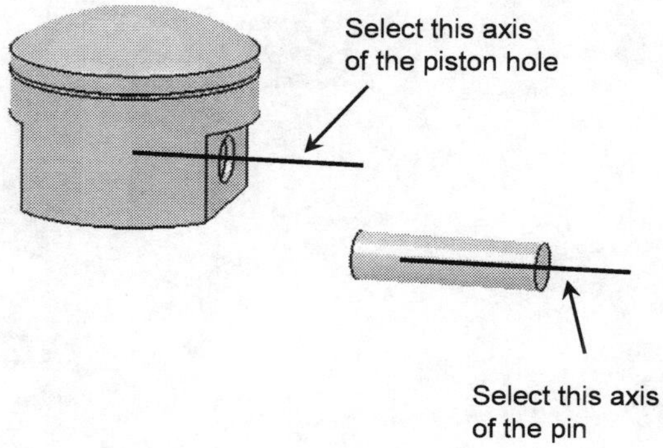

Note that the rotation of the **pin** inside of the **piston** should be removed. To do so, pick The **Angle Constraint** icon, and select the planes shown below. Note that you have other choices for this plane selection. The objective is to maintain the same angle between these planes and therefore prevent relative rotation between the pin and the piston. Close the pop up box.

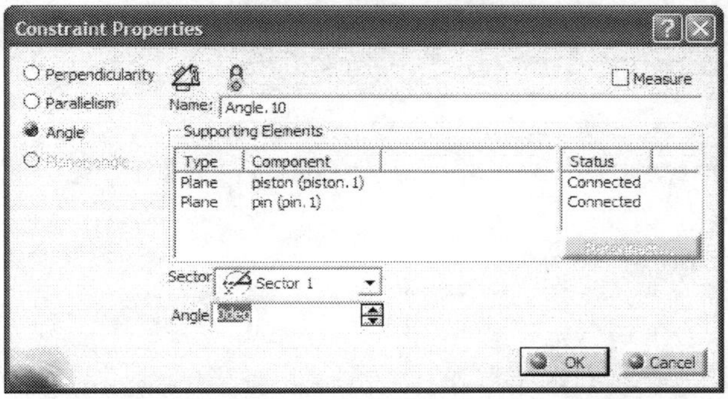

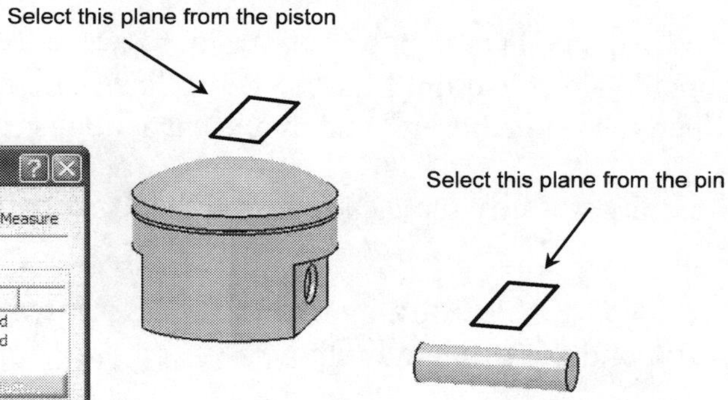

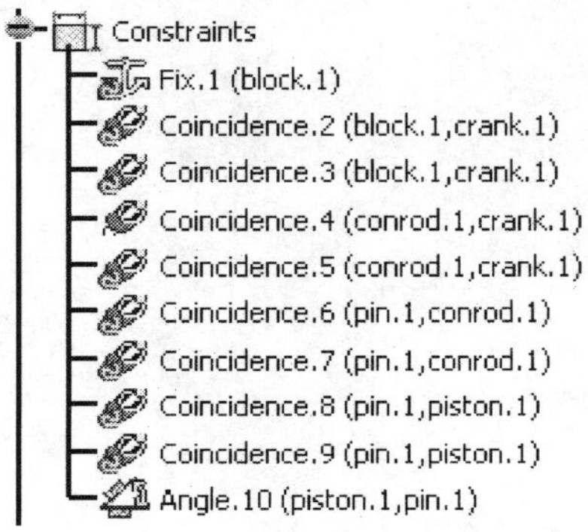

Use **Update** icon to enforce the two constraints just created resulting in relative position the two parts similar to as shown below.

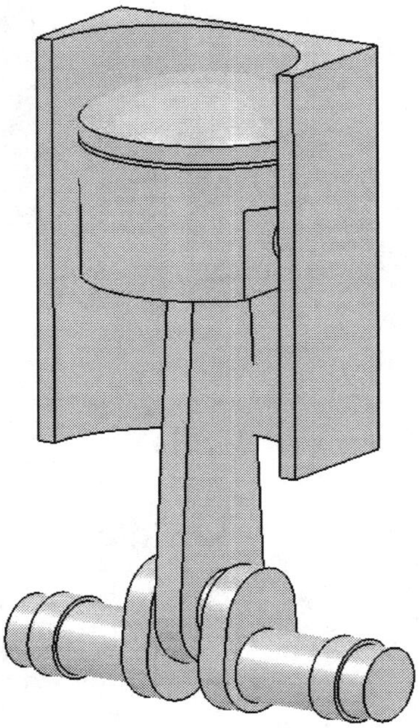

The final step is to create a constraint between the **piston** and the **block**. A single coincidence constraint between centerlines suffices here since the rotation of the piston is effectively already removed by the earlier constraints.

You may simplify the task by using the **Manipulation** icon to separate the parts first.

Pick the **Coincidence** icon from **Constraints** toolbar and select the axes of the **block** and the **piston** as shown.

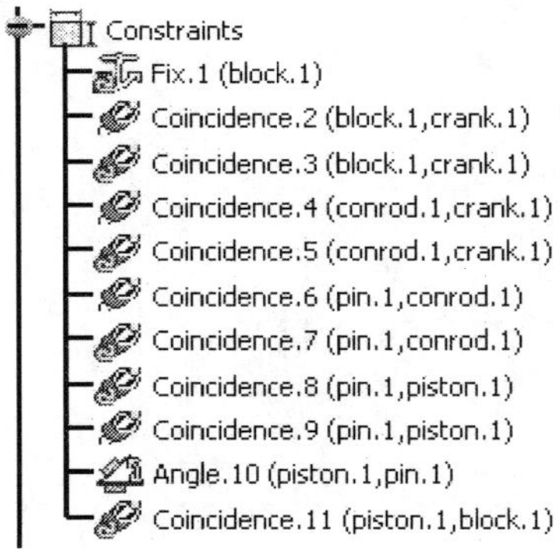

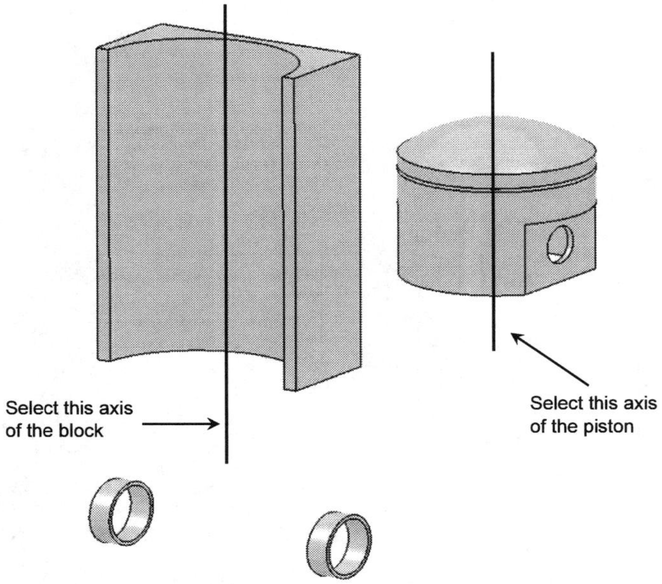

Use the **Update** icon  to enforce the two constraints just created resulting in relative position of the two parts similar to as shown below. Your final relative positions may look slightly different, but should represent a valid engine position.

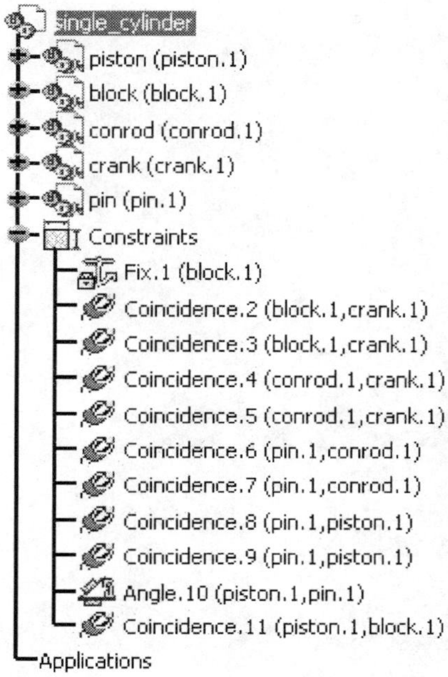

The assembly is complete and we can proceed to the **Digital Mockup** workbench.

4 Creating Joints in the Digital Mockup Workbench

The **Digital Mockup** workbench is quite extensive but we will only deal with the **DMU Kinematics module**. To get there you can use the standard Windows toolbar as shown below: **Start > Digital Mockup > DMU Kinematics**.

We will begin by converting our assembly constraints into mechanism joints. Select the **Assembly Constraints Conversion** icon 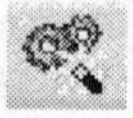 from the **DMU Kinematics** toolbar

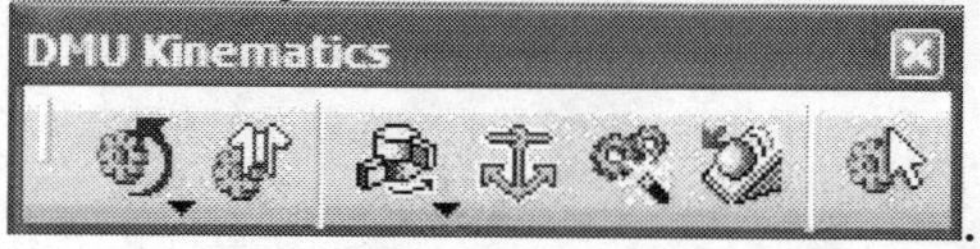

. This icon allows you to create most common joints automatically from the existing assembly constraints.
The pop up box below appears.

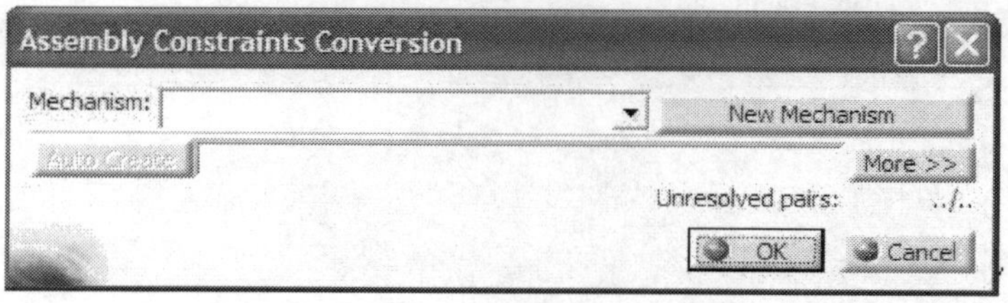

Select the **New Mechanism** button 

.
This leads to another pop up box which allows you to name your mechanism.
The default name is **Mechanism.1**. Accept the default name by pressing **OK**.

Note that the box indicates **Unresolved pairs: 5/5**

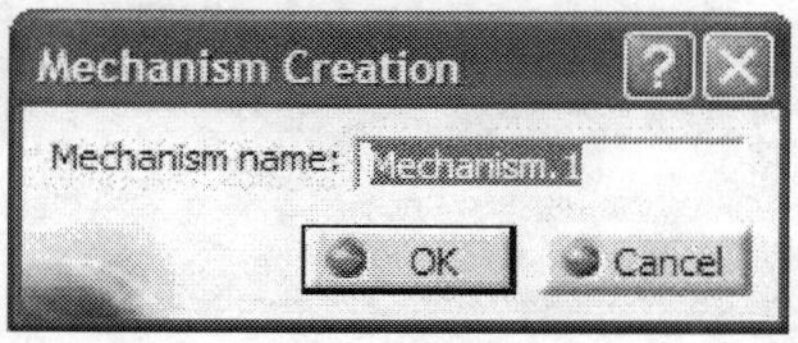

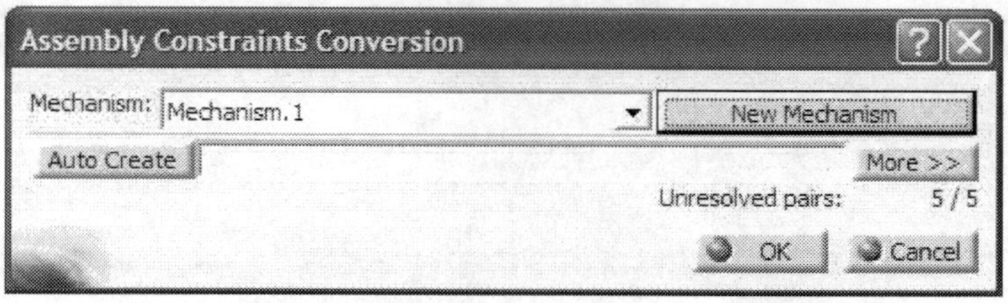

Select the **Auto Create** button 

. Then if the **Unresolved pairs** becomes **0/5**, things are moving in the right direction.

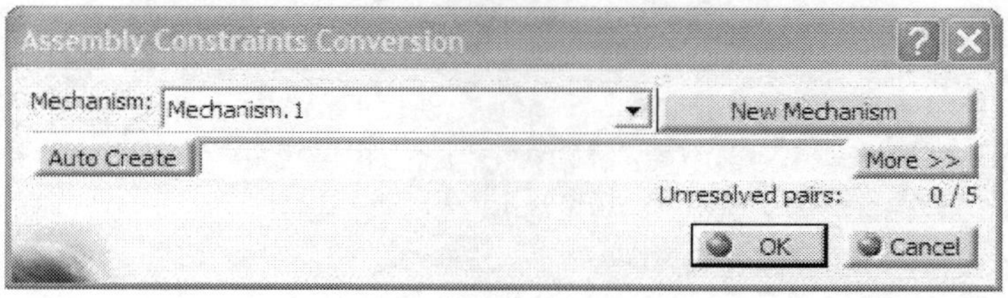

The joints, displayed below, are exactly as planned. The block is also fixed since it was anchored in the assembly. The remaining one dof is representative of the fact that the mechanism position is not fully defined until we specify a crankshaft position (or piston position).

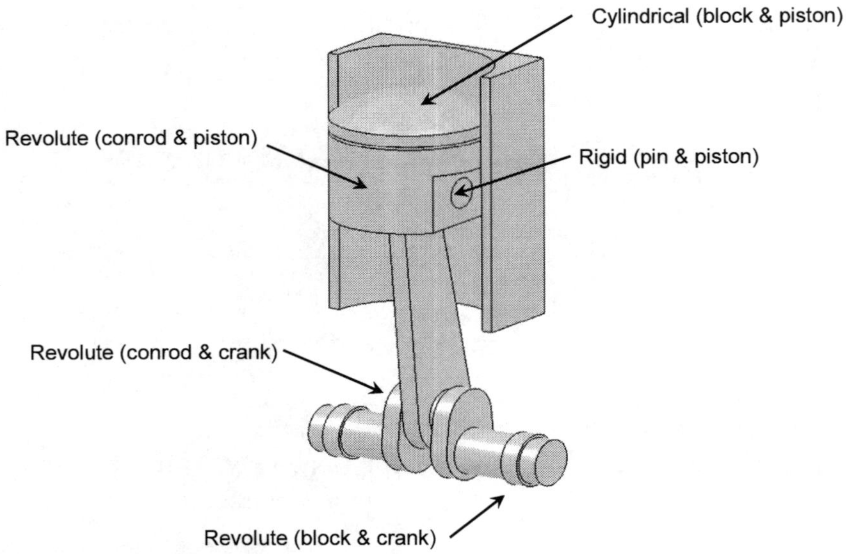

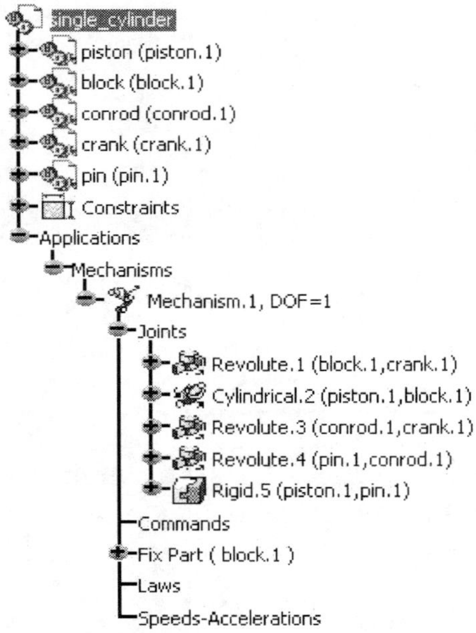

In the event that automatic assembly constraints conversion does not produce the desired joint or joints, a revolute joint (and any other joint) can be created directly using the **Kinematics Joints** toolbar shown below.

In order to animate the mechanism, we need to remove the one degree of freedom present. This will be achieved by turning **Revolute.1** into an **Angle driven** joint. Double click on **Revolute.1** in the tree. The pop up box below appears.

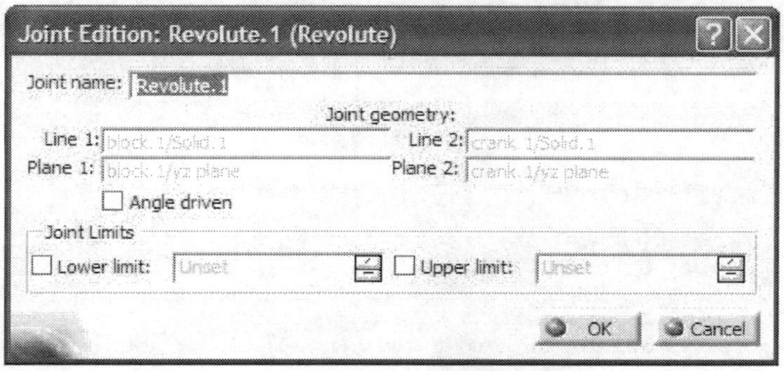

Check the **Angle driven** box and change the **Lower limit** and **Upper limit** to read as indicated below. Keep in mind that these limits can also be changed elsewhere.

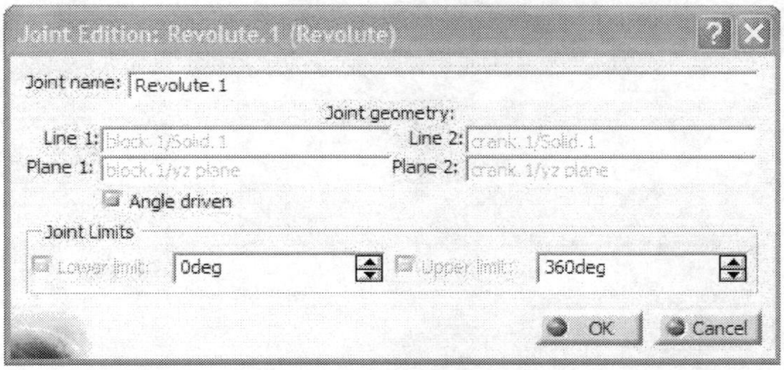

Upon closing the above box and assuming that everything else was done correctly, the following message appears on the screen.

This indeed is good news.

Next we will animate the mechanism without regard to time based motion.

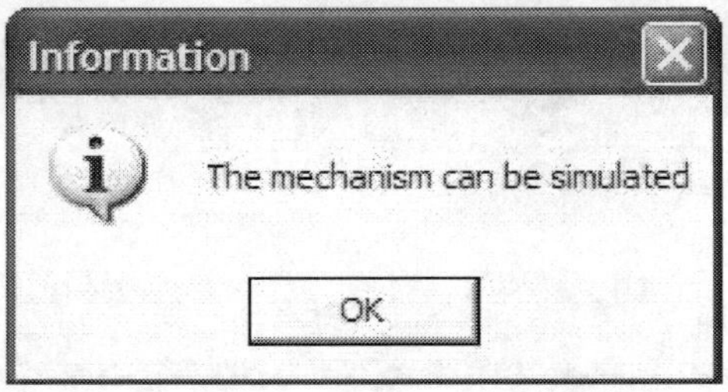

Select the **Simulation** icon 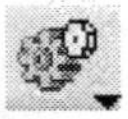 from the **DMU Generic Animation** toolbar 

. This enables you to choose the mechanism to be animated if there are several present. In this case, select Mechanism.1 and close the window.

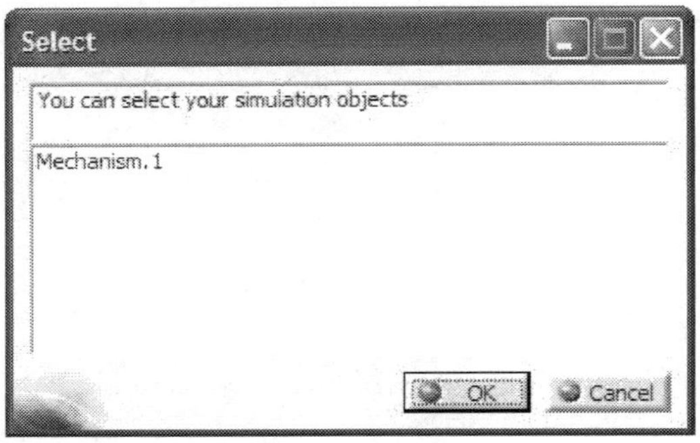

As soon as the window is closed, a Simulation branch is added to the tree.

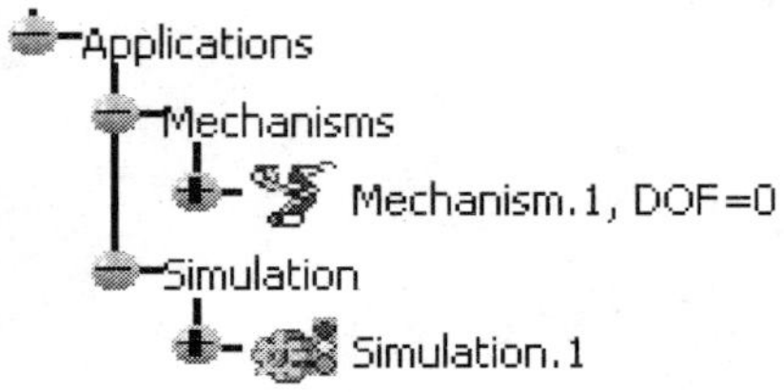

In addition, the two pop up boxes shown below appear.

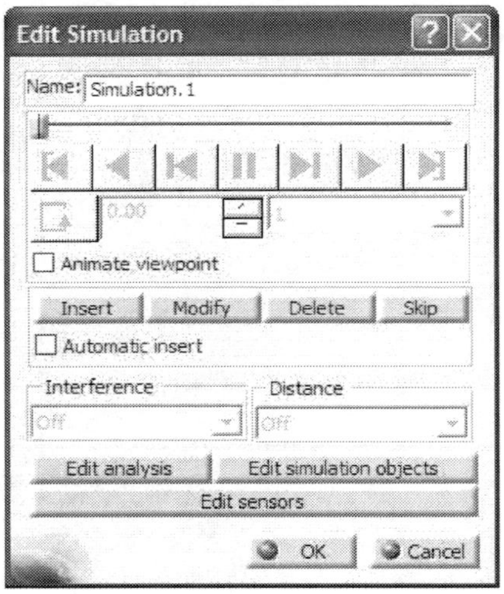

As you scroll the bar in this toolbar from left to right, the crank begins to rotate about the bearing.

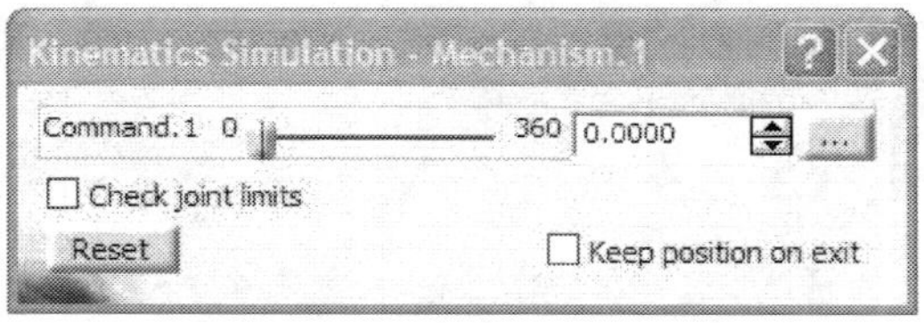

When the scroll bar in the **Kinematics Simulation** pop up box reaches the right extreme end, select the **Insert** button 

in the **Edit Simulation** pop up box shown above. This activates the video player buttons shown .

Return the arm to its original position by picking the **Jump to Start** button .

Note that the **Change Loop Mode** button  is also active now.

Upon selecting the **Play Forward** button , the crank makes such a fast jump to the end that there does not seem to be any motion.

In order to slow down the motion of the crank, select a different **interpolation step**, such as 0.04.

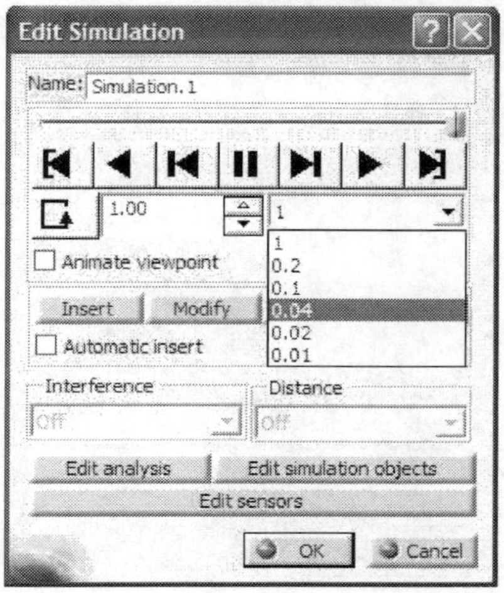

Upon changing the interpolation step to 0.04, return the crank to its original position by picking the **Jump to Start** button . Apply **Play Forward** button  and observe the slow and smooth rotation of the crank.

Select the **Compile Simulation** icon  from the **Generic Animation** toolbar

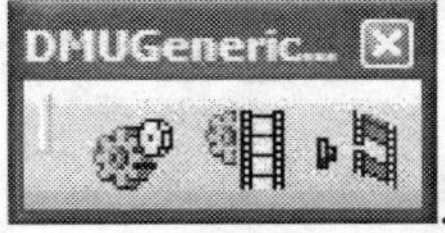

. Pressing the **File name** button File name ... allows you to set the location and name of the animation file to be generated as displayed below.

Select a suitable path and file name and change the **Time step** to be 0.04 to produce a slow moving arm in an AVI file.

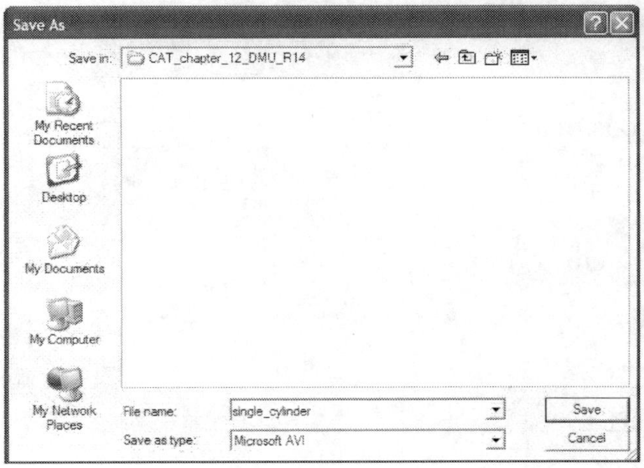

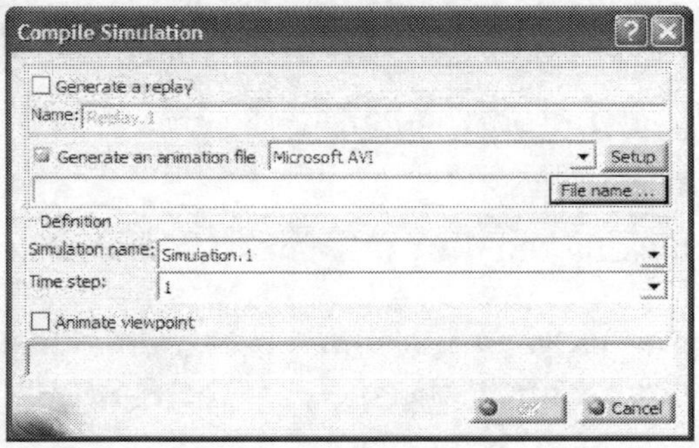

The completed pop up box is displayed for your reference.

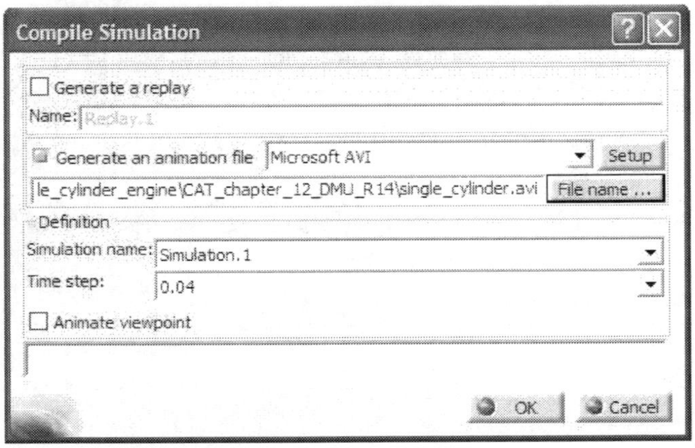

AS the file is being generated, the arm slowly rotates. The resulting AVI file can be viewed with the Windows Media Player.

In the event that an AVI file is not needed, but one wishes to play the animation, repeatedly, a **Replay** needs to be generated. Therefore, in the **Compile Simulation** box, check the **Generate a replay** button.

Note that in this case most of the previously available options are dimmed out. A **Replay.1** branch has also been added to the tree.

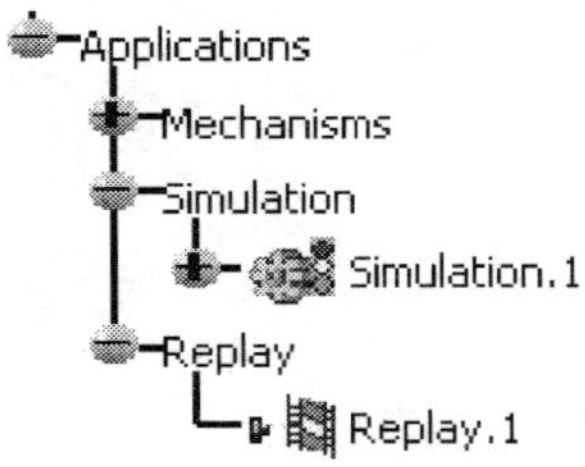

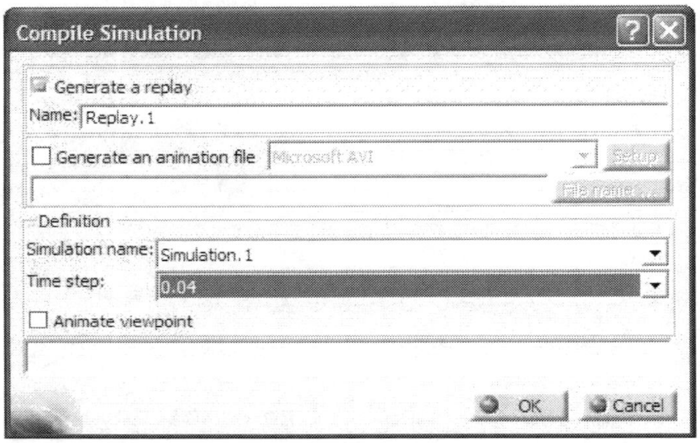

Select the **Replay** icon  from the **Generic Animation** toolbar 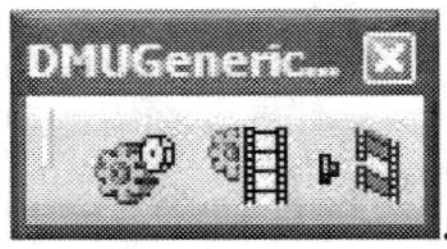.

Double clock on **Replay.1** in the tree and the **Replay** pop up box appears. Experiment with the different choices of the **Change Loop Mode** buttons , , .
The crank can be returned to the original position by picking the **Jump to Start** button .

The **skip ratio** (which is chosen to be x1 in the right box) controls the speed of the **Replay**.

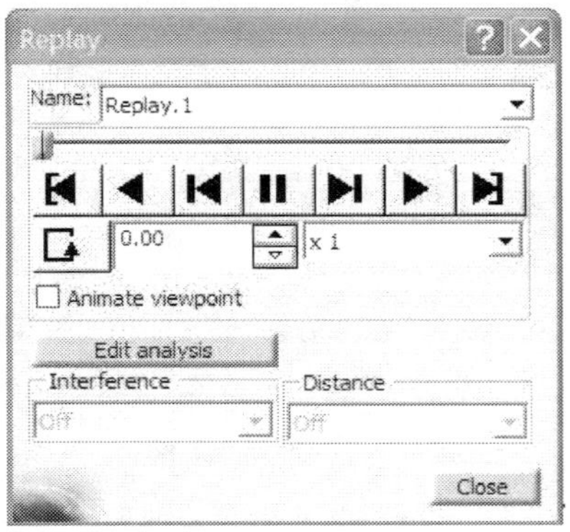

5 Creating Laws in the Motion and Simulating the Desired Kinematics

The motion animated this far was not tied to the time parameter or the angular velocity given in the problem statement. You will now introduce some time based physics into the problem.

Since you will be plotting the position, velocity, and acceleration of the piston as a function of time, you will need a point on the piston to be monitored. You could use the origin of the part, but since sometimes you want motion of a particular point and sometimes the body of concern involves both translation and rotation, we will create a point on the piston to illustrate the process of creating a point to monitor.

Load **piston** into the **Part Design** workbench .

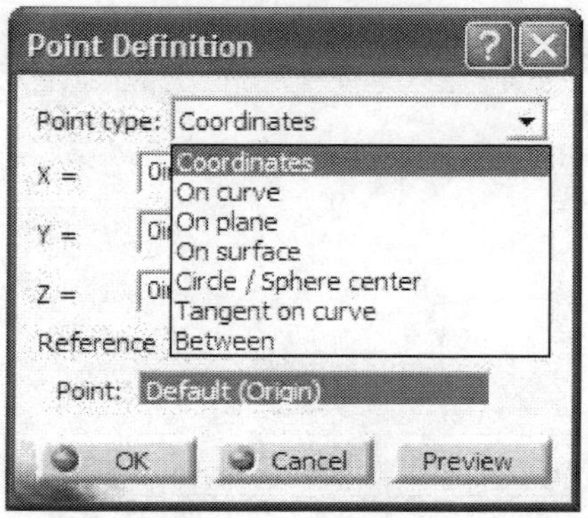

Pick the **Point** icon 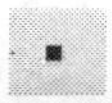 from the **Reference Element** toolbar 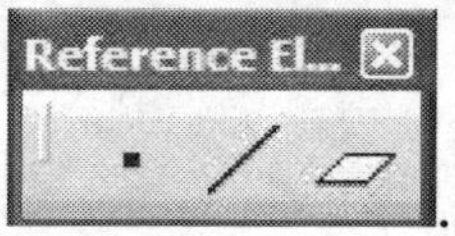. In the pop up box, use the pull down menu and choose **Circle/Sphere center**.

Select the circle shown below. This leads to the creation of point at its center location.

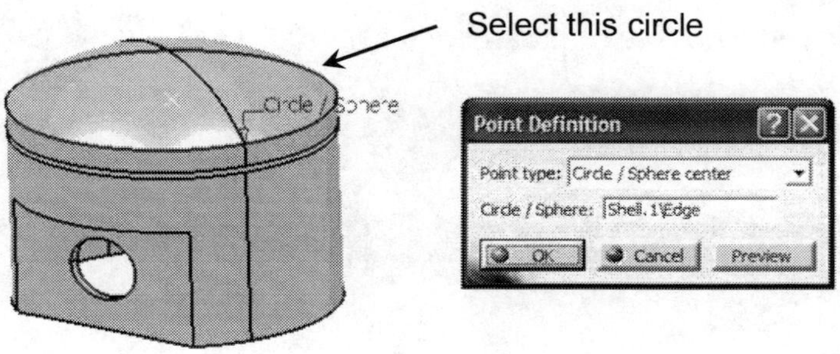

Click on **Simulation with Laws** icon  in the **Simulation** toolbar .

You will get the following pop up box indication that you need to add at least a relation between a command and the time parameter.

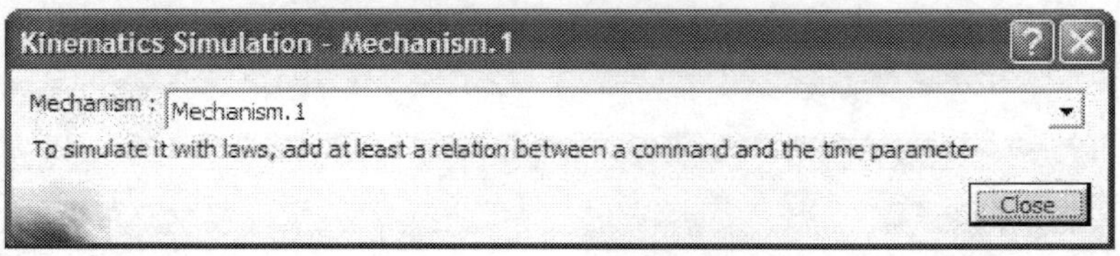

To create the required relation, select the **Formula** icon  from the **Knowledge** toolbar 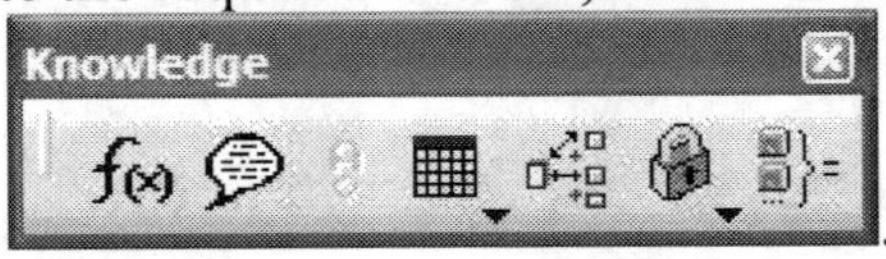

. The pop up box below appears on the screen.

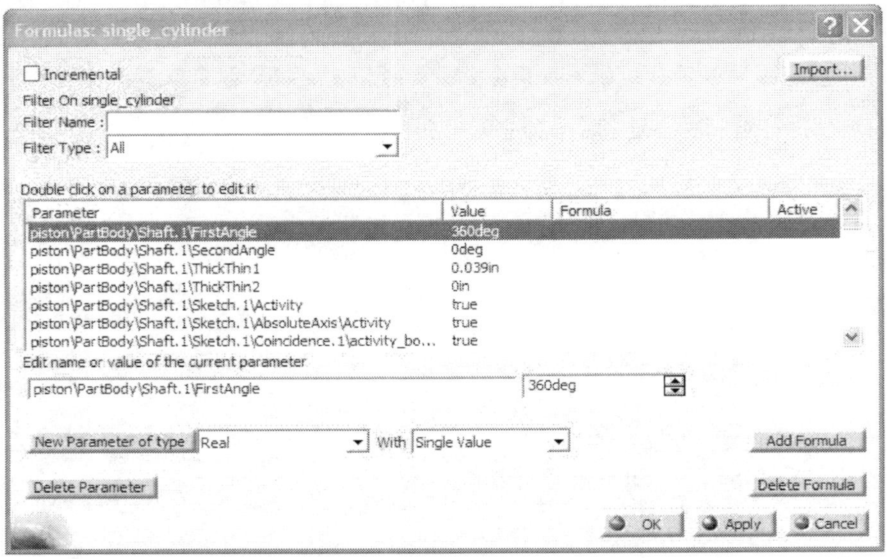

Point the cursor to the **Mechanism.1, DOF=0** branch in the tree and click. The consequence is that only parameters associated with the mechanism are displayed in the **Formulas** box.

The long list is now reduced to two parameters as indicated in the box.

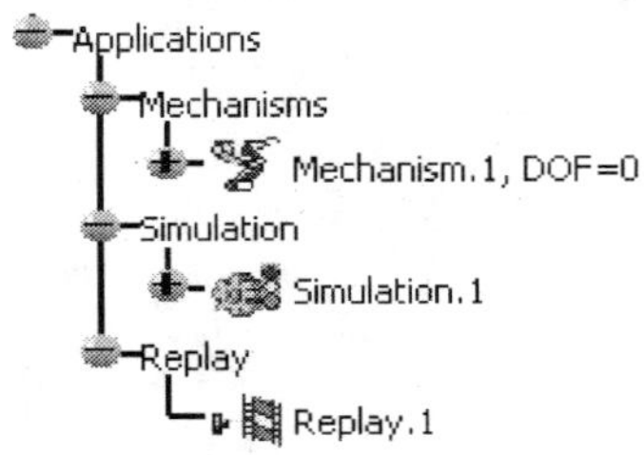

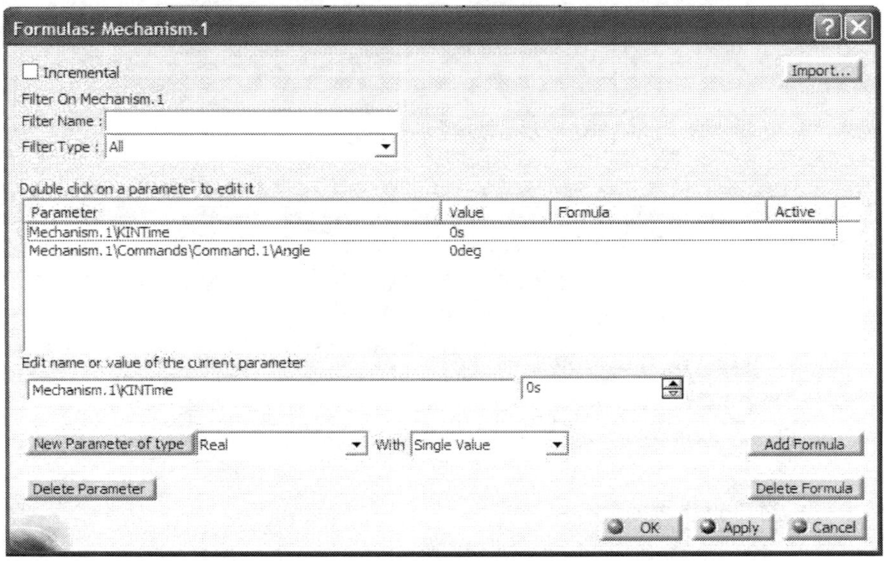

Select the entry **Mechanism.1\Commands\Command.1\Angle** and press the **Add Formula** button Add Formula. This action kicks you to the **Formula Editor** box.

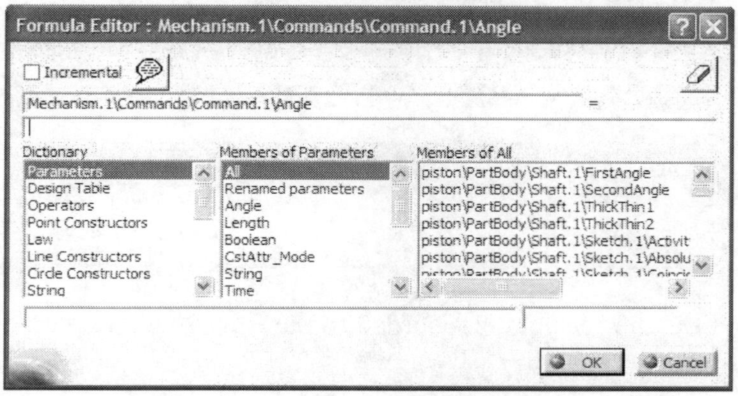

Pick the **Time** entry from the middle column (i.e. **Members of Parameters**) then double click on **Mechanism.1\KINTime** in the **Members of Time** column.

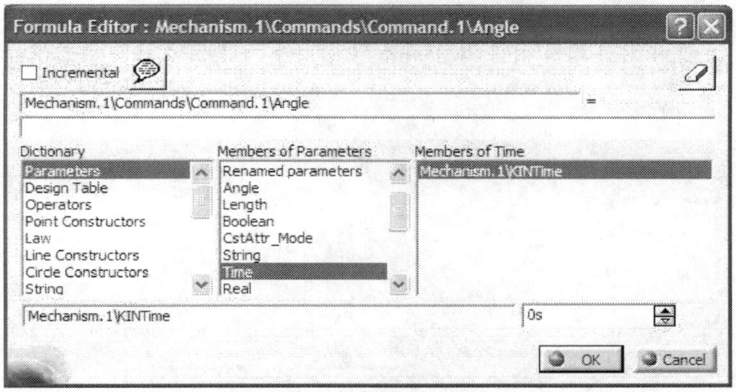

Since angle can be computed as the product of angular velocity (3600deg)/(1s) in our case and time, edit the box containing the right hand side of the equality such that the formula becomes:

$$Mechanism.1 \setminus Commands \setminus Command.1 \setminus Angle =$$
$$(3600\,\mathrm{deg}) * (Mechnism.1 \setminus KINTime)/(1s)$$

The completed **Formula Editor** box should look as shown below.

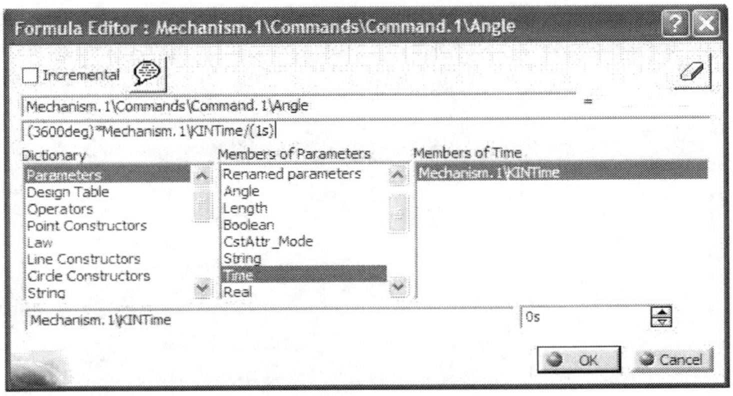

Upon accepting **OK**, the formula is recorded in the **Formulas** pop up box as shown below.

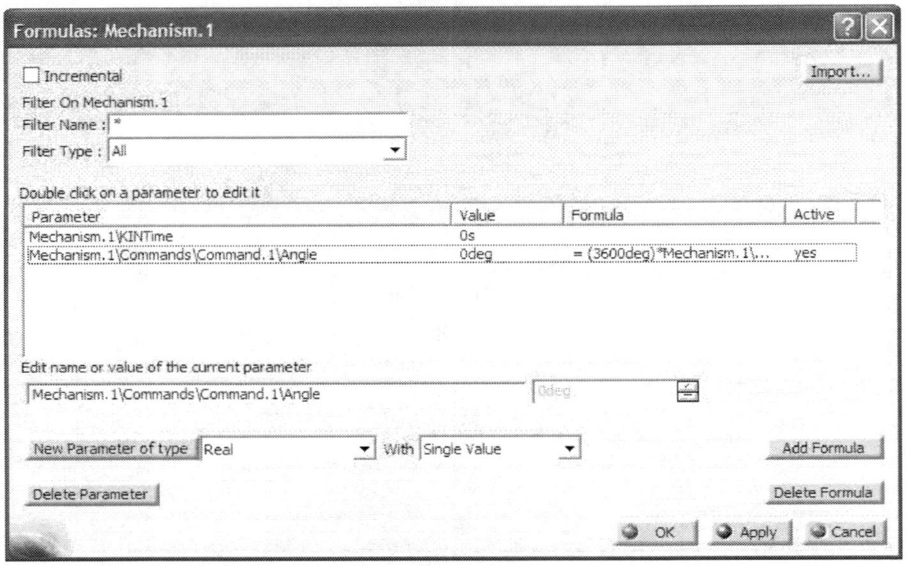

Careful attention must be given to the units when writing formulas involving the kinematic parameters. In the event that the formula has different units at the different sides of the equality you will get **Warning** messages such as the one shown below.

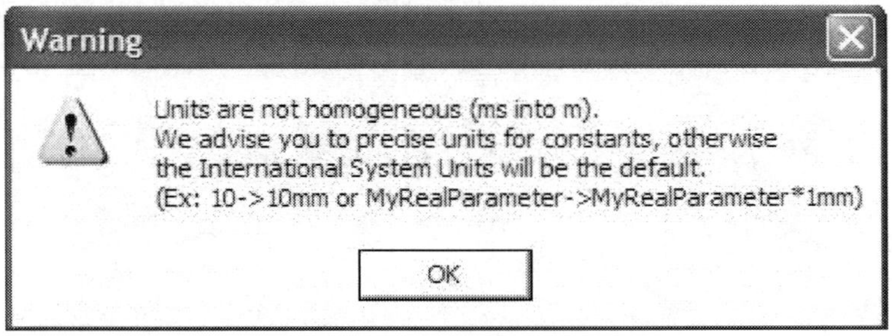

We are spared the warning message because the formula has been properly inputted. Note that the introduced law has appeared in **Law** branch of the tree.

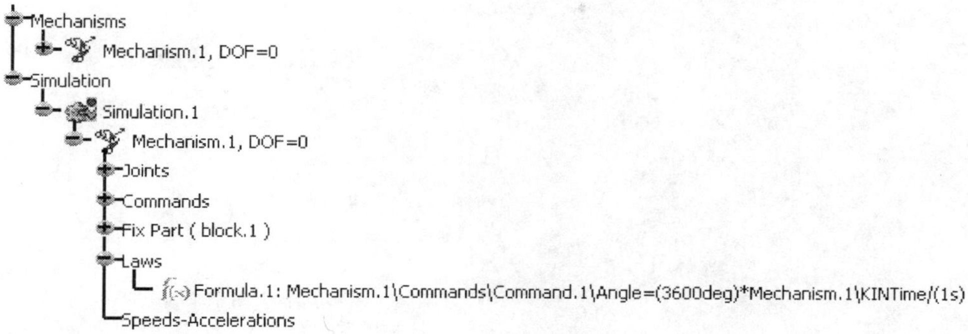

Keep in mind that our interest is to plot the position, velocity and accelerations generated by this motion. To set this up, select the **Speed and Acceleration** icon  from the **DMU Kinematics** toolbar 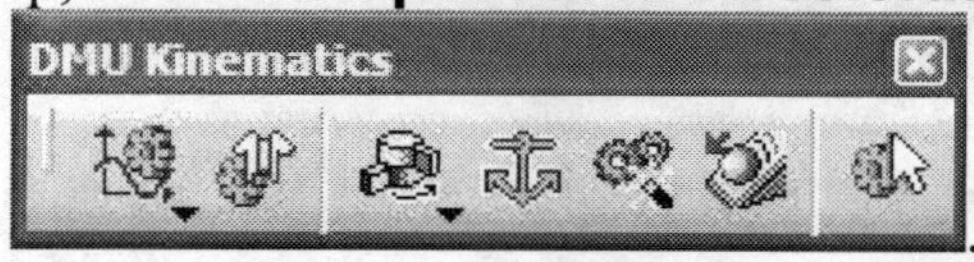

. The pop up box below appears on the Screen.

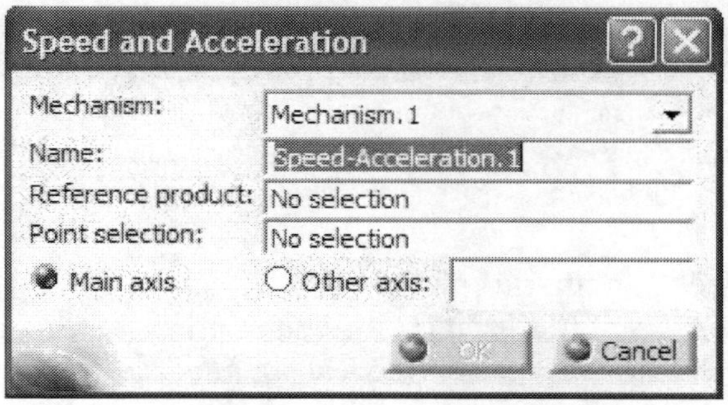

For the **Reference product,** select the **block** from the screen or the tree. For the **Point selection**, pick the point on the piston which was created earlier. This will set up the sensor to record the movement of the chosen point relative to the block (which is fixed).

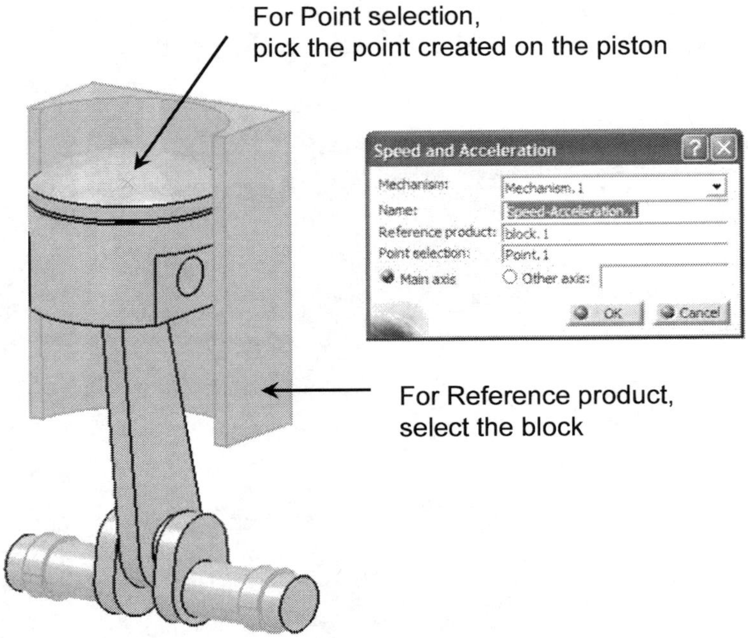

Note that the **Speed and Acceleration.1** has appeared in the tree.

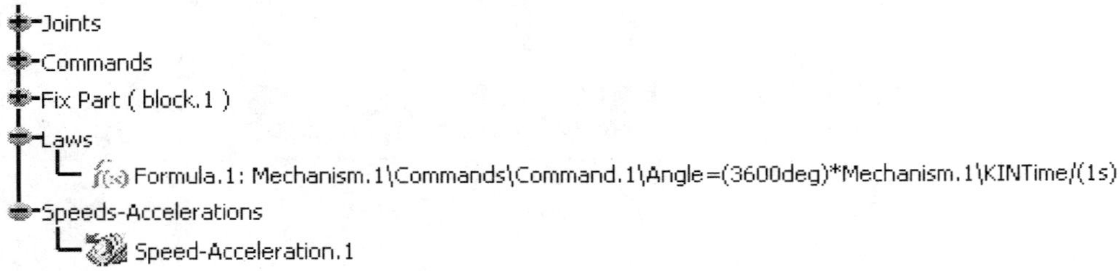

Having entered the required kinematic relation and designated the point on the block as the point to collect data on, we will simulate the mechanism. Click on **Simulation with Laws** icon  in the **Simulation** toolbar 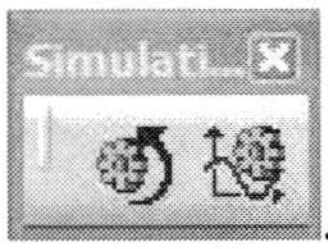

.
This results in the **Kinematics Simulation** pop up box shown below.

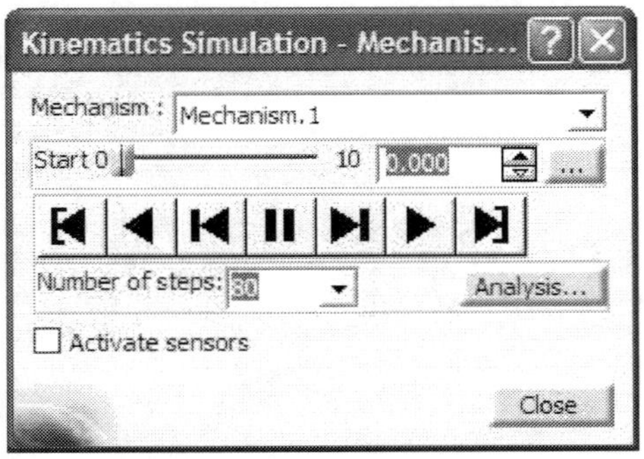

Note that the default time duration is 10 seconds.
To change this value, click on the button 

. In the resulting pop up box, change the time duration to 1s. This is the time duration for the crank to make ten full revolutions.

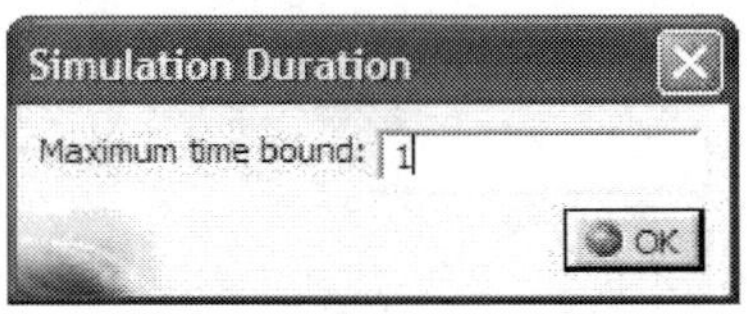

The scroll bar now moves up to 1s.

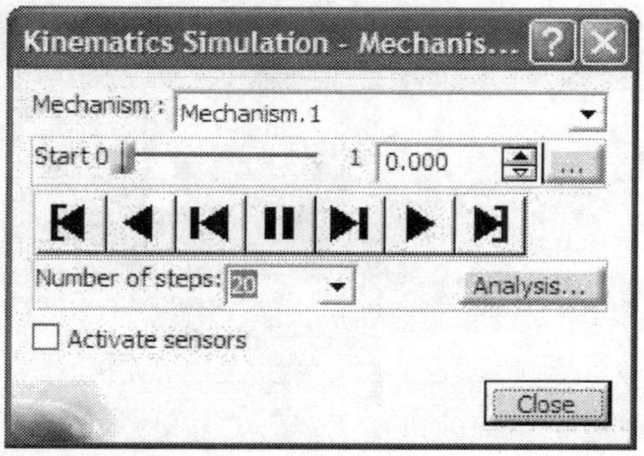

Check the **Activate sensors** box, at the bottom left corner. (Note: CATIA V5R15 users will also see a **Plot vectors** box in this window).

You will next have to make certain selections from the accompanying **Sensors** box.

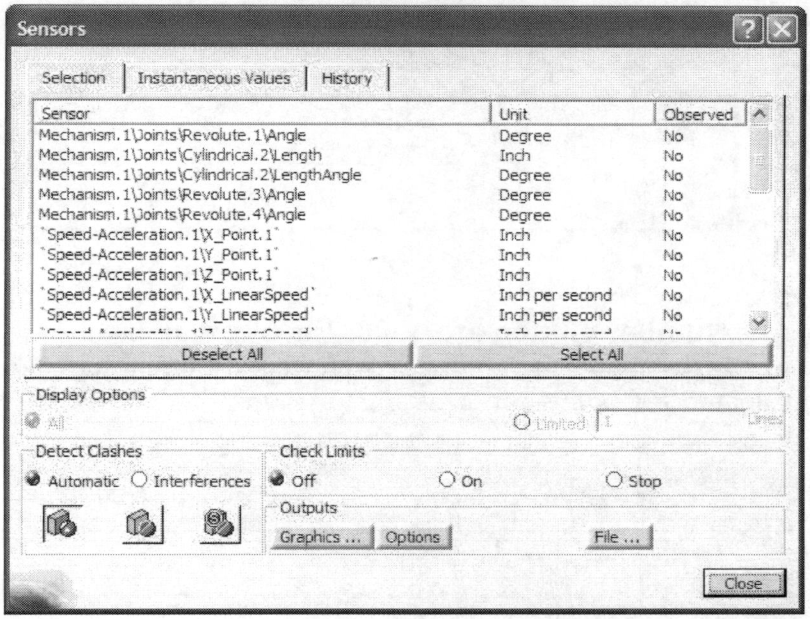

Observing that the coordinate direction of interest is Z, click on the following items to record position, velocity, and acceleration of the piston:

Mechanism.1\Joints\Cylindrical.1\Length
Speed-Acceleration.1\Z_LinearSpeed
Speed-Acceleration.1\Z_LinearAcceleration

Note: An equivalent way to get the results we want is to pick **Speed-Acceleration.1\Z_Point.1** instead of **Mechanism.1\Joints\Cylindrical.1\Length**.

As you make selections in this window, the last column in the **Sensors** box, changes to **Yes** for the corresponding items. This is shown on the next page. Do not close the **Sensors** box after you have made your selection (leave it open to generate results).

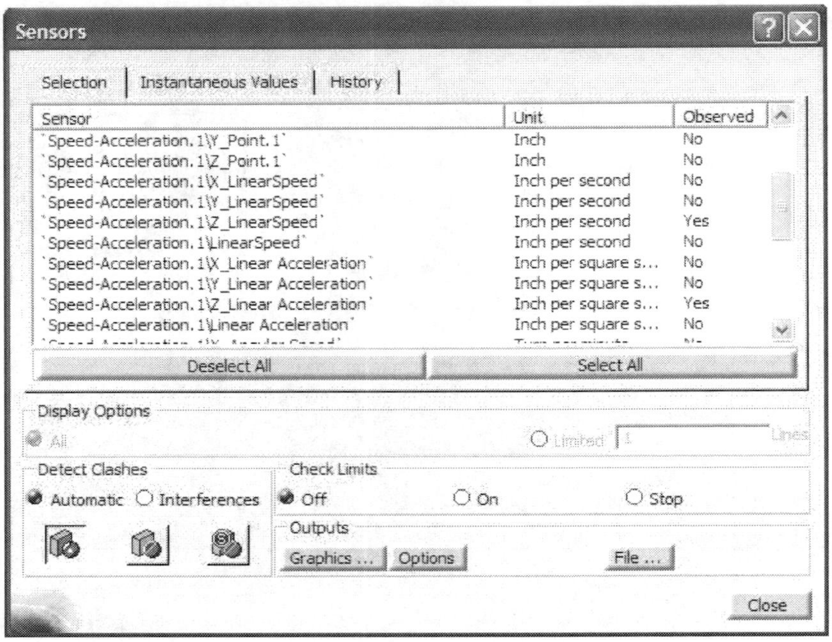

Also, change the **Number of steps to 1000**. The larger this number, the smoother the velocity and acceleration plots will be, and given we are plotting for 10 revolutions, 1000 steps is equivalent to 100 points per crank rotation.

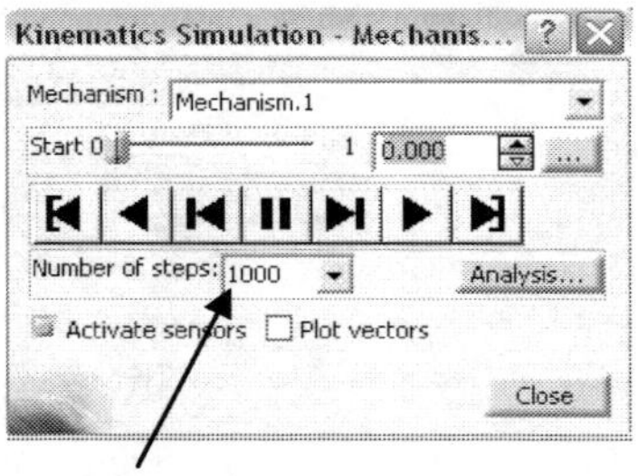

The larger this number the smoother the plots.

Note: If you haven't already done so, change the default units on position, velocity and acceleration to in, in/s and in/s^2, respectively. This is done in the **Tools, Options, Parameters and Measures** menu shown on the next page.

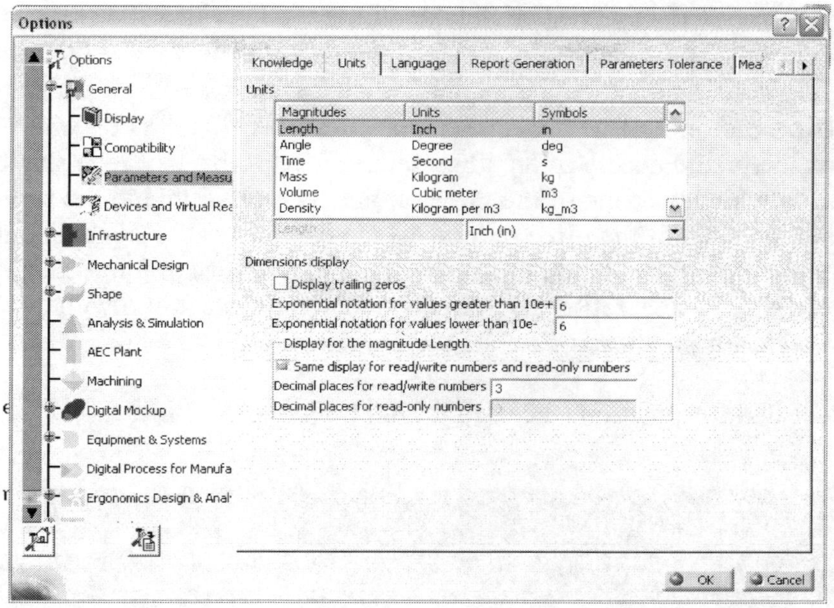

Finally, drag the scroll bar in the **Kinematics Simulation** box (or click the **Forward Play** button ▶). As you do this, the crank rotates and the block travels along the base. Once the bar reaches its right extreme point, the crank has made one full revolution. This corresponds to 1s.

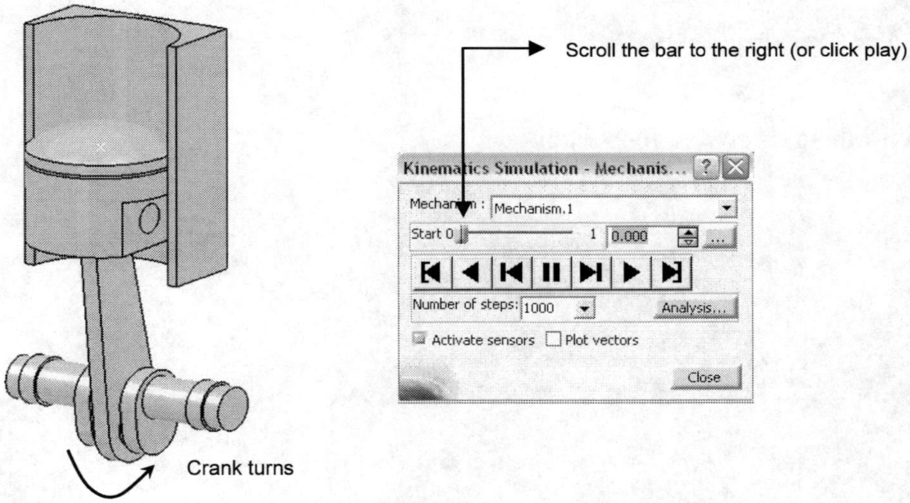

Once the crank reaches the end (this will take a little while with 1000 steps, but since it is ten crank revolutions, significantly fewer steps would result in very choppy plots), click on the **Graphics** button 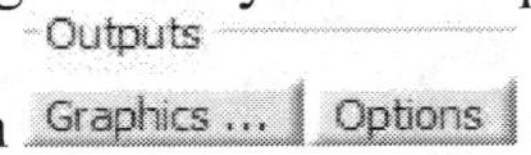

in the **Sensor** box. The result is the plot of the position, velocity and acceleration all on the same axis (but with the vertical axis units corresponding to whichever one of the three outputs is highlighted in the right side of the window). Click on each of the three outputs to see the corresponding axis units for each output. The three plots for position (corresponding to cylindrical joint Length), velocity (Z_LinearSpeed), and acceleration (Z_Linear_Acceleration) are shown below with the vertical axis scaled for position, velocity, and acceleration.

With the axis scaled for position (the stroke can be seen to be 2 in):

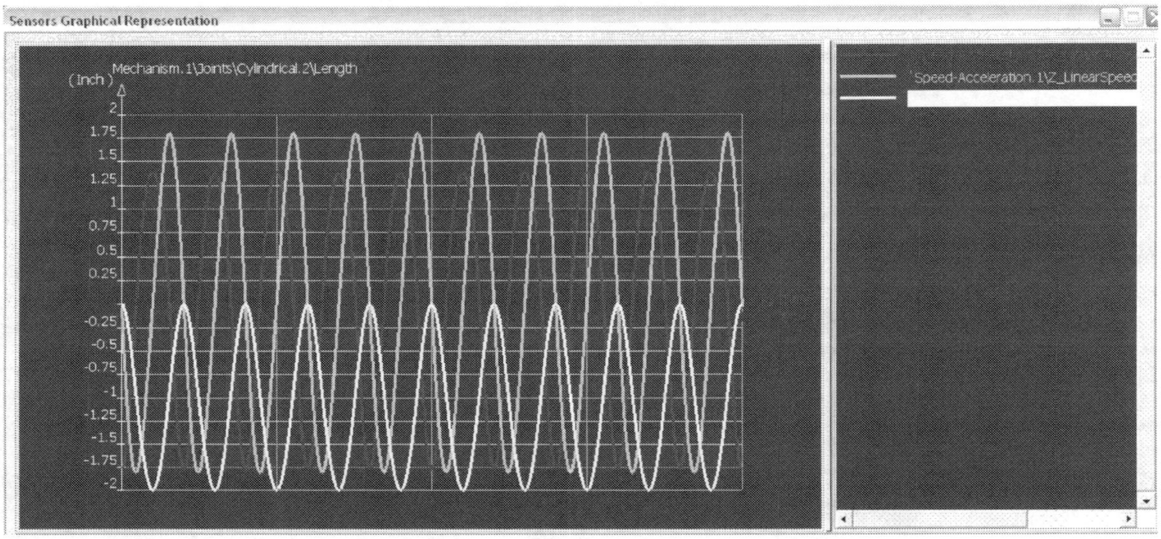

With the axis scaled for velocity:

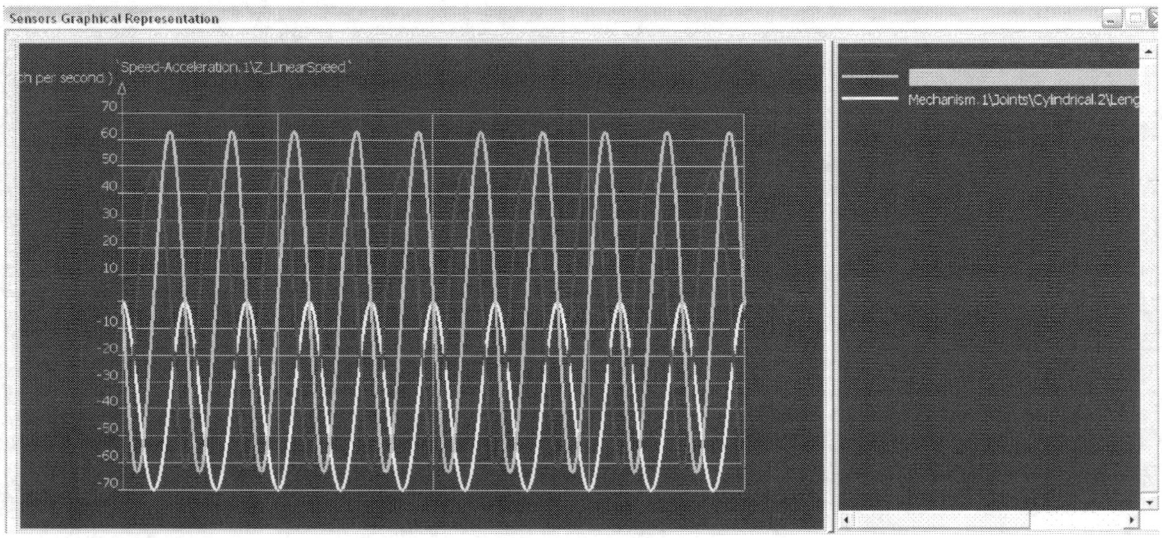

With the axis scaled for acceleration:

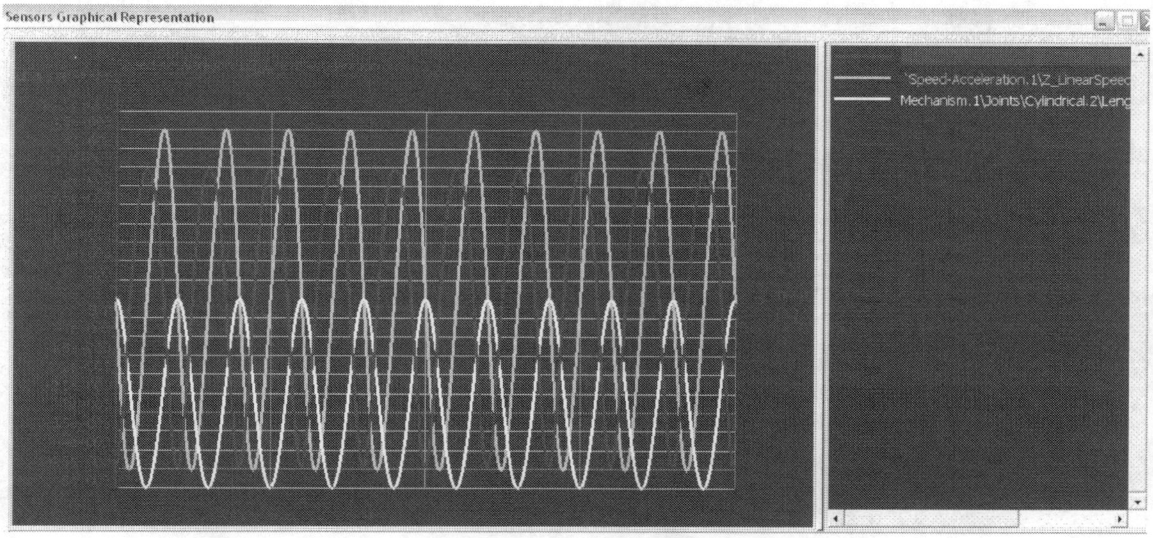

The above graph corresponds to ten revolutions of the crank. Let us now plot the data corresponding to one revolution of the crank (which is t = 0.1 second). We'll use 80 steps for these plots.

Use the **Start** video button  to return the crank to the original position.
To change the time value, click on the button . In the resulting pop up box, change the time duration to 0.1s. This is the time duration for the crank to make one full revolution.

Note: If the scroll bar jumps all the way to the right, you need to use the **Start** video button  to return the scroll bar to the time 0.

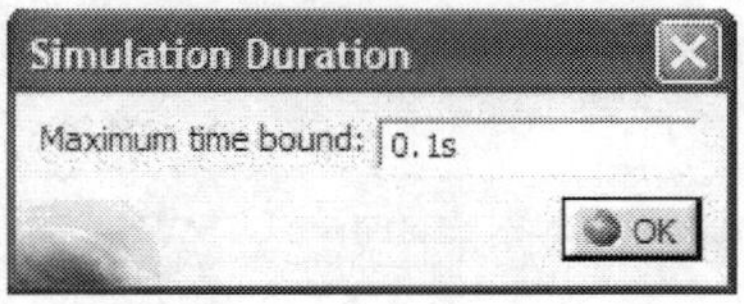

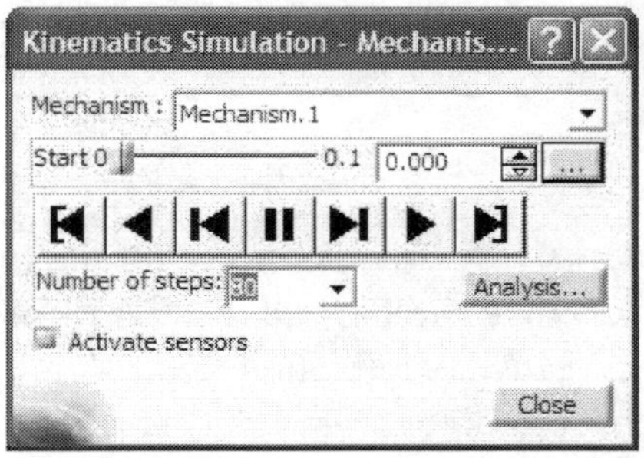

<u>Very important</u>:

Click on the **History** tab History of the **Sensors** box.

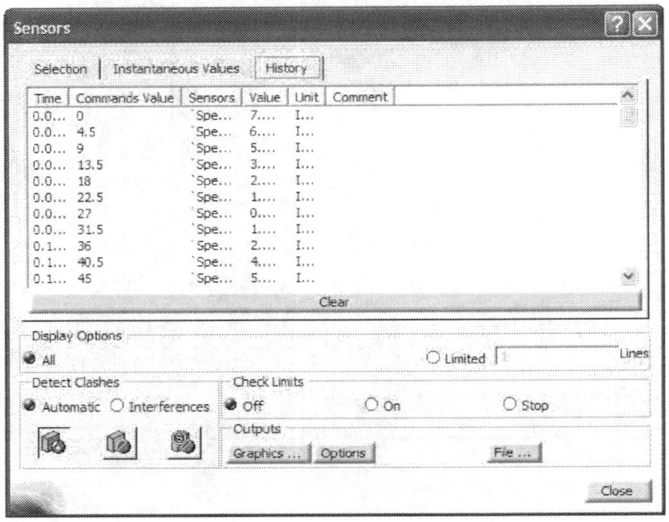

Use the **Clear** key Clear to erase the previous values generated.

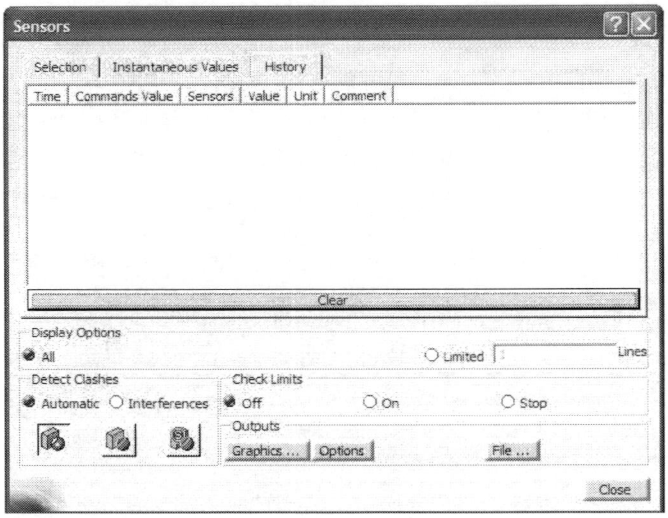

Drag the scroll bar in the **Kinematics Simulation** box. As you do this, the crank rotates and the piston travels along the block. Once the bar reaches its right extreme point, the crank has made one full revolution. This corresponds to 0.1s.

Once the crank reaches the end, click on the **Graphics** button Outputs Graphics ... Options in the **Sensor** box. The result is the plot of the position, velocity and acceleration all on the same axis during one revolution of the crank. The resulting plots are shown on the next two pages.

With the axis scaled for position (again the stroke can be seen to be 2 in):

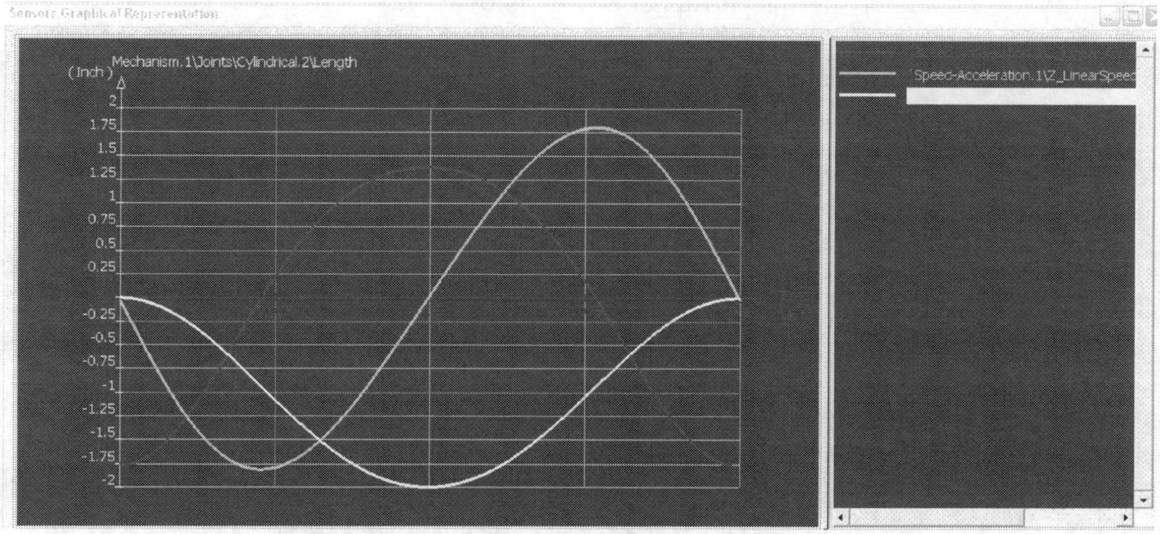

With the axis scaled for velocity one can see some things we already should know, such as zero velocity at top dead center or bottom dead center (the two extremes of the length plot), and maximum velocity midway on the stroke:

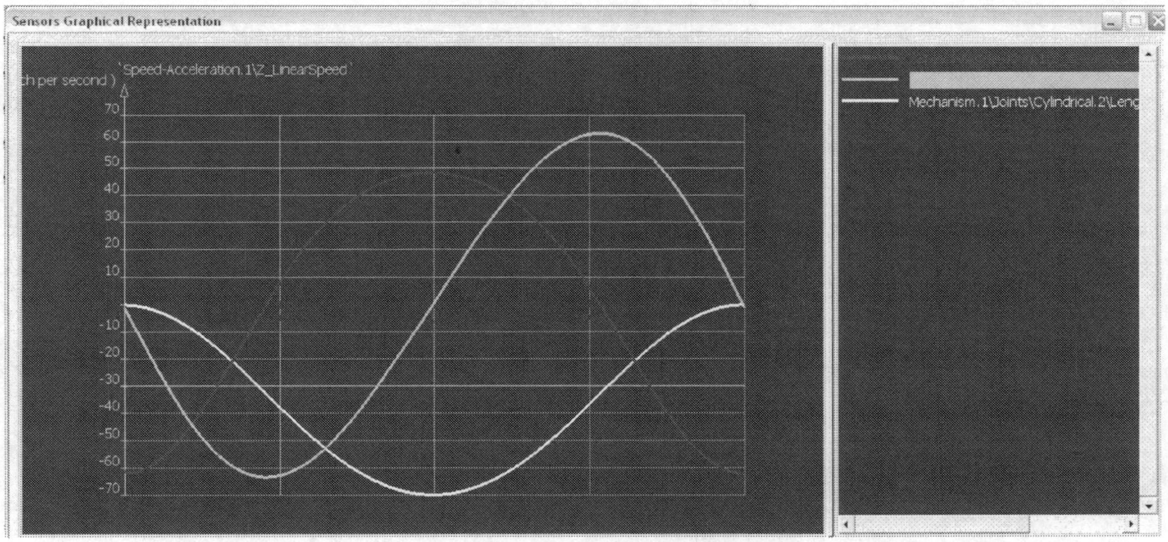

With the axis scaled for acceleration we note that acceleration peaks at top dead center and bottom dead center for this particular engine geometry:

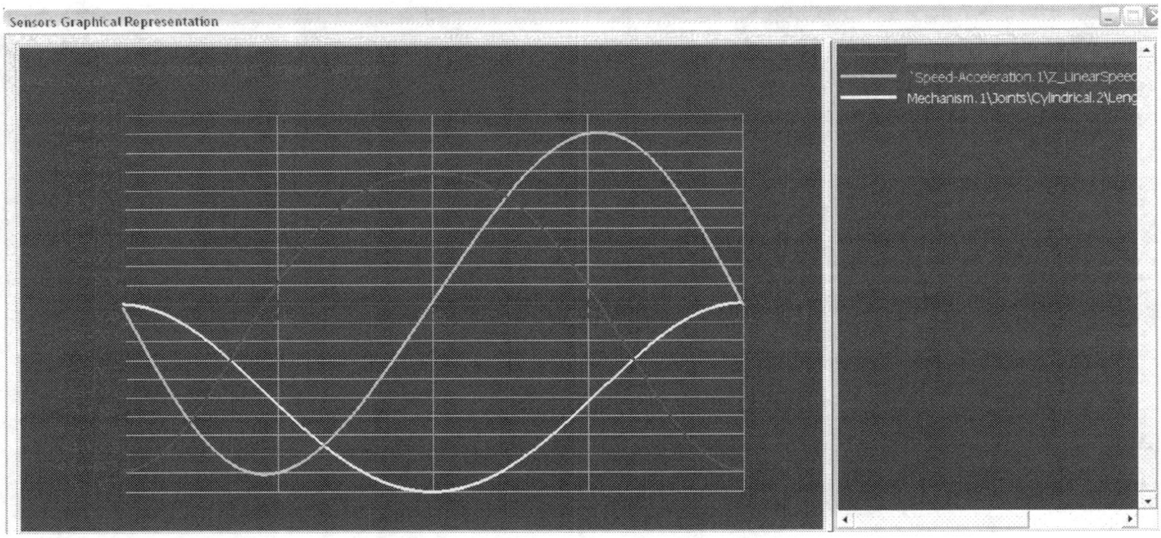

A good exercise left to the reader is to use Customized plots to generate these kinematic results versus crank angle instead of versus time. The results should be as shown below.

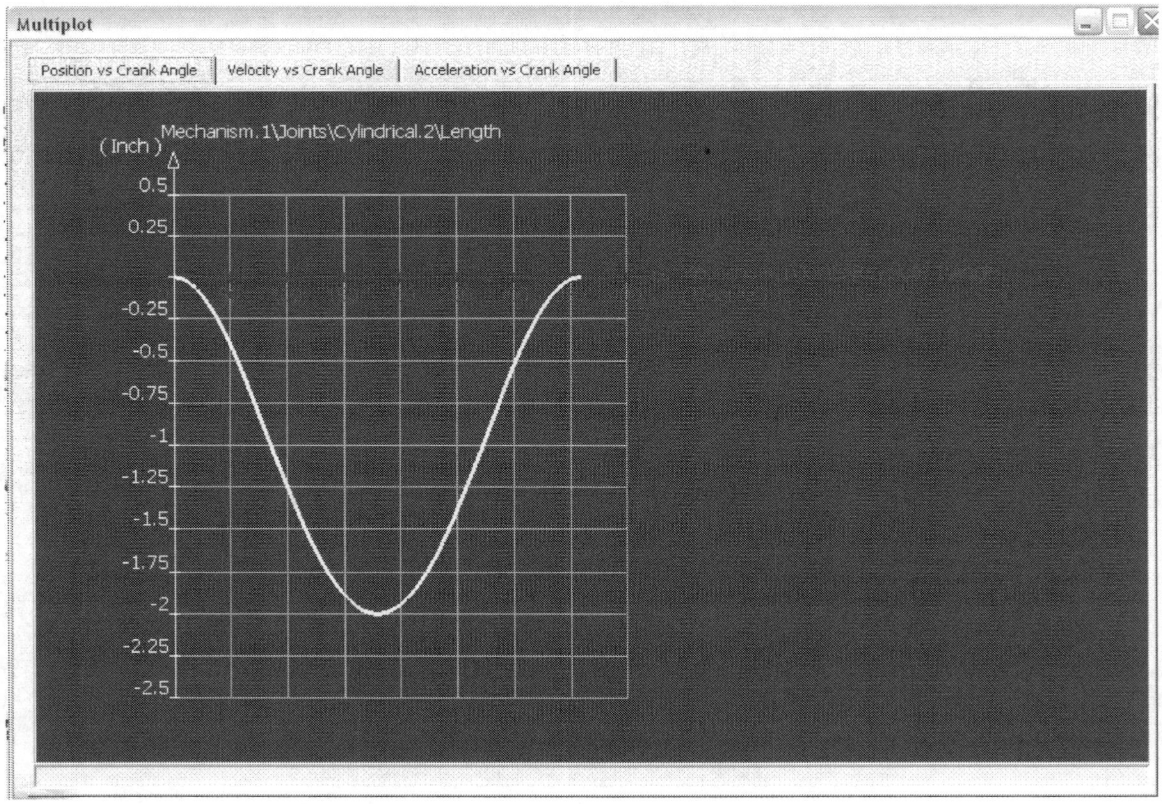

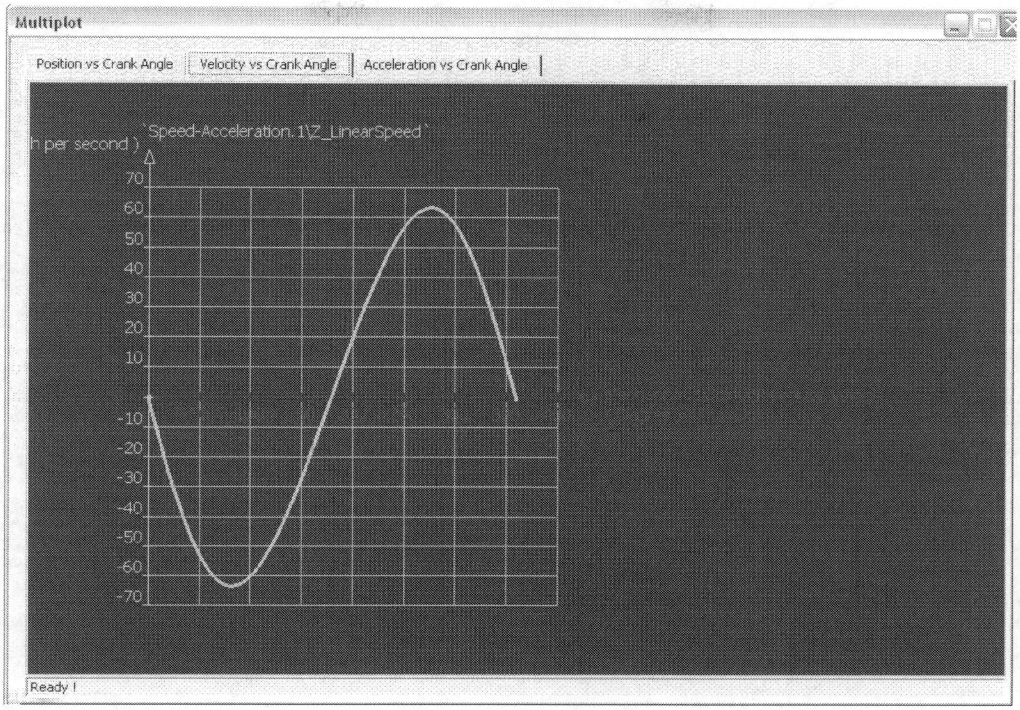

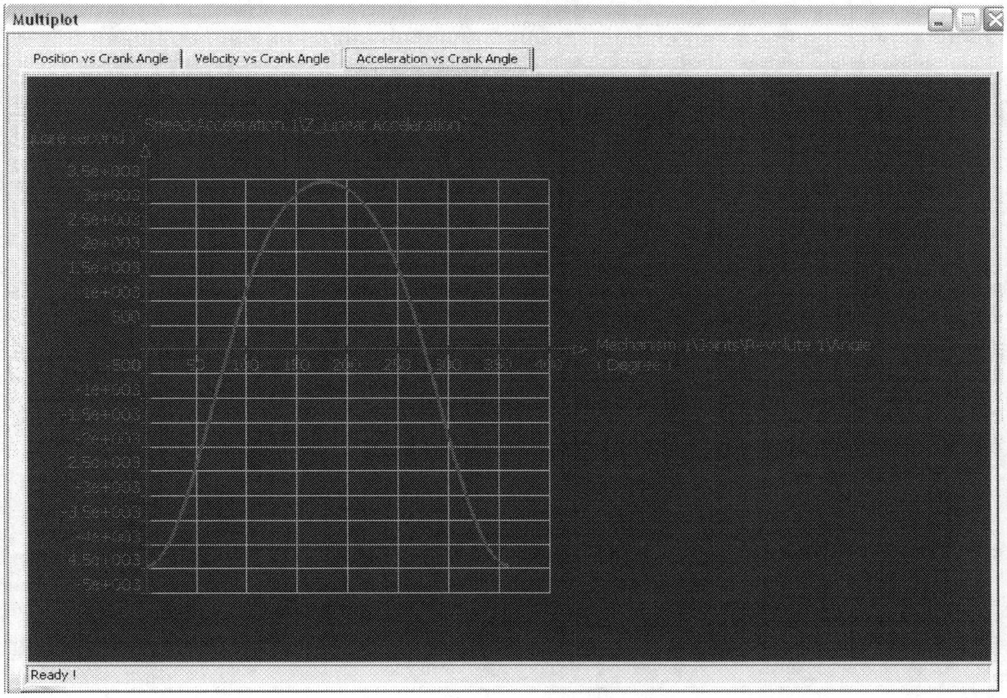

This concludes this tutorial.

NOTES:

Chapter 13

Universal Joint Mechanism

Introduction

In this tutorial, a universal joint similar to the type commonly used in automotive drive train applications is modeled. A primary shaft, a secondary shaft, a pin, and dummy part for setting up the orientation of shafts are involved. The simulation will show that constant angular velocity of the primary (input) shaft leads to a fluctuating angular velocity for the secondary (output) shaft.

1 Problem Statement

It is well established that for a constant input shaft angular velocity (ω_{in}), the output shaft has a fluctuating angular velocity (ω_{out}). The range of the velocity is given by

$$\cos\gamma \leq \frac{\omega_{out}}{\omega_{inp}} \leq \frac{1}{\cos\gamma}.$$

The parameter γ in this expression is the acute angle between the two shafts.
The objective of this tutorial is to simulate a universal joint with $\omega_{in} = 60\ rpm$ and $\gamma = 30^\circ$. We would like to make a plot of the output angular velocity and angular acceleration and show that the result for angular velocity is consistent with the range $52\ rpm \leq \omega_{out} \leq 69\ rpm$ as per the earlier equation.

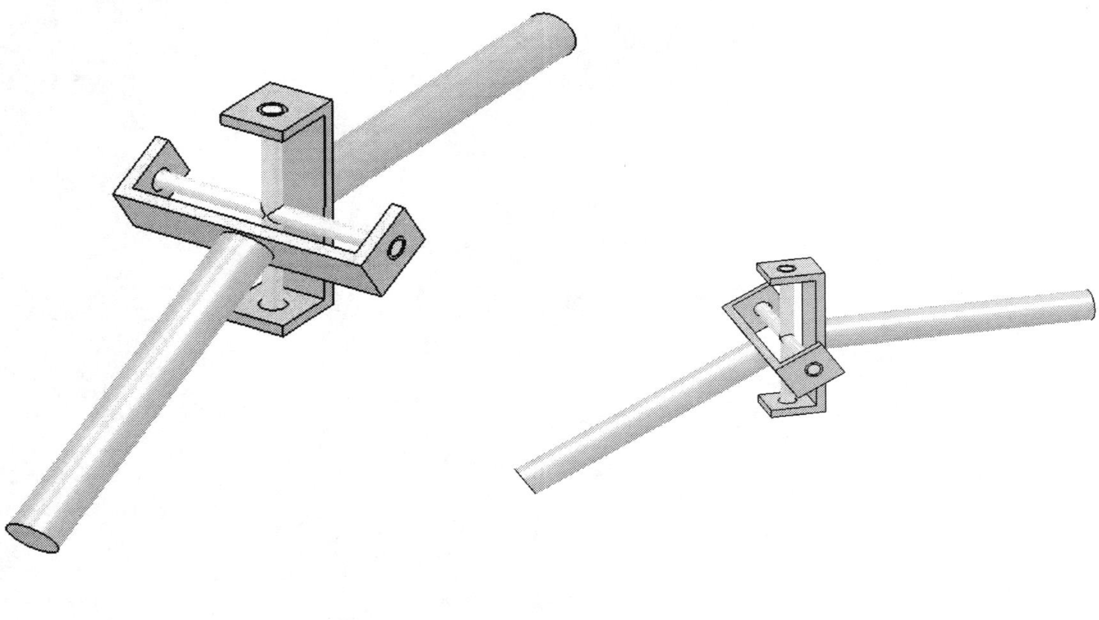

2 Overview of this Tutorial

In this tutorial you will:

1. Model the three CATIA parts required.
2. Create an assembly (CATIA Product) containing the parts.
3. Constrain the assembly in such a way that the constraints on each of the shafts are consistent with a cylindrical joint and the constraints on the pin locate the two shafts relative to each other.
4. Enter the **Digital Mockup** workbench and convert the assembly constraints into a three cylindrical joints and a revolute; delete two of these and manually create the universal joint.
5. Simulate the motion of the universal joint mechanism without consideration to time (in other words, without implementing the time based angular velocity given in the problem statement).
6. Add a formula to implement the time based kinematics associated with constant angular velocity of the primary shaft.
7. Simulate the desired constant angular velocity motion and generate plots of the kinematic results for the secondary shaft.

3 Creation of the Assembly in Mechanical Design Solutions

In this tutorial you need to create three parts: **shaft**, **pin,** and **shaft_orientation** as shown below. The **shaft_orientation** is a dummy part consisting of only two lines intersecting each other at 30°. The sole purpose of this dummy part is to easily orient the **shaft** and its instance aligned correctly.
The dimensions of the parts in this tutorial are arbitrary and do not affect the calculations, so use any dimensions that look reasonable to you. However, make sure your pin lengths are such that the ends of the pin will be flush with the outer surfaces of shaft when installed into position. We assume you are sufficiently familiar with the basics of part modeling in CATIA to generate these parts without any difficulties.

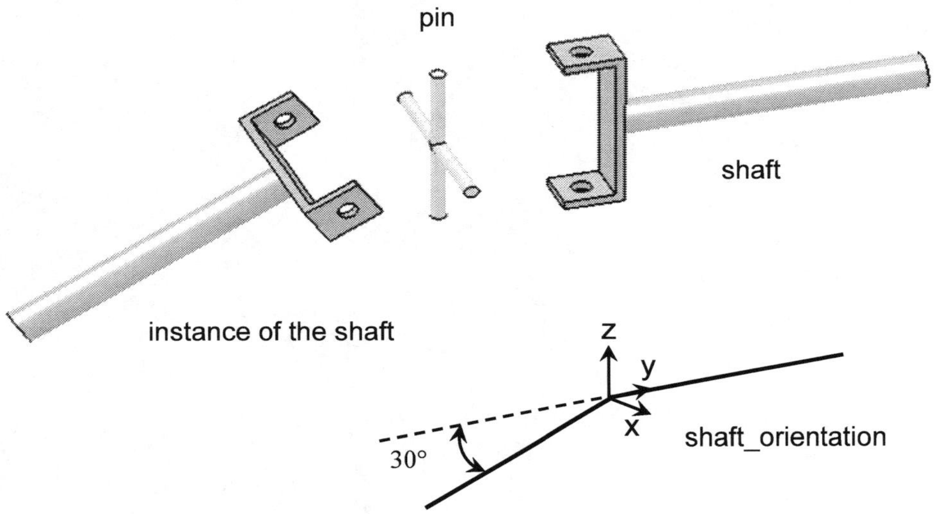

Once your parts are modeled, enter the **Assembly Design** workbench which can be achieved by different means depending on your CATIA customization. For example, from the standard Windows toolbar, select **File > New**.
From the box shown on the right, select **Product**. This moves you to the **Assembly Design** workbench and creates an assembly with the default name **Product.1**.

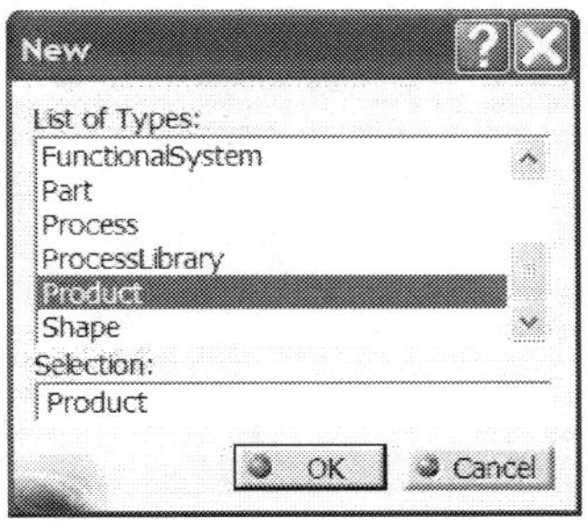

In order to change the default name, move the cursor to **Product.1** in the tree, right click and select **Properties** from the menu list.

From the **Properties** box, select the **Product** tab and in **Part Number** type **Universal_Joint_Mechanism**.

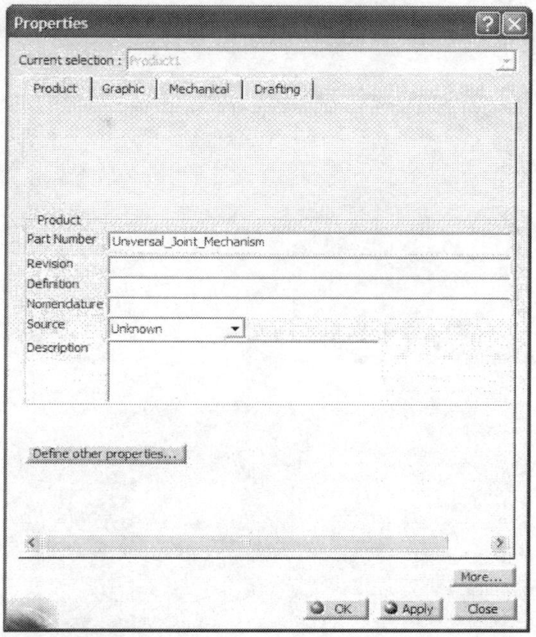

This will be the new product name throughout the chapter. The tree on the top left corner of your computer screen should look as displayed below.

The next step is to insert the three parts into the assembly just created. From the standard Windows toolbar, select **Insert > Existing Component**. From the **File Selection** pop up box choose **shaft**, **pin**, and **shaft_orientation**. Remember that in CATIA multiple selections are made with the **Ctrl** key.
The tree is modified to indicate that the parts have been inserted.

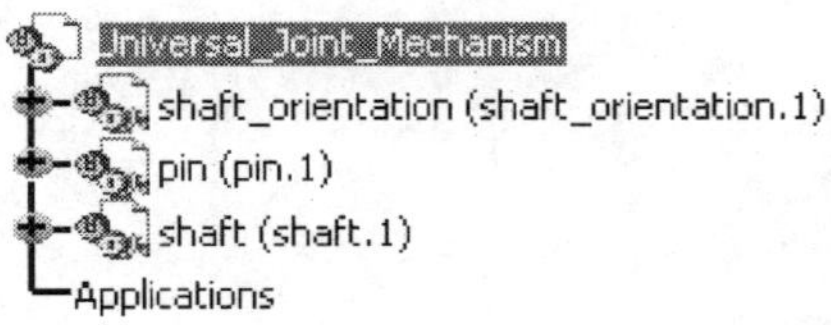

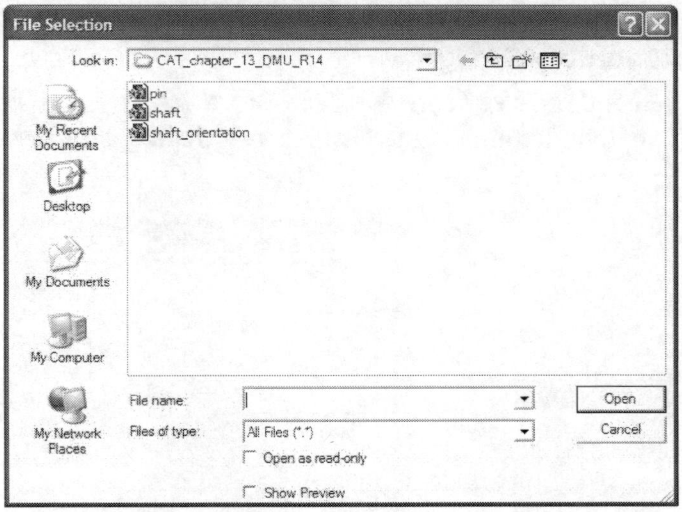

Note that you need another instance of the shaft. From the standard Windows toolbar, select **Insert > Existing Component**.

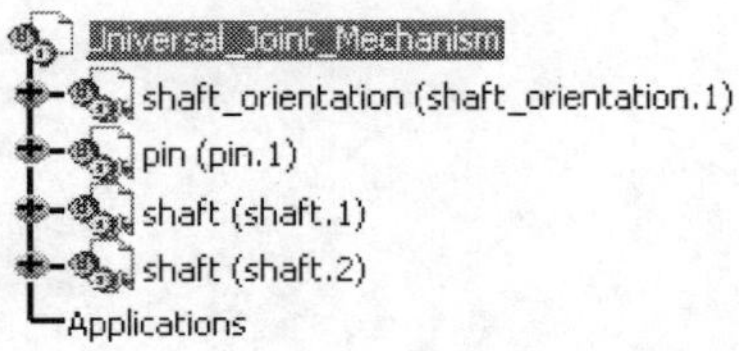

From the **File Selection** pop up box choose **shaft** and close the **File Selection** window.
This introduces the branch **shaft (shaft.2)** in the tree. (Alternatively, you could also have copied the instance already in the assembly.)

The four parts in your model may overlap and in such a case, use the **Manipulation** icon  to separate them.

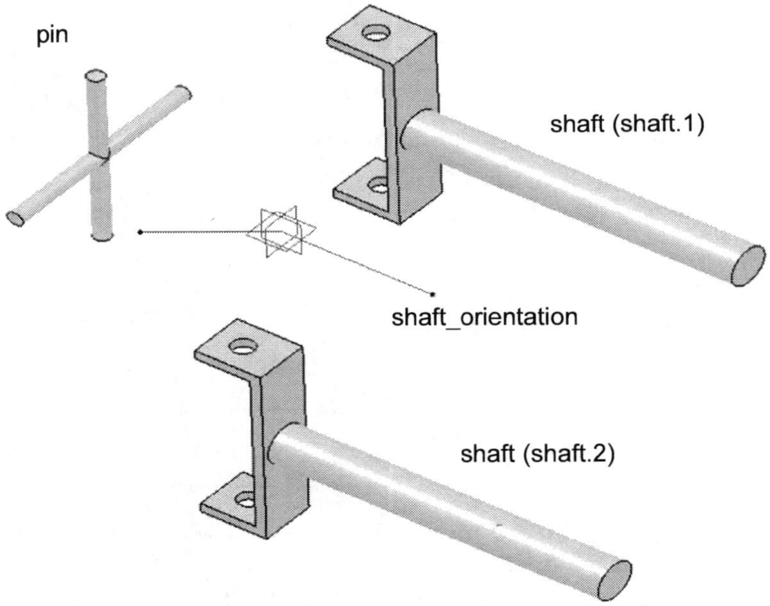

The best way of saving your work is to save the entire assembly.
Double click on the top branch of the tree. This is to ensure that you are in the **Assembly Design** workbench.
Select the **Save** icon . The **Save As** pop up box allows you to rename if desired.
The default name is the **Universal_Joint_Mechanism**.

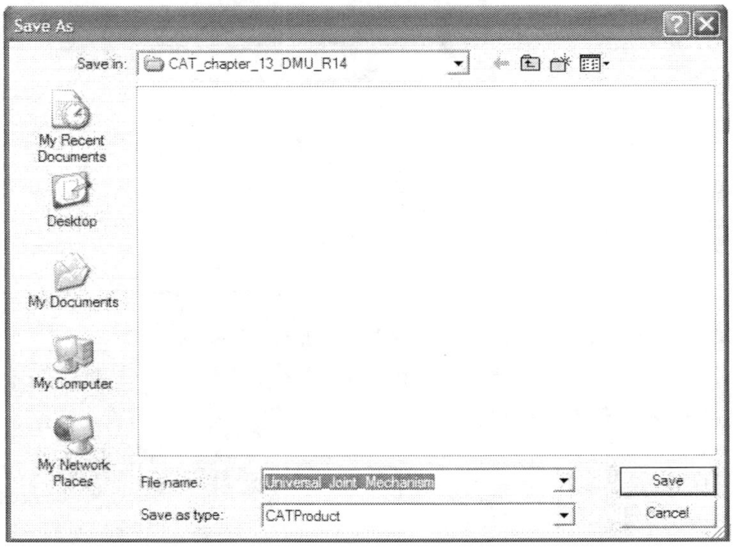

We will begin the constraining process by anchoring the **shaft_orientation** part so it cannot move as we apply the remaining constraints. Pick the **Anchor** icon from the **Constraints** toolbar and select the **shaft_orientation**.

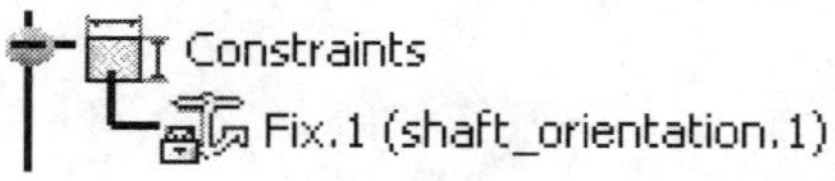

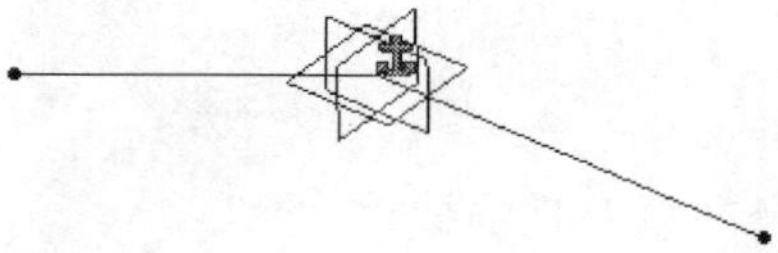

Next you will position the primary shaft (which we will take to be instance **shaft.1**) by creating a coincidence constraint between the axis of the shaft and the horizontal line on **shaft_orientation**.

Pick the **Coincidence** icon from **Constraints** toolbar and select the lines described below.

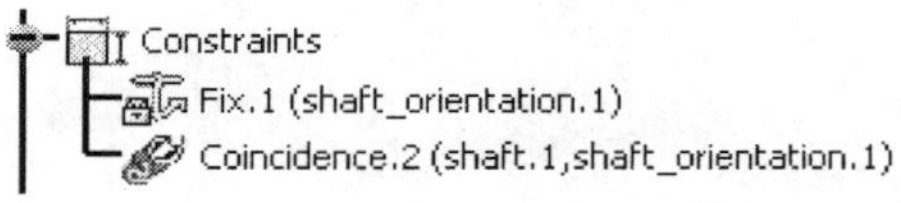

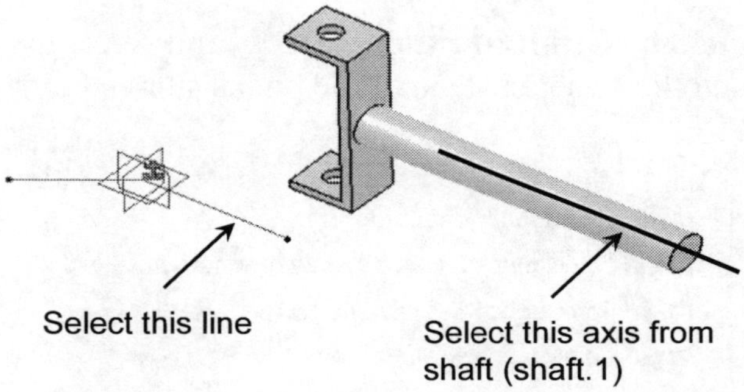

Use the **Update** icon to enforce the constraint just created resulting in relative position of the two parts similar to as shown below. If your shaft is not located in approximately the correct position, use the **Manipulation** icon followed by the **Update** icon to position the shaft approximately where ultimately desired (exact positioning will occur with a subsequent constraint).

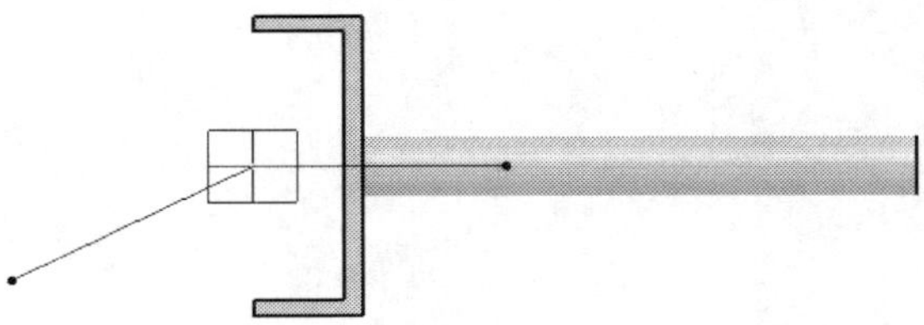

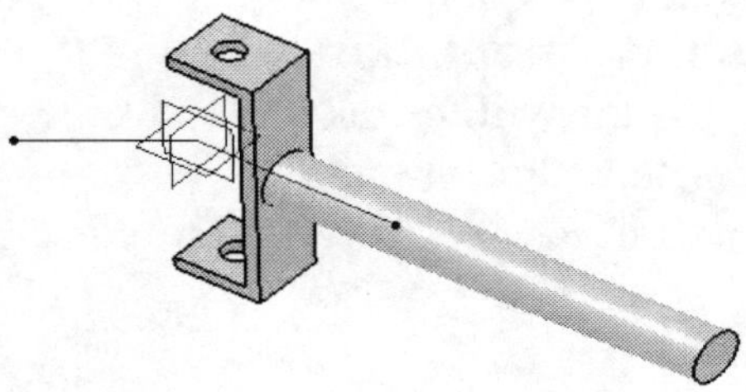

You will next position the **pin** with respect to **shaft (shaft.1)** using two coincidence constraints.

Pick the **Coincidence** icon and select the axes of the hole and the pin as shown below.

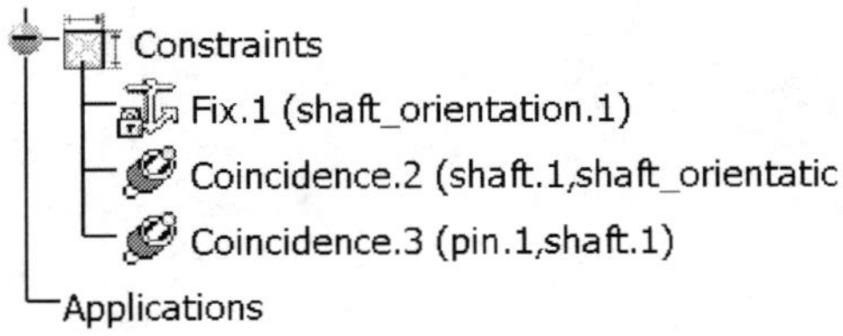

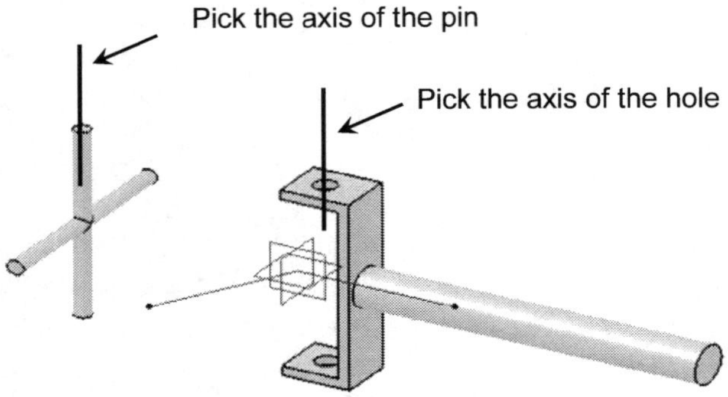

The pin is still free to slide along this axis of coincidence. To remove this translation, pick the **Coincidence** icon and select the upper surface of the shaft near the hole and the upper surface of the pin as shown below.

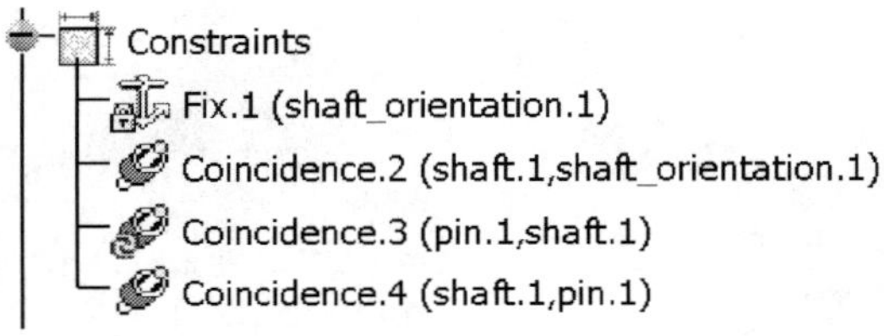

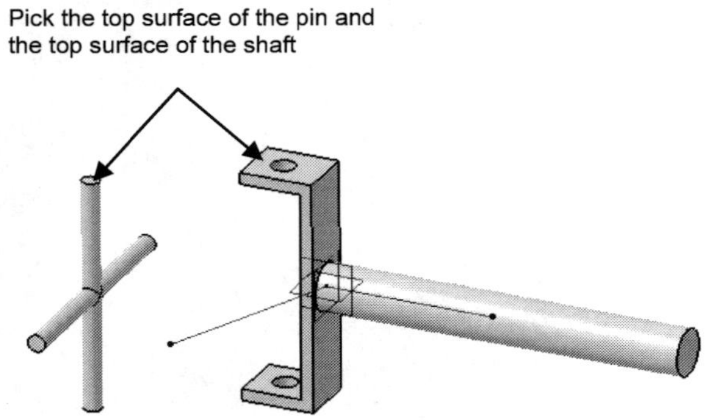

Use the **Update** icon to enforce these constraints. The shaft is not necessarily in its final position along the **shaft_orientation** part, but this will be taken care with an upcoming constraint.

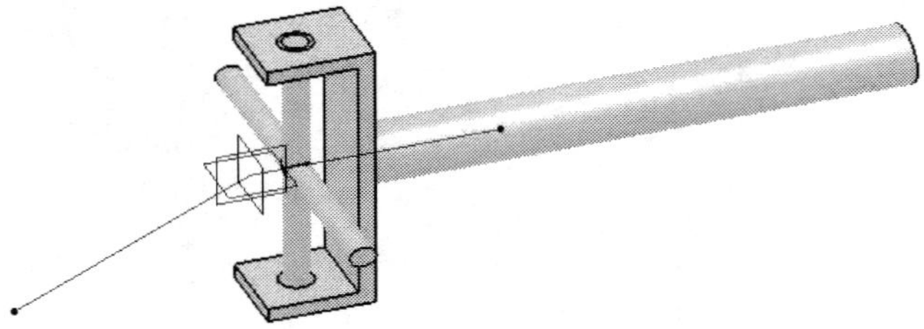

Use the Manipulation icon  to position **shaft (shaft.2)** to approximately the desired orientation as displayed below. This may require a combination of translation and rotation.

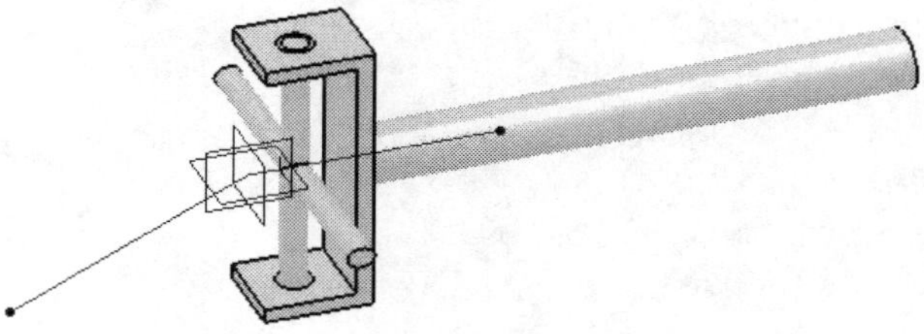

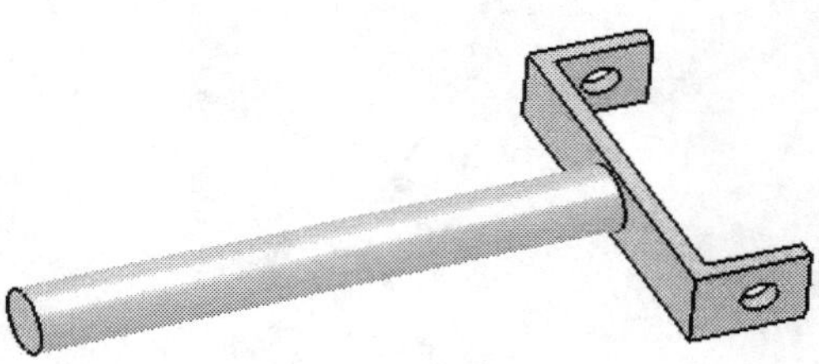

Two coincidence constraints will be used to locate this instance of the shaft, one to locate it on **shaft_orientation** and one to locate it to the **pin**. Pick the **Coincidence** icon  from **Constraints** toolbar and make the line selections shown to locate **shaft.2** to **shaft_orientation**.

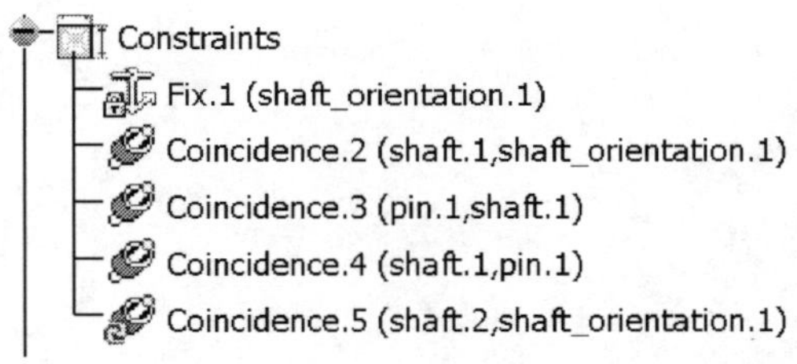

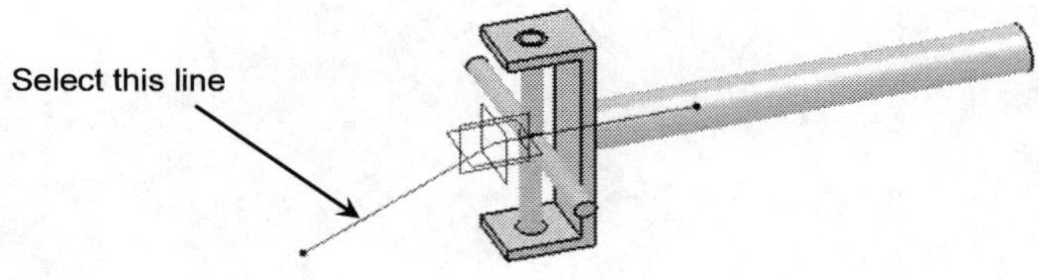

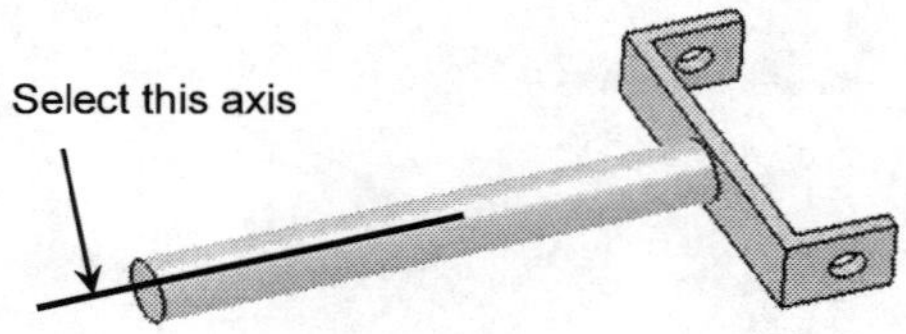

Pick the **Coincidence** icon from **Constraints** toolbar and make the line selections shown to locate **shaft.2** to the axis of the **pin**.

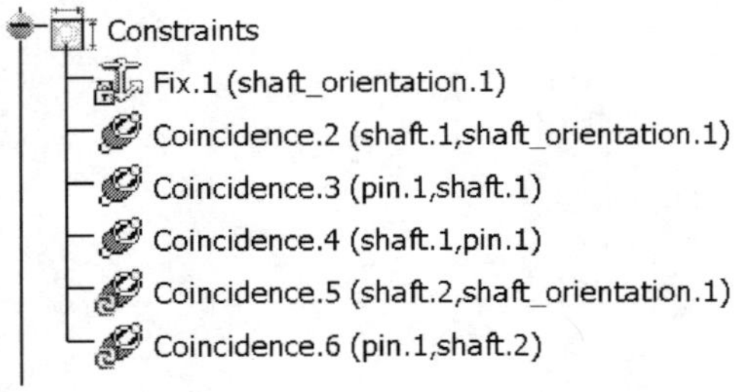

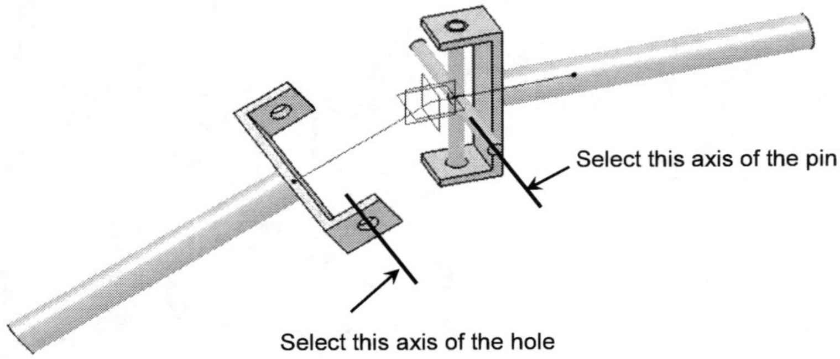

Note that we do not need to locate the pin along the length of the hole on this shaft as it must be correct based on the other constraints applied.

Use the **Update** icon to enforce the latest constraints and position the mechanism to its assembled condition.

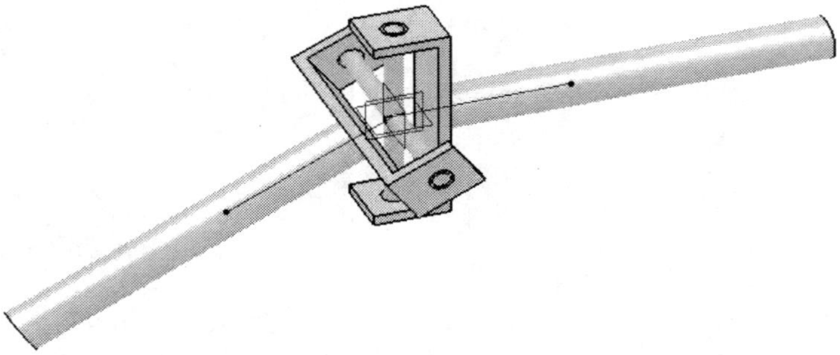

Note that the dummy part **shaft_orientation** has served its purpose and can be hidden for the rest of the tutorial.

The assembly is complete and we are ready to proceed to **Digital Mockup**.

4 Creating Joints in the Digital Mockup Workbench

The **Digital Mockup** workbench is quite extensive but we will only deal with the **DMU Kinematics module**. To get there you can use the standard Windows toolbar as shown below: **Start > Digital Mockup > DMU Kinematics**.

Select the **Assembly Constraints Conversion** icon  from the **DMU Kinematics** toolbar 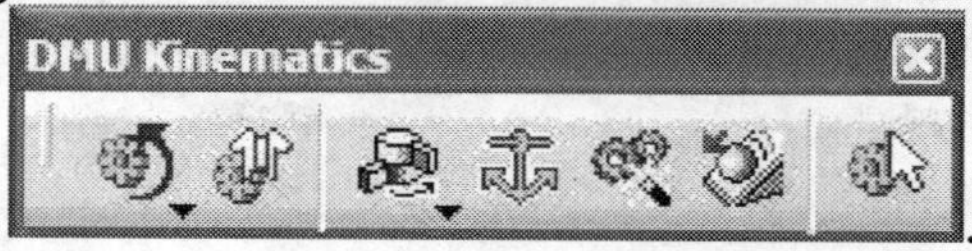

. This icon allows you to create most common joints automatically from the existing assembly constraints. The pop up box below appears.

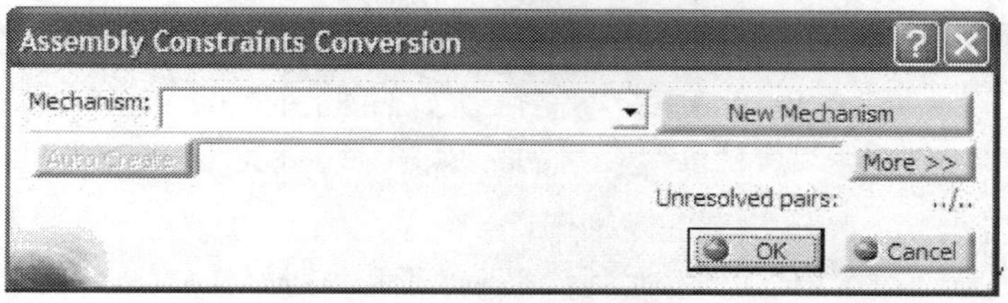

Select the **New Mechanism** button 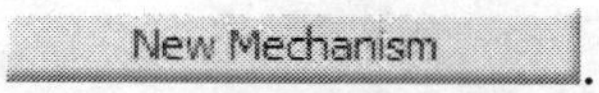

.
This leads to another pop up box which allows you to name your mechanism. The default name is **Mechanism.1**. Accept the default name by pressing **OK**.

Note that the box indicates **Unresolved pairs: 4/4**.

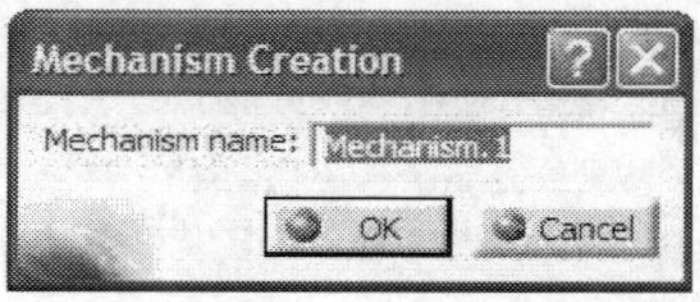

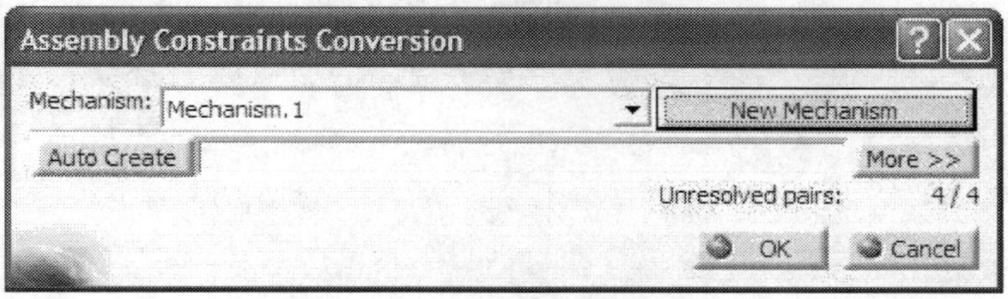

Select the **Auto Create** button 

. Then if the **Unresolved pairs** becomes **0/4**, things are moving in the right direction.

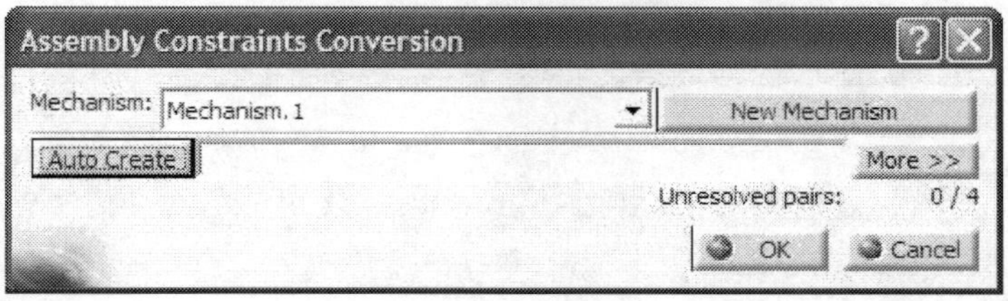

Note that a Mechanisms branch has been added to your tree as shown below (expand the tree as necessary to view it).

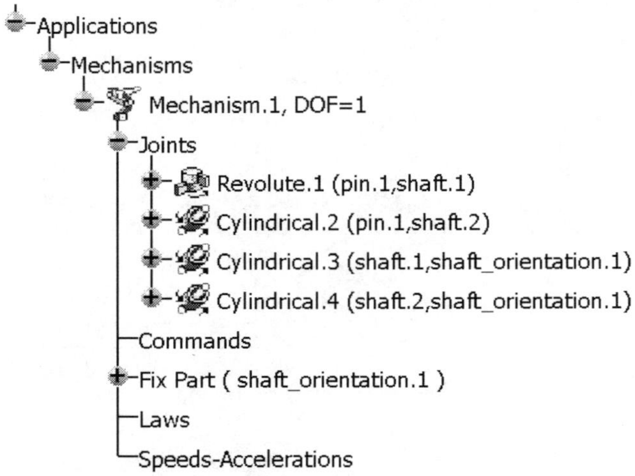

In this tutorial, you will not be concerned with the motion of the **pin**. This part was helpful in locating the parts in the assembly, but the mechanism universal joint functionally takes the place of the pin in the mechanism simulation. Therefore, the revolute joint and cylindrical joint pertaining the **pin** should deleted by highlighting them in the tree and pressing **delete** on your keyboard. Upon deleting these joints, the tree takes the following form. Prior to adding the universal join the mechanism degrees of freedom (dof) are 4.

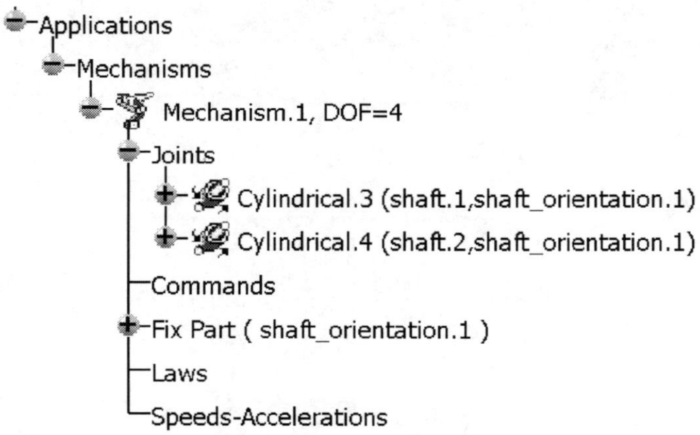

The universal joint needs to be created manually. To do so, select the **Universal Joint** icon  from the **Kinematics Joints** toolbar

.

The associated pop up box shown on the next page is displayed.

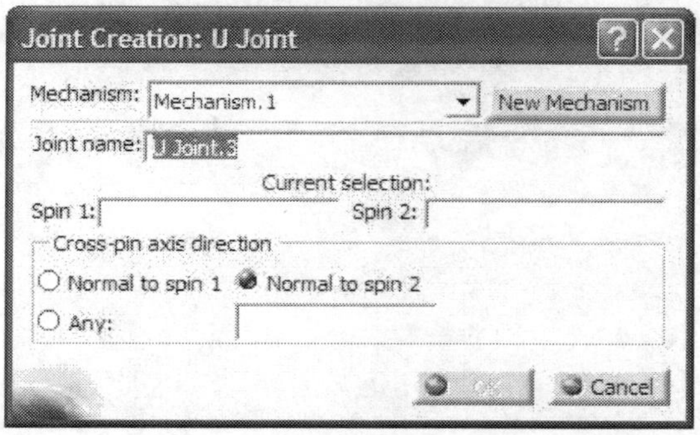

The **Spin 1** and **Spin 2** should be selected as displayed below. Finally, use the radio button **Normal to spin 1** since the pin axes are normal to this spin axis. The completed pop up box is also shown.

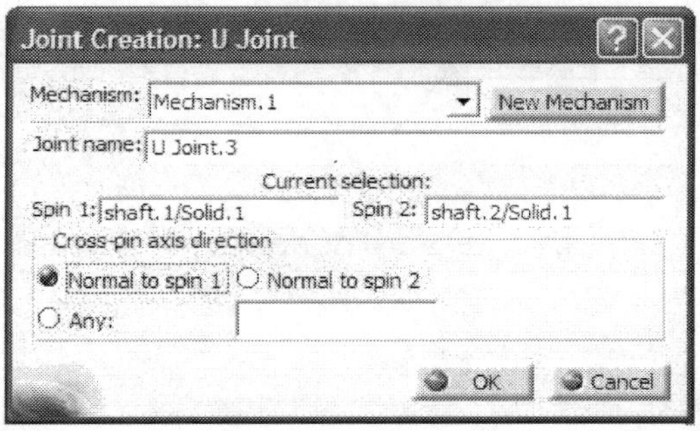

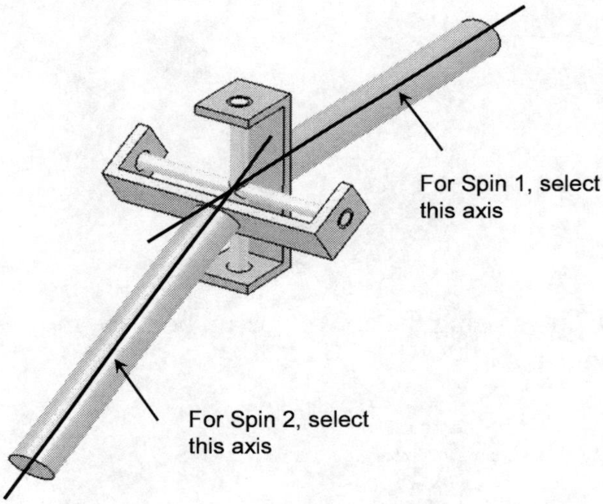

The universal joint is reflected in the tree and the dof is reduced to 1.

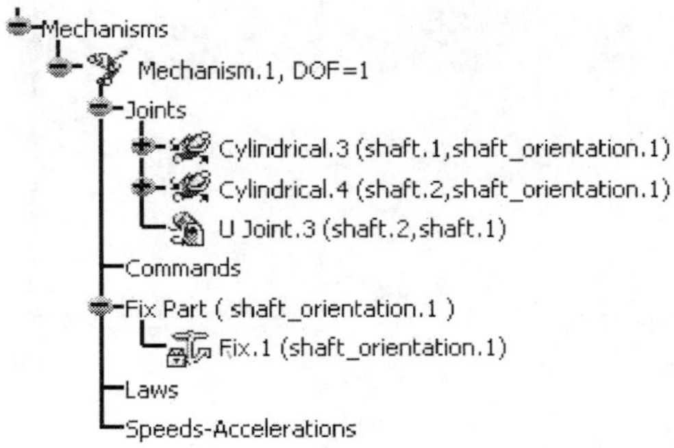

The remaining 1 dof will be removed by making the cylindrical joint corresponding to our intended input shaft angle driven. Double click on the cylindrical joint **Cylindrical.3** and make this joint angle driven by selecting the appropriate box.

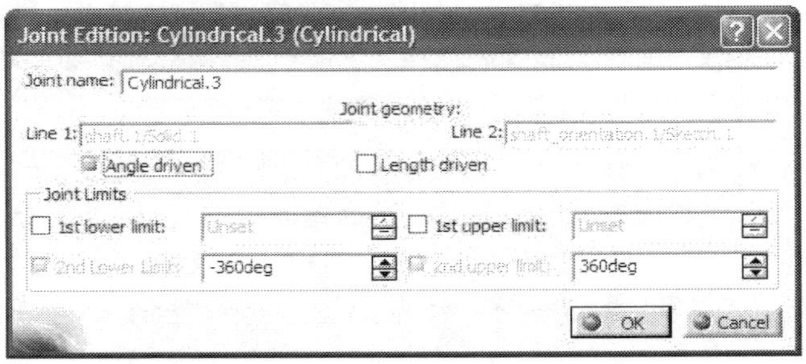

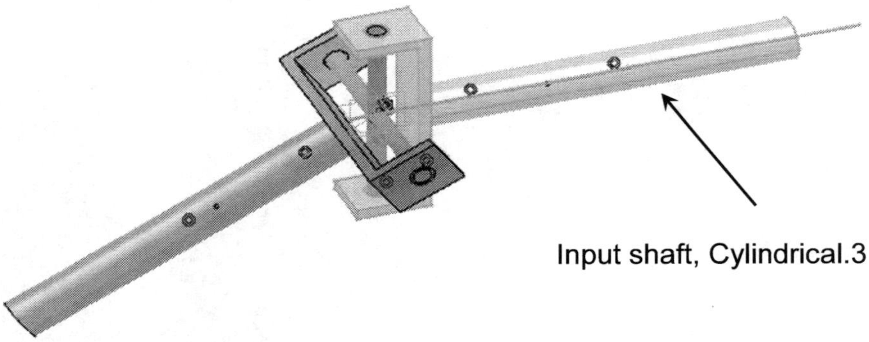

Upon closing the above pop up box, the message “**Mechanism can be simulated**” appears.

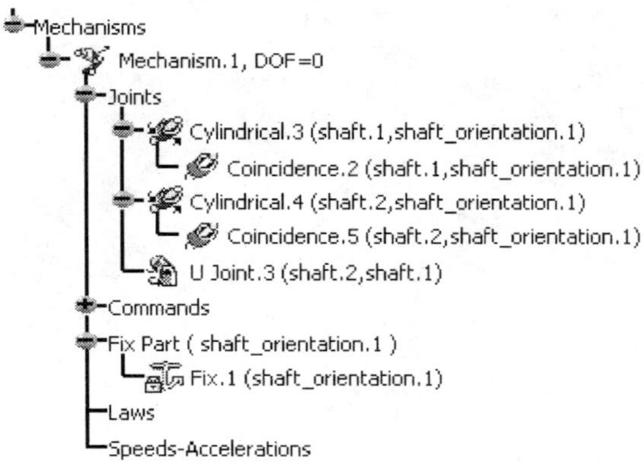

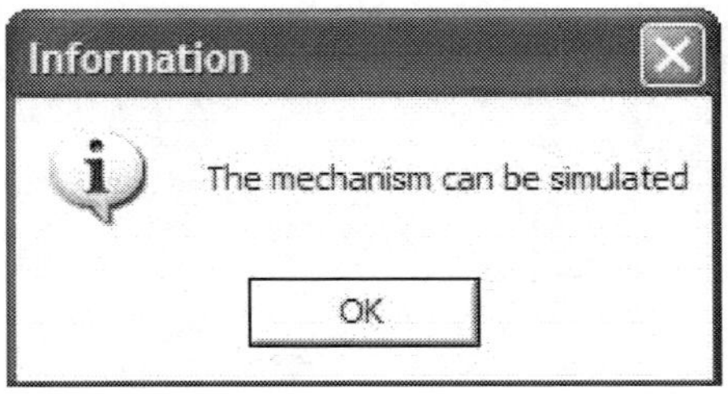

The **pin** plays no role in this simulation and therefore can be hidden.

To simulate the motion without regard to time, select the **Simulation** icon  from the **DMU Generic Animation** toolbar 

. This enables you to choose the mechanism to be animated if there are several present. In this case, select Mechanism.1 and close the window.

As soon as the window is closed, a Simulation branch is added to the tree.

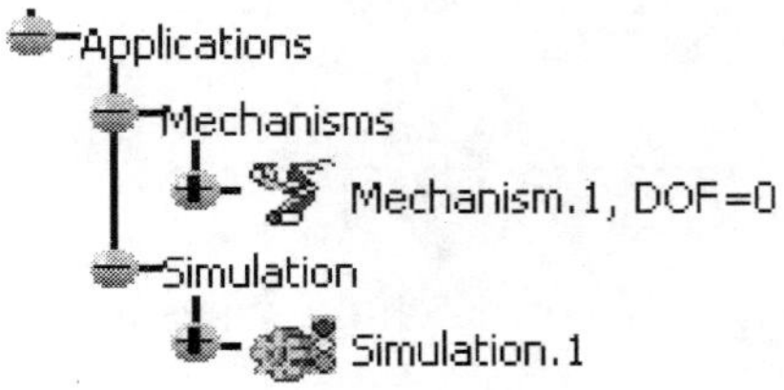

In addition, the two pop up boxes shown below appear.

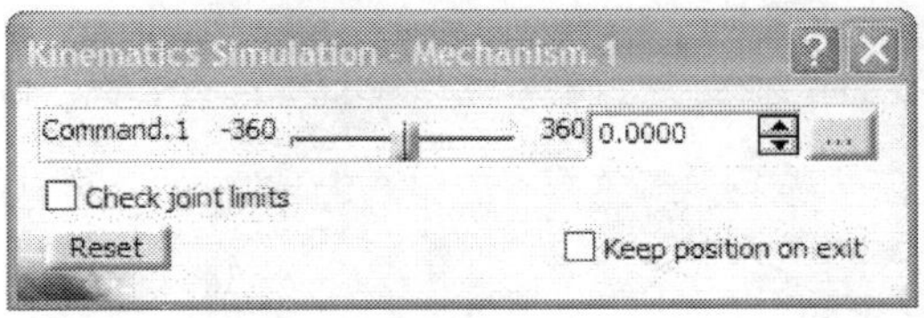

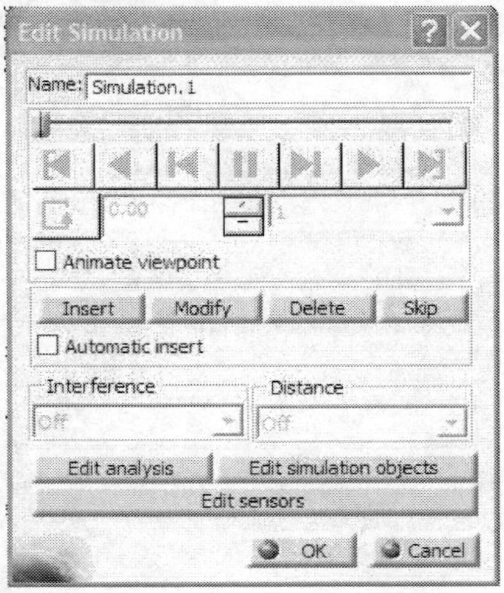

Click on  to change of the input shaft rotation range.

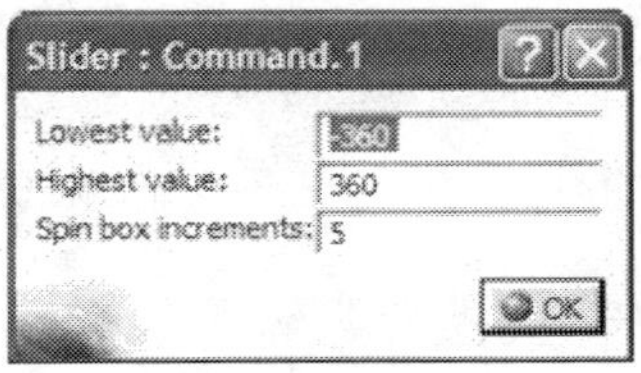

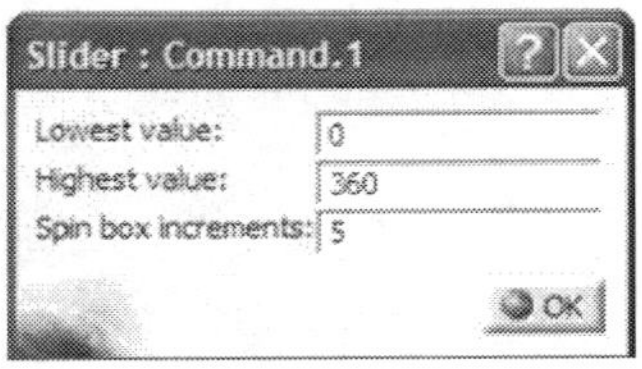

original range modified range

The scroll bar in the Kinematics Simulation box now spans (0,360) as shown.

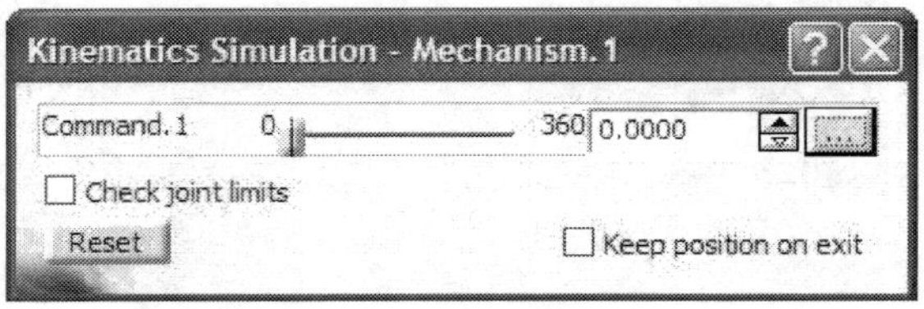

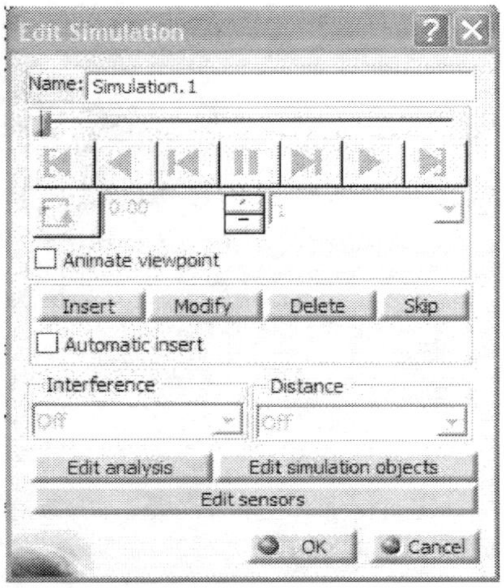

As you scroll the bar from left to right, the input shaft begins to rotate and causes the output shaft to track accordingly.

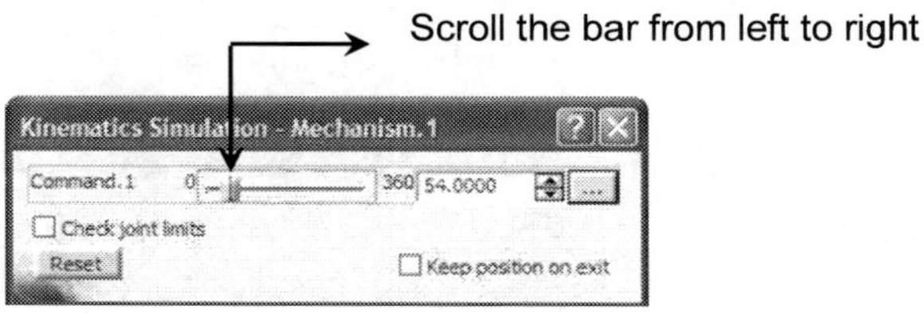

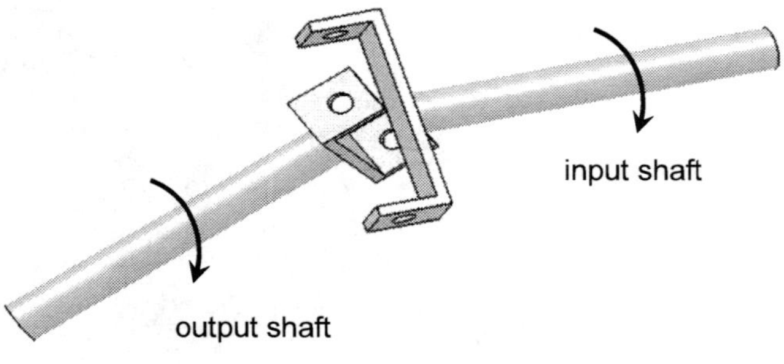

When the scroll bar in the **Kinematics Simulation** pop up box reaches the right extreme end, select the **Insert** button Insert in the **Edit Simulation** pop up box shown above. This activates the video player buttons shown

.

Return the input shaft to its original position by picking the **Jump to Start** button.
Note that the **Change Loop Mode** button is also active now.

Upon selecting the **Play Forward** button, the shaft makes such a fast jump to the end that there does not seem to be any motion.

In order to slow down the motion of the shaft, select a different **interpolation step**, such as 0.04.

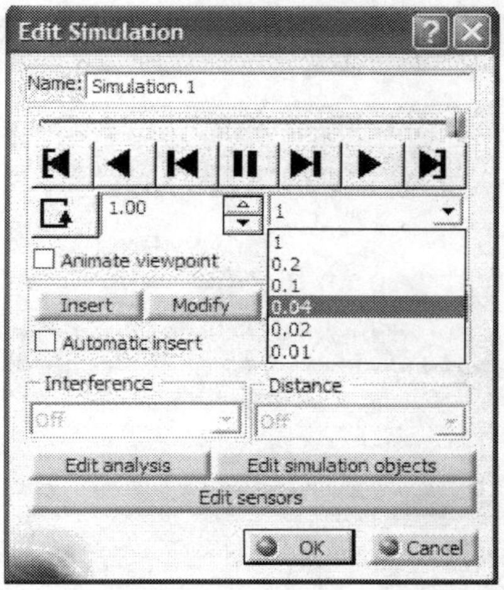

Upon changing the interpolation step to 0.04, return the shaft to its original position by picking the **Jump to Start** button. Apply **Play Forward** button and observe the slow and smooth rotation of the shaft.

Now we are ready to simulate the time based motion given in the problem statement.

5 Creating Laws in the Motion and Simulating the Desired Kinematics

The motion animated this far was not tied to the time parameter or the angular velocity given in the problem statement. You will now introduce some time based physics into the problem. The objective is to specify a constant input shaft angular velocity of 360 deg/s.

Click on **Simulation with Laws** icon  in the **Simulation** toolbar 

. You will get the following pop up box indication that you need to add at least a relation between the command and the time parameter.

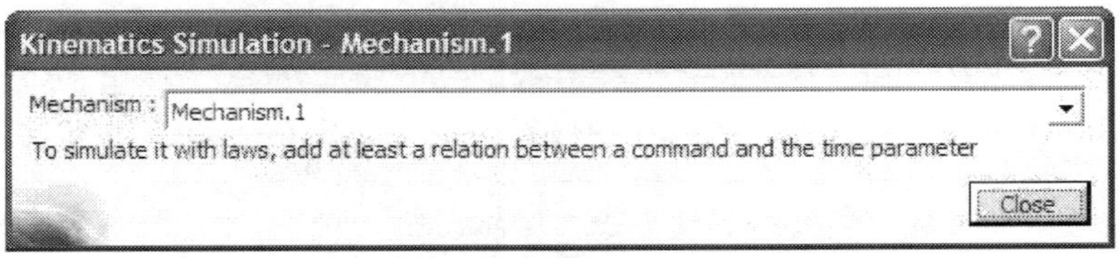

Select the **Formula** icon  from the **Knowledge** toolbar

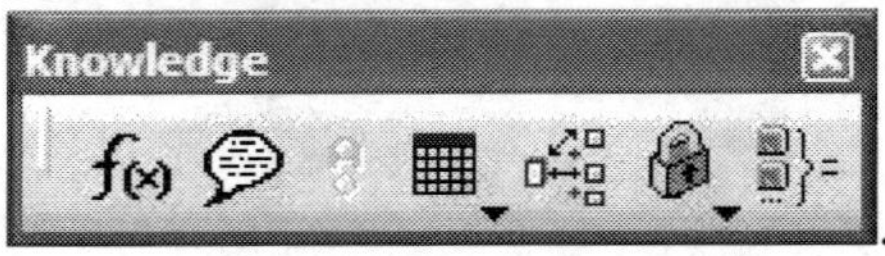

. The pop up box below appears on the screen.

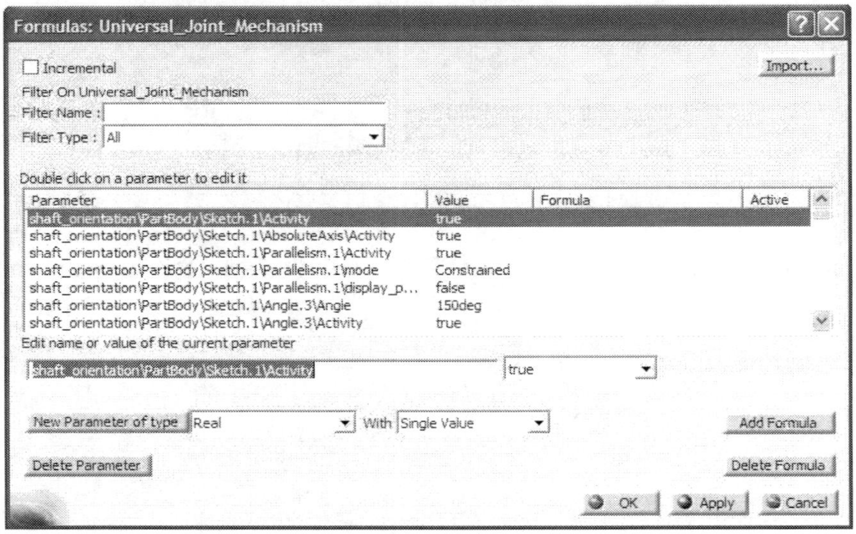

Point the cursor to the **Mechanism.1, DOF=0** branch in the tree and click. The consequence is that only parameters associated with the mechanism are displayed in the **Formulas** box.
The long list is now reduced to two parameters as indicated in the box.

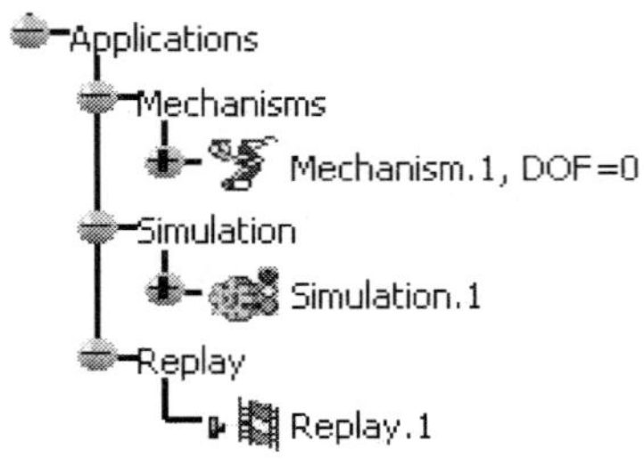

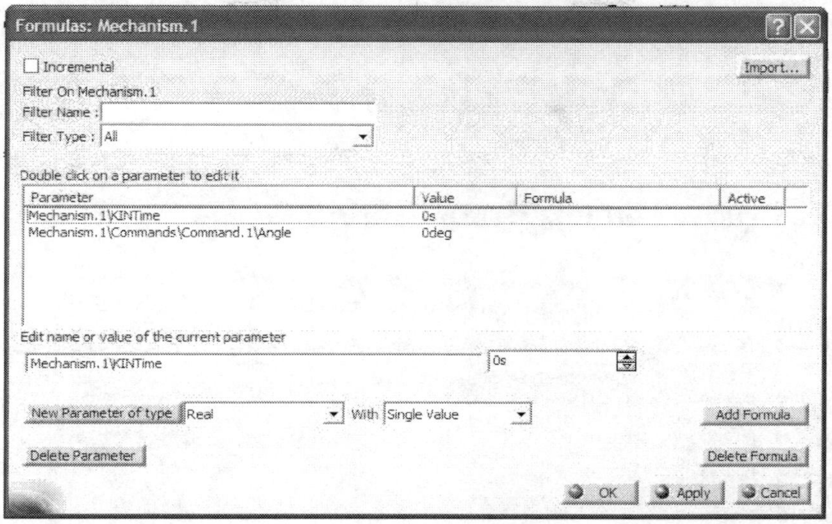

Select the entry **Mechanism.1\Commands\Command.1\Angle** and press the **Add Formula** button 

. This action kicks you to the **Formula Editor** box.

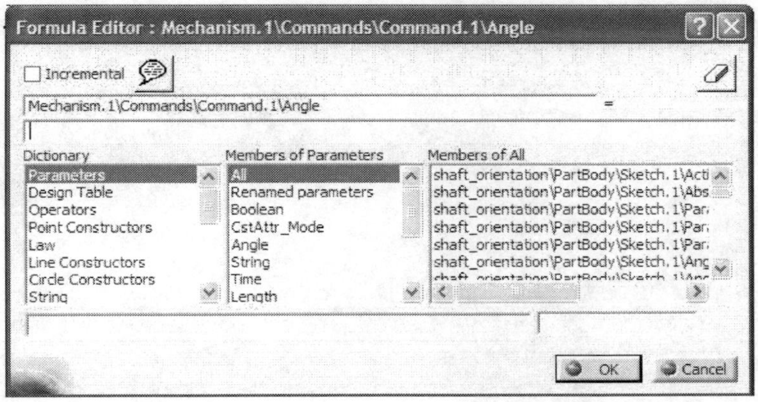

Pick the **Time** entry from the middle column (i.e. **Members of Parameters**).

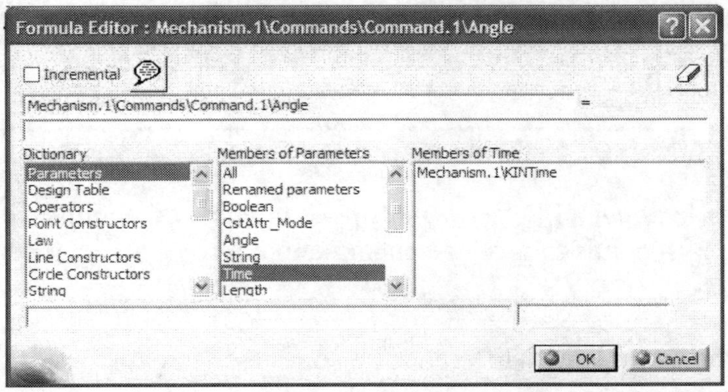

The right hand side of the equality should be such that the formula becomes

$$Mechanism.1 \backslash Commands \backslash Command.1 \backslash Angle =$$
$$(360\,\mathrm{deg}/1s) * Mechanism.1 \backslash KINTime$$

Therefore, the completed **Formula Editor** box becomes

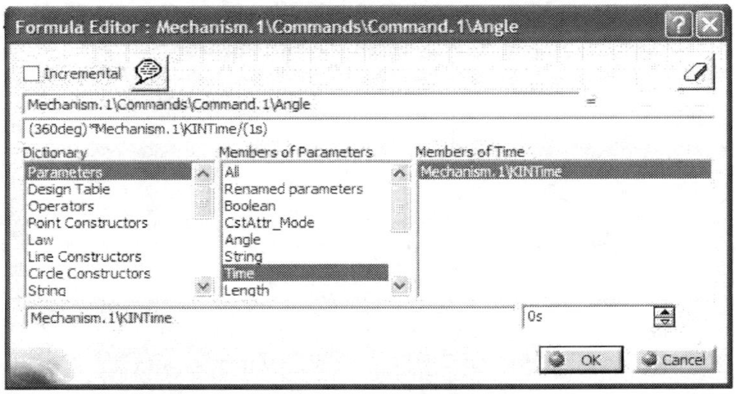

Upon accepting **OK**, the formula is recorded in the **Formulas** pop up box as shown below.

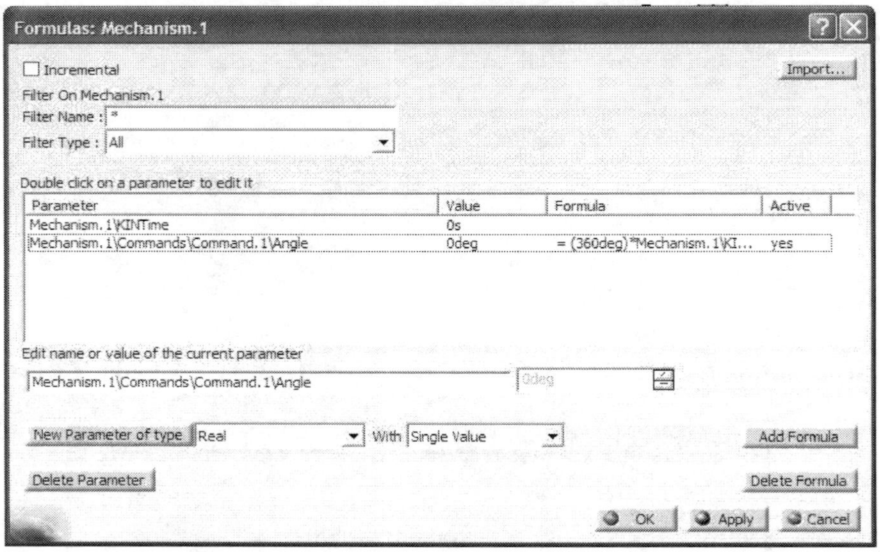

Note that the formula above effectively multiplies the desired angular velocity of 360 deg/s by time in seconds to produce an angle in degrees.

In the event that the formula has different units on the different sides of the equality you will get **Warning** messages such as the one shown below.

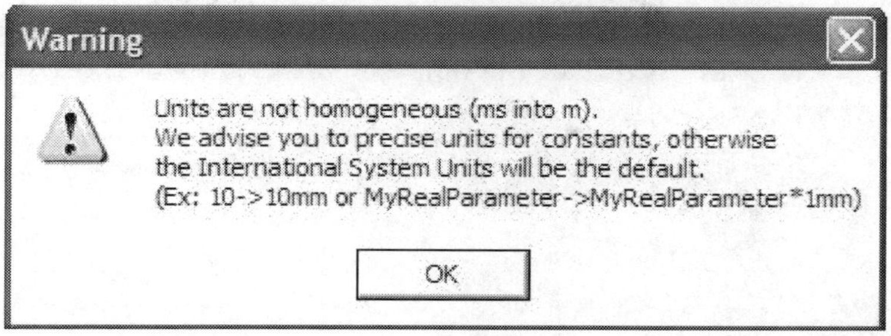

We are spared the warning message because the formula has been properly inputted. Note that the introduced law has appeared in the **Law** branch of the tree.

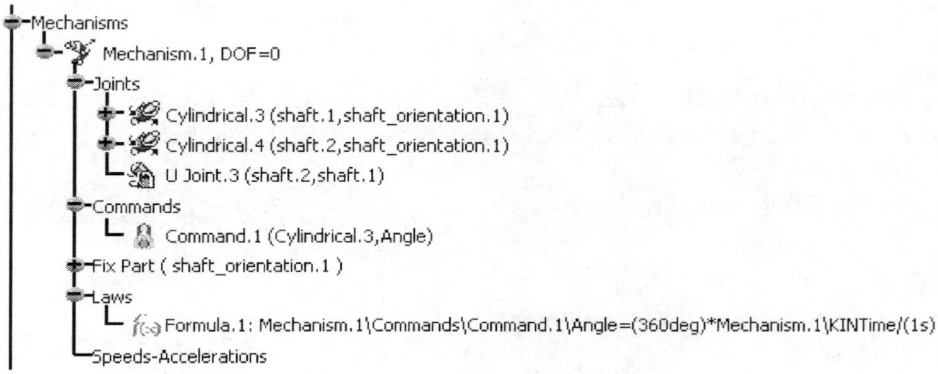

Keep in mind that our interest is to plot the angular velocity and angular acceleration of the output shaft generated by the constant angular velocity of the input shaft. This requires creating a speed and acceleration sensor.

Select the **Speed and Acceleration** icon  from the **DMU Kinematics** toolbar 

. The pop up box below appears on the Screen.

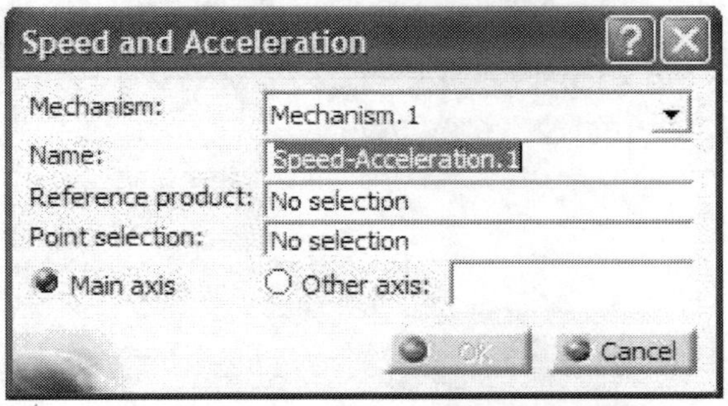

For the **Reference product,** select the **shaft_orientation** from the tree. For the **Point selection**, pick the vertex of the output shaft as shown in the sketch below. (Any point on the part will suffice).

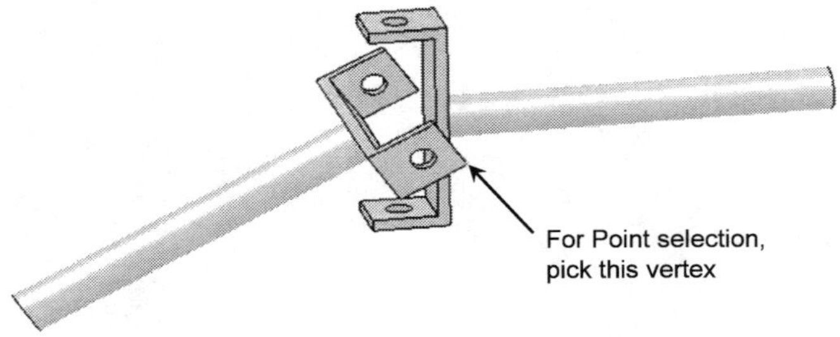

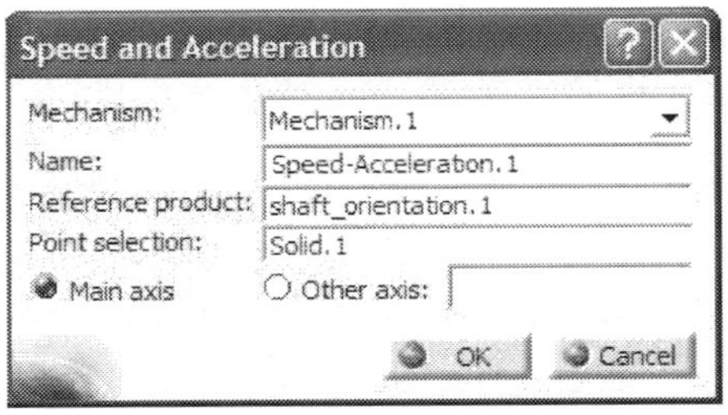

Click on **Simulation with Laws** icon  in the **Simulation** toolbar .

This results in the **Kinematics Simulation** pop up box shown below.

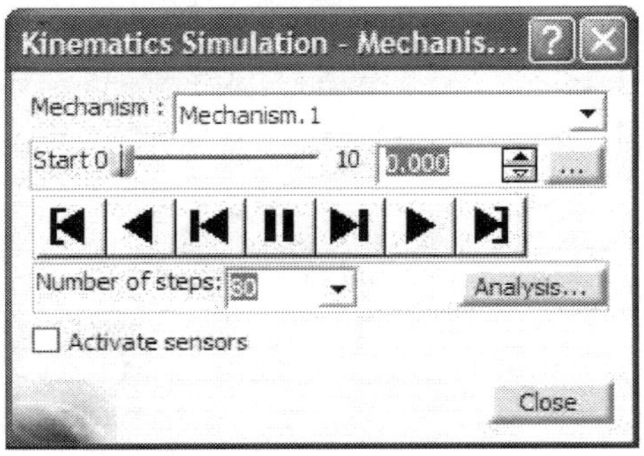

Note that the default time duration is 10 seconds.
To change this value, click on the button . In the resulting pop up box, change the time duration to 1s.

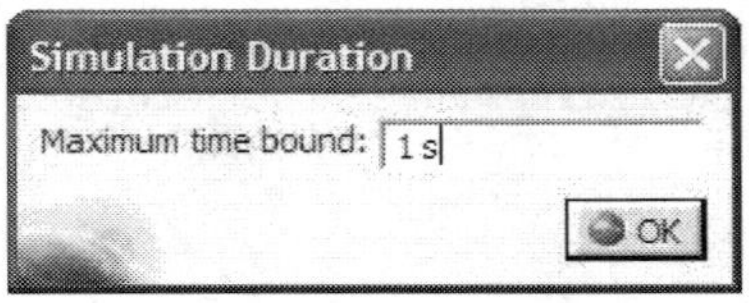

The scroll bar now moves up to 1s.

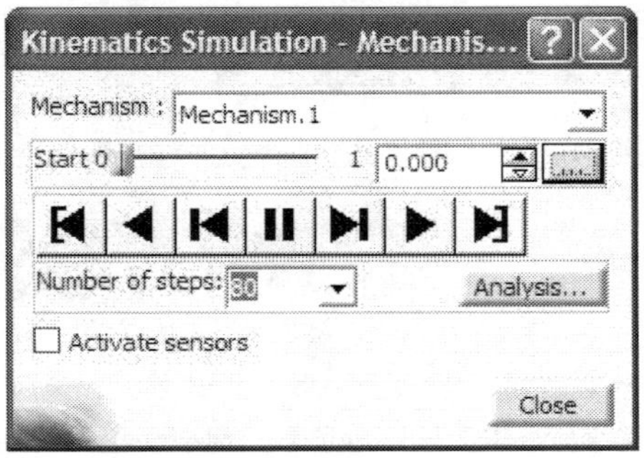

Check the **Activate sensors** box, at the bottom left corner.

You will next have to make certain selections from the accompanying **Sensors** box to indicate the kinematics parameters you would like to compute and store results on.

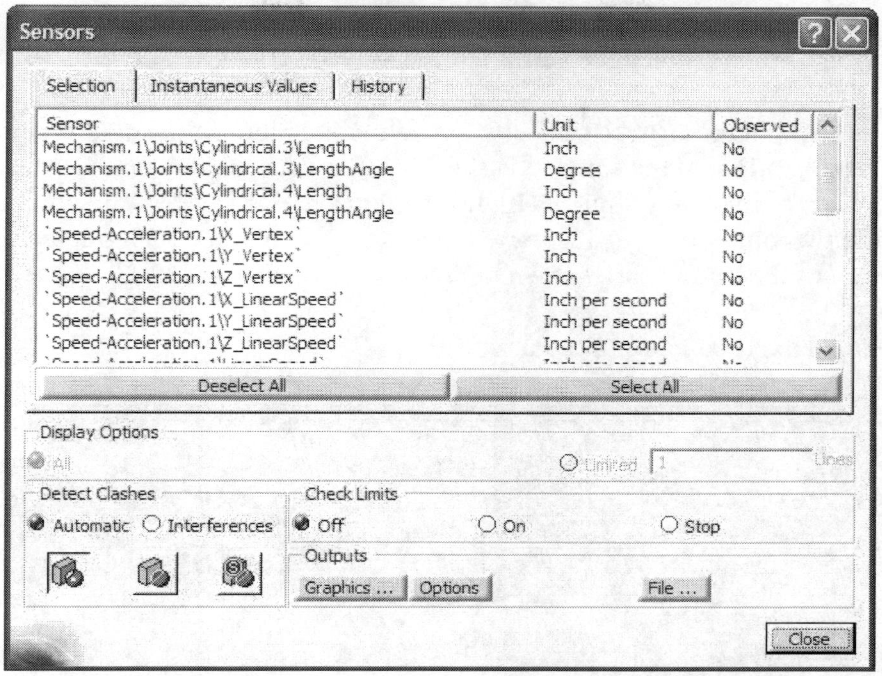

Click on the following items

Speed-Acceleration.1\Angular Speed
Speed-Acceleration.1\Angular Acceleration

As you make these selections, the last column in the **Sensors** box, changes to **Yes** for the corresponding items. This is shown below.

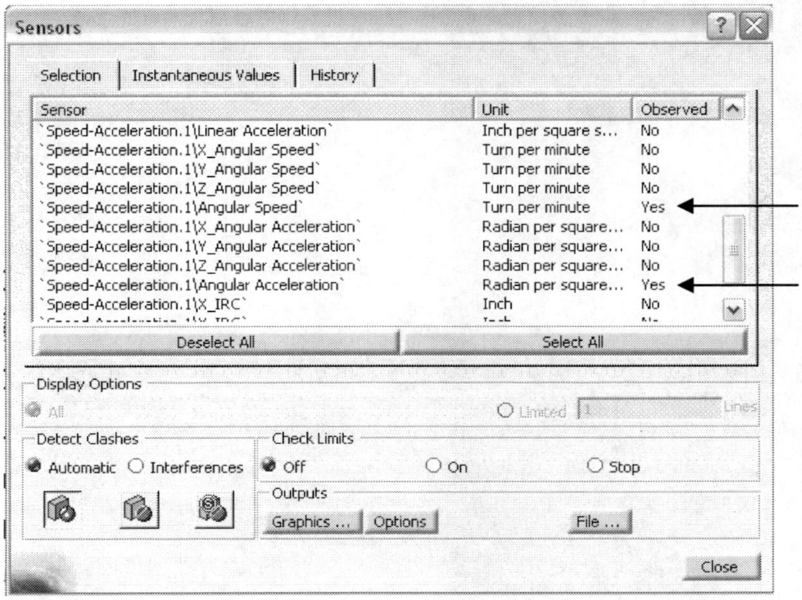

At this point, drag the scroll bar in the **Kinematics Simulation** box. As you do this, the shafts begin to rotate. Once the scroll bar reaches the end, click on **Graphics** button

in the **Sensor** box. The result is the plot of the angular velocity and the angular acceleration on the same axis (but with the vertical axis units corresponding to whichever one of the two outputs is highlighted in the right side of the window). Click on each of the two outputs to see the corresponding axis units for each output. The plots scaled for each of the outputs are shown below.

With the vertical axis scaled for angular speed:

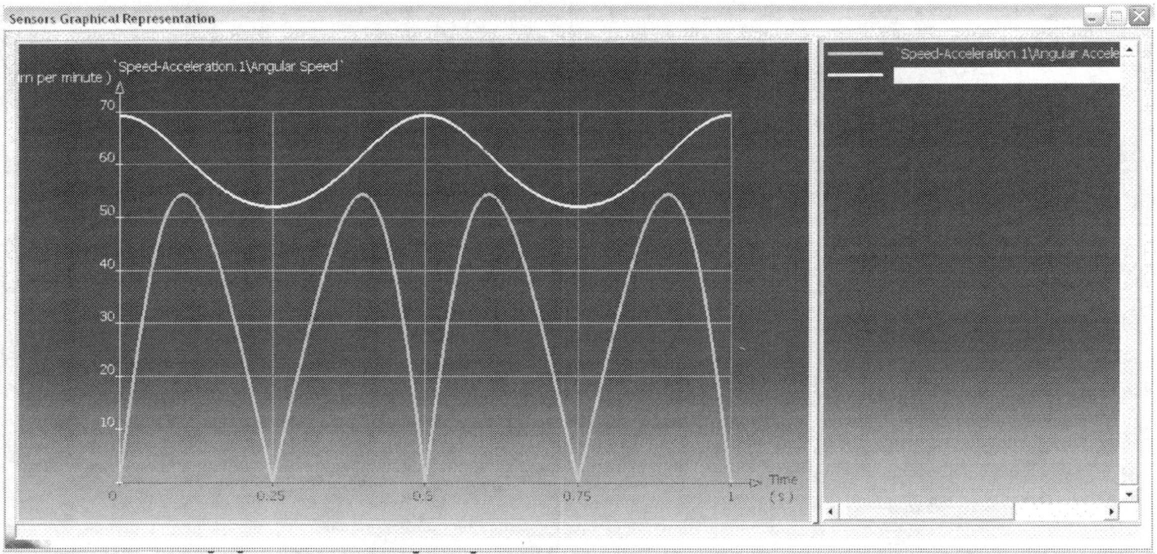

We can see that the range of the fluctuating output shaft angular speed agrees with the theoretical range of 52 to 69 rpm with the input shaft rotating at 60 rpm.

The plot with the vertical axis scaled for angular acceleration is show below.

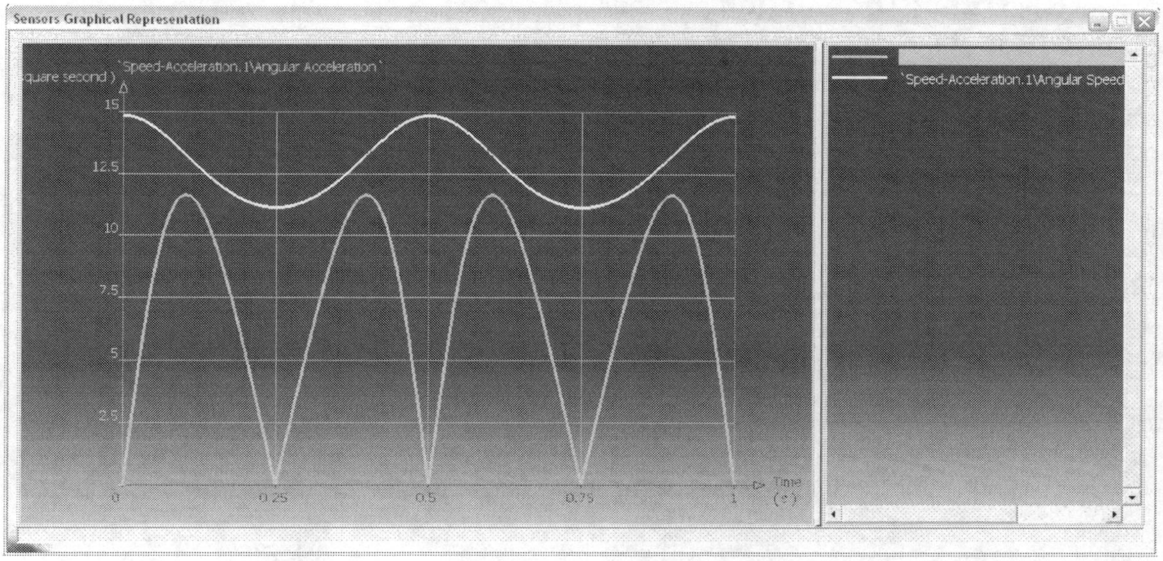

Note that net angular acceleration is always positive (it is computed as the square root of the sum of squares of the three perpendicular components).

In order to get magnitude and sign of the angular acceleration we could create an axis system on the **shaft_orientation** part with one of the principle axis directions being along the axis of the output shaft, and then we would choose that axis system when creating the sensor. If the appropriate components of angular velocity and angular acceleration are chosen, the signed angular acceleration plot can be produced. The detailed steps for this activity are not provided herein, but the following plot (with the vertical axis called for angular acceleration) shows the result one would obtain.

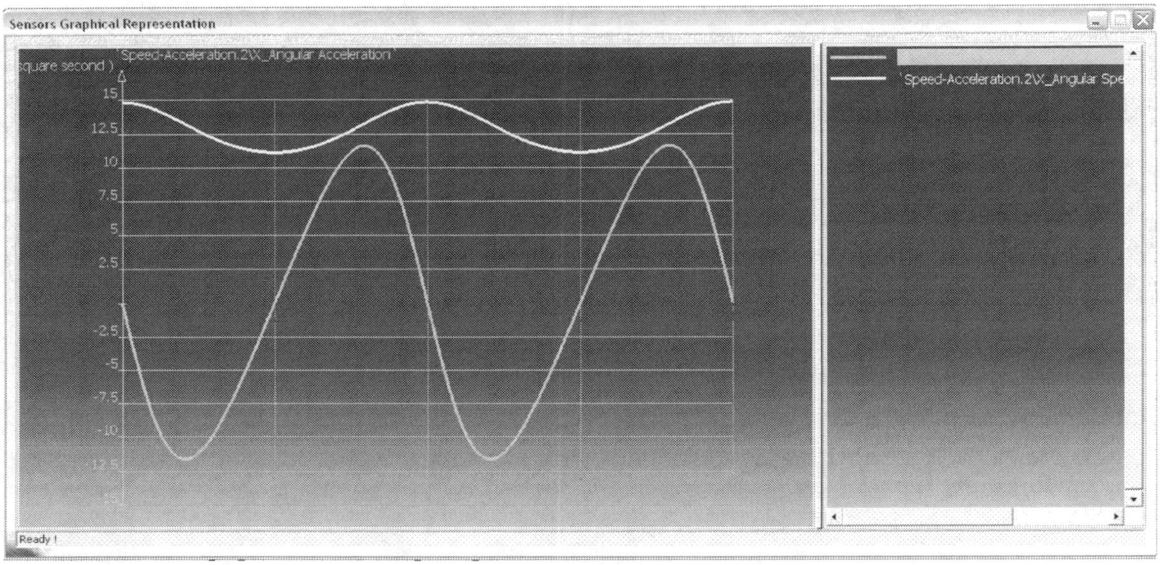

This concludes the tutorial.

Chapter 14

C-Clamp Mechanism

Introduction

In this tutorial you will model a C-clamp mechanism consisting of a fixed frame and a moving screw part.

1 Problem Statement

The purpose of this tutorial is to familiarize the reader with the screw joint. The joint is modeled as a part of a C-clamp mechanism as shown below. The parts are so simple that you can easily model them and therefore there is no need to specify dimensions. For our purposes, there is no need to attempt to model the actual threads.

The screw joint requires a line on each of the two parts where the translation takes place. Furthermore, you need to define the pitch in inches. The pitch variable is the distance that the screw tip advances upon one turn of the screw. A screw joint can be defined as either length driven or as angle driven. The objective here is to simulate the motion of the clamp through several turns of the handle.

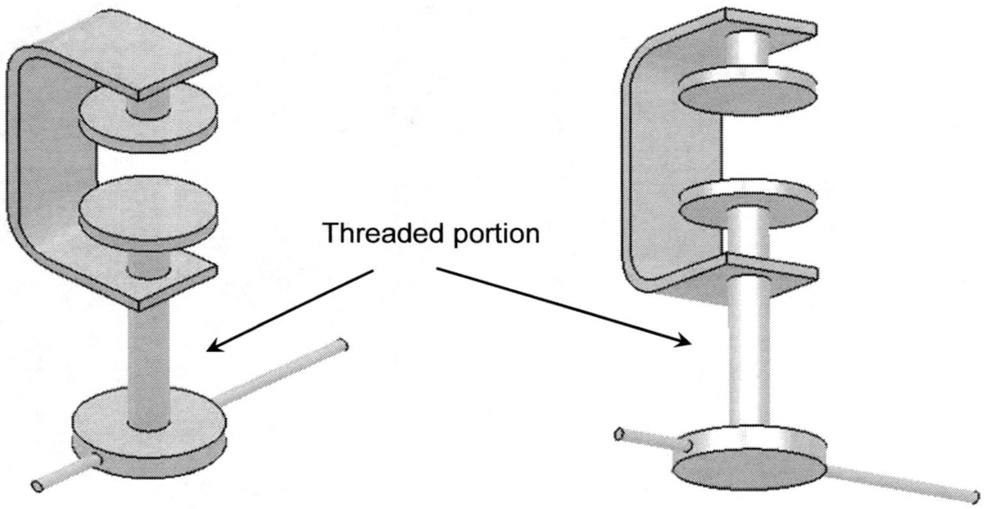

2 Overview of this Tutorial

In this tutorial you will:

1. Model the two CATIA parts required.
2. Create an assembly (CATIA Product) containing the parts.
3. Constrain the assembly to a position representing the full open position of the clamp.
4. Enter the **Digital Mockup** workbench and manually create the screw joint.
5. Simulate the relative motion of the screw without consideration to time.

3 Creation of the Assembly in Mechanical Design Solutions

In CATIA, model two parts named **frame** and **screw** as shown below. The detailed dimensions of the parts are not important. In an actual C-clamp, the upper disc on the screw is typically a separate part connected by a ball and socket type of joint. Since our emphasis in this tutorial is on the screw joint, we simply model that disc as part of the screw. The handle is added to aid in the visualization as the screw rotates and advances.

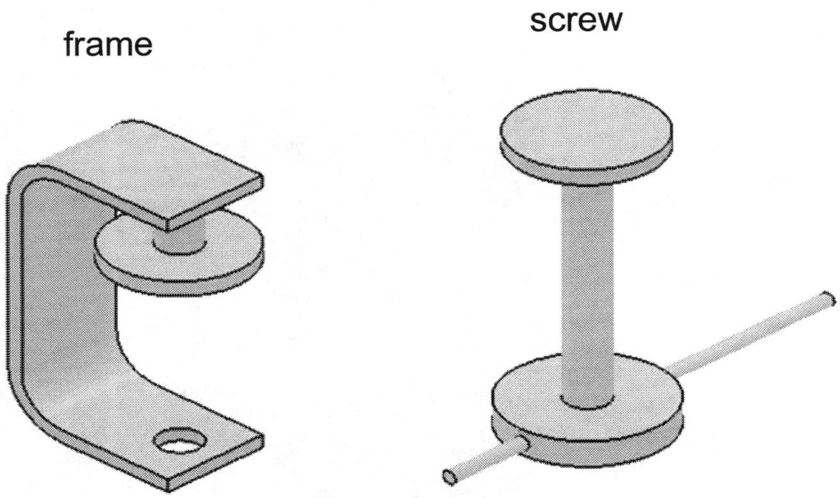

Once the parts are modeled, the next step is to create the assembly (CATIA Product).

Enter the **Assembly Design** workbench which can be achieved by different means depending on your CATIA customization. For example, from the standard Windows toolbar, select **File > New** . From the box shown on the right, select **Product**. This moves you to the **Assembly Design** workbench and creates an assembly with the default name **Product.1**.

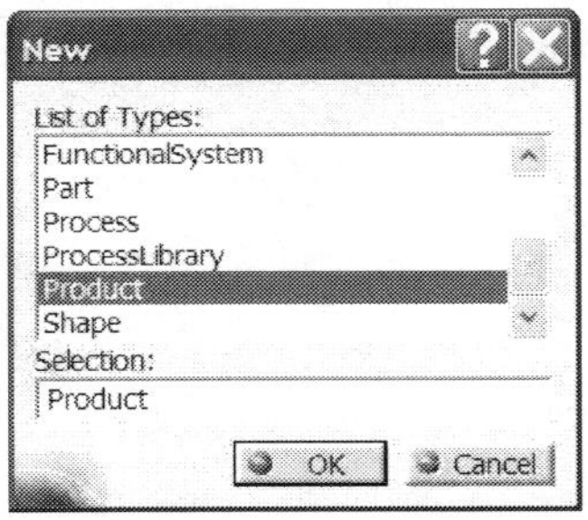

In order to change the default name, move the cursor to **Product.1** in the tree, right click and select **Properties** from the menu list.

From the **Properties** box, select the **Product** tab and in **Part Number** type **C-clamp**.

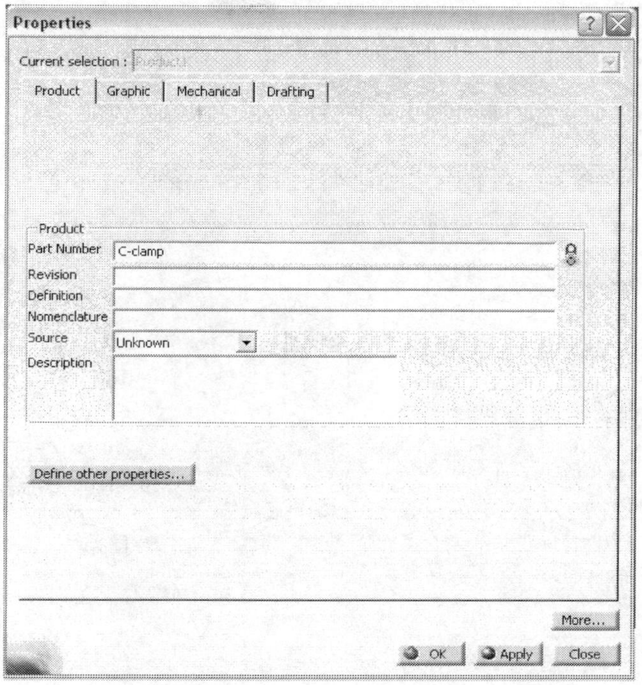

This will be the new product name throughout the chapter. The tree on the top left corner of your computer screen should look as displayed below.

To add the two parts to the assembly, select **Insert > Existing Component** or the corresponding icon .

From the **File Selection** pop up box choose **frame**, and **screw**. Remember that in CATIA multiple selections are made with the **Ctrl** key.
The tree is modified to indicate that the parts have been inserted.

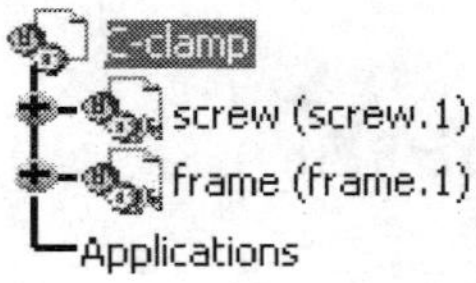

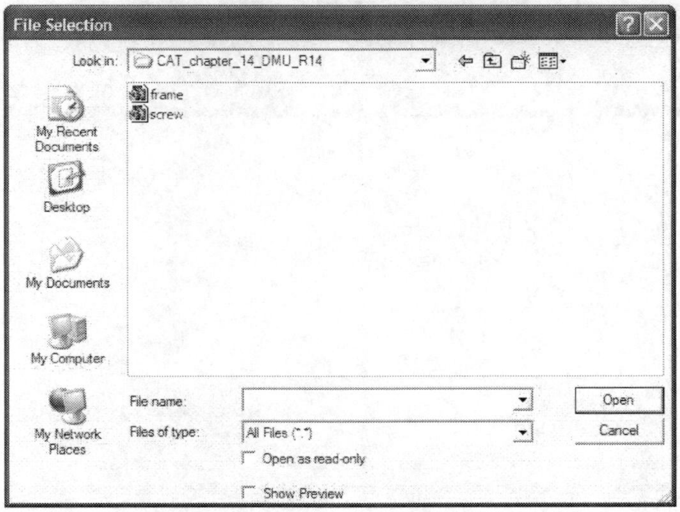

Depending on how the parts were created, they may appear overlapping with each other. This can make the picks during the constraining process difficult.

To make the tasks easier, you can use the **Manipulation** icon  from the **Move** toolbar 

to rearrange them to a more convenient configuration.

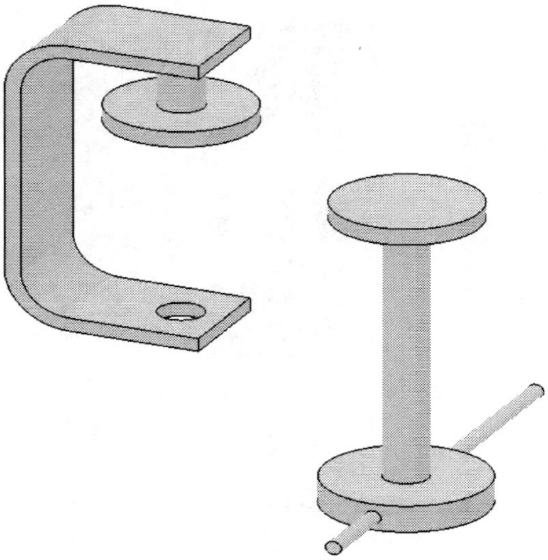

The next task is to impose assembly constraints. We will begin by anchoring the frame. This part will serve as our inertial reference.

Select the **Fix Component** icon  from the **Constraints** toolbar 

. Pick the **frame** from the screen or from the tree.

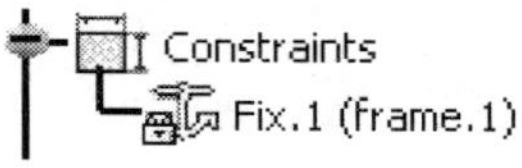

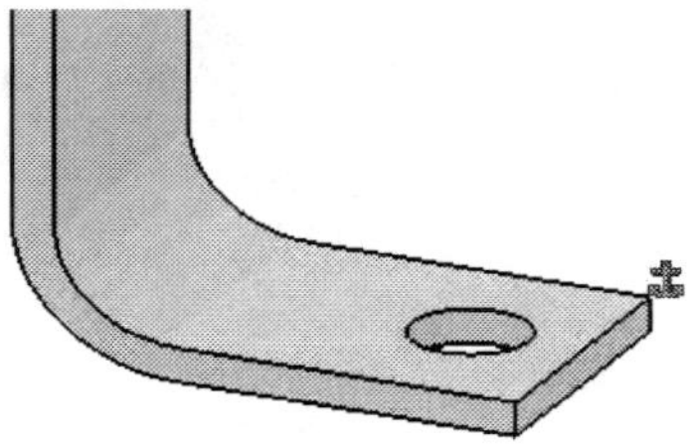

We would like to constrain the screw into the location it would be in at the full open position of the clamp. This will be done with two constraints: a coincident constraint between the centerline of the screw and the centerline of the lower hole in the frame, and a contact constraint to locate the position along the coincident centerlines. To apply the coincident constraint, pick the **Coincidence** icon  from **Constraints** toolbar and select the axes of the **frame** and the **screw** as shown.

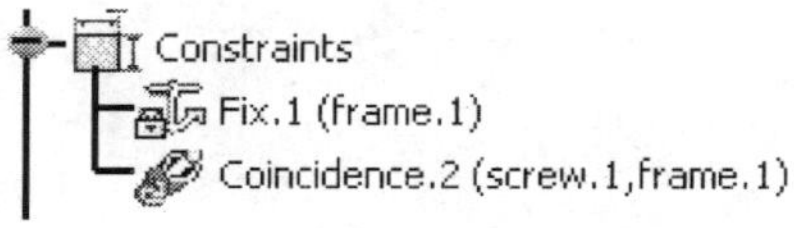

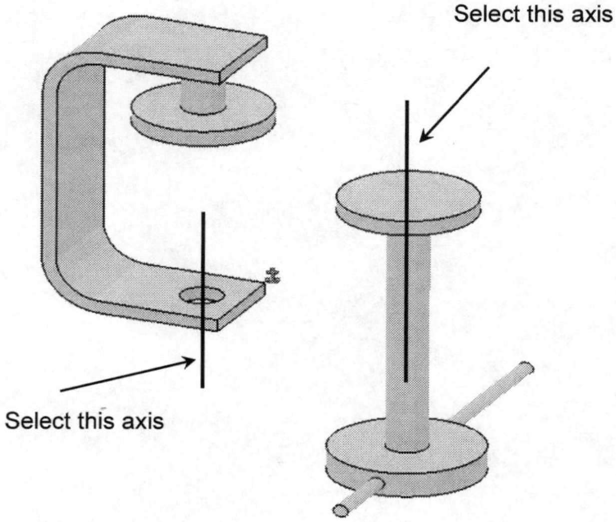

Use the **Update** icon  to check your constraints.

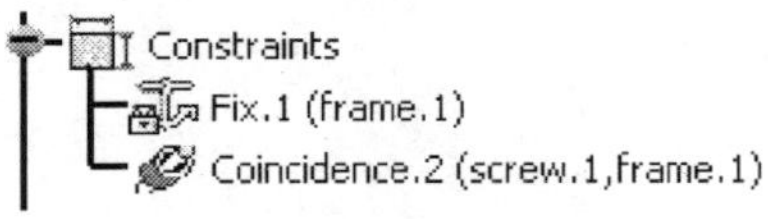

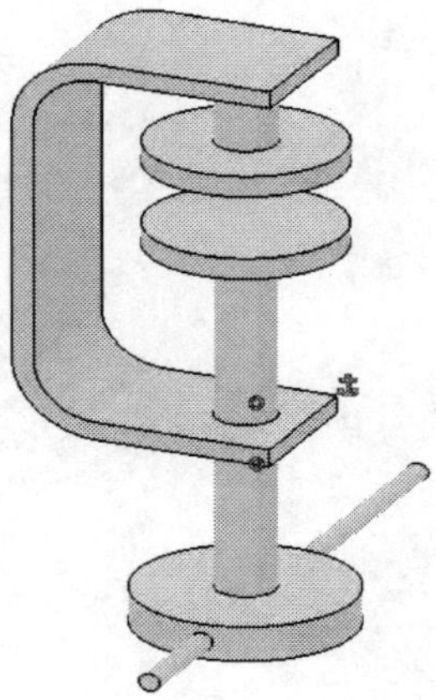

Now pick the **Contact** icon  from the **Constraints** toolbar and select the surfaces of the **frame** and the **screw** as shown on the right.

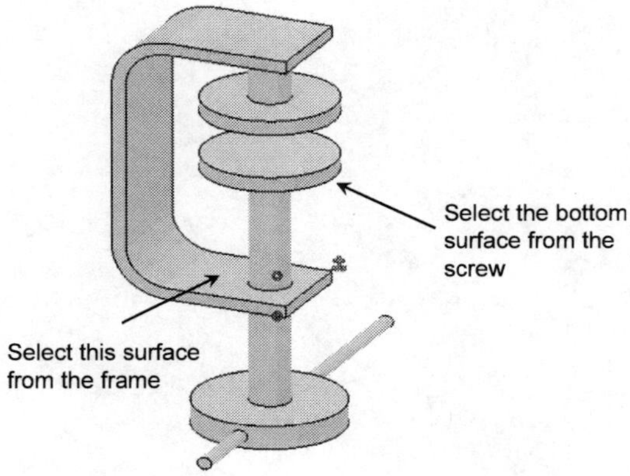

Use the **Update** icon  to check your constraints.

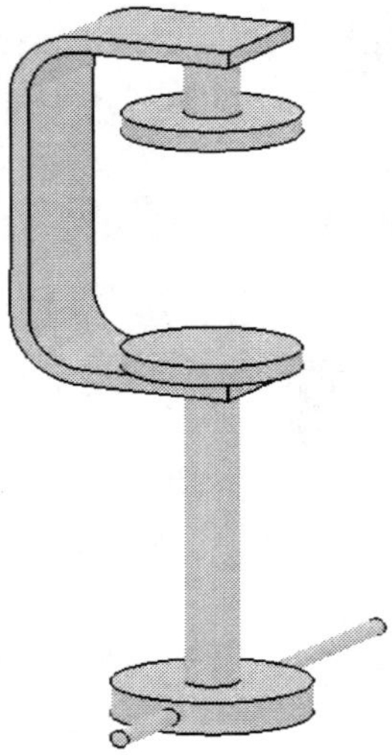

The purpose of the constraints applied was to position the parts to the appropriate position so that we can manually create the **Screw Joint** in the **Digital Mock Up**. The screw joint cannot be made by automatic assembly constraints conversion, but does require the two parts involved in the joint to be located in a feasible starting position.

4 Creating Joints in the Digital Mockup Workbench

The **Digital Mockup** workbench is quite extensive but we will only deal with the **DMU Kinematics module**. To get there you can use the standard Windows toolbar as shown below: **Start > Digital Mockup > DMU Kinematics**.

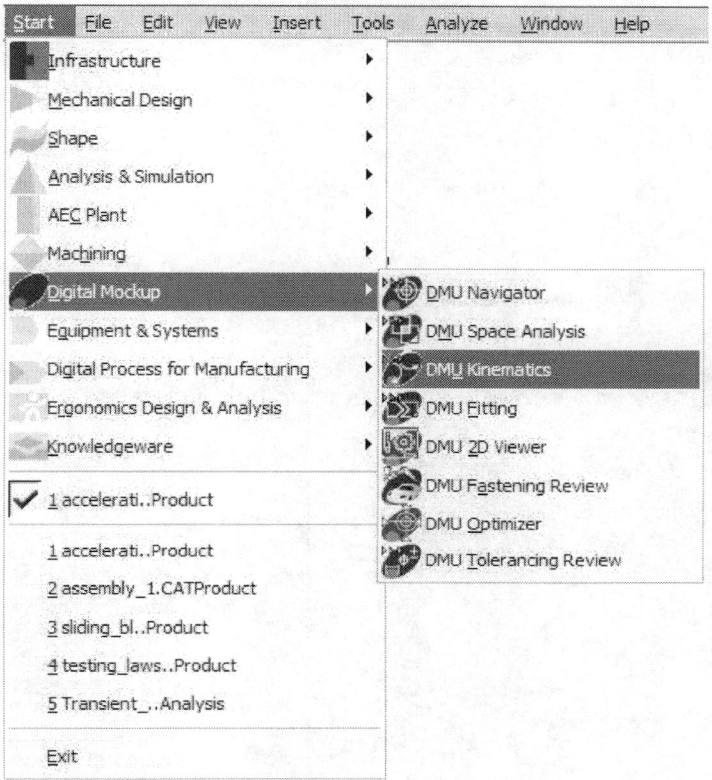

As mentioned earlier, we will create the screw joint manually. To do so, select the

Screw Joint icon  from the **Kinematics Joints** toolbar

.

The pop up box shown below allows you to specify the joint characteristics.

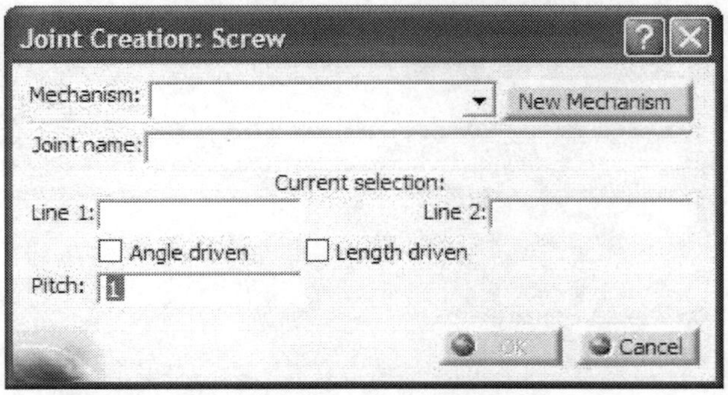

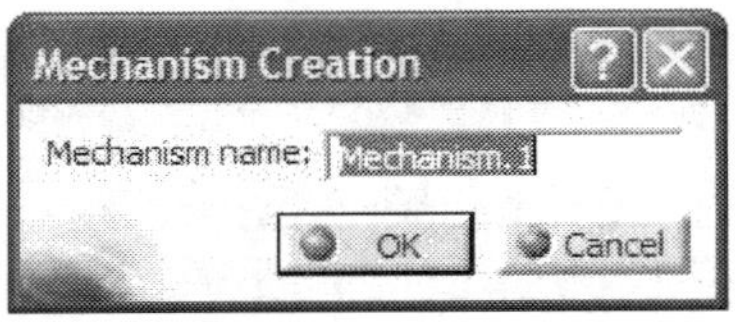

Click on the **New Mechanism** button  in this box. At this point you have the option of naming the mechanism. Keep the default name **Mechanism**.1 and close the box.

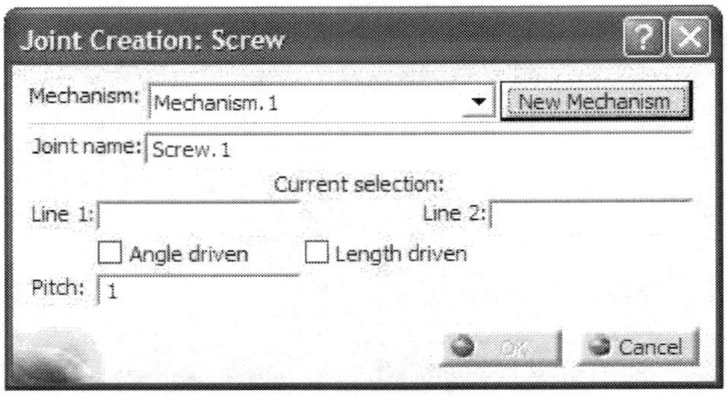

For **Line 1** and **Line 2** make the selections shown below and use a reasonable **Pitch** value for the dimensions of your parts.

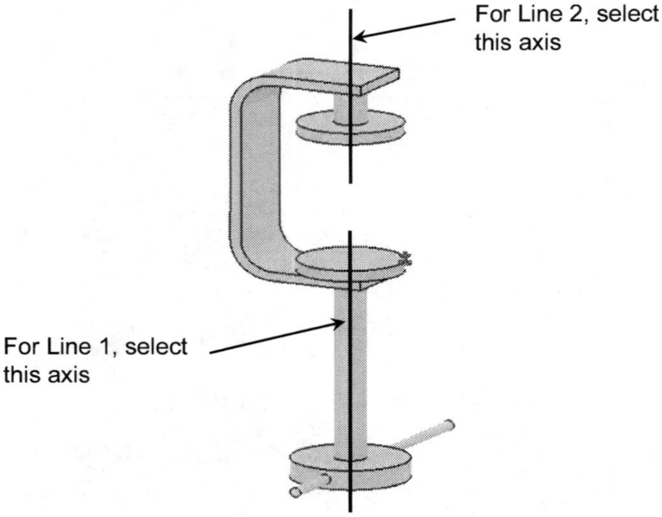

Keep in mind that pitch represents the number of inches per turn. However, as far as the authors can determine, CATIA will assume units on the pitch of mm/turn regardless of your choice of length units or units on Angular feed rate. We will select a pitch of 10mm/turn (equivalent to 0.3937 in/turn).

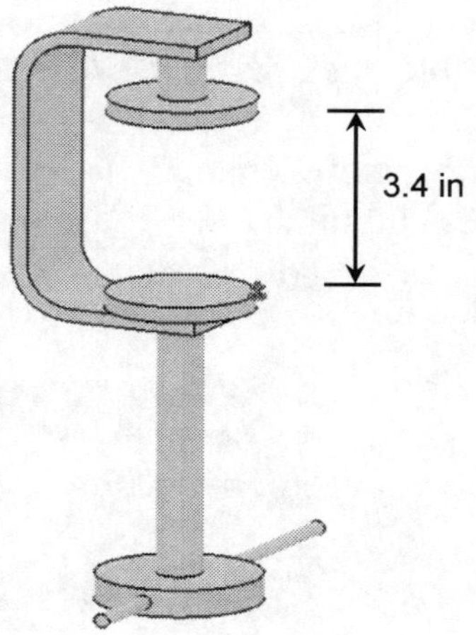

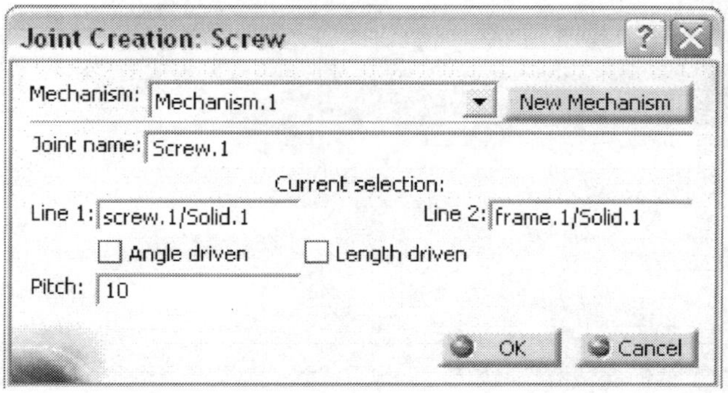

Note that although the frame was anchored at the assembly level, this information is not reflected in the joints.

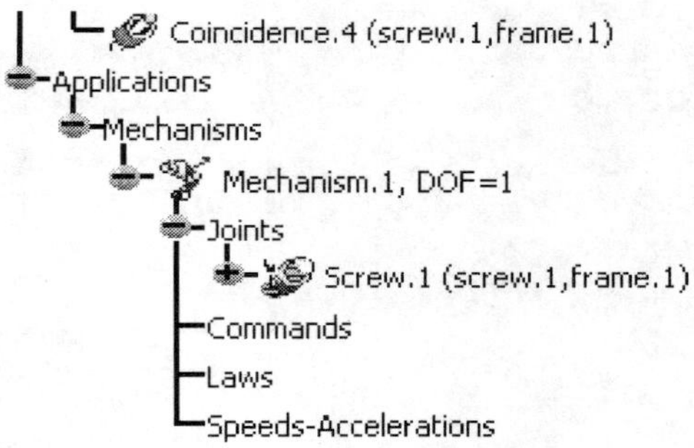

Pick the **Fixed Part** icon  from the **DMU Kinematics** toolbar

and select the **frame**.

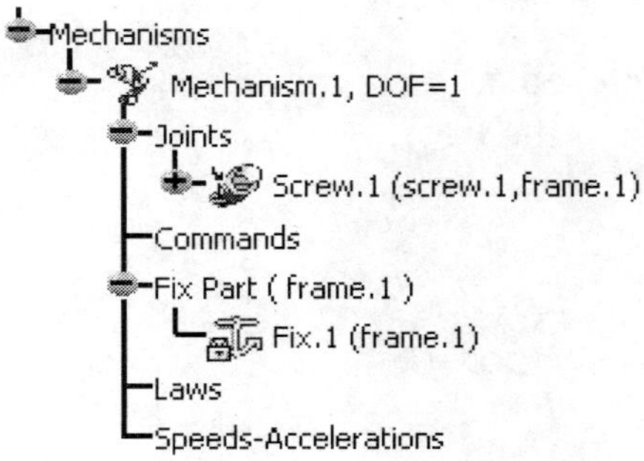

At this point, the degree of freedom is one and by specifying a command the mechanism can be simulated. This can be done by making the screw and **Angle driven** joint. Double click on the **Screw.1 Joint** branch and select the angle driven option.

Furthermore, change the limits to represent a reasonable number of turns for your part sizes and pitch. We'll use 6 turns (2160 degrees) of the screw.

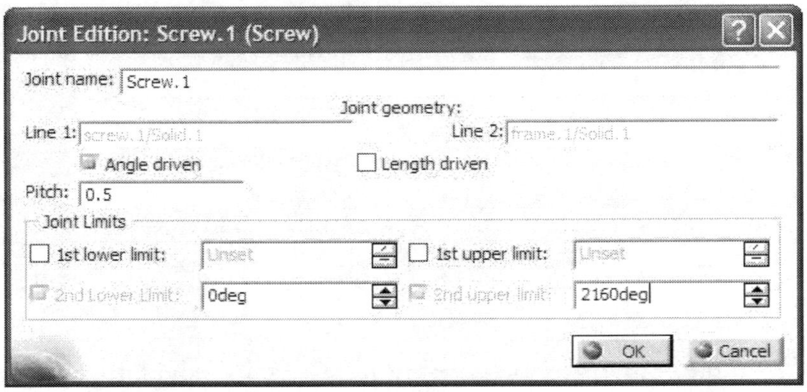

Upon closing the above box, you get the message "**The mechanism can be simulated**".

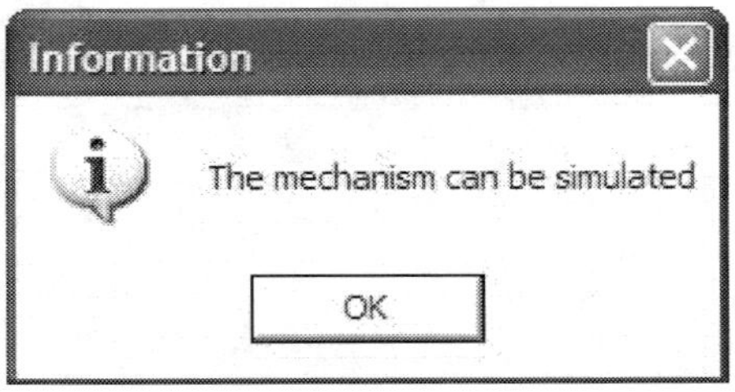

To simulate the C-clamp motion, select the **Simulation** icon  from the **DMU Generic Animation** toolbar 

. This enables you to choose the mechanism to be animated if there are several present. In this case, select Mechanism.1 and close the window.

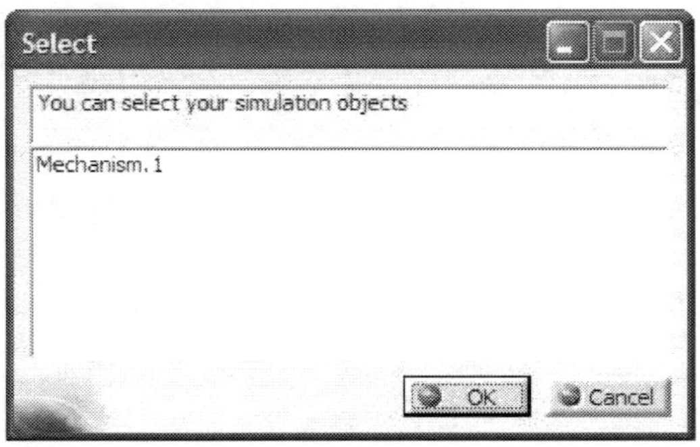

As soon as the window is closed, a Simulation branch is added to the tree.

In addition, the two pop up boxes shown below appear.

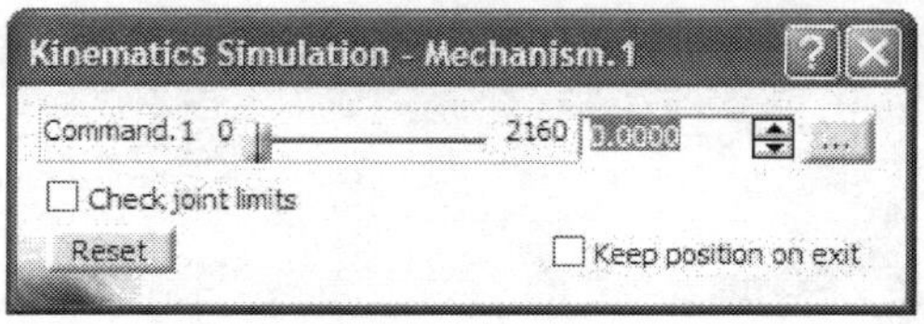

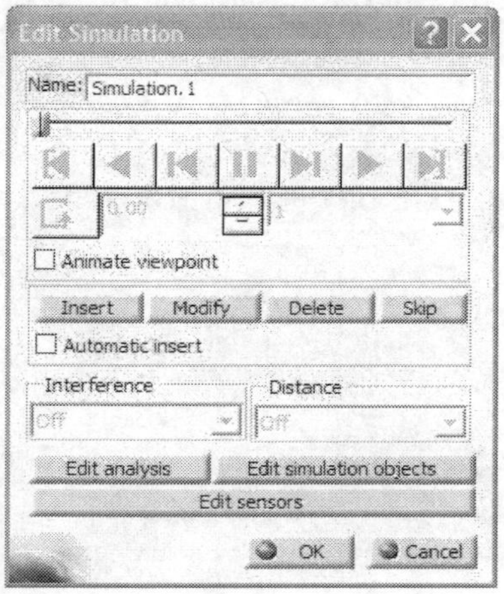

As you scroll the bar from left to right, the screw begins to turn, however, it may be moving in the wrong direction as indicted below.

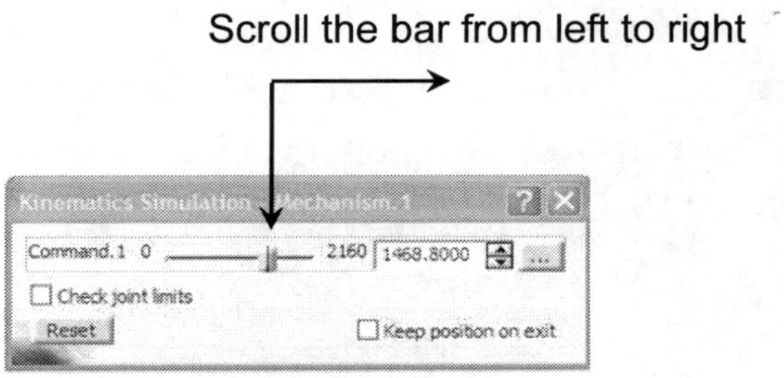

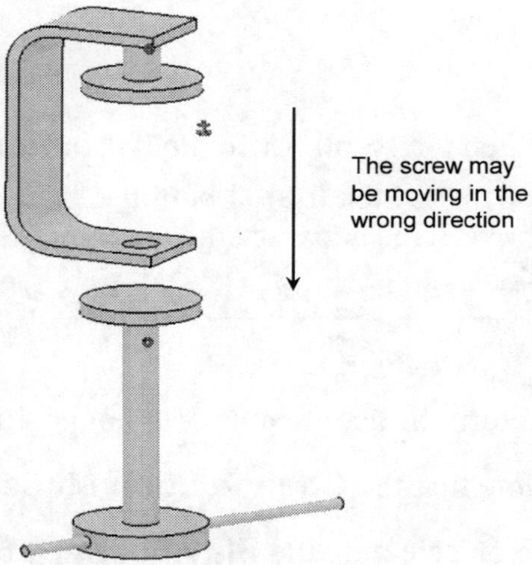

If this happens, double click on the **Screw.1 Joint** branch in the tree and click on the arrow on the screw to change the positive direction of the joint. Also key in the lower limit of 0 deg if this is no longer the value shown.

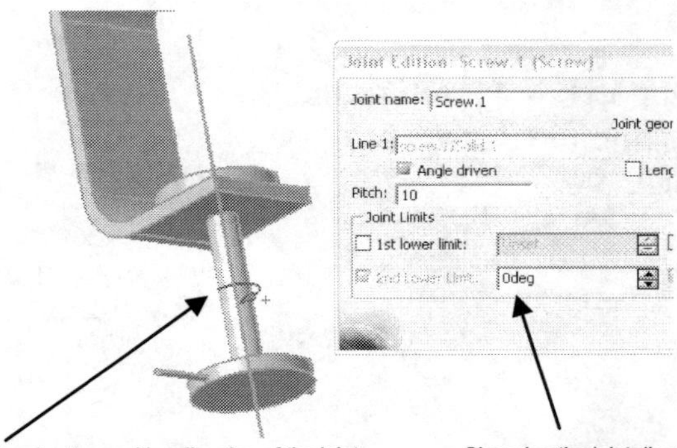

Clicking on this arrow toggles the positive direction of the joint. A positive value of pitch is consistent with a right hand thread (you would use a negative pitch for a left thread).

Changing the joint direction may cause the lower limit to read Unset. If so, change it to 0 deg.

Now if you open the simulation again and scroll the bar from left to right, the screw begins to turn and advances in the proper direction.

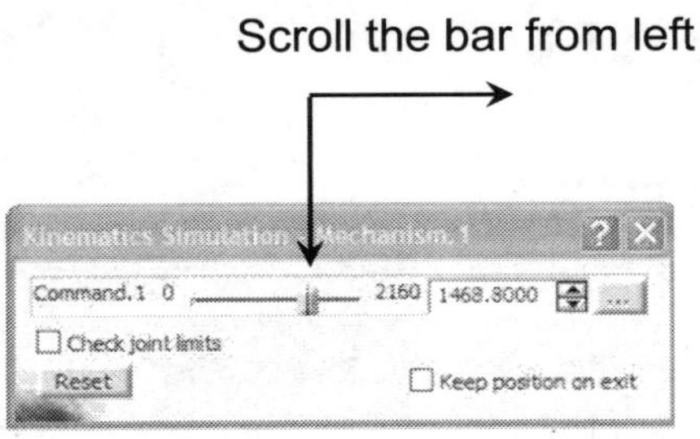

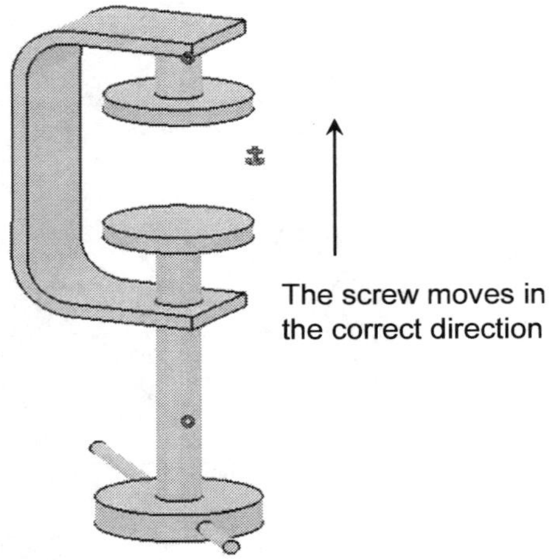

When the scroll bar in the **Kinematics Simulation** pop up box reaches the left extreme end, select the **Insert** button [Insert] in the **Edit Simulation** pop up box shown above. This activates the video player buttons shown

.

Return the screw to its original position by picking the **Jump to Start** button.

Note that the **Change Loop Mode** button is also active now.

Upon selecting the **Play Forward** button, the screw makes a fast jump to the frame.

In order to slow down the motion of the screw, select a different **interpolation step**, such as 0.04.

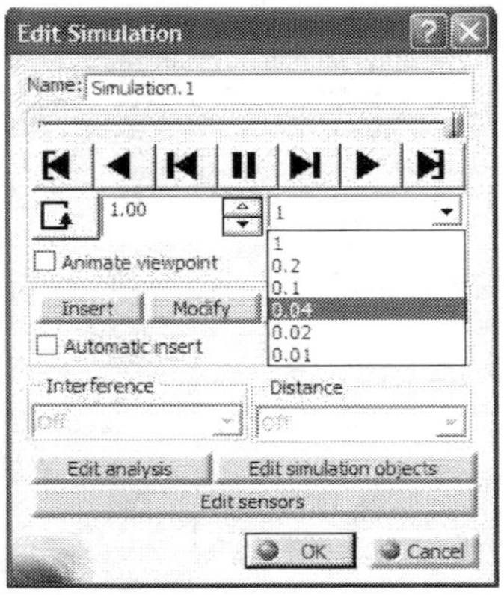

Upon changing the interpolation step to 0 0.04, return the block to its original position by picking the **Jump to Start** button. Apply **Play Forward** button and observe the slow and smooth translation of the screw.

This concludes the tutorial.

Chapter 15

A Mechanism Involving Coriolis Acceleration

Introduction

This tutorial deals with a two degree of freedom mechanism which involves a Coriolis acceleration. This problem is analogous to a person walking radially outward on a spinning carousel. The two degrees of freedom (one can be thought of as representing the spinning of the carousel and one as representing the walking motion radially outward) are tied to the time variable resulting in a mechanism that can be simulated. For simplicity's sake, we'll model a sliding collar on a rotating arm rather than a person on a carousel.

1 Problem Statement

A collar is sliding along a bar which is itself rotating about one end. The linear velocity of the bar along the arm is 6 in/s and the angular velocity of the arm is 360 deg/s (or 60 rpm). The collar experiences Coriolis acceleration throughout the motion. The dimensions of the problem are irrelevant to the goal of merely simulating such a mechanism. The goal is to plot the X and Y components of acceleration of a point on the collar for the first 1 s of motion.

The two degrees of freedom in this mechanism are the radial location of the collar along the arm and the angular position of the arm. The joints involved in this mechanism are a revolute joint due to the rotation of the arm and a prismatic joint due to the translation of the collar along the arm. By making the revolute joint angle driven, and the prismatic joint length driven, the degrees of freedom are reduced to zero.

Although at this point the mechanism can be simulated, two scroll bars are present in Kinematics Simulation pop up box. Each of the commands (angle driven and length driven) can be imposed individually but not simultaneously. By bringing in the time parameter, the two motions are tied together.

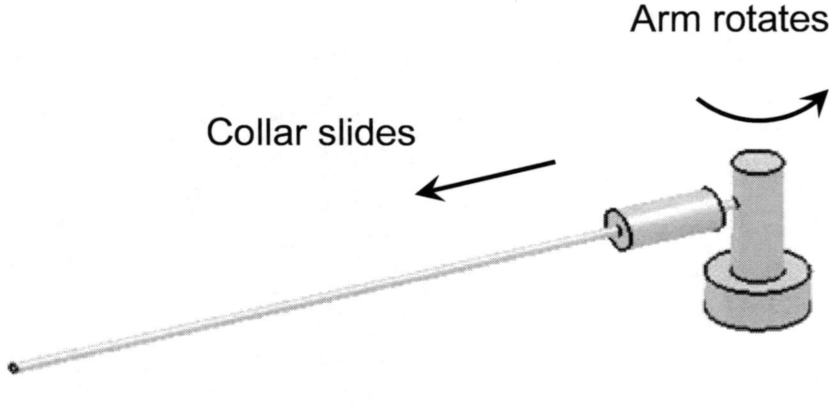

2 Overview of this Tutorial

This tutorial will involve the following steps:

1. Modeling the three CATIA parts required.
2. Creating an assembly (CATIA Product) containing the parts and constraining them consistent with the desired revolute and prismatic joints.
3. Entering the **Digital Mockup** workbench and converting the assembly constraints into a revolute and a prismatic joint.
4. Simulating the relative motion of the assembly without consideration to time (in other words, without implementing the time based linear velocity given in the problem statement) and with separate control (sliders) of the two joints.
5. Adding a formula to implement the time based kinematics.
6. Simulating the desired simultaneous constant angular velocity of the revolute and constant linear velocity of the prismatic joint.
7. Generating a plot of the resulting X and Y components of acceleration and velocity of a desired point vs. time.

3 Creation of the Assembly in Mechanical Design Solutions

Model three parts named **base**, **arm** and **collar** as shown below. The only suggested dimension is the length of the arm which is 8 inches. It is assumed that you are sufficiently familiar with CATIA to model these parts fairly quickly.

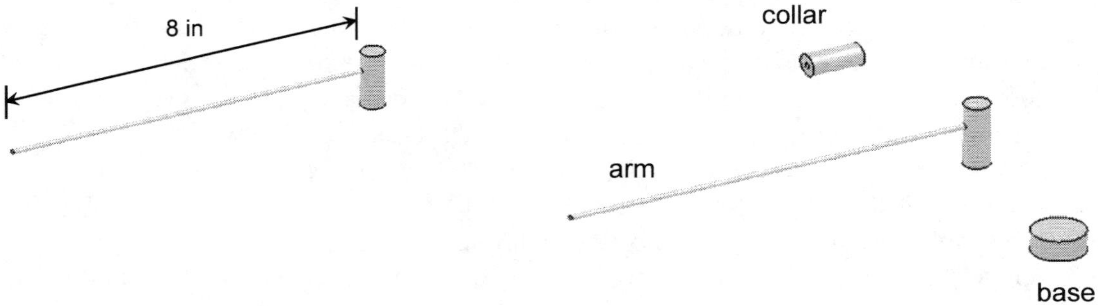

Once the parts are modeled, it is time to assemble them.

Enter the **Assembly Design** workbench which can be achieved by different means depending on your CATIA customization. For example, from the standard Windows toolbar, select **File > New** .
From the box shown on the right, select **Product**. This moves you to the **Assembly Design** workbench and creates an assembly with the default name **Product.1**.

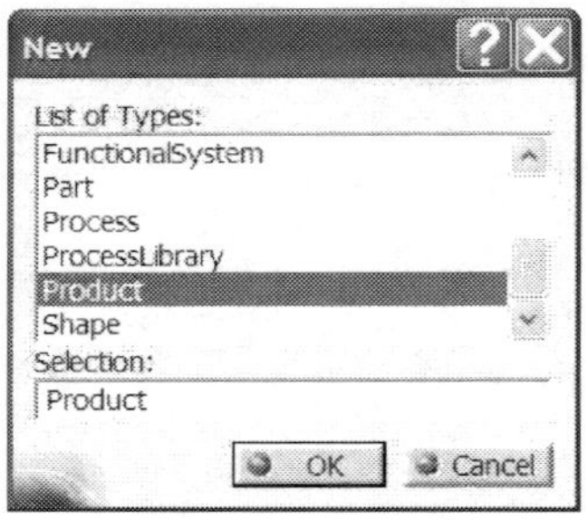

In order to change the default name, move the cursor to **Product.1** in the tree, right click and select **Properties** from the menu list.

From the **Properties** box, select the **Product** tab and in **Part Number** type **Coriolis_Acceleration**.

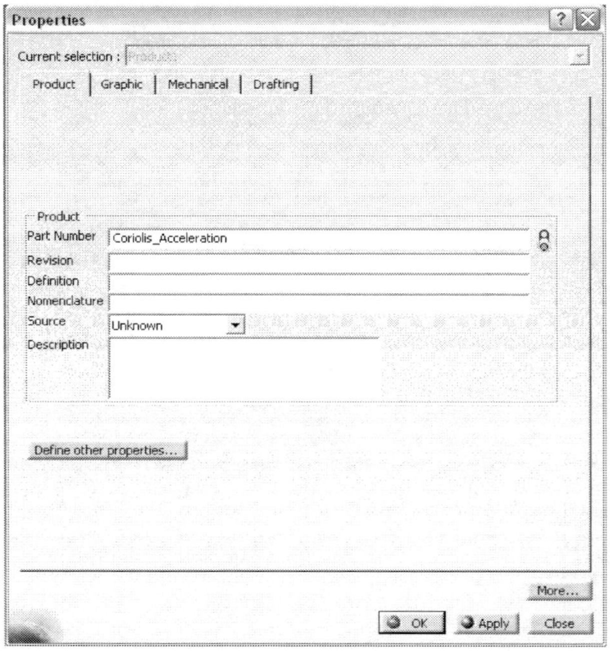

This will be the new product name throughout the chapter. The tree on the top left corner of your computer screen should look as displayed below.

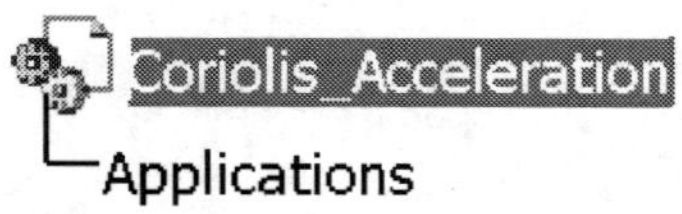

The next step is to insert the three parts into the assembly just created. From the standard Windows toolbar, select **Insert > Existing Component**. From the **File Selection** pop up box choose **arm**, **base** and **collar**. Remember that in CATIA multiple selections are made with the **Ctrl** key.
The tree is modified to indicate that the parts have been inserted.

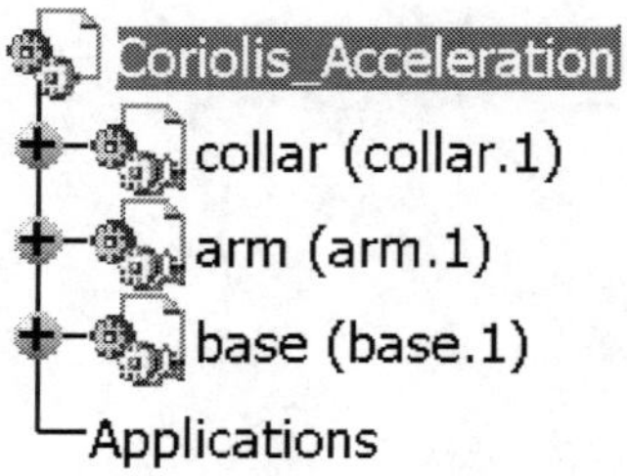

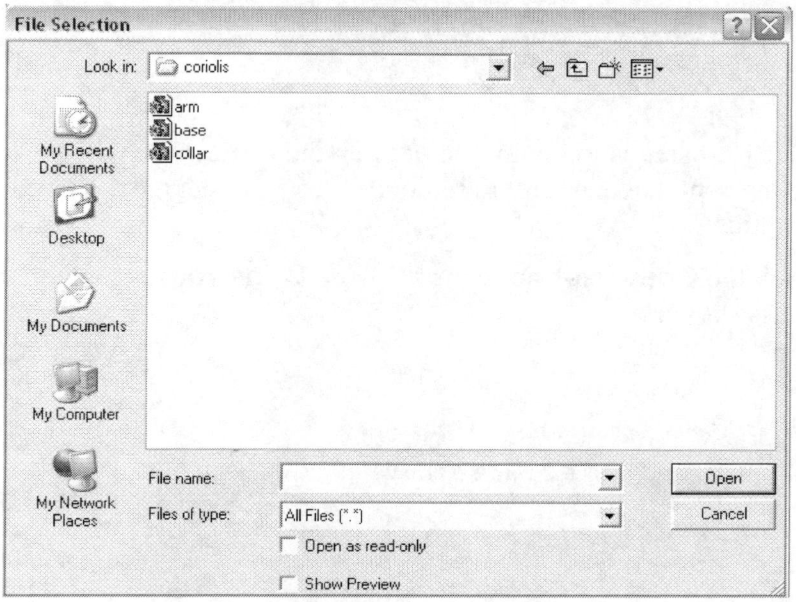

The three parts will appear on your screen. Keep in mind that the relative positioning of the parts on your screen depends on how they were generated. Most probably your parts overlap as is the case on the right.

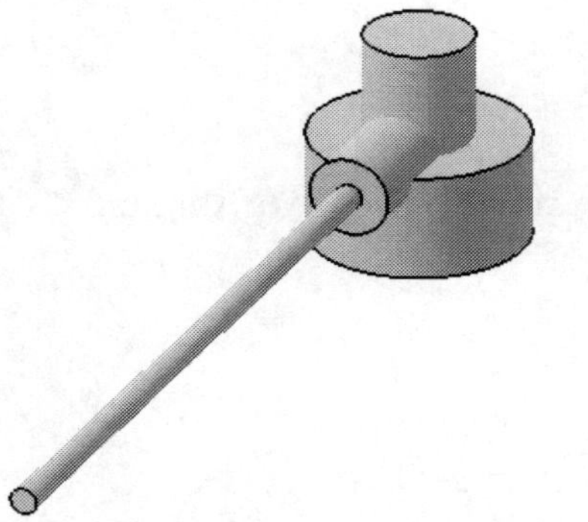

You can use the **Manipulation** icon  to separate the parts to make it easier to apply assembly constraints.

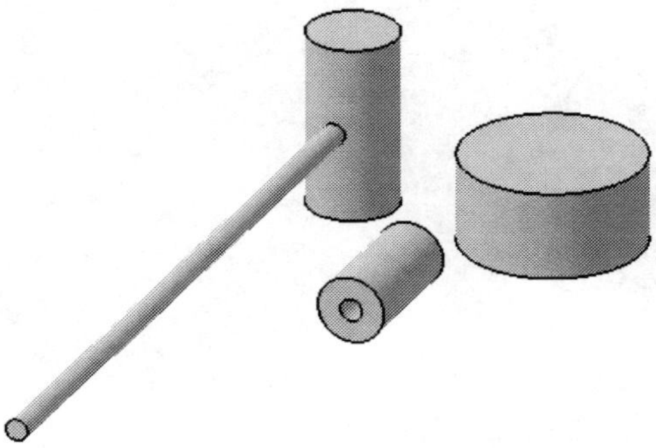

To fix the location and orientation of the base, pick the **Anchor** icon  from the **Constraints** toolbar and select the **base** part from the tree or from the screen.

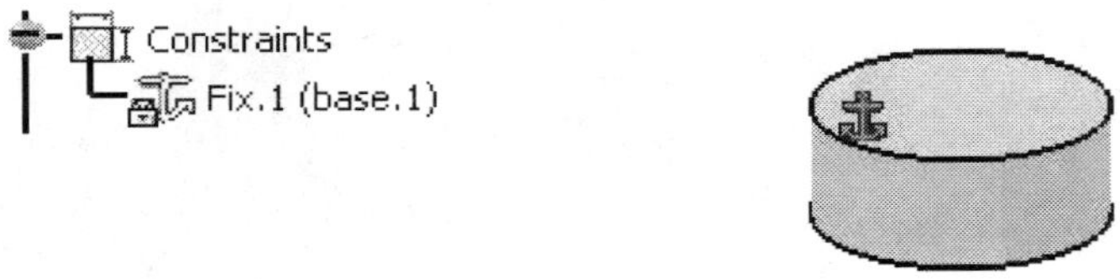

The next step is to mount the **arm** on the **base**. We will use a coincidence constraint and a contact constraint to remove all relative degrees of freedom (dof) except the desired rotation.

Pick the **Coincidence** icon  from **Constraints** toolbar and select the axes of the parts shown.

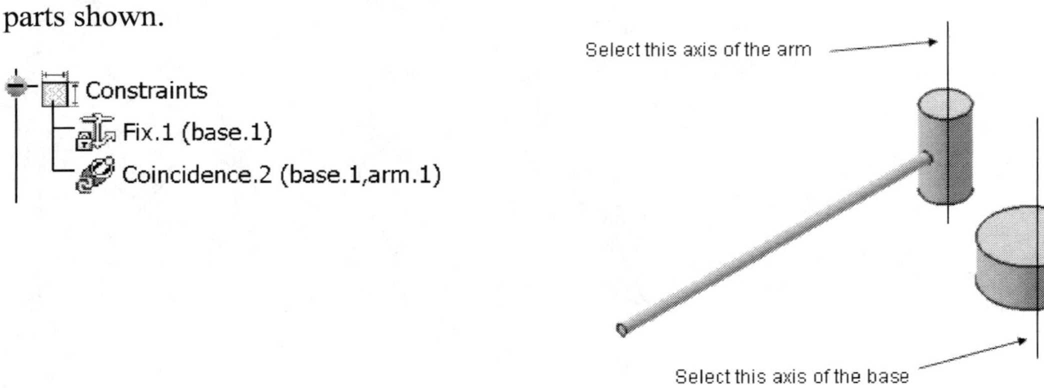

Next pick the **Contact** icon  and make the surface selections as displayed below.

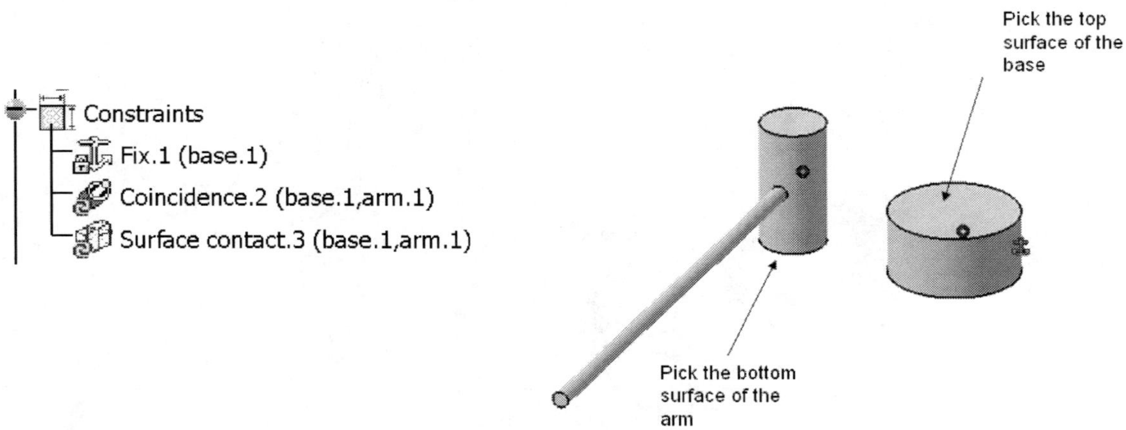

Use **Update** icon  to enforce constraints.

To mount the collar to the arm, we want to remove all of the relative degrees of freedom (dof) between the collar and the arm except for translation along the length of the arm. This can be done using two constraints as described below. First, pick the **Coincidence** icon from **Constraints** toolbar and select the axes of the parts shown.

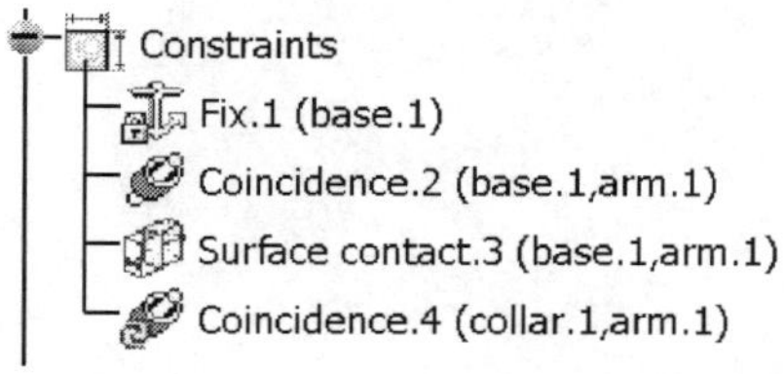

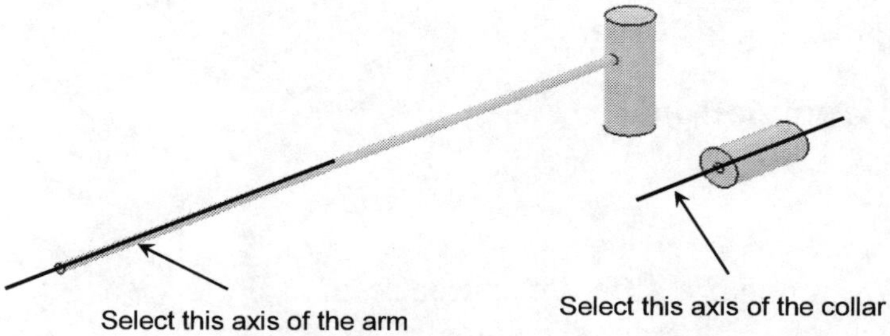

The next step is to prevent the rotation of the **collar** as it slides along the **arm**. Pick the **Angle Constraint** icon from the **Constraints** toolbar

and make the plane selections as shown below. There are other choices for plane selection which will serve just as well.

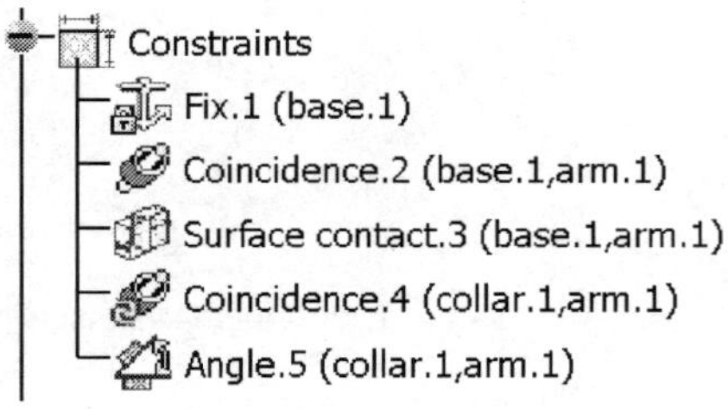

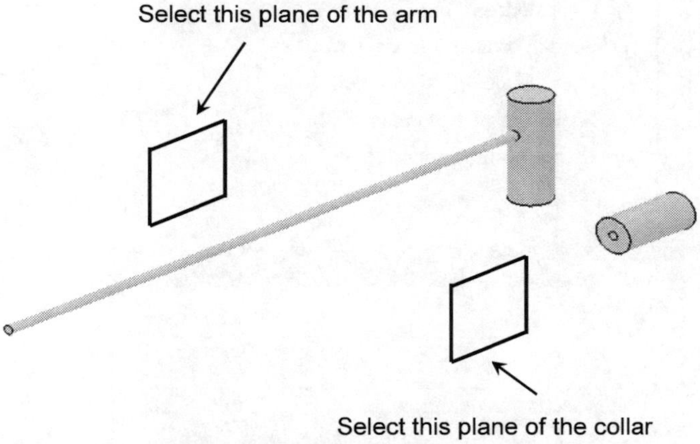

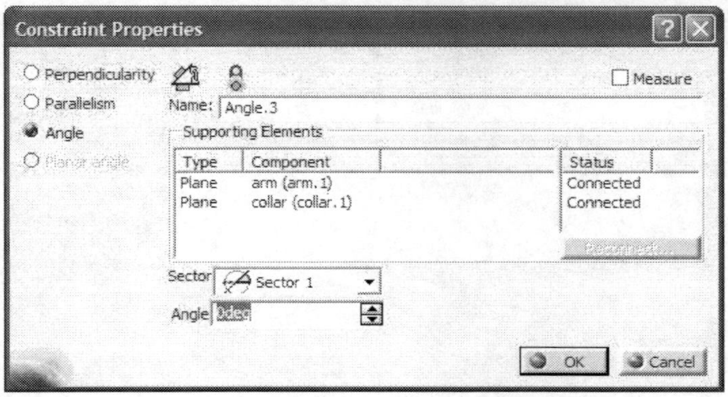

Use **Update** icon  to enforce the latest constraints.

Note that depending on how the parts were created, once updated they may overlap. This can be corrected by relocating the collar using the **Manipulation** icon .

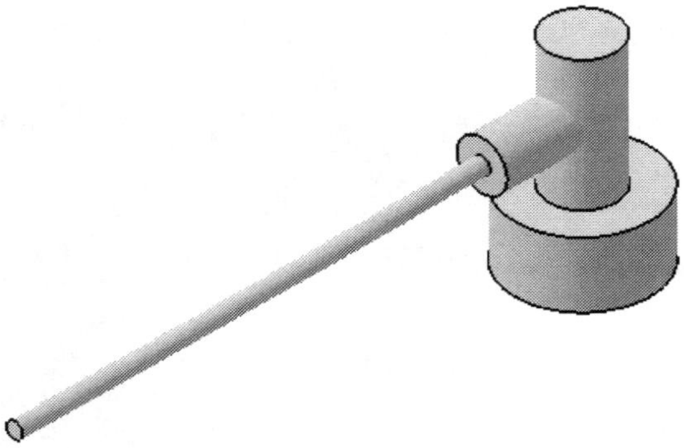

We propose a different approach to accurately position the collar along the arm so that the starting position is precisely known.

Pick the **Offset Constraint** icon  and select the planes from the arm and the collar. Specify the desired value as the separation distance. In the associate pop up box we have prescribed a value of 0.5 in. Depending upon the sizes of your parts, you might choose a different offset.

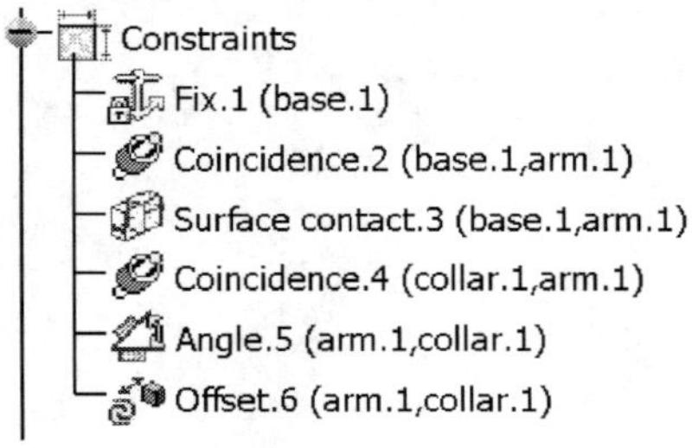

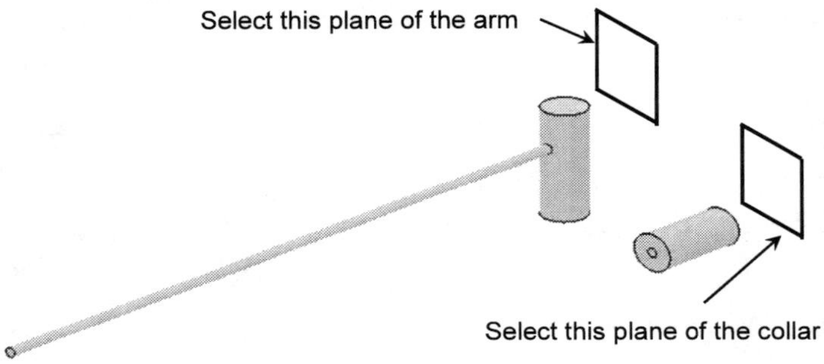

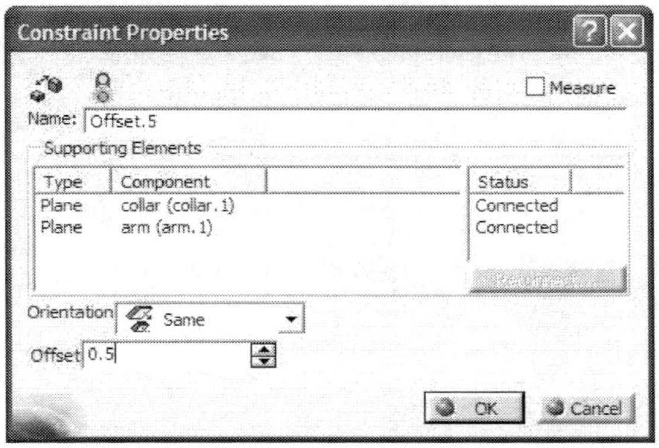

Use the **Update** icon  to enforce the latest constraints. Your assembly should look similar to the one shown below.

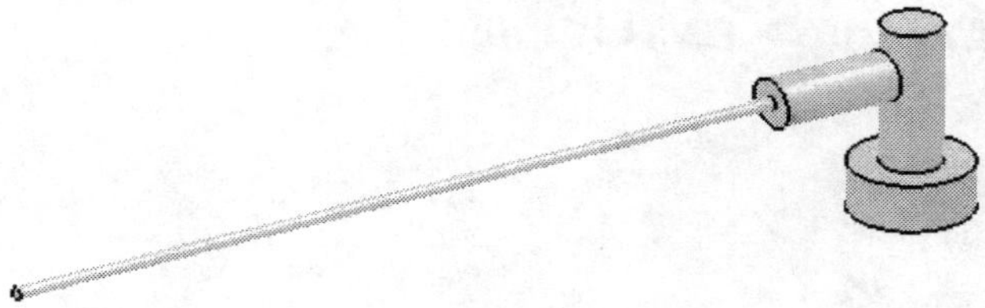

Important: This **Offset Constraint** has to be deleted otherwise it will lead to a **Rigid Joint** in the Digital Mock Up.

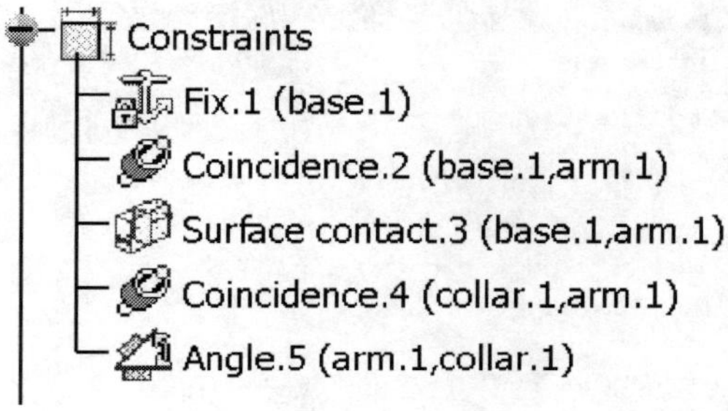

The assembly is complete and we can proceed to the **Digital Mockup** workbench.

4 Creating Joints in the Digital Mockup Workbench

The **Digital Mockup** workbench is quite extensive but we will only deal with the **DMU Kinematics module**. To get there you can use the standard Windows toolbar as shown below: **Start > Digital Mockup > DMU Kinematics**.

Select the **Assembly Constraints Conversion** icon 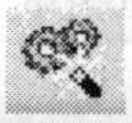 from the **DMU Kinematics** toolbar 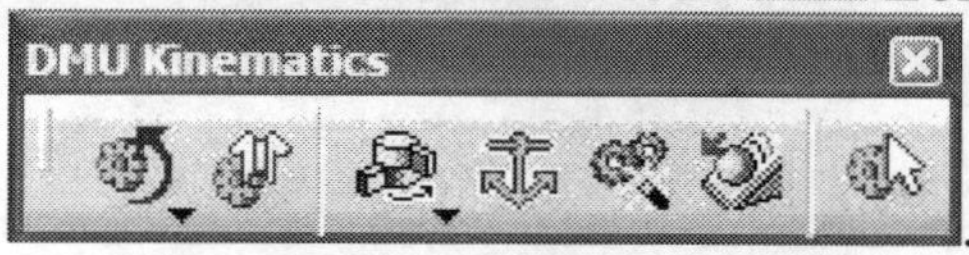

. This icon allows you to create most common joints automatically from the existing assembly constraints. The pop up box below appears.

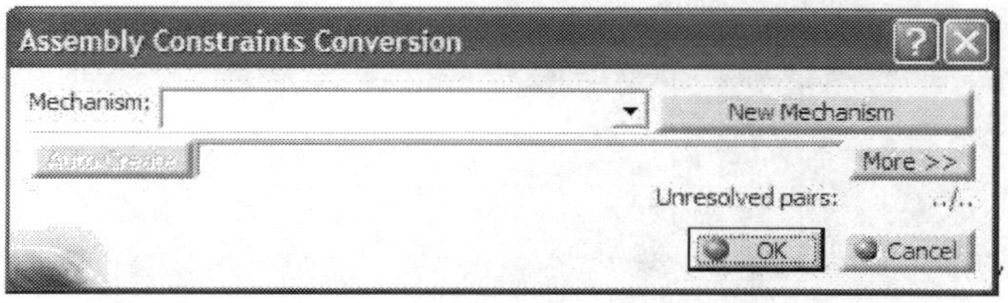

Select the **New Mechanism** button 

.
This leads to another pop up box which allows you to name your mechanism. The default name is **Mechanism.1**. Accept the default name by pressing **OK**.

Note that the box indicates **Unresolved pairs: 2/2**.

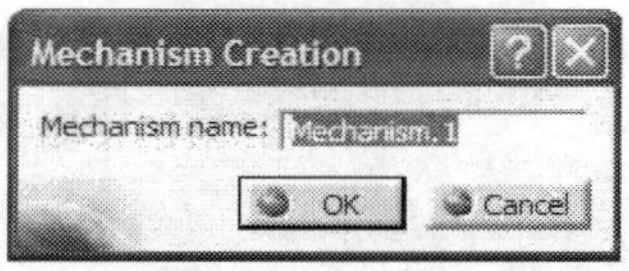

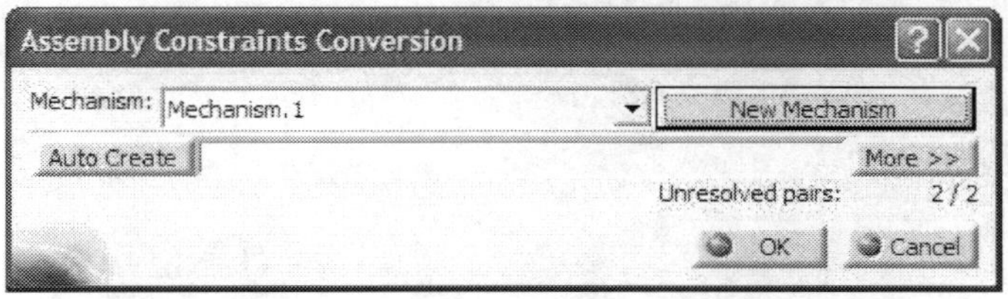

Select the **Auto Create** button 

. Then if the **Unresolved pairs** becomes **0/2**, things are moving in the right direction.

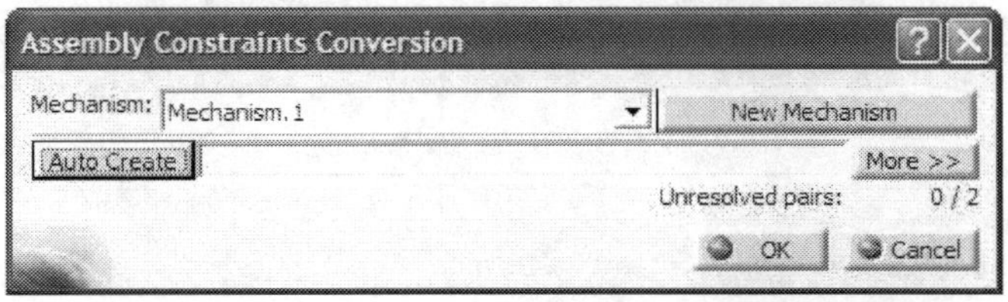

The tree is modified to reflect the created joints. Note that a revolute and a prismatic joint have been created and the degree of freedom is 2.

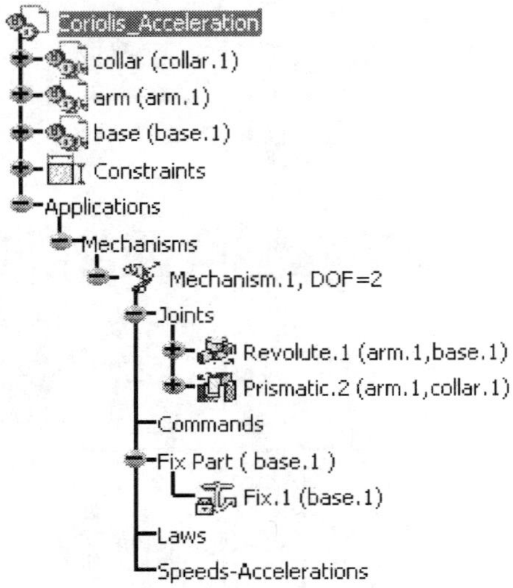

Double click on the **Revolute.1** branch of tree to open the pop up box for the joint. Check the box to make this joint **Angle Driven**. Close the box.

Make Revolute.1 an Angle driven joint

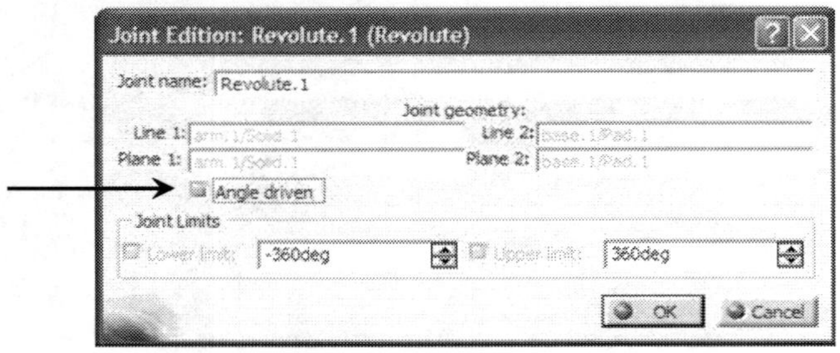

The **Command.1** in the tree corresponds to the Angle driven **Revolute.1** joint.

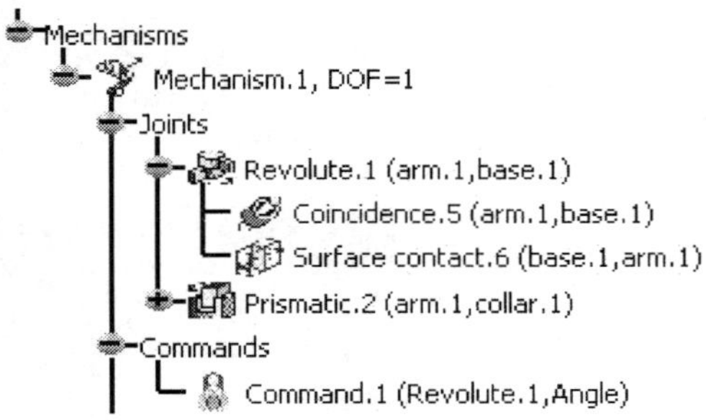

Double click on the **Prismatic.2** branch of tree to open the pop up box for the joint. Check the box to make this joint **Length Driven**, and change the **Lower Limit** to 0 and the **Upper Limit** to 6. Close the box. The reason behind a value of 6 in is that the length of the arm is 8 in.

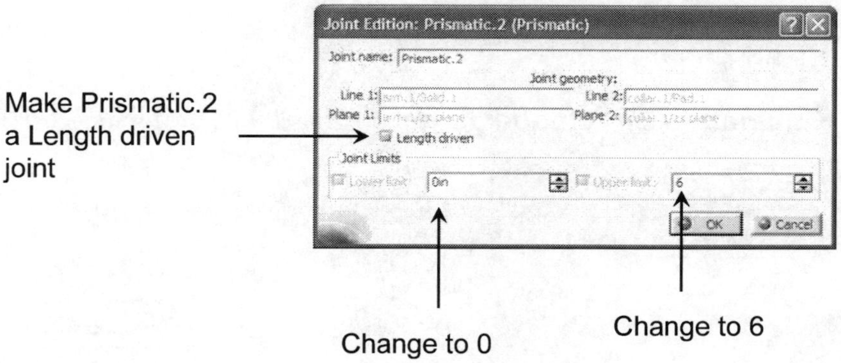

The **Command.2** in the tree corresponds to the Angle driven **Prismatic.2** joint.

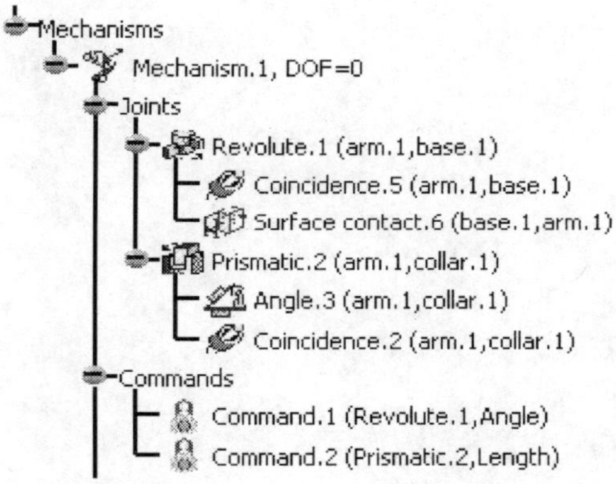

Upon closing this box, the degree of freedom is reduced to 0. The message "**Mechanism can be simulated**".

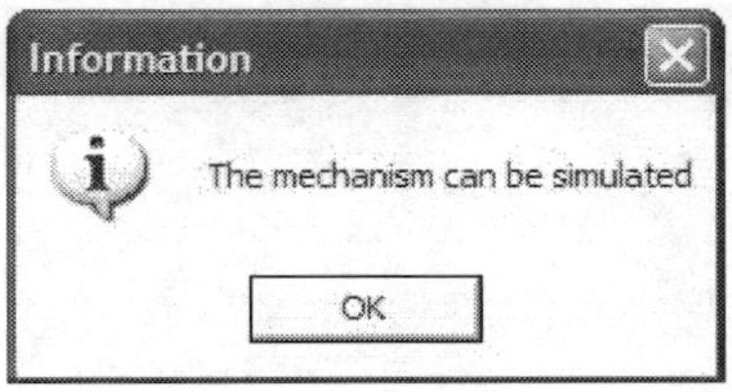

We are now ready to simulate the mechanism with one slider devoted to each joint's motion. Select the **Simulation** icon  from the **DMU Generic Animation** toolbar

.

This enables you to choose the mechanism to be animated if there are several present. In this case, select Mechanism.1 and close the window.

As soon as the window is closed, a Simulation branch is added to the tree.

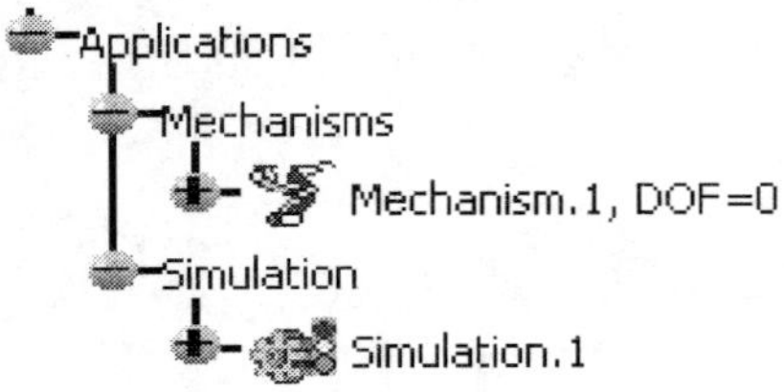

Note that the **Kinematics Simulation** pop up box has two scroll bars.

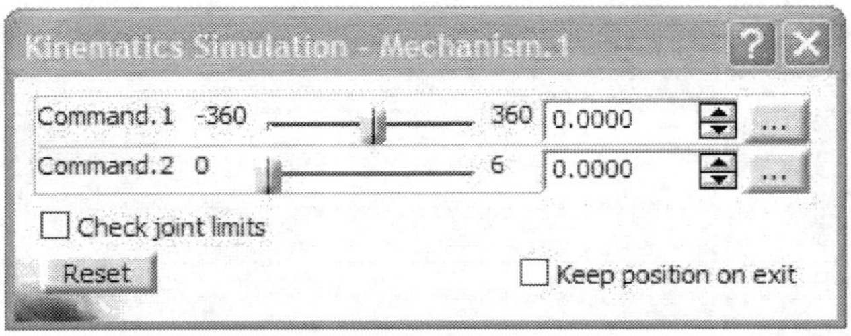

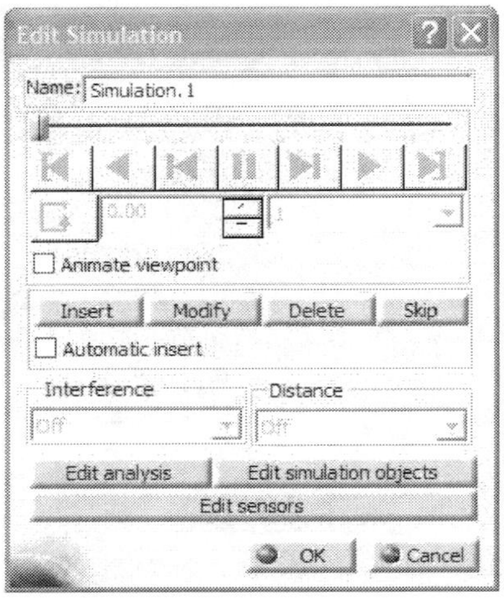

As you scroll the bottom bar, the collar slides along the arm, whereas, scrolling the top bar causes the arm to rotate about the base.

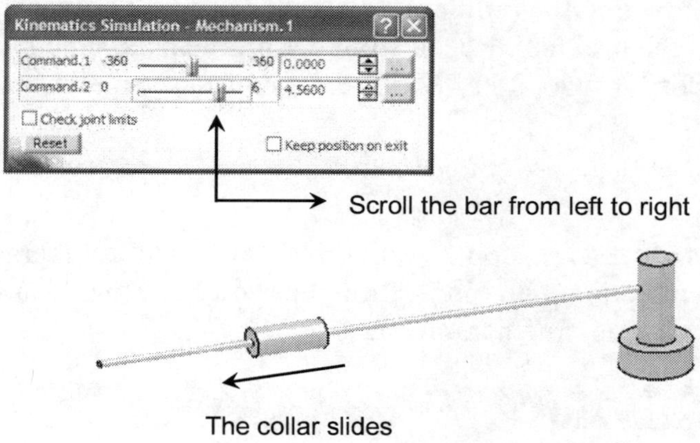

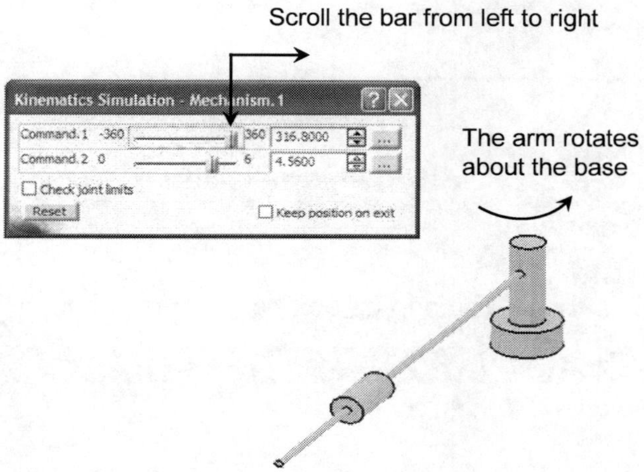

5 Creating Laws in the Motion and Simulating the Desired Kinematics

The simulation thus far did not enable simultaneous motion of the two joints. In addition, the motion animated this far was not tied to the time parameter or the rotational translational velocities given in the problem statement. You will now introduce some time based physics into the problem. Recall from the problem statement that the objective is to specify a constant linear velocity of 6 in/s and a constant angular velocity of 360 deg/s.

Click on **Simulation with Laws** icon  in the **Simulation** toolbar 

. You will get the following pop up box indication that you need to add at least a relation between the command and the time parameter.

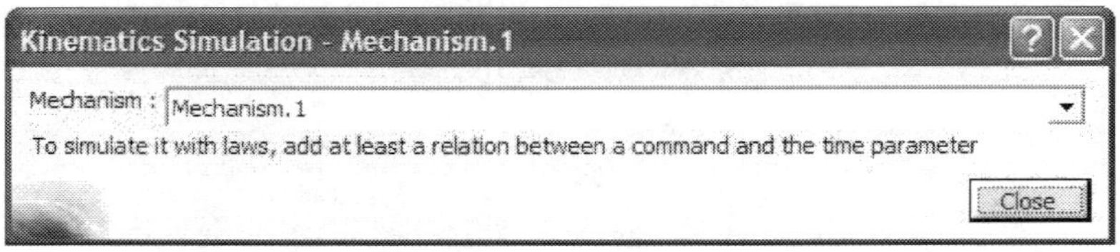

Select the **Formula** icon  from the **Knowledge** toolbar 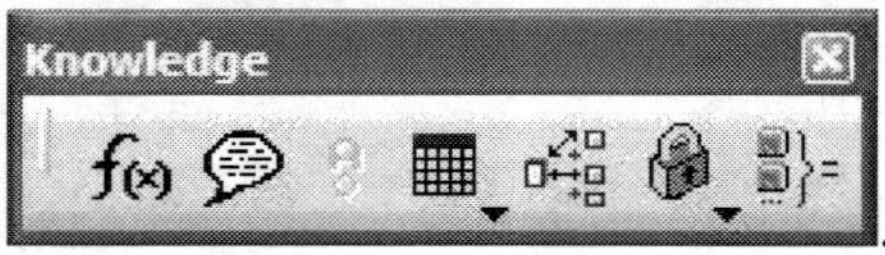

. The pop up box below appears on the screen.

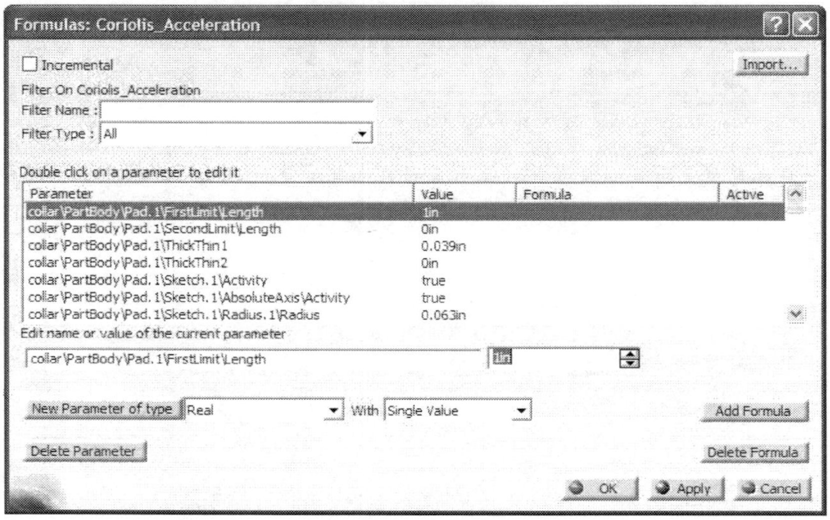

Point the cursor to the **Mechanism.1, DOF=0** branch in the tree and click. The consequence is that only parameters associated with the mechanism are displayed in the **Formulas** box.

The long list is now reduced to three parameters as indicated in the box shown on the next page.

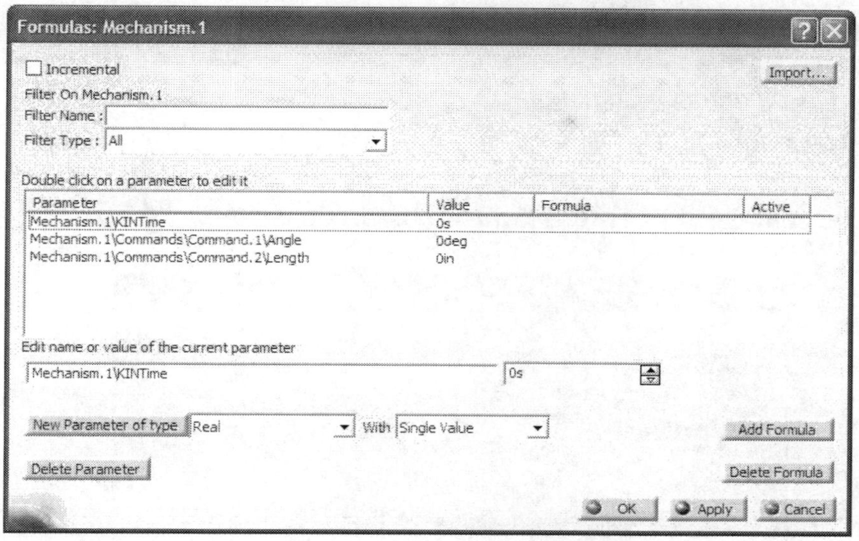

Select the entry **Mechanism.1\Commands\Command.1\Angle** and press the **Add Formula** button . This action kicks you to the **Formula Editor** box.

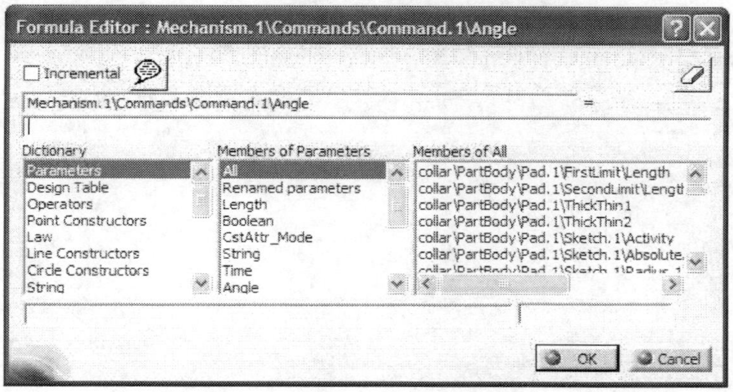

Pick the **Time** entry from the middle column (i.e. **Members of Parameters**).

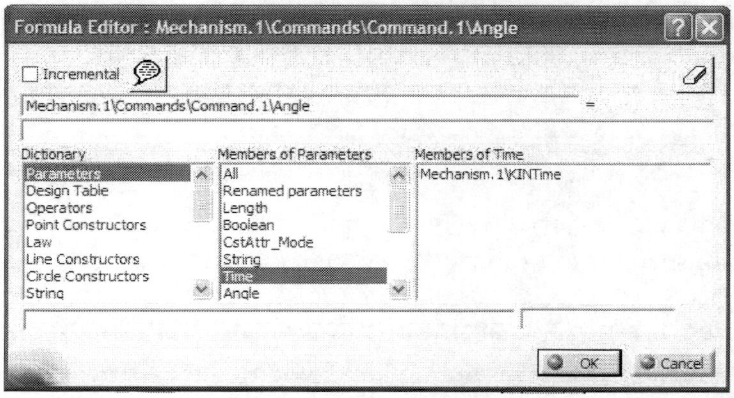

The right hand side of the equality should be such that the formula becomes

$$Mechanism.1 \backslash Commands \backslash Command.1 \backslash Angle = \\ (360\,\text{deg}) * Mechanism.1 \backslash KINTime / (1s)$$

Therefore, the completed **Formula Editor** box becomes

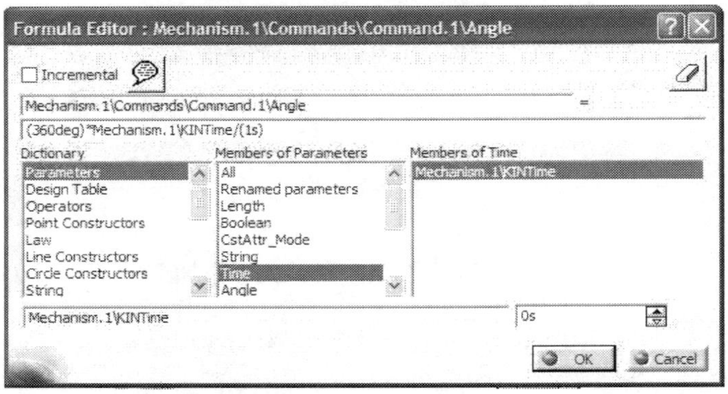

Upon accepting **OK**, the formula is recorded in the **Formulas** pop up box as shown below.

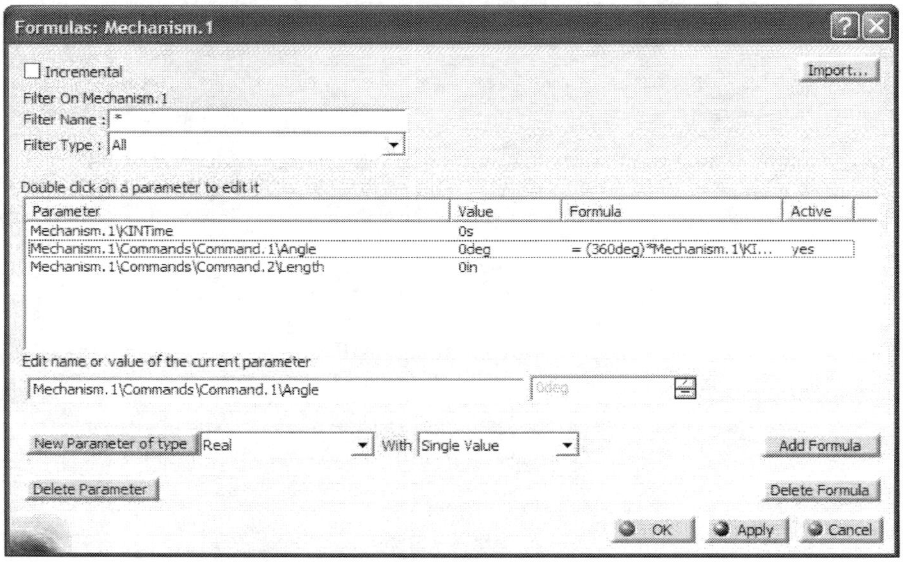

Note that the formula entered effectively multiplies the desired angular velocity of 360deg/s by time in seconds to produce an angle in degrees.

Select the entry **Mechanism.1\Commands\Command.2\Length** and press the **Add Formula** button 

. This action kicks you to the **Formula Editor** box.

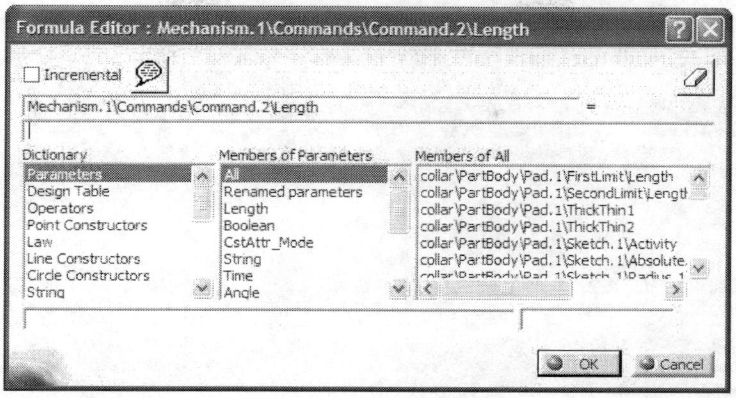

Pick the **Time** entry from the middle column (i.e. **Members of Parameters**).

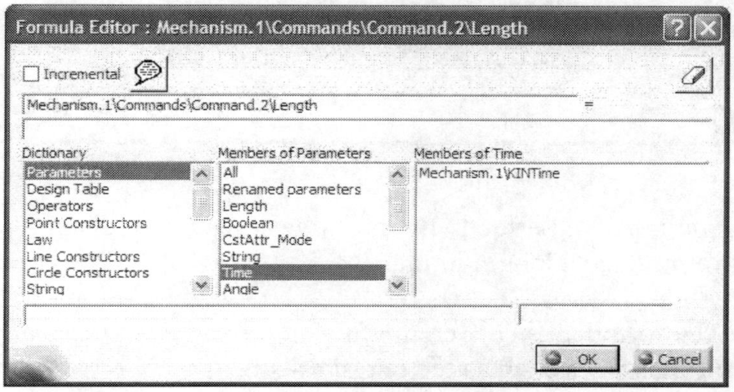

The right hand side of the equality should be such that the formula becomes

$$Mechanism.1 \backslash Commands \backslash Command.2 \backslash Length =$$
$$(6in) * Mechanism.1 \backslash KINTime / (1s)$$

Therefore, the completed **Formula Editor** box becomes

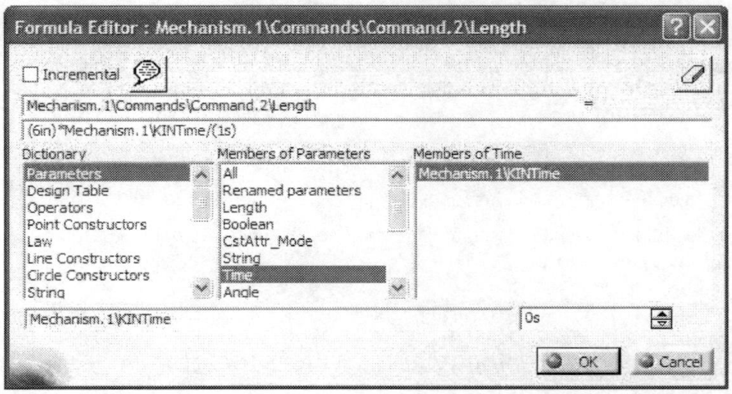

Upon accepting **OK**, the formula is recorded in the **Formulas** pop up box as shown below.

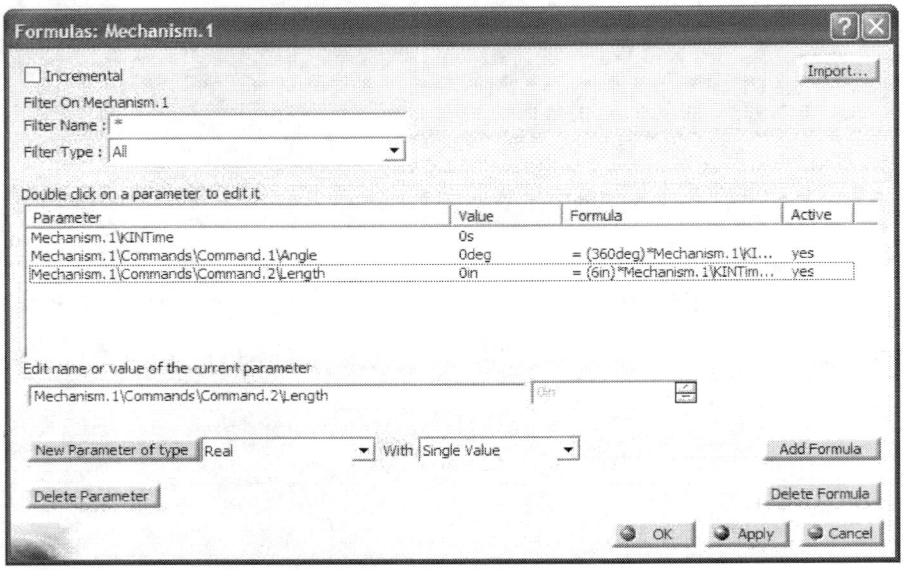

Note that the formula entered effectively multiplies the desired linear velocity of 6in/s by time in seconds to produce a length in inches.

In the event that the formula has different units on the different sides of the equality you will get **Warning** messages such as the one shown below.

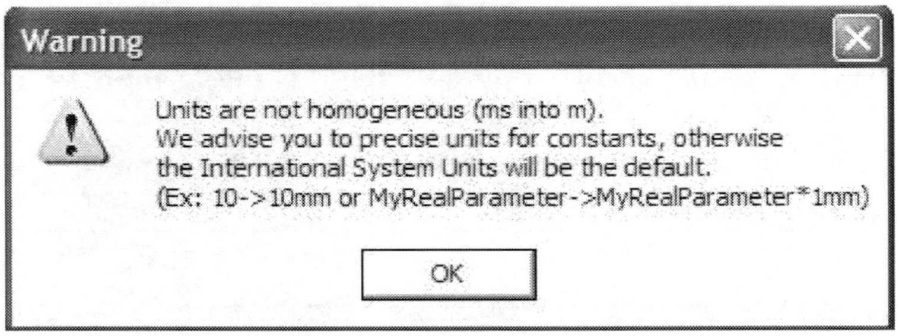

We are spared the warning message because the formula has been properly inputted. Note that the introduced law has appeared in the **Law** branch of the tree.

Since you will be plotting the velocity and acceleration of the collar, you must create a point on the collar which can be used for that purpose. You could use the part's origin or open the collar in **Part Design** and create a reference point on the collar as shown below.

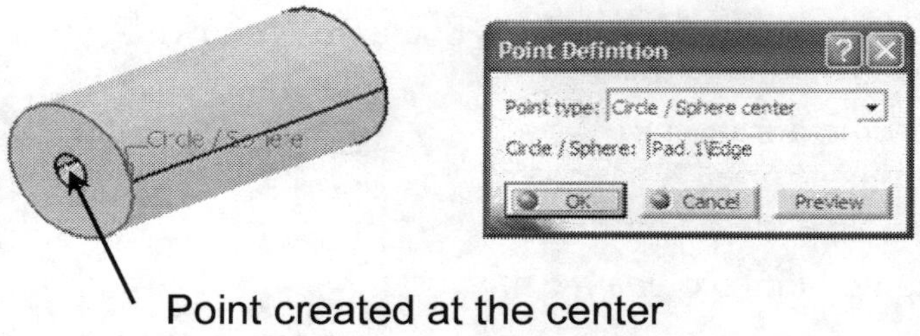

Now that we have a point to monitor, we will set up a speed and acceleration sensor. To do so, select the **Speed and Acceleration** icon  from the **DMU Kinematics** toolbar 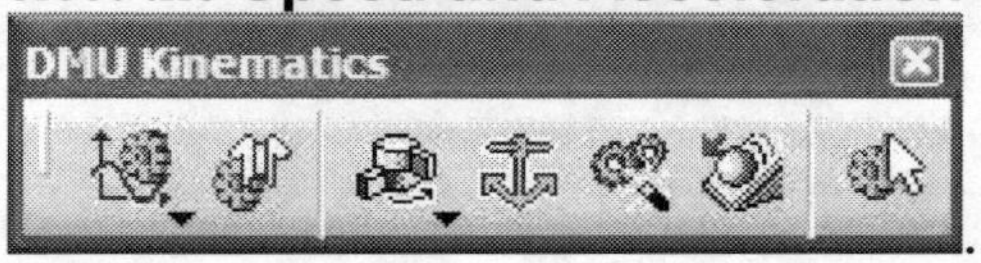

. The pop up box below appears on the Screen.

Make the selections as indicated.

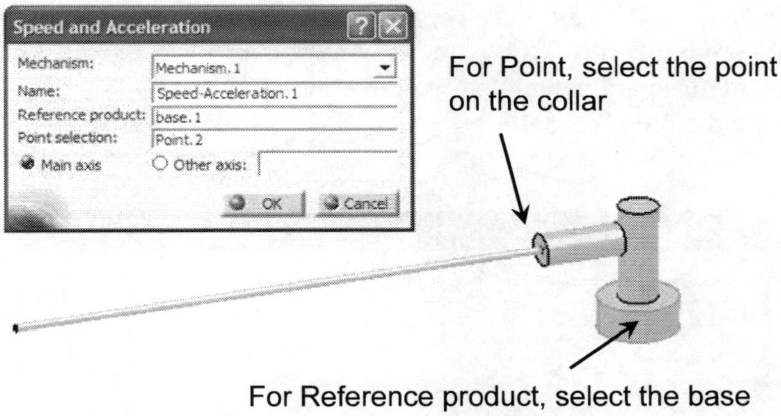

Note that the **Speed and Acceleration.1** has appeared in the tree.

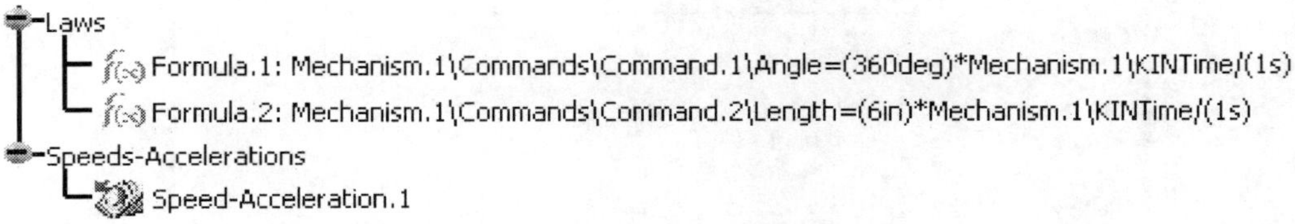

The time has come to simulate the desired time based motion. Click on **Simulation with Laws** icon  in the **Simulation** toolbar 

.
This results in the **Kinematics Simulation** pop up box shown below.

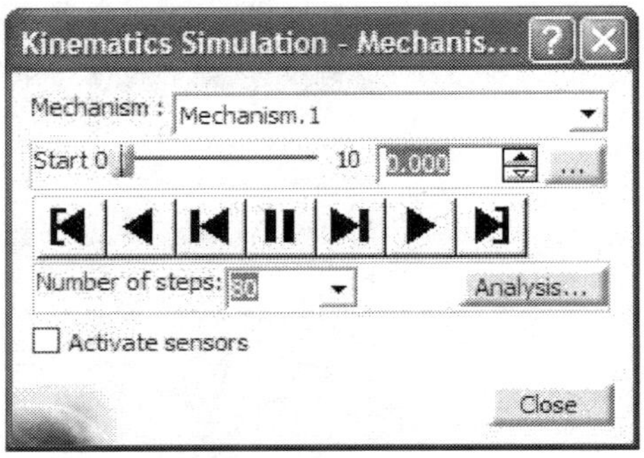

Note that the default time duration is 10 seconds.
To change this value, click on the button . In the resulting pop up box, change the time duration to 1s.

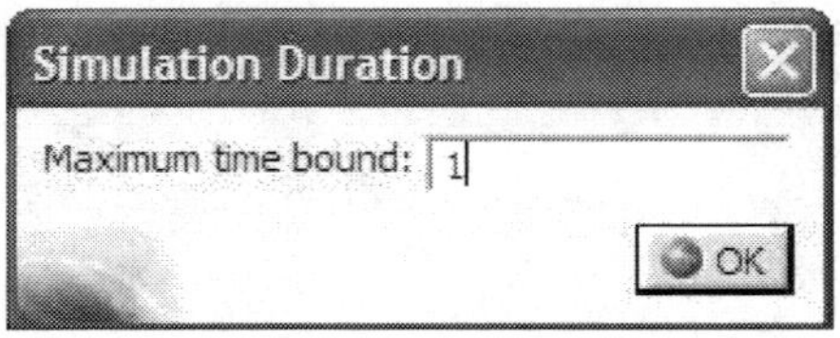

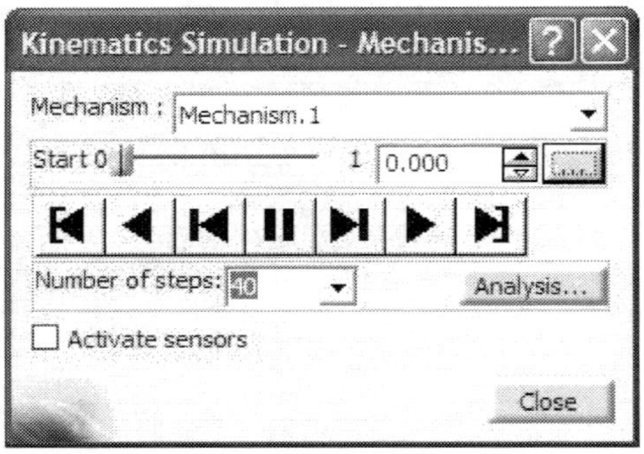

The scroll bar now moves up to 1s.

Check the **Activate sensors** box, at the bottom left corner.

You will next have to make certain selections from the accompanying **Sensors** box to indicate the kinematics parameters you would like to compute and store results on.

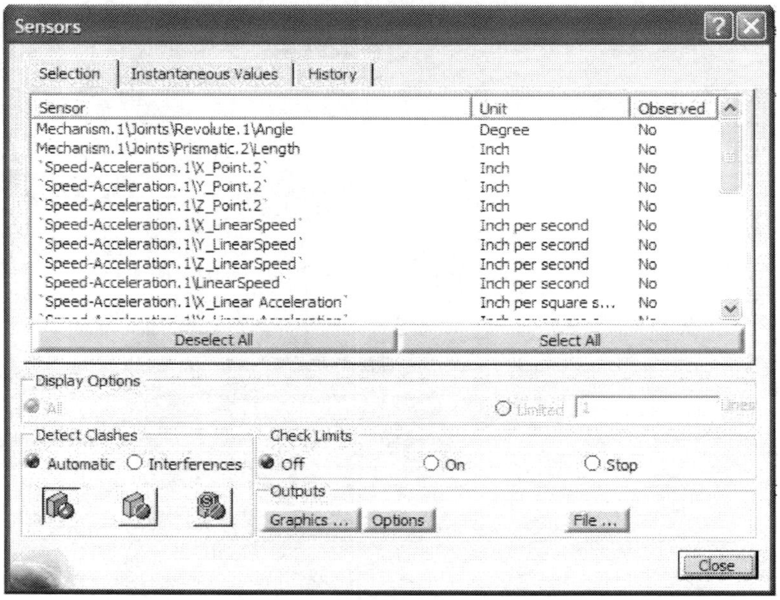

Click on the following items

Speed-Acceleration.1\X_LinearSpeed
Speed-Acceleration.1\Y_LinearSpeed
Speed-Acceleration.1\X_LinearAcceleration
Speed-Acceleration.1\Y_LinearAcceleration

Note: If your assembly is not oriented with the axis of rotation of the revolute joint in the world z direction, you will need to pick the appropriate components of velocity and acceleration for your layout.

As you make these selections, the last column in the **Sensors** box, changes to **Yes** for the corresponding items.

At this point, drag the scroll bar in the **Kinematics Simulation** box. As you do this, the collar travels along the arm and the arm makes a full rotation. Once the bar reaches its

Once the collar makes a full trip, click on **Graphics** button 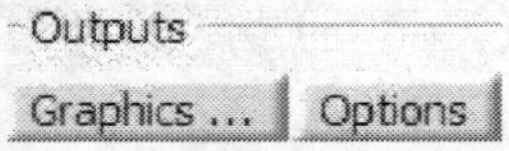

in the **Sensor** box. This results in the plots of the X and Y components of linear velocity and linear acceleration as shown on the next two pages. You need to toggle on each curve in the right portion of the dialog box to have the y axis scale appropriately for each plot.

The plot scaled for the X component of velocity:

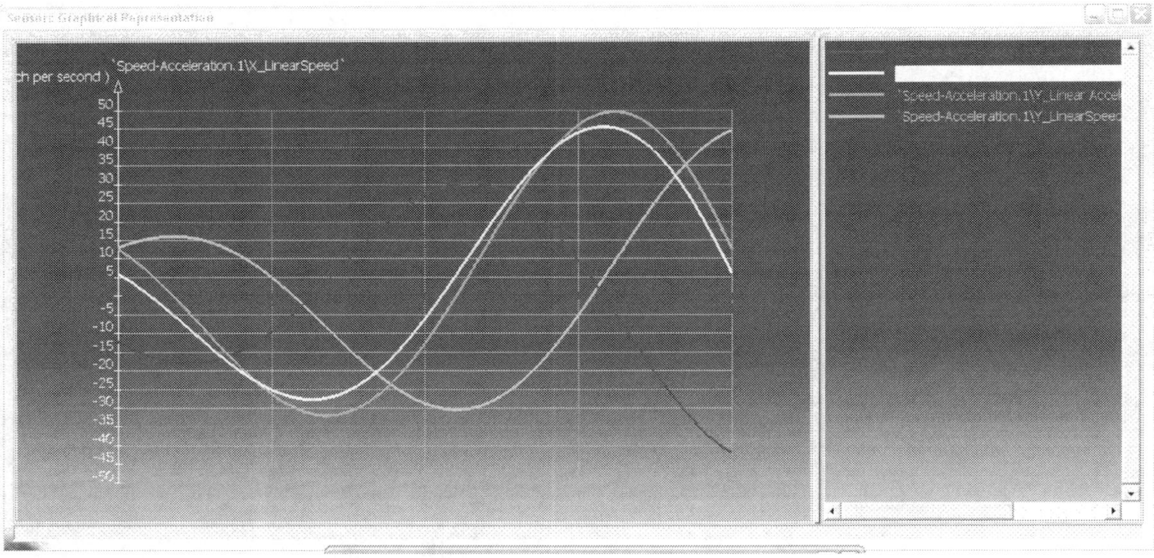

The plot scaled for the Y component of velocity:

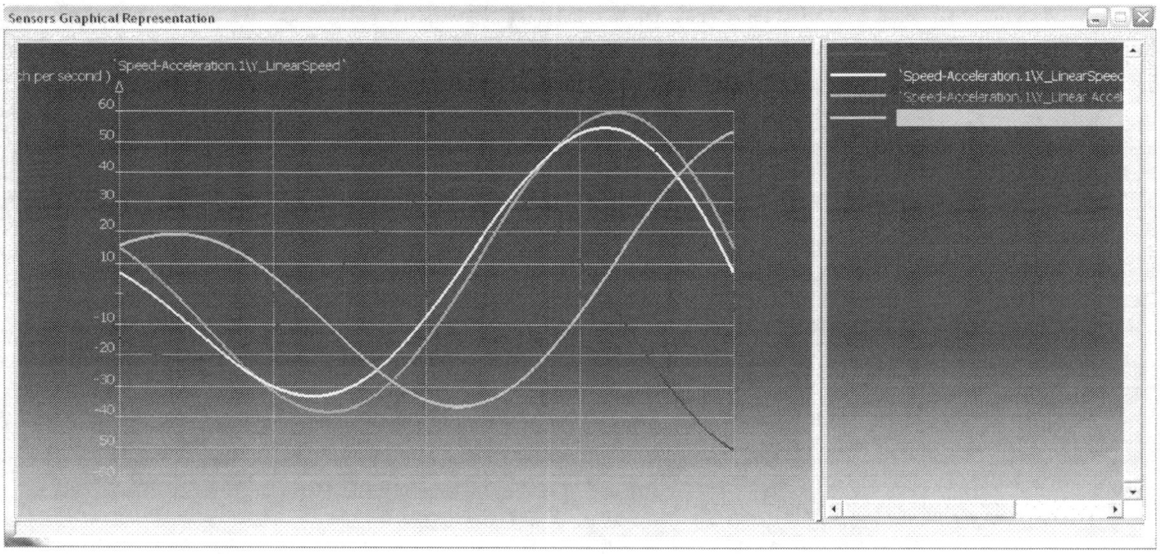

The plot scaled for X component of acceleration:

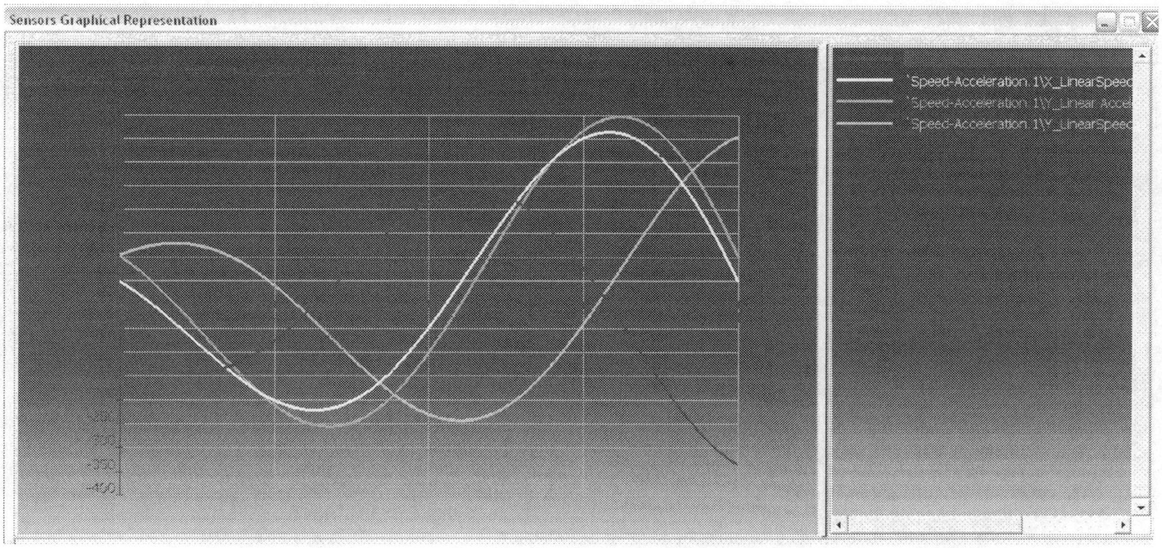

And finally the plot scaled for Y component of acceleration:

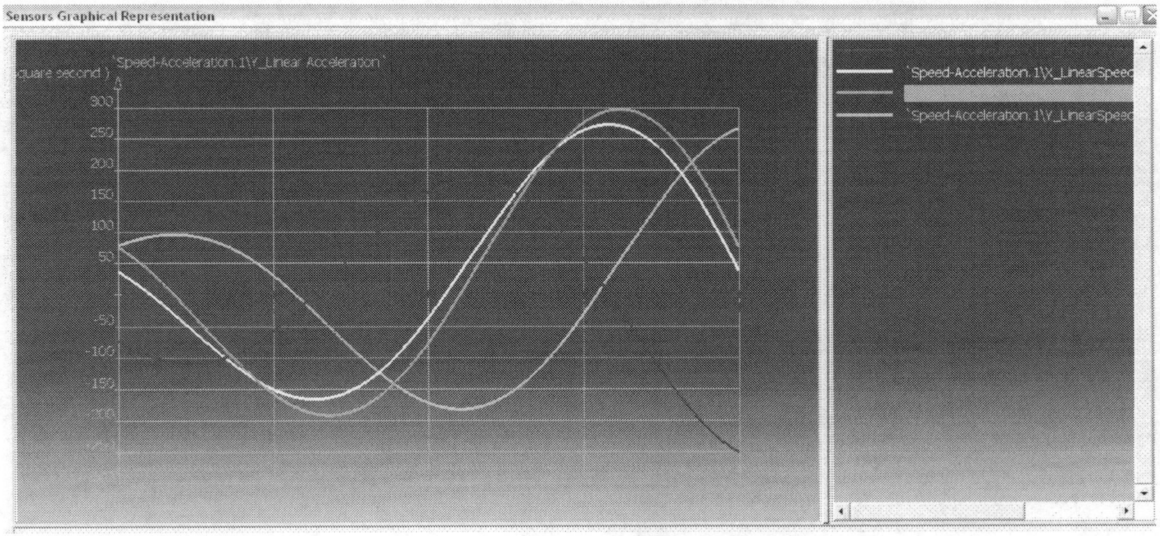

Note that at time t=0s and time t=0.5 s, the Y component of acceleration is not zero. Since the arm is rotating at constant angular velocity, this nonzero acceleration in the Y direction is due solely to the Coriolis acceleration. For the geometry and values used in this simulation, a hand calculation of the Coriolis acceleration at time t=0s gives:

$$ac = 2\,\omega \; x \; v_{rel} = 2[2\pi k]x[6i] = 75.4\vec{j}\,\frac{in}{s^2}$$

This result agrees with the simulation results.

This concludes this tutorial.

NOTES:

Chapter 16

A Prelude to the Human Builder Workbench

This chapter is intended to provide a brief introduction to the **Ergonomic Design & Analysis** workbench in **CATIA V5**. It shows how to create a manikin and a few of the basics as to how the manikin can be manipulated.

The **Ergonomic Design & Analysis** workbench is quite extensive but we will only deal with the **Human Builder** module . To get there you can use the standard Windows toolbar as shown below: **Start > Ergonomic Design & Analysis > Human Builder**.

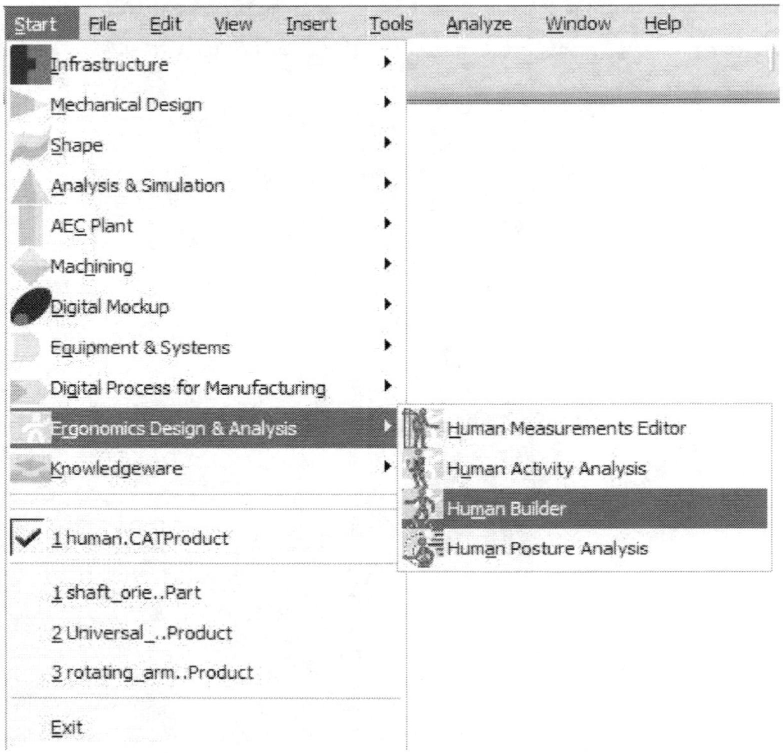

A default product named **Product1** will appear in the tree. Right click on **Product1** and choose **Properties**. In the resulting dialog box shown on the next page, choose the **Properties** tab and type **human** for the product name and **OK** the box.

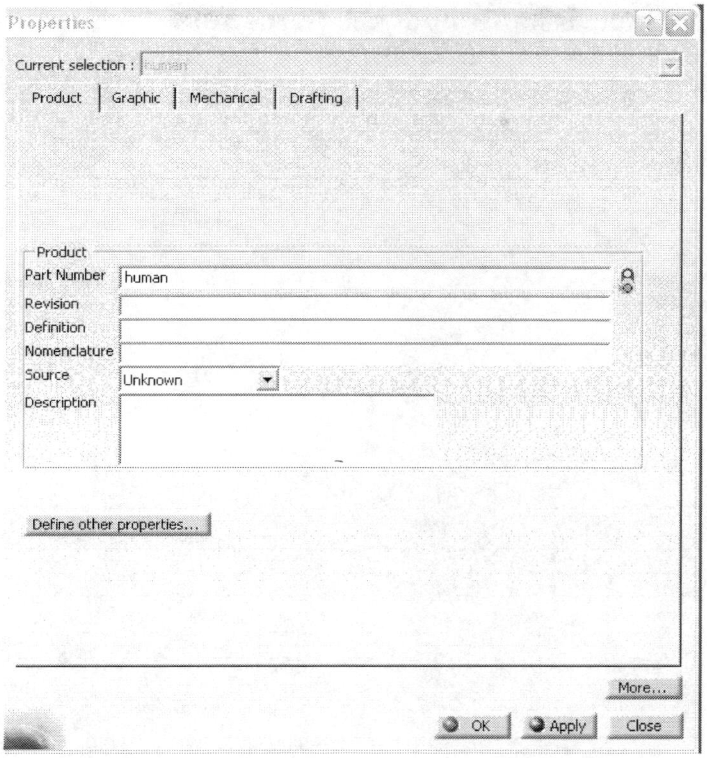

Now we will insert a manikin. Pick the **Inserts a new manikin** icon  from the **Manikin Tools** toolbar 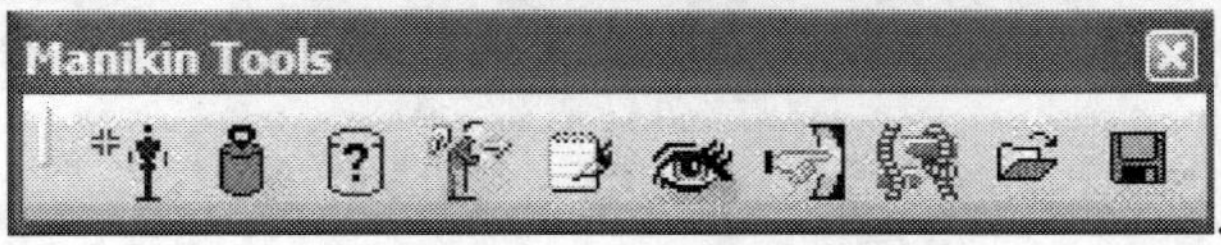

.

The pop up box appears as shown.
For the **Father product**, select the **human** product from the tree.

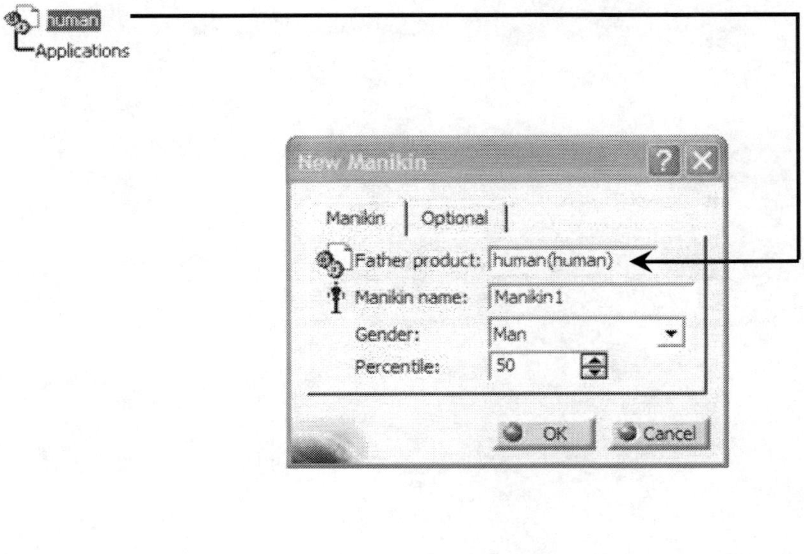

Use the default specifications for **Gender** and **Percentile**. Choose the **Optional** tab and for **Population**, select **Canadian** or whatever you desire.

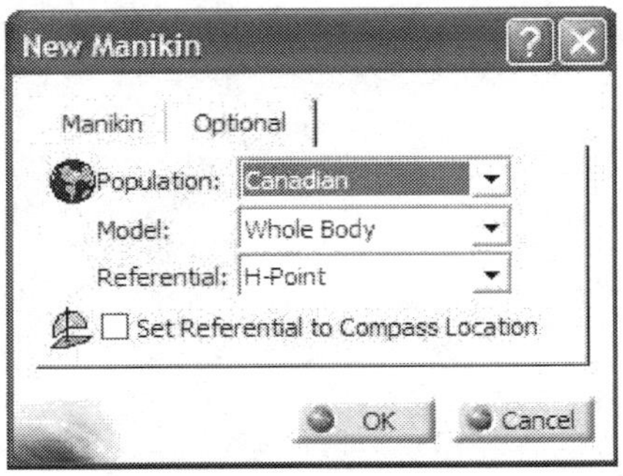

Upon closing the **New Manikin** box, the manikin appears on your screen.

To investigate one way to manipulate the manikin's position, click on the **Posture Editor** icon 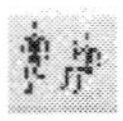 in the **Manikin Posture** toolbar 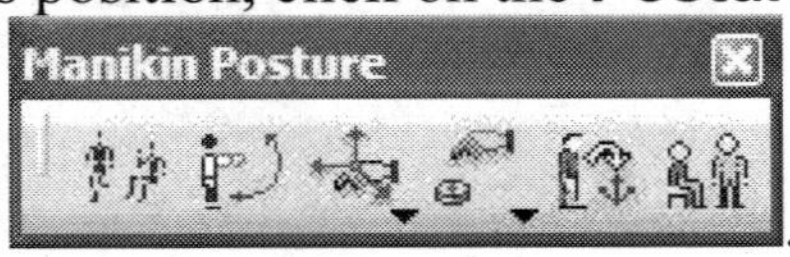

. With the cursor, click on the right thigh. The resulting pop up box shown on the next page allows you to input the desired information.

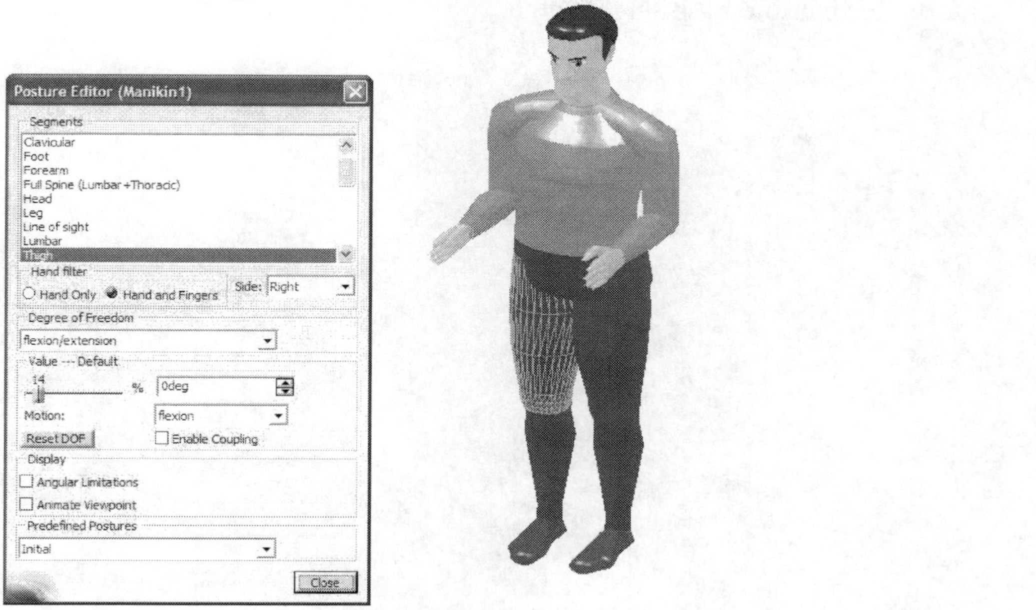

Change the **Predefined Posture**, from **Initial** to **Sit**.

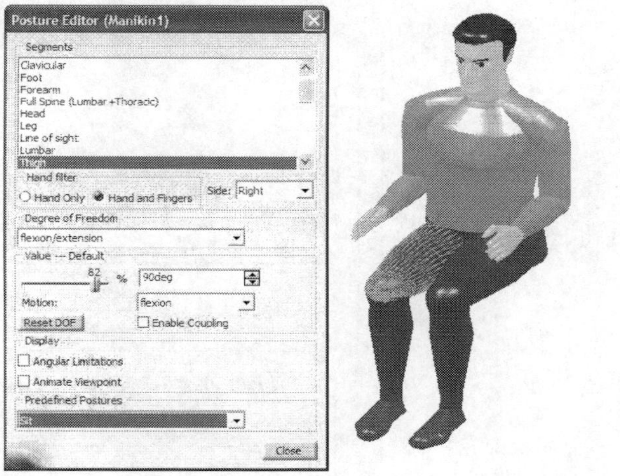

By dragging the bar shown you can change the thigh configuration.

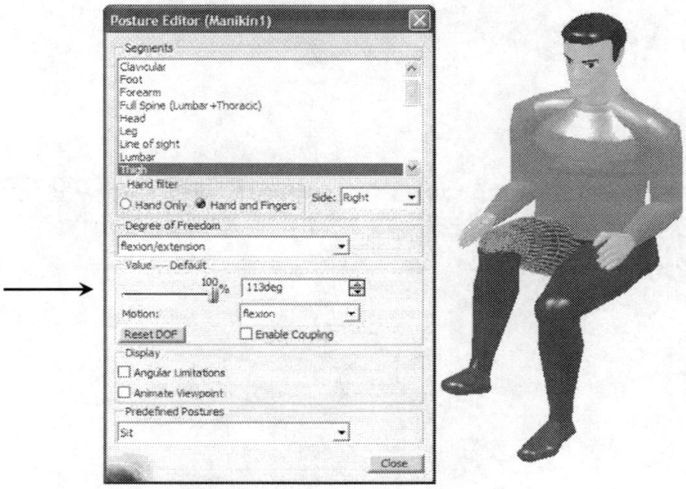

Drag the bar to reposition the thigh.

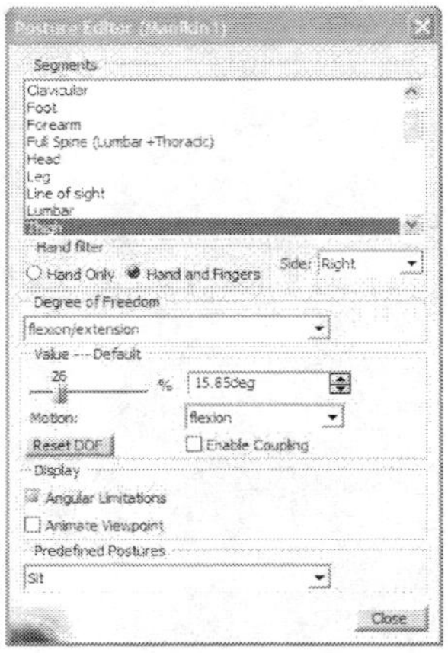

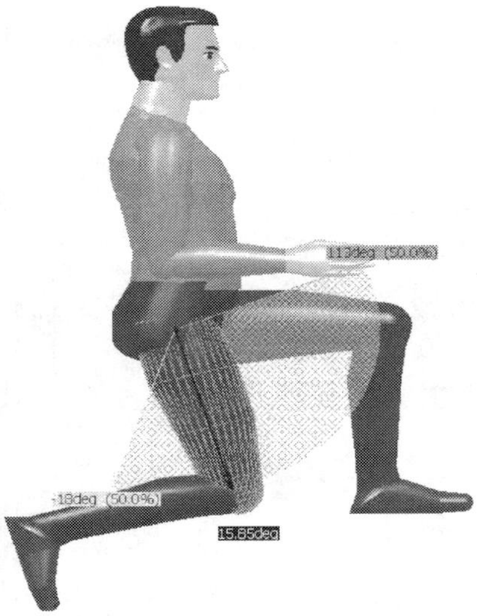

Close the box to finalize the posture of the manikin.

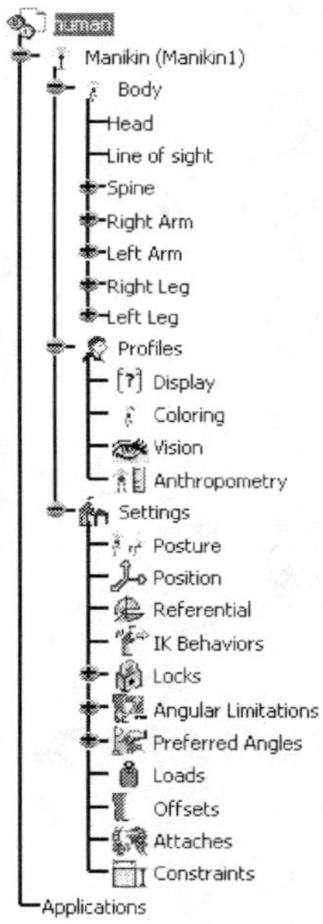

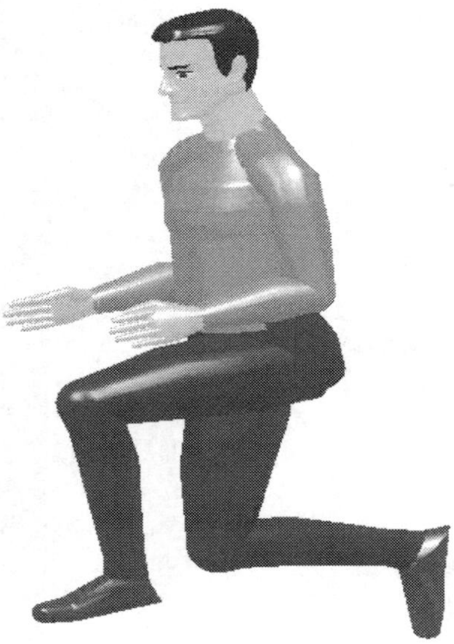

You are through with this manikin. Next we will introduce another manikin and explore some additional capabilities of the software.

Insert a female manikin with characteristics of your choice.

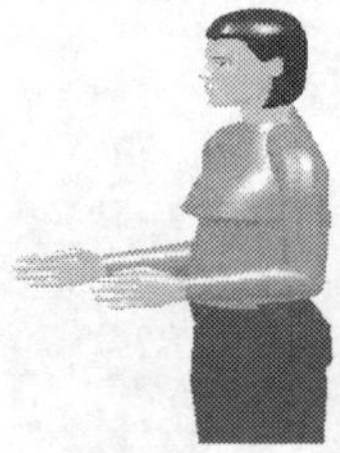

Double click on the manikin on the screen and you are transferred to

the **Human Posture Analysis** workbench 

.

This can also be achieved by selecting the icon .

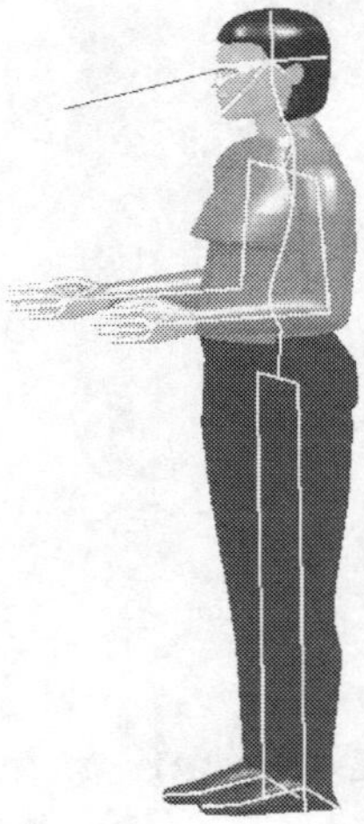

Exit the workbench .

Select the **Human Measurements Editor** icon  from the **Manikin** toolbar 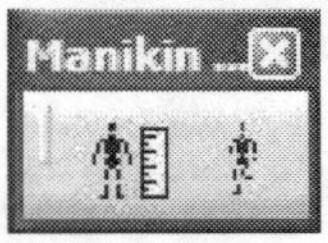

and click on your manikin if necessary to transfer you to a new workbench 

. The following display is shown.

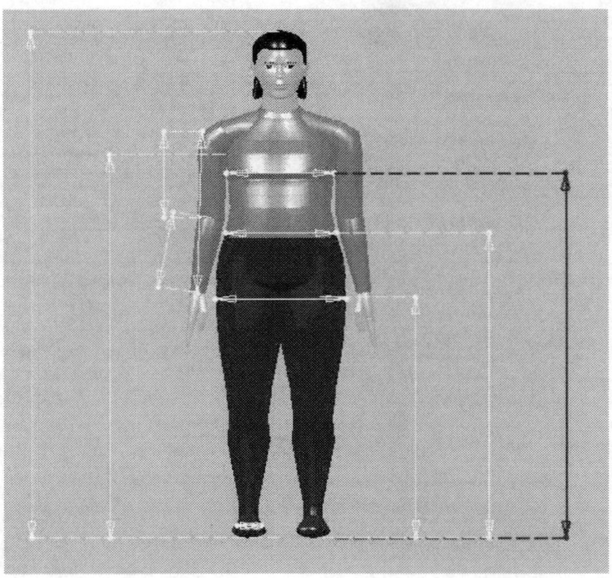

Double click on the dimension of interest and the measurements are displayed in the pop up box.

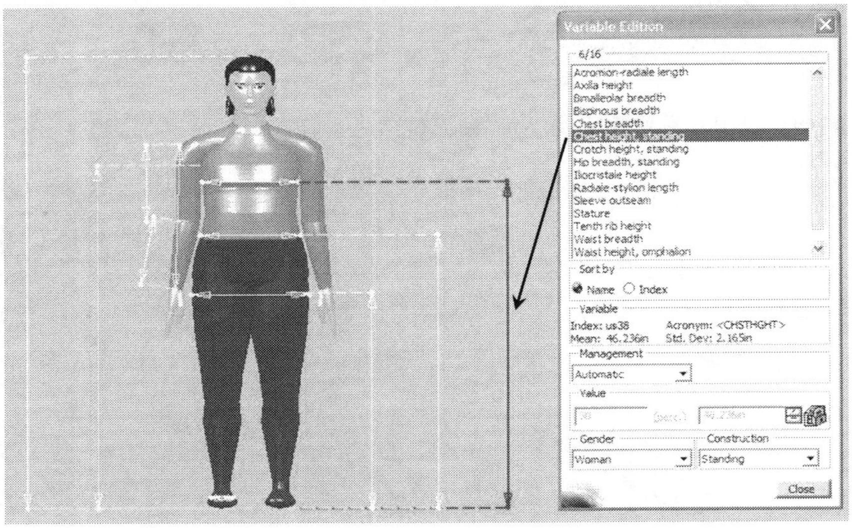

Change the **Construction** to **Sitting** and the corresponding dimensions become available.

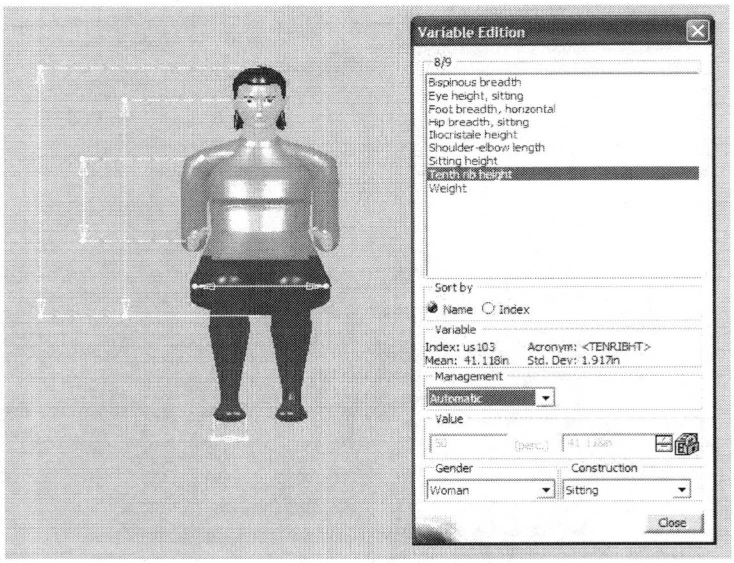

Exit the workbench . Next we'll explore a simple interaction between a manikin and an object.

Insert a simple part in the product file that the manikin resides in. This can be a block as shown below.

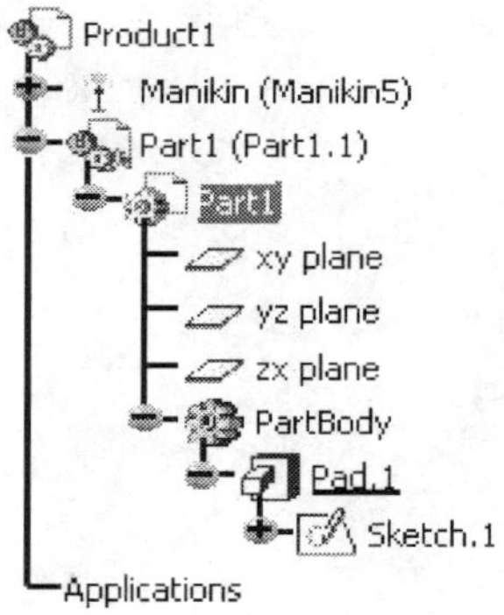

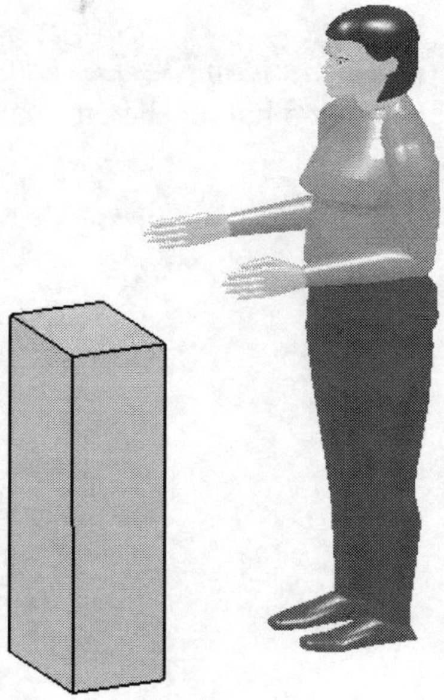

Pick the **Reach (position only)** icon  from the **Reach** toolbar 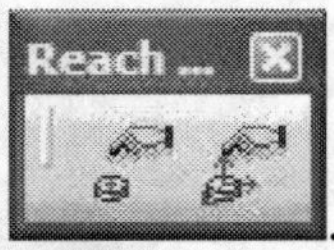

.
The prompt area becomes Place the compass at the target location and select a segment... . Move the compass and place it on the block.
Then select the right hand. The manikin's hand moves toward the compass.

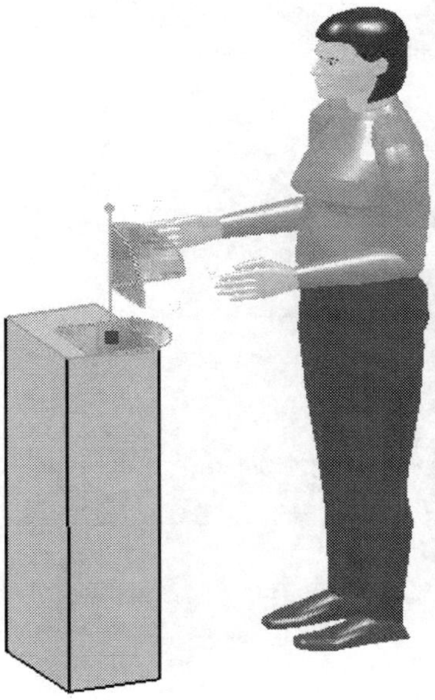

To compute a reach envelope, select the **Computes a reach envelope** icon  from the **Manikin Tools** icon 

. You are prompted to select a hand. The envelope is computed and displayed as shown below.

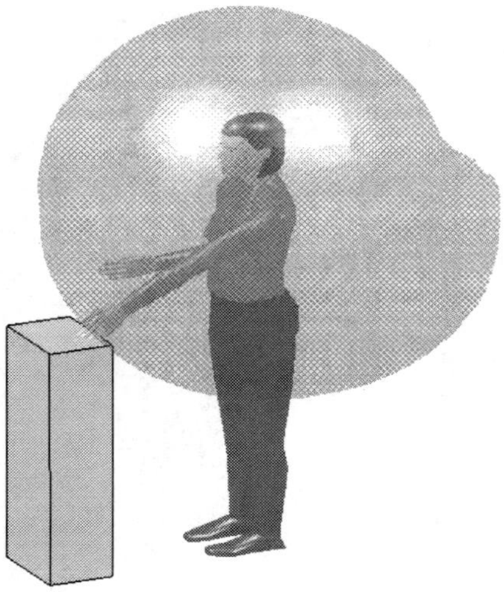

Select the **Standard Pose** icon  from the from the **Manikin Posture** toolbar 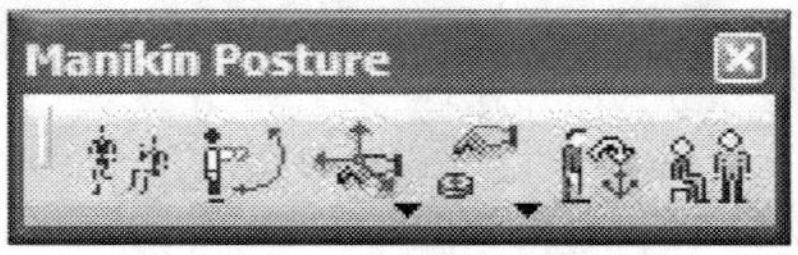

. The pop up box below allows you to change posture such as twist. Modify the **Twist** angle.

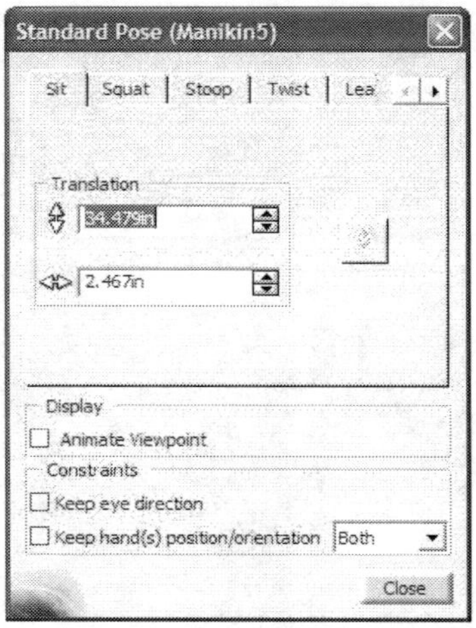

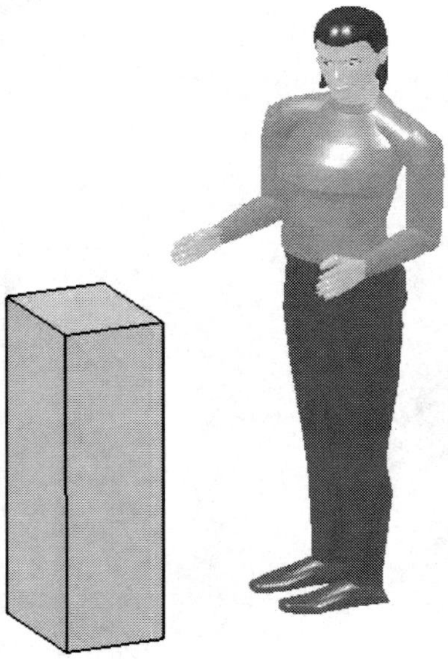

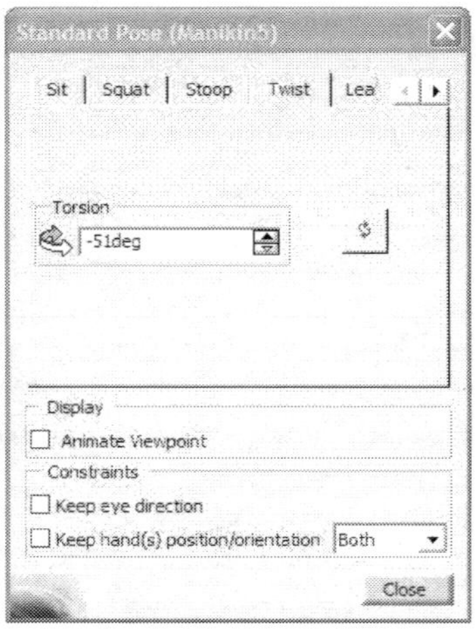

Experiment with the **Lean** Parameter.

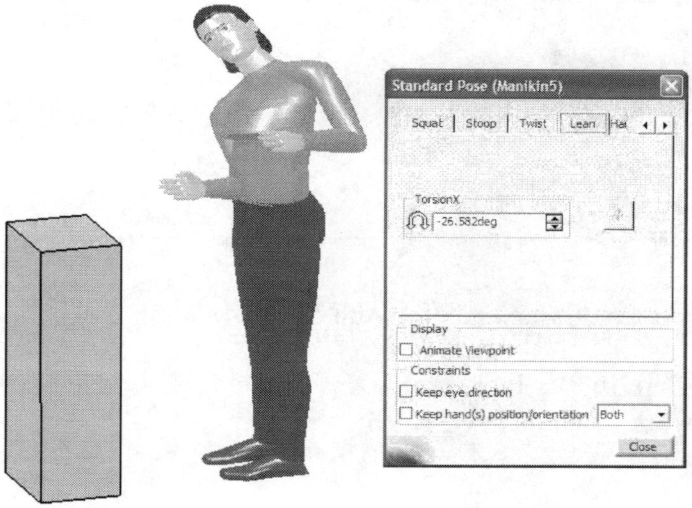

Select the **Changes the display of manikin** icon  from the **Manikin** toolbar and check the **Center of gravity** box. The location of the CG is displayed as shown.

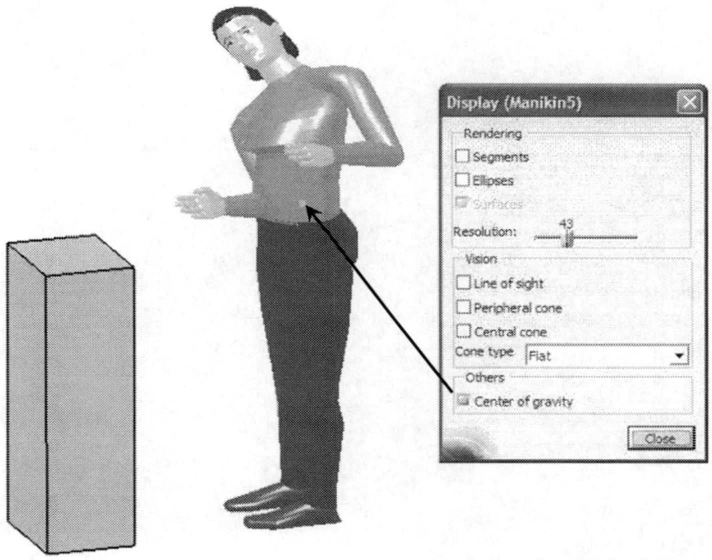

Close the **Display** box.

Pick the **Adds the description to a manikin** icon  from the **Manikin Tools** toolbar 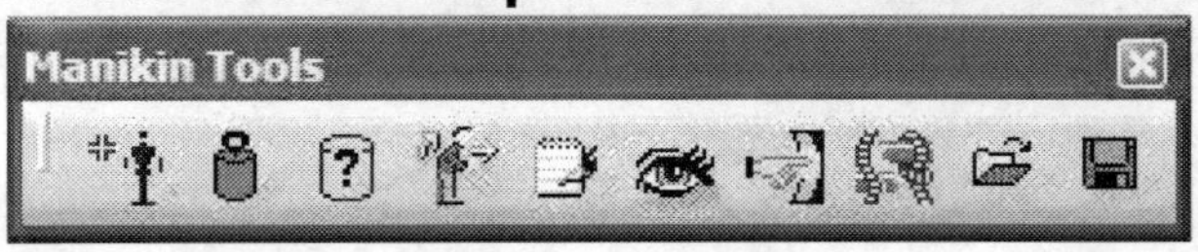

and the pop up box enables you to write your description of the manikin.

Enter any description you would like and close the box by picking **OK**.

This concludes this tutorial briefly illustrating a few of the basics in the **Ergonomic Design & Analysis** workbench in **CATIA V5**.

Chapter 17

Additional Exercises

These 15 exercises supplement the tutorials provided in Chapters 2-16.

Problem 1: Folding Garage Door Mechanism

Using a combination of revolute joint and point curve joints, model a folding garage door mechanism as shown below. You can ignore the details of the track and the wheels which are typically present in an actual garage door. Note that if your parts are modeled similar to what is shown below, you need only model one door panel and one track, and the assembly will involve four instances of the door panel and one instance of the track. Furthermore, for parts modeled similar to what is shown here, the simulation is possible without any mechanism joints made involving the second track.

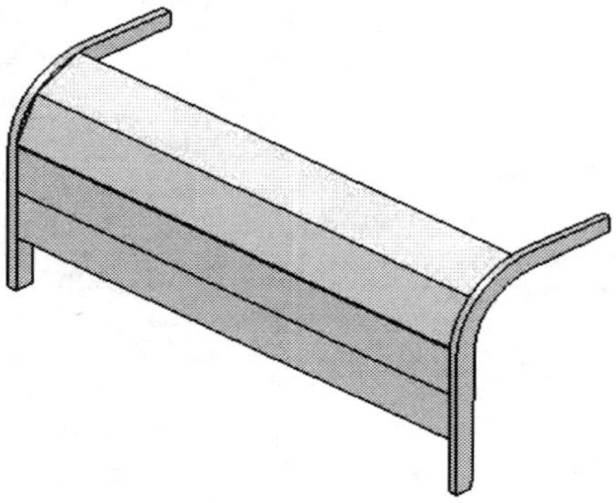

Problem 2: The Instant Center of the Sliding Ladder

This problem involves an extension to the sliding ladder tutorial of Chapter 5 with the ladder modeled as a rigid right triangular part as shown. From basic mechanics, at the instant displayed on the left below, the instant center of the rigid part (or instantaneous center of zero velocity) is easily seen to be at the vertex of the right angle of the triangle as denoted below by IC. At this instance, the entire rigid triangle seems to be purely rotating about IC.

Model the mechanism in CATIA and plot the speed of the vertex as a function of time. By inspecting the plot, convince yourself that the speed is in fact zero at the stated orientation. Repeat plotting speed of the vertex versus angle of the ladder (the triangle's hypotenuse).

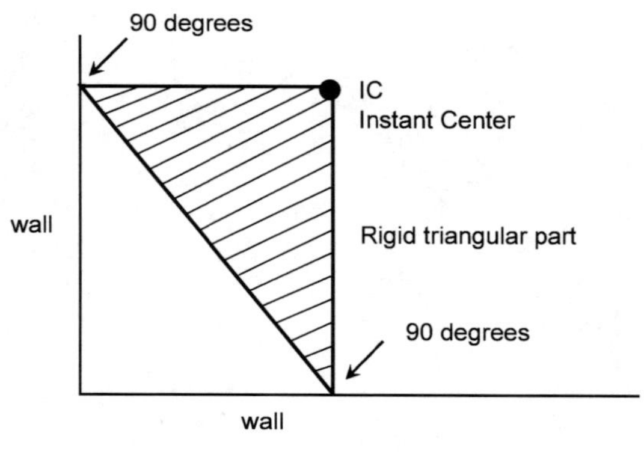

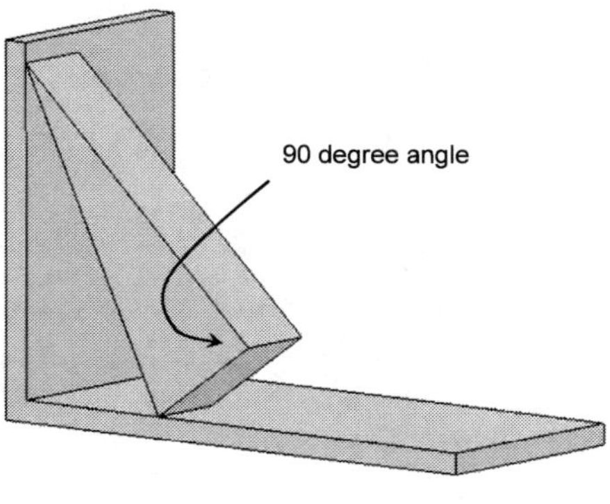

Problem 3: A Compound Gear Train

Using dimensions of your choice, model the compound gear train shown and simulate the mechanism by making one of the side gears the driven gear. This is potentially more challenging than it may first appear since creating a gear joint effectively consumes the involved revolute joints precluding their use in another gear joint.

Problem 4: A Simple Gear Train

Using dimensions of your choice model the simple gear train shown and simulate the mechanism by making one of the side gears the input device.

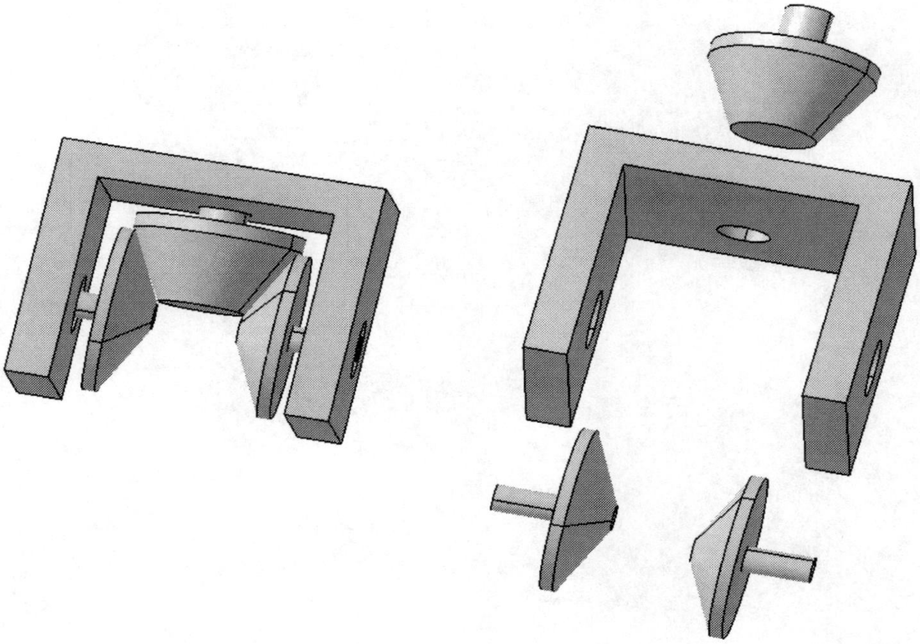

Problem 5: A Revised Planetary Gear

The planetary gear shown below has a fixed ring and a pinion which rotates at 1000 rpm. The number of teeth in the system is shown in the figure. Model the mechanism as suggested in this tutorial and let CATIA estimate the angular velocity of the carrier.

Partial answer:

The carrier rotates at 200 rpm in the opposite direction to the pinion.

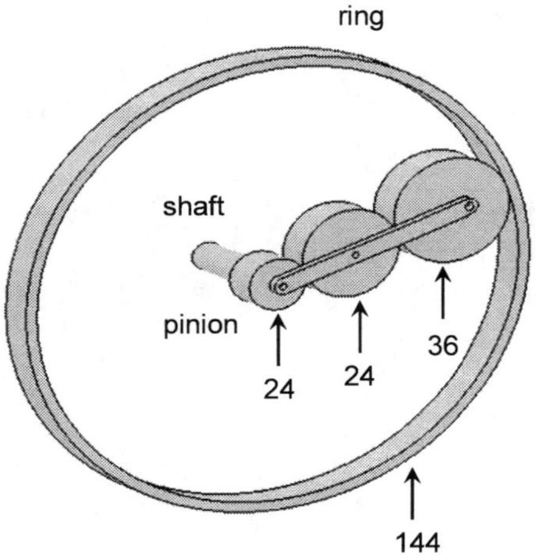

Problem 6: A Primitive Bicycle

Use the Roll-Curve joint to model a primitive bicycle frame travel along a track as shown below. The exploded view is also displayed for your convenience.

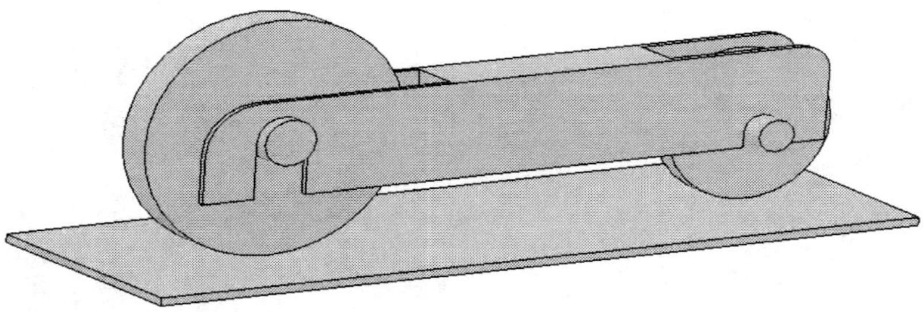

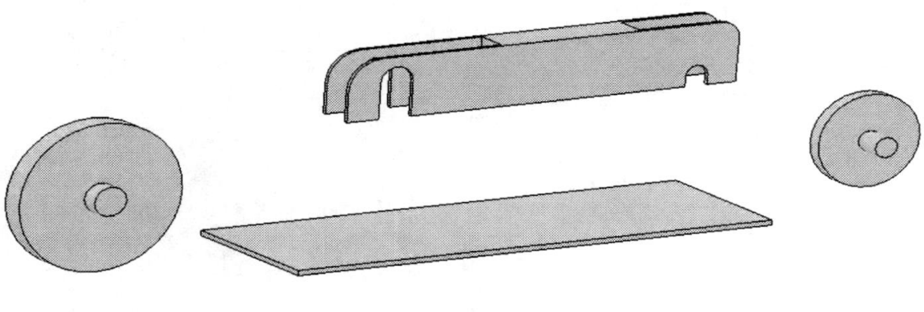

Problem 7: A Cam Follower Mechanism

Model the cam follower mechanism shown below and plot the linear acceleration of the follower. Assume a constant angular velocity for the cam.

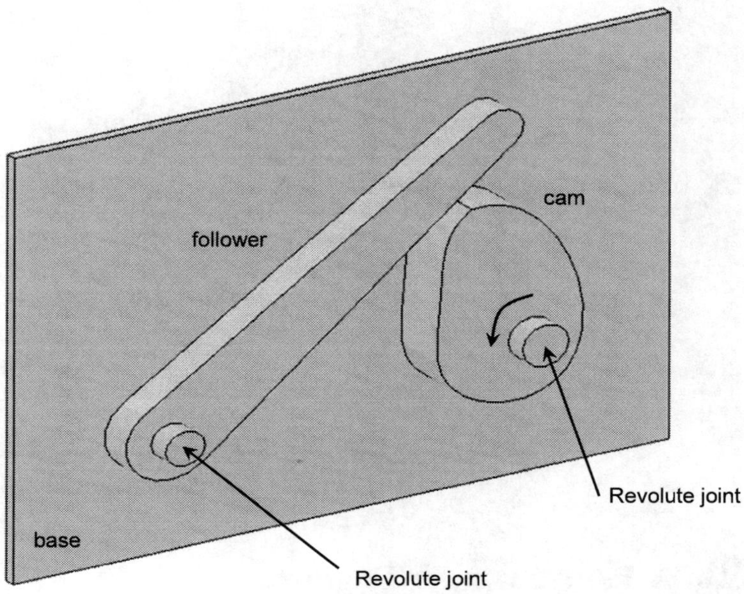

Problem 8: A Translating Part along a Track

Model the two problems shown below. The rigid part is translating along the indicated track at a constant linear velocity.

Problem 9: A Two Cylinder Engine

Use instances of the one cylinder engine assembly created earlier to create the assembly shown below. Animate the mechanism.

Problem 10: A Four Cylinder Engine

Extend the above problem to a four cylinder engine similar to that shown below.

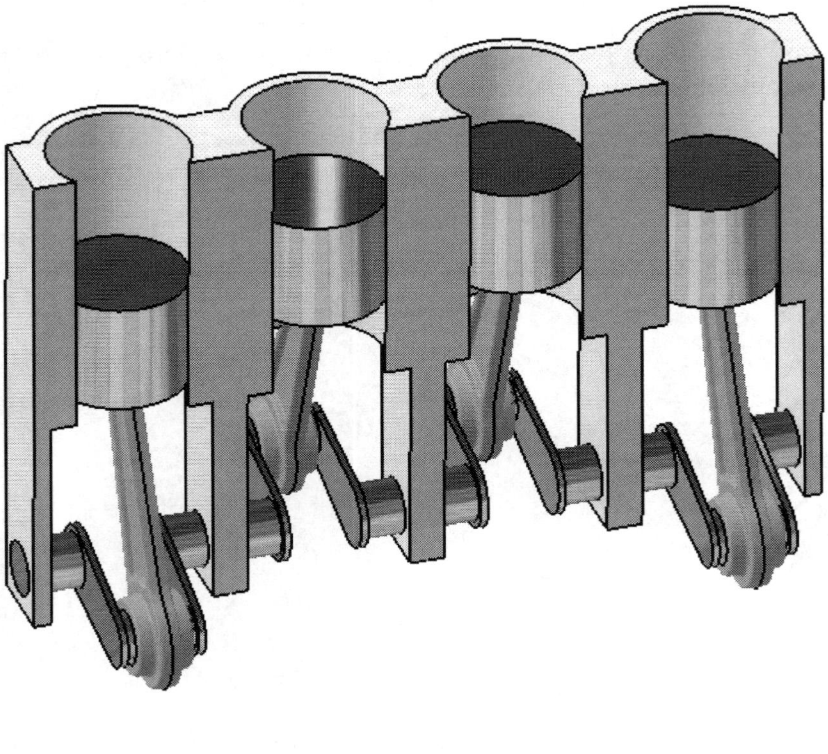

Problem 11: Complete Motion of the Universal Joint

In the tutorial on universal joint, the motion of the pin was not included. It was for this reason that the pin was hidden during the simulation. In this exercise, you are asked to rethink the joints so that both shafts and the pin participate in the motion.
Hint: Do not use the universal joint; instead, make a total of three cylindrical joints and one revolute joint involving a shaft.

Problem 12: Extension of the Coriolis Acceleration Tutorial

Compare the CATIA generated velocity and acceleration of the collar, at a few different positions of your choice with the results you obtain applying the theoretical formulae provided below.

$$\vec{v}_{collar} = \vec{\Omega} \times \vec{r}_{collar/arm} + \vec{v}_{collar/arm}$$

$$\vec{a}_{collar} = \vec{\Omega} \times (\vec{\Omega} \times \vec{r}_{collar/arm}) + 2\vec{\Omega} \times \vec{v}_{collar/arm}$$

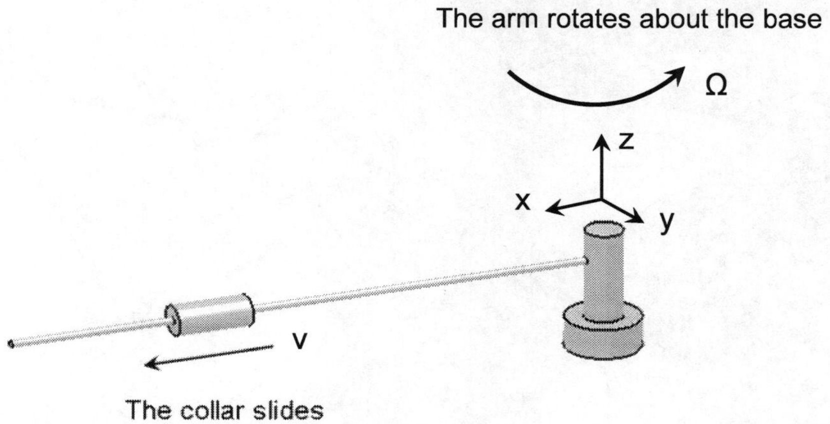

Problem 13: A Gear Mechanism

Model the gear mechanism shown below. Note that the three parts on the left side constitute a four-bar linkage mechanism.

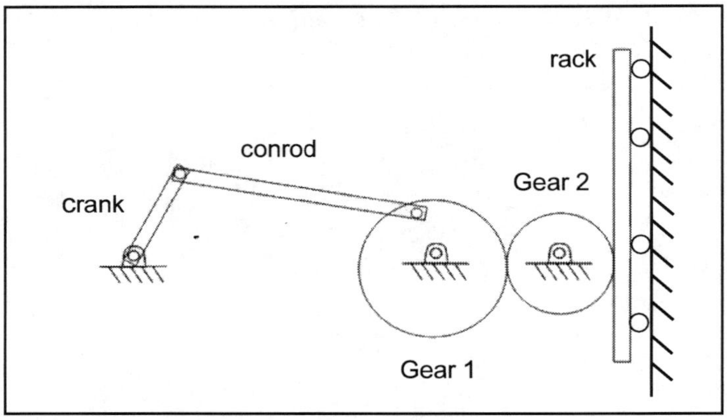

Problem 14: A Rolling Contact Mechanism

In the mechanism shown, link AB is turning with a constant angular velocity of 200 rpm CCW. Use CATIA to determine the angular velocity and acceleration of link DC at the position shown.

Answer: $\omega_{DC} = 6.133$ rad/s (CCW), $\alpha_{DC} = -625.98$ rad/s^2

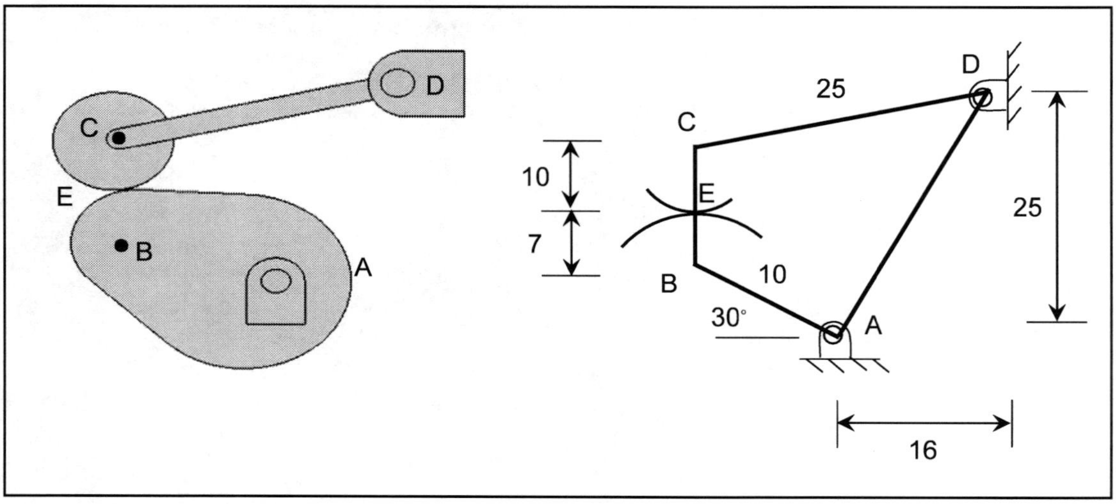

Problem 15: A Differential

The differential model shown below is similar to that in a typical automotive application. Simulate this mechanism for the following scenarios: (1) both wheels (axles) turning at the same speed (driving straight), (2) one wheel turning slightly faster than the other (cornering), and (3) one wheel stopped while the other turns (loss of traction situation with a non-locking differential). You may find it helpful to create an inertial reference part consisting of no more than an axis system similar to the one shown in the assembly below.

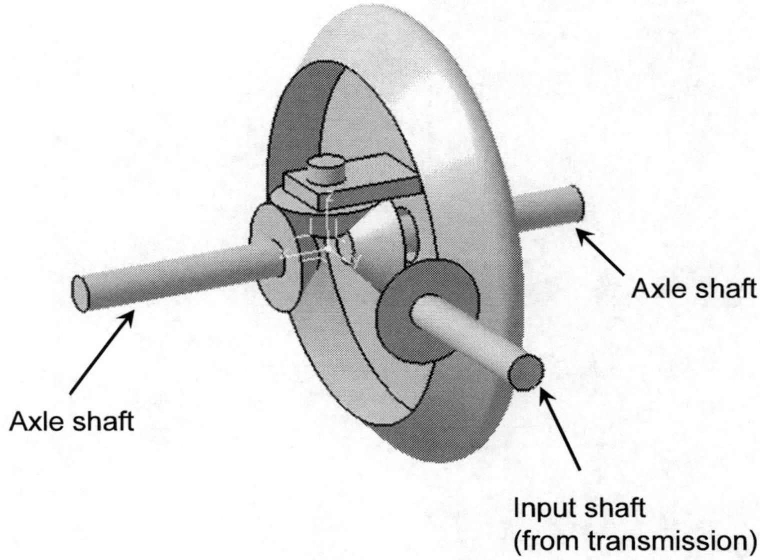

NOTES:

Appendix I

Additional Functionalities, Tips and Tricks

Section 1. Determining the Positive Sense of a Joint

When you manually create a joint in **DMU**, the resulting arrow shown on the mechanism shows the positive sense of the joint. *Positive sense* can be thought of as meaning that the second part picked in the joint creation process moves in that direction with respect to the first part picked in the joint creation process when the joint's command value increases.

Many times it may be helpful to determine the positive sense of a joint. This is often the case for joints which were automatically created from assembly constraints or if the user simply forgets the order the parts were picked when making the joint.

The following steps summarize how the positive sense of a joint can be determined (and, for most joint types, changed):

Step 1. Double-click on the desired joint in the tree to open that joint's **Command Edition** dialog box, color code the parts involved in the joint in orange, and show an arrow (either green or blue) indicating the sense of motion for the joint. An example is shown below for the cylindrical joint between the crank and the base from the slider crank mechanism of Chapter 4. Note that the joint must have a command defined on it (e.g., angle driven, length driven) in order to have a sense defined. As an alternative, you can open the joint's **Command Edition** dialog box by double-clicking on the joint's Command in the tree.

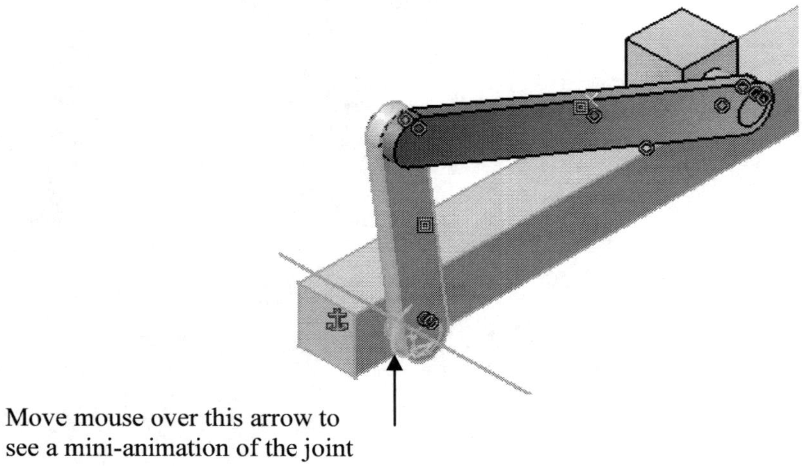

Step 2. If you move your mouse over the arrow, you will see a mini-animation showing movement in the positive direction of the joint. Note: A green arrow indicates that the selected joint is involved in a loop. A blue arrow indicates that the command motion is fully determined (such as in an open chain mechanism).

Step 3. (optional): To flip the positive direction, simply click on the arrow. Note that for **Roll Curve** and **Point Curve** joint types, you can check, but not change, the orientation.

Section 2: Common Reference Parts on Cable and Gear Joints

A Cable Joint is a relationship imposed between two prismatic joints such that the motions are coupled according to the user-defined ratio. Similarly, a Gear Joint is a relationship imposed between two revolute joints such that the motions are coupled according to the user-defined ratio.

A key restriction when defining a Cable Joint or a Gear Joint is that both joints must share a common reference part. In many cases, this condition is met by the nature of the design and no further consideration is warranted. In other cases, the natural way to build the mechanism may not meet the restriction. For example, in an engine mechanism, it would be typical to define a Revolute Joint between the crankshaft and block, and another revolute joint between the camshaft(s) and the cylinder head(s). In this case, creation of a Gear Joint to drive the camshaft rotation as a function of crankshaft rotation is not supported since the two joints do not share a common reference part. In a case such as this, wherein one part used in defining one of the revolute joints (the block) would not move with respect to one of the parts used in defining the other revolute joint (the cylinder head), then a workaround would be as follows: Create a dummy part consisting of axis systems sufficient to define the two revolute joints relative to that dummy part. In the engine example, the dummy part would require a crankshaft axis and an axis for each camshaft. Of course, this dummy part would need to either be parametrically defined to update with changes to the engine parts, or would need to be updated manually if a change is made affecting the axes' locations.

Section 3: Mechanism Analysis Dialog Box

The **Mechanism Analysis** dialog box provides a nice summary of the overall makeup and properties of the mechanism.

To access the **Mechanism Analysis** dialog box, click on the **Mechanism Analysis**

icon. The resulting dialog box for the robot mechanism of Chapter 11 is shown below.

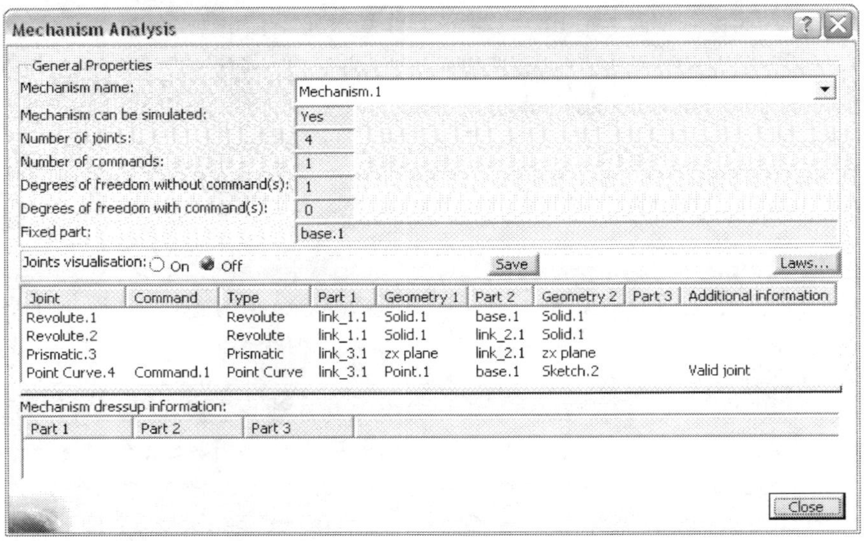

The information in this dialog box can be very useful when diagnosing a problem with a mechanism. Toggling the **Joints visualization** radio button to **On** overlays a graphic representation of all the joints onto the mechanism model such as is shown below for the robot mechanism.

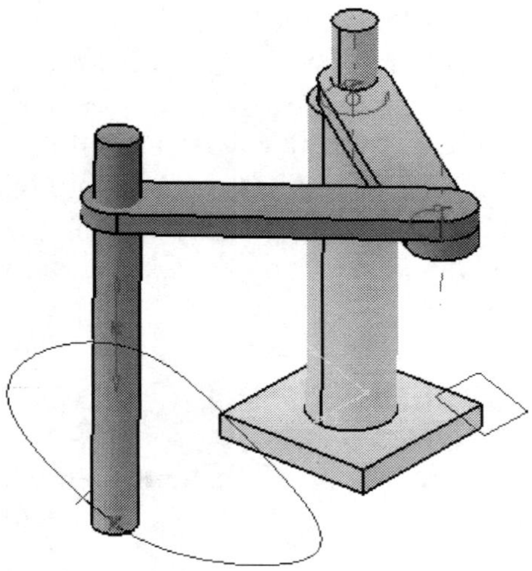

Section 4: Positioning Part for a Point-Surface Joint

Creating a Point-Surface joint requires that the two involved parts must be pre-positioned with the point on the surface. For example, if it is desired to create a Point-Surface joint between the two parts shown below so that the tip of the pencil shaped part rides on the top surface of the wavy part, it will first be necessary pre-position the parts.

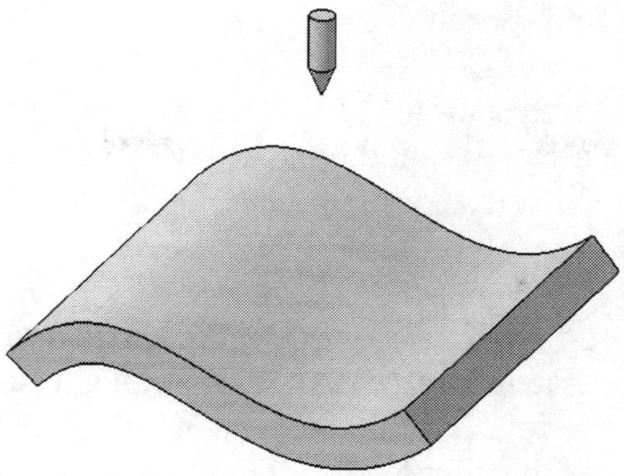

An easy way to preposition the parts is as follows:

Step 1. From the **Start** menu, pick **Digital Mockup > DMU Navigator**

Step 2. Use the **Snap** icon  to reposition the parts (the first part picked will move to the second).

Section 5: Using Sub-Mechanisms

Sub-Mechanisms in V5 appear to suffer from a substantial drawback, namely that the sub-mechanism motion may be animated within a larger mechanism, but only as a stand-alone motion within that larger mechanism.

For example, you may have a *clock* mechanism consisting of a clock face, hour hand and minute hand. A simulation could be developed showing the proper relative motion of the hands with respect to the face. You could then create a larger *complete clock* mechanism (product) consisting of, say, the *clock* mechanism, a housing, and a pendulum. If you were to import the sub-mechanism for the clock mechanism, you could animate the motion of the hour and minute hands with respect to the clock face, but apparently cannot integrate the motion of that mechanism with motion at a higher product level, say to include the pendulum motion.

As another example, assume that you are modeling a multi-cylinder engine. It would be natural to want to create a sub-mechanism consisting of the power elements (meaning the piston, wrist pin, connecting rod, piston rings, etc.) and to then plan to import that mechanism into a larger assembly (and mechanism) in the various cylinder locations. As far as the authors can tell, such an approach will not allow those various submechanisms to properly move in an integrated fashion with crankshaft motion.

A perhaps more significant restriction is that, as far as the authors can tell, a joint cannot be made in **DMU Kinematics** that is between components within a sub-product of the top level assembly. For example, if a conrod and piston subassembly is made, and that subassembly is used in multiple cylinder locations in an engine assembly, **DMU** will not permit creation of a revolute joint between the conrod and piston since they are within a subassembly.

Section 6: Swept Volume and Trace

The **Trace** functionality generates a trace of the path of a point or edge of a product element as it moves through a path defined by a replay. The resulting trace may be useful for a number of purposes, such as verifying the intended kinematic path or in designing a cam.

To create a trace, you need to first simulate your mechanism and define a **Replay** for which you would like to generate the trace. As an example, a **Replay** has been defined for a full crank rotation for the four bar linkage shown below. We would like to generate a trace of a point on the end of the coupler as shown below.

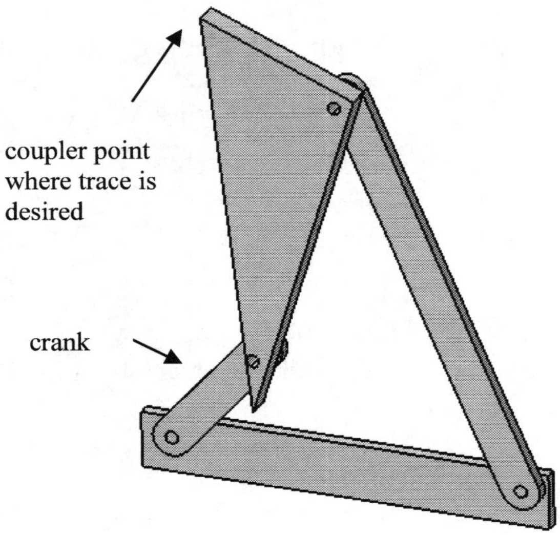

The steps to define the trace are summarized below:

Step 1. After you have defined the **Replay** for which you would like to generate a **Trace**, select the **Trace** icon  from the **DMU-Generic Animation** toolbar. This will open the **Trace** dialog box shown below.

Step 2. In the **Trace** dialog box, choose your **Replay** as the **Object to trace out**.

Step 3. In the **Trace** dialog box, choose the **Elements to trace out** by selecting points or edges on the geometry or in the specification tree. For our example, the upper front vertex of the **coupler** is selected.

Step 4. For the **Reference product**, you may leave the default reference product, choose another reference product, or choose a part as the reference product. If your reference product is a product, the **Trace Destination** will be a new part. If your reference product is a part, you may choose the **Trace Destination** to be either a **New Part** or **Reference Product**. For our example, the **ground** part is chosen as the **Reference Product** and the **Trace Destination** is set as **Reference Product** (meaning the resulting points and spline generated as the trace will be appended to the ground part). The completed **Trace** dialog box for our example is shown below. The **Number of steps** is pre-determined by the number of steps in the **Replay**.

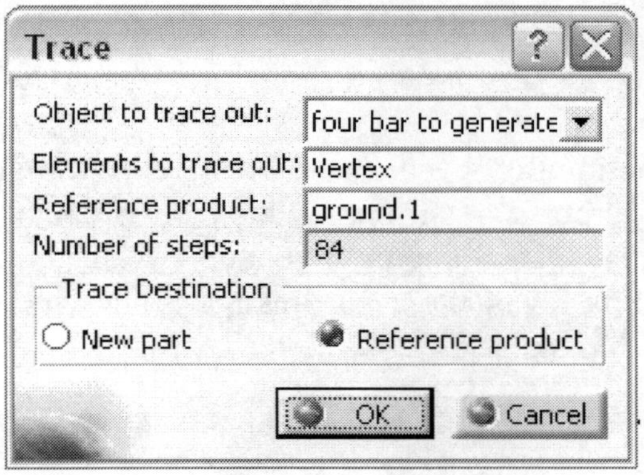

Step 5. **OK** the dialog box. The geometry resulting from the **Trace** will be automatically created. In our case, the points and spline created are added to the specification tree as part of the **ground** part. The results for this example are shown below.

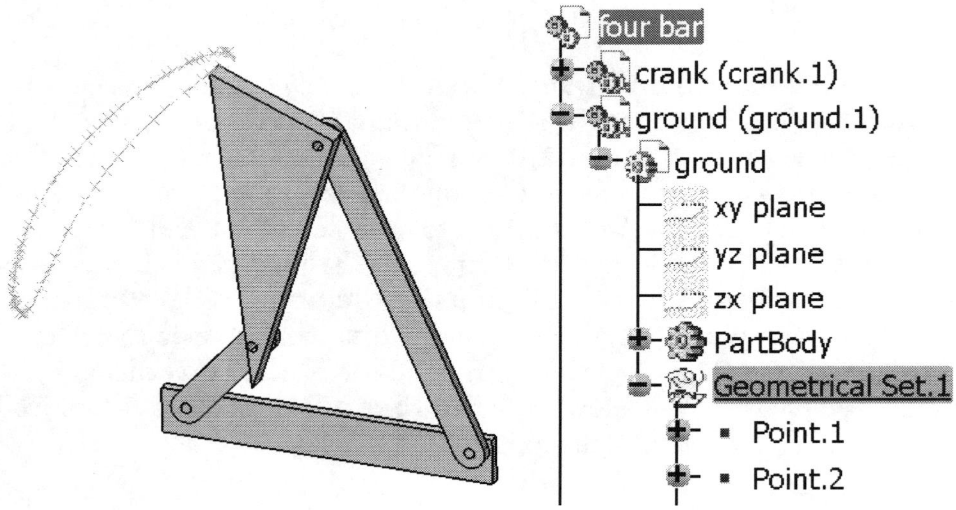

The **Swept volume** functionality behaves similarly, except that products are chosen to sweep, and the resulting output is a .cgr part. This part can be added to the existing assembly to visualize the swept volume in the context of the assembly. The **Swept volume** for the coupler link for our four bar linkage is shown below.

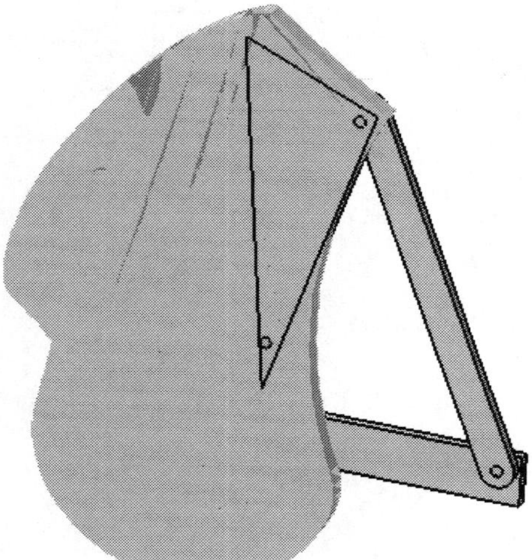

Section 7: Making Mechanisms More Robust to Part Updates

As with general parametric modeling, some simple techniques can make it much more likely that your mechanism will properly update upon changes to the parts making up the product. Problems tend to arise when using part geometry to define assembly constraints and mechanism joints; these tend to get renamed/renumbered under certain types of part changes resulting in loss of assembly constraint and/or mechanism joint information upon updates to the parts.

The authors have found the following to be good practice to minimize such loss of information upon updates: When modeling the parts, try to use axis systems and other reference geometry to define all the key interfaces to mating parts. Model the part to be associative to that reference geometry, and use the reference geometry when creating assembly constraints and/or mechanism joints. In this way, changes to the geometry do not affect the entities involved in the constraint and joint definition.

NOTES:

Appendix II

Introduction to Parametric Modeling

Introduction:

While the focus of this text is on mechanism modeling and simulation, the authors feel that the subject of parametric modeling given its potential to significantly improve design times in digital product creation activities warrants a brief exercise to introduce the topic to those readers not already familiar with it.

In the context of mechanism design, there are tremendous opportunities to take advantage of parametric design. As one example, consider the design of a typical piston engine. As digital design tools continue to mature, more and more analytical models are driving the design and development process. The outputs of those models often relate to the key geometric parameters of the design. In the engine case, these outputs may include things like bore, stroke, vee angle, compression ratio, etc. An organization that can develop a parametric CAD model of an engine can easily, quickly, and accurately update the model as key parameters change.

The following exercise provides a very simple introduction to parametric modeling

Problem Statement:

Suppose it is desired to design a box (rectangular solid) which maintains a constant 3:1 length to width ratio. In this exercise, a model of the box displayed on the right will be parameterized to maintain the prescribed relation; the user would be able to set the parameters H and W at will and the constraint L=3W will automatically hold.

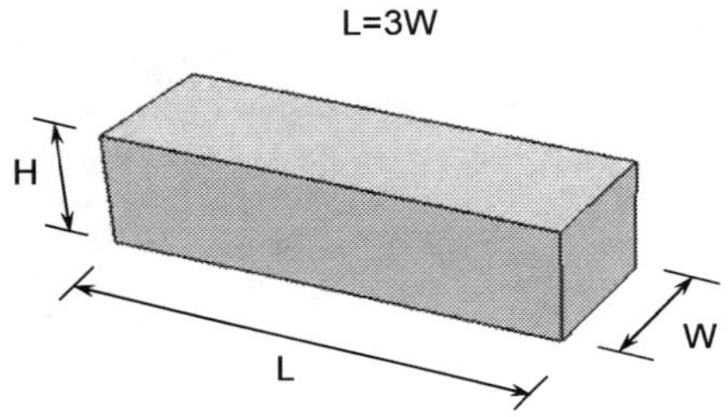

Development of the model:

Enter the **Part Design** workbench. Select the **New** icon  from the **Standard** toolbar 

. Select the **Part** type in the **New** dialogue box shown below. Click on **OK** to close the dialogue box. In the resulting **New Part** dialogue box, accept the default part name of **Part1** (or enter your own name) and choose **OK**. The history tree is shown on the screen.

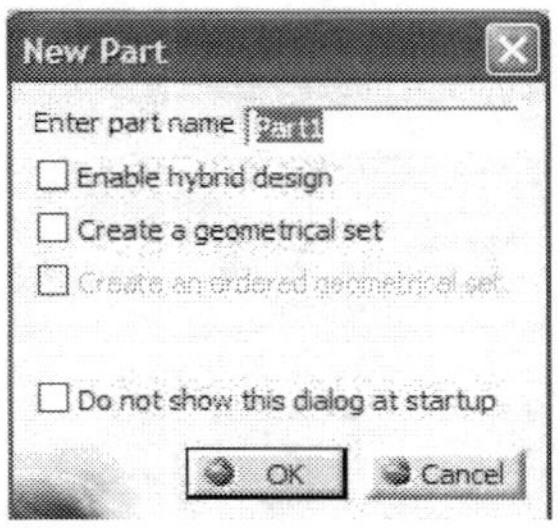

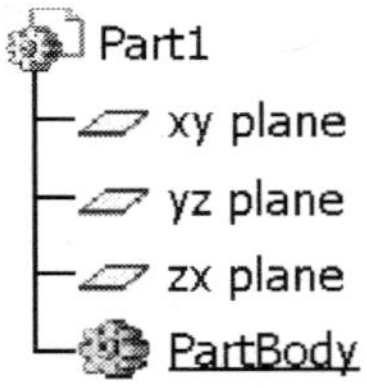

To create the box, we will draw a rectangle on the xy plane and Pad it. The steps to do so follow.

Select the **xy** plane from the tree and click on the **Sketch** icon 

to enter the **Sketcher** workbench.

Use the **Rectangle** icon 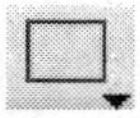 from the **Profile** toolbar 

to draw a rectangle (any rectangle will do).

Using the **Constraint** icon 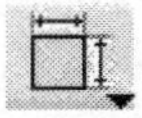 dimension the sides shown. Do not be concerned with the actual values of the dimensions.

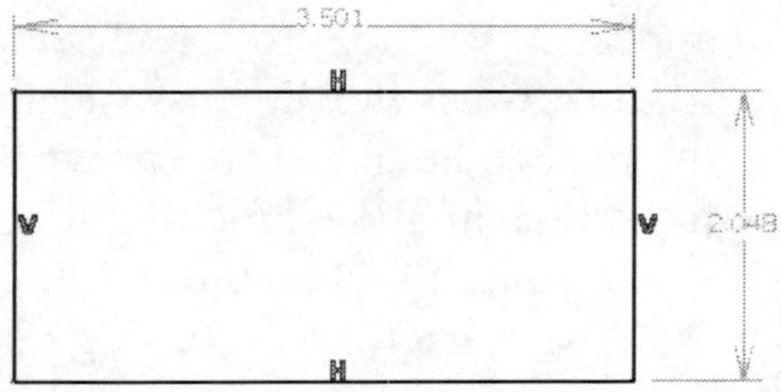

Exit the **Sketcher** by selecting the **Exit Workbench** icon 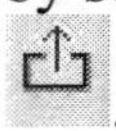.
The rectangle is displayed in isometric view.

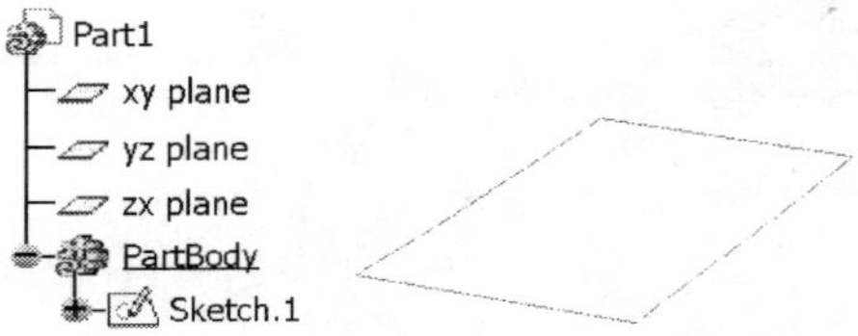

Now, select the **Pad** icon  from the **Sketch-Based Feature** toolbar .

In the resulting dialogue box, select **Sketch.1** and accept the default **Length** value. You need not be concerned with the actual value of the pad.

Close the **Pad Definition** box by clicking on **OK**.

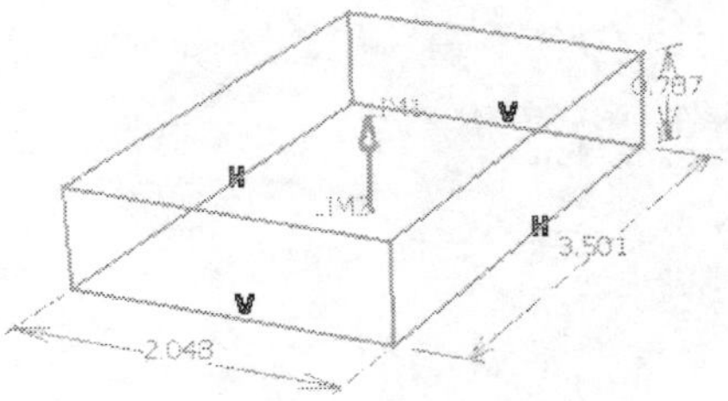

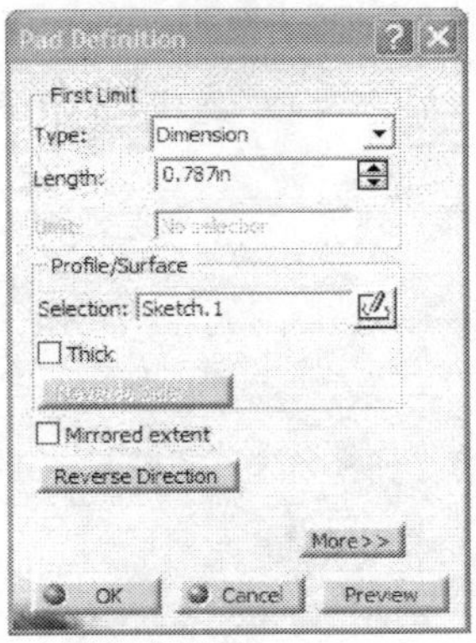

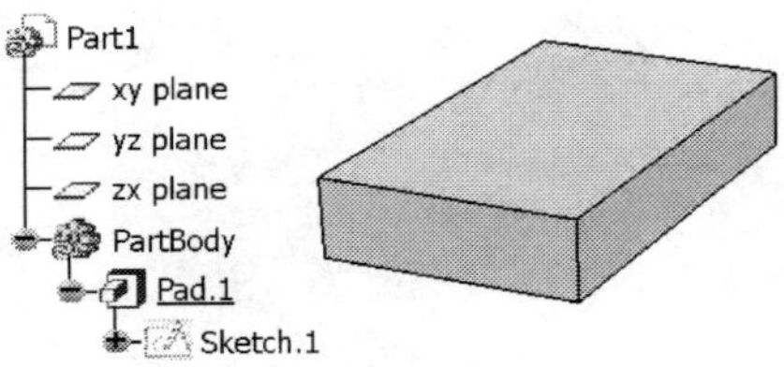

The constructed box appears on the screen.

Renaming the Dimensions:

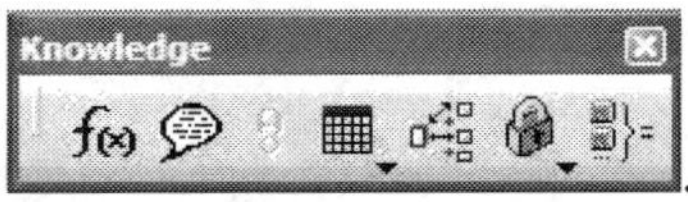

Select the **Formula** icon  from the **Knowledge** toolbar. The **Formulas: Part1** dialogue box appears on the screen.

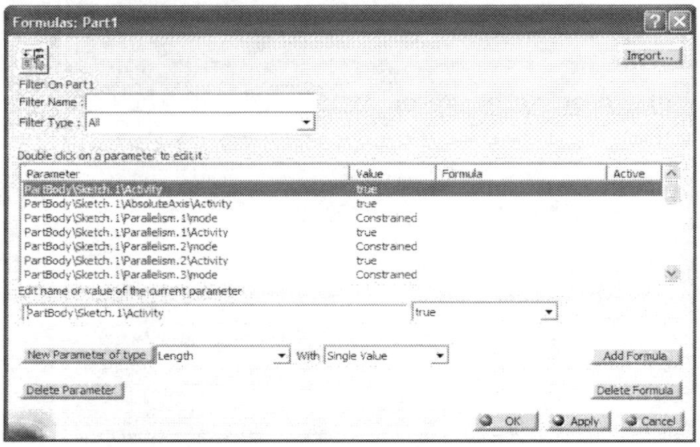

Point the cursor to the block appearing on the screen and select it. This forces the dimensions and the padded height to appear on the screen as shown making it much easier to relate the dimension list to the resulting solid.

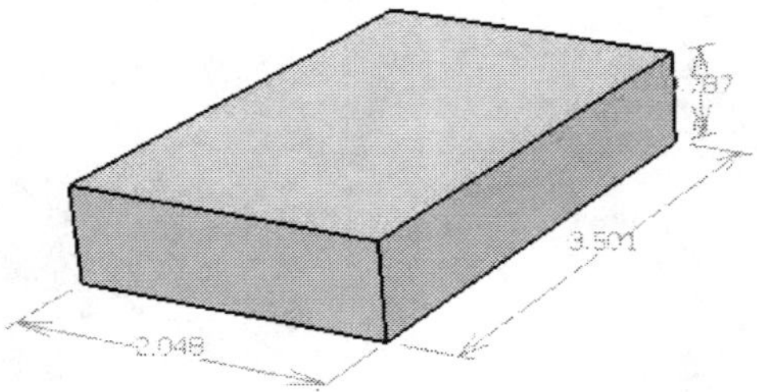

Point the cursor to the padded height dimension on the screen and select it. This locates the actual entity in the CATIA database which is then highlighted in the **Formulas: Part1** dialogue box.

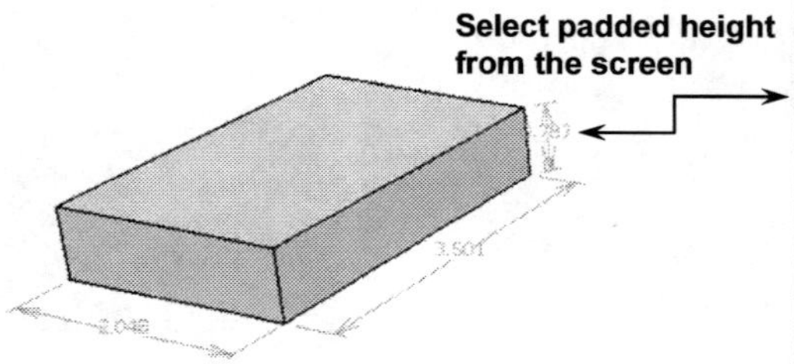

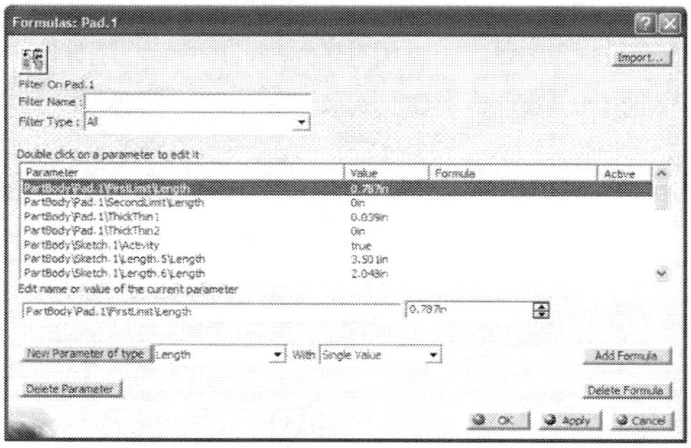

Next we will rename the dimensions to **H**, **W** and **L** corresponding to the box's height, width, and length, respectively.

Select the default name shown **PartBody/Pad.1/firstLimit/Length** in the list of parameters.

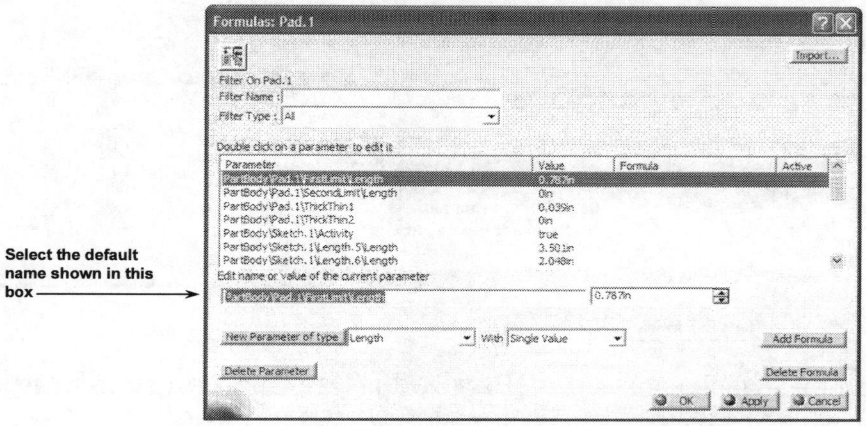

Now, highlight the current name in the **Edit name or value of the current parameter** area and type **H** for the new name.

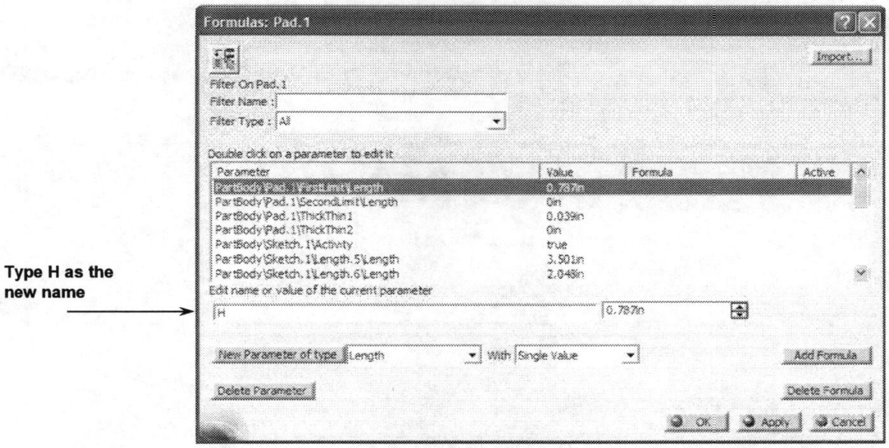

Point the cursor one of the horizontal dimensions on the screen and select it. This locates the actual entity in the CATIA database which is then highlighted in the **Formulas: Part1** dialogue box.

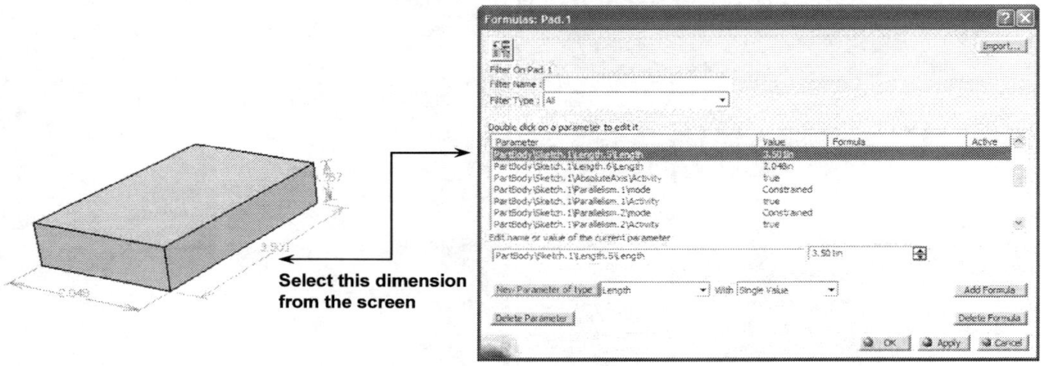

Select the default name shown **PartBody/Sketch.1/Length.5/Length** in the data base. <u>Note that the name in your model may not be **Length.5**.</u>

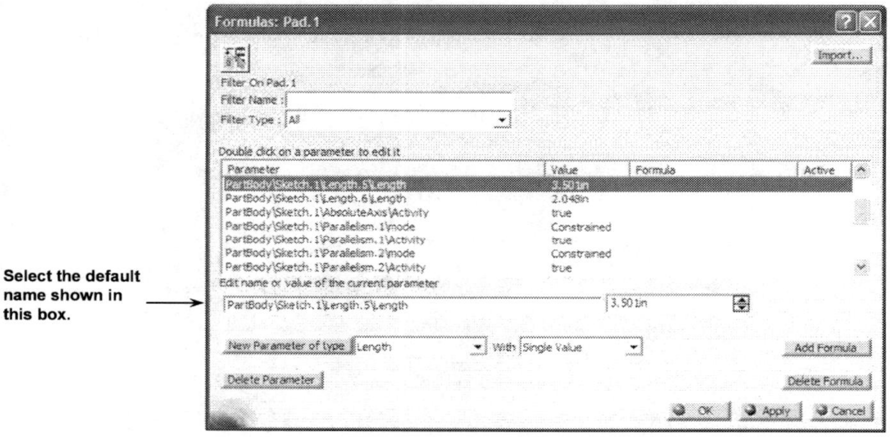

Type **L** as the new name.

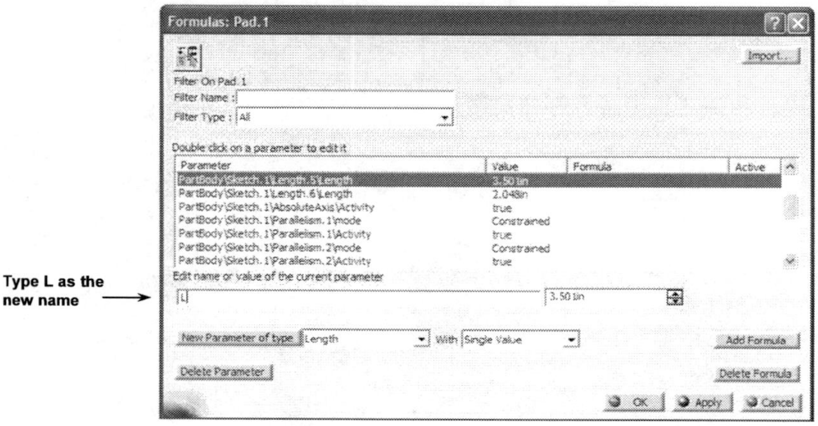

Point the cursor to the remaining horizontal dimension on the screen and select it. This locates the actual entity in the CATIA database which is then highlighted in the **Formulas: Part1** dialogue box.

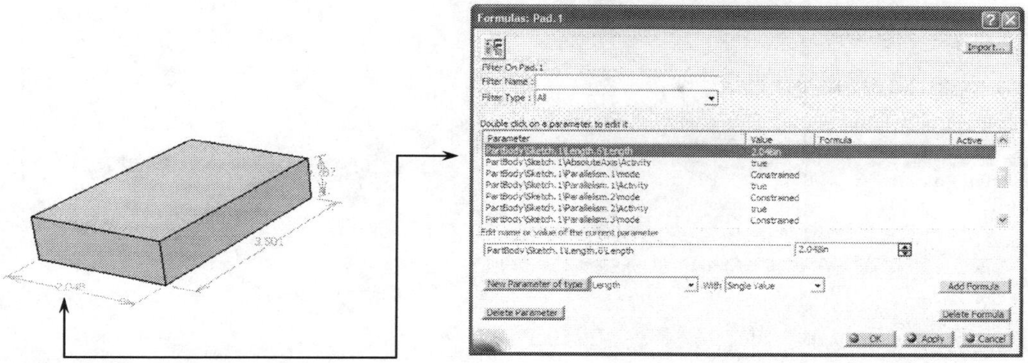

Select the remaining dimension

Select the default name shown **PartBody/Sketch.1/Length.6/Length** in the data base. <u>Note that the name in your model may not be **Length.6**.</u>

Select the default name shown in this box

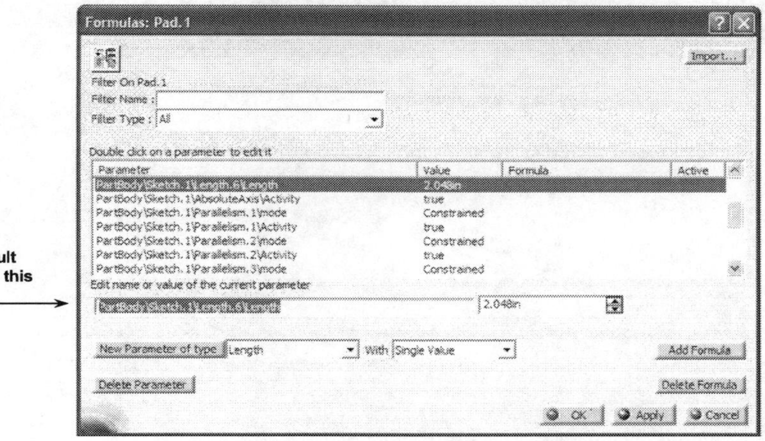

Type W as the new name.

Type W as the new name

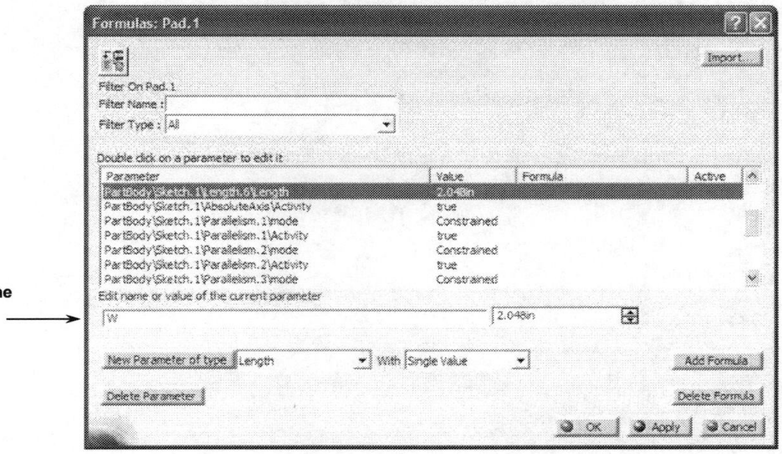

Use the box **Filter Type** pull-down menu to select **Renamed Parameters**. This will help reduce visual clutter as we proceed.

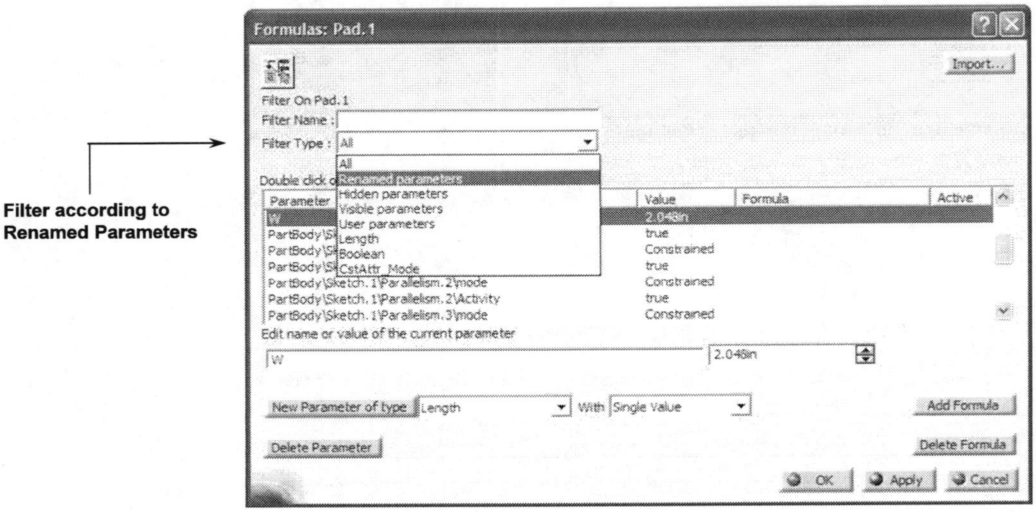

This displays the renamed parameters as shown below.

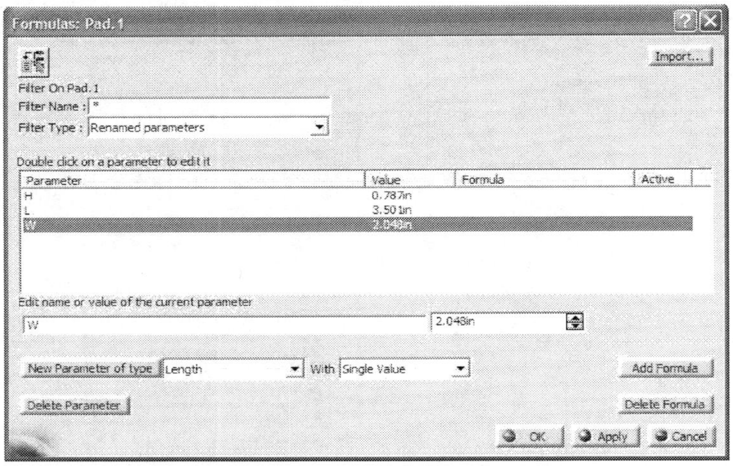

Creating the Parametric Relation:

Select the line indicating the variable **L**.

Select L

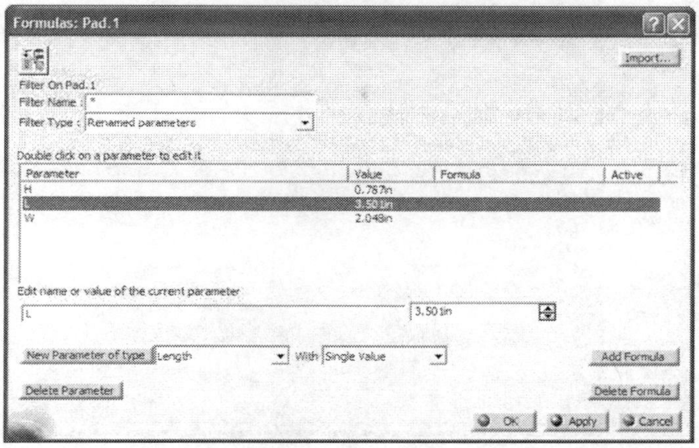

Select the box **Add Formula** Add Formula.

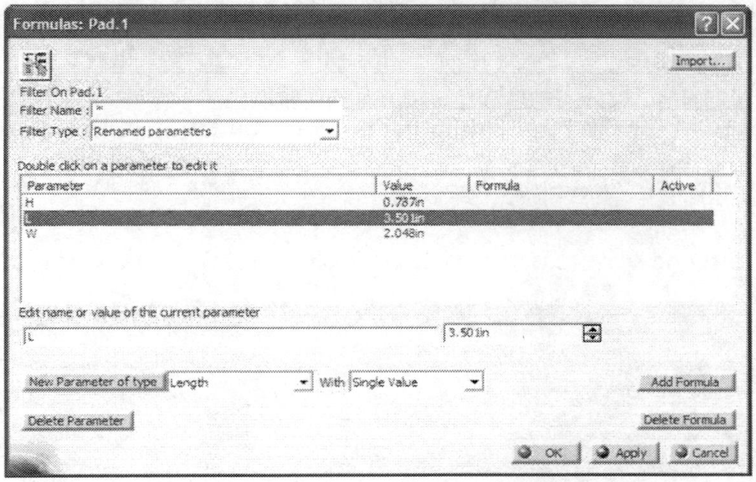

Select Add Formula

In the **Formula Editor: L** dialogue box type **3*W** as shown below.

Type 3*W

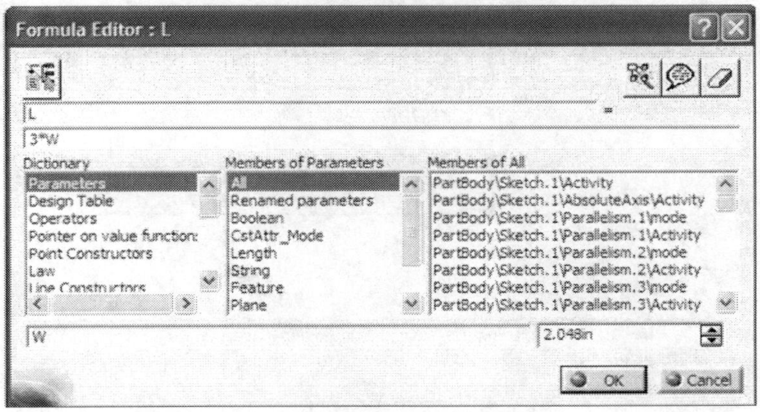

Press **OK** to close the **Formula Editor: L** dialogue box.

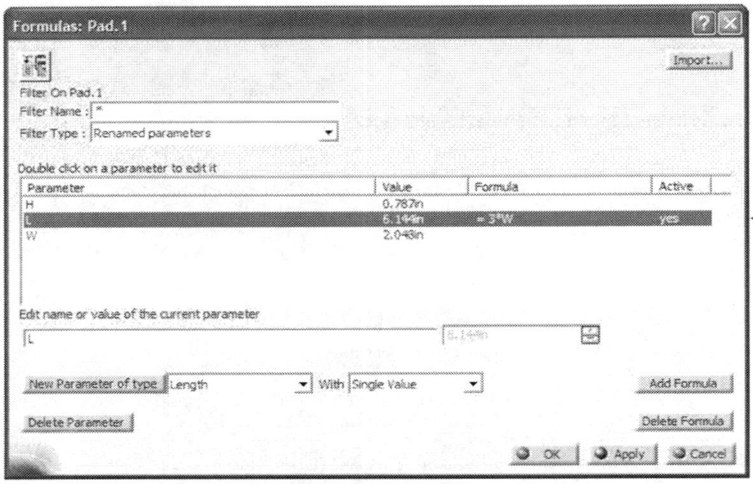

Equation is enforced

Important:

<u>To ensure that your work in defining the variables is not lost (accidentally), click on **Apply** Apply button. In doing so, even if you close the **Formula:Part1** dialogue box, the renamed variables and the defined equation is preserved.</u>

The part in your model could turn red indicating the need for updating. Click on the **Update** icon . The new part geometry appears.

Now to experiment with the newly created parametric relation, select the variable **W**.

Select W

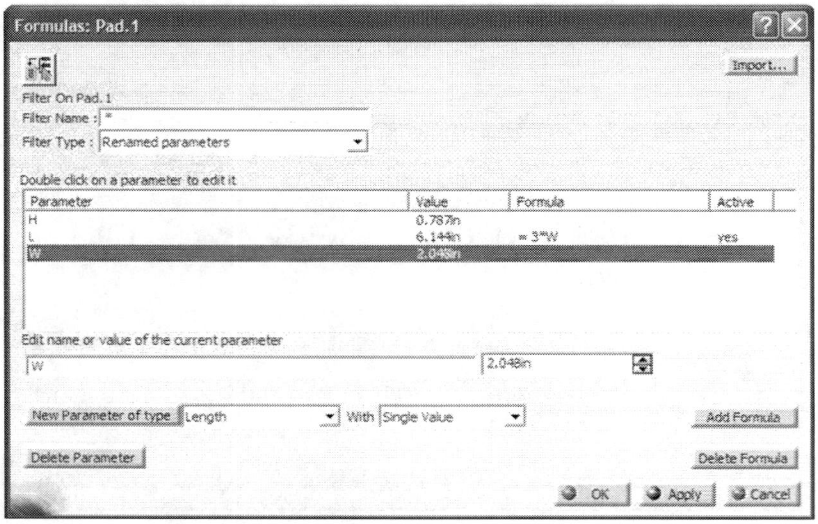

Change the value of **W** to a new value (in our case, we have changed it to 4)

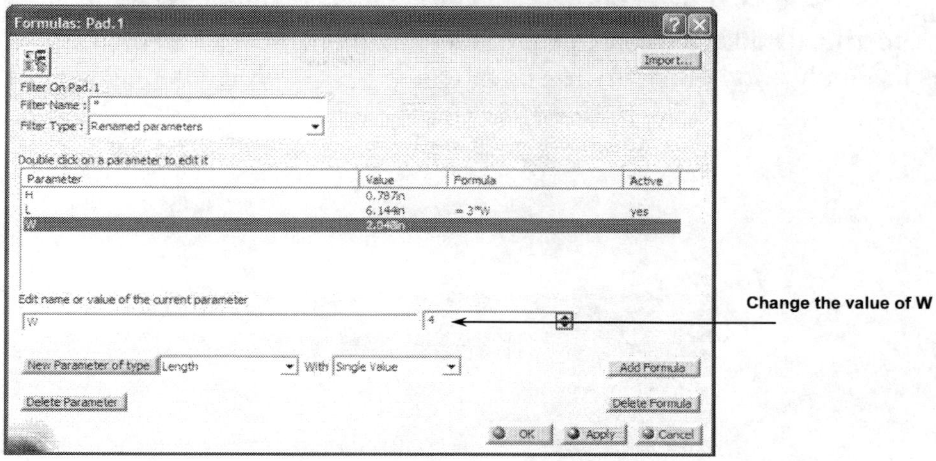

Click on **Apply**  and note that your part changes dimension subject to the equation **L=3W**.
Depending on your CATIA setup, you may have to update. This can be achieved by Clicking on the **Update** icon .

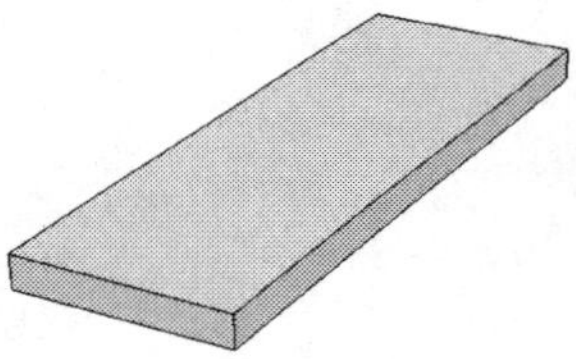

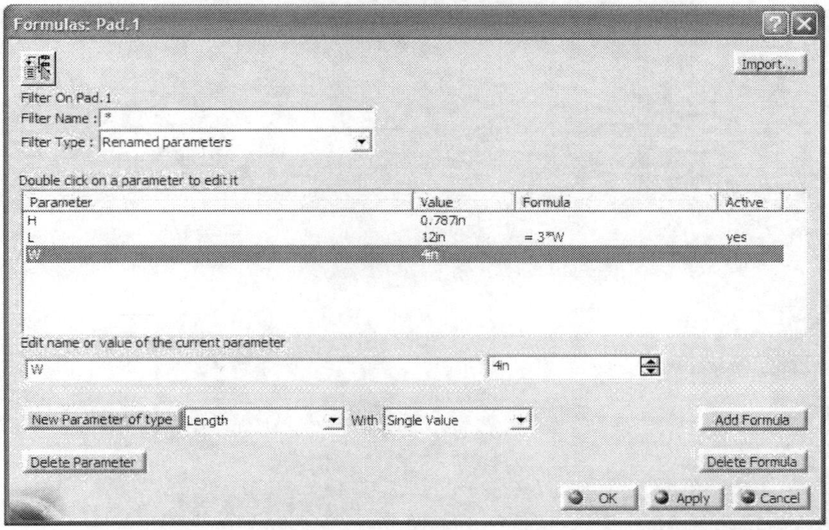

Similarly, you can change the variable **H**.

Further Suggestions:

One idea for further practice extending this parametric model is to create a variable named **V** representing the desired volume of the box. Then, for a specified **V** and **W**, write parametric equations to determine **H** as necessary while maintaining the 3:1 **L** to **W** ratio. Of course, one must be careful to ensure dimensional homogeneity.

The authors routinely introduce the concept of parametric modeling to their students through project work. For example, the students may be required to design a flashlight which parametrically adapts to one, two, or three batteries of sizes AAA, C, or D. This illustrates the application of parametric equations across several components in an assembly.